Thomas Budd Van Horne, Edward Ruger

History of the Army of the Cumberland

Vol. II

Thomas Budd Van Horne, Edward Ruger

History of the Army of the Cumberland
Vol. II

ISBN/EAN: 9783743399938

Manufactured in Europe, USA, Canada, Australia, Japa

Cover: Foto ©ninafisch / pixelio.de

Manufactured and distributed by brebook publishing software (www.brebook.com)

Thomas Budd Van Horne, Edward Ruger

History of the Army of the Cumberland

HISTORY

OF THE

ARMY OF THE CUMBERLAND

ITS

ORGANIZATION, CAMPAIGNS, AND BATTLES

WRITTEN AT THE REQUEST OF

MAJOR-GENERAL GEORGE H. THOMAS

CHIEFLY FROM HIS PRIVATE MILITARY JOURNAL AND OFFICIAL AND OTHER
DOCUMENTS FURNISHED BY HIM

BY

THOMAS B. VAN HORNE, U. S. A.

ILLUSTRATED WITH

CAMPAIGN AND BATTLE MAPS

COMPILED BY

EDWARD RUGER

LATE SUPERINTENDENT TOPOGRAPHICAL ENGINEER'S OFFICE, HEADQUARTERS
DEPARTMENT OF THE CUMBERLAND

TWO VOLUMES AND ATLAS

VOL. II

CINCINNATI
ROBERT CLARKE & CO
1875

Entered according to Act of Congress, in the year 1875,
THOS. B. VAN HORNE AND EDWARD RUGER.
In the Office of the Librarian of Congress, at Washington.

Stereotyped by OGDEN, CAMPBELL & Co., Cincinnati.

CONTENTS VOL. II.

CHAPTER XXIII.
CAMPAIGN IN EAST TENNESSEE, AND MINOR OPERATIONS IN THE DEPARTMENT OF THE CUMBERLAND.. 1

CHAPTER XXIV.
GENERAL VIEW OF THE STATUS OF THE CONFLICT AT THE CLOSE OF 1863. 8

CHAPTER XXV.
OPERATIONS IN THE DEPARTMENT DURING JANUARY, FEBRUARY, AND MARCH, 1864, AND PREPARATIONS FOR AGGRESSION......................... 13

CHAPTER XXVI.
THE TURNING OF DALTON... 44

CHAPTER XXVII.
BATTLE OF RESACA... 64

CHAPTER XXVIII.
ADVANCE TO THE ETOWAH RIVER—THE TURNING OF ALATOONA—BATTLES NEAR NEW HOPE CHURCH.. 71

CHAPTER XXIX.
OPERATIONS NEAR KENESAW MOUNTAIN, INCLUDING THE BATTLE AT KULP'S HOUSE, ASSAULT OF THE MOUNTAIN, AND THE FLANK MOVEMENT.. 86

CONTENTS.

CHAPTER XXX.
ADVANCE UPON ATLANTA—BATTLE OF PEACHTREE CREEK...... 109

CHAPTER XXXI.
SIEGE OF ATLANTA...... 123

CHAPTER XXXII.
THE FLANK MOVEMENTS, CULMINATING IN THE BATTLE OF JONESBORO AND THE FALL OF ATLANTA...... 140

CHAPTER XXXIII.
THE MARCH OF THE OPPOSING ARMIES TO THE NORTH, AND THE EVOLUTION OF NEW CAMPAIGNS...... 155

CHAPTER XXXIV.
THE RESISTANCE TO GENERAL HOOD'S ADVANCE FROM THE TENNESSEE RIVER, CULMINATING IN THE BATTLE OF FRANKLIN...... 186

CHAPTER XXXV.
BATTLE OF NASHVILLE, AND PURSUIT OF THE ROUTED ENEMY...... 222

CHAPTER XXXVI.
MINOR OPERATIONS HAVING RELATION MORE OR LESS INTIMATE WITH THOSE OF THE MAIN ARMY DURING NOVEMBER AND DECEMBER 270

CHAPTER XXXVII.
THE MARCH TO THE SEA AND THE CAPTURE OF THE CITY OF SAVANNAH, GEORGIA...... 278

CHAPTER XXXVIII.
MARCH THROUGH THE CAROLINAS, FROM SAVANNAH TO GOLDSBORO AND RALEIGH—THE BATTLES OF AVERYSBORO AND BENTONVILLE........ 306

CHAPTER XXXIX.
GENERAL GEORGE STONEMAN'S CAVALRY OPERATIONS IN TENNESSEE AND NORTH CAROLINA...... 337

CHAPTER XL.

GENERAL J. H. WILSON'S CAVALRY OPERATIONS IN ALABAMA AND
GEORGIA 347

CHAPTER XLI.

CAPTURE OF THE CONFEDERATE PRESIDENT............................ 362

CHAPTER XLII.

THE DISSOLUTION OF THE ARMY—SUMMARY OF ITS ACHIEVEMENTS..... 369

CHAPTER XLIII.

THE DEAD AND THEIR DISPOSITION.. 377

APPENDIX.

ORGANIZATION OF DEPARTMENT OF THE CUMBERLAND................. 381
ORGANIZATION OF DEPARTMENT OF THE OHIO............................ 385
LIST OF OFFICERS OF ARMY OF THE CUMBERLAND WHO WERE KILLED
   IN ACTION OR DIED OF WOUNDS OR DISEASE DURING THE WAR... 386
THE ENGINEER SERVICE IN THE ARMY OF THE CUMBERLAND............ 439

HISTORY

OF THE

ARMY OF THE CUMBERLAND.

CHAPTER XXIII.

CAMPAIGN IN EAST TENNESSEE AND MINOR OPERATIONS IN THE DEPARTMENT OF THE CUMBERLAND.

GENERAL BURNSIDE had been informed that he should have help as soon as practicable, when first it was known that General Longstreet had been sent against him. General Grant said to him that he could hardly conceive the necessity of retreating from East Tennessee. But as the issue at Chattanooga, though glorious in its coming, had been delayed, it became imperative at once to make effort to raise the siege of Knoxville.

November 29th, General Howard marched from Parker's Gap to Cleveland, taking the lead in the movement upon Knoxville. He was followed immediately by General Sherman's three divisions, under General F. P. Blair, and General Davis' division of the Fourteenth Corps. On the 30th, General Granger left Chattanooga with two divisions of the Fourth Corps for the same destination.

Brigadier-General Elliot, who had recently been appointed chief of cavalry in the Department of the Cumberland, and who had concentrated the troops of his first division at Sparta, moved in conjunction with the infantry forces. Colonel

VOL. II—1

Long's brigade moved to the head of the column, and on the 2d of December, the Fifteenth Pennsylvania and Tenth Ohio Cavalry left Chattanooga for Kingston. Colonel Spears' brigade, that had been previo..sly stationed on the north bank of the Tennessee river above Chattanooga, also moved toward Knoxville. General Sherman's command embraced more than eight divisions of infantry, while five were left to garrison Chattanooga. Supplies for the troops in motion were sent up the river on the steamer Dunbar, but the main dependence was upon the country.

On the 30th, General Howard advanced from Cleveland to Charleston, on the Hiawassee river. As he approached the town, the enemy's cavalry retreated toward Athens. They had previously partially destroyed the railroad bridge, and had made effort to destroy the pontoons also. But a large number of the boats were saved, and during the following night the railroad bridge was repaired and planked over, so that in the morning the Eleventh Corps passed over, followed by the rear forces. The head of column reached Athens the next evening. The march of the infantry was resumed on the 2d and Colonel Long hurried on to Loudon to save the bridge, if possible. He, however, found the enemy in such force that he could not make a dash, as had been anticipated. The town was well fortified, and was held by infantry and artillery, under General Vaughan, and he could only skirmish until General Howard should get up. The latter reached the position on the 3d, but the enemy had evacuated it the night previous, having first destroyed the bridge, three locomotives, and from sixty to seventy-five cars containing commissary stores, clothing, and ammunition. The pontoon bridge had also been partially destroyed. Notwithstanding the immense destruction of supplies, three days' rations were found uninjured. From this point, Colonel Long was sent with picked men to communicate with General Burnside. On the 4th, Colonel Hecker's brigade crossed the river, skirmished with the cavalry, and took possession of four rifled cannon, which the enemy could remove, and captured a flag. Here General Howard found about thirty wagons partially destroyed, which he repaired for use in forming a temporary bridge, in anticipation of crossing the Little Tennessee river at Davis' ford. The route by this ford was not the one which had been designated, but it was ascertained that time could be saved, and the march shortened by advancing upon it rather than upon the road to Morgantown, and General Sherman permitted General Howard to use it.

Before leaving Loudon, General Howard received an order to command the left wing of the army, while the center and righ twere placed respectively under Generals Granger and Blair. These divisions of the army were to act independently, but to march to each other's support when called by the noise of battle.

December 5th, General Howard crossed the Little Tennessee river, at Davis' ford, by means of an extemporized bridge formed of wagons and movable trestles, and reached Louisville at dark. At night, the three heads of column communicated at Marysville. Here information was received that Longstreet had raised the siege of Knoxville, and retreated eastward. He assaulted Fort Sanders, the key to the position, on the 29th, and was repulsed with heavy loss. Aware, subsequently, of the proximity of Sherman's army, he sought safety in timely retreat. All the forces were now ordered to halt, and the day following, General Sherman met General Burnside at Knoxville. It was then agreed that the Fourth Corps should remain and the other forces return to Chattanooga.

The countermarch was commenced on the 7th. A halt was made at Athens, with the various columns so disposed as to cover a movement of Colonel Long, who had gone toward North Carolina to cut off one of Longstreet's trains. Upon his return, the infantry forces marched to Chattanooga. Howard's corps and Davis' division resumed their old relations in the Army of the Cumberland, and Sherman's divisions returned to the West.

Though the march to East Tennessee involved no serious fighting with Longstreet's command, which was lost to General Bragg in his emergency at Chattanooga, it nevertheless thoroughly accomplished its object, as it forced the former from Knoxville toward the East, in what proved to be perpetual separation from the Confederate Army of the Tennessee. It was a hard march, as the troops commenced it immediately after a series of engagements, and Sherman's forces after a long march from the West. The latter had "stripped for the fight" at Bridgeport, and they, with many from other commands, were destitute of suitable clothing for a winter campaign. Besides, their supplies were drawn mainly from the country, and in a hurried movement this source is exceedingly precarious. Supplies were sent up the river in boats it is true, but the army was not always near the river; and, on the whole, the circumstances were such as none but veteran soldiers would easily overcome. The mills were seized in advance, and run night and day; and a broad belt of country in the march and countermarch paid exhaustive contributions. There were some excesses which were reprehensible, especially as the march was through a region whose inhabitants were mainly loyal. General Davis' division, by its order on the march and its restraint from pillage, elicited special praise from General Sherman. In this commendable and conspicuous bearing, this division represented the Army of the Cumberland, which, throughout its existence, was systematically restrained from pillage and irresponsible foraging.

The objects now were to hold all the territory which had been gained, to maintain and perfect communications, reinforce, recuperate, and reorganize the army, and accumulate supplies and material, all looking to offensive movements, as early as practicable. The enemy was in no condition for aggression on a grand scale, but great vigilance and skillful dispositions were necessary to maintain communications and prevent cavalry raids and guerrilla depredations.

Upon the withdrawal of the troops from Ringgold, General Hooker resumed the occupation of Lookout valley. General Cruft was directed, with his two brigades, to stop on the way and bury the national dead on the battle-field of Chickamauga,* and then to take position on the railroad between

---

* War's visage, despite the glory of heroism and victory, and all the gentle courtesies which enemies may extend at all times, except when the rage of battle brooks no restraint, is grim and forbidding; but when the ordinary usages of civilized and Christian nations in the conduct of

Whitesides and Bridgeport. Colonel Watkins' brigade of the First division of cavalry was directed to take post at Rossville; and the Ninety-second Illinois Mounted Infantry was sent to Caperton's ferry, to guard and observe at that point. A pioneer brigade, composed of detachments from various regiments, Colonel G. P. Buell commanding, was employed in the construction of a double-track macadamized road over the nose of Lookout Mountain, to serve as a communication between Lookout valley and Chattanooga, without dependence upon pontoon bridges. Beyond this primary use, this road was essential to overland communications with Bridgeport. The repair of the railroad commanded immediate attention, but as two long and high bridges were to be built—one over the Tennessee river at Bridgeport, and the one over Falling Water, near Whitesides—much time was required.

When the army returned from East Tennessee, the Eleventh Corps went into camp at Whitesides; two brigades of Davis' division, east of Missionary Ridge, near Rossville; and the third at the mouth of the North Chickamauga. General Elliott was ordered to establish his headquarters at Athens, and post pickets at Calhoun, Columbus, and Tellico Plains.

During the months of November and December, there were several brilliant contests in resisting the enemy's cavalry, repressing guerrillas, and scouting to the front to ascertain the strength and movements of the enemy. And in most cases the national troops were victorious.

November 2d, Brigadier-General R. S. Granger, command-

---

war are ignored, then are its features forbidding in the extreme. The carnage and suffering are appalling when cool reflection and the kindly sympathies have play; but all strong terms are inadequate to express the wanton barbarities of war, either in cruelty to the living or dishonor to the dead, and on both counts the leaders of the rebellion must be convicted. Andersonville and other prisons, where starvation and want of room for captives entailed the intensest suffering and fearful mortality, and Chickamauga, with its hundreds of unburied dead, give proof of the most revolting inhumanity. General Bragg accepted an exchange of prisoners who were wounded, but he denied burial to multitudes of the slain. The national dead upon that part of the field occupied by General Longstreet were buried; but very many on their right, where General Polk commanded, lay upon the ground for two months.

ing at Nashville, sent a mixed command, under Lieutenant-Colonel Sculley, First Middle Tennessee Infantry, to look after Hawkins, and other guerrilla chiefs, near Piner's factory. Sculley met them, and having routed the party, pursued to Centerville. At this point, as he was crossing the river, Hawkins attacked in turn, but was again routed, and his partisans were dispersed. His loss was from fifteen to twenty killed, and sixty-six prisoners.

November 4th, Major Fitzgibbon, of the Fourteenth Michigan Infantry, fought near Lawrenceburg the guerrilla bands of Cooper, Kirk, Williams, and Scott. After a hand-to-hand contest, Fitzgibbon defeated them, killing eight, wounding seven, and capturing twenty-four men. Among the captured were a captain and two lieutenants. The victor had three men slightly wounded, and eight horses killed.

On the 13th, Captain Cutler, with one company of mounted infantry from the garrison at Clarksville, and a section of Whitmore's battery, had a contest with Captain Gray's company of guerrillas, near Palmyra. He killed two, wounded five, and captured one. The same day, fifteen prisoners were captured near Lebanon, and forty by Missener, near Columbia.

On the 16th, General Payne sent parties from Gallatin and La Vergne. Five guerrillas were killed, and twenty-six were captured, also horses, cattle, sheep, and hogs, which had been collected for the Confederate army.

The next day, Colonel Coburn sent an expedition from Murfreesboro against the enemy's irregular cavalry. A detachment of the Fourth Tennessee Cavalry captured nineteen guerrillas and twenty horses, without loss.

On the 21st, an expedition was sent down the Tennessee river, which destroyed nine boats for local use, some of them being sixty feet long. They were wrested from the enemy.

On the 26th, the First Tennessee Cavalry and Ninth Pennsylvania Cavalry, under Colonel Brownlow, attacked Colonel Murray, at Sparta. He killed one man, wounded two, and captured ten. Extensive salt-works were destroyed, and some horses and ammunition were taken.

The same day, Captain Brixie's scouts encountered a party

of guerrillas near Bathsheba Springs, capturing fifteen or twenty, and dispersing the remainder.

December 12th, Colonel Watkins, with two hundred and fifty men, from the Fourth and Sixth Kentucky Cavalry, made a dash upon Lafayette, Georgia, and captured a colonel of the Georgia home guard, six officers of the signal corps, and thirty horses and mules, and returned to his camp at Rossville, without loss. On the 27th, the colonel sent Major Willing, with one hundred and fifty men from the same regiments, to McLemore's Cove and Lafayette. The major captured one lieutenant, sixteen men, and thirty-eight horses and mules.

On the 15th, General Dodge captured a small party of cavalry, under command of Major Joe Fontaine, General Roddy's adjutant, not far from Pulaski, Tennessee. This party had made a reconnoissance on the Nashville and Chattanooga and Nashville and Decatur railroads, which doubtless had some relation to projected movements or raids. It suggested greater vigilance along these important roads.

December 27th, General Wheeler, with fifteen hundred men, appeared at Calhoun, Tennessee, with evident expectation of capturing a train under escort of Laiboldt's brigade. Colonel Laiboldt charged this force, and routed it speedily, and Colonel Long, with one hundred and fifty men, having come from the opposite side of the river, in support, moved in pursuit, believing that a small force had been cut off from the main body. By a saber charge, this force was scattered in all directions. One hundred and thirty-one prisoners were taken, including five officers, one a division inspector and one a surgeon. The number of killed and wounded was not ascertained. Colonel Long lost two killed, twelve wounded, and one missing. Wheeler commanded in person, and anticipated rich booty with slight trouble, but failed in his object, with heavy loss.

CHAPTER XXIV.

GENERAL VIEW OF THE STATUS OF THE CONFLICT AT THE CLOSE OF 1863.

THE year 1863 was crowded with disaster to the insurgents. They were victorious in some of the great battles in Virginia, but lost fearfully in the battle of Gettysburg. So that, at the East, where only they had been at all successful, their strength was relatively less than at the beginning of the year. In the West, their losses in men, material of war, and territory were immense. In their effort to maintain their hold upon the Mississippi river, they lost two armies, and when subsequently the "Father of Waters" flowed "unvexed to the sea," and the supremacy of the national navy upon this great river and its tributaries was unquestioned, all contiguous portions of the insurgent states were at the mercy of the national armies. At the close of the year the central offensive line was resting upon the northern limits of Alabama, Georgia, and North Carolina. The loss of so much territory, the complete division of what remained by the navy moving at pleasure upon the Mississippi river, and the immense diminution of men and means, gave new conditions to the campaigns of the next year.

Besides the effect of numerous defeats during the year, two proclamations of the President of the United States greatly alarmed the insurgents. On the 1st day of January, 1863, he proclaimed freedom to all the slaves in the revolted states, and in the last month he promised pardon to all below a given grade, in the insurgent armies.

As a sequence of the freedom of the slaves, and as a war measure of great moment, arms were soon put in their hands.

(8)

At first, however, the enrollment of the freedmen as soldiers was only occasionally undertaken by individual department commanders in absence of any general plan or explicit authority from Washington. Though slavery directly and indirectly was the dominant cause of the war, there was manifest reluctance for nearly three years to lay hands upon it, and after its abolition was decreed, the national authorities hesitated to make soldiers of those whose bondage they had broken. The slaves had aided the enemy not only by their productive labor, but also by the construction of defenses, and contributed to the strength of the rebellion in greater measure, than they had previously given political weight to the Southern States, in Congress. The more moderate and far-seeing men of the South anticipated, from the first, that sooner or later the African race would be involved in the war. And later than many of this class anticipated, and a growing party in the North demanded, the President pronounced the freedom of the negroes in the seceded states. Their enlistment as soldiers was so plainly a legitimate consequent that it was not long delayed. Both measures were repugnant to the traditional and inveterate prejudices of the Southern people, and of many in the North as well. In the official utterances of the Confederate President, the reprehension of the civilized world was invoked upon those who proposed these measures, and the total destruction of the Africans in America was predicted. But the argument in their support was so simple and forcible that serious opposition to either soon ceased in the North. As the slaves were a source of strength to the rebellion, the logic of war first declared them contraband, and then demanded their employment as soldiers. The fact that their freedom was contingent upon the overthrow of the Southern Confederacy, not only justified their grasp of the musket, but enforced its obligation. And the results vindicated the policy, as colored regiments greatly augmented the national armies for the campaigns of 1864.

The President's offer of pardon to the masses in the Confederate armies, had marked effect. It gave assurance that peace could ensue without the entailment of penal criminality upon those in arms against the government below the rank of brigadier-general, and hence removed the necessity that mere desperation should keep them under the standards of treason. And as this promise of amnesty involved no hard conditions, and was made at a time of general despondency in the South, and when such was the depreciation of Confederate money, that no poor man could give even partial support to a family from his pay as a soldier, it prompted numerous desertions. Desertion being added to the drain of active campaigns, the diminution of the insurgent armies became alarming to the leaders. But they still claimed that the independence of the Southern States was assured, and on this ground, in part justified a conscription of widest compass. The people did not bear this patiently. Murmurs of discontent became general. Occasionally there was open protest and severest criticism. But as nothing but counter-revolution could remedy the evil, and as this step plainly led through anarchy to submission to the general government, the relentless conscription of young and old, and the sweeping appropriation of private property was endured. As a result, sullenness and discouragement took the place of cheer and hope in their armies, and outward restraint rather than moral force kept multitudes in the ranks; while the certainty of pardon, in the event of the failure of the rebellion, induced those not ready to desert to weigh the cost of protracting a contest when success was extremely doubtful. But the leaders, after a year of gigantic reverses, standing upon the threshhold of new campaigns with diminished armies, as boldly as ever declared that subjugation was impossible. President Davis, in his annual message to his congress, announced that "grave reverses had befallen the Confederate armies," and that the hope of a speedy termination of the war, entertained at the beginning of the year, had not been realized, and yet asserted that peace could only come with the acknowledgment of the independence of the Confederate States. Even after General Lee's defeat at Gettysburg, the fall of Vicksburg and Port Hudson, and the retreat of General Bragg's army over Cumberland Mountains, M. T. Maury assured the world, in a paper published in the "London Times," that the prospect of success to the South was brighter than at any former period of the war. Whether

GENERAL VIEW AT THE CLOSE OF 1863. 11

this assurance was real or assumed, on the part of the leaders, and whether they had to any great extent the sympathy of the masses in their avowed hopes, such was the power of the Confederate government and the momentum of the rebellion, that armies of fair defensive proportions were maintained, and some of the Southern generals even entertained projects of aggression.

The events of the year as affecting the national cause, viewed from a military or political stand-point, were cheering in the extreme. The victories of the national armies and the support of war measures as evinced by the elections, equally indicated that the crisis of the nation's destiny had been safely passed. The strength of the rebellion had culminated, and the general situation gave encouragement to the government and those who supported it, to strike blow after blow until the final one should be given. The elections declared the nation's approval of the President's proclamation of freedom to the slaves, and the policy of making them soldiers, and universal freedom was now as firmly established as a condition of peace as the surrender of the Confederate armies.

The maintenance of the full strength of the national armies was now the grand problem. The term of enlistment of very many regiments would expire early in 1864. Their retirement during active operations would endanger the success of all plans of aggression which might be formed. In fact, the speedy suppression of the rebellion turned upon their retention in the service, and yet there was no law to hold them. Fortunately for the country her citizen soldiers were equal to the emergency, and their voluntary re-enlistment, more stringent drafting, and the enrollment of the freedmen, gave promise of adequate armies.

It was evident at the close of the year that the Army of the Cumberland was again to confront its old enemy, the Army of the Tennessee. After its defeat at Chattanooga, this army took position at Dalton, with a heavy detachment at Buzzard's Roost, and forces also at the strong positions between Dalton and Atlanta. The Western and Atlantic railroad courses through the hills and mountains of Northern Georgia, which give marked advantage to an army acting on the defensive, against another

12   GENERAL VIEW AT THE CLOSE OF 1863.

dependent upon the railroad for supplies. And before the exact character of the next central campaign could be determined, the Confederate generals exerted themselves to give additional strength to the fortresses which nature had provided. Whether they should be able to take the offensive or not, their past experience suggested the propriety of making provision for defense as far to the rear as practicable, while maintaining a strong defensive front.

CHAPTER XXV.

OPERATIONS IN THE DEPARTMENT DURING JANUARY, FEBRUARY, AND MARCH, 1864, AND PREPARATIONS FOR AGGRESSION.

At the beginning of the year 1864, and during the first months of the year, the troops of the Army of the Cumberland were disposed from Knoxville to Bridgeport, and on the railroad from the latter place to Louisville, Kentucky. The attitude of the army was mainly defensive. In fact, it was in no condition for aggression. At least ten thousand animals had died during the siege of Chattanooga, and those which survived were so reduced in strength as to be unfit for service. The army, too, was temporarily weakened by the absence of numerous regiments that had been granted furloughs upon re-enlistment; and previous to the completion of the railroad between Chattanooga and Bridgeport, it was hardly possible to supply the troops at rest on the defensive line, including the Army of the Ohio in East Tennessee. Thus restrained from active operations, its chief duty was preparation for future aggression.

As the primary step, it was imperative to make Chattanooga a reliable proximate base of supplies for an army advancing toward Atlanta. The Confederate army being in winter-quarters in Northern Georgia, could destroy all the productions of that region which it did not consume or transport. So that the accumulation of supplies at Chattanooga, and the continued maintenance of railroad communications with Nashville and Louisville, were conditions of a southward advance; and the practicability of making Chattanooga a base for offensive operations, hinged upon the capacity of a single railroad.

Two railroads from Nashville meet at Stevenson, Alabama, but from their junction to Bridgeport, and thence to Chattanooga, there is only a single track. As the bridges at Bridgeport and Falling Waters were not completed until the 14th of January, half the winter was gone before there was the slightest accumulation of supplies; and though subsequently this single railroad was pressed to its utmost capacity, such were the immediate wants of the armies, and so numerous were the veteran regiments passing over the road, that the large storehouses which had been built at Chattanooga were very slowly filled.

During the first half of January, the enemy was not active. General Thomas sent scouting parties in all directions, but no indications of aggression were discerned. Apart from the exhaustion which the preceding campaigns had produced, a change of commanders was doubtless one cause of inaction. Soon after his defeat before Chattanooga, General Bragg had been removed from command in Georgia, and General Joseph E. Johnston, while charged with the administration of a military division corresponding in extent to the one which had been created for General Grant, assumed personal command of the forces immediately south of Chattanooga. His presence at Dalton indicated his appreciation of the importance of the center of his line, either to regain what had been so recently lost, or to neutralize Chattanooga, as far as possible, as a base for aggressive operations.

By this time, the foreshadows of the campaign which General Grant had projected began to appear. Mobile was his next objective, with Atlanta and Mongomery as important intermediate points.* Not being ready to advance upon the direct line to his objective, he proposed a movement from his right flank by General Sherman, while General Thomas should make effort to hold Johnston's forces at Dalton, and General Foster, commanding in East Tennessee in room of General Burnside, should neutralize Longstreet's army. The objects proposed for General Sherman were the destruction of the railroads from Vicksburg to Meridian, and the capture of Mobile, should its practicability be developed as he advanced. But before he was ready to move, rumors were current that

---

* Statement of plan by General Badeau, in "Life of General Grant."

Longstreet was receiving reinforcements from Virginia. This deranged the plans with regard to the center and left. General Thomas was desirous of recalling his troops from East Tennessee, to be able to demonstrate strongly against Dalton; but it now became necessary that he should have regard to the contingency of sending additional troops to General Foster.

General Longstreet's attitude had been ambiguous since his abandonment of the siege of Knoxville, upon the approach of General Sherman, in December. His presence was a menace, even in absence of operations of direct offense; and as it was possible for reinforcements to reach him from Dalton and from Virginia, an effort to regain the mountain fortresses of East Tennessee was probable, especially if General Johnston could entertain the hope of keeping the war out of Georgia by carrying it to the North. Any plan of aggression on his part would involve the possession of a route to the northeast of Chattanooga, and for a time such a course was plainly indicated or feigned.

When, on the 15th of January, General Wood advanced to Dandridge and drove the rebel cavalry from the town, an offensive return was provoked, which for a time threatened to change General Grant's plans very materially. Though General Wood was joined by General Sheridan's division and McCook's cavalry at Dandridge, it was not deemed safe to hazard a general engagement. For two days there was skirmishing, and late in the afternoon of the 18th, there was a brisk conflict mainly between McCook's cavalry and Longstreet's advance. Three Ohio regiments—the First, Ninety-third, and One Hundred and Twenty-fifth—were holding the front as pickets, and were severely pressed by a tentative advance of the enemy, but they fought bravely to cover the preparations for a retreat. McCook, by a saber charge, cleared the field and captured two steel rifle-guns, and over one hundred prisoners. This action and the darkness permitted the safe retreat of the national troops. They fell back, first to Strawberry Plains, and subsequently to Marysville, followed by Longstreet.

Simultaneously with this movement, General Roddy crossed the Tennessee river near Florence, Alabama, with two brigades of cavalry. General Dodge, commanding troops of General Sherman's army at Pulaski, Tennessee, received information on the 20th, that he was preparing boats and concealing them with the evident purpose of crossing his command for a raid upon the railroads. General Grant at once advised General Thomas of the fact, and directed him to organize an expedition to drive Roddy back, and destroy his boats and all material which could be used in effecting the passage of the river. But he was across two days before these instructions were communicated, and General Thomas could only make arrangements to defeat his purpose. He directed the detachments guarding the roads to watch against attacks, and ordered General Crook commanding cavalry at Huntsville, Alabama, to advance against Roddy and drive him across the river.

Colonel H. O. Miller, Ninety-second Indiana, commanding one expedition, defeated Johnson's brigade near Florence on the 26th, killing fifteen, and wounding and capturing a large number. Among the prisoners were three officers. His own loss was ten wounded. General Gillem also sent parties from the line of the Northwestern railroad against Roddy, as soon as he heard that he had crossed the river. These parties returned on the 30th with Lieutenant-Colonel Brewer, two captains, three lieutenants, and twenty men as prisoners. Having thus met forces between him and the railroad in all directions, Roddy recrossed the river, having effected no damage that compensated for his losses.

January 27th, the cavalry under General Elliott, in a brilliant action at Mossy Creek, East Tennessee, defeated General Martin, commanding two divisions of cavalry, Morgan's and Armstrong's, and followed his routed forces until darkness terminated the pursuit. Campbell's and La Grange's brigades were engaged, and they put the enemy to rout by a saber charge, capturing one hundred and twelve prisoners, including two regimental commanders and seven other officers, two rifled guns, eight hundred small arms, Morgan's battle-flag, and two regimental flags, which the enemy had previously captured from the national troops, and killed and wounded over two hundred men, exclusive of prisoners. Morgan's division was thoroughly broken, and Armstrong's was thrown into rapid re-

OPERATIONS FROM JANNARY TO MARCH, 1864. 17

treat. Guerrillas were also active. January 20th, one hundred and fifty guerrillas attacked Tracy City, and having three times summoned the garrison to surrender, were handsomely repulsed.

The next day, Colonel T. J. Harrison, Thirty-ninth Indiana Mounted Infantry, sent two hundred men on an expedition to Sparta, Tennessee, to look after the guerrillas infesting that region. This party in five subdivisions scoured the country occupied by the bands of Curtis, Ferguson, Bledsoe, and Murray. Remaining out several days, they killed four men, wounded five or six, and captured fifteen, including a captain and lieutenant. They also captured thirty horses and twenty stand of arms.

On the 24th, Colonel Boone, commanding the Twenty-eighth Kentucky Mounted Infantry, with four hundred and forty-six men, moved through McLemore's Cove, crossed to Broomtown valley, and proceeded through Summerville, across Taylor's ridge, to Dirt Town. Beyond the latter place he destroyed a camp of the Georgia militia, captured fifteen men, including Captain Hubbard, and returned without loss.

Upon the completion of the railroad from Bridgeport to Chattanooga, General Thomas transferred the working parties to the road leading to Knoxville, and on the 24th directed General Stanley, commanding the First division of the Fourth Corps, to dispose his command from Chickamauga Station to the Hiawassee river, to protect the workmen on the road. As it had been suggested that troops might be sent to East Tennessee to support Foster against Longstreet, these troops were thus in readiness to meet this contingency while guarding the railroad, and watching against the direct movement of troops from Dalton to Longstreet.

' As deserters concurred in asserting that General Johnston was sending troops south from Dalton, General Thomas directed General Palmer to make a reconnoissance with a portion of his command to ascertain, if possible, whether these representations were true. The latter having accomplished his office by developing a strong force at Tunnel Hill, returned to Chattanooga.

February 10th, General Grant directed General Thomas to prepare for an advance to Knoxville, with such forces as could be spared from the protection of Chattanooga and its communications, to assist General Foster to drive Longstreet from East Tennessee. Such a movement was no part of the original plan, but concurrent reports had convinced General Grant that there had been a heavy concentration of troops under Longstreet to secure East Tennessee, and he determined to prevent it, and relieve that flank from pressure. General Foster had prepared to assume the offensive if he could get at least ten thousand men from General Thomas. It was deemed safe to diminish the forces at Chattanooga, as there was reason to believe that Johnston had detached heavily from Dalton to reinforce Polk against Sherman in Alabama, as well as to strengthen Longstreet for offense against Foster in East Tennessee.

The Army of the Cumberland was not in condition to enter upon a winter campaign, and General Thomas found it difficult to make such preparations as he deemed essential. His army was greatly diminished by the absence of regiments having re-enlisted as veterans. Artillery horses and train animals had not been supplied in room of the thousands that had died from starvation during the siege, and he advised a postponement of the movement until the railroad would be in running order to Loudon. On the 12th, however, the day previous to the one designated for starting, he was informed by General Grant that a conversation with General Foster, who, on account of ill-health, had been superseded by General Schofield, and dispatches from the latter, induced him to doubt the propriety of moving against Longstreet, and suggested that should he not be required to go into East Tennessee, he should make a formidable reconnoissance toward Dalton, and if possible occupy that place, and repair the railroads to it. This order was given on the 17th, and at the time there was some probability that it might be successful, as it was supposed that Johnston had weakened his center, especially to strengthen Polk against Sherman. Two days later, however, General Thomas received information that Johnston had in hand six divisions, comprising from thirty to forty thousand men, and that no troops had been sent away, except one brigade of infantry. This intelligence did not, however, induce General Grant to recall the movement, though it rendered General Thomas hopeless of success.

The troops were put in motion toward Dalton, February 22d. General Thomas threw General Stanley's division, General Cruft commanding, with such cavalry as he could safely withdraw from Calhoun, Tennessee, forward on the Spring Place road, and Johnston's and Baird's divisions, with cavalry in advance and on the right flank, directly to Ringgold. At night, Cruft's division was at Red Clay, with Long's cavalry in advance, having been instructed to observe the enemy well toward Dalton, and give timely warning of any effort to turn Cruft's left flank, or to notify him to advance should Johnston retire. The other divisions were at Ringgold, in position on the ridge west of East Chickamauga, with a regiment of mounted infantry on each flank, and Carlin's brigade thrown toward Taylor's ridge.

During the evening, General Palmer advised General Thomas that he had received intelligence that Johnston had dispatched Cheatham's and Cleburne's divisions to reinforce General Polk, who was falling back before General Sherman, in Alabama. All available troops were now moved up to dislodge General Johnston, should this report prove to be true. Davis' division advanced to Ringgold on the 23d, and General Matthias was directed to send six regiments from Cleveland to support General Cruft, at Red Clay. Colonel Long advanced toward Dalton, on the Spring Place road; first drove in the enemy's videttes, and when within four miles of Dalton, attacked and routed from camp a regiment of infantry. The enemy then forming in force, he withdrew to Russell's Mills. Cruft's division advanced to Lee's house, on the road from Red Clay to Tunnel Hill. The four divisions were now well concentrated in the vicinity of Ringgold, and after a thorough reconnoissance on each flank, General Palmer advanced, on the 24th, to develop the enemy's strength at Tunnel Hill. After skirmishing three or four miles with Wheeler's cavalry, he gained possession of the town, when the enemy formed a new line, and opened with his batteries from a hill, one mile beyond. General Palmer then withdrew, and encamped three miles to the northwest. The following morning he decided to feel the enemy's position more fully. Baird's division was south of Taylor's Ridge near Ringgold, and Cruft's was well closed up on its left. Davis'* and Johnson's divisions were in the advance toward Tunnel Hill, with Harrison's mounted infantry in front, and Boone's on the left flank, and Long's brigade, supported by Grose's brigade of Cruft's division, was at Varnell's station, on the Dalton and Cleveland railroad. These pairs of divisions were ordered to advance on different lines, the former upon Tunnel Hill, and, if practicable, directly upon Dalton; the latter, with Long's cavalry, to move down the valley, along the eastern base of Rocky Face Ridge, to threaten the right and rear of the enemy.

In compliance, the troops on the right advanced in three columns. After the right and left had moved some distance, the center advanced, but was soon checked by a battery of Parrott guns planted on the summit beyond the town of Tunnel Hill, and skillfully handled. The right and left columns, Morgan's and Hambright's brigades, again advanced, and flanking this battery, forced its retirement. Davis' division, with Johnson's in support, pursued and found the enemy at Buzzard's Roost, a gap in Rocky Face Ridge, whose precipitous acclivities and salient summits forbade assault. Baird and Cruft also encountered the enemy as they moved down Rocky Face valley. Giving ground at first, he soon offered resistance upon a central hill. An attack was here necessary to develop his strength; and General Turchin, with four regiments, the Eleventh, Eighty-ninth, and Ninety-second Ohio, and the Eighty-second Indiana, was directed to advance. Advancing boldly, these troops pressed back the enemy and reached the summit, but were unable to hold it, as the routed troops met reinforcements, and returned in overwhelming force. The conflict was sharp, but it was too unequal to be maintained, and Turchin yielded the hill. Spirited skirmishing and cannonading were continued until nightfall, when the national troops were withdrawn. Colonel Harrison spent

---

* General Davis' division had previously closed up from the rear.

the night at a gap six miles south of Buzzard's Roost, nearly opposite Dalton, whence he was driven the following morning by Cleburne's division, one of the two that had been dispatched to Alabama.

As it had been ascertained that General Johnston was holding his strong positions with forces superior to his own, General Thomas deemed it futile to attempt to dislodge him, and that it was even impracticable to maintain his threatening attitude. The country was stripped of provisions, and his transportation was not sufficient to supply his command. He therefore advised General Grant of his embarrassment, and suggested the abandonment of the enterprise. In reply, General Grant urged him to maintain his position, and make the impression upon Johnston that an advance into the heart of the South was intended, until the fate of General Sherman should be known. Compliance, however, was not considered practicable, and as it was known that Johnston had recalled his divisions from Polk's support, orders were issued for the withdrawal of the troops. Baird's division was posted on a line of hills north of the town of Tunnel Hill, to cover the retirement of Johnson and Davis, and then took permanent post at Ringgold. Davis' division returned to his former position near Rossville. Two brigades of Johnson's division were posted at Tyner's Station, and the third at Graysville, with a strong guard at Parker's Gap, to protect Baird's left flank. Cruft's division returned to Ooltawah and Blue Springs, the commander sending a detachment to Cleveland to guard his supplies, where Colonel Long also took post to patrol the left flank of the army. Colonels Harrison and Boone were stationed at Leet's tanyard, to observe the enemy toward Lafayette.

This movement to Dalton involved a loss of more than three hundred men killed and wounded. Among the wounded was Colonel Mihalotzy, of the Twenty-fourth Illinois, who died a few days later at Chattanooga. The enemy's loss was probably two hundred. As a reconnoissance it was successful, though there were no such results as General Grant mentioned as probable. It seemingly recalled the two divisions that General Johnston had sent against General Sherman, but as the latter had retreated from Meridian on the 20th, six days previous to their return, the demonstration had no effect upon their movements. The chief advantages were the development of the strength of General Johnston's position before Dalton, and the suggestion to General Thomas of a plan to turn it by a movement through Snake Creek Gap. He was so impressed with the feasibility of this plan, that upon his return to Chattanooga, he requested permission from General Grant to make preparation to accomplish it.

Having disposed his troops for defense, General Thomas addressed himself to preparation for the spring campaign. He ordered General Butterfield to make a careful examination of the Nashville and Chattanooga railroad, and Captain Merrill, chief engineer of the department, to examine other roads, to ascertain the minimum force necessary to hold them securely. He also ordered a thorough examination of the railroad to Tunnel Hill, with a view to its repair, as an important step in provision for an advance.

These examinations resulted in a more economical protection of railroad communications, by means of a system of block-houses at the bridges and other important points, which became an element of power to the close of the war. And the conclusion having been reached that six thousand infantry and two thousand cavalry could hold securely the railroads to Nashville, General Thomas recommended that the railroad guards, as far as practicable, should be drawn from the local Tennessee militia.

The month of February closed with the military situation by no means developed. General Sherman destroyed railroads extensively in Mississippi, but otherwise his expedition was not compensative. It was not known what Longstreet would do, whether give further trouble in East Tennessee, return to Virginia, or join Johnston. Neither were General Johnston's plans at all indicated. One day would bring rumors from deserters, and from sources more reliable, that he was under orders to withdraw his army from Dalton, followed on the next by contradictions from sources equally entitled to credence. But ignorance of the purposes of the enemy did not prevent preparation for aggression. Reconstruction of railroads was pressed westward and southward, and material and supplies were accumulated as rapidly as possible. Steamboats and large storehouses were built. Horses were provided for the artillery, and efforts were made to recuperate those of the cavalry worn down by hard winter service. Eight companies of the First Michigan Engineers and Mechanics, and two regiments of colored troops, were ordered to commence the construction of block-houses and other defenses along the line of the Nashville and Chattanooga railroad, and the first Missouri Engineers and Mechanics were detailed for similar duty on the Nashville and Decatur railroad. In anticipation of a campaign designed to bisect the Gulf States east of the Mississippi river, the secure defense of railroad communications from Chattanooga to the North with the least possible draft upon the strength of the aggressive columns, was a matter of great moment. With strong block-houses at all the bridges, and with earthworks, in addition, at all of the more important points, a comparatively small force could hold the roads securely—at least, could prevent all damage that could not be quickly repaired. One of the greatest embarrassments to Generals Buell and Rosecrans, had been the necessity of scattering their troops in heavy detachments on their lines of supply. The plan now adopted promised better security, both to the railroads and to the troops guarding them, while employing a small portion of the force formerly assigned to this service. Besides, it transferred the cavalry almost entirely from the rear to the front, and relieved the veteran infantry from guard duty, as new regiments and local militia could be trusted to hold the block-houses and earthworks.

At the beginning of March there were indications that General Johnston was receiving reinforcements at Dalton, and General Grant was not free from apprehension that Longstreet's army might join him, in addition to other forces, for an attack upon Chattanooga. To provide against such a contingency, the two divisions of the Fourth Corps in East Tennessee were ordered to be constantly ready for quick movement to support General Thomas. On the 3d, Wagner's brigade of Sheridan's division was moved to Calhoun, Tennessee, to relieve the first brigade of the first division of cavalry, Colonel Campbell commanding, that it might take post at Cleveland. Five days later, Colonel Daniel McCook, commanding second brigade of Davis' division, was ordered to Lee and Gordon's Mills, to give strength to the front, and observe the enemy upon a line of former approach. The same day, Colonel Harrison was driven from Leet's tanyard by a strong force of cavalry. This advance, coupled with rumors that Johnston had been joined by ten thousand men from South Carolina and by Roddy's cavalry, that Longstreet's cavalry was in motion toward him, and that his troops were under orders to carry three days' rations on their persons, intensified somewhat the apprehension that an offensive movement was meditated. There were no changes of troops, however, except that McCook's division of cavalry was ordered to Cleveland, since it was not yet deemed safe to withdraw the Fourth Corps from East Tennessee, as Longstreet's action was still uncertain.

On the 17th of March, General Grant, having been appointed lieutenant-general, in command of the entire army, advised General Thomas that Major-General W. T. Sherman had been assigned to the command of the Military Division of the Mississippi. The assumption of general command by General Grant gave the contemplated campaign into Georgia a closer relation to operations against General Lee's army in Virginia than had previously existed between movements east and west.

Soon after his assignment to the command of the military division, General Sherman went to Chattanooga to confer with General Thomas with regard to future movements. At this conference, General Thomas suggested that the armies of the Tennessee and Ohio, under the respective commands of Major-Generals McPherson and Schofield, should demonstrate against Johnston's position before Dalton, by the direct roads to Buzzard's Roost, and from Cleveland, while he should throw the entire Army of the Cumberland through Snake Creek Gap, which he knew to be unguarded, and fall upon Johnston's communications between Dalton and Resaca, and thereby turn his position completely, and either force him to retreat toward the east, through a difficult country poorly supplied with provisions and forage, with a strong probability of the total disorganization of his army, or attack him, in which event he felt confident of being able to beat him, especially as he hoped to gain position in his rear before he should be aware of his movement. General Sherman objected to this suggestion, for the reason that he desired the Army of the Cumberland to form the reserve of the united armies, and to serve as a rallying point from which the two wings, the armies of the Tennessee and Ohio, could operate.

The union of the armies of the Cumberland, Tennessee, and Ohio in a campaign from Chattanooga as a base, having been determined upon, preparations of the grandest dimensions possible were at once inaugurated with vigor. The most difficult problem was that of supplies. Its solution turned upon the capacity of a single railroad track from Stevenson to Chattanooga, and thence toward Atlanta. There was steamboat transportation from Bridgeport to Chattanooga; but there was dependence alone upon the track from the former place to Stevenson. As the accumulation of supplies at Chattanooga had hitherto been slight, General Sherman restricted railroad transportation to dead freight, and forbade passage to citizens or private property. He also forbade the further issue of rations to the destitute citizens of the country. The people complained of these measures; but such was the necessity for the accumulation of supplies, that he persisted in their maintenance, against the protests of the citizens, remonstrances from Washington, and what under other circumstances would have been the demands of humanity.

During the month of April, again, as before the battles in November, Chattanooga was the scene of the greatest activity. Troops were constantly coming up from the rear and moving to position in the front. The quartermaster and commissary departments were pressed to extreme exertion building steamboats, erecting and filling vast storehouses, bringing forward artillery and cavalry horses, mules, and cattle; while the railway was almost constantly trembling under the long trains heavily loaded with supplies and munitions.

General Johnston, in the meantime, was not idle, though he was restrained in his preparation for an offensive movement, which it was expected in the South he would be able to make in such force as to change the theater of war again to the North. He waited for preparation for well-sustained aggression, and thus lost an opportunity for partial success. Cleveland was the weak point in the national line. General Thomas could not hold this vital point strongly while the Fourth Corps remained with General Schofield, and this corps could not be safely withdrawn until it was known that Longstreet had abandoned East Tennessee. But before Johnston was well prepared even for defense, the opportunity was lost for forcing any concentration of troops which was not required by General Sherman's plan of operations. General Johnston was fully alive to the importance of successful aggression to change the tone of feeling in the South, and sought such reinforcements as he thought were necessary. A little later he learned that he needed more troops than were available in all the South, upon the plan of defense which was adopted. In the light of subsequent events, it is plain that in failing to give adequate reinforcements to Johnston, while General Grant's armies were widely separated and weakened by the temporary absence of veteran regiments, the Confederate authorities at Richmond rendered impossible the aggression for which they subsequently clamored. In December previous, General Beauregard suggested, as the only hope of success, that Richmond and other important places should be fortified and garrisoned for defense, and that an immense army should be concentrated against Grant, at Chattanooga, or thrown in bold offense from Knoxville. Later, General Johnston's suggestions were somewhat similar, but were unheeded, by Mr. Davis and his advisers. The Western army remained in diffusion, until concentration, as a necessity of defense rather than a condition of aggression, was hurriedly effected. Longstreet's army was sent to General Lee, and from all of the troops that so long menaced Knoxville, only Martin's division of cavalry joined General Johnston; while almost all the national troops that wintered in East Tennessee were free to join the combination against him. The impracticable President had entertained visions of successful aggression from Dalton, but had been, from choice or necessity, so sparing in provision for such enterprise, that the thought of it, except in wildest vagary, could not be entertained. To require Johnston to advance with less than fifty thousand men against a combination of armies, which in defense would greatly exceed one hundred thousand, was to exact defeat. The fact that the Confederate President did not discern this, revealed his incapacity as a revolutionary leader, and his subsequent criticisms of his ablest general, for the non-accomplishment of a palpable impossibility, manifested the inveteracy of his self-conceit and his utter misapprehension of the situation in Georgia. His general had no choice of methods, but was confined to the defense of his positions between his enemy and the campaign region south of Resaca. Had he been able to assume the offensive, he could not have reached any vital point in the rear of Chattanooga, without a long detour, in dependence for supplies upon a devastated country, or on wagon transportation from a remote base. In his weakness and his restriction from movement by mountain barriers right and left, he could make no flank movements or threatening dashes, with infantry or cavalry; and any expectation of a general advance from Dalton, except with an immense army, through East Tennessee or Northern Alabama, Bridgeport or Decatur—was groundless.

Having now, from necessity, accepted the defensive, General Johnston could only make effort to embarrass Sherman's communications with his cavalry, and await the approach of the armies combining against him. He threw his cavalry into Northern Alabama, in constant menace, but accomplished no interruption to communications. General Thomas sent General Geary, with two regiments and one piece of artillery, on a steamboat, to destroy the boats used by the cavalry in crossing and recrossing the river, as far to the west as possible. General Geary was only partially successful; he destroyed a great many boats in going and coming, but was prevented by forces on each side of the river from going a great distance.

On the 29th of April, a tentative advance was made by General Baird, having reference to the general movement of the united armies. He sent three hundred cavalry, under General Kilpatrick, supported by Vanderveer's brigade, to feel the enemy's position at Tunnel Hill. These troops encountered the enemy and drove him some distance, when developing a greatly superior force, they were compelled to withdraw. At Davis' house the enemy pressed them, when they turned and repulsed him handsomely. The day following, General Johnston gave indications of greater strength in front of Ringgold, and General Thomas instructed General Baird to call upon General Johnson for help in the event of an advance against his position.

During the month, important changes were made in the Army of the Cumberland. The reorganization of the Fourth and Fourteenth Corps having been of recent date, they remained intact, except some changes in general officers. On the 11th, the cavalry, under the general command of Brigadier-General W. L. Elliott, was organized into four divisions; Colonel Edward McCook, and Brigadier-Generals Kennard Garrard, Judson Kilpatrick, and A. C. Gillem, commanding respectively, according to numerical designation. There were three brigades in each division, and an average of three regiments in each brigade. On the 15th, orders were received from Washington, requiring the consolidation of the Eleventh and Twelfth Corps as the Twentieth, under the command of Major-General Hooker. Major-General Gordon Granger was relieved from the command of the Fourth Corps, and Major-General O. O. Howard assigned, and Major-General P. H. Sheridan having been transferred to the Army of the Potomac, Major-General John Newton was assigned to the position made vacant by his vacation of the command of the Second division, Fourth Corps.

There were now in the Army of the Cumberland a large number of re-enlisted troops. During the winter and spring there re-enlisted eighty-eight regiments of infantry, three of mounted infantry, sixteen of cavalry, eighteen batteries of artillery, and twenty-six detachments of all arms, and eight thousand one hundred and thirty-six recruits in the aggregate were added to these organizations while on furlough. The importance of the re-enlistment of these troops can not be overestimated. Without them and the "veterans" of the other two co-operative armies, the Atlanta campaign could not have been safely undertaken; the war would have been greatly postponed, and its issue might have been different. The slow movement of the draft, and the provisional measure of short enlistments could

OPERATIONS FROM JANUARY TO MARCH, 1864. 29

not have furnished such troops as were demanded in the spring of 1864. Without the veterans, aggression could not have been entertained, and the feeble armies, during the summer, might have been compelled to relax their grasp upon the heart of the rebellious states. It is then the plainest duty of the historian to mention the regiments and other organizations, whose members, in whole or in part, re-enlisted as " veteran volunteers," and ever after bore the grandest name which the war originated. Of the regiments and batteries whose organization was maintained under re-enlistment, were the Thirteenth, Fifteenth, Seventeenth, Nineteenth, Twenty-first, Twenty-sixth, Thirty-first, Thirty-third, Thirty-sixth, Fortieth, Forty-first, Forty-ninth, Fifth-first, Fifty-fifth, Sixty-first, Sixty-fifth, Sixty-ninth, Seventy-first, Seventy-fourth, and Eighty-second Ohio Infantry; the First, Third, and Fourth Ohio Cavalry, and batteries " B," " C," " F," and " G," First Ohio Artillery; the Twenty-second, Thirtieth, Thirty-first, Thirty-fifth, Fortieth, Forty-second, Forty-fourth, Fifty-first, Fifty-seventh and Fifty-eighth Indiana Infantry; Seventy-ninth Mounted Infantry, and Thirteenth Indiana battery; the Tenth, Twenty-first, Thirty-sixth, Thirty-eighth, Forty-second, Forty-fourth, Fifty-first, Fifty-ninth, and Sixtieth Illinois Infantry, and batteries " H "and " I," Second Illinois Artillery; the Fourth, Eighteenth, Twenty-first, and Twenty-third Kentucky Infantry; the Second, Third, Fourth, and Sixth Kentucky Cavalry, and the Twenty-eighth Kentucky Mounted Infantry; the Forty-sixth, Seventy-third, Seventy-ninth, and One Hundred and Ninth Pennsylvania Infantry, and the Seventh Pennsylvania Cavalry; the Forty-fifth, Fifty-eighth, and Sixtieth New York Infantry, and the New York Independent Battery; the Tenth and Thirteenth Michigan Infanty; the Fourteenth Michigan Mounted Infantry, and the First Michigan battery; the Thirteenth Wisconsin Infantry, and the Fifth Wisconsin battery; the Fifteenth Missouri Infantry, and battery " G," First Missouri Artillery; the Second Minnesota Infantry; the Fifth Iowa Cavalry; the Eighth Kansas Infantry, and Third Maryland Infantry. Of the detachments, there were representatives in greater or less numbers from the Fifth, Seventh, Eleventh, Eighteenth, and Twenty-fourth Ohio Infantry, and the Tenth Independent battery; the Tenth, Fifteenth, Twenty-seventh, and Thirty-seventh Indiana Infantry; the Twenty-first, Twenty-second, and Twenty-seventh Illinois Infantry, and battery "C," First Illinois Artillery; the Eighth Kentucky Infantry; the Seventy-ninth Pennsylvania Infantry; batteries "F" and "M," New York Artillery; the First Michigan Engineers, and battery "E," First Michigan Artillery; the Third Wisconsin battery; the First Missouri Engineers; the Tenth Maine Infantry, and battery "3," Maine Artillery; battery "F," Fourth United States Artillery, and battery "K," Fifth United States Artillery.

On the 1st of May, the Army of the Cumberland was well in hand, awaiting orders to advance. The Fourth Corps, Major-General O. O. Howard commanding, was at Cleveland. The Fourteenth, Major-General J. M. Palmer commanding, was before Chattanooga, and the Twentieth Corps, Major-General Joseph Hooker commanding, was mainly in Lookout valley. The divisions of the Fourth Corps, in numerical order, were commanded by Major-Generals D. S. Stanley and John Newton and Brigadier-General T. J. Wood; those of the Fourteenth, Brigadier-Generals R. W. Johnson, J. C. Davis, and A. Baird, and those of the Twentieth, Brigadier-General A. S. Williams and J. W. Geary and Major-Generals D. Butterfield and Lovell H. Rousseau. The division of the latter, and other troops of infantry, cavalry, and artillery, assigned as garrisons, comprising thirty-two regiments of infantry, nine of cavalry, and thirty-nine batteries, were disposed at all important points from Chattanooga to Nashville, on the direct road, and at Clarksville and Fort Donelson. The cavalry comprised four divisions, under Brigadier-General W. L. Elliott—the first, Colonel McCook commanding, was with the Fourth Corps, at Cleveland; the second under Brigadier-General Garrard, was ordered to report to General McPherson, commanding the Army of the Tennessee; the third under Brigadier-General Kilpatrick, was at Ringgold, and the Fourth, under Brigadier-General Gillem, was at Nashville. The army for the field comprised 54,568 infantry, 3,238 cavalry, and 2,377 artillery, with 130 guns; total, 60,773 effective men.

OPERATIONS FROM JANUARY TO MARCH, 1864. 31

Organization of the Army of the Cumberland, Major-General George H. Thomas commanding, April, 1874.

Fourth Army Corps.
MAJOR-GENERAL O. O. HOWARD COMMANDING.

First Division.
MAJOR-GENERAL D. S. STANLEY *commanding.*

First Brigade.	*Second Brigade.*
GEN. CHARLES CRUFT *commanding.*	GEN. W. C. WHITTAKER *commanding.*
1st Kentucky Infantry.	21st Kentucky Infantry.
2d " "	35th Indiana "
21st Illinois Infantry.	84th " "
38th " "	40th Ohio "
31st Indiana "	51st " "
81st " "	99th " "
90th Ohio "	96th Illinois "
101st " "	115th " "

Third Brigade.
COLONEL WM. GROSE *commanding.*
9th Indiana Infantry.
30th   "   "
36th   "   "
59th Illinois   "
75th   "   "
80th   "   "
84th   "   "
77th Pennsylvania Infantry.

Artillery.
5th Indiana Battery.   Battery " B," Independent Penn.

Second Division.
MAJOR-GENERAL JOHN NEWTON *commanding.*

First Brigade.	*Second Brigade.*
COL. F. T. SHERMAN *commanding.*	GEN. G. D. WAGNER *commanding.*
2d Missouri Infantry.	40th Indiana Infantry.
15th " "	57th " "
24th Wisconsin "	26th Ohio "
28th Kentucky "	97th " "
36th Illinois "	100th Illinois "
44th " "	
73d " "	
74th " "	
88th " «	

Third Brigade.

Colonel C. G. Harker *commanding.*

- 3d Kentucky Infantry.
- 64th Ohio "
- 65th " "
- 125th " "
- 22d Illinois "
- 27th " "
- 42d " "
- 51st " "
- 79th " "

Artillery.

Battery "G," 1st Missouri.   Battery "M," 1st Illinois.

Third Division.

Brigadier-General T. J. Wood *commanding.*

First Brigade.
General A. Willich *commanding.*

- 8th Kansas Infantry.
- 15th Wisconsin Infantry.
- 15th Ohio "
- 49th " "
- 32d Indiana "
- 25th Illinois "
- 35th " "
- 89th " "

Second Brigade.
General W. B. Hazen *commanding.*

- 1st Ohio Infantry.
- 6th " "
- 41st " "
- 93d " "
- 124th Ohio "
- 5th Kentucky Infantry.
- 6th " "
- 23d " "
- 6th Indiana "

Third Brigade.
General Samuel Beatty *commanding.*

- 9th Kentucky Infantry.
- 17th " "
- 13th Ohio "
- 19th " "
- 59th " "
- 79th Indiana "
- 86th " "

Artillery.

6th Ohio Battery.   Bridge's Illinois Light Battery.

Fourteenth Army Corps.
Major-General JOHN M. PALMER commanding.

First Division.
Brigadier-General R. W. Johnson *commanding.*

OPERATIONS FROM JANUARY TO MARCH, 1864.

First Brigade.
GENERAL W. P. CARLIN commanding.
2d Ohio Infantry.
33d "   "
94th "   "
10th Wisconsin Infantry.
15th Kentucky   "
38th Indiana   "
42d   "   "
88th   "   "
104th Illinois   "

Second Brigade.
GENERAL J. H. KING commanding.
15th U. S. Infantry, 1st Battalion.
15th "   . "   2d   "
16th "   "   1st   "
18th "   "   1st   "
18th "   "   2d   "
19th "   "   1st   "
11th Michigan Infantry.
19th Illinois   "
69th Ohio Infantry.

Third Brigade.
COLONEL JAS. M. NEIBLING commanding.
1st Wisconsin Infantry.
21st   "   "
21st Ohio   "
74th "   "
24th Illinois   "
37th Indiana   "
78th Pennsylvania Infantry.
79th   "   "

Artillery.
Battery "A," 1st Michigan.   Battery "C," 1st Illinois.

Second Division.
BRIGADIER-GENERAL JEFF. C. DAVIS commanding.

First Brigade.
GEN. J. D. MORGAN commanding.
10th Illinois Infantry.
16th "   "
60th "   "
10th Michigan "
14th   "   "

Second Brigade.
COL. JOHN G. MITCHELL commanding
98th Ohio Infantry.
108th "   "
113th "   "
121st "   "
34th Illinois "
78th   "   "

Third Brigade.
COLONEL DAN. MCCOOK commanding.
52d Ohio Infantry.
85th Illinois Infantry.
86th   "   "
110th   "   "
125th   "   "
22d Indiana   "

Artillery.

2d Minnesota Battery.* Battery "I," 2d Illinois.
5th Wisconsin Battery.

Third Division.

BRIGADIER-GENERAL A. BAIRD *commanding.*

First Brigade.	*Second Brigade.*
GEN. J. B. TURCHIN *commanding.*	COL. F. VANDERVEER *commanding.*
11th Ohio Infantry.	2d Minnesota Infantry.
17th " "	9th Ohio Infantry.
31st " "	35th " "
36th " "	105th Ohio "
89th " "	75th Indiana Infantry.
92d " "	87th " "
82d Indiana Infantry.	101st " "

Third Brigade.

COLONEL GEO. P. ESTE *commanding.*

4th Kentucky Infantry.
10th   "   "
18th   "   "
10th Indiana   "
74th   "   "
14th Ohio   "
38th   "   "
92d Illinois   "

Artillery.

7th Indiana Battery.   19th Indiana Battery.

Twentieth Army Corps.

MAJOR-GENERAL JOSEPH HOOKER COMMANDING.

Company "K," 15th Illinois Cavalry.
Independent Company, 8th N. Y. Infantry.

First Division.

BRIGADIER-GENERAL A. S. WILLIAMS *commanding.*

First Brigade.	*Second Brigade.*
GEN. JOSEPH KNIPE *commanding.*	GEN. THOS. H. RUGER *commanding*
3d Maryland Infantry.	2d Massachusetts Infantry.
20th Connecticut Infantry (5).	3d Wisconsin "
46th Pennsylvania "	13th New Jersey "
123d New York "	27th Indiana "
141st " " "	107th New York "
	150th " " "

---

* Absent on veteran furlough.

OPERATIONS FROM JANUARY TO MARCH, 1864.

Third Brigade.
GENERAE H. TYNDALE *commanding.*
61st Ohio Infantry.
82d   "   "
45th New York Infantry.
143d   "   "   "
82d Illinois Infantry.
101st   "   "

Artillery.
Battery "M," 1st New York.   Battery "I," 1st New York.

Second Division.
BRIGADIER-GENERAL JOHN W. GEARY *commanding.*

First Brigade.	*Second Brigade.*
COL. CHARLES CANDY *commanding.*	COL. A. BUSCHBECK *commanding.*
5th Ohio Infantry.	27th Pennsylvania Infantry.
7th " "	73d " " "
29th " "	109th " " "
66th " "	33d New-Jersey "
28th Pennsylvania Infantry.	119th New York "
147th " "	134th " " "
	154th " " "

Third Brigade.
COLONEL D. IRELAND *commanding.*
29th Pennsylvania Infantry.
111th   "   "
60th New York   "
78th   "   "   "
102d   "   "   "
137th   "   "   "
149th   "   "   "

Artillery.
Battery "E," Independent Pennsylvania.   13th New York Battery.

Third Division.
MAJOR-GENERAL D. BUTTERFIELD *commanding.*

First Brigade.	*Second Brigade.*
GENERAL W. T. WARD *commanding.*	COLONEL JOHN COBURN *commanding.*
70th Indiana Infantry.	5th Connecticut Infantry.
79th Ohio "	20th " " "
102d Illinois "	19th Michigan "
105th " "	22d Wisconsin "
129th " "	33d Indiana "
	85th " "

Third Brigade.
COLONEL J. WOOD, JR., *commanding.*
26th Wisconsin Infantry.
33d Massachusetts "
55th Ohio "
73d " "
136th New York "

Artillery.
Battery "C," 1st Ohio Artillery.   Battery "I," 1st Michigan Artillery.

Fourth Division.
MAJOR-GENERAL L. H. ROUSSEAU *commanding.*

First Brigade.
GENERAL R. S. GRANGER *commanding.*
10th Tennessee Infantry
13th Wisconsin "
18th Michigan "
73d Indiana "
102d Ohio "

Not Brigaded.
58th New York Infantry.   83d Illinois Infantry.
68th   "   "   71st Ohio   "
75th Pennsylvania "   106th "   "
23d Missouri   "   115th "   "
81st Wisconsin   "

Artillery.
9th Ohio Battery.   20th Indiana Battery.

Cavalry.
BRIGADIER-GENERAL W. L. ELLIOTT COMMANDING.
15th Pennsylvania Cavalry, attached to Department Headquarters.

First Division.
COLONEL E. M. MCCOOK *commanding.*

First Brigade.   *Second Brigade.*
COL. A. P. CAMPBELL *commanding.*   COL. O. H. LA GRANGE *commanding.*
1st Tennessee Cavalry.   1st Wisconsin Cavalry.
2d Michigan   "   2d Indiana   "
8th Iowa   "   4th   "   "

Third Brigade.
COLONEL L. D. WATKINS *commanding.*
4th Kentucky Cavalry.
6th   "   "
7th   "   "
18th Indiana Battery.

OPERATIONS FROM JANUARY TO MARCH, 1864.

Second Division.
BRIGADIER-GENERAL K. GARRARD *commanding.*

First Brigade.
COL. WM. B. SIPES *commanding.*
4th U. S. Cavalry.
7th Pennsylvania Cavalry.
4th Michigan Cavalry.

Second Brigade.
COLONEL R. H. G. MINTY *commanding.*
1st Ohio Cavalry.
3d   "   "
4th "   "

Third Brigade.
COLONEL A. O. MILLER *commanding.*
17th Indiana Mounted Infantry.
72d   "   "   "
98th Illinois   "   "
123d   "   "   "
Chicago Board of Trade Battery.

Third Division.
COLONEL W. W. LOWE *commanding.*

First Brigade.
5th Iowa Cavalry.
9th Pennsylvania Cavalry.
3d Indiana Cavalry (1 battal.)

Second Brigade.
8th Indiana Cavalry.
2d Kentucky "
10th Ohio   "

Third Brigade.
3d Kentucky Cavalry.
5th   "   "

Fourth Division.
BRIGADIER-GENERAL A. C. GILLEM *commanding.*

First Brigade.
2d Tennessee Cavalry.
3d   "   "
4th   "   "

Second Brigade.
5th Tennessee Cavalry.
*10th   "   "
*12th   "   "

Third Brigade.
*8th Tennessee Cavalry.
*9th   "   "
*13th   "   "

Unassigned Troops.
10th Ohio Infantry, Department Headquarters.
1st   "   Sharpshooters,   "
9th Michigan Infantry.
1st Michigan Engineers and Mechanics; headquarters at Bridgeport, Ala.

---

* Not mustered.

Garrison of Chattanooga.
GENERAL JAS. B. STEEDMAN *commanding.*

First Separate Brigade.

8th Kentucky Infantry.	3d Ohio Infantry.
15th Indiana "	24th " "
29th " "	44th Indiana Infantry.
51st " "	68th " "

Engineer Brigade. *Pioneer Brigade.*

18th Ohio Infantry, Chattanooga, Tenn.	1st Battalion, Chattanooga, Tenn.
13th Michigan " " "	2d " " "
21st " " " "	Pontoon " " "
22d " " " "	58th Indiana Infantry.

Artillery.

Reserve Artillery.

First Division. *Second Division.*

Battery "F," 4th U. S. Art.	Battery "A," 1st Ohio Art.
" "G," " "	" "F," " "
" "H," " "	" "G," " "
" "M," " "	" "M," " "
" "H," 5th U. S. "	18th Ohio Battery.
" "K," " "	1st Kentucky Battery.

Garrison Artillery.

Chattanooga, Tenn

4th Indiana Battery.	3d Wisconsin Battery.
8th " "	20th Ohio "
10th " "	Battery "I," 1st Ohio Artillery.
11th " "	" "C," 1st Wisconsin Heavy Art.
Battery "K," 1st Michigan Artillery.	

Bridgeport, Ala.
Battery "E, 1st Ohio Artillery.   Battery "B," 1st Ohio Artillery.

Stevenson, Ala.
Battery "K," 1st Ohio Artillery.

Murfreesboro, Tenn.
Battery "D," 1st Michigan Artillery.   12th Ohio Battery.
8th Wisconsin Battery.

Nashville, Tenn.

12th Indiana Battery.	Battery "C," 1st Tennessee Artillery.
Battery "E," 1st Michigan Artillery.	" "D," " "
" "I," 4th U. S. Artillery.	" "F," " "

Fort Donelson, Tenn.
Battery "C," 2d Illinois Artillery.

Clarksville, Tenn.
Battery "H," 2d Illinois Artillery.

OPERATIONS FROM JANUARY TO MARCH, 1864.

Detached Artillery.
10th Wisconsin Battery, Calhoun, Tenn.
18th Indiana Battery, Gallatin, Tenn.
21st Indiana Battery, Columbia, Tenn.
1st Kansas Battery, Waverly, Tennessee (N. & N. W. R. R.)
2d Kentucky Battery, Tullahoma, Tenn.
Battery "A," 1st Tennessee Artillery, La Vergne, Tenn.

Colored Troops.
12th U. S. Colored Troops, Waverly, Tenn. (N. & N. W. R. R.)
13th U. S. Colored Troops, Waverly, Tenn. (N. & N. W. R. R.)
14th U. S. Colored Troops, Chattanooga, Tenn.
15th U. S. Colored Troops, Nashville, Tenn.
16th U. S. Colored Troops, Chattanooga, Tennesee (*en route*).
17th U. S. Colored Troops, Murfreesboro, Tenn.
42d U. S. Colored Troops, Chattanooga, Tenn.
44th U. S. Colored Troops, Chattanooga, Tenn.
Battery "A," 1st U. S. Colored Light Artillery.

KNOXVILLE, *January* 31, 1864—2 P. M.

General Geo. H. Thomas, Chattanooga:

I am preparing to take the offensive. To do do this with effect, in the face of Longstreet's reinforcements, will require at least ten thousand infantry from you. In addition, that you place working gangs on the road to the Hiawassee bridge, so as to increase our supplies, which may be boated over the Tennessee, at Loudon, and afterward sent by rail to this place. I also require a pontoon train of twelve hundred feet length. Colonel Babcock will come down in the first boat, to attend to this. The cavalry from Atlanta is reported to be moving into East Tennessee, through North Carolina. Seven regiments started on the 13th instant. Please telegraph what is the extent of the assistance you can give me. . . . .

J. G. FOSTER,
Major-General Commanding.

NASHVILLE, TENN., *February* 6, 1864—2.30 P. M.

Major-General Thomas:

Reports of scouts make it evident that Joe Johnston has removed most of his force from your front, two divisions going to Longstreet. Longstreet has been reinforced by troops from the East. This makes it evident that they intend to secure East Tennessee, if they can, and I intend to drive them out, or get whipped this month. For this purpose, you will have to detach at least ten thousand men, besides Stanley's division (more will be better). I can partly relieve the vacuum at Chattanooga by troops from Logan's command. It will not be necessary to take artillery or wagons to Knoxville, but all the serviceable artillery horses should be taken to use on artillery there. Six mules to each one hundred men should also be tak̄en, if you have them to spare. Let me know how soon you can start.

MAJOR-GENERAL GRANT.

NASHVILLE, *February* 10, 1864.

Major-General Thomas:

Prepare to start for Knoxville on Saturday. I will order Logan to send to Chattanooga all the troops he can, and still hold his line of the road. The number will probably be about five thousand men. One division of your command will have to move out to hold the road to the Hiawassee.

MAJOR-GENERAL GRANT.

NASHVILLE, *February* 17, 1864.

Major-General Thomas:

Longstreet can not afford to place his force between Knoxville and the Tennessee. If he does, it will then be time to move against him. The work of a raid on the road can soon be repaired, if it can not be prevented. Make your contemplated move as soon as possible.

MAJOR-GENERAL GRANT.

CHATTANOOGA, TENN., *February* 19, 1864.

Major-General Grant, Nashville, Tenn.:

Assistant Surgeon Jacob Miller, Sixth Missouri Volunteer Infantry, arrived here yesterday, from Dalton. He was captured at Lebanon, Alabama, when General Logan sent out an expedition toward Rome. He reports Cleburne's division at Tunnel Hill, Stewart's division between Tunnel Hill and Dalton; Walker, two miles out from Dalton, toward Spring Place; Cheatham at Dalton; and Stevenson's and Bate's divisions to the west of Dalton two miles. He saw all of the camps, and estimates their force between thirty and forty thousand. He moreover states that no troops have been sent away, except one brigade of infantry, which went to Rome, about the 1st of this month.

GEO. H. THOMAS,

Major-General U. S. V.

TUNNELL HILL, *February* 26, 1864—7½ P. M.

Major-General U. S. Grant, Nashville:

I arrived here last night. Davis and Johnson occupy the pass at Buzzard's Roost. They have a force equal to theirs in their front, who outnumber them in artillery. It is not possible to carry this place by assault. General Palmer made the attempt to turn yesterday, with Baird's and Cruft's divisions, but was met by an equal force, exclusive of their cavalry, and in an equally strong position as at Buzzard's Roost. After expending nearly all of his ammunition, he retired during the night, to Catoosa Platform. Our transportation is poor and limited; we are not able to carry more than sixty rounds per man. Artillery horses so poor, that Palmer could bring but sixteen pieces. The country is stripped entirely of subsistence and forage. The enemy's cavalry is much superior to ours. Prisoners taken yesterday report that a portion of Cleburne's division has returned. I will wait the development of this day, and advise you further.

          GEO. H. THOMAS,
           Major-General U. S. V.

NASHVILLE, *February* 27, 1864.

Major-General Geo. H. Thomas:

It is of the utmost importance that the enemy should be held in full belief that an advance into the heart of the South is intended, until the fate of General Sherman is fully known. The difficulties of supplies can be overcome by keeping your trains running between Chattanooga and your position. Take the depot trains at Chattanooga, yours and General Howard's wagons; these can be replaced temporarily, by yours returning. Veterans are returning daily. This will enable you to draw reinforcements constantly to your front. Can General Schofield not also take a division from Howard's corps? It is intended to send Granger to you the moment Schofield is thought to be safe without him.

          U. S. GRANT,
           Major-General.

NASHVILLE, *February* 27—6 P. M.

Brigadier-General Whipple, Chief of Staff:

Information has reached Washington, that orders have been given for Johnston's army to fall back. General Thomas should watch any such movement and follow it up closely. Can't you draw teams from Bridgeport and Stevenson, to send supplies to the front? They have teams in great numbers at those places. Every energy should be exerted to get supplies and reinforcements forward. Troops will leave here at the rate of two or three thousand a day, for the front. Many of them go to Chattanooga.

          U. S. GRANT,
           Major-General.

CHATTANOOGA, *March* 5, 1864—11 P. M.

Major-General Schofield, Knoxville:

I have just received reliable information that Johnston has been reinforced by ten thousand men from South Carolina, and by Roddy, and that he contemplates making an offensive movement in this direction. Can you spare Granger's corps? If so, please direct them to concentrate at Cleveland, leaving a brigade of infantry and battery at Calhoun, to guard the railroad at that place.

          GEORGE H. THOMAS,
           Major-General U. S. V.

CHATTANOOGA, *March* 5, 1864.
Major-General John M. Schofield, Knoxville:

It has been reported to Major-General Thomas to-day, and also two days since, that the enemy were heavily reinforcing at Dalton. General Grant thinks it is not improbable that he may advance against us here. In that case we shall need the Fourth Corps, and wish you to hold it in readiness to send, if it be needed. Can not send you any assistance while this contingency is hanging over us.

WILLIAM D. WHIPPLE,
Brigadier-General and Chief of Staff.

EXTRACTS FROM THE OFFICIAL REPORT OF GENERAL JOS. E. JOHNSTON.

On the 17th of February, the President ordered me, by telegraph, to detach Lieutenant-General Hardee with the infantry of his corps, except Stevenson's division, to aid Lieutenant-General Polk, against Sherman in Mississippi. This order was obeyed as promptly as our means of transportation permitted.

* * * * * * * * *

On the 27th of February, I suggested to the executive by letter, through General Bragg, that all preparations for a forward movement should be made without delay. In a letter, dated 4th of March, General Bragg desired me "to have all things ready at the earliest practicable moment, for the movement indicated." In replying, on the 12th, I reminded him that the regulations of the war department do not leave such preparations to commanders of troops, but to officers who receive their orders from Richmond.

On the 18th, a letter was received from General Bragg, sketching a plan of offensive operations, and enumerating the troops to be used in them under me. I was invited to express my views on the subject. In doing so, both by telegraph and mail, I suggested modifications, and urged that the additional troops named should be sent immediately, to enable us, should the enemy advance, to beat him, and then move forward; or, should he not advance, do so ourselves. General Bragg replied, by telegraph, on the 21st: "Your dispatch of 19th does not indicate acceptance of plan proposed. Troops can only be drawn from other points for advance. Upon your decision of that point, further action must depend.

I replied, by telegraph, on the 22d: "In my dispatch of the 19th, I expressly accept taking offensive, only differ with you as to details. I assume that the enemy will be prepared for an advance before we are, and will make it to our advantage. Therefore I propose, both for offensive and defensive, to assemble our troops here immediately." This was not noticed. Therefore, on the 25th, I again urged the necessity of reinforcing the Army of the Tennessee, because the enemy was collecting a larger force than that of the last campaign, while ours was less than it had been then.

OPERATIONS FROM JANUARY TO MARCH, 1864. 43

On the 8th of April, Colonel B. S. Ewell, A. A. G., was sent to Richmond, to represent to the President my wish to take the offensive, with proper means, and to learn his views. A few days after, Brigadier-General Pendleton arrived from Richmond, to explain to me the President's wishes on the subject. I explained to him the modification of the plan communicated by General Bragg, which seemed to me essential, which required that intended reinforcements should be sent to Dalton. I urged that this should be done without delay, because our present force was not sufficient even for defense, and to enable us to take the offensive, if the enemy did not.

———

BY TELEGRAPH FROM CHATTANOOGA, *February* 28, 1864.
Major-General Grant, Nashville:

General Butterfield, by my direction, has recently examined the line between here and Nashville, and reports that he thinks six thousand men will be sufficient to guard that line, two regiments of which force should be cavalry. From what I know of the road between Nashville and Decatur, two thousand infantry and two thousand cavalry will be sufficient to protect that line. One thousand infantry will be sufficient to protect the line from Athens to Stevenson. Probably both lines of communication can be guarded by six thousand infantry and two thousand cavalry, a great portion of which should be made up from the local militia of Tennessee, or troops organized especially for the preservation of order in the state. I believe if I can commence the campaign with the Fourteenth and Fourth Corps in front, with Howard's corps in reserve, that I can move along the line of the railroad and overcome all opposition as far at least as Atlanta. I should want a strong division of cavalry in advance. As soon as Captain Merrill returns from his reconnoissance along the railroad lines, I can give you a definite estimate of the number of troops required to guard the bridges along the road.

GEO. H. THOMAS, *Major-General U. S. V.*

———

EXTRACT FROM GENERAL THOMAS' REPORT TO THE COMMITTEE ON THE CONDUCT OF THE WAR.

The above proposition was submitted to General Grant for his approval, and if obtained it was my intention (having acquired by the reconnoissance of February 23d, 24th, and 25th, a thorough knowledge of the approaches direct upon Dalton from Ringgold and Cleveland) to have made a strong demonstration against Buzzard's Roost, attracting Johnston's whole attention to that point, and to have thrown the main body of my infantry and cavalry through Snake Creek Gap, upon his communications, which I had ascertained from scouts he had up to that time neglected to observe or guard. With this view, I had previously asked for the return to me of Granger's corps and my cavalry from East Tennessee, and had already initiated preparations for the execution of the above movement as soon as the spring opened sufficiently to admit of it.

CHAPTER XXVI.

THE TURNING OF DALTON.

THE first of May, 1864, was a crisis of the war. Two of the largest armies hitherto assembled East or West were in readiness to move against the enemy at the bidding of the Lieutenant-General. The local objectives of these armies were distinct, but the common general object was the immediate suppression of the rebellion. It was proposed to accomplish this grand aim, by crushing General Lee's army covering Richmond and General Johnston's standing before Dalton. These two armies embodied the life of the rebellion.

Generals Grant and Sherman were to move on lines too remote to admit direct co-operation, but they proposed to be mutually helpful by simultaneous aggression. General Grant was to forbid the transfer of troops from Virginia to Georgia, by vigor of attack, and General Sherman was to engage Johnston in such a manner that he could not send supporting columns from Georgia to Virginia. Volunteers were invited for one hundred days, to hold the important points in the rear of the two great armies, that all the available veteran troops East might be massed against General Lee, and all in the West concentrated at Chattanooga, that General Sherman, with three armies in one, should dash upon General Johnston at Dalton. Campaigns, East or West, had never been undertaken under conditions of similar promise, and the loyal people were hopeful of early and complete success.

The conditions of the Georgia campaign were exceedingly favorable to General Sherman, as compared with the ruling features of all preceding campaigns in the central theater of war. The superiority of the national army at Chattanooga had been far greater than in any previous battle in this region, and in some of the anterior engagements, as at Chickamauga, the enemy had been superior. But General Sherman's preponderance of strength was greater than General Grant's when General Bragg was hurled from Lookout Mountain and Missionary Ridge. Then the strength of the opposing armies was perhaps as three to two; it was now to be as two to one. Besides, General Johnston could not now have, as his predecessor had always had, when on the defensive, the advantage of interior lines. The possession of Chattanooga and Cleveland, with roads converging at Dalton, gave direct lines for General Sherman's first advance, and with the railroad and river from Knoxville to Decatur well guarded, and a fortified line of supply from the north, he could move southward without endangering flank or rear, so long as he could so engage the enemy as to keep him before him. In the projected campaign, neither General Sherman nor General Johnston could have the advantage of interior lines, only so far as the defensive could give to either, shorter lines for maneuver and array, within a limited range only. The general line of maneuver being north and south, forbade great advantage of lines to either.

But General Johnston had other advantages. He had choice of positions and could always resist behind battlements with good management, and in giving ground would be constantly gathering to him his reserves; while General Sherman, in advancing, would be compelled to detach more and more from his offensive forces to guard his constantly lengthening line of supply. So, therefore, the relative conditions of the campaign were by no means expressed by the comparative proportions of the opposing armies.

The 2d day of May was first named by General Grant for the advance of the great armies, but finally the 5th was announced in orders. General Thomas, however, commenced his dispositions and movements on the 2d. On this day, General Davis' division joined General Baird's at Ringgold, and General Butterfield's advanced from Lookout valley to Lee and Gordon's Mills. During the day, General Baird sent infantry and cavalry detachments to reconnoiter toward Tunnel Hill, and developed the enemy in force at that point.

May 3d, General Johnson's division closed upon the other two of the Fourteenth Corps at Ringgold. On the day following, the Fourth Corps, with McCook's division of cavalry on its left flank, advanced to Catoosa Springs, and Butterfield's division advanced to Pleasant Grove, and General Williams' division to Lee and Gordon's Mills. The next day, General Geary's division, having marched across the mountain from Bridgeport, closed up on the other divisions of the Twentieth Corps at Leet's tanyard, completing the concentration of the Army of the Cumberland.

General Sherman originally designed that the Army of the Tennessee, Major-General McPherson commanding, should advance from Decatur by Gunter's Landing and Lebanon, Alabama, to Lafayette, Georgia; but subsequently, he ordered it to move upon Chattanooga. This army was not as strong as had been anticipated, as two of its veteran divisions under General A. J. Smith were detained by the protraction of General Banks' expedition west of the Mississippi river. With two corps, General McPherson attained position at Lee and Gordon's Mills on the 6th, and the same day the Army of the Ohio, Major-General Schofield commanding, reached Red Clay. At the close of this day the armies representing the controlling strength of the contending powers in the West, lay confronting each other on the eve of one of the greatest campaigns of a war, made memorable in the annals of the world by the magnitude of armies, the frequency of great battles, and immense compass of military operations.

General Sherman's three armies for offense now numbered nearly one hundred thousand men. There were sixty thousand seven hundred and seventy-three men in the Army of the Cumberland; twenty-four thousand and sixty-five in the Army of the Tennessee; and thirteen thousand five hundred and fifty-nine in the Army of the Ohio. The Army of the Cumberland comprised fifty-four thousand five hundred and sixty-eight infantry, two thousand three hundred and seventy-seven artillery, three thousand two hundred and twenty-eight cavalry, and one hundred and thirty guns; the Army of the Tennessee, twenty-two thousand infantry, one thousand four hundred and four artillery, six hundred and twenty-four cavalry, and ninety-six guns; and the Army of the Ohio, eleven thousand one hundred and eighty-three infantry, six hundred and seventy-nine artillery, one thousand six hundred and ninety-seven cavalry, and eighty-two guns. The grand aggregates were eighty-eight thousand one hundred and eighty-eight infantry, four thousand four hundred and sixty artillery, five thousand five hundred and forty-nine cavalry, and two hundred and fifty-four guns. General Johnston's army embraced forty-four thousand nine hundred infantry, artillery, and cavalry; two corps, commanded by Lieutenant-Generals Hardee and Hood, and four thousand cavalry, by Major-General Wheeler.

General Sherman proposed first to carry Tunnel Hill, and then threaten a direct attack upon Johnston's main position before Dalton, while McPherson's army should move through Snake Creek Gap to operate against Resaca. He accordingly gave orders, May 6th, requiring General Thomas, on the day following, to move his center, the Fourteenth Corps, directly upon Tunnel Hill; his right, the Twentieth Corps, to Trickum, and his left, the Fourth Corps, to Lee's house, in support of the Fourteenth: General McPherson to advance with his army first upon Ship's Gap and Villanow, and thence to Snake Creek Gap, and through it as soon as practicable; and General Schofield to move forward to Catoosa Springs, feeling toward General Thomas' left flank.

The Army of the Cumberland moved on the 7th, in compliance with orders. The enemy made a show of resistance to General Palmer, with infantry and artillery, at Tunnel Hill, but on the appearance of General Howard's corps upon his left, his troops fled to Buzzard's Roost. General Hooker, upon reaching Trickum, threw out detachments toward Buzzard's Roost on the left, and Villanow on the right, to observe the enemy. General Kilpatrick's cavalry remained at Gordon's Springs, in readiness to establish communications with the Army of the Tennessee, expected at Villanow on the morning of the 8th.

The next day, Harker's brigade of Newton's division of the Fourth Corps advanced along Rocky Face ridge to a point within a mile and a half of the enemy's signal station.

Meeting here with obstructions forbidding farther advance, Harker made preparations to hold the position. Skirmish lines were then thrown forward from Wood's, Davis', and Butterfield's divisions, and the enemy was pressed into his intrenchments at Buzzard's Roost, or "Mill Creek Gap,"* and the three divisions advanced to the entrance.

As General McPherson was now moving upon Snake Creek Gap, it was imperative that a strong feint should be made, to create the impression that it was the intention to carry the position by assault. Accordingly, General Geary was directed to scale Chattooga Mountain with his division, if practicable, at the point known as Dug Gap, where the road from Lafayette to Dalton ascends from Mill Creek valley. Chattooga Mountain is separated from Rocky Face ridge by Mill Creek at Buzzard's Roost, and from that point trends southward.

At the point selected for Geary's ascent, the mountain side is steep and rough, and the summit is crowned with a palisade of rocks, with occasional openings that admit passage to the top. With the One Hundred and Nineteenth New York deployed as skirmishers, and Buschbeck's and Candy's brigades formed on right and left, in two lines of battle, Geary moved up the mountain. Midway, his skirmishers became hotly engaged, but the enemy was pressed upward until the main lines reached the base of the palisades. After resting for a few minutes, to recover from the exhaustion produced by excessive heat and protracted exertion, an effort was made to reach the summit. A few men only succeeded, and they were either killed or forced back. The position was such that defense was easy, even by rolling stones from the summit. A second attempt, however, was made, soon after the first failed, but with similar issue. General Geary then brought McGill's rifled battery to bear upon the enemy in his front, to cover an effort of the Thirty-third New Jersey to reach the summit a half mile to the right, where the enemy made less show of strength. As in the other cases, a few men gained the crest, and their shouts invited the advance of the whole line, but

---

* So designated by General Johnston.

THE TURNING OF DALTON.   49

again there was emphatic failure. By this time, General Hardee was present with reinforcements, and further effort would have been madness. Geary 'ost heavily, but his action being regarded by the enemy as the initiative to carry the position by assault, it was in some degree compensative, as such impression was the object of the movement. Night and the third repulse coming together, the division was withdrawn to the valley, out of reach of the enemy's guns.

During the afternoon, Johnson's and Baird's divisions were advanced to Davis' support, and Butterfield's was ordered to join General Hooker. General Kilpatrick communicated with General McPherson, and then moved to Trickum. McCook's division was thrown on Schofield's left flank, to cover the extremity of the general line, until General Stoneman should come up. The position for General Garrard's cavalry division was to be with General McPherson, but it was yet in the rear, en route from Pulaski, Tennessee.

The next day, the Army of the Cumberland was somewhat heavily engaged on the east, north, and west of Buzzard's Roost. The action was intended as a feint, unless it should be ascertained that General Johnston was withdrawing his army. Such, however, was the position, by nature and art, that emphatic feints subjected the national forces to great exposure, and there was considerable loss throughout the line. The character of the feints may be inferred from the fact that General Johnston reported that five assaults upon "Rocky Face Mountain" were repulsed on the 9th of May. His troops holding Buzzard Roost were Stewart's and Bate's divisions, supported by Stevenson's and Anderson's. The defenses for infantry were at right angles to the roads, and batteries, covered with abatis, were placed on the adjacent summits to throw a converging fire upon the valley, which was flooded by means of well-concealed dams. Carlin's brigade, supported by the remainder of Johnson's division, felt the enemy's lines on the west; Morgan's brigade of Davis' division, on the north, and Grose's brigade of Stanley's division, on the east. The loss in killed was slight, but a great many were wounded. The heaviest loss, in comparison with the number of troops engaged, was in McCook's division on the extreme left. Under instructions from General Schofield, Colonel McCook made demonstrations on all the roads leading to Dalton on the east. Colonel La Grange, commanding his second brigade, encountered Wheeler, with twenty-two hundred men, on the road from Varnell's Station. He was at first successful, and pressed Wheeler back to intrenchments near Poplar Place, but was there repulsed with heavy loss. He and fourteen officers were captured, and one hundred and thirty-six of his men were either killed, wounded, or captured. Wheeler's loss was supposed to be greater. During the day, Hooker's corps was at Trickum to support McPherson in passing through Snake Creek Gap.

The action the next day was less severe, though the feint was vigorously maintained with a view to prevent any concentration against General McPherson. To give him support, Kilpatrick's cavalry was ordered to join him, and Williams' division of the Twentieth Corps was sent to his rear. In the evening, General Hooker was directed to send a division on the following day to widen the road through the gap, to facilitate the passage of troops and trains.

General McPherson passed through Snake Creek Gap, and reached the vicinity of Resaca at 2 P. M. on the 9th. Finding the place "fortified and manned," and no roads through the forest to the railroad, while his flank was exposed to attack from the direction of Dalton, he withdrew to the debouche of the gap through which he had passed. During the afternoon of the 9th, General Johnston learned that two corps of the national army were in the gap, and sent General Hood to Resaca with three divisions.

When General Sherman learned that McPherson had not touched Johnston's communications and had withdrawn to the gap, he made a change of plan. He desired, from the first, to hold Johnston at Dalton, and entertained the hope that McPherson's movement would so interrupt his communications that he would be forced to give battle at Dalton—an issue that was preferred to operations "far down into Georgia." His instructions to General McPherson were to secure Snake Creek Gap, and from it make a bold attack on the enemy's flank or his railroad at any point between Tilton and Dalton. He said: "I hope the enemy will fight at Dalton; in which case he can have no force there that can interfere with you; but should his policy be to fall back along the railroad, you will hit him in flank. Do not fail in that event to make the most of the opportunity, by the most vigorous attack possible, as it may save us what we have most reason to apprehend—a slow pursuit, in which he gains strength as we lose it. In either event, you may be sure the forces north of you will prevent his turning on you alone. In the event of hearing the sounds of heavy battle about Dalton, the greater necessity for your rapid movement on the railroad. If broken to an extent that would take some days to repair, you can withdraw to Snake Creek Gap, and come to us or await the development, according to your judgment or the information you may receive." As soon as he learned that General McPherson had failed to accomplish any of these objects, except to attain position at the debouche of the gap, he determined to attack with his armies through the gap, and issued orders for the movement.

It was plain to General Sherman, as it had been to General Thomas, in February, that no effort should be made to dislodge the enemy from Buzzard Roost, by direct attack; but he continued the feint, in order to still hold Johnston at Dalton, that he might throw his armies upon his rear. Snake Creek Gap made it easy to turn Dalton, by an army strong enough to uncover its communications, or to detach sufficient forces to risk an engagement with the enemy's whole army. Through this gap all the fortresses north of Dalton could be evaded, and the army in passage be under the cover of the mountains. Had Johnston's army been strong enough for division to hold the positions north of Dalton, and the lower mouth of the gap, he could have defied a hundred thousand men. But as his safety demanded the concentration of his army on his lines of retreat and supply, he was compelled to leave the passage undefended, and make roads for the quick transfer of his army from Dalton to Reseca, should his antagonist use the gap for a flank movement. General Sherman's orders to effect this measure required the concentration of his armies in Snake Creek Gap, on the 12th.

When General Johnston first learned that General McPherson had retired from Resaca, he recalled Hood's three divisions, and on the 11th his army was again concentrated at Dalton. On the morning of the 12th, he was confronted by Howard's corps and Stoneman's cavalry, the remainder of the national forces being in motion to concentrate in Snake Creek Gap. Stanley's division was before Buzzard's Roost Gap; Newton's was holding the north end of Rocky Face ridge, and the roads around it; Wood's was in reserve on Tunnel Hill, and Stoneman's troopers were on Newton's left flank. From the signal station on the ridge, the movements of the enemy were plainly visible. About 10 A. M. a heavy column was seen to advance toward Newton's left, as if to turn it. The menace was of such positive expression that Wood's division moved to Newton's support. But the enemy, after driving back Newton's skirmishers, withdrew. General Johnston's object, doubtless, was to ascertain whether the national forces had withdrawn from his front, as he had heard the day previous that Resaca was again threatened. The evening before, he had ordered General Polk, who had just arrived with Loring's division, to defend the place with that division, and Canty's brigade. But as his safety depended upon his knowledge of General Sherman's movements, his reconnoissance was directed to this end. During the day, he was so fully assured of the flank movement, that, by a night march, he transferred his infantry and artillery to Resaca, leaving his cavalry to cover his rear.

This result was not in harmony with the plans and expectations of General Sherman, his object being to hold Johnston's army at Dalton, until his own armies could pass through Snake Creek Gap; but the opportunity to accomplish it was lost between the 9th and the morning of the 13th. On the 9th, Resaca was held by Canty's brigade. The day following, General Hood was there with three divisions. On the 11th, Canty's brigade again held the place, and from the evening of the 11th until the morning of the 13th, General Polk was there with Loring's division in addition to Canty's brigade.

THE TURNING OF DALTON. 53

General McPherson passed through Snake Creek Gap on the 9th, and was on that day with his army within a mile of Resaca, and from the 9th to the 13th, he was south of the gap. On the 11th, Hooker's corps was in supporting distance, and on the 12th, Palmer's corps and Schofield's two divisions were close in the rear of Hooker.

Johnston remained in ignorance of Sherman's grand flank movement until the evening of the 12th, and then he was at Dalton with his army. After the national armies had gained Snake Creek Gap, he was unable to ascertain how many troops passed through it. An army, there, could pass as secretly as a brigade. He said in his official report, that "Rocky Face Mountain, and Snake Creek Gap, at its south end, completely covered for the enemy the turning of Dalton." His ignorance, then, of the movement until the evening of the 12th, was a condition of its success. Had McPherson's army and the forces in his rear, on that day, moved rapidly into position between Resaca and Tilton, Johnston would have been thrown from his communications, or been compelled to give battle upon conditions of great disadvantage.

It was unfortunate that Resaca was not gained at the same time that Dalton was turned, as the campaign did not furnish a similar opportunity to defeat Johnston, or press him from his communications. The grandest possibility between Tunnel Hill and Lovejoy's Station invited a prompt advance in force from the debouche of Snake Creek Gap. General Thomas' plan differed from the one adopted by General Sherman. He proposed that the Armies of the Tennesse and the Ohio should hold General Johnston at Dalton, by a feint upon his position at Buzzard's Roost, while the Army of the Cumberland, sixty thousand strong, should pass rapidly through Snake Creek Gap, and fall upon Johnston's communications between Dalton and Resaca, and thus cut him off from his communications, and either drive him eastward into a mountain region, or force him to give battle on unequal conditions. General Sherman's first plan proposed to demonstrate against Resaca, so as to hold him at Dalton to give battle, or induce General Johnston to abandon Dalton, and then strike his army in flank, while in motion between that place and Resaca.

This first series of operations in offense and defense gave the types of the campaign. The offensive compelled a choice between the direct attack of fortified positions and the flank movement. The adopted methods of defense were the maintenance of fortified positions as long as practicable, a constant outlook for opportunities to strike insulated columns, and retreat when necessary to save communications. General Johnston's leading idea was to fight under cover, and thus reduce the national army until he could meet it on equal conditions of battle, and at Dalton, and almost daily while he held command, he gave it revelation. General Sherman's leading object was to entrap or force his enemy into ·battle under circumstances which would not neutralize his superior strength, and of this, his zigzag lines of aggression were the expression.

EXTRACT FROM GENERAL GRANT'S OFFICIAL REPORT OF OPERATIONS FROM MARCH, 1864, TO JULY, 1865.

The enemy had concentrated the bulk of his forces east of the Mississippi into two armies, commanded by Generals R. E. Lee and J. E. Johnston, his ablest and best generals. The army commanded by Lee occupied the south bank of the Rapidan, extending from Mine run westward, strongly intrenched, covering and defending Richmond, the rebel capital, against the Army of the Potomac. The army under Johnston occupied a strongly intrenched position at Dalton, Georgia, covering and defending Atlanta, Georgia, a place of great importance as a railroad center, against the armies under Major-General Sherman.

* * * * * * * * *

These two armies and the cities covered by them and defended by them, were the main objective points of the campaign.

* * * * * * * *

General Sherman was instructed to move against Johnston's army to break it up, and to go into the interior of the enemy's country as far as he could, inflicting all the damage he could upon their war resources. If the enemy in his front showed signs of joining Lee, to follow him up to the full extent of his ability, while I would prevent the concentration of Lee upon him, if it was in the power of the Army of the Potomac to do so.

CULPEPPER, *April* 25—10.30 A. M.

Major-General Sherman :

Will your veterans be back to enable you to start on the 2d of May? I do not want to delay later.

U. S. GRANT,
Lieutenant-General.

THE TURNING OF DALTON. 55

HEADQUARTERS MILITARY DIVISION OF THE MISSISSIPPI,
NASHVILLE, *April* 27, 1864.

Lieutenant-General Grant, Culpepper:

In view of the fact that I will have to take the initiative with twenty thousand less men in McPherson's army than I estimated, I intend to order all McPherson's disposable force, twenty thousand (20,000), and Garrard's cavalry, five thousand (5,000), to Chattanooga, to start from a common center. I go forward to-morrow.

W. T. SHERMAN,
Major-General.

CULPEPPER, VA., *April* 28, 1864.

Major-General Sherman:

Get your forces up so as to move by the fifth (5th) of May.

U. S. GRANT,
Lieutenant-General.

HEADQUARTERS MILITARY DIVISION OF THE MISSISSIPPI,
IN THE FIELD, TUNNEL HILL, GA., *May* 8, 1864.

Major-General, Halleck, Washington, D. C.:

*   *   *   *   *   *   *   *

I have been all day reconnoitering the mountain range through whose gap the railroad and common road pass. By to-night, McPherson will be in Snake Creek Gap, threatening Resaca, and to-morrow will move to the attack. Army in good condition. I hope Johnston will fight here, instead of drawing me far down into Georgia.

W. T. SHERMAN,
Major-General.

HEADQUARTERS MILITARY DIVISION OF THE MISSISSIPPI,
IN THE FIELD, TUNNEL HILL, GA., *May* 9, 1864—8 P. M.

General Halleck, Chief of Staff, Washington, D. C.:

We have been fighting all day against precipices and mountain gaps to keep Johnston's army busy, whilst McPherson could march to Resaca to destroy the railroad behind him. I heard from McPherson up to two (2) P. M., when he was within a mile and a half of the railroad. After breaking the road good, his orders are to retire to the mouth of Snake Creek Gap, and be ready to work on Johnston's flank in case he retreats south. I will pitch in again early in the morning. Fighting has been mostly skirmishing, and casualties small. McPherson has the Army of the Tennessee, twenty-three thousand (23,000), and only encountered cavalry, so that Johnson did not measure his strength at all.

W. T. SHERMAN,
Major-General.

HEADQUARTERS MILITARY DIVISION OF THE MISSISSIPPI,
IN THE FIELD, TUNNEL HILL, GA., *May* 10, 1864—7 A. M.
Major-General Halleck, Washington, D. C.:

I am starting for the extreme front in Buzzard Roost Gap, and make this dispatch that you may understand Johnston acts purely on the defensive. I am attacking him on his strongest fronts—viz., west and north—till McPherson breaks his line at Resaca, when I will swing round through Snake Creek Gap, and interpose between him and Georgia. I am not driving things too fast, because I want two columns of cavalry that are rapidly coming up to me from the rear—Stoneman on my left and Garrard on my right—both due to-day. Yesterday I pressed hard to prevent Johnston detaching against McPherson, but to-day I will be more easy, as I believe McPherson has destroyed Resaca, when he is ordered to fall back to the mouth of Snake Creek Gap, and act against Johnston's flank when he does start. All are in good condition.

W. T. SHERMAN,
Major-General.

HEADQUARTERS MILITARY DIVISION OF THE MISSISSIPPI,
IN THE FIELD, TUNNEL HILL, *May* 10, 1864.

GENERAL:—I propose to leave hereabouts one (1) of your corps—say Howard's—the cavalry of Colonel McCook, and the cavalry of General Stoneman, to keep up the feint of a direct attack on Dalton through Buzzard Roost, as long as possible, and with all the remainder of the three armies to march to and through Snake Creek Gap, and attack the enemy in force from that quarter.

You may at once commence your preparations, and give orders that the force left here is to be under the command of the senior officer, who will strip his command light, sending all spare wagons to Ringgold; that the cars run daily to this point with daily supplies, but the main stores to be at Ringgold; that the cavalry watch well the passes north of Tunnel Hill, and at Ray's Gap; and that in case the enemy detect the diminution of force, and attack, gradually withdraw in the direction of Ringgold, but defend that point at all costs; that a locomotive and construction train be kept here with orders, and prepared, if this retrograde movement be made necessary; that the party shall take up, at intervals, rails, so as to make a repair train necessary to replace them—this, that the enemy may not have the track to facilitate his movement in pursuit. A few rails should at once be removed at some point east of the tunnel, that can again be put down when we want it done.

The pass at Snake creek is represented as very narrow. Please instruct a division to be there to-morrow, provided with axes and spades, so as to widen the road as to enable the passage of wagons; also to facilitate the march of troops by roads and paths outside the wagon track.

General Stoneman will be at Varnell's to-night, and by to-morrow night all his command will be in, so that we will calculate all to go to Snake creek, and close up on General McPherson *during* the day after to-morrow. As soon as General Stoneman comes, I will cause him to relieve Colonel McCook on that flank, so that you may send him to replace General Geary at Ray's road. Let the troops move as much under cover as possible; wagons going round by Villanow, and troops by Mill Creek road.

General Schofield will either go round by Villanow or follow General Newton.

I am, etc.,
W. T. SHERMAN,
Major-General.

Major-General Thomas, Commanding Army of the Cumberland.

HEADQUARTERS MILITARY DIVISION OF THE MISSISSIPPI,
IN THE FIELD, TUNNEL HILL, *May* 10, 1864.

GENERAL:—I think you are satisfied that your troops can not take Rocky Face ridge, and also the attempt to put our columns into the jaws of Buzzard Roost would be fatal to us.

Two plans suggest themselves:

1. By night, to replace Schofield's 'present command by Stoneman's cavalry, which should be near at hand, and to move rapidly your entire army, the men along the base of John's Mountain by the Mill Creek road to Snake Creek Gap, and join McPherson while the wagons are moved to Villanow. When we are joined to McPherson, to move from Sugar valley on Resaca, interposing ourselves between that place and Dalton. Could your army and McPherson's surely whip Joe Johnston?

2. I cast loose from the railroad altogether, and move the whole army on the same objective point, leaving Johnston to choose his course.

Give orders for all your troops to be ready with three days' provisions, and to be prepared to march to-night. I expect to hear from McPherson and Schofield as to their situation, also as to the near approach of Stoneman. He was at Charleston yesterday, and is apprized of the necessity for haste. Do you think any danger to McPherson should make us delay one day?

Please give me the benefit of your opinion on these points.

Yours, etc.,
W. T. SHERMAN,
Major-General Commanding.

Major-General Thomas, present.

HEADQUARTERS MILITARY DIVISION OF THE MISSISSIPPI,
IN THE FIELD, TUNNEL HILL, GA., *May* 10, 1864.

Major-General Halleck, Washington, D. C.:

General McPherson reached Resaca, but found the place strongly fortified and guarded, and did not break the road. According to his instructions, he drew back to the debouche of the gorge, where he has a strong defensive position, and guards the only pass into the valley of the Oostanaula, available to us. Buzzard Roost Gap, through which the railroad passes, is naturally and artificially too strong to be attempted. I must feign on Buzzard Roost, but pass through Snake Creek Gap, and place myself between Johnston and Resaca, where we will have to fight it out. I am making the preliminary move. Certain that Johnston can make no detachments, I will be in no hurry. My cavalry is just approaching from Kentucky and Tennessee, detained by difficulty of getting horses, and even now it is less than my minimum.

W. T. SHERMAN,
Major-General Commanding.

HEADQUARTERS MILITARY DIVISION OF THE MISSISSIPPI,
IN THE FIELD, TUNNELL HILL, GA., *May* 11, 1864.

GENERAL:—I received by courier in the night yours of 5 and 6.30 P. M. of yesterday. You will also, during the night, come to the same conclusion.

You have now your twenty-three thousand, and General Hooker is close in support, so that you can hold all Joe Johnston's army in check should he abandon Dalton. He can't abandon Dalton, for he has fixed it up so well for us, and he observes we are close at hand, waiting for him to quit. He can't afford a detachment strong enough to fight you, as his army will not admit of it.

Strengthen your position, fight anything that comes, and threaten the safety of the railroad all the time. But to tell the truth, I would rather he would stay in Dalton two more days, when he will find a larger party than he expects, in an open field. At all events we can then choose our ground, and he will be forced to move out of his works. I do not intend to put a column into Buzzard Roost Gap at present.

See that you are in easy communication with me and all headquarters. After to-day supplies will be at Ringgold.

Yours,
W. T. SHERMAN,
Major-General Commanding.

Major-General McPherson, Commanding Army of the Tennessee, Sugar Valley, Georgia.

HEADQUARTERS MILITARY DIVISION OF THE MISSISSIPPI,
IN THE FIELD, TUNNELL HILL, GA., *May* 11, 1864.

GENERAL:—The indications are that Johnston is evacuating Dalton. In that event, Howard's and the cavalry will pursue, and all the rest will follow your route. I will be down early in the morning.

Try to strike him, if possible, about the forks of the roads.

Hooker must be with you now, and you might send General Garrard by Somerville, to threaten Rome and that flank. I will cause all the lines to be felt at once.

W. T. SHERMAN,
Major-General Commanding,

General McPherson, Sugar Valley.

THE TURNING OF DALTON. 59

[SPECIAL FIELD ORDERS, NO 3.]

HEADQUARTERS MILITARY DIVISION OF THE MISSISSIPPI,
IN THE FIELD, SNAKE CREEK GAP, GA., *May* 12, 1864.

The object of the movement for to-morrow is to interpose between the enemy and Resaca, and to break his communications.

I. Major-General McPherson will move his column directly on Resaca, occupying in force the hills on this side of Camp creek, and his left extending along up Camp creek. He will prepare to advance a part of his force from his left to the railroad, and break it, and then fall back to his line.

II. Major-General Thomas will follow close to General McPherson, and when he reaches a main road crossing to the Resaca road, about two miles this side of town, viz., the Dalton and Calhoun road, he will turn to the left toward Dalton, prepared to deploy forward and connect on his right with General McPherson's left, choosing strong positions to cover the movement on the railroad.

III. Major-General Schofield will follow General Thomas, and at the first Dalton road, known as the Dalton and Rome road, will turn to the left and advance to abreast of General Thomas, and connect with him. General Schofield will leave one brigade in Snake Creek Gap, about five miles east of Villanow, and the balance of the one division in General McPherson's intrenched camp at this point.

IV. The cavalry of General Garrard will picket all roads to our rear and in case of being threatened from the north, will come into Snake Creek Gap, and cover the rear of the army and the wagon train. The cavalry of General Kilpatrick will move south of the main road to Resaca, and be held in reserve near the forks of the road, and be subject to the orders of the commander-in-chief.

V. All trains will be brought in Snake Creek Gap, and be placed in convenient order off the road. Great care must be observed in keeping the road clear, and ambulances and wagons when not traveling the road, must invariably turn out and leave all the road clear. Each army commander will leave his own wagon guards, and the men should leave their knapsacks in camp.

VI. The movement will begin at six (6) o'clock A. M. to-morrow.

By order of Major-General W. T. Sherman.   L. M. DAYTON,
Aid-de-Camp.

HEADQUARTERS MILITARY DIVISION OF THE MISSISSIPPI,
IN THE FIELD, NEAR RESACA, *May* 13, 1864—2.15 P: M.

General Thomas, Commanding Army of the Cumberland:

Until I hear that Joe Johnston is south of the Oostanaula, I would not cross at Lay's. We must first interpose between Dalton and Resaca, threatening the latter all the time. I want Hooker's right and McPherson's left strong, until we encounter Johnston, who has not yet got below Resaca, I think. If he retreat east, we have the advantage. I want the pontoons up, and to secure the railroad on Hooker's right. Palmer should join on to Hooker, and Hooker should be strong.

W. T. SHERMAN, *Major-General Commanding.*

HEADQUARTERS MILITARY DIVISION OF THE MISSISSIPPI,
IN THE FIELD, SNAKE CREEK GAP, *May* 13, 1864.

General Stoneman, Commanding Cavalry:

Your note of to-day was received. Very good, indeed. Press down the valley strong, and communicate with me. Your messenger will find me where there is most noise of artillery, or near Resaca. You can safely move on parallel roads, by brigades. Let your packs follow on the heels of the column. Pick up whatever of provisions and plunder you can.

W. T. SHERMAN, *Major-General Commanding.*

EXTRACT FROM GENERAL SHERMAN'S REPORT.

Speaking of the demonstration against Rocky Face ridge, he says:

"This, however, was only designed as a demonstration, and worked well, for General McPherson was thereby enabled to march within a mile of Resaca unopposed. He found Resaca too strong to be carried by assault, and although there were many good roads from north to south, endangering his left flank from the direction of Dalton, he could find no road by which he could rapidly cross over to the railroad, and accordingly he fell back and took strong position near the west end of Snake Creek Gap. I was somewhat disappointed at the result; still, appreciated the advantage gained, and on the 10th ordered General Thomas to send General Hooker's corps to Snake Creek Gap in support of General McPherson, and to follow with another corps, the Fourteenth, General Palmer's, leaving General Howard, with the Fourth Corps, to continue to threaten Dalton in front, while the rest of the army moved rapidly through Snake Creek Gap. On the same day General Schofield was ordered to follow by the same route, and on the 11th the whole army, excepting General Howard's corps and some cavalay left to watch Dalton, was in motion on the west side of Rocky Face ridge, for Snake Creek Gap and Resaca. The next day we moved against Resaca, General McPherson on the direct road, preceded by General Kilpatrick's cavalry; General Thomas to come up on his left, and General Schofield on his. General Kilpatrick met and drove the enemy's cavalry from a cross-road within two miles of Resaca, but received a wound which disabled him and gave the command of his brigade to Colonel Murray, who according to his orders wheeled out of the road, leaving General McPherson to pass. General McPherson struck the enemy's infantry pickets near Resaca, and drove them within their fortified lines, and occupied a ridge of bald hills, his right on the Oostanaula, about two miles below the railroad bridge, and his left abreast the town. General Thomas came up on his left, facing Camp creek, and General Schofield broke his way through the dense forest to General Thomas' left. Johnston had left Dalton, and General Howard entered it, and pressed his rear. Nothing saved Johnston's army at

Resaca but the impracticable nature of the country, which made the passage of troops across the valley almost impossible. This fact enabled his army to reach Resaca from Dalton along the comparatively good roads constructed beforehand, partly from the topographical nature of the country, and partly from the foresight of the rebel chief. At all events on the 14th of May, we found the rebel army in a strong position behind Camp creek, occupying the forts of Resaca, and his right on some high chestnut hills to the north of the town."

EXTRACT FROM GENERAL THOMAS' REPORT TO THE "COMMITTEE OF CONGRESS ON THE CONDUCT OF THE WAR."

Shortly after his assignment to the command of the Military Division of the Mississippi, General Sherman came to see me at Chattanooga, to consult as to the position of affairs, and adopt à plan for a spring campaign. At that interview, I proposed to General Sherman that if he would use McPherson's and Schofield's armies to demonstrate on the enemy's position at Dalton, by the direct roads through Buzzard Roost Gap, and from the direction of Cleveland, I would throw my whole force through Snake Creek Gap, which I knew to be unguarded, fall upon the enemy's communications between Dalton and Resaca, thereby turning his position completely, and force him either to retreat toward the east, through a difficult country, poorly supplied with provisions and forage, with a strong probability of total disorganization of his force, or attack me, in which latter event, I felt confident that my army was sufficiently strong to beat him, especially as I hoped to gain position on his communications before he could be made aware of my movement. General Sherman objected to this plan, for the reason that he desired my army to form the reserve of the united armies, and to serve as a rallying point for the two wings, the Army of the Ohio and that of the Tennessee, to operate from.

EXTRACT FROM GENERAL THOMAS' OFFICIAL REPORT.

General Hooker was directed to send another division of his command to Snake Creek Gap, with instructions to repair the road through the gap, so as to facilitate the passage of infantry and wagons. On the 11th, it was decided to leave one corps, Howard's, supported by Stoneman's and McCook's divisions of cavalry, and move to Snake Creek Gap with the balance of the army, attacking the enemy in front from that quarter, whilst Howard was keeping up the impression of a direct attack at Buzzard's Roost. This movement was to commence on the 12th. Instructions were given to corps commanders to provide their commands with ten days' rations and a good supply of ammunition, sending all surplus wagons back to Ringgold. At 9 A. M. on the 13th, General Howard's command occupied Dalton, it having been evacuated by the enemy on the evening of the 12th. Concentrating his troops in Dalton, General Howard pursued the enemy along the railroad, in the direction of Resaca.

capturing a considerable number of prisoners. The concentration of the balance of the army in Snake Creek Gap having been completed by the night of the 12th, at 8 A. M. on the 13th, Hooker's corps, preceded by Kilpatrick's cavalry, moved out on the Resaca road in support of McPherson's troops threatening Resaca.

EXTRACT FROM GENERAL HOWARD'S REPORT.

May 11th, the troops of the corps were disposed as follows: General Stanley to hold the gap; General Newton to hold Rocky Face, and the roads leading around the north end of it, with General Stoneman's cavalry covering his left flank; and General Wood in reserve on Tunnel Hill. During the evening of this day, and on the morning of the 12th, the general movement was progressing, and the Fourth Corps found itself alone confronted by the whole rebel army.

EXTRACTS FROM GENERAL JOS. E. JOHNSTON'S REPORT.

At Dalton, the great numerical superiority of the enemy made the chances of battle much against us, and even if beaten, they had a safe refuge behind the fortified pass of Ringgold, and in the fortress of Chattanooga. Our refuge, in case of defeat, was in Altanta, one hundred miles off, with three intervening rivers. Therefore, victory for us could not have been decisive, while defeat would have been utterly disastrous.

On the 5th of May, this army was in line between Ringgold and Tunnel Hill, and after skirmishing on that day and the following day, on the 7th, pressed back our advanced forces to Mill Creek Gap. On the same day, Canty reached Resaca with his brigade, and was halted there. On the 8th, at 4 P. M., a division of Hooker's corps attacked Dug Gap, which was bravely held by two regiments of Reynolds' Arkansas brigade and Grigsby's brigade of Kentucky cavalry, fighting on foot, until the arrival of Lieutenant-General Hardee, with Granbury's brigade, when the enemy was put to flight. On the 9th, five assaults were made on Lieutenant-General Hood's troops on Rocky Face Mountain. All were repulsed. In the afternoon, a report was received that Logan's and Dodge's corps were in Snake Creek Gap. Three divisions, under Lieutenant-General Hood, were therefore sent to Resaca. On the 10th, Lieutenant-General Hood reported the enemy retiring. Skirmishing to our advantage continued all day, near Dalton. Major-General Bate repulsed a vigorous attack at night. On the 11th, Brigadier-General Canty reported that the enemy was again approaching Resaca. Lieutenant-General Polk arrived in the evening with Loring's division, and was instructed to defend the place with those troops and Canty's. The usual skirmishing continued near Dalton.

Rocky Face Mountain and Snake Creek Gap, at its south end, completely covered for the enemy the operation of turning Dalton. On the

12th, the Federal army, covered by the mountain, moved by Snake Creek Gap toward Resaca. Major-General Wheeler, with 2,200 of ours, attacked and defeated more than double that number of Federal cavalry, near Varnell's Station. At night, our artillery and infantry marched for Resaca. The cavalry followed on the 13th. On that day, the enemy approaching on the Snake Creek Gap road was checked by Loring's troops, which gave time for the formation of Hardee's and Hood's corps, just arriving. As the army was formed, the left of Polk's corps was on the Oostanaula, and the right of Hood's on Connasauga. There was brisk skirmishing during the afternoon on Polk's front and Hardee's left.

CHAPTER XXVII.

BATTLE OF RESACA.

EARLY on the morning of the 13th, General Howard discovered that General Johnston had withdrawn from Dalton, and he at once occupied the town, having driven his cavalry from it. He then moved in pursuit, and skirmishing as he advanced, encamped eight miles toward Resaca. In the morning, General Johnston reached Resaca, Loring's division having moved out to check General McPherson and give time for the formation of Hood's and Hardee's corps upon their arrival from Dalton. He formed his army, now stronger by several thousand men than at Dalton, with Polk's corps on the left, resting on the Oostanaula river below the town, Hardee's in the center, and Hood's on the right, his right flank resting on the Connasauga river.

At 8 A. M., Hooker's corps, preceded by Kilpatrick's cavalry, moved out upon the Resaca road, in support of McPherson, who was advancing against the town. Kilpatrick encountered Wheeler and drove him nearly to the town, when, being wounded, he turned over the command to Colonel Murray. Palmer's corps moved from Snake Creek Gap, two miles northeast of Hooker, and then moved parallel with the Resaca road, under orders to proceed as far as the railroad. On reaching the vicinity of the railroad, his skirmishers encountered those of the enemy, strongly posted on the hills, immediately west of the railroad, and warmly engaged them until nightfall. Butterfield's division of Hooker's corps moved forward to support Palmer's right. Schofield's two divisions advanced upon Palmer's left. Howard advanced to the vicinity of Resaca, and when communications were established throughout the line, it was found that his right was but a mile from Schofield's left.

General Johnston's position was a strong one, with Camp creek in front, and heavy intrenchments in the immediate vicinity of the town—the strongest to defend the bridges across the Oostanaula, and cover the retreat of his army. His outer defenses consisted of detached redoubts, and extensive rifle-trenches, and the ground beyond was favorable for defense. His army was disposed partly in the inner defenses, but mainly on the high hills north and west of the town, which were fortified.

Before delivering battle, General Sherman ordered a pontoon bridge to be thrown across the Oostanaula at Lay's ferry, in the direction of Calhoun, Sweeny's division of the Fifteenth Corps to cross and threaten that place, and Garrard's division of cavalry to move from Villanow toward Rome, to cross the Oostanaula, and if possible break the railroad below Calhoun and above Kingston. On the 14th, General McPherson crossed Camp creek, near its mouth, and forced Polk's corps from the hills commanding the railroad bridges from the west, and secured a lodgment close to his works. This done, it became necessary to swing round the whole line formed the previous evening, from Hooker's left to the extreme left. This movement was made with the right of Johnson's division, which was the right of the Fourteenth Corps, as a pivot, and each division advanced until it encountered the enemy.

As Johnson's right was in proximity to the enemy, the divisions to the left met the enemy in succession. Baird's division was in line on Johnson's left, and Davis in reserve. General Howard, in compliance with orders from General Thomas, moved in the morning, to form his corps on the left of Schofield, and advance upon the main roads to Resaca. Newton's division, followed by Wood's, moved toward Schofield's left, and Stanley's toward the enemy's extreme right, on the Fulton and Resaca road. When Newton gained Schofield's left, Wood changed direction to the left, upon a road between Newton and Stanley.

Carlin's brigade of Johnson's division was the first to encounter the foe. General Carlin crossed Camp creek and advanced some distance over the open ground in front of the enemy's position, under a severe fire of artillery and musketry. The passage of the creek disordered his lines somewhat, and being hopeless of holding the enemy's works should he succeed in an assault, he withdrew, and found shelter and a parapet at the bank of the stream. Here he maintained position all day, and delivered a desultory but destructive fire. General King, perceiving Carlin's repulse, halted his brigade to the left and rear. The ground over which the left of Baird's division and the right of Schofield's line advanced, was thickly wooded, rendering it difficult to maintain lines, and the troops farther to the left having gained ground, those having been delayed moved forward rapidly as they emerged from the woods upon the open space before the enemy's intrenchments; but such was the severity of the musketry and artillery fire to which they were exposed, that they were soon compelled to retreat. Some isolated squads had passed Camp creek, and were driven back; others were so delayed by the miry banks that they could not withdraw with the main line, and were compelled to seek cover at the stream. To cover the retreat and re-formation of Turchin's brigade, and Schofield's right, Mitchell's brigade of Davis' division, in reserve, moved quickly to the left, and was severely engaged, while the broken lines were reformed upon the high ground west of the creek. As the lines of advance of Howard's corps were converging, the three divisions made close connection before reaching the enemy's position, and as the convergence of the roads shortened the battle front continually, the greater portion of Newton's division fell in rear of Schofield's right, in reserve, and when his left carried the position in its front, Newton moved to the relief of his left center, and grasped firmly all the ground that had been gained. In the meantime, Wood came abreast of Newton, and drove the enemy from his rifle-pits, and Stanley formed his division on Wood's left, with one brigade across the Fulton road, to protect his flank. These movements were all slowly made, in consequence of dense woods and rough ground, and the resistance of the enemy. But an advanced line was gained, and from it artillerists poured a fire so destructive as in some cases to drive the enemy temporarily from his works.

General Johnston, fearing that the lines of investment were closing around him, determined to assume the offensive, and if possible turn General Sherman's left flank. General Stanley soon observed indications of the movement. As General Howard had no reserves to direct to the endangered flank, he communicated in person with General Thomas and secured immediate assistance from the Twentieth Corps. In compliance with orders, General Hooker promptly dispatched Williams' division, under the guidance of Colonel Morgan,* of the Fourteenth Colored regiment, and preceeded it to the point of danger. Williams moved rapidly on the most direct route, and arrived on the extreme left just as that flank had been turned and pressed back. Stanley had exhausted all his reserves in extending his line against the overlapping of the enemy. Simonson's battery, by effective execution, was retarding the advance of the enemy to double up the line, when Williams deployed his division and advanced to the support of the battery. His terrific fire first checked and then routed the enemy, and completely defeated this attempt at flanking. The other divisions of the Twentieth Corps, Geary's and Butterfield's, followed Williams, later in the evening, and McCook's cavalry passed to Hooker's left.

The enemy's troops engaged against the left flank were Stevenson's and Stewart's divisions and two brigades of Walker's—a strong column in view of the length of Johnston's lines and the relative inferiority of his army. Another fact evinced his estimate of the importance of the movement. After its failure he gave orders for its repetition the next morning, but was subsequently led to revoke them, when he learned that the national infantry were crossing the Oostanaula river, near Calhoun, on a pontoon bridge. To provide against this menace to his rear, he dispatched General Walker to Calhoun.

Such advantages had been gained during the day as promised success in forcing Johnston to abandon his position, and

---

*Colonel T. J. Morgan was volunteer aid to General Howard.

orders were issued for a general advance the next morning. Notwithstanding this aggressive purpose, the troops covered themselves with the usual defenses. There was no change in the line, except that Schofield was directed to withdraw from the center and pass to Hooker's left.

There was delay in making the attack in the morning, to await the result of a reconnoissance by General Geary, from the left flank. Full preparations were not completed until noon. At this hour the Twentieth Corps advanced—Geary on the right, Butterfield on the left, and Williams in reserve. Before the enemy's works were reached, General Hooker directed General Williams to deflect to the left to cover and protect that flank, again threatened by the enemy, as General Johnston, having learned that there was no immediate danger from infantry at Calhoun, had repeated his order to General Hood to advance against the national left. Facing to the east, Williams' division moved to the point menaced—Knipe's brigade on the right, Ruger's in the center, and Robinson's on the left. The ground traversed by the advancing columns was hilly, with woods and open spaces alternating. Williams' brigades formed lines on a series of hills west of the railroad and running parallel to it; batteries were planted with supports to command the ground in front of the line.

The enemy before Hooker, occupied intrenched hills, having spurs extending in all directions, and batteries were so placed on the higher points as to enfilade assaulting lines. Geary's and Butterfield's divisions advanced with spirit, and though receiving a heavy fire from artillery and musketry, carried the nearest hills. Then Butterfield's division—Ward's, Coburn's, and Wood's brigades—supported by Ireland's brigade on Geary's left, drove the enemy from a battery, which from a ruling position was pouring an exceedingly destructive fire; but another line of intrenchments was so near that the captors could neither remove the guns nor remain with them. But, withdrawing to tenable ground, they covered the guns so fully with their fire that the enemy could not approach them, and during the remainder of the day the guns remained between the lines. They were taken during the night by a detachment of the Fifth Ohio under Colonel Kilpatrick.

In the meantime, the entire line became engaged, from Howard's right to Hooker's left; while throughout the whole front of the "Army of the Cumberland," heavy skirmishing and artillery action was maintained. General Howard, being nearest the assaulting corps, kept up a constant fire of artillery and musketry, and in one instance made a positive attack, and although he did not succeed in holding any point of the enemy's line, he prevented the diversion of troops from his front, to sustain their comrades before General Hooker, against whose left they were maintaining the offensive with great determination. Near the railroad, in front of Williams, he massed his forces and advancing as much as possible under cover, made repeated assaults, but was unable to disturb the line. Williams' artillery was used with most destructive effect in the repulsion of these assaults. In front of Williams' right and Geary's left, there was a long cleared field, compassing two hills and a ravine, and extending to a wooded hill, upon which rested the enemy's main line. This field was flanked on the right by wooded hills, which extended to the captured battery. About 5 P. M. Stevenson's division left the main line and charged in column to gain possession of these lateral hills.

This movement, if successful, would have insulated one-half of Geary's division, which had been concentrated under Colonel Cobham, in the rear of the guns wrested from the enemy. But Stevenson was repulsed mainly through the concentration of fire from Williams' right and Geary's left. His leading regiments were almost annihilated. On both sides, artillery charged with canister and schrapnel was freely used. Stevenson's repulse closed the general contest. This attack of Stewart's and Stevenson's divisions was made after General Johnston had decided to evacuate Resaca, but his order forbidding the assault was not received in time to prevent it.

During the night of the 15th, General Johnston abandoned Resaca. It was observed by those on the outlook the preceding day, that he was sending his material to the rear. He had lost positions on his right and left, and had been pressed throughout his lines by two days of fighting, and the exposure of his communications in the event of a flank movement, which had been foreshadowed, made his retreat necessary. He had attacked the brigade across the river below Resaca on the

BATTLE OF RESACA.

15th, and had been repulsed, and as General Sherman's front now presented defenses as well as his own, the transfer of heavy forces across the river was plainly practicable. He therefore retreated before embarrassments crowded upon him.

The action at Resaca, though presenting different features from the one before Dalton, was not essentially different in type or result. In the latter one, the two armies more fully confronted each other, and there was more fighting and heavier losses. The champaign region of Georgia was now before General Sherman, offering freedom for maneuver and strategy, which the mountain region had denied.

As the aggregate monthly losses of the Army of the Cumberland were reported by General Thomas, it is impossible to ascertain definitely the casualties at Resaca. The Twentieth Corps lost seventeen hundred and forty-six men, and the other two corps lost nearly as many in the aggregate. General Johnston's losses were also heavy, especially when he assumed the offensive.

CHAPTER XXVIII.

ADVANCE TO THE ETOWAH RIVER, THE TURNING OF ALLATOONA, BATTLES NEAR NEW HOPE CHURCH.

RESACA was occupied by the Army of the Cumberland on the morning of May 16th, and General Sherman gave orders for rapid pursuit. There was delay, however, in passing the river, as it was necessary to throw a pontoon bridge at Resaca and at points above. During the day, the Army of the Tennessee crossed at Lay's ferry, and Howard's corps at Resaca. As in the pursuit the Army of the Cumberland was to follow the enemy's line of retreat, General Howard moved forward toward Calhoun. His progress was slow, as stubborn resistance was offered by the rear-guard of Johnston's army.

The next day, the three armies advanced. Palmer's corps followed Howard's; Hooker's having crossed above, moved on the left. On his left, was the Army of the Ohio, and the Army of the Tennessee advanced on lines on the right of the central army. Stoneman's cavalry was on the extreme left, and Garrard's on the extreme right, under instructions to reach the enemy's rear if practicable.

Early in the day, General Howard found the rear-guard of the enemy, formed of cavalry and artillery, and at times supported by infantry. Three lines were presented at short intervening distances, and generally behind barricades in woods, with open ground in front. When the first line was pressed from position, the troops forming it passed to the rear of the third and reformed. Thus, not only was the rear of the army covered, but two of the three lines of the rear-guard itself. The Fourth Corps advanced in two columns abreast, and pressed the enemy so strongly in the evening that a battle seemed imminent. The skirmish lines were reinforced until they had the weight of lines of battle, and artillery was freely used. The action terminated as darkness approached, and during the night, General Johnston abandoned a position which he had intrenched. His reasons were, that a portion of Polk's corps was yet in the rear; that, as he thought, the expiration of service of the regiments in the national armies confronting him that had not re-enlisted, would soon reduce their strength, and he hoped that some blunder would give him an opportunity to strike a blow without risking a general battle, or to enter such a contest with advantages to counterbalance the inferiority of his army.

General Sherman's object now was to compel Johnston to fight north of the Etowah river, divide his army, or give up Rome or Allatoona. In the event of his attempt to hold both these places, he proposed to break his line at Kingston; or should he concentrate at Kingston, to break his railroads right and left, and "fight him square in front." To give support to the cavalry on the right, he directed General Thomas to send a division from Resaca toward Rome, and Davis' had been put in motion.

On the 18th, the armies moved forward without change of order, and at night the Fourth and Fourteenth Corps encamped near Kingston. At 8 A. M. the next day, the central column, Stanley's division leading, advanced toward Cassville. Midway to that place the enemy opened upon Stanley with a six-gun battery, from an eminence, but yielded, under the pressure of an attack with infantry and artillery. Moving in pursuit nearly four miles, Stanley was again arrested. This time there was a formidable combination before him, and the enemy was observed to be advancing in two lines of battle. General Howard promptly deployed his corps—Stanley's and Wood's divisions in front, and Newton's in support of the left. As soon as the enemy observed these dispositions, his lines were halted and their front covered with barricades. When Howard's artillery opened, the first line retreated in some confusion, and the Fourth Corps advanced and occupied the position. Here a junction with Hooker's corps was made, which had engaged the enemy during the day on the direct road from Adairsville to Cassville. Skirmishing was maintained until dark, when the three corps bivouacked in close proximity. During the day, General Schofield approached Cassville, and General McPherson moved from Woodland to Kingston.

As reports had reached General Sherman that General Johnston had been reinforced, he thought it probable that he would now give battle in the vicinity of Cassville, and in such expectation he threw his armies from their parallel lines of march, toward the head of the central column. His cavalry was on right and left, in effort to break the railroad in Johnston's rear to force him to battle, or to subject a portion of his army and trains to capture, before he could cross the Etowah river. General Schofield was under instructions to support the cavalry on the left, in the accomplishment of this object, and during the day, McCook's division of cavalry had a brilliant passage of arms with Stevenson's division of infantry.

It was General Johnston's purpose to give battle at Cassville. He had been joined by French's division of Polk's corps, and the lines which Howard first encountered were Hood's, who had orders to attack. His lieutenant, however, under the impression that the columns on the east had turned his position, refrained until it was too late to overpower the head of column. Even after this failure, General Johnston meditated delivering battle, but was dissuaded by his lieutenants, Polk and Hood, though General Hardee gave counter advice. During the night he crossed the Etowah with all his trains, and moved to his strong position at Allatoona Pass. This step was a matter of subsequent regret to him, though it is probable that his sorrow would have been more profound, had he engaged Sherman's three armies at Cassville.

Pending these greater movements, General Davis with his division captured Rome. His orders did not require him to go so far from the line of march, but as circumstances, in his judgment, justified the step, and having advised General Thomas of his purpose, he passed beyond all co-operation with the cavalry, and hurried Mitchell's brigade in advance, on the 17th, drove back the rebel cavalry, and deployed within range of the artillery, on De Soto hill, on the west side of the Oostanaula. McCook's brigade and Morgan's moved forward, and the enemy,

74 ETOWAH—ALLATOONA—NEW HOPE CHURCH.

at first assuming the aggressive, was driven within his fortifications. The next morning the city was abandoned in too much hurry to destroy machine-shops and iron-works of great value, and vast quantities of stores and cotton, and six pieces of artillery. General Davis lost in killed and wounded one hundred and fifty men.

BEYOND THE ETOWAH.

General Sherman did not pursue beyond the Etowah. The rough hills and gorges around Allatoona presented such obstacles to maneuver and attack as to deter him from a direct advance. He chose rather to make a detour to the right, to turn Allatoona, or throw his armies upon Johnston's communications at Marietta or the Chattahoochee river. He accordingly gave orders for a few days of rest, and time to repair the railroad to Cassville, and accumulate supplies at Resaca.

At this period, General Johnston was calling to him infantry from the Southwest and cavalry from Mississippi, and General Sherman was making effort to maintain his relative superiority. His losses and constantly lengthening line of supply were reducing his offensive strength, and he called all available troops from the rear. May 23d, he ordered General Blair, with two divisions of infantry of the Seventeenth Corps, and Long's brigade of cavalry of Garrard's division, to move on Rome and Kingston, from Huntsville, Alabama.

On this day, he put his armies in motion south of the Etowah. The Army of the Tennessee crossed the river at the mouth of Conasene creek, on a bridge which had been saved from destruction, and advanced toward Dallas by Van Wert. General Thomas crossed four miles south of Kingston, and moved through Euharley and Stilesboro. General Schofield crossed near Etowah cliffs, and kept on the left of General Thomas. Each army had supplies for twenty days in wagons.

McCook's division of cavalry preceded the central columns, and reached Stilesboro in the afternoon, and finding the enemy there in force, with cavalry and infantry, skirmished until dark. Hooker, Howard, and Palmer encamped south of Euharley creek. Kilpatrick's division, Colonel W. W. Lowe commanding, was left to guard the line of the Etowah—an im-

ETOWAH—ALLATOONA—NEW HOPE CHURCH. 75

portant duty, as Wheeler's cavalry had been sent to interrupt communications north of that river. Garrard's division was covering General McPherson's right flank.

At daylight on the 24th, by direction of General Thomas, General Hooker sent Geary's division to Euharley creek, to hold the Alabama road toward Allatoona, and cover the left flank of the corps, until relieved by General Schofield. The remainder of the Twentieth Corps was directed to advance to Burnt Hickory, preceded by McCook's cavalry. The cavalry commander, upon arrival, was instructed to picket strongly the roads leading toward Alatoona, and cover the movements of the army. McCook reached Burnt Hickory at 2 P. M., having skirmished with the enemy for several miles. In this skirmish he captured a rebel courier, bearing dispatches from General Johnston to a division commander of cavalry, requiring him to observe the movements of the national forces toward Burnt Hickory, and advising him that his army was moving toward Dallas and Powder Springs. Later in the day, General Garrard informed General Thomas that in moving upon Dallas, he had been attacked by Bate's division, the advance of Hardee's corps. Thus, from two sources, the fact was ascertained that General Johnston had divined General Sherman's purpose in time to throw his army before him near Dallas. At night, the Fourth and Twentieth Corps encamped at Burnt Hickory; the Fourteenth, impeded by trains, halted some distance in the rear.

The next morning, the march was resumed. McCook's cavalry moved on the road to Golgotha, followed by Butterfield's division. Hooker's other two divisions, and Howard's corps, advanced on roads running south of Butterfield's line of march. General Howard sought roads to the right, to avoid the main roads, upon which the trains of Johnson's division and the Twentieth Corps were advancing. Baird's division was left at Burnt Hickory, to protect trains and the rear of the army. The divisions of the Army of the Cumberland, marching upon four roads, were under orders to converge upon Dallas, as it was not expected that Johnston's army would be met nearer than that place. But at 11 A. M. Geary's division, the central one of the Twentieth Corps, came upon the enemy in considerable force. A cavalry outpost had been previously found near Owen's Mill, where a burning bridge had caused some delay. After crossing this bridge, General Geary had deployed the Fifth Ohio as skirmishers in advance of Candy's brigade, and when within four and a half miles of Dallas, this regiment became heavily engaged, and soon after, a charge was made by the enemy. Candy's brigade was then rapidly deployed, and after a sharp conflict repulsed the foe. General Geary immediately extended his skirmish line, formed Candy's brigade in line of battle, and brought up Ireland's and Buschbeck's in support. Advancing again, the division drove the enemy a half mile. From prisoners, it was now ascertained that Hood's corps was in front, and that Hardee's was not far distant, in the direction of Dallas. The situation was now critical, as no supporting forces were near. General Hooker, who was with his central division, now directed that it should be formed upon a hill affording advantages for defense, that the skirmish line should be extended, and make a show of strength by maintaining an aggressive fire, and that barricades should be constructed. He sent orders immediately to Williams and Butterfield to hasten to Geary's support, and informed General Thomas of the posture of affairs.

As Williams and Butterfield were several miles distant, they did not reach Geary's position until late in the afternoon. Upon arrival, their divisions advanced against the enemy with Geary's in reserve, under instructions from General Sherman to drive him beyond New Hope Church, a point where roads from Marietta, Dallas, and Ackworth meet.

Though the country was hilly and covered with trees and undergrowth, Williams' and Butterfield's division, dashed at the enemy at double-quick, and drove him back a mile and a half, to New Hope Church; but here they received his artillery fire at short range, and were arrested. Geary moved to the front again, and though the attack was vigorously made, the enemy was not dislodged. General Johnston had thrown his army directly across General Sherman's line of advance, and was ready for defensive battle. His position was a strong one, and his troops were under cover. The engagement which defined his position resulted in heavy losses to both armies.

When General Sherman first learned that the enemy was before him in force, he divined that he was on Johnston's right flank, and proposed to turn it. With this object in view, he directed General McPherson to move to the left, if he could not dislodge the eneny in his front. But General McPherson did not move to the left as projected, and the opportunity to pass round General Johnston's right to Ackworth and Marietta was lost.

General Hooker at night intrenched a line in close proximity to the enemy. The Fourth Corps, ordered by General Thomas to his support during the day, came up by divisions in the evening and after night, and formed on his left. Davis' division of the Fourteenth Corps, having left Rome on the 24th, was now in supporting distance; but Johnson's and Baird's divisions, having been delayed by the trains on the roads in advance of them, were still in the rear.

The following day was spent in the concentration of the armies. General McPherson's army advanced to Dallas, and General Schofield's was directed to the left of General Thomas, to turn Johnston's right flank. Garrard's cavalry formed the extreme right, Stoneman's the left, and McCook's covered the rear.

The Twentieth Corps maintained the position assumed the previous evening. The Fourth was slightly changed by swinging round to occupy a line of hills, trending at right angles to Hooker's line. This change of front threatened the enemy's right flank more directly. General Schofield, on Howard's left, covered the road leading from Allatoona to Dallas, by New Hope Church. Both Howard and Schofield skirmished into position; and so close were they to the enemy that not only their skirmishers, but their main lines maintained a continuous fire.

In the forenoon, General Davis, by direction of General Thomas, made a reconnoissance to Dallas, to determine the position of Johnston's left flank and open communications with General McPherson. He advanced on the Burnt Hickory road with Morgan's brigade in front, drove the enemy's pickets through the town, and deployed his division on the east of the Marietta road. Soon after, the Army of the Tennessee came abreast, and was formed in lines extending across the Villa Rica road.

During the day, McCook, on the left, struck a column of cavalry in flank, broke it in two, and captured fifty-two prisoners. From his prisoners he learned that Wheeler's cavalry corps was on Johnston's right flank. In the afternoon, Johnson's division of the Fourteenth Corps came up in the rear of the Fourth Corps.

The opposing armies were now in closest proximity. Hardee's corps was on Johnston's left, Hood's on his right, and Polk's in the center. The batteries of the two armies were placed on the commanding positions in the opposing lines, and nothing was needed to precipitate the work of death but a word from either of the commanding generals.

As General Johnston had twice withdrawn his army under circumstances not radically different, General Sherman did not feel confident that he would maintain his position even for a day, and gave such orders as would compass the issues of battle or the retreat of the enemy. He directed General McPherson to connect his left with Hooker's right, so that he could then move his whole line by the left flank beyond Johnston's right, and interpose between him and the railroad. In addition to McPherson's movement, a strong demonstration by Hooker and Howard, and a positive attack upon Johnston's right flank, were ordered.

The effort to turn this flank commanded the personal attention of Generals Sherman and Thomas, in addition to General Howard, who was ordered to furnish the assaulting column. In the beginning, General Sherman designated the point in the enemy's line upon which the assault should be made, but Generals Thomas and Howard, upon special examination, perceived that there the enemy could bring a cross-fire of artillery and musketry to bear upon the approaches, and General Howard was directed to move his column to the left, beyond all the troops in line, and endeavor to strike the enemy's flank.

General T. J. Wood's division of the Fourth Corps was

selected to make the assault, to be supported on the left by General R. W. Johnson's division of the Fourteenth Corps, and by General McLean's brigade of General Schofield's Twenty-third Corps, on the right. The column was formed in the rear of the extreme left of the Twenty-third Corps—Wood's division in column of six lines deep, Johnson's on the left, with a brigade front. After moving a mile to the east, General Howard supposed that he had reached the enemy's flank, and directed General Wood to wheel his command so as to face the south, and advance. The enemy's works were soon discovered, and upon examination of their strength, the column was moved another mile to the east. Here, Generals Howard and Wood reconnoitered the ground, and ascertained that the line of works did not cover the whole division front, and preparation was made for attack. Johnson's division was slightly refused on Wood's left, with Scribner's brigade in front, and McLean's brigade was sent to a point in full view from the enemy's works, a little to the right of the place of attack, to attract his attention and draw his fire.

At 5 P. M. the entire column marched briskly forward, Hazen's brigade of Wood's division leading, and having driven back the enemy's skirmishers, assaulted his main line with great vigor. Hazen at first was without support from Johnson's division on his left, and was so heavily engaged that General Wood was compelled to move up his supporting lines. Scribner's brigade was also hurried forward on Hazen's left, but, before getting abreast of Hazen, was struck in flank from the opposite side of a creek on the left. Colonel Scribner halted, to throw out troops to cover his flank, at the crisis of the assault, and it was soon evident that it had failed. The Confederate general, Cleburne, threw his reserves and an enfilading fire upon Wood's left flank, and forced it back, and his right at the same time was subjected to a cross-fire of artillery and musketry, and was also without support, as McLean had not shown himself to the enemy nor opened fire. As both of Wood's flanks were melting away under a most destructive fire, General Howard ordered the withdrawal of the column. The retirement was made with such deliberation as permitted the removal of the wounded. General Johnson withdrew to the left and rear of the main line, and General Wood to a ridge farther to the front and right. General McLean withdrew entirely, and left the two divisions in complete isolation.

General Wood lost over fourteen hundred men killed, wounded, and missing. General Johnson's loss was slight in comparison, but was himself severely wounded. The reported loss of the enemy was four hundred and fifty.

Two advantages resulted from this unsuccessful assault, though dearly purchased. A position was secured far on the enemy's right, which was of importance to subsequent movements, and it was clearly developed that Johnston's right would be found in strength wherever a column might go to turn it. At night, Wood and Johnson intrenched their respective positions.

During the day, the enemy came out of his works in front of Newton's division, but was handsomely repulsed by Wagner's and Kimball's brigades. Colonel Daniel McCook's brigade of General Davis' division seized a mountain pass in the rebel center, and held it against a night attack by troops from Polk's corps.

General McPherson found it impracticable to move to the left, in compliance with General Sherman's orders. General Johnston was meditating offensive action, and pressed the national lines throughout their length in search for an opportunity to strike an effective blow. Each commander was watching for an advantage, and yet each was "duly cautious in the obscurity of the ambushed ground." During the 28th, there was brisk skirmishing from flank to flank. General Sherman was waiting for McPherson's movement to the left, to make effort to turn General Johnston's position, and the latter was planning a battle for the next day. At night, General Hood was instructed to attack the national left the next morning at dawn, and the remainder of the army was ordered to join in the action, successively from right to left.

General Hood advanced, but finding an intrenched flank, refrained from attack and asked for instructions. As this delay defeated the surprise, that was intended, in the initiative, Hood was recalled. But in the evening General Johnston attacked McPherson, as he was in effort to leave position to close up on the center of the national line. Fortunately the Army of the Tennessee had not moved far from the defenses, and repulsed Hardee's corps with great loss. As a feint, to cover the assault upon McPherson, the enemy demonstrated in front of Stanley and Newton, and at intervals during the day there was artillery action and skirmishing throughout the battle front.

As General McPherson did not change position, there were only slight changes at other points in the line. A brigade of Stanley's division was thrown between Schofield and Wood, and Colonel J. G. Mitchell's brigade of Davis' division was placed in position about half-way toward General Hooker. The chasm here was three miles wide. Colonel Mitchell intrenched thoroughly, and cut roads to his rear to facilitate the closing up of the right wing upon the center at New Hope Church.

The purpose to move the whole line to the left was not abandoned by General Sherman, though the repeated attempts of General McPherson to leave position, during the last days of the month, invited the enemy's attacks.

During the month of May, the Army of the Cumberland lost about nine thousand men. Sixty-six officers and ten hundred and ninety enlisted men were killed; three hundred and one officers, and six thousand four hundred and fifty-one enlisted men were wounded, and eight officers and eight hundred and fifty-eight men were missing from the three corps of infantry. Colonels A. S. McDougall, One Hundred and Twenty-third New York, and John H. Patrick, Fifth Ohio, fell at New Hope Church, and Colonel Gilbert, Nineteenth Michigan, was mortally wounded; Lieutenant-Colonel E. F. Lloyd, One Hundred and Nineteenth New York, was killed at Resaca. The army captured one thousand four hundred and seventy-seven prisoners, and received five hundred and fifty deserters.

As General Sherman had held his armies before General Johnston, near Dallas, he had not made effort to ascertain with what force Allatoona was held, to turn which stronghold was his primary object in moving his armies to the right. He had ordered General Blair to move to that point, but on the first of June he was still far in the rear. But as at this time General McPherson effected his own dislodgment from the position that had been so closely watched by the enemy, and the united armies could move by the left flank, General Sherman ordered General Garrard to move to the east end of Allatoona Pass, and General Stoneman to the west with, instructions to fight cavalry with cavalry, and infantry with dismounted cavalry.

As General McPherson's army, by divisions, approached New Hope Church, the divisions of the Twentieth Corps moved to the left of Johnson's division, which had held the extreme left since the 27th of May. Davis' division relieved Hovey's of the Twenty-third Corps, and Baird's advanced from Burnt Hickory to Johnson's rear. Schofield's troops passed to Hooker's left. At night, Garrard and Stoneman were at Allatoona.

On the 2d, Hooker moved to the left of Schofield, and Baird moved to Johnson's left, when Hooker, Schofield, and Baird moved on a right wheel, drove back the enemy's skirmishers, and threw General Johnston farther from the roads leading to Ackworth and Allatoona; and yet, in front of the new positions on the left, finished defenses were found. The movements of the day were embarrassed by a rain-storm, which flushed the creeks and softened the ground.

During the 4th and 5th, the national line was gradually extended to the left, and by successive steps was advanced to Johnston's immediate front. From first to last, each army fortified as it advanced, and the field-works from Dallas far toward Ackworth revealed to the future the proximity and nature of the belligerence of the two armies. When at last General Johnston perceived that General Sherman's movement to the left had given him an open way to Ackworth, he abandoned the position and threw his army upon the mountains and hills north and west of Marietta.

The Army of the Cumberland rested on the 5th, and on the next day moved leisurely into position southwest of Ackworth: Hooker's corps, near the junction of the Sandtown road with the one leading from Burnt Hickory to Marietta; Palmer's on his left, and Howard's at Durham's house, three miles from Ackworth. McPherson was now on the left and Schofield on the right. As all the troops had been under fire for several consecutive days, though there had been no general battle, a rest until the 10th was declared. During this period, the repair of the railroad was hastened, and Allatoona was fortified as a secondary base of supplies.

June 8th, General Blair reached Ackworth with nine thousand men, having left fifteen hundred as a garrison at Allatoona. This reinforcement restored the grand aggregate of the armies again.

HEADQUARTERS MILITARY DIVISION OF THE MISSISSIPPI,
IN THE FIELD, KINGSTON, GA., *May* 20, 1864.

Major-General Halleck, Washington, D. C.:

We have secured two good bridges and an excellent ford across the Etowah. Our cars are now arriving with stores. I give two days' rest, to replenish and fit up. On the 23d, I will cross the Etowah and move on Dallas. This will turn the Allatoona Pass. If Johnston remain at Allatoona, I shall move on Marietta; but if he fall behind the Chattahoochee, I will make for Sandtown and Campbellton, but feign at the railroad crossing.

General Davis' division occupies Rome, and finds a good deal of provisions and plunder—fine iron-works and machinery. I have ordered the Seventeenth Corps, General Blair's, to march from Decatur to Rome. My share of militia should be sent at once, to cover our lines of communication. Notify General Grant that I will hold all of Johnston's army too busy to send anything against him.

W. T. SHERMAN,
Major-General.

[SPECIAL FIELD ORDERS, NO. 10.]

HEADQUARTERS MILITARY DIVISION OF THE MISSISSIPPI,
IN THE FIELD, KINGSTON, GA., *May* 22, 1864.

* * * * * * * *

II. The several armies will move punctually to-morrow morning, provided as heretofore ordered, by separate roads, aiming to reach the positions hereinafter assigned them in the course of the third day, and in the meantime each wing communicating freely with the center by cross-roads.

The Army of the Cumberland will move on Dallas by Euharley and Stilesboro; the division of General Jeff. C. Davis, now at Rome, marching direct for Dallas by Van Wert. The Army of the Ohio will move for position on the left, via Richland creek and Burnt Hickory or Huntsville.

The Army of the Tennessee will move, via Van Wert, to a position on the right, at or near the head of Pumpkin Vine creek, south of Dallas.

III. Marietta is the objective point, and the enemy is supposed to be in force at Allatoona, but with cavalry all along the line of the Etowah. Henceforth great caution must be exercised to cover and protect trains.

* * * * * * * * *

By order of Major-General W. T. Sherman.

L. M. DAYTON,
Aid-de-Camp.

HEADQUARTERS MILITARY DIVISION OF THE MISSISSIPPI,
IN THE FIELD, KINGSTON, GA., *May* 23, 1864.

General Blair, Huntsville, Ala.:

We are now all in motion for the Chattahoochee. Colonel Long telegraphs from Pulaski, and should overtake you at Decatur, or soon after leaving. Although you must move on Rome and Kingston by the direct road, still you can make believe you have designs on Gadsden and Talladega. Keep silent, and the enemy will exaggerate your strength and purposes. Johnston has called to him all the infantry of the Southwest, and also the cavalry of Mississippi, so you must look out for them. If they hang around you, keep Long close in, and watch the opportunity for him to charge with sabers.

W. T. SHERMAN,
Major-General Commanding.

HEADQUARTERS MILITARY DIVISION OF THE MISSISSIPPI,
IN THE FIELD, NEAR DALLAS, GA., *May* 27, 1864—11 A. M.

GENERAL:—If you can't drive the enemy from his position, work to the left, so as to connect with Hooker.

We are working on the left of the line in front of us, and as soon as you are in connection with General Hooker, I will strengthen the left, and work round in that direction, so we may, if we choose, march round their extreme right, and reach Marietta or Ackworth.

Yours, etc.,
W. T. SHERMAN,
Major-General Commanding.

General McPherson, Dallas, Ga.

HEADQUARTERS MILITARY DIVISION OF THE MISSISSIPPI,
NEAR DALLAS, *May* 28, 1864.

General Halleck, Washington, D. C.:

The enemy discovered my move to turn Allatoona, and moved to meet us here. Our columns met about one mile east of Pumpkin Vine creek, and we pushed them back about three miles, to the point where the road forks to Allatoona and Marietta. Here Johnston has chosen a strong line, and made hasty but strong parapets of timber and earth, and has thus far stopped us. My right is at Dallas, center about three miles north, and

ETOWAH—ALLATOONA—NEW HOPE CHURCH. 85

I am gradually working around by the left, to approach the railroad anywhere in front of Ackworth.

Country very densely wooded and broken; no roads of any consequence. We have had many sharp encounters, but nothing decisive. Both sides duly cautious in the obscurity of the ambushed ground.

W. T. SHERMAN,
Major-General.

HEADQUARTERS MILITARY DIVISION OF THE MISSISSIPPI,
IN THE FIELD, NEAR DALLAS, *May* 30, 1864.

General Halleck, Washington, D. C.:

To move General McPherson up to the center, he has had to make a retrograde of a mile or so, owing to difficult ground. Every time he attempted to withdraw division by division, the enemy attacked his whole line; it may be on the theory that we wanted to draw off altogether.

These assaults were made in the night, and were all repulsed with comparatively small loss to us, but seemingly heavy to the enemy. If we can induce the enemy to attack us, it is to our advantage.

Do n't expect us to make much progress toward the Chattahoochee till Blair comes up, and moves into Allatoona Pass.

* * * * * * * *

W. T. SHERMAN,
Major-General.

HEADQUARTERS MILITARY DIVISION OF THE MISSISSIPPI,
IN THE FIELD, ACKWORTH, *June* 8, 1864.

Major-General Halleck, Washington, D. C.:

General Blair arrived to-day, with two divisions of the Seventeenth Army Corps, about nine thousand (9,000) strong, having left about fifteen hundred (1,500) in the Allatoona Pass, to fortify and hold it. Colonel Wright, railroad superintendent, reports he will have the Etowah bridge done by the 12th instant.

To-morrow I will feel forward with cavalry, and follow with infantry the moment the enemy develops his designs.

If he fights at Kenesaw Mountain, I will turn it; but if he selects the line of the Chattahoochee, then I must study the case a little before I commit myself.

W. T. SHERMAN,
Major-General Commanding,

CHAPTER XXIX.

OPERATIONS NEAR KENESAW MOUNTAIN, INCLUDING THE BATTLE AT KULP'S HOUSE, ASSAULT OF THE MOUNTAIN, AND THE FLANK MOVEMENT.

JUNE 9th, General E. M. McCook, commanding the First division of cavalry, made a reconnoissance in front, and having driven back the enemy's pickets, formed a heavy line three miles in front of General Hooker, and observed the enemy in force on Pine Mountain. General Johnston's army now rested with its left on Lost Mountain, its center at Gilgath Church, and its right extended across the railroad. On the 10th, Palmer's corps advanced southeasterly and confronted Pine Mountain, and skirmishing, gained an eminence within artillery range. Howard's corps, with Hooker's in rear, came abreast. The next day, Palmer and Howard advanced slightly, and moved by the left flank until Palmer's left touched McPherson's right at the railroad. General Johnston's position was now fully discovered. His lines extended over a series of hills from Kenesaw Mountain to Lost Mountain, with Pine Mountain fortified in front. Before him, the ground was so broken by ravines and so densely wooded as greatly to embarrass the advance of the national armies.[1]

Two days of constant rain prevented all motion; but on the 14th, active overations were resumed. The Fourteenth Corps, carrying with it the left of the Fourth, advanced a mile. The right of the Fourth still rested in proximity to Pine Mountain, with the Twentieth Corps closed compactly upon it. During the day, Lieutenant-General Polk was killed upon the mountain by a cannon shot from one of the guns of Simonson's Indiana battery. The advanced position being now well turned by the forward movement of the left of the national line, was abandoned the following night, and the troops withdrawn to the main line of intrenchments between Kenesaw and Lost Mountain.

It was not known that General Johnston had a second intrenched line, and that he might not have time to construct one, General Sherman ordered an advance of his armies the next day. General Schofield was directed to threaten Lost Mountain; General McPherson to turn Kenesaw Mountain on the left, and General Thomas to press the center with a view to its rupture. General Schofield carried a line of works in his immediate front, which had been left exposed by the abandonment of Pine Mountain. General McPherson gained a hill on his left front, and General Thomas advanced a mile and a half in the center; but as in all other cases, General Johnston had his key-points well fortified and strongly defended. Newton's and Geary's divisions, supported by the remaining divisions of the Fourth and Twentieth Corps, carried an intrenched skirmish line and advanced nearly to the main line. General Howard, deeming it unsafe to assault without a reconnoissance, restrained Newton; but Geary penetrated the abatis and maintained a conflict under the enemy's guns until dark, losing five hundred and thirty-four men. During the night, the two corps intrenched a line a short distance from the enemy, and in the morning cannon responded to cannon, while the usual skirmishing prevailed between the armies. It being now evident to General Johnston that an assault could be made with fair prospect of success, he abandoned six miles of good field-works and fell back to an intrenched line on the Marietta side of Mud creek.

Early on the morning of the 17th, General Thomas ordered an advance of his army. The Fourth and Twentieth Corps and the right of the Fourteenth moved over the abandoned fortifications in a southeasterly direction, and encountered a skirmish line in front of a series of hills extending southwest from Kenesaw Mountain. The ground was so favorable to the enemy that it was not until night that his skirmishers were driven across Mud creek, and during the night he made two attempts to dislodge the skirmishers of the Fourth Corps intrenched on the west side of the stream. The next morning Generals Wood and Newton threw forward a strong line of skirmishers, and partially surprising the enemy, secured a portion of his main line. General Harker, of Newton's division, without waiting for orders, deployed two regiments to hold the position. Perceiving the advantage, General Howard ordered General Newton to move up his entire division in support. General Wood gained the ridge across the creek on the right and intrenched, and General Baird moved his division promptly on General Newton's left. As soon as it was dark, Newton's division intrenched within less than one hundred yards of the enemy's works. The advantage gained was decisive. General Johnston's new line was nearly perpendicular in direction to his old one, and that portion of the latter which he had lost was so related to the former that a successful assault was practicable. This General Thomas ordered for the next day, but the enemy withdrew before morning.

Early the following morning, General Thomas ordered an advance to ascertain how far General Johnston had receded. The Fourth Corps, Stanley's division leading, moved forward, and driving the enemy across Nose's creek, halted on the west bank; the Twentieth Corps crossed the creek late in the day, and formed with its left in proximity to the right of the Fourth; and the Fourteenth advanced toward Kenesaw Mountain and rested in line in proximity to its base, touching with its right the left of the Fourth. General Johnston's position was now well defined. Hood's corps was covering Marietta on the northeast; Loring's was holding Kenesaw Mountain, and Hardee's extended from the mountain to the road from Lost Mountain to Marietta. His lines were in view running along the base of the large mountain over the small one, and thence on the hills to the southwest. The large mountain was his salient, and from it right and left he drew back his flanks to cover Marietta and his communications. The position was one of great strength, thoroughly intrenched, and covered against approach by entanglements of every type.

Through three weeks of rain, General Sherman had been pressing the enemy from position to position, but it was now apparent that General Johnston must maintain his ground or defend Atlanta much nearer its gates. That he might reach round his army toward his communications, General Sherman determined to move his armies by the right flank, but not at first to uncover his depot of supplies at Big Shanty, and while he put the Army of the Cumberland in motion to the right, he held the Army of the Tennessee east of the railroad, in readiness, at call, or when the noise of battle should reveal the necessity to move also to the right.

On the morning of the 20th, General Wood's division and one brigade of General Stanley's moved to the right to relieve General Williams' division, that the latter might co-operate with General Schofield whose advance was resisted on the Sandtown road. During the forenoon, General Stanley, with Whittaker's and Kirby's brigades, crossed Nose's creek and intrenched a line, and in the afternoon Whittaker carried a wooded hill in his front and Kirby a bald one before him. The former barricaded at once, and held his position against repeated and furious assaults of the enemy, but the latter having been less prompt in constructing defenses, was driven back. At dark, the extended right of the Fourteenth Corps touched the left of the Fourth, and Williams' division was in connection with General Schofield's left.

The next morning, General Newton's division was relieved by a division from General Palmer's corps, when it moved to the right of General Wood. This accomplished, General Howard ordered Kirby's brigade and Nodine's, the left brigade of General Wood's division, to regain the hill which Kirby had lost the evening previous. It had been intrenched by the enemy during the night, and his artillery bore upon it, but these brigades carried it handsomely and intrenched its crest, under the fire of two of the enemy's batteries. General Wood then pushed two regiments to the front and right, and gained an eminence which commanded a long intrenched skirmish line, and permitted the advance of the right of the Fourth Corps a distance of five hundred yards. General Hooker advanced with his left abreast of General Howard's right, against all the resistance the enemy could offer. This movement was so threatening, that General Johnston transferred Hood's corps from his right to his left, leaving only

Wheeler's cavalry in front of the Army of the Tennessee, and made three unsuccessful assaults during the night to dislodge General Wood.

The removal of this corps from General McPherson's front was so thoroughly covered by the activity of Wheeler's troopers, that he was led to believe that there was a concentration rather than a vacuum behind their bold front. But though General Johnston succeeded in hiding the uncovering of his right, and the heavy concentration on his left, his subsequent aggression resulted in signal defeat. He gained, however, in defensive strength at the very point it was most needed, and defeated the combination to turn his left, and in fact defeated for a time all efforts to dislodge him. General Sherman's plan proposed that General McPherson should, " at the first possible chance, push forward on the line of the railroad and main Marietta road, break through the enemy and pursue him, or secure a position on the commanding ridge over which these roads pass," while the movement of the Army of the Cumberland toward General Schofield, who was searching for the enemy's left flank, should cause him to lengthen his line "beyond his ability to defend," and give an opportunity to break it, by a quick and energetic blow. This manœuver entirely failed in its final development through the transfer of Hood's corps from the right to the left, so secretly that it was in battle against Hooker's corps, on the Powder Spring road, before it was ascertained that it was not still before McPherson.

The movements ordered by General Sherman for the 22d, had reference to preparation for attack upon Johnston's left flank. He directed General Schofield to cross Nose's creek, and turn the head of his column up toward Marietta until he reached Hooker, and deploy south of the Marietta and Powder Spring road; while General Hooker was ordered to get possession of the ground, if practicable, up to Mrs. Kulp's, and deploy with his right resting on the Powder Spring road. This accomplished, the remainder of General Thomas' line was to be advanced in conformity. General McPherson was instructed to press the enemy in his front, to cover Big

Shanty, and hold his rear massed in readiness to support General Thomas, should he become heavily engaged.

At 3 A. M. on the 22d, Cobham's detachment of Geary's division drove the enemy from the hill a mile in front of the center of the Twentieth Corps. The whole division soon followed, and intrenched a commanding ridge, reversing the works of the enemy, and covering artillery as well as infantry lines. Subsequently, Williams' division advanced to Geary's right, and Butterfield's to his left, each skirmishing into position. The corps did not form a continuous line, but each division occupied a hill with slopes to right and left, and between Williams' left and Geary's right there was a swampy ravine. Williams' right rested on the Powder Spring road, at Kulp's house, and his division was formed with Ruger's brigade on the right, Knipe's in the center, and Robinson's on the left. In front of Robinson, who held a lateral hill, slightly refused, there was an open space extending to Geary's front. The ground was open before Knipe, except in front of his left, and almost entirely wooded in Ruger's front. General Williams' placed Winegar's and Woodbury's batteries before his center and left so as to command all the open ground. When the Twentieth Corps had attained this advanced position, General Howard moved his line forward in correspondence.

At 3 P. M., General Williams was informed that Hood's corps was massed before him. Reporting the fact to General Hooker, he was directed to deploy his division and construct breastworks without delay. He had, however, no time to construct defenses, and barely enough for array, before the enemy was seen to emerge from the woods beyond the open space in his front and dash toward his lines. The formation in triple lines and the peculiar shout of the troops forming them, alike, presaged an assault. The movement was begun with the enemy's usual spirit, but Woodbury's canister swept the open ground with such destructive effect that the enemy was soon thrown into confusion and retreat. A portion of the column was driven directly back, and the remainder was forced by volleys from Knipe's line and Ruger's left, to seek cover in a ravine and dense clump of trees and underbrush, on Knipe's left front.

A second column moved directly against Robinson's position, but being exposed in the open ground to a direct fire from Winegar's battery, and an enfilading one from Geary's guns on the left, was also thrown into confusion and rout. As a final effort, the rebel troops who had taken shelter in the ravine and woods, having been reinforced from the rear, attempted to turn Knipe's left flank by a stealthy advance under cover; but the movement having been perceived, Winegar's battery and Geary's artillery again opened. The Sixty-first Ohio of Robinson's brigade advanced to support the endangered flank, and the concentric fire of artillery and musketry soon completed the repulse of the enemy. While Hood's attack was in progress, heavy cannonading was maintained throughout the front of the Army of the Cumberland.

In the repulse of Hood's attack, General Hooker's artillery was so remarkably effective, that General Johnston admitted in his official report that his troops, Stevenson's and Hindman's divisions, were compelled to withdraw by the fire of fortified artillery. His loss was exceedingly heavy; General Hooker's very light. General Williams, who alone was directly assailed, lost only one hundred and thirty men, including nineteen captured on the picket line by the sudden advance of the enemy. Major D. C. Becket, of the Sixty-first Ohio, was killed.

As soon as the character of the attack upon General Hooker was developed, General Thomas made provision for his support. The reserve regiments of the Fourth Corps were immediately thrown to the right, and as soon as practicable, Butterfield's division was relieved by Stanley's, and moved to the rear of Williams' right. These dispositions were sufficient for defense, but the transfer of Hood's corps to General Johnston's left flank, necessitated a new combination, either to turn his position or break through his lines. General Thomas suggested that General McPherson should attack Marietta from the east side of Kenesaw Mountain; but General Sherman decided to attack General Johnston's fortified lines near his center, and on the 24th, directed Generals McPherson and Thomas to make preparations to assault on the 27th—the former near Little Kenesaw, and the latter about a mile to the south, in front of the Fourth Corps.

OPERATIONS NEAR KENESAW MOUNTAIN.

General Thomas designated Davis' and Newton's divisions to form the assaulting column, and during the night of the 25th, Davis' and Baird's divisions having been relieved on the left of the Army of the Cumberland by General McPherson's troops, moved to the rear of the Fourth Corps. On the morning of the 27th, Morgan's brigade of Davis' division occupied the intrenchments thrown up by Whittaker's brigade of Stanley's division. Stanley moved to the left to support Newton, and Baird held his division in direct support on Davis' right. Hooker's whole corps was held in readiness to support Palmer's and Howard's.

At 8 A. M. the preparations were complete. The brigades of Colonels Daniel McCook and J. G. Mitchell were massed in rear of the intrenchments held by Morgan's brigade, as there was no cover for formation in front. Their point of attack was a salient in the enemy's works, conforming to a projection in the ridge, around whose summit his fortifications were built, and was selected in consequence of the absence of obstructions in front. Newton's division was formed with Harker's and Wagner's brigades in line, slightly separated for better cover, and Kimball's in echelon with Wagner's. For fifteen minutes all the artillery available, poured a concentrated fire upon the points of attack, and then the columns moved forward. From the moment that McCook's and Mitchell's brigades bounded over their intrenchments, they were subjected to a galling fire of artillery and musketry. The distance to the enemy's works was about six hundred yards, and the ground was rough and partially covered with trees and undergrowth; but disregarding the fire of the enemy and the difficulties of the way, these brigades advanced rapidly until they were under the guns of the enemy. They reached his works, but such was their strength, and the spirit of the heavy forces behind them, and such their own exhaustion, that they were compelled to halt. At this juncture, their situation was exceedingly critical. To carry the works was impracticable; to retreat, threatened almost total destruction, and the maintenance of position likewise involved great hazard and loss. As, however, it was soon ascertained that it was possible to so far restrain the fire of the enemy by a vigorous response that defenses could be constructed, General Thomas directed

General Davis to hold the position and fortify it. Intrenching tools were at once sent forward, and works were thrown up within a few yards of the enemy. The loss in the advance and during the day was very great. Colonel McCook fell early mortally wounded; Colonel Harmon, the next in rank, was soon after killed, when the command fell to Colonel Dilworth. Lieutenant-Colonel James Shane and Major John Yager of Mitchell's brigade received fatal wounds, and from both brigades a very large number of officers and men were killed and wounded.

The conditions of Newton's assault were somewhat different, and so was the result. His troops were less exposed in the advance, but the formidable obstructions and entanglements held them to a terrific fire under circumstances that forbade its restraint. As a consequence, he was compelled to withdraw his division altogether as soon as it was evident that the assault could not be successful. At the moment of making a second effort to advance, General Harker was mortally wounded, and in his brigade and in Wagner's the loss was very great. Some were killed on the enemy's parapet.

The aggregate loss to Davis and Newton, in nearly equal division, was fifteen hundred and eighty killed, wounded, and missing. The compensation was the lodgment of troops in proximity to works too strong to be assaulted, and the infliction of a loss to the enemy of two hundred and thirty-six men, including one hundred captured. The officers and men engaged in this assault "went to their work with the greatest coolness and gallantry," as General Thomas testified, but their valor and sacrifice brought no adequate reward.

During the progress of the action in the center, Generals McPherson and Schofield demonstrated strongly on the enemy's flanks. The former threw a portion of his army against a spur of Little Kenesaw, and though he attained position near the enemy, did not disturb his line. The latter gained some advantage at Olley's creek, as opening the way for another flank movement to the right.

Thus far in the campaign, Generals Sherman and Johnston had each kept up the most persistent belligerence to keep the other from detaching troops to Virginia. But on the 28th, General Grant authorized General Sherman to make his movements without reference to the retention of General Johnston's forces where they were. This independence and the necessity of active offense induced immediate preparation for an effort to reach General Johnston's communications. As the accomplishment of this project necessitated the temporary abandonment of the railroad, General Sherman proposed, should the development of his movement cause General Johnston to abandon Marietta, to swing in upon the road in his rear, but should he hold that position, to strike it between him and the Chattahoochee bridge.

The Army of the Cumberland lost during the month five thousand seven hundred and forty-seven men—sixty-seven officers killed, two hundred and fifty-nine wounded, and eight missing, and eight hundred and seventy-three enlisted men killed, four thousand three hundred wounded, and forty missing. The army captured seven hundred and forty-two prisoners, including thirty-seven officers, and received five hundred and two deserters at Nashville and Chattanooga.

During the month, the enemy's cavalry in small parties, assisted by guerrillas and disloyal citizens, was exceedingly active along the railroad south of Dalton, but wrought no damage beyond slight interruptions and the destruction of a few cars. On the 10th, the "District of the Etowah" was created, with General Steedman in command, who was charged with the protection of the line of supply south from Chattanooga. Soon after, the district commander sent Colonel Watkins' brigade of cavalry to Lafayette, and a few days later it was attacked by General Pillow with about two thousand men. Colonel Watkins refused to surrender, and with four hundred men defended the town until reinforced by Colonel Croxton, commanding the Fourth Kentucky Mounted Infantry, whose vigorous attack routed the enemy. Pillow's loss was about three hundred men, including eighty captured. Watkins and Croxton lost sixty. On the 28th, Brigadier-General Smith's division of the Fifteenth Corps arrived at Chattanooga, and was soon after disposed to protect the railroad north from Allatoona.

As these troops gave assurance of secure communications, and as supplies had been accumulated in such quantity as to warrant the temporary abandonment of the railroad, General Sherman gave orders, July 1st, for the movement of his armies to the right, to turn the position he had failed to carry by assault. His orders required that General Thomas should hold his intrenchments and observe the enemy until General McPherson should pass to the right in menace to Johnston's rear. General McPherson moved his army on the 2d, and the night following General Johnston withdrew his army, and when morning dawned, was far on his way to other intrenchments. In the pursuit, the Army of the Cumberland first converged upon Marietta, and then moved on the direct roads to Atlanta. The enemy's rear-guard was overtaken four miles from Marietta, and driven forward to Ruff's station, where his forces were found in strong earthworks, constructed long before in provision for retreat. The lines of the Army of the Cumberland were speedily formed, and at midnight were again in closest proximity to the enemy. General Sherman urged his army commanders to extreme activity and vigor to press the enemy in confusion upon the bridges across the Chattahoochee. But General Johnston was secure against direct attack. His forecast of the possibilities of the unequal warfare had been so exhaustive that his steps from one intrenched position to another had all been anticipated. He held his works at Ruff's station and on his left flank against General McPherson, until Hood's and Loring's corps were across the Chattahoochee, and then placed Hardee's corps in his intrenchments on the right bank of the river to cover the bridges.

General Sherman's plans were soon formed, though their execution was deferred to give rest to his armies, perfect his communications, and accumulate supplies in proximate depots, that he might be free from daily dependence upon the continuity of his communications in the next stage of his campaign. He proposed to make the next advance from his left, and the initial dispositions were such as at the same time to protect his communications against an anticipated cavalry raid north of Marietta. While holding the main portion of the Army of the Cumberland firmly against Hardee's corps in his defenses, and feigning with the Army of the Tennessee and Stoneman's cavalry far down to the right, he threw Garrard's cavalry to Roswell, and disposed the Army of the Ohio, and portions of the Fourth Corps, to secure and fortify the crossings from Roswell to Paice's ferry. Between the 6th and 9th, two heads of column crossed the river, one at Roswell and the other at Phillips' ferry; and to give security to the crossings, strong defenses were thrown up on the enemy's side of the river.

[SPECIAL FIELD ORDERS, NO. 20.]

HEADQUARTERS MILITARY DIVISION OF THE MISSISSIPPI,
IN THE FIELD, ACWORTH, GA., *June* 9, 1864.

The armies will move forward to-morrow morning.

I. Major-General Thomas, the center, on the Burnt Hickory and the Marietta road, and such other roads as he may choose between it and the Acworth and Marietta road, aiming to strike the northern end of Kenesaw Mountain.

II. Major-General McPherson will move by the Acworth and Marietta road, with a column following the railroad, and his cavalry well to the left after passing Big Shanty.

III. Major-General Schofield will cover his wagons well about Mount Olive Church, and feel well with cavalry and skirmishers down the road past Hardshell Church, to ascertain the enemy's strength about Lost Mountain and the ridge connecting it with Kenesaw Mountain. He will not pass position about Hardshell Church in force until he is certain Major-General Thomas has reached some point on Kenesaw.

IV. The object will be to develop the enemy's position and strength, and to draw artillery fire from his intrenched works. . . .

V. Major-General Stoneman's cavalry will cover the right, and Brigadier-General Garrard's the left flanks. Brigadier-General McCook's cavalry should be kept to the rear, or to keep up communications.

VI. The movement will begin at six (6) o'clock A. M., and continue until some one of the columns reaches Kenesaw Mountain, or until the center is checked.

By order of Major-General W. T. Sherman.

R. M. SAWYER
Aid-de-Camp.

HEADQUARTERS MILITARY DIVISION OF THE MISSISSIPPI,
IN THE FIELD, BIG SHANTY, *June* 11, 1864.

General Halleck, Washington, D. C.:

Johnston is intrenched on the hills embracing Lost Mountain, Pine Hill, and Kenesaw. Our lines are down to him, but it has rained so hard, and the ground is so boggy, that we have not developed any weak point or flank.

I will proceed with due caution, and try and make no mistake. The Etowah bridge is done, and the construction train has been to our very camps. Supplies will now be accumulated at Allatoona Pass, or brought right up to our lines.

One of my chief objects being to give full employment to Joe Johnston, it makes no difference where he is, so he is not on his way to Virginia.

W. T. SHERMAN,
Major-General.

HEADQUARTERS MILITARY DIVISION OF THE MISSISSIPPI,
IN THE FIELD, BIG SHANTY, *June* 13, 1864.

Major-General Halleck, Washington, D. C.:

We have had hard and cold rains for about ten days. A gleam of sunshine this evening gives hope of a change. The roads are insufficient here, and the fields and new ground are simply impassable to wheels. As soon as possible I will study Johnston's position on Kenesaw and Lost Mountain, and adopt some plan to dislodge him or draw him out of his position. We can not risk the heavy losses of an assault at this distance from our base. Cars now run to our very front camps. All well.

There are troops enough in Kentucky to manage Morgan, and in Tennessee to watch Forrest should he make his appearance, as Johnston doubtless calculates.

W. T. SHERMAN,
Major-General.

HEADQUARTERS MILITARY DIVISION OF THE MISSISSIPPI,
IN THE FIELD, BIG SHANTY, *June* 16, 1864.

General Halleck, Washington, D. C.:

General Thomas did not make the progress last night I expected. He found the enemy strongly intrenched on a line slightly advanced from a straight line connecting Lost and Kenesaw Mountain. I have been along it to-day, and am pressing up close. Shall study it, and am now inclined to feign on both flanks, and assault the center. It may cost us dear, but in result would surpass an attempt to pass round. The enemy has a strong position, and covers his road well, and the only weak point in the game is in having the Chattahoochee in his rear. If, by assaulting, I can break his line, I see no reason why it should not produce a decisive effect. I know he shifts his troops about to meet our

OPERATIONS NEAR KENESAW MOUNTAIN. 99

supposed attacks, and thereby fatigues his men, and the woods will enable me to mask our movements.

W. T. SHERMAN,
Major-General Commanding.

HEADQUARTERS MILITARY DIVISION OF THE MISSISSIPPI,
IN THE FIELD, BIG SHANTY, *June* 21, 1864.

Major-General Halleck, Washington, D. C.:

This is the nineteenth day of rain, and the prospect of clear weather as far off as ever. The roads are impassable, and fields and woods become quagmires after a few wagons have crossed, yet we are at work all the time. The left flank is across Novaday, and the right across Nose's creek. The enemy holds Kenesaw, a conical mountain, with Marietta behind it, and has retired his flanks to cover that town and his railroad. I am all ready to attack the moment the weather and roads will permit troops and artillery to move with anything like life.

W. T. SHERMAN,
Major-General Commanding.

HEADQTARTERS MILITARY DIVISION OF THE MISSISSIPPI,
IN THE FIELD, *June* 22, 1864.

GENERAL:—I will start early to look at the position of McPherson as near the north base of Kenesaw as I can safely do, and then come to Wallace's, or the house in front, and then over to Hooker. I have ordered Schofield to cross his whole command over Nose's creek, and turn the head of his column up toward Marietta, until he reaches Hooker, to support and co-operate on his right, but to keep his cavalry and a part of his rear infantry on the Sandtown road, prepared to regain it in case the enemy shows signs of let go. I fear we will get our commands too close, but I suppose Schofield can find room to deploy south of the Powder Springs and Marietta road. You may order Hooker to extend to that road and leave Schofield beyond. If he can get possession of the ground up to Mrs. Kulp's house, I wish him to do so, and the balance of your line to conform. I will explain McPherson's orders when I meet you.

W. T. SHERMAN,
Major-General Commanding.

Major-General Thomas, Commanding Army of the Cumberland.

HEADQUARTERS MILITARY DIVISION OF THE MISSISSIPPI,
IN THE FIELD, BIG SHANTY, *June* 22, 1864—9 P. M.

GENERAL:—When on the hill in front of your center to-day, waiting for you, I signaled General Hooker:

" How are you getting along ? Near what house are you ?
" W. T. SHERMAN,
"*Major-General.*"

At this hour (9½) I have received this answer:

"KULP HOUSE—5.30 P. M.

"We have repulsed two heavy attacks, and feel confident, our only apprehension being from our extreme right flank. Three (3) entire corps are in front of us.

"MAJOR-GENERAL HOOKER."

I was at the Wallace house at 5.30 P. M., and the Kulp house was within two miles; and though I heard some cannonading, I had no idea of his being attacked, and General Hooker must be mistaken about three (3) corps being in his front. Johnston's army has only three corps, and I know there was a respectable force along McPherson's front; so much so, that this general thought the enemy was massing against him. I know there was some force in front of Palmer and Howard, for I was there. Still, it is very natural the enemy should meet Hooker at that point in force, and I gave Schofield orders this morning to conduct his column from Nose's creek, on the Powder Spring road, toward Marietta, and support Hooker's right flank, sending his cavalry down the Powder Spring road toward Sweetwater, and leaving some infantry from his rear to guard the fords. Captain Dayton says that General Schofield received my orders, which were in writing. If later information shows that Schofield is not up, send a staff officer and notify him of the necessity, and, if need be, call off all of Palmer's, and notify McPherson, who has orders for this very contingency. To-morrow, if need be, we must bring things to a crisis.

Cars and telegraph now all right. Some of John E. Smith's men are at Chattanooga, so that I think our road will be better guarded. The cavalry of Lowe should be out on the Tennessee road, patrolling from Cartersville to Spring Place.

W. T. SHERMAN,
Major-General Commanding.

Major-General Thomas, Commanding Army of the Cumberland

HEADQUARTERS MILITARY DIVISION OF THE MISSISSIPPI,
IN THE FIELD, BIG SHANTY, *June* 22, 1864.

GENERAL:—General Hooker, this P. M., advanced to the Kulp house, two and half miles southwest of Marietta, and reports finding three (3) corps. He was attacked twice, and successfully repulsed the enemy. General Thomas thinks that that will be the enemy's tactics, and that you ought to attack Marietta from that side of Kenesaw, but I judge the safer and better plan to be the one I indicated, viz., for you to leave a light force and cover that flank, and throw the remainder rapidly, and as much out of view as possible, to our right.

You may make the necessary orders, and be prepared for rapid action to-morrow. So dispose matters that the big guns of Kenesaw will do you as little mischief as possible. Yours, etc.,

W. T. SHERMAN,
Major-General.

Major-General McPherson, Commanding the Army of the Tennessee.

[SPECIAL FIELD ORDERS, NO. 28.]

HEADQUARTERS MILITARY DIVISION OF THE MISSISSIPPI,
IN THE FIELD, NEAR KENESAW MOUNTAIN, *June* 24, 1864.

The army commanders will make full reconnoissances and preparation to attack the enemy in force on the 27th instant, at eight (8) o'clock A. M. precisely. The commanding general will be on "Signal Hill," and will have telegraphic communication with all the army commanders.

I. Major-General Thomas will assault the enemy at any point near his center, to be selected by himself, and will make any changes in his troops necessary, by night, so as not to attract the attention of the enemy.

II. Major-General McPherson will feign by a movement of his cavalry and one (1) division of infantry on his extreme left, approaching Marietta from the north, and using artillery freely; but will make his real attack at a point south and west of Kenesaw.

III. Major-General Schofield will feel to his extreme right, and threaten that flank of the enemy with artillery, and display, but attack some one point of the enemy's line as near the Marietta and Powder Spring road as he can with prospect of success.

IV. All commanders will maintain reserve and secrecy, even from their staff officers, but make all proper preparations and reconnoissances. When troops are to be shifted to accomplish this attack, the movements will be made at night. At the time of the general attack, the skirmishers at the base of Kenesaw will take advantage of it, to gain, if possible, the summit, and hold it.

V. Each attacking column will endeavor to break a single point of the enemy's line, and make a secure lodgment beyond, and be prepared for following it up toward Marietta and the railroad, in case of success.

By order of Major-General W. T. Sherman.

L. M. DAYTON,
Aid-de-Camp.

HEADQUARTERS MILITARY DIVISION OF THE MISSISSIPPI,
IN THE FIELD, NEAR KENESAW, *June* 24, 1864.

GENERAL:—I am directed by the major-general commanding to acknowledge the receipt through you of Rousseau's communication in copy, the original of which also came to hand. The general commanding thinks quite favorably of the suggestion therein, and desires you to instruct General Rousseau to gradually collect his available force of cavalry and infantry at Pulaski, Athens, and Decatur, upon the representation of protecting our roads against Forrest, but really to strike as proposed; the cavalry to be well fed, and the infantry stripped for light, rapid movements, and to be ready to move at telegraphic notice from us. The time to do it will be when we have forced Johnston across the Chattahoochee. . . . .

L. M. DAYTON,
Aid-de-Camp.

Major-General G. H. Thomas, Commanding, etc.

HEADQUARTERS MILITARY DIVISION OF THE MISSISSIPPI,
IN THE FIELD, NEAR KENESAW MOUNTAIN, *June* 25, 1864.

General Halleck, Washington, D. C.:

I have nothing new to report; constant skirmishing and cannonading. I am making some changes in the disposition of our men, with a view to attack the enemy's left center. I shall aim to make him stretch his line until he weakens it, and then break through.

* * * * * * * * *

W. T. SHERMAN,
Major-General Commanding.

HEADQUARTERS MILITARY DIVISION OF THE MISSISSIPPI,
IN THE FIELD, *June* 27, 1864—11.45 A. M.

General Schofield:

Neither McPherson nor Thomas has succeeded in breaking through, but each has made substantial progress, at some cost. Push your operations on the flank, and keep me advised.

W. T. SHERMAN,
Major-General Commanding.

HEADQUARTERS MILITARY DIVISION OF THE MISSISSIPPI,
IN THE FIELD, *June* 27, 1864—11.45 A. M.

General Thomas:

McPherson's column marched near the top of the hill through very tangled brush, but was repulsed; it is found almost impossible to deploy, but they still hold the ground. I wish you to study well the positions, and, if it be possible, break through the line to do it; it is easier now than it will be hereafter. I hear Leggett's guns well behind the mountain.

W. T. SHERMAN,
Major-General Commanding,

HEADQUARTERS MILITARY DIVISION OF THE MISSISSIPPI.
IN THE FIELD, *June* 27, 1864—1.30 P. M.

General Thomas:

McPherson and Schofield are at a dead lock. Do you think you can carry any part of the enemy's main line to-day? McPherson's men are up to the abatis, and can't move without direct assault. I will order an assault, if you think you can succeed at any point. Schofield has one division close up on the Powder Spring road, and the other across Olley's creek, about two miles to his right and rear.

W. T. SHERMAN,
Major-General Commanding.

HEADQUARTERS MILITARY DIVISION OF THE MISSISSIPPI,
IN THE FIELD, *June* 27—2.25 P. M.

General Thomas:

Secure what advantageous ground you have gained; but is there anything in the enemy's present position, that, if we should approach by regular saps, he could not make a dozen new parapets before our saps are completed? Does the nature of the ground warrant the time necessary for regular approaches?

W. T. SHERMAN,
Major-General Commanding.

HEADQUARTERS DEPARTMENT OF THE CUMBERLAND,
June 27—10.45 A. M.

Major-General Sherman:

Yours received. Harker's brigade advanced to within twenty paces of the enemy's breastworks, and was repulsed with canister at short range, General Harker losing an arm. General Wagner's brigade of Newton's division, supporting General Harker, was so severely handled that it is compelled to reorganize. Colonel Mitchell's brigade of Davis' division captured one line of rebel breastworks, which they still hold. McCook's brigade was also severely handled, nearly every colonel being killed or wounded. It is compelled to fall back and reorganize. The troops are all too much exhausted to advance, but we hold all that we have gained.

GEO. H. THOMAS,
Major-General U. S. V.

HEADQUARTERS DEPARTMENT OF THE CUMBERLAND, *June 27.*

General Sherman:

Your dispatch of 2.25 received. We still hold all the ground we have gained, and the division commanders report their ability to hold. They also report the enemy's works exceedingly strong; in fact, so strong that they can not be carried by assault, except by immense sacrifice, even if they can be carried at all. I think, therefore, the best chance is to approach them by regular saps, if we can find a favorable approach to batter them down. We have already lost heavily to-day, without gaining any material advantage. One or two more such assaults would use up this army.

GEO. H. THOMAS,
Major-General U. S. V.

HEADQUARTERS MILITARY DIVISION OF THE MISSISSIPPI,
IN THE FIELD, NEAR KENESAW, *June* 27, 1864.

General Halleck:

Pursuant to my orders on the 24th, a diversion was made on each flank of the enemy, especially on the Sandtown road, and at 8 A. M. General McPherson, at the southwest end of the Kenesaw, and General Thomas at a point about a mile further south; at the same time, skirmishers and artillery along the whole line kept up a sharp fire. Neither attack succeeded, though both columns reached the enemy's works, which are very strong. General McPherson reports his loss about five hundred, and General Thomas about two thousand; the loss particularly heavy in generals and field officers. General Harker is reported mortally wounded; also, Colonel Dan. McCook, commanding brigade; Colonel Rice, Fifty-seventh Ohio, very seriously. Colonels Barnhill, Fortieth Illinois, and Augustine, Fifty-fifth Illinois, are killed.

The facilities with which defensive works of timber and earth are constructed, gives the party on the defensive great advantage

I can not well turn the position of the enemy without abandoning my railroad, and we are already so far from our supplies that it is as much as the road can do to feed and supply the army. There are no supplies of any kind here. I can press Johnston, and keep him from reinforcing Lee, but to assault him in position will cost us more lives than we can spare.

McPherson took, to-day, one hundred prisoners, and Thomas about as many, but I do not suppose that we have inflicted heavy loss on the enemy, as he kept close behind his parapets.

W. T. SHERMAN,
Major-General.

HEADQUARTERS MILITARY DIVISION OF THE MISSISSIPPI,
June 27, 1864—9 P. M.

General Thomas:

Are you willing to risk the move on Fulton, cutting loose from our railroad? It would bring matters to a crisis, and Schofield has secured the way.

W. T. SHERMAN,
Major-General Commanding.

HEADQUARTERS DEPARTMENT OF THE CUMBERLAND, *June* 27.

General Sherman:

What force do you think of moving with? If with the greater part of the army, I think it decidedly better than butting against breastworks twelve feet thick, and strongly abatised.

GEO. H. THOMAS,
Major-General U. S. V.

HEADQUARTERS MILITARY DIVISION OF THE MISSISSIPPI,
NEAR KENESAW MOUNTAIN, *June* 27, 1864.

General Thomas:

Let your troops fortify as close up to the enemy as possible. Get good positions for artillery, and group as conveniently as you can by corps and divisions, keeping reserves. Schofield has the Sandtown road within eleven miles of the Chattahoochee, and he could move by that flank. The question of supplies will be the only one. I regret beyond measure the loss of two such young and dashing officers as Harker and McCook.

McPherson lost two or three of his young and dashing officers, which is apt to be the case in unsuccessful assaults. Had we broken the line to-day, it would have been most decisive; but as it is, our loss is small compared with some of those east. It should not in the least discourage us. At times, assaults are necessary and inevitable. At Arkansas Post we succeeded; at Vicksburg we failed. I do not think our loss to-day greater than Johnston's, when he attacked Hooker and Schofield the first day we occupied our present ground.

W. T. SHERMAN,
Major-General Commanding.

HEADQUARTERS MILITARY DIVISION OF THE MISSISSIPPI,
IN THE FIELD, NEAR KENESAW, *June* 27, 1864.

General McPherson:

Is General Blair back? Report to me fully his operations for to-day. Schofield's right division (Cox) has gained a good position on the other side of Olley's creek and at the head of Nickajack. If we had our supplies well up, I would move by the right flank; but suppose we must cover our railroad for a few days.

W. T. SHERMAN,
Major-General Commanding.

WASHINGTON, *June* 28, 1864—4 P. M.

Major-General Sherman:

General Grant directs me to say that the movements of your army may be made entirely independent of any desire to retain Johnston's forces where they are. He does not think that Lee will bring any more additional troops to Richmond, on account of the difficulty of feeding them.

H. W. HALLECK,
Major-General.

HEADQUARTERS MILITARY DIVISION OF THE MISSISSIPPI,
IN THE FIELD, NEAR KENESAW, *June* 30, 1864.

General Schofield:

General Thomas is here. He will study the ground well, and prepare to relieve Hascall's division to-night, in which event I want you with your whole force to occupy between Olley's creek and Nickajack, to drive the enemy from the forks of the road, and picket as far down as Nickajack creek, and as far down on the Sandtown road as possible. At the same time, General Stoneman's cavalry, supported by McCook, should move across Sweetwater by Powder Springs, and down the west side of Sweetwater creek to Sweetwater town, which crossing once secured, Stoneman to hold it, and McCook to return to Lost Mountain.

General McPherson's command to remain where it is until our stores are complete, when his cavalry will guard the roads from Marietta toward Allatoona, while McPherson moves with his whole command down the Sandtown road to the Chattahoochee. If Johnston holds on to

Kenesaw, then we must strike some point on the railroad, between Marietta and the bridge; but if he lets go of Marietta, then we will swing across the railroad, to a position that gives us again the use of the railroad.

W. T. SHERMAN,
Major-General Commanding.

[SPECIAL FIELD ORDERS, NO 31.]

HEADQUARTERS MILITARY DIVISION OF THE MISSISSIPPI,
IN THE FIELD, NEAR KENESAW MOUNTAIN, *July* 1, 1864.

The object of the contemplated movement is to deprive the enemy of the great advantage he has in Kenesaw, as a watch-tower from which to observe our every movement, to force him to come out of his intrenchments, or move further south. To attain this end:

I. All army commanders will fill up their wagons at Big Shanty depot, to their utmost, with provisions, ammunition, and forage. The chief quartermaster and commissary will give all necessary orders to clean out the depots in front of Allatoona, and so instruct that the locomotives and cars will come forward of Allatoona with great caution, and only when ordered by chief commmissary.

II. Major-General Thomas will hold the ground below Kenesaw, as far as Olley's creek, near Mount Zion; Major-General Schofield that from Olley's creek to Nickajack, and General McPherson will move his train and troops rapidly in a single march, and as little observed from Kenesaw as possible, to the Sandtown road, and down it to the extreme right, with one corps near the Widow Mitchell's, another near Ruff's mill on the Nickajack, and the the third in reserve, near the forks of the road.

III. General Garrard's cavalry will cover the roads out of Marietta which pass north of Kenesaw, and General Stoneman's cavalry will occupy Sweetwater (old town), coincident with the movement of McPherson. General McCook will receive orders from General Thomas. In case the enemy presses Garrard back by superior and overwhelming forces, he will send one of his brigades to the flank of General Thomas, and will, with the others, fall back gradually toward Allatoona, disputing every foot of ground.

IV. Major-General McPherson will threaten the Chattahoochee river and also the railroad, and General Thomas will press the enemy close, and, at the very earliest possible moment, break his lines, and reach the railroad below Marietta. All movements must be vigorous and rapid, as the time allowed is limited by the supplies in our wagons.

By order of Major-General W. T. Sherman.

L. M. DAYTON,
Aid-de-Camp.

HEADQUARTERS MILITARY DIVISION OF THE MISSISSIPPI,
MARIETTA, GA., *July* 3, 1864—10 A. M.
General Halleck, Washington, D. C.:
    The movement on our right caused the enemy to evacuate. We occupied Kenesaw at daylight, and Marietta at 8½ A. M. Thomas is moving down the main road toward the Chattahoochee; McPherson toward the mouth of Nickajack, on the Sandtown road. Our cavalry is on the extreme flank. Whether the enemy will halt this side of the Chattahoochee or not will soon be known. Marietta is almost entirely abandoned by its inhabitants, and more than a mile of the railroad iron is removed betwen the town and the foot of Kenesaw. I propose to press the enemy close till he is across the Chattahoochee river, when I must accumulate stores and better guard my rear.
                                        W. T. SHERMAN,
                                      Major-General Commanding,

---

HEADQUARTERS MILITARY DIVISION OF THE MISSISSIPPI,
IN THE FIELD, NEAR CHATTAHOOCHEE, *July* 9, 1864.
General Halleck, Washington, D. C.:
    I telegraphed to you, and Mr. Secretary Stanton answers. Drop me a word now and then of advice and encouragement. I think I have done well to maintain such an army in this country, fighting for sixty (60) days, and yet my losses are made up by the natural increase. The assault I made was no mistake. I had to do it. The enemy, and our own army and officers, had settled down into the conviction that the assault of lines formed no part of my game, and the moment the enemy was found behind anything like a parapet, why everybody would deploy, throw up counter-works, and take it easy, leaving it to to the "Old Man" to turn the position. Had the assault been made with one-fourth more vigor (mathematically), I would have put the head of George Thomas' whole army right through Johnston's deployed line on the best ground for " go ahead," while my entire forces were well in hand on roads converging to my then object, Marietta. Had Harker and McCook not been struck down so early, the assault would have succeeded, and then the battle would have all been in our favor, on account of our superiority of numbers and initiative. Even as it was, Johnston has been much more cautious since, and gave ground more freely. His next fighting line (Smyrna camp-ground) he only held one day.
    *   *   *   *   *   *   *   *   *
    Write me a note occasionally, and suggest anything that may occur to you, as I am really in the wilderness down here; but I will fight any and all the time on anything like fair terms, and that is the best strategy, but it would not be fair to run up against such parapets as I find here.
                                          W. T. SHERMAN,
                                            Major-General.

HEADQUARTERS MILITARY DIVISION OF THE MISSISSIPPI,
IN THE FIELD, NEAR CHATTAHOOCHEE RIVER, *July* 13, 1864.

DEAR GENERAL :—I have written you but once since the opening of the campaign, but I report by telegraph to General Halleck daily, and he furnishes you copy. My progress was slower than I calculated, from two chief causes—an uninterrupted rain from June 2d to the 22d, and the peculiar submountainous nature of the country from the Etowah to the Chattahoochee. But we have overcome all opposition, and whipped Johnston in every fight when we were on anything like fair terms, and I think the army feels that way, that we can whip the enemy in anything like a fair fight; but he has uniformly taken shelter behind parallels of strong profile, made in advance for him by negroes and militia. I regarded an assault on the 27th of June necessary for two good reasons: 1. Because the enemy, as well as my own army, had settled down into the belief that "flanking" alone was my game; and, 2. That on that day and ground, had the assault succeeded, I could have broken Johnston's center, and pushed his army back in confusion, and with great loss, to his bridges over the Chattahoochee. We lost nothing in morale in the assault, for I followed it up on the extreme right, and compelled him to quit the very strong lines of Kenesaw, Smyrna camp-ground, and the Chattahoochee, in quick succession. . . .

I have now fulfilled the first part of the "grand plan." Our lines are up to the Chattahoochee, and the enemy is beyond.

* * * * * * * *

I feel certain we have killed and crippled for Joe Johnston as many as we have sent of our men to the rear; have sent back about six or seven thousand prisoners; have taken eleven (11) guns of Johnston, and about ten (10) in Rome; have destroyed immense iron, cotton, and wool mills; and have possession of all the entire country. My operations have been rather cautious than bold, but, on the whole, I trust are satisfactory to you.

* * * * * * * * *

W. T. SHERMAN,
Major-General Commanding.

Lieutenant-General Grant near Petersburg, Va.

CHAPTER XXX.

ADVANCE UPON ATLANTA, AND BATTLE OF PEACHTREE CREEK.

ACTING upon the belief that two corps were across the river, and intrenched, General Johnston withdrew Hardee's corps the night of the 9th, and the smoke of the burning bridges was the first revelation of his action. He selected as his next line, Peachtree creek and the Chattahoochee below its mouth, and placed his army on the high ground south of the creek in waiting to attack the national armies whenever they should attempt to cross. Should he be unsuccessful in preventing their passage, he proposed to delay their approach to Atlanta until his defenses between the Marietta and Decatur roads could be intrusted to the state troops, and then sally out with his whole army, and strike the flank most exposed. He was under the impression that his method of defense, covering continually, not only his main line, but his skirmishers, with intrenchments, had enabled him to inflict losses fivefold greater than his own, and that such had been the reduction of General Sherman's superiority that he could now safely deliver offensive battle, especially as he had the fortifications of Atlanta for refuge in the event of defeat, which, in his estimation, were "too strong to be assaulted, and too extensive to be invested." But as his estimation of the reduction of General Sherman's strength was radically erroneous, there was no ground for his faith in his ability to meet him in general battle. He confessed a loss of ten thousand killed and wounded of infantry and artillery, and though General Sherman's loss in the same arms were probably one-half more, the relative strength of the armies had not materially changed since the battle of Resaca, and now, as then, he had fifty thousand against a hundred thousand men for an open battle. In the defense of fortifications, he was relatively stronger, as he had gradually received accessions of militia, to be used only in constructing and holding intrenchments, so that his purpose to act offensively before Atlanta was formed in ignorance of the fact that General Sherman had maintained a hundred thousand men on his offensive front, against all his losses and the demands of an ever-lengthening line of supply.

To General Sherman, the outlook from the Chattahoochee was promising in the main, but there were contingencies productive of no slight anxiety. He had been able thus far to maintain his communications against all the forces that General Johnston could detach against them; but Forrest, the bold raider, had given remote menace from East Tennessee, and the possibility of a dash by him from Mississippi was not yet entirely removed. And he looked anxiously, though hopefully, to Major-General Canby, commanding the newly created military division of West Mississippi, to so engage the enemy's forces in the West and Southwest as to prevent their approach to his rear. Before him, the city of Atlanta, his next objective, was in view. Its importance as a railroad and manufacturing center, and the moral effect of its successful defense, might justly be regarded as overmastering incentives to the enemy to fortify, and to fight to hold it. To sever its railroad connection with the states west, and cut off supply and reinforcement from that quarter, General Rousseau, with a mounted force, was in motion from Decatur, Alabama, to Opelika, and Stoneman had been sent to strike the same road nearer Atlanta. But another general advance could not be delayed in waiting for the issues of remote operations, and with the completion of preparations for it, there came, as an incentive to prompt motion, the announcement from General Grant that the transfer of Confederate troops from Virginia to Georgia was not improbable, and that provision for such a contingency should be made.

On the 16th, the date of General Grant's dispatch, General Sherman gave orders for the advance toward Atlanta on the following day. McPherson's army had been previously transferred from the extreme right to Roswell; Schofield's was across in front of Phillip's ferry, and Howard's corps on the south side, before Power's ferry. The next morning, General McPherson crossed at Roswell, and moved toward the Augusta railroad, east of Decatur; General Schofield advanced toward Cross Keys, and Palmer's and Hooker's corps passed the river on pontoon bridges, at Paice's ferry, covered by Wood's division, which marched down the left bank of the river from Power's ferry, and subsequently rejoined the Fourth Corps, and with it moved toward Buckhead. Garrard's cavalry acted with General McPherson, and Stoneman's and McCook's watched the river and roads below the railroad.

The movement was a right wheel, with Palmer's corps of the Army of the Cumberland as a pivot. The night of the 17th, the Army of the Cumberland rested on Nancy's creek, a tributary of Peachtree creek, having pressed back the enemy's skirmishers from the bank of the Chattahoochee. The next day it advanced until Palmer's right rested at the junction of Nancy's and Peachtree creeks, and Howard's corps at Buckhead. General Schofield approached Decatur, and General McPherson broke up a section of the Augusta railroad a few miles east of the town. The line was now a long one, but the movements prescribed for the 19th were designed to unite the armies before Atlanta, or in that city.

Early in the morning, Woods' division leading, the Fourth Corps reached Peachtree creek on the Buckhead and Atlanta road, finding the bridge burned and a heavy fortification on the high ground beyond, manned with infantry and artillery. In the afternoon, General Wood constructed a bridge and forced the passage, and drove the enemy from his defenses. General Stanley crossed the north fork of the creek some distance to the left, against strong opposition. To the right, Davis' and Geary's divisions fought their way over the stream. General Geary covered the construction of a foot-bridge with a heavy artillery fire, and gained a strong position beyond. General Davis first threw over Dilworth's brigade, which soon became warmly engaged, and after a sharp conflict repulsed the enemy. Mitchell's brigade moved promptly in support, and participated in the action near its close. All the troops on the south side intrenched during the night.

Early the next morning the remaining divisions of the Army of the Cumberland passed the stream. This army was now compactly formed, and was under orders to advance to develop the enemy's purpose with respect to Atlanta. Between General Thomas' left and General Schofield's right there was, however, a wide interval, and General Sherman ordered two divisions of the Fourth Corps to move to the left to connect with General Schofield. Their movement to the left did not fill the interval nor greatly diminish its length, but changed its location in the general battle front, and gave the preponderance of strength to the left wing. When Stanley and Wood had moved to the left and faced toward Atlanta, in harmony with General Schofield's column, there was still an interval of nearly two miles* between the right of their line and General Thomas' left on the Buckhead road.

When General Williams crossed the creek, he advanced beyond General Geary to an eminence abreast of one Johnson had taken for his division on the left of the Fourteenth Corps, and separated from it by a depression. Here he halted, by direction of General Hooker, as he was near an extensive intrenched outpost of the enemy, and his front was covered by dense woods and thickets. At 10 A. M. General Geary moved forward to the hill on the left of General Williams, and formed his division several hundred yards in advance. Later, General Newton advanced and attained a good position in open ground on the Buckhead road, a division interval from Geary's left. General Hooker for a time held Ward's division opposite this interval, but concealed behind a hill. The resistance offered to the skirmishers that covered the advance of these divisions, and other circumstances, indicated the presence of the enemy in strong force, and both Newton and Geary made dispositions for defense. The former placed two brigades in line—Wagner's, Colonel Blake commanding, on the left of the road, and Kimball's on the right—and held Bradley's in column for support. Between the two deployed brigades, he placed a four-gun battery, and constructed slight rail barricades. General Geary formed his division with Candy's brigade on the left,

---

* Statement in General Howard's report.

Jones' on the right, and Ireland's massed in rear of Jones'. As the ground in front of Jones was wooded, but open before Candy and on his left, General Geary planted his guns on Candy's line. Here also barricades of rails were constructed.

A new army commander had been observing the movements of the national forces since the 17th, as on that day General Johnston, by order of the Confederate President, had given his army and his immediate projects to General Hood. General Johnston had proposed to himself attack General Sherman's armies as they should cross Peachtree creek, in hopes of pressing them in confusion upon the creek and the river beyond, but he had not anticipated such favorable conditions as now existed. He had determined to assume the offensive against Sherman's combined armies, and to make flanks to turn, by breaking lines; but his successor had been permitted to see the wide separation of the two smaller armies from the Army of the Cumberland, and then to see the latter cross Peachtree creek bereft of the two divisions which extended its flank between the forks of the stream, and then advance with its shortened left flank thrown forward almost to the hills upon which his forces were massed for sudden attack, while its right was wedged in between his works and the creek. And now to add surprise to exposure, that his success might be assured, he called in his skirmishers in semblance of entire withdrawal, and sent soldiers into the national lines, under the pretense of capture, who should say that there were no heavy bodies of their troops within two miles. So when, after formation, the most exposed divisions threw forward their skirmishers to develop the state of things in their front, there was no resistance, and no enemy in view until the moment that the massed forces were ready to spring from concealment, in boldest attack. The blow was well concealed, and it was well delivered under the most favorable conditions. It was nevertheless as complete a failure as any assault of the war.

At 3 P. M. the enemy in masses rushed from the woods. A division attacked Newton in front; another passed his left flank altogether, and thrust itself between Peavine and Peachtree creeks, and a third attacked his right flank. As the menace to his left flank involved the greatest danger, General Newton first repulsed the column on his left, and drove it to the woods, with Bradley's brigade and his reserve artillery. Wagner's and Blake's brigades next repelled the front attack, and drove back the enemy with heavy loss. The latter changed front at right angles, and engaged the enemy's third division. While this division had advanced between Newton and Geary, in evident belief that then there was a complete opening in the line, and had faced to the east to engage Newton, Ward's division advanced from cover, and the heavy skirmish line, far in advance, composed of the Twenty-second Wisconsin and One Hundred and Thirty-sixth New York, Lieutenant-Colonel Bloodgood commanding, held the enemy in check until the whole division had reached a hill to the right and rear of Newton. The unexpected appearance of this division and its destructive fire threw the enemy into confusion, and he fell back with shattered ranks. General Ward then advanced to another eminence abreast of Newton and Geary, and formed his division so as to connect with the right of the one and the left of the other. The hill he occupied commanded the open space for six hundred yards in front, and the enemy for a time refrained from attack. During this interval, General Ward fortified his position. The enemy first attacked the right of Geary's line, then passed round to attack him in flank and rear. Williams' division not being fully abreast, this advantage was possible. Geary was therefore compelled to change front to the right with almost all of his division, and extend his line to connect with Williams, leaving only five regiments, with his artillery, on his first line. When the noise of severe battle was first heard by General Williams, he was in the act of moving artillery to his skirmish line, to dislodge the enemy from his fortified outpost; but warned by the heavy volleys of musketry on his left, he deployed his division at double-quick—Knipe's brigade on the right, Robinson's on the left, and Ruger's in reserve—to await the development of the attack. He placed his batteries by sections, to command his front and flanks, and held three sections in reserve. Hardly had these dispositions been made before the enemy advanced upon Williams in great force, and having driven in his skirmishers, with his line of battle under cover of the thickets and undergrowth, approached very near without being seen. His attack, as in other cases, was direct in part, but heavy masses swept down the ravines to right and left. Hearing heavy firing on his right, General Williams sent the Twenty-seventh Indiana to reinforce Knipe's right. This regiment and the Forty-sixth Pennsylvania speedily checked and drove back the enemy, and held the ground until the close of the action. On the left, the attack was more threatening, because made with stronger columns; but Robinson's brigade, the artillery, and Geary's line upon the other hill, poured a destructive fire upon the enemy, and here, too, he was completely repulsed. This first attack swept from Newton's position to Colonel Anson McCook's brigade of Johnson's division of the Fourteenth Corps; but though signally repulsed, General Hood did not desist, and soon again, from Newton to Johnson, the battle raged furiously.

The second general action was commenced upon Newton's left in effort to double up the line by taking it in reverse as well as in flank. This time General Thomas sent the artillery of Ward's division, and in person urged the artillery horses to the greatest possible speed to meet the emergency, and then directed their action. These guns, and all of Newton's, with all kinds of metal most destructive at short range, opened upon the heavy assaulting columns, and they were again repulsed. Again the battle raged to the right; but as the national line was now compact, the enemy exhausted himself in direct attacks. His infantry assaults, as at first, extended from Newton to Johnson, and further to the right his fortified artillery was most active, but charge after charge from left to right was repulsed, until at 6 P. M., when he abandoned his effort to turn or break the line. In this action, artillery was used with fearful effect, and so skillfully was it posted, and so bravely defended, that the enemy did not reach a single gun.

When it is considered that four divisions and one brigade, in open field, repulsed an attack of the army which was intended to initiate such offense as should destroy Sherman's armies, the grandeur of this victory becomes apparent. Not General Hood alone, but General Johnston also, was defeated in the "Battle of Peachtree Creek." A new policy demanded by the authorities at Richmond, and by the Southern people, and a plan of battle elaborated by an able general and put upon trial under conditions far more favorable than had been anticipated, was defeated by less than half of the infantry and artillery of the "Army of the Cumberland." Four divisions, and a third of another, parried a blow intended to initiate the ruin of three armies, comprising more than five times as many men, and the significance of the miscarriage should have been accepted as the prophecy of the doom of the rebellion. The national troops fought great odds, introducing aggression as the policy of a new commander, to stop the further advance of General Sherman and save Atlanta. It was seemingly a grand opportunity, but the issue was positive defeat and immense loss. An opportunity for the enemy, it was an emergency for the exposed flank and the fraction of the national army subjected to attack. But there were those in chief and subordinate command, who, by personal direction and vigor, inspirited the troops made veteran by participation in numerous battles. Generals Thomas and Hooker were with their troops at the points of extreme danger, and officers and men in proportionate service contributed to the emphatic repulse of the enemy in a combination planned for grandest effect.

General Hood lost from three to five thousand men. He left over six hundred dead on the field, and several hundred of his men were captured. Ward's division captured seven battle flags and two hundred and forty-six prisoners.

The total loss of the Army of the Cumberland was sixteen hundred. Colonel Cobham, One Hundred and Eleventh Pennsylvania; Colonel Logie, One Hundred and Forty-fourth New York; Lieutenant-Colonel Randall, One Hundred and Forty-ninth New York, and many other officers were killed; and Lieutenant-Colonel W. H. H. Brown, Sixty-first Ohio, and Major Lathrop Baldwin, One Hundred and Seventh New York, were mortally wounded. A number of field and line officers were severely wounded. General Newton's loss was only one hundred, though his division was on the flank and in extreme exposure.

ADVANCE UPON ATLANTA, ETC.

Generals Stanley and Wood were somewhat heavily engaged during the afternoon and evening, the enemy using artillery freely. They drove in his outposts, and came up in sight of intrenchments, with the usual skirmish line in front. Late in the evening, General Stanley captured a portion of the pickets, drove in the remainder, and worked up close to the enemy.

The night following, the enemy withdrew from General Newton's left. The next morning, General Wood advanced his right a mile and a half, and during the day, the Army of the Cumberland, from left to right, advanced close to the enemy's works. Heavy skirmishing was maintained; batteries were put in position and kept in continuous action wherever there was probability of effect, and the new front was strongly intrenched.

In the night, the enemy retired to the immediate defenses of the city; comprising a strong line of redoubts, connected by curtains, covered by abatis and cheveau de frise. The next morning, General Thomas advanced his line and intrenched as close as practicable to the enemy's works. The Fourteenth Corps fortified a line west of the railroad, the Twentieth Corps from the railroad to the Buckhead road, and the Fourth Corps from that road to General Schofield's right—the contraction of the line now permitting the reunion of the three divisions in continuous front. General Thomas' position was strong, affording commanding points for batteries within easy range of the city, and bearing directly upon the fortifications of the enemy. Constant skirmishing and cannonading were maintained. General McCook's cavalry was thrown on General Thomas' right, along Proctor's creek, and covering the Macon and Turner's Ferry roads.

On the 22d, while the Army of the Tennessee was changing position to close in upon Atlanta, General Hood put upon trial General Johnston's suggestion to sally from the fortifications and strike the most exposed flank. This time he gained a temporary advantage, but in the final issue was defeated with heavy loss.

General McPherson was killed early in the engagement, while making dispositions to save his left flank.

The same day, General Rousseau arrived at Marietta, having

accomplished his raid through Alabama and Georgia. He suggested the expedition, and had organized and commanded it by permission of General Sherman. He destroyed over thirty miles of railroad, several trestle-bridges, many station-buildings, and quantities of supplies and materials. He met and defeated General Clanton at the Coosa river, and another force at Chehaw station, and having suffered a loss of about forty men from a command of twenty-five hundred, reached the theater of war at a time when cavalry reinforcements were much needed.

EXTRACTS FROM THE OFFICIAL REPORT OF GENERAL JOS. E. JOHNSTON.

The character of Peachtree creek, and the numerous fords in the Chattahoochee above its mouth, prevented my attempting to defend that part of the river. The broad and muddy channel of the creek would have separated the two parts of the army. It and the river, below its mouth, were therefore taken as our line. A position on the high ground south of the creek was selected for the army, from which to attack the enemy while crossing. The engineer officers, with a large force of negroes, were set to work to strengthen the fortifications of Atlanta, and mount on them seven heavy rifles, borrowed from General Maury. The chief engineer was instructed to devote his attention, first, to the works between Marietta and Decatur roads, to put them in such condition that they might be held by state troops, so that the army might attack the enemy in flank when he approached the town. This, in the event that we should be unsuccessful in attacking the Federal army in its passage of Peachtree creek.

* * * * * * * * *

In transferring the command to General Hood, I explained my plans to him. First, to attack the Federal army while crossing Peachtree creek. If we were successful, great results might be hoped for, as the enemy would have both it and the river to intercept his retreat. Second, if unsuccessful, to keep back the enemy by intrenching, to give time for the assembling of the state troops promised by Governor Brown; to garrison Atlanta with those troops, and when the Federal army approached the town, to attack it on its most exposed flank with all the Confederate troops.

These troops, who had been for seventy-four days in the immediate presence of the enemy, laboring and fighting daily, enduring toil, exposure, and danger with equal cheerfulness, more confident and high spirited than when the Federal army first presented itself near Dalton, were then inferior to none who ever served the Confederacy.

* * * * * * * * *

ADVANCE UPON ATLANTA, ETC. 119

I commenced the campaign with General Bragg's army of Missionary Ridge, with one brigade added (Mercer's), and two taken away (Baldwin's and Quarles'). That opposed to us was Grant's army of Missionary Ridge, then estimated at eighty thousand by our principal officers, increased, as I have stated, by two corps, a division, and several thousand recruits—in all, at least thirty thousand men. The cavalry of that army was estimated by Major-General Wheeler at fifteen thousand.

The reinforcements which joined our army amounted to fifteen thousand infantry and artillery, and four thousand cavalry. Our scouts reported much greater numbers joining the United States army—the garrisons and bridge-guards from Tennessee and Kentucky relieved by "one hundred days' men," and the Seventeenth Corps, with two thousand cavalry.

The loss of our infantry and artillery, from the 5th of May, had been about ten thousand in killed and wounded, and four thousand seven hundred from all other causes, mainly slight sickness produced by heavy cold rains, which prevailed in the latter half of June. These and the slightly wounded were beginning to rejoin their regiments. For want of reports, I am unable to give the loss or the services of the cavalry, which was less under my eye than the rest of the army. Its effective strength was increased by about two thousand during the campaign.

The effective force transferred to General Hood was about forty-one thousand infantry and artillery, and ten thousand cavalry.

According to the opinions of our most experienced officers, daily reports of prisoners, and statements of Northern papers, the enemy's loss in action could not have been less than five times as great as ours. In the cases in which we had the means of estimating it, it ranged from seven to one to ninety to one, compared to ours, and averaged thirteen to one. The Federal prisoners concurred in saying that their heaviest loss was in the daily attacks made in line of battle, upon our skirmishers in their rifle-pits. Whether they succeeded in dislodging our skirmishers or not, their loss was heavy and ours almost nothing.

Between Dalton and the Chattahoochee, we could have given battle only by attacking the enemy intrenched, or so near intrenchments that the only result of success to us would have been his falling back into them, while defeat would have been our ruin.

In the course pursued, our troops always fighting under cover, had very trifling losses compared with those they inflicted, so that the enemy's numerical superiority was reduced daily and rapidly, and we could reasonably have expected to cope with the Federal army on equal ground by the time the Chattahoochee was passed. Defeat on this side of that river would have been its destruction. We, if beaten, had a place of refuge in Atlanta, too strong to be assaulted, and too extensive to be invested.

EXTRACT FROM GENERAL SHERMAN'S COMMUNICATION TO GENERAL GRANT, OF JULY 12, 1864.

As soon as I hear from General Stoneman, I will shift all of General McPherson's army to Roswell, and cross General Thomas three (3) miles above the railroad bridge, and move against Atlanta—my left well to the East, to get possession of the Augusta road about Decatur or Stone Mountain. I think all will be ready in three (3) days. I will have nearly one hundred thousand (100,000) men.

I feel certain we have killed and crippled for Joe Johnston as many as we have sent to the rear; have sent back six or seven thousand prisoners.

CITY POINT, VA., *July* 16, 1864—10 A. M.

Major-General Sherman:

The attempted invasion of Maryland having failed to give the enemy a firm foothold north, they are now returning with possibly twenty-five thousand (25,000) troops. All the men they have here beyond a sufficiency to hold their string of fortifications, will be an element of weakness by eating up their supplies. It is not improbable, therefore, that you will find in the next fortnight, reinforcements on your front to the number indicated above. I advise, therefore, that if you get Atlanta, you set about destroying the railroad as far to the east and south of you as possible. Collect all stores of the country for your own use, and select a point that you can hold until help can be had. I shall make a desperate effort to get a position here which will hold the enemy without the necessity of so many men. If successful, I can detach from here for other enterprises. looking much to your assistance, or anything elsewhere.

U. S. GRANT,
Lieutenant-General.

WASHINGTON, *July* 16, 1864—4.30 P. M.

Major-General Sherman:

Lieutenant-General Grant wishes me to call your attention to the possibility of Johnston's being reinforced from Richmond, and the importance of your having prepared a good line of defense against such an increase of rebel force. Also, the importance of getting as large an amount of supplies collected at Chattanooga as possible.

H. W. HALLECK,
Major-General and Chief of Staff.

HEADQUARTERS MILITARY DIVISION OF THE MISSISSIPPI,
IN THE FIELD, ON CHATTAHOOCHEE, *July* 16, 1864.

Generals Thomas and McPherson:

Dispatches from General Grant and Halleck to-day speak of the enemy having failed in his designs in Maryland, and cautioning me that Lee may, in the next fortnight, reinforce Johnston by twenty thousand (20,000) men. It behooves us therefore to hurry, so all will move to-morrow as far as Nancy's creek.

W. T. SHERMAN,
Major-General Commanding.

[SPECIAL FIELD ORDERS, NO. 36.]
HEADQUARTERS MILITARY DIVISION OF THE MISSISSIPPI,
IN THE FIELD, CHATTAHOOCHEE, *July* 17, 1864.

The operations of the army for to-morrow, the 18th July, will be as follows:

I. Major-General Thomas will move forward, occupy Buckhead, and the ridge between Nancy's creek and Peachtree, also all the roads toward Atlanta as far as Peachree creek.

II. Major-General Schofield will pass through Cross Keys, and occupy the Peachtree road where intersected by the road from Cross Keys to Decatur.

III. Major-General McPherson will move toward Stone Mountain, to secure strong ground within four (4) miles of General Schofield's position, and push Brigadier-General Garrard's cavalry to the railroad, and destroy some section of the road, and then resume position to the front and left of General McPherson.

IV. All armies will communicate with their neighbors. The commander-in-chief will be near General Thomas' left, or near General Schofield.

By order of Major-General W. T. Sherman.

L. M. DAYTON,
Aid-de-Camp.

HEADQUARTERS MILITARY DIVISION OF THE MISSISSIPPI,
IN THE FIELD, AT SAN HOUSE, PEACHTREE ROAD,
FIVE MILES NORTHEAST OF BUCKHEAD, GA., *July* 18, 1864.

GENERAL:—I have reports from General McPherson to 2 P. M. He has reached the railroad at a point two (2) miles from Stone Mountain and seven (7) miles from Decatur; had broken the telegraphs and road, and by 5 P. M. will have four (4) or five (5) miles broken. To-morrow I want a bold push for Atlanta, and have made my orders, which I think will put us in Atlanta or very close to it. Hold on about Howell's mill and the main road, and let your left swing across Peachtree creek, about south fork, and connect with General Schofield, who will approach Decatur from the north, whilst General McPherson moves down from the East. It is hard to realize that Johnston will give up Atlanta without a fight, but it may be so. Let us develop the truth.

W. T. SHERMAN,
Major-General Commanding.

Major-General Thomas, Buckhead.

ADVANCE UPON ATLANTA, ETC.

[SPECIAL FIELD ORDERS, NO. 39.]

HEADQUARTERS MILITARY DIVISION OF THE MISSISSIPPI,
IN THE FIELD, NEAR DECATUR, *July* 19, 1864.

The whole army will move on Atlanta by the most direct roads to-morrow, July 20th, beginning at five (5) o'clock A. M., as follows:

I. Major-General Thomas from the direction of Buckhead, his left to connect with General Schofield's right, about two (2) miles northeast of Atlanta, about lot 15, near the houses marked as Howard and Colonel Hooker.

II. Major-General Schofield, by the road leading from Dr. Powell's to Atlanta.

III. Major-General McPherson will follow one or more roads direct from Decatur to Atlanta.

Each army commander will accept battle on anything like fair terms, but if the army reach within cannon range of the city without receiving artillery or musketry fire, he will halt, form a strong line, with batteries in position, and await orders. If fired on from the forts or buildings of Atlanta, no consideration will be paid to the fact that they are occupied by families, but the place must be cannonaded without the formality of a demand.

The general-in-chief will be with the center of the army, viz., with or near General Schofield.

By order of Major-General W. T. Sherman.

L. M. DAYTON,
Aid-de-Camp.

CHAPTER XXXI.

SIEGE OF ATLANTA.

AFTER the 22d, the situation at Atlanta conformed in the main to the type of the campaign developed north of the Oostanaula. The two armies presented to each other fortified fronts, each inviting the attack of the other. The stronger not being able to secure a general battle on fair terms, was restricted again to a choice between assault and flank movement. As the issue of previous assaults did not warrant the attempt to carry the defenses of Atlanta, the alternative of a movement by the flank was inevitable. The railroad on the east having been greatly damaged by General Garrard to Covington, and nearer Atlanta by the Army of the Tennessee, there remained but one railroad—that from Macon to Atlanta—which had not been greatly damaged. If this road were held by the national forces or damaged beyond use, General Hood could no longer remain in the city. General Sherman resolved to change the Army of the Tennessee from the left to the right, and to reach toward the Macon road from his right flank, and at the same time throw his cavalry in two heavy columns upon it—five thousand under General Stoneman to pass to the east of the city to McDonough, and four thousand under General McCook to the west to Fayetteville, to meet at Lovejoy's Station and there destroy the road effectually. This accomplished, General Stoneman had permission to make effort with his own division to liberate the prisoners—two thousand at Macon, and twenty thousand at Andersonville. The object of these movements was to force the enemy to come out of Atlanta to fight or be invested, or force him to extend his lines to the south, and choose between Atlanta and East Point.

The cavalry started on the 27th. General McCook crossed the Chattahoochee at Riverton, and moved rapidly on Palmetto station, on the West Point road. Here he destroyed a section of the track two and a half miles long, and advanced to Fayetteville. There he burned a hundred bales of cotton, destroyed two railroad trains, burned a train of four hundred wagons, killed eight hundred mules, saving a large number, and captured two hundred and fifty prisoners. He then moved to Lovejoy's Station to meet General Stoneman. He there burned the depot and having commenced the destruction of the railroad, only desisted when there was such an accumulation of the enemy that he was forced to defend himself. Hearing nothing of General Stoneman and being strongly opposed on the east, he turned south and west to Newnan, on the West Point road. At Newnan he encountered an infantry force that had been stopped on its way to Atlanta by the break he had made in the road at Palmetto. The pursuing cavalry and the infantry now hemmed him in completely, and he was compelled to drop his captives and fight. He cut his way out with a loss of five hundred, and reached Marietta in safety with the remainder of his command.

General Stoneman went farther and fared worse. He sent Garrard's cavalry to Flat Rock, and moved through Covington, down the Ocmulgee, to East Macon. In endeavoring to return, he was hemmed in and captured with seven hundred of his command, the remainder escaping. General Garrard engaged successfully two divisions of cavalry at Flat Rock, and then returned to Atlanta. These cavalry expeditions in the main were failures, and made no impression upon the situation at Atlanta.

On the 27th, General Howard was assigned to the command of the "Army of the Tennessee." by order of the President, and General Stanley, by seniority of rank, to the command of the Fourth Corps. At this time the Army of the Tennessee was in motion to the right, and the next morning went into position on the right of General Thomas, with its line trending to the south. As a support to this movement, General Davis' division was ordered to make a detour to Turner's ferry on the Chattahoochee, and thence to Howard's right, to take the enemy in flank should he sally forth as on the 22d. This change of the Army of the Tennessee was so threatening that General Hood threw two corps upon it—Hardee's and Lee's—with great impetuosity. Attacking again and again, they were repulsed with immense loss. To create a diversion during the progress of this action, there was heavy skirmishing on the whole front of the "Army of the Cumberland;" but Davis' division, General Morgan commanding, was unable, through absence of a direct road, to reach the enemy's flank in time to participate in the action.

General Morgan was not only embarrassed in not finding such roads as had been anticipated, but he was left in ignorance of the object of his movement—his orders, which were received late in the morning, not being explicit as to his duty nor definite in description of the road which he was to pursue, and the consequence was, that the movement so far miscarried that he did not reach his camp until very late at night. The next day he was joined by General Ward's division of the Twentieth Corps, when the two divisions advanced, and driving back the enemy, ascertained that he had strong intrenched lines in their front. Strong reconnoissances from the Fourteenth and Twentieth Corps developed the fact that General Hood's lines were still strong on his right, although he had greatly extended his left.

On the 30th, the picket line of the Twentieth Corps was advanced to high ground, and captured one hundred and twenty of the enemy, including eight officers. The dash was a bold one, but the ground was permanently held. The next day General Davis made a reconnoissance toward the Macon railroad, and found the enemy within a mile, posted in earthworks, from which his artillery opened with canister. It was the old story of extension and counter-extension of lines and intrenchments, and the weaker army having inner lines could keep fully abreast, and at the same time have easy concentration for sally or defense.

During the month the Army of the Cumberland lost forty commissioned officers, one hundred and sixty wounded, and seventeen missing; five hundred and forty-seven enlisted men killed, two thousand five hundred and ninety-two wounded, and three hundred and forty-four missing—total, three thousand seven hundred and nine. General Hooker was relieved of the command of the Twentieth Corps, at his own request, and General Williams was assigned to temporary command. The President gave General Stanley the permanent command of the Fourth Corps.

On the first of August, General Schofield moved from the left to relieve Davis and Ward, and the "Army of the Cumberland" was holding the left of the investing line. The Fourth Corps refused its left to cover the Buckhead road; two divisions of the Twentieth were in the center and two divisions of the Fourteenth between the railroad and Turner's Ferry road; Garrard's division was on the left of the Fourth Corps, guarding the approaches from Decatur, and Roswell's and Kilpatrick's divisions, having been relieved on the line of the Etowah by McCook's, was on the railroad from Chattahoochee bridge to Marietta. When Davis and Ward gave room for Schofield on Howard's right, and then moved to the right of Schofield, the former was on the left in line, and the latter refused, to form a strong flank.

After the failure of General Hood's third effort at aggression, he relapsed into the defensive, and General Sherman was again forced to choose between assault and the "turning movement." The investing line had been moved far to the west and south, and yet Hood's left flank had not been found. The supposition was that the main portion of his army was on his left, extending his intrenchments as far or farther than General Sherman's, and that his main works on the north of Atlanta were held by state troops or a slender line of regular troops. General Sherman's armies had been on a strain for three months, in frequent battles, and perpetual skirmishing and watching. But though the enemy had been roughly handled during July, his army was yet as much out of reach as at any period of the campaign. General Sherman decided to again extend his line still farther to the right, so as at least to reach the Macon railroad with artillery at short range, and force General Hood to fight or abandon the city. In the execution of this plan it was necessary that his right flank should be kept exceedingly strong, while his line throughout its length should have such firmness as would insure its safety and at the same

SIEGE OF ATLANTA.

time menace Atlanta from the north so strongly as to prevent an overwhelming concentration against the advancing right flank.

On the 3d, Johnson's and Baird's divisions of Palmer's corps were moved to the right in support of Schofield, while Ward's division moved to the right of the Fourth Corps, and assisted in covering the space previously held by the Fourteenth. The Fourth and the Twentieth now held a line of intrenchments five miles long. During the day, while General Schofield was rushing to reach the railroad, there was great activity along the whole line from General Thomas' left to General Howard's right, in skirmishing and cannonading, to relieve the pressure upon the right flank in its aggression. General Schofield succeeded in getting two divisions, one of his own, and General Baird's, across the head of Utoy creek. General Baird formed his division on the right of General Hascall's, with his right swung back toward the creek.

The next morning, General Baird readjusted his line in expectation of supporting the divisions of General Schofield in an assault. But no movement was made of a general character, and late in the day General Palmer directed him to feel the enemy's works in his front with a brigade. He designated Colonel Gleason's brigade for this service, which advanced in double lines with skirmishers in front. Colonel Gleason carried the first and second line of rifle-pits, and approached so near the enemy's main line, as to develop its location and character, and drew from it an artillery and musketry fire. At night he withdrew his brigade, but held with shirmishers the outer line of rifle-pits which he had carried.

The next morning at 8 A. M. General Baird's division was in line ready to advance. He was instructed to pay no attention to his connections on his left, as General Cox's division was to fill the space between him and General Hascall, and was informed that the latter was already so near the enemy that he would not advance during the day. He was promised support on his right by the other two divisions of his own corps, although he was not yet in communication with them. Regarding his orders to advance as imperative, he threw forward skirmishers in double the usual strength, and moved forward in perilous insulation. As he advanced, he found that the enemy had reoccupied the inner line of rifle-pits which Colonel Gleason had carried the evening previous. This line he again carried against stubborn resistance, capturing one hundred and forty prisoners. He was then within short musket range of the enemy's main works. He could advance no farther, unless he assaulted without support, but held the position, refusing two regiments on his right, and intrenched himself as rapidly as possible under the fire of musketry and artillery. The main lines were now four hundred yards apart, while only thirty yards separated the skirmishers. Baird lost in this engagement, five officers, and seventy-eight enlisted men killed and wounded. Lieutenant-Colonel Myron Baker, commanding Ninety-fourth Indiana, was killed.

Soon after General Baird attained position near the enemy, General Davis' division, General Morgan commanding, formed on his right, and later, General Johnson's division took position in the rear of Morgan. As on the 3d, there was great activity along the line of the left to divert attention from the advance on the right.

Thus there was just sufficient extension and action on the right to advise the enemy of what was intended, without gaining any advantage that promised ultimate success. The line had only been extended by one division. General Sherman's orders required that the attack on the right should be pressed, and he had given promise that if it was too hard pressed, Generals Thomas and Howard should attack somewhere, but the indications were emphatic that General Hood was rapidly extending his intrenchments toward East Point, and yet General Sherman was so shut up to counter-movement, that he said to General Thomas in the evening, "We will try again to-morrow, and proceed to the end."

Accordingly, the next morning a new effort was made to reach beyond the enemy's left flank. The Fourteenth Corps, under command of Brigadier-General R. W. Johnson, by virtue of seniority, General Palmer having been relieved at his own request, held its own line and that occupied by the Twenty-third Corps, and the latter moved to the right, beyond what appeared the day before to be the left flank of the enemy. General Schofield then threw forward Reilly's brigade, but it was found impossible to penetrate the obstructions before the enemy's parapets. General Schofield then made a still larger circuit to the right, for the purpose of "breaching" his line at a point not protected by abatis, but he found his lines extended beyond the main Utoy creek. While General Schofield was operating against General Hood's left, the latter evinced great activity on his right. He felt General Thomas' line from right to left, and was so demonstrative against General Stanley, as to make it evident that he was either looking for a weak point to assault, or was endeavoring to ascertain the strength of his line, as throwing light upon General Schofield's movements. General Hood was now holding his works north of the city by state troops, supported by movable divisions of regular troops. The main portion of the army was on his left, extending his defenses to hold the Macon railroad. General Sherman's line was also greatly attenuated, and as a compensation for it, the defenses on the north were made exceedingly strong, and from them shells were constantly thrown to the city.

In the evening of the 6th, General Sherman said to General Schofield: "There is no alternative but for you to continue to work on that flank with as much caution as possible, and it is possible the enemy may attack us, or draw out." To General Thomas, he said: "Instead of going round East Point, I would prefer the enemy to weaken, so we may break through at some point, and wish you to continue to make such effort. I will instruct General Howard to do the same at the head of Utoy creek, his right." But General Thomas did not deem it prudent to assault such works, as there was a certainty of great loss, and with such a column, as he could form from his attenuated line, there was little probability of success. His response was: "I will keep the attention of the enemy fully occupied by threatening all along my front; but I have no hopes of breaking through his lines anywhere in my front, as long as he has a respectable force to defend them. My troops are so thinned out that it will be impossible to form an assaulting column sufficiently strong to make an attack sure." In the emergency, General Sherman ordered heavy rifled guns from Chattanooga to "batter the town."

On the 7th, General Hood withdrew his troops from the intrenchments assaulted by General Schofield, which, though strong and well protected by entanglements, formed no part of his main line, and their abandonment did not greatly endanger his possession of the Macon railroad. During the day the Fourteenth Corps advanced, carried a line of rifle-pits in front of the position previously occupied by the Twenty-third Corps, and established a line close to the enemy's works. The loss of the corps was seventy men killed, and four hundred and thirteen wounded. One hundred and seventy-two prisoners were taken.

From the 8th to the 10th, General Sherman continued his effort to reach the Macon road, by the extension of his line to the right. He thought it impossible that the enemy could reach much farther in that direction, but it was finally ascertained that his well-fortified line extended from the Decatur road, on the east of Atlanta, to East Point, a distance of fifteen miles. And as the farther attenuation of the investing line was not considered safe, and as the enemy's works were too strong to be assaulted, General Sherman began to cast about for a new plan. In the meantime, the heavy guns were at work throwing solid shell into the city with great frequency, night and day, in expectation that their agency would reduce the value of Atlanta as a "large machine-shop and depot of supplies."

On the 11th, General Sherman received intelligence through General Garrard, that General Hood was collecting an immense force of cavalry to operate upon his communications. It was important to General Hood to cut short General Sherman's supplies, but in the effort to do it, by breaking his railroad far to the north, he was depriving his own communications of protection. As soon as General Sherman learned that Wheeler, with eight or ten thousand troopers, was moving to the north, he determined to throw his cavalry upon the railroad south of Atlanta.

The news from the north on the 14th gave confirmation to

previous reports of Wheeler's intended raid. Early in the morning of that day he attacked a party guarding a large herd of cattle near Calhoun, dispersed a portion of the guard and captured a large number of the cattle, some portions of which were recaptured by Colonel Faulkner, who pursued upon receipt of the news. At 3 P. M. General Steedman, at Chattanooga, was informed that Wheeler was going toward Dalton. He at once relieved all the troops that could be spared from the garrison to prepare to move to Dalton. Being delayed by trains running on unusual time, General Steedman did not reach the vicinity of Dalton until midnight; and having been informed that the garrison had surrendered, he awaited daylight, and then moved forward and engaged the enemy's skirmishers. Hearing firing in Dalton, and learning that the garrison was still holding out, he dashed into the town and cleared it of the enemy. He remained for a day, and learning that the enemy had moved off, through fear for the bridges over the Chickamauga, he hastened back to Chattanooga. Colonel Laiboldt had held his position against a superior force, and General Steedman's quick relief gave him final safety. The troops under General Steedman were the Second Missouri, Twenty-ninth, Fifty-first, and Sixty-eighth Indiana, Seventy-eighth Pennsylvania, One Hundred and Eighth Ohio, and the Fourteenth United States Colored troops, in all about eighteen hundred effective men. Wheeler's loss was about two hundred. He left thirty-three dead and fifty-seven badly wounded on the field. Steedman's, was one officer and eight men killed, one officer and twenty-nine men wounded, and twenty-three men missing.

From Dalton, General Wheeler moved north, injured the railroad slightly at Graysville, threatened Cleveland with a detachment, and then turned to the northeast. Soon after, however, he changed his course to meet in Middle Tennessee another cavalry force under General Roddy. The latter had crossed the Tennessee river, near Decatur, to strike the Nashville and Decatur railroad. General Wheeler's primary object was to damage the Nashville and Chattanooga railroad. About the same time, the enemy was active near Fort Donelson, thus giving a third intimation of purpose to disturb the communications of the national armies before Atlanta. There was, however, less force in the raiding columns or more in the troops defending the railroads than had been anticipated, as little injury was effected. The failure resulted from the combined opposition of General Rousseau, commanding at Nashville, General Steedman at Chattanooga, and General R. S. Granger at Decatur.

General Granger sallied forth from Decatur and encountered Roddy near Athens, Alabama, which place he was besieging. The garrison had been upon the defensive previously, but upon his arrival the barricades were removed, and the enemy was attacked and routed. General Granger then marched up the Nashville and Decatur railroad to Pulaski, to intercept Wheeler, who was moving to the west, followed by General Rousseau. From Pulaski he moved upon Linnville with three regiments of infantry, expecting General Starkweather to join him with a brigade of cavalry in time to give battle. He met his advance and drove it back, but his cavalry did not arrive in time to engage the enemy. During the night, Wheeler abandoned the line of the railroad and moved in the direction of Lawrenceburg. Granger then left his infantry to guard the railroad, and assuming personal command of his cavalry went in pursuit; and overtaking the enemy as he was leaving Lawrenceburg, he fell upon Wheeler's rear-guard and harassed him as he retreated. At this juncture, General Rousseau ordered General Granger to halt and form a junction with his own force. For a time the order was not obeyed, upon the supposition that General Rousseau was ignorant of the fact that he was up with the enemy and was retarding his retreat. A second order was received, requiring him to discontinue the pursuit and move upon Athens to intercept Roddy. The result was that both Wheeler and Roddy succeeded in crossing the Tennessee river without loss or embarrassment. The enemy thus escaped serious punishment, but utterly failed to interrupt General Sherman's communications.

Having despaired of flanking Hood out of Atlanta, on the 16th General Sherman announced his new plan of operations, but suspended them first to learn the results of a raid by Kilpatrick to Fairburn, and subsequently until his cavalry could make one more effort to break up General Hood's communications and compel him to fight or abandon the city. General Kilpatrick drove back Jackson's division of cavalry from Fairburn on the 15th, destroyed the station and public buildings, and the telegraph and railroad for about three miles. On the 18th, he, with his own division and two brigades from General Garrard's, in all about five thousand cavalry, dashed out from his camp at Sandtown to the West Point road, and broke it near Fairburn, and thence moved to Jonesborough, defeated Ross' cavalry, and commenced the destruction of the road; but while thus engaged he was attacked by Jackson's cavalry and a brigade of infantry, which had hurried up from the south, and he was compelled to draw off toward McDonough. He then made a circuit to Lovejoy's Station, where again, while breaking the road, he was attacked by the same force. Perceiving that he was almost surrounded, he charged the cavalry and cut his way through, capturing four guns and many prisoners; but being hard pressed could not incumber himself with all of his captives, and brought in but seventy men, three flags, and one gun. He then returned by McDonough and Decatur.

EXTRACT FROM GENERAL MORGAN'S REPORT OF HIS ACTION ON THE 28TH OF JULY.

July 28th, received orders to be ready with my brigade at 8 A. M.; reported to General Davis for orders; was informed by him that he was too unwell to take command of the division in the field. At 9 A. M. took command of the division on the Turner Ferry road, to move under the following order:

"*July* 28, 1864.

Major-General G. H. Thomas:

"Order General Davis to leave camp and move to Turner's ferry, and then by a road leading toward East Point, to feel forward for Howard right back with some known point at Turner's ferry. I will be over on that flank all day, and await to reach out as far as possible.

(Signed,) "W. T. SHERMAN."

In compliance with above order, I did move to Turner's ferry, halted an hour for rest and dinner. Having no guide, no correct map of the country, I had to rely upon such information as I could obtain from residents. Returning from the ferry, turned to the right at the church, one mile from the river, and took the road leading toward East Point. The enemy's pickets were soon met upon the road; they were well posted and in good numbers, requiring the deployment of a whole regiment to clear the front. After moving upon this road about one and a half miles, a staff officer of the general commanding division overtook the command, and I received verbal orders to return as soon as possible to the Turner's Ferry road, the enemy having attacked General Howard's right. Heavy skirmishing continuing in front, I determined to advance and take the first road to the left. This was done, and the division was moved with all possible dispatch to Turner's Ferry road, arriving late in evening, and owing to a bad swamp and a very dark night, was nearly all night in getting into camp.

HEADQUARTERS MILITARY DIVISION OF THE MISSISSIPPI,
IN THE FIELD, NEAR ATLANTA, GA., *July* 30, 1864.

Generals Thomas and Howard:

I am just back from an interview with General Schofield. . . .

I think General Stoneman has gone to Macon, east of Yellow river, and that is well. I have ordered General Garrard in on our left, and to-morrow night will let him fill with a skirmish line General Schofield's position, and move all of Schofield's to the right of General Howard, and with the divisions of General Davis and Ward kept in reserve on the right, to strike a blow beyond our new right flank when intrenched. Our right flank must be advanced in close and absolute contact with the enemy; and with General Schofield on that flank, I think we can make him quit Atlanta, or so weaken his line that we can break through somewhere, the same as our Kenesaw move. . . .

(Signed,)   W. T. SHERMAN,
Major-General Commanding.

[SPECIAL FIELD ORDERS, NO. 48.]

HEADQUARTERS MILITARY DIVISION OF THE MISSISSIPPI,
IN THE FIELD, NEAR ATLANTA, GA., *August* 1, 1864.

I. During the next series of operations, General Thomas will be the left, General Howard the center, and General Schofield the right army. The two divisions of Generals Davis and Ward will continue to be held in reserve toward the right, and in case the enemy attack that flank, these divisions will report to, and during the action, obey General Schofield's orders. When not engaged, General Thomas will post them so as to cover his communications from danger coming from the Southeast.

II. Brigadier-General Garrard's cavalry will relieve General Schofield on the left, and occupy in part his trenches, patrol the road about Decatur, and picket toward Roswell. He will report to General Thomas, and be prepared to sally out as cavalry from his trenches in case of necessity.

III. All trains of wagons going to and from the depots of Vining's and Marietta will follow roads converging at the railroad bridge, and never go north of Buckhead or south of Turner's.

SIEGE OF ATLANTA.

IV. General Thomas will cause a new infantry flank to be prepared on the left, north of the Buckhead road, connecting General Stanley's lines with the old rebel parapet near Peachtree creek.

By order of Major-General W. T. Sherman.

L. M. DAYTON,
Aid-de-Camp.

[SPECIAL FIELD ORDERS, NO. 51.]

HEADQUARTERS MILITARY DIVISION OF THE MISSISSIPPI,
IN THE FIELD, NEAR ATLANTA, GA., *August* 4, 1864.

The order of movement of the army to-day will be as follows:

I. Major-General Schofield, with his own command and General Palmer's corps, will move directly on the railroad which leads south out of Atlanta, at any point between Whitehall and East Point, and will not stop until he has absolute control of the railroad, but must not extend more to the right than is absolutely necessary to that end.

II. Major-Generals Thomas and Howard will press close on the enemy at all points, and reinforce well the points of the line where the enemy is most likely to sally—viz., on the Decatur, Buckhead, and Turner's Ferry roads; but more especially watch the outlet along the railroad—viz., General Williams' front.

III. On the right we must assume the offensive, and every man be prepared to fight, leaving knapsacks, etc., in present trenches. Wagons will not be taken east of Utoy creek, until General Schofield has secured position on the railroad, or so near it that it can be reached by musket-balls and canister. If necessary to secure this end, ordinary parapets must be charged and carried, and every hour's delay enables the enemy to strengthen; therefore, let it be done to-day.

By order of Major-General W. T. Sherman.

L. M. DAYTON,
Aid-de-Camp.

HEADQUARTERS MILITARY DIVISION OF THE MISSISSIPPI,
IN THE FIELD, NEAR ATLANTA, GA., *August* 4, 1864.

General Palmer:

You will, during the movement against the railroad, report to and receive orders from General Schofield. General Thomas will personally look to the front of Atlanta. General Howard will co-operate with General Schofield, and General Schofield, reinforced by your corps, is charged to reach the railroad. Obey his orders and instructions. Acknowledge receipt.

W. T. SHERMAN,
Major-General Commanding.

HEADQUARTERS MILITARY DIVISION OF THE MISSISSIPPI,
IN THE FIELD, NEAR ATLANTA, GA., *August* 5, 1864.
General Schofield:
Dispatch received. All right. Press the attack on the right. I will judge by the sound; and if I judge you are too hard pressed, will order Generals Thomas and Howard to assault somewhere. Get some part of your command where you can easily reach the railroad with short-range guns, and then intrench a strong flank. It is worth a battle, and the closer the first advantages are followed up, the better. The weakest point of the enemy must be mathematically at some point between Atlanta and East Point. Keep me often advised of your progress, and I will come over any minute you say, but can better handle the whole army from here by telegraph.

W. T. SHERMAN,
Major-General Commanding.

HEADQUARTERS MILITARY DIVISION OF THE MISSISSIPPI,
IN THE FIELD, NEAR ATLANTA, GA., *August* 6, 1864.
General Thomas:
General Schofield has been at work to-day with his two divisions, and holds Johnson's in support. . . .
He tried to break through the enemy's lines by a brigade to-day, but failed, losing five hundred (500) men. Instead of going round East Point, I would prefer the enemy to weaken, so we may break through at some point, and wish you to continue to make such an effort. I will instruct General Howard to do the same about the head of Utoy creek—his right.

W. T. SHERMAN,
Major-General Commanding.

HEADQUARTERS MILITARY DIVISION OF THE MISSISSIPPI,
IN THE FIELD, NEAR ATLANTA, GA., *August* 6, 1864.
General Schofield:
I have your dispatch. There is no alternative but for you to continue to work on that flank with as much caution as possible, and it is possible the enemy may attack us or draw out. He must defend that road.

W. T. SHERMAN,
Major-General Commanding.

HEADQUARTERS DEPARTMENT OF THE CUMBERLAND, *August* 7, 1864.
Major-General Sherman:
I will keep the attention of the enemy fully occupied by threatening all along my front as long as he has a respectable force to defend them. My troops are so thinned out that it will be impossible to form an assaulting column sufficiently strong to make an attack sure.

GEO. H. THOMAS,
Major-General.

SIEGE OF ATLANTA. 137

HEADQUARTERS MILITARY DIVISION OF THE MISSISSIPPI,
IN THE FIELD, NEAR ATLANTA, GA., *August* 7, 1864.

General Halleck, Washington:

* * * * * * * * *

I do not deem it prudent to extend more to the right, but will push forward daily by parallels, and make the inside of Atlanta too hot to be endured.

I have sent to Chattanooga for two (2) 30-pounder Parrotts, with which I can pick out almost any house in the town. I am too impatient for a siege, but I do n't know but here is as good a place to fight it out as further inland. One thing is certain—whether we get inside of Atlanta or not, it will be a used-up community by the time we are done with it.

W. T. SHERMAN,
Major-General Commanding.

HEADQUARTERS MILITARY DIVISION OF THE MISSISSIPPI,
IN THE FIELD, NEAR ATLANTA, GA., *August* 10, 1864.

General Howard:

I thank you for the suggestion. I am studying all the combinations possible, and beg you to think also, and communicate to me; but be careful to keep your own confidence. I spoke of the same thing to-day to General Thomas, and he goes to look at the railroad bridge, to see to a proper cover there for the wagons and a corps. I want to expend four thousand (4,000) heavy rifle shots on the town before doing anything new, and then will be prepared to act quick. General Schofield has been reconnoitering the right all day, and after he has answered a few more of my questions, I will give you the substance of his report.

W. T. SHERMAN,
Major-General Commanding.

HEADQUARTERS MILITARY DIVISION OF THE MISSISSIPPI,
IN THE FIELD, NEAR ATLANTA, GA., *August* 10, 1864.

General Thomas:

I have your last dispatch. I hear the guns. I hear the guns and shells also. The enemy's battery of 32-pounders, rifled, are firing on us here from the Whitehall fort, to draw off or divert our fire. Keep up a steady, persistent fire on Atlanta with the 4½-inch guns and 20-pounder Parrotts, and order them to pay no attention to the side firing, by which the enemy may attempt to divert their attention. I think those guns will make Atlanta of less value to them as a large machine-shop and depot of supplies. The inhabitants have, of course, got out.

W. T. SHERMAN,
Major-General Commanding.

SIEGE OF ATLANTA.

HEADQUARTERS MILITARY DIVISION OF THE MISISSIPPI,
IN THE FIELD, NEAR ATLANTA, GA., *August* 16, 1864.

General Thomas:

* * * * * * * * *

I do think our cavalry should now break the Macon road good. If we can save our rations at Marietta and Allatoona, and break the Macon road for many miles, we can wait as long as Hood.

* * * * * * * *

W. T. SHERMAN,
Major-General Commanding.

HEADQUARTERS MILITARY DIVISION OF THE MISSISSIPPI,
IN THE FIELD, NEAR ATLANTA, GA., *August* 16, 1864.

Generals Thomas, Howard, and Schofield:

We will commence the movement against the railroad about Jonesboro, Thursday night, unless something occurs in the meantime to mar the plan. I will make my orders, and the preliminary preparations may be begun.

If Wheeler interrupts our supplies, we can surely cut off those of Hood, and see who can stand it best.

W. T. SHERMAN,
Major-General.

[SPECIAL FIELD ORDERS, NO. 57.]

HEADQUARTERS MILITARY DIVISION OF THE MISSISSIPPI,
IN THE FIELD, NEAR ATLANTA, GA., *August* 16, 1864.

The movement of the army against the Macon railroad will begin Thursday night, August 18th, and will be continued on the following general plan:

I. All army commanders will send across the Chattahoochee river, and within the old rebel works at the bridge, and down as far as Turner's ferry, all surplus wagons, horses, men, and materials not absolutely necessary to the success of the expedition, and will collect in their wagons, with best teams, bread, meat, sugar, coffee, etc., for fifteen (15) days, after the nineteenth (19th) instant, and ammunition, and park them near Utoy creek.

First move.—General Kilpatrick's cavalry will move to Camp creek; General Schofield will cover the Campbelton road, and General Thomas will move one corps (General Williams') to the Chattahoochee bridge, with orders to hold it; Paice's ferry bridge, and pontoon bridge (Captain Kossack's) at Turner's ferry, ready to be laid down if necessary. The other corps (General Stanley's) will move south of Proctor's creek, to near Utoy, behind the right center of the Army of the Tennessee, prepared to cover the Bell's Ferry road. General Garrard's cavalry will fall behind Peachtree creek, and act against the enemy should he sally against General Williams or General Stanley's corps during the movement.

Second move.—The Army of the Tennessee will withdraw cross Utoy creek, and move by most direct road toward Fairburn, going as far as Camp creek. General Thomas will mass his two corps (General Stanley's and Johnson's) below Utoy creek, and General Garrard's cavalry will join General Thomas by most direct road, or by way of Sandtown bridge, and act with him during the rest of the move.

General Schofield will advance abreast of and in communication with the Army of the Tennessee as far as Camp creek.

Third move.—The Armies of the Ohio and Tennessee will move direct for the West Point road, aiming to strike it between Red Oak and Fairburn. General Thomas will follow, well closed up into two columns, the trains between. General Kilpatrick will act as advance, and General Garrard will cover the rear, under direction of General Thomas.

The bridges at Sandtown will be kept and protected by a detachment of cavalry, detailed by General Elliott, with a section of guns or four (4) gun battery.

II. During the movement, and until the army returns to the river, the utmost care will be taken to expose as little as possible the trains of cars and wagons. The depots at the bridge, at Allatoona and Marietta, will be held against any attack, and communication kept up with the army as far as possible by way of Sandtown. On reaching any railroad, the troops will at once be disposed for defense, and at least one-third put to work to tear up track and destroy iron, ties, and all railroad material.

By order of Major-General W. T. Sherman.

L. M. DAYTON,
Aid-de-Camp.

HEADQUARTERS DEPARTMENT OF THE CUMBERLAND, *August* 17, 1864.
Major-General Sherman:

Information from all sources seems to confirm the report that Wheeler has taken off the greater part of his cavalry. I therefore think this will be as good a time as could be taken to make another raid on the Macon railroad; but if you send Kilpatrick, I would insist on his taking the most practicable route, and avoid the enemy's infantry as much as possible.

GEO. H. THOMAS,
Major-General.

HEADQUARTERS MILITARY DIVISION OF THE MISSISSIPPI,
IN THE FIELD, NEAR ATLANTA, GA., *August* 19, 1864—10.45 A. M.
General Grant, City Point:

I have your dispatches of 14th and 16th, and also that of 18th. I will never take a step backward, and have no fears of Hood. I can whip him outside of his trenches, and, I think, in time can compel him to come out. I think at this time I have a fine cavalry force on the only road which can feed him, and, if necessary, will swing my whole army across it also.

W. T. SHERMAN,
Major-General Commanding.

CHAPTER XXXII.

THE FLANK MOVEMENT CULMINATING IN THE BATTLE OF JONESBORO AND THE FALL OF ATLANTA.

PENDING General Kilpatrick's movements the shelling of Atlanta was actively maintained, and feints of various kinds were employed by General Stanley on the left to confuse the enemy and lead to the belief that a movement was intended in that direction; but when, after General Kilpatrick's return, it was ascertained that the damage to the railroads was not such as to greatly embarrass the enemy, General Sherman repeated his order for the grand movement by the right flank, which involved the necessity of raising the siege of Atlanta, and using his armies against the communications of the enemy rather than against his intrenchments around the city. To take the place by siege would require too much time, and to take it by assault would cost too many lives. His sick, and all surplus supplies, wagons, and incumbrances, having been sent to the intrenchments beyond the Chattahoochee, the Fourth Corps was, on the 25th, withdrawn to the high ground, in the rear of the Twentieth Corps, to cover the retirement of the latter to the farther side of the Chattahoochee, to hold the railroad bridge and the bridges at Paice's and Turner's ferries, and guard the material there accumulated. Garrard's cavalry covered the movement of the Twentieth Corps to the rear, and that of the Fourth Corps to the right, to take position on the high ground along Utoy creek. This change was effected on the 26th with but slight molestation, and the night following, the Fourteenth Corps, now in permanent command of Brevet Major-General J. C. Davis, was withdrawn from position and formed on the right of General Stanley, on Utoy creek. The same night the Army of the Tennessee moved rapidly by a circuit toward Sandtown. General Schofield alone remained in position.

The next day the Fourth Corps advanced to Mount Gilead Church, and, forming line of battle on the road to Fairburn, skirmished with the enemy's cavalry. The Fourteenth Corps remained in position, as it was necessary that one corps should cover another until out of reach of the enemy. General Garrard's cavalry operated upon the rear and left of the armies during these movements, and Kilpatrick's having crossed the Chattahoochee, at Paice's ferry, and recrossed at Sandtown, was charged with similar service on the right. The Twentieth Corps, at the Chattahoochee, passed to the command of Major-General H. W. Slocum.

On the 28th, the Fourteenth Corps passed the Fourth at Mount Gilead, and reached its designated camp, near Red Oak, late in the afternoon. General Morgan's division, in the advance, skirmished with the enemy's cavalry during the day. The Fourth Corps followed, and the two corps encamped in line across the West Point railroad, facing east. The Army of the Tennessee was on the same road above Fairburn, and General Schofield was on this road below East Point. Shortly after dark, orders were received to destroy the railroad, by heating and twisting the rails and burning the ties. The work of destruction was continued through the night and a portion of the following day, by each army, and twelve and a half miles of the road were thoroughly dismantled. But this was not the road of most importance to the enemy. The Macon road passes to Jonesboro, from Atlanta, on the ridge dividing the waters of the Flint and Ocmulgee rivers, and offered a good position as a strategic base for ulterior movements, and on the 30th the armies advanced eastward to reach it, more directly in rear of Atlanta.

The Fourth and Fourteenth Corps moved to Couch's house, formed a line trending to the northwest, and went into camp. The leading divisions of each corps skirmished with infantry and cavalry, and at night it was ascertained that there was a force of the enemy at Morrow's mill, on Crooked creek, three-fourths of a mile from General Stanley's left. General

Thomas was in communication with General Howard beyond Renfrew's, but not with General Schofield on the left. General Garrard was guarding the left and rear, at Red Oak, and General Kilpatrick was on General Howard's right.

General Sherman having ascertained that General Howard was near Jonesboro, directed General Thomas to send Stanley's corps toward Rough and Ready, in connection with Schofield, and to send forward a strong detachment from the Fourteenth Corps to "feel for the railroad." In compliance, General Baird, with his own division, and Mitchell's brigade of Morgan's division, was sent forward from the center, and an early advance discovered that the enemy's trains were in motion on a road to the east toward Jonesboro, and later in the day it was ascertained from captured stragglers that Hardee's and Lee's corps had passed.

In the afternoon General Baird's leading detachment reached the railroad about four miles from Jonesboro. Although greatly in advance of other columns, General Baird determined to hold the railroad by strengthening Colonel Carleton's party in the advance, and sending Colonel Gleason's brigade forward in support. The Fourth Corps formed a junction with the Twenty-third, at the railroad, and rested on the road southeast of Rough and Ready, in a barricaded line facing Jonesboro. Carlin's division, formerly Johnson's, moved to Renfrew's to cover the trains, and late in the afternoon was ordered to support General Howard, who had been attacked by Hardee's and Lee's corps. Carlin moved as ordered, but did not reach the field until after General Howard had completely repulsed the enemy.

The situation was now partially developed. Two corps of Hood's army were at Jonesboro. It was not known that Stewart's corps had left Atlanta, but as the army was in force at Jonesboro, General Sherman determined to move against that place, and if Stewart was not there to thrust his forces between the two portions of Hood's army. Deeming it probable that the third corps would abandon Atlanta, he directed General Thomas to order General Slocum to make a reconnoissance toward Atlanta to determine the state of affairs, and also to send a cavalry force toward Decatur to observe the enemy in that direction. Circumstances now indicated a speedy solution of all problems having connection with Atlanta.

General Sherman's orders for September 1st required all the forces to turn upon Jonesboro. General Howard was already before it, and General Davis, with Morgan's and Carlin's divisions, joined Baird's on the railroad, and the whole corps was soon on Howard's left. Generals Schofield and Stanley, having a longer march, and owing to railroad destruction and other causes, were greatly delayed. General Garrard was still in the rear, and General Kilpatrick was sent down the west bank of Flint river to threaten the railroad below Jonesboro, and General Blair's corps of the Army of the Tennessee was sent in the same direction. This immense combination had been directed against Hardee's corps alone, which had been left behind to cover the retreat to a point where the dissevered army could be reunited.

After occupying the position vacated by General Blair's corps, General Davis directed General Carlin to send a brigade to explore the ground toward the railroad upon which General Stanley was advancing. The reconnoissance was made by Edie's brigade of regulars, and was strongly resisted by the enemy. It was, however, pressed until a commanding hill beyond Moker's creek was carried, from the front of which the enemy's works could be attacked with advantage.

At this juncture General Thomas reached the head of column, to whom General Davis reported the condition of affairs, and suggested a plan of operations. Having received permission to make the attack directly before the hill which Edie had gained, General Davis pushed his troops in column to that point, and deployed for action. Carlin's second brigade was formed on the right of Edie's. General Morgan crossed the creek and connected the left of his division with Carlin's right. General Baird formed his division in rear of Carlin's left, which rested on the railroad. General Morgan's movement was executed over rough ground, and in exposure to the enemy's artillery. About the time that the formation of the Fourteenth Corps was completed, General Stanley's head of column appeared on Carlin's left, and Grose's and Kirby's brigades of Kimball's division were deployed, under instructions to push the enemy vigorously on the left of the railroad.

The troops of the Fourteenth Corps designated for the attack, were General Carlin's two brigades and General Morgan's entire division, and were formed in double lines, and as nearly contiguous as the ground would permit. The distance to the enemy from Morgan's division, when deployed, was about one thousand yards; the intervening space was open, but swampy, and cut with ditches. The distance to the enemy's works in General Carlin's front could not be determined, as a dense thicket interposed. The defenses of the enemy were in the woods on a ridge, at various distances from the edge of the wooded ground, but in no case exceeding one hundred yards. Morgan's division was formed by brigades in column of regiments in echelon, from left to right—Lum's, Mitchell's, and Dilworth's—and were ordered to assault with the bayonet alone.

At 4 P. M., after a heavy cannonade from Prescott's and Gardner's batteries on Carlin's ridge, the troops moved forward, but owing to the thickets in Carlin's front, and the swampy ground and ditches before Morgan, their progress was slow, and there was difficulty in maintaining alignments and direction. When the whole line had advanced to the slope of a hill, and an open field within three or four hundred yards of the enemy's position, it was halted for readjustment, the ground offering some protection. Thus far the enemy's fire had been only slightly felt, except by Edie's brigade, which was some distance in advance of the troops on the right, and had already carried a projection of the enemy's works, and was exposed to a most galling fire. To give Edie support, or rather to relieve him from position in the line, Este's brigade of Baird's division was thrown forward, and took part in the general attack which followed. The other two brigades of Baird's division were retained on the left, to push the advantage on that flank, should a general assault prove successful.

At 5 P. M., the rectified lines again moved forward, and the attack was quickly and vigorously made along the whole battle front. There had been so many unsuccessful assaults made by both armies during the campaign, that the enemy regarded this attempt to carry his intrenchments, so strongly defended, as an exhibition of folly and harmless audacity. But it was soon revealed that the most determined resistance could not arrest or defeat the bold assault.

Morgan's division carried its entire front, and gloriously reversed the issue of its assault near Kenesaw Mountain on the 27th of June. The brigades of Mitchell and Dilworth there clung to the hillside under the enemy's guns, having failed in assault; here they leaped the fortifications, and under sword and bayonet held captive the troops set for their defense.

Este's brigade was successful at once on its right, the Tenth Kentucky and Seventy-fourth Indiana gaining the intrenchments in their front; but the Fourteenth and Thirty-eighth Ohio, on the left, met such obstructions, as compelled them to halt. They, however, held their ground under a fire of fearful effect. Colonel Este, who had been in the charge on his right, now turned his attention to his left, and meeting with Colonel W. T. C. Grower, Seventeenth New York, of General Morgan's left brigade, requested him to put in his regiment, which he did with great gallantry and success, though he was himself one of the first to fall. Joined by this regiment, Este's left carried the works in front, and captured a large number of prisoners. Moore's brigade, Carlin's left, encountered such obstructions as held it in check for a time, but finally joined the remainder of the assaulting troops in the enemy's works.

Equal success on the part of the Fourth Corps might have resulted in the capture of Hardee's command; but Kimball's and Newton's divisions were so delayed by the thick undergrowth, and the enemy's skirmishers, that they did not get before his main lines until 5 P. M., and then Grose and Kirby only succeeded in breaking through the entanglements in front of his barricade, while Newton, who was compelled to make a larger circuit, passed beyond the right flank of the enemy, when it was too dark to take advantage of his position.

Although Hardee's corps was neither captured nor annihilated—a conjectural result, had the troops on the left reached the field earlier—the action was the most brilliant and successful of its type during the campaign. All other assaults of main lines by either army had resulted in failure, and, as a general rule, the defensive in positive battle had been successful; but here a strongly intrenched line was carried, with the capture of nearly a thousand men, including one general officer, and many of inferior grades, also eight guns, and seven battle flags. During the night, about one thousand men in addition either surrendered or were captured.

The contest closed so late in the evening that pursuit was impossible, and the troops bivouacked in the enemy's works connecting with the Fourth Corps at the railroad. During the night, Hardee fell back to Lovejoy's Station. The next morning the national forces followed, except the Fourteenth Corps, left behind to bury the dead and collect the material abandoned by the enemy. The troops in pursuit reached the vicinity of the station at noon. The Fourth Corps formed line of battle, and made preparations to attack the enemy who was busy fortifying a line across the railroad, a mile north. The necessity of resistance at this point had not been anticipated, and the enemy was extemporizing defenses. General Stanley's line was formed with Wood's division in the center, and Newton's and Kimball's on the right and left. As his attack was to be co-operative with the Army of the Tennessee, he waited for General Howard to fix the time, and at $3\frac{1}{2}$ P. M. as directed, advanced his line. Upon reaching the immediate vicinity of the enemy, he did not deem it advisable to attack at the railroad, as Hood's artillery swept this point completely. Supposing that the Army of the Tennessee would so hold the enemy by attack, that he could reach his right flank, General Stanley advanced his center and left. The ground, however, was so unfavorable, on account of roughness, streams, and marshes, that Wood's and Kimball's divisions did not get near the position until nearly 6 P. M. While General Wood was selecting a point for attack, he received a wound which obliged him to relinquish his command. However, his left brigade, Knefler's, charged and carried the enemy's works, but could not maintain its hold, as it was subjected to an enfilading fire on both flanks. Kimball's column was exposed to a sweeping artillery fire, and the ground before them being open, the order to charge was countermanded. Both divisions intrenched. General Sherman did not deem it advisable subsequently to press the attack, as he was led to believe that Hood had halted merely to cover the roads to McDonough and Fayetteville, and that it was then too late to intercept Stewart's corps, reported to be in retreat from Atlanta upon McDonough.

Pending the movement south of Atlanta, General Slocum strengthened the position at the Chattahoochee, and watched the enemy closely toward Atlanta. The explosions during the night of the 1st called forth a special reconnoissance. As Colonel Coburn, commanding the advance, approached the city on the 2d, he was met by the mayor, who made to him a formal surrender of the place. After entering Atlanta, Colonel Coburn exchanged a few shots with Ferguson's cavalry, acting as a rear-guard of the retreating army, and captured one hundred men. General Slocum soon after occupied the city with seven brigades, and found twenty pieces of artillery and several hundred small arms; but General Hood had destroyed almost all valuable material which he could not remove, including eight locomotives and eighty-one cars loaded with ammunition and supplies. The explosion of the ammunition had been heard at Jonesboro, and was the first indication of the total abandonment of the place. As General Sherman had interposed between Stewart's corps at Atlanta, and Hardee's and Lee's on the Macon road, the retreat of the former was the only condition of safety.

The losses in the engagements south of Atlanta amounted in the aggregate to twelve hundred men. Fifteen hundred of the enemy were captured, and he left three hundred dead on the field of battle.

September 3d, General Sherman announced the conclusion of the campaign, and gave orders for the return of his armies to Atlanta, to rest and recuperate until the enemy's movements or some new plan of his own should call them again to action. As the enemy remained in his intrenchments at Lovejoy's Station, General Sherman did not withdraw his army at once. Both commanding generals sent their trains to the rear; and thus indicated a mutual disposition to widen the breach between them for a time at least.

On the 5th, the Fourth Corps quietly withdrew from position and joined the Fourteenth at Jonesboro, at daylight on the 6th. Though the general withdrawal was impeded by a rain-storm and consequent bad roads, it was successfully conducted. The enemy manifested a disposition to annoy the two corps at Jonesboro, but there was no action beyond the exchange of a few shots. The next day, the army moved to Rough and Ready, the enemy refraining from pursuit, and went into camp on the 8th, on the outskirts of Atlanta—the Fourteenth Corps on the right of the Campbellton road, and the Twentieth and Fourth Corps to the east in reserve. Pickets were thrown out well to the front upon commanding positions. Thus, Atlanta was gained after a campaign of four months, involving strategical and tactical combinations on a grand scale, but without a general decisive battle. General Sherman did not risk a general assault, and the Confederate generals did not offer battle with a broad front, except with intrenched lines; but there were many engagements of great severity, and constant skirmishing on a scale that produced great waste of life.

The fall of Atlanta was hailed by the Northern people as a result of great moment. The noise of cannon all over the land, orders of congratulation from Washington and army commanders gave expression to the general appreciation of the campaign and its issue. The moral effect of the consummation was indeed great North and South, and yet, as no army had been destroyed or signally defeated, the possession of Atlanta was only a partial solution to the war problem in the West. The march southward of Sherman's armies, despite the heaviest concentration that could be made in resistance, the destruction of extensive manufactories of materials of war, and the palpable diminution of the central insurgent forces, were grand results indeed; but the Confederate Army of the Tennessee was not annihilated, and until it and the one in Virginia should be, the end of the war could not come. The end was indeed foreshadowed by the fact that the national armies could force their way into the South anywhere, subject to the one condition of supplies. But this war, beyond most wars, was a conflict of ideas, and the persistence of the parties to it revealed the overmastering force of the antagonistic opinions. The protraction of the war had intensified the original antagonisms, and had, besides, involved the two sections in debt to such an enormous extent that financial ruin was inevitable in the defeat of either. The success of the North would restore the Union and place its debt upon the whole country. The success of the South would be a division of the country, with a burden of debt to each portion of crushing weight. So that now, not only the primal causes of the war and the extreme reluctance of a proud people to yield to an enemy, but financial considerations, precluded peace so long as the South could maintain armies. The campaigns of the summer had made a heavy draft upon the strength of the Confederate armies; but the two which unfurled their banners before Grant and Sherman in May were intact, though one had been shut up in Richmond and the other had been battled and flanked out of Atlanta. General Canby and Admiral Farragut had neutralized Mobile, though the former had been bereft of the corps intended for its complete reduction to reinforce the Army of the Potomac. There were troops yet in the Gulf States, east of the Mississippi, to raise Hood's army to its maximum strength, though their accretion would reveal the desperate straits of the insurgents. There were forces beyond the Mississippi, whose isolation hitherto, through the viligance of General Canby, had prevented a more potential combination against General Sherman in Georgia. These troops were raiding in Missouri, and by predatory warfare were doing local mischief without affecting the general issue. The rebellion, then, was palpably resting upon the armies of Lee and Hood. The former, by political considerations, if not by purely military ones, was restricted to the defense of the Confederate capital. Hood's army alone had freedom of motion, and to determine how best to use that freedom was to the insurgent leaders the great problem of the hour.

The aggregate casualties of the Army of the Cumberland, during the campaign, from the 1st of May to the 6th of September, were as follows: One hundred and ninety-six officers and two thousand eight hundred and forty-five men enlisted were killed; eight hundred and ten officers and fourteen thousand nine hundred and seventy-three enlisted men were wounded; one hundred and four officers and two thousand six hundred and three enlisted men were captured—in all, twenty-one thousand five hundred and thirty-four men. During the campaign forty-three thousand one hundred and fifty-three were reported sick to Major George E. Cooper, surgeon United States army, medical director of the department. Of these, twenty-six thousand one hundred and eighty-four were sent to the rear; two hundred and seven died from disease, and one thousand and sixty-seven died from wounds. Almost all others, sick or wounded, were returned to duty.

General J. M. Brannan, chief of artillery, reported the capture of four guns by the Twentieth Corps, at Resaca, in battle, and four left by the enemy in his fortifications; ten guns captured by General J. C. Davis, at Rome; twenty left by the enemy in Atlanta, and eight captured by the Fourteenth Corps, at Jonesboro. He also reported the expenditure of 86,611 rounds of artillery ammunition, 11,815,299 rounds of infantry ammunition, and the loss of 1,489 artillery horses.

During the period the army captured 8,067 men from the enemy and received 2,162 deserters, as reported by Colonel Parkhurst, provost marshal general of the department. These statistics reveal the cost of war.

HEADQUARTERS MILITARY DIVISION OF THE MISSISSIPPI,
IN THE FIELD, NEAR ATLANTA, GA., *August* 13, 1864—8 P. M.
General Halleck, Washington, D. C.:

We have now pressed the enemy's lines from the east around to East Point on the south. The nature of the ground, with its artificial defenses, makes it too difficult to assault, and to reach the road by a further extension will be extra hazardous. I have ordered army commanders to prepare for the following plan: Leave one corps strongly intrenched at the Chattahoochee bridge in charge of our suplus wagons and artillery; with sixty thousand (60,000) men reduced to fighting trim, to make circuit of devastation around the town, with a radius of fifteen or twenty miles.

To do this, I go on faith that the militia in Atlanta are only good for the defense of its parapets, and will not come out.

I would like the utmost activity to be kept up in Mobile Bay, and if possible, about the mouth of Apalachicola; also, to be assured that no material reinforcements have come here from Virginia.

If ever I should be cut off from my base, look out for me about St. Marks, Florida, or Savannah, Georgia.

W. T. SHERMAN,
Major-General.

HEADQUARTERS MILITARY DIVISION OF THE MISSISSIPPI,
IN THE FIELD, NEAR ATLANTA, GA., *August* 13, 1864.
General Halleck, Washington, D. C.:

In making the circuit of Atlanta, as proposed in my dispatch of to-day, I necessarily run some risk. If there be any possibility of Admiral Farragut and the land forces of Gordon Granger taking Mobile (which rebel prisoners now report, but the report is not confirmed by Macon papers of the 11th, which I have seen), and further, of pushing up to Montgomery, my best plan would be to wait awhile as now, and, at proper time, to move down to West Point, and operate into the heart of Georgia from there.

Before cutting loose, as proposed, I would like to know the chances of our getting the use of the Alabama river this campaign: I could easily break up the railroads back to Chattanooga, and shift my whole army down to West Point and Columbus, a country rich in corn, and make my fall campaign from there.

I know Fort Morgan must succumb in time.

W. T. SHERMAN,
Major-General.

HEADQUARTERS MILITARY DIVISION OF THE MISSISSIPPI,
IN THE FIELD, NEAR ATLANTA, GA., *August* 17, 1864.
Generals Thomas, Schofield, and Howard:

I now have positive and official information that General Wheeler has gone up into East Tennessee, beyond Spring Place. We will repair all damages to railroad and telegraph to-night. I will not move our infantry now, but break the Macon road all to pieces with our cavalry to-morrow night. Therefore, be active, and demonstrate against Atlanta, to occupy the entire front, and make them believe we will attack them in their trenches during to-morrow and next day.

W. T. SHERMAN,
Major-General Commanding.

HEADQUARTERS MILITARY DIVISION OF THE MISSISSIPPI,
IN THE FIELD, NEAR ATLANTA, GA., *August* 24, 1864—8 A. M.
Generals Thomas, Schofield, and Howard:

I will ride down to the bridge to-day, to see the lay of the ground and the character of the redoubts there. Go on and make all preparations possible, so that our movement, when begun, may proceed rapidly and safely. Our maps should be compiled, and as many roads laid down between Red Oak and Jonesboro as we can be sure of existence.

W. T. SHERMAN,
Major-General Commanding.

HEADQUARTERS MILITARY DIVISION OF THE MISSISSIPPI,
August 24, 1864.

Major-General Sherman:

A fire seems to be raging in Atlanta, direction ten (10) degrees south of east from my tree. Can see heated air rising in dense columns; seems to be spreading. Town is filled with smoke.

I have directed my heavy guns to fire on the town.

O. O. HOWARD,
Major-General.

HEADQUARTERS MILITARY DIVISION OF THE MISSISSIPPI,
IN THE FIELD, NEAR LOVEJOY'S STATION, GA., *September 2, 1864—8 P. M.*

Major-General Thomas:

Until we hear from Atlanta the exact truth, I do not care about your pushing your men against breastworks. Destroy the railroad well up to your lines. Keep skirmishers well up, and hold your troops in hand for anything that may turn up. As soon as I know positively that our troops are in Atlanta, I will determine what to do.

I have ordered General Schofield to feel for the McDonough road, to prevent reinforcements coming to the enemy from that direction.

Yours, etc., W. T. SHERMAN,
Major-General Commanding.

[SPECIAL FIELD ORDERS, NO. 63.]

HEADQUARTERS MILITARY DIVISION OF THE MISSISSIPPI,
IN THE FIELD, NEAR LOVEJOY'S, *September 3, 1864.*

I. Army commanders will, during to-day, send to Jonesboro all sick and wounded men, all empty wagons and prisoners of war, also all surplus wheels not needed for a five days' stay in front, ready to start to-morrow morning, at 6 o'clock, from Jonesboro to Atlanta. Each army will send a regiment to escort these wagons, and General Thomas will send an experienced colonel to conduct the train into Atlanta, there to wait further orders.

II. The army will be prepared to move back to-morrow or next day—the Army of the Cumberland to Atlanta and Chattahoochee bridge, the Army of the Tennessee to East Point, and the Army of the Ohio to Decatur. Major-General Thomas will have General Garrard's cavalry ready to act as rear guard.

By order of Major-General W. T. Sherman.

L. M. DAYTON,
Aid-de-Camp.

[SPECIAL FIELD ORDERS, NO. 66.]

HEADQUARTERS MILITARY DIVISION OF THE MISSISSIPPI,
IN THE FIELD, NEAR JONESBORO, GA., *September 6, 1864.*

I. The General-in-Chief communicates, with a feeling of just pride and satisfaction, the following orders of the President of the United States.

FALL OF ATLANTA, ETC.   153

and telegram of Lieutenant-General U. S. Grant, on hearing of the capture of Atlanta:

EXECUTIVE MANSION,
WASHINGTON, D. C., *September* 3, 1864.

The national thanks are rendered by the President to Major-General W. T. Sherman, and the gallant officers and soldiers of his command before Atlanta, for the distinguished ability, courage, and perseverance displayed in the campaign in Georgia, which, under Divine favor, has resulted in the capture of the city of Atlanta. The marches, battles, sieges, and other military operations that have signalized the campaign, must render it famous in the annals of war, and have entitled those who have participated therein to the applause and thanks of the nation.

(Signed,)   ABRAHAM LINCOLN,
President of the United States.

EXECUTIVE MANSION,
WASHINGTON CITY, *Septmber* 3, 1864.

Ordered:
1st. . . . .
2d. That, on Wednesday, the 9th day of September, commencing at the hour of 12 M., there shall be fired a salute of one hundred (100) guns, at the arsenal at Washington, and at New York, Boston, Philadelphia, Baltimore, Pittsburg, Newport, Kentucky, St. Louis, New Orleans, Mobile, Pensacola, Hilton Head, and Newbern, or the day after the receipt of this order, for the brilliant achievements of the army under command of Major-General Sherman, in the State of Georgia, and the capture of Atlanta. The Secretary of War will issue directions for the execution of this order.

(Signed,)   ABRAHAM LINCOLN,
President of the United States.

CITY POINT, VA., *September* 4, 1864—9 P. M.

Major-General Sherman:

I have just received your dispatch, announcing the capture of Atlanta. In honor of your great victory, I have ordered a salute to be fired with shotted guns from every battery bearing upon the enemy. The salute will be fired within an hour, amidst great rejoicing.

(Signed,)   U. S. GRANT,
Lieutenant-General.

II. . . . . All the corps, regiments, and batteries composing this army, may, without further orders, inscribe "Atlanta" on their colors. By order of Major-General W. T. Sherman.

L. M. DAYTON,
Aid-de-Camp.

[GENERAL ORDERS, NO. 134.]

HEADQUARTERS DEPARTMENT OF THE CUMBERLAND,
ATLANTA, GA., *September* 9, 1864.

Soldiers of the Army of the Cumberland:

The major-general commanding, with pride and pleasure, congratulates you upon the fact that your achievements during the campaign which has just closed, in connection with those of the Armies of the Tennessee and Ohio, have received such distinguished marks of appreciation as the thanks of the President of the United States, and of the major-general commanding the Military Division of the Mississippi.

Your commander now desires to add his to those you have already received, for the tenacity of purpose, unmurmuring endurance, cheerful obedience, brilliant heroism, and all those high qualities which you have displayed to an eminent degree, in attacking and defeating the cohorts of treason, driving them from position after position, each of their own choosing, cutting their communications, and in harassing their flanks and rear, during the many marches, battles, and sieges of this long and eventful campaign.

It is impossible, within the limits of an order like this, to enumerate the many instances in which your gallantry has been conspicuous, but among them may be mentioned the actions of Rocky Face Mountain and before Dalton, fought between the 8th and 13th of May; of Resaca, on the 14th and 15th; of Adairsville, on the 17th, and of New Hope Church, on the 25th of the same month; of Culp's Farm, June 22d; Peachtree creek, July 20th, and the crowning one of Jonesboro, fought September 1st, which secured the capture of the city of Atlanta, the goal for which we set out more than four months ago, and furnished a brilliant termination to your struggles for that long period.

Let these successes encourage you to the continued exercise of those same high qualities, and to renewed exertions in the cause of our country and humanity when you shall again be called upon to meet the foe; and be assured, the time is not far distant when your prowess will conquer what territory now remains within the circumscribed limits of the rebellion. A few more fields like those whose names now crowd your standards, and we can dictate the terms of a peace alike honorable to yourselves and our country. You can then retire to your homes amid the plaudits of your friends, and with the proud consciousness that you have deserved well of the country.

Our rejoicings are not unmixed with a proud regret for our brave comrades who have fallen. Their graves mark the spots where they went down amid the din and roar of battle, dotting every field and hillside, or lying beneath the spreading boughs of the forest along our route; they will, in future days, serve like finger-boards, to point out to the traveler the march of your victorious columns. Those silent mounds appeal to us to remain true to ourselves and the country, and to so discharge the high duty devolving upon us that their lives, which they so freely offered up, may not prove a useless sacrifice.

By command of Major-General Thomas.

WM. D. WHIPPLE,
Assistant Adjutant-General.

CHAPTER XXXIII.

THE MARCH OF THE OPPOSING ARMIES TO THE NORTH AND THE EVOLUTION OF NEW CAMPAIGNS.

WHEN General Sherman, August 18th, informed General Halleck that he would make the circuit of Atlanta with his armies, he suggested that it might be prudent to break up the railroad to Chattanooga, and shift his armies to West Point and Columbus, and there make his base for the fall campaign. To this General Grant replied, advising that there should be no backward movement, even if his roads should be so cut as to preclude the possibility of supplies from the North, and said: "If it comes to the worst, move South as you suggest." After General Sherman had taken the city, without overthrowing the army which had so long defended it, he was occupied with the question of its use in future operations. That he might hold it for purely military purposes, he banished the citizens, giving them choice to go North or South; and as the defenses constructed by the enemy were so extensive that only an army could utilize them, he established an inner line of works, which, held by an ordinary garrison, would protect his depots. That he might accumulate supplies for future enterprise, he restricted the railroads to persons connected with the army, and the transportation of military stores. But underlying these essential preparations, even to hold Atlanta defensively, there was the grand problem of farther aggression. To hold Atlanta and the long railroad to his primary base, and have forces to advance, in the manner of his previous movement, required an impracticable augmentation. As the enemy was now free to detach heavily, to break his communications, he was compelled to send troops to the rear, and, besides this draft, he was constantly losing regiments by expiration of term of service. Despairing of being able to cling to the railroads in advancing from Atlanta, he, in common with General Grant, was looking for a southern base to which he might leap, without intervening communications. General Grant suggested that General Canby should act upon Savannah, and General Sherman upon Augusta. General Sherman in reply expressed his willingness " to move upon Milledgeville, and compel Hood to give up Macon and Augusta, and then turn upon the other," if he could be assured of finding provisions at Augusta or Columbus; but without such assurance he would risk his army by going far from Atlanta. The country, in any direction southward, would supply an army that could maintain motion and freedom to forage, but the contingency of slow maneuvers or stopping to dislodge an intrenched enemy, coupled with constraint in foraging, was the barrier to a campaign having a remote objective. The questions of the direction and object of an advance, though discussed at length by Generals Grant and Sherman, remained unsettled until General Hood's movements gave a turn to affairs which had not been anticipated by either.

Soon after the fall of Atlanta, the Southern President left Richmond to confer with his western generals with regard to the next campaign, and to use his eloquence to rouse the people from despondency. His removal of General Johnston from command had not averted disaster. He had watched the closing in of the national lines around his capital, but the conditions of warfare were there inveterately defined, and he sped to the West to give shape to some new enterprise in solution of the problems imposed by the issue of the preceding disastrous campaign.

It would have been well had he called General Johnston to Palmetto, and this he doubtless would have done, had his sole object been to give a successful issue to a new campaign; but even in this supreme moment, personal considerations were dominant, and the justification of his removal of his ablest western general from command, took rank with the projects which involved the fate of the Confederacy. He now needed judicious counsel, for another campaign of dire issue would be fatal. Nearly one hundred thousand national troops were holding Atlanta, and preparing to utilize all the advantages gained in the previous campaign. It was not possible to increase Hood's army promptly to such an extent as to justify direct offense in open field, much less against Atlanta. The Confederate leaders were then restricted to the continuance of the defensive, wherever General Sherman should invite defense, or to some diversion that would retard or avert the blow which he was meditating. It was decided that Hood's army should be thrown upon General Sherman's communication, and the forces under Smith and Magruder called over the Mississippi river for conjunction in Northern Alabama; that the united armies, gathering recruits as they advanced, should sweep through Tennessee and Kentucky, and stand a hundred thousand strong upon the banks of the Ohio. Critics have been swift to condemn Hood's advance to the North, and considered as an independent movement, it is seemingly, at least, open to criticism; but regarded as a part of a comprehensive plan, it is not apparent that his army could have been used to better advantage. That the expectation of gathering a vast army on the Tennessee river was the inspiration of Hood's movement, which in itself promised no mean results, is plainly true; for before he had crossed the Chattahoochee, the Confederate President sent an order (which General Canby intercepted) to Smith and Magruder to cross the Mississippi river with their forces. The assumption of the practicability of their conjunction with Hood, is the explanation of Mr. Davis' prophetic declarations in speeches throughout the South, that should the absent soldiers return to their colors, General Sherman should be forced into a retreat as disastrous as that of Napoleon from Moscow, and the Confederate army would advance in triumph to the Ohio river. The precedents of the war were against the plan itself, as even in the first flush of the rebellion all aggression with remote objectives had resulted in failure; while in no case during the conflict, had a Confederate army been thrown with ultimate advantage upon the communications of a national army whose aggressive pressure could not be resisted. Latterly, all defense in the West had been unsuccessful, and the disparity of aggregate forces forbade all sober-minded Southerners the hope that any plan could be devised whose execution would arrest, much less avert the downfall of the rebellion.

General Hood remained at Lovejoy's Station, quietly recuperating and reinforcing his army, until the 20th of September, when those on the outlook informed General Sherman that he was in motion. General Sherman's first thought was that he was drawing back to Macon, and would send reinforcements to Richmond. The next day, however, it was apparent that General Hood had only shifted his army to Palmetto Station, and was there intrenching. This movement, and the appearance of Forrest with a force of six or eight thousand men in Tennessee, were the first steps in the execution of the new plan of operations. General Sherman now surmised that General Hood had resolved to throw his army on his flanks, to prevent the accumulation of supplies, and made dispositions to thwart him. He sent General Newton's division to Chattanooga, and ordered General Corse to unite his division at Rome, to act against any force that might threaten Bridgeport from the direction of Gadsden. Having provided for the defense of these important points, he left the disposition of Forrest to the district commanders—Generals Steedman, Granger, and Rousseau.

A raid from Forrest into Middle Tennessee had been expected by those in the rear, though not by those in the front. About the 12th of the month, General Granger received through his scouts information, which he deemed reliable, that such was his purpose, if the corps of General A. J. Smith had been removed from West Tennessee. He therefore expressed his convictions to General Sherman, and asked if Smith's corps had left Tennessee. General Sherman directed General Thomas to inform him that he need feel no uneasiness about Forrest, as he had gone to Mobile. Notwithstanding this positive assurance that there was no danger, General Granger sent a force to reconnoiter in the direction of Forrest's anticipated approach. In obedience to his order, Lieutenant-Colonel Elliott, commanding the Sixth Tennessee Cavalry, advanced toward Florence, and having returned to the main road, after a short detour, found himself in the rear of a cavalry force of eight or ten thousand men. And thus was positively revealed the first of a series of aggressive movements on the part of the enemy, which gave a new complexion and unexpected issues to military operations in Tennessee and Georgia.

September 25th, it was supposed that General Hood was moving toward the Alabama line, and this opening of the way for a march to the sea, turned General Sherman to the consideration of a movement thither without an intermediate base of supplies. General Grant, however, suggested that his attention should first be given to affairs in his rear, and appreciating the situation in Tennessee, and knowing that desperate efforts would be made to force Sherman to relax his grasp upon Georgia, ordered all the spare troops in the West to Nashville, that no further reduction of forces at Atlanta might be necessary. On the 28th, General Sherman said to General Grant: "I want Apalachicola arsenal taken, also Savannah, and if the enemy does succeed in breaking my road, I can fight my way to one or the other place, but I think it better to hold on to Atlanta and strengthen to my rear, and therefore I am glad that you have ordered troops to Nashville." And to President Lincoln, he said: "It would have a bad effect, if I am forced to send back any material part of my army to guard roads, so as to weaken me to an extent that I could not act offensively, if the occasion calls for it." Clinging thus to Atlanta, he was nevertheless so apprehensive with regard to his communications, that he sent General Thomas to the north to provide for their security, having previously ordered General Morgan's division to Chattanooga, and a brigade of the Army of the Tennessee, and the cavalry from Memphis, to Eastport, to operate against the flank of any force going into Tennessee by any of the fords near Florence. General Thomas started on the 29th, and the same day there came to General Sherman the first intimation that Hood was crossing the Chattahoochee. The day following it was known that a portion of his army was across, and by the first of October the movement was well developed, except in respect to its ultimate object. The direction of the march did not indicate an advance to Blue Mountain, but toward General Sherman's communications, and citizens reported that Rome was General Hood's destination. In doubt of his purpose and destination, General Sherman made provision for two contingencies—the enemy swinging across to the Alabama line and thence into Tennessee, or striking the railroad south of Kingston. In the one case, he proposed to send back to Chattanooga all the troops from Kingston north, and with all south of Kingston to move to the sea-board, and in the other, he would turn upon Hood and attack him.

To ascertain the direction of the enemy's march before putting his own armies in motion, General Sherman sent General Garrard to Powder Springs, General Kilpatrick to Sweetwater, General Howard to reconnoiter to Fairburn, and General Cox, commanding the Twenty-third Corps in absence of General Schofield, to send a division to Flat Rock. His object, in addition, was to get the bridges over the Chattahoochee, and then place his armies between them and General Hood. But the latter was indifferent to all such designs, as he had cut loose from all connections in his rear. General Sherman regarded his movement as ostentatious, but it was one of desperation rather, and right boldly did he and his army dash on to the issues involved. He was vigorously executing his part of the grand combination which had been projected, to change, if possible, the theater and the issue of the war in the West. Having crossed the Chattahoochee, he threw Stewart's corps upon the railroad north of Marietta, and with the remainder of his infantry forces, moved toward Dallas, his cavalry, under Wheeler, being already in Northern Georgia. Stewart reached the railroad, and commenced its destruction, October 2d, and citizens reported that it was General Hood's purpose to attack Acworth and Allatoona, afterward Rome, and in the event of repulse, to retreat to Blue Mountain, Jacksonville, and Selma. General Sherman now ordered General Stanley to move with ten days' rations to Ruff's Station, and open communications with General Elliott, who, with his cavalry divisions, was over toward Sweetwater and Nose's creek. The next day, he ordered all his remaining forces, except the Twentieth Corps, which was left to hold Atlanta and the railroad bridge over the Chattahoochee, to follow Stanley. In the evening of the 4th, the advance of the latter encamped near Little Kenesaw Mountain. General Hood's infantry was then advancing upon Allatoona, having captured the garrisons at Big Shanty and Acworth, and destroyed the track of the road for several miles. The same day, General Elliott found the enemy between Dallas and Big Shanty, occupying the old works of the national army, in more force than could be dislodged by dismounted cavalry.

General Sherman had been convinced of General Hood's audacity too late to protect his communications, and was now anxious with regard to his depot of supplies at Allatoona. He had previously ordered General Corse to reinforce the garrison from Rome, should the enemy approach from the south; and this provision saved the place. General Corse reached Allatoona with a few regiments, on the 4th, and the next morning he was attacked by French's division of Stewart's corps. General Sherman, while signaling his presence at Kenesaw Mountain, and his purpose to give the earliest possible support, witnessed the repeated repulse of the enemy. The gallant resistance of the garrison, and the movement of General Cox to his left, induced General French to withdraw entirely during the afternoon, having lost at least a thousand men. This was not a promising initiative for General Hood, and its probable bearing upon his plans was added to other circumstances of positive character to conceal again, for a few days, his ultimate purpose. French's division remained in the rear of the army, and offered such resistance to General Elliott, that it was impossible to ascertain in what direction the enemy's standards were pointing. From the 5th to the 10th, it was not known whether they were pointing northward or westward.

During this period, General Sherman again proposed to General Grant to break up the railroad to Chattanooga, and move with wagons to Savannah, entertaining the opinion that Hood would move to the West. But on the 10th, learning that he was marching toward Rome, he ordered his generals to move upon Kingston with a view to support General Corse at Rome, should the enemy approach in force. General Hood crossed the Coosa river twelve miles below, in feint upon

Rome, to cover another dash upon the railroad and his march northward. General Sherman's forces were concentrated in the vicinity of Kingston on the 11th, but again General Hood's movements were in doubt, as he disappeared from the vicinity of Rome without indicating where he was going. General Sherman, on the 12th, made effort to develop his movements, by sending Garrard's division* and the Twenty-third Corps across the Oostanaula, while a brigade from Hazen's division moved down the Coosa from Rome. In the meantime, Hood moved rapidly toward Resaca with his whole army. Here, again, provision had been made to reinforce the garrison, as, in compliance with General Sherman's contingent orders, the troops at Cassville, Colonel Watkins' brigade of cavalry, and General Baum, with three hundred and fifty infantry, moved forward before the place was invested. Colonel Watkins left his horses on the left bank, and placed his men in the intrenchments on the other side. General Hood demanded the surrender of the place on the 11th, under the threat that no prisoners would be taken if he should be compelled to carry the works by assault. But though General Baum refused to capitulate, and General Hood had a heavy force, probably two corps present, and threw a line around the town from the river above to the river below, he may have been deterred from attack by the uncertainty of the issue, or may have considered the temporary possession no compensation for the cost of taking it.

While halting before Resaca, General Hood sent detachments to destroy the railroad toward Dalton, and having himself withdrawn on the 12th, he demanded the surrender of the latter place the next day. Colonel Johnson, commanding the Forty-fourth Colored regiment, was convinced that resistance was useless, and accepted terms. The garrison at Tilton was also captured. Early in the day, General Schofield had reached Dalton on his way to join General Sherman, but not being able to go farther, and learning that the enemy was advancing, he returned to Cleveland with his train and what

---

* General Garrard drove a brigade of the enemy through the entrance to Chattooga valley, and captured two guns.

public property it was practicable to save. From Dalton, General Hood, with Lee's and Cheatham's corps, passed into Snake Creek Gap. Stewart's corps destroyed the railroad to Tunnel Hill. General Sherman reached Resaca on the 14th, and disposed his forces to strike the enemy in flank, or force him to fight by shutting him up in Snake Creek Gap. He sent General Howard to the southern entrance, and General Stanley, with his own and Davis' corps, by Tilton, to the northern entrance. But though General Howard skirmished to hold General Hood in the pass until General Stanley should reach his rear, his effort was ineffectual, as he retreated to the north before Stanley could intercept him by closing the Gap. Having emerged from the pass, General Hood had freedom of motion north and west. On the 16th, General Sherman threw his columns to Lafayette to cut off his retreat, but he was able to unite his forces in time to attain a safe position between the Coosa and Lookout-Mountain.

Reference should here be made to operations by which Forrest was expelled from Tennessee. This bold trooper crossed the Tennessee river at Waterloo, September 20th, and two days afterward appeared before Athens, Alabama. Colonel Campbell, commanding the post, after skirmishing with the enemy for a short time, withdrew from the town to the fortifications. This step exposed the public buildings and stores, and Forrest immediately applied the torch. The next day he invested the fort, which had been constructed for defense by a small force, and opened with his artillery. Colonel Campbell responded with spirit, and refused two calls to surrender, but finally, through a personal interview with Forrest, was induced to conclude that resistance was useless. Forrest adopted the policy, which in many instances was successful, to make a show of force to induce surrender, when there was no intention to attack, or at least a great reluctance to do so, in view of inevitable loss or uncertain issue. The garrison surrendered consisted of four hundred and fifty men of the One Hundred and Sixth, One Hundred and Tenth, and One Hundred and Eleventh Colored regiments, and one hundred and thirty men of the Third Tennessee Cavalry. A half hour later, the Eighteenth Michigan and One Hundred and Third Ohio arrived, and were surrendered after an engagement. This was an auspicious beginning for Forrest, but fortunately proved to be his only important success.

From Athens he advanced toward Pulaski, and destroyed the Nashville and Decatur railroad for several miles. At Pulaski, General Rousseau was awaiting his coming with such force that Forrest withdrew after a skirmish. The same day, the 29th, one of his detachments appeared on the Nashville and Chattanooga road, north and south of Tullahoma, cut the telegraph wires, and injured the track. The road was soon repaired, but the party having touched it, was the advance of Forrest's main force, which passed Fayetteville the night following, moving toward Decherd. Having learned, however, that heavier forces were before him than he wished to meet, he changed direction and divided his forces. General Rousseau had moved by rail, the day previous, to Tullahoma, and General Steedman had crossed the Tennessee river, and was advancing north upon the road with five thousand men, and in the face of the two columns, Forrest turned back, sending Buford with four thousand men to Huntsville, and moving himself with three thousand toward Columbia. Buford reached Huntsville the night of the 30th, and made an ineffectual demand for the surrender of the place. Remaining during the night, he repeated his demand with similar issue the next morning, and then moved off toward Athens. Here he made an attack at 3 P. M., and was repulsed by the Seventy-third Indiana, Lieutenant-Colonel Slade commanding, which had been sent thither by General Granger to regarrison the post, immediately after Colonel Campbell's surrender. Buford anticipated an easy victory, but was twice repulsed, and was pursued after withdrawal, by a small party of General Granger's cavalry. He crossed the Tennessee, at Brown's ferry, on the 3d of October.

General Forrest succeeded no better. He reached Columbia on the 1st, but refrained from attack. He remained in the vicinity until the 3d, and then moved in the direction of Mount Pleasant, destroying five miles of railroad between Cartersville and Spring Hill. By this time, four columns were converging upon him, under the direction of General Thomas. General Morgan's division having arrived at Huntsville the night of the 1st, moved through Athens to secure the crossing at Bainbridge; General Rousseau was on his way from Nashville with four thousand men, who had been hastily mounted; Croxton was advancing through Lawrenceburg, and General Washburne, with three thousand infantry and fifteen hundred cavalry, was passing up the Tennessee river, under instructions to leave his infantry at Johnsonville and join General Rousseau at Pulaski, with his cavalry. In addition to these dispositions, Lieutenant-Commander Forrest, commanding the naval force on the Upper Tennessee, was requested to send gunboats to Florence, if the stage of water would permit. This combination might have resulted in Forrest's capture, had not the high water in Elk river detained Morgan, who did not reach Rogersville until the night of the 4th, while Forrest passed through Laurenceburg the same night, and crossed at Bainbridge on the 6th, his rear forces having been reached by Washburne's advance. But if Forrest was neither captured nor defeated, the main line of railroad was saved from serious damage, and to break it was doubtless the chief object of his raid.

As soon as General Thomas was advised of Hood's northward march, he made dispositions to offer resistance on the line of the Tennessee river, and especially to defend Chattanooga and Bridgeport—the most important points on the direct line of supply. He first directed General Rousseau to destroy all ferry-boats and other means of crossing the river below Decatur, and then take post at Florence, Alabama, and ordered General Morgan to return to Athens. When the direction of General Hood's march was clearly indicated, he directed General Croxton, with his brigade of cavalry, to cover the crossings of the river from Decatur to Eastport, and hurried Morgan's division from Athens to Chattanooga, Steedman's from Decatur to Bridgeport, and Rousseau's from Florence to Athens. The garrisons at Decatur, Huntsville, and Stevenson were not reinforced, that there might be the heaviest concentration possible, should the enemy advance toward Chattanooga or Bridgeport.

The northward march of Hood's army, on General Sherman's communications, created an intense alarm all over the North, from which the highest military circles were not free.

As a consequence, all available troops in the Department of the Ohio, and all, in fact, far and near, were directed to General Thomas; and so threatening was the emergency in the estimation of the lieutenant-general, that he advised the withdrawal of all the forces on the railroad "from Columbia to Decatur, and thence to Stevenson." General Thomas, however, did not adopt the suggestion, and subsequent events justified his action.

When, on the 13th, General Thomas ascertained that Hood's advance was at Lafayette, Georgia, he directed General Wagner, in command at Chattanooga, to call in all the detachments from Tunnel Hill, north, and make preparations to hold his important post. Accordingly, a very large number of guns were mounted in the fortificatious, which had been made exceedingly strong by Colonel Merrill, with his engineer regiment and the forces left as a garrison, while all the outlying troops were concentrated for the defense of the town and supplies.

Upon General Schofield's return from Dalton to Cleveland, General Thomas directed him to assume command at Chattanooga, and add to the garrison all the troops within reach.

But though General Hood was so near, he had no thought of putting his army between the mountains, south of Chattanooga, at least while General Sherman was in his immediate rear, and soon moved westward to avoid battle and pursue the accomplishment of the ultimate object of his march to the north. As soon as he turned westward, General Thomas sent General Schofield, with Morgan's and Wagner's divisions, up Will's valley to watch against the approach of the enemy toward Bridgeport, but soon recalled him, having gained knowledge of General Hood's movement upon Gadsden.

When General Sherman learned that Hood had turned westward, he proposed to follow him wherever he might go, but did not believe that he meditated the invasion of Tennessee, though the declarations of the Confederate President and General Hood gave assurance of this design. The pursuit of Hood was maintained by various routes to Gaylesville, and there General Sherman halted his armies to await the repair of the railroad and the developments of the enemy. He stationed the Army of the Tennessee near Little river, to support the cavalry and observe the enemy toward Will's valley; the Army of the Ohio at Cedar Bluffs, to feel forward to Center and in the direction of Blue Mountain; and the Army of the Cumberland at Gaylesville. While in this region the armies drew their supplies from the country.

Although General Hood had not achieved the grand results which the sanguine President had predicted, he had nevertheless been so far successful as to perplex the national commanders and give hope to the insurgents. He had not forced General Sherman into a disastrous retreat, but he had drawn him to the north, not in abandonment of Atlanta and his fortified positions, but with nearly all his forces. He had twice thrown his armies between General Sherman and his base; had maneuvered with skill; had captured the garrisons at Big Shanty, Acworth, Tilton, and Dalton; had destroyed nearly thirty miles of railroad, and, except in his attack upon Allatoona, had received no harm. He had moved in boldest disregard of railroads and communications, contrary to the precedents of the previous campaign, and, in fine, his northward march had been brilliantly executed. The resulting problems were freighted with the gravest issues. The insurgents were now too far exhausted to bear the overthrow of his army in its perilous adventure to the north, and yet Hood held boldly to his plan, as though assured of success. A new base, with railroad communications, was in preparation for him in Northern Mississippi, under the direction of General Beauregard, now in supreme command in the West, not for defense, but for aggression of the boldest type, whose explanation is found in the expectation that the trans-Mississippi forces would swell Hood's army for its resistless sweep through Tennessee and Kentucky. General Canby's dispatch to General Sherman, dated October 18th, gives evidence of the effort to reinforce Hood's army from the West; as, without heavy reinforcements, aggression, in the face of General Sherman's armies, was palpably impossible. No doubt the minor object was to decoy General Sherman from the Chattanooga and Atlanta railroad, and the undoing of the campaign on that line; but the main one was the invasion of Tennessee and Kentucky. Subsequently, General Sherman's movement to the south so changed the situation that this invasion was attempted without the trans-Mississippi forces.

While the rebel generals were preparing to invade Tennessee and Kentucky, General Sherman was engrossed with the project which he first suggested as a contingency when about to make the circuit of Atlanta, in August, and which he had since repeatedly brought to the attention of General Grant. At Atlanta, Allatoona, Kingston, and now, while awaiting, at Gaylesville, the repair of the railroad, he made suggestions to General Grant, from day to day, concerning the "march to the sea." He was unwilling to follow Hood farther west, as in this way, it had been planned that he should be decoyed from Georgia. By the 20th of October his plans for a counter-movement were well matured, and his utterances and orders foreshadowed their early execution. He proposed to leave General Thomas in command of the military division in his absence—which at first he thought would be ninety days, as in that time he could go to the sea and return—giving him as an army for defense the Fourth Corps, the garrisons in Tennessee and Alabama, and the new troops that had been ordered to Nashville. For himself he would retain the Fourteenth, Fifteenth, Seventeenth, Twentieth, and Twenty-third Corps, and a cavalry corps of three divisions, comprising twenty-five hundred men each, under the command of Brevet Major-General J. H. Wilson, recently sent by General Grant to be chief of the cavalry of the military division. These troops were to be trimmed to perfect efficiency. The railroad was to be repaired to Atlanta, for use in preparation for the march beyond, and then to be destroyed.

Telegraphic communication between Chattanooga and Atlanta was established October 20th, and on the 28th the railroad was in running order. In the meantime General Hood assumed the offensive. Advancing from Gadsden, he appeared before Decatur on the 26th and made an attack, but not with such force as indicated a purpose to storm the place—his three corps of infantry being near, and his cavalry being disposed on the south bank of the river, from Guntersville to Eastport. General Thomas sent two regiments to General

Granger, from Chattanooga, and instructed him to hold his post at all hazards. This was a feeble reinforcement, but he had no other spare troops to throw before the enemy. The divisions of Morgan and Wagner had been recalled from Tennessee by General Sherman, and for the defense of the line of the Tennessee river there were the usual garrisons, and General Croxton's brigade of cavalry spread out on the north bank. In the emergency General Sherman ordered General Stanley to report with his corps to General Thomas, and, by order, placed the latter in command of all troops and garrisons in his military division, not in his own presence, contingent upon his separation from his division " by military movements or the accidents of war."

On the 27th, General Hood intrenched his position before Decatur, skirmished during the day, but used no artillery, though he put guns in position. Under the cover of darkness, he drove in General Granger's pickets with a strong force, and established a new line within five hundred yards of the town. The next day, General Granger made a successful sortie. . His troops advanced, under cover of the guns of the fort, down the river bank and round to the rear of the enemy's rifle-pits, and by a bold charge cleared them, killing a large number of men and capturing one hundred and twenty. A battery above the town was also captured by the Fourteenth United States Colored troops, Colonel T. J. Morgan commanding, but the position being too much exposed to be held, the guns were spiked and the regiment under orders retired to the fort. In the charge, Colonel Morgan lost forty men killed and wounded, including three officers killed. This resistance to the establishment of his investing lines, and his lack of provisions, induced General Hood to withdraw his forces altogether at 4 A. M. on the 29th. He could neutralize the place by passing to the west and meet his supplies, while he could secure crossings at less cost down the river; and these considerations doubtless induced his withdrawal. He lost several hundred, perhaps more than a thousand men, while inflicting a loss of eighty, and kept his troops in action in almost utter destitution of provisions.

General Hood has not reported his objects in the various

movements of his campaign, and hence his purpose in operating against Decatur has not been authentically revealed. All circumstances, except his own statement of his plan, lead to the belief that he expected to cross the Tennessee river at Decatur and move rapidly upon General Sherman's communications in Middle Tennessee, and cut off his supplies entirely. The press in the South, and his own officers, entertained and expressed the opinion that this extreme aggression was meditated. The opposition of General Granger's small force at Decatur was so positive, even showing the purpose of offense, that he was deterred from the effort to carry the position by assault. There was a diversity of opinion among his general officers as to the wisdom of his withdrawal from Decatur, as it involved the abandonment, for a time, of his advance to Nashville.

During the 29th, General Croxton discovered that the enemy was crossing the Tennessee river at the mouth of Cypress creek, two miles below Florence. He concentrated his forces as far as practicable, but was unable to regain the north bank. Having been informed of this turn of affairs, General Thomas directed General Hatch, at Clifton, commanding a cavalry division of General Howard's army, and under orders to join General Sherman in Georgia, when ready for the field, to move to General Croxton's support, and urged both commanders to keep the enemy from crossing other forces, if possible, until the Fourth Corps could arrive from Georgia and get into position to meet him. It was, however, too late to defend the line of the Tennessee river, as Hood was master of too many crossings; and when General Wood's division, the advance of the corps, arrived at Athens, on the 31st, General Thomas ordered General Stanley to unite his command at Pulaski and await further instructions. The same day, General Schofield was ordered to move from Resaca, Georgia, to Columbia, Tennessee, to combine with General Stanley and the cavalry to resist the advance of the enemy into Middle Tennessee. That an invasion was meditated had become evident from Southern newspapers, and prisoners and deserters from Hood's army bore testimony to this purpose. The conjecture that he could not supply his army on the Tennessee or north of it was now plainly groundless, as he had established communications by the repair of the Ohio and Mobile railroad, and supplies were coming to him from Selma and Montgomery, through Corinth, and thence eastward to Cherokee Station, on the Memphis and Charleston railroad. And while he had thrust the heads of infantry columns over the river at Florence and at points above and below, he had sent Forrest with his bold troopers up the Tennessee river to break up General Thomas' line of supply by the river and the Northwestern railroad.

Forrest appeared at Fort Heiman, an earthwork on the west bank of the Tennessee, about seventy-five miles from Paducah, where, three days later, he captured gunboat No. 55, and two transports, having previously burned the steamer Empress. On the 2d of November, he planted his batteries above and below Johnsonville, the western terminus of the Northwestern railroad, and an important depot of supplies. His guns blockaded the river, and shut in before the town three gunboats, eight transports, and about a dozen barges. The garrison comprised a thousand men from the Forty-third Wisconsin and the Twelfth United States Colored regiment, and a detachment of the Eleventh Tennessee cavalry, under the command of Colonel C. R. Thompson, of the Twelfth Colored regiment. The naval forces, under Lieutenant E. M. King, attacked the enemy's guns below the town, but though repulsed after a severe conflict, they recaptured a transport having on board two 20-pounder Parrott guns and quartermaster's stores, and forced Forrest to burn the gunboat captured on the 31st of October. On the 4th, the enemy opened fire upon the gunboats from the opposite bank. The guns on boats and land responded briskly, but were soon disabled, and for fear that they would fall into the hands of the enemy, both gunboats and transports were fired. The flames reached the stores on the levee, and property worth a million of dollars was consumed. It was fear rather than necessity that caused this waste, as Forrest withdrew soon after altogether, having delivered a furious cannonade. He crossed the river above the town, by means of extemporized flat-boats, and moved toward Clifton, with evident design of co-operating with the main army.

On the evening of the 5th, General Schofield reached Johnsonville with a portion of his command, having moved rapidly by rail, in compliance with instructions from General Thomas to save the gunboats and supplies. Having left a sufficient force to defend the place, he then proceeded to join General Stanley at Pulaski, to assume command of the forces before the enemy. He was assigned to this position, by reason of his rank as a department commander, though General Stanley was his senior as a major-general.

General Hood was now free to invade Tennessee, as the low stage of water in the river prevented the effective use of the gunboats against his pontoon bridges, and General Thomas could not offer a strong army on the north bank. He was also free to move to the southwest should General Sherman concentrate his armies against him; but General Sherman was unwilling to do this. His preparations for his march through Georgia were nearly completed, and he was unwilling to take a step backward, to pursue Hood. He made provision, however, for reinforcing General Thomas, by calling two divisions, under General A. J. Smith, from Missouri, and by sending back General Wilson, and the cavalry of McCook's and Garrard's divisions to give a good remount to Kilpatrick's division, retained by himself.

General Hood's threatening attitude called forth a fresh discussion of General Sherman's projected march between him and General Grant, but induced no change of plan. The conclusions reached were these, that turning back would undo the work of the preceding campaign, give up the territory which had been gained, and fulfill the predictions of Mr. Davis with regard to the effect of Hood's advance to the North, and that he could not be overtaken if followed; and on the other hand, going forward would destroy the railroads of Georgia, inflict immense damage, and produce a most potent moral effect, in illustrating the vulnerability of the South. In his last communication to General Grant, General Sherman said: "If we can march a well-appointed army right through this territory, it is a demonstration to the world—foreign and domestic—that we have a power which Davis can not resist. This may not be war, but rather statesmanship. Nevertheless it is overwhelming to my mind, that there are thousands of people abroad and in the South who will reason thus: If the North can march an army right through the South, it is proof positive that the North can prevail in this contest, leaving only its willingness to use that power." This moral effect was, indeed, the justification of the movement, as General Sherman proposed to use the territory which he had gained in Georgia as a track simply for his march, and not hold any part of Georgia except his objective on the Atlantic shore, while he left behind him one of the two great armies upon which the existence of the rebellion depended. It is true, however, that even in his last dispatches before starting, he expressed the conviction that Beauregard and Hood would be forced by public clamor to follow him. He retained for himself from his three armies the Fourteenth, Fifteenth, Seventeenth, and Twentieth Corps, and one large division of cavalry, in all sixty thousand infantry, and five thousand five hundred cavalry, and one piece of artillery to every thousand men.

CITY POINT, VA., *September* 10, 1864.

Major-General Sherman:

As soon as your men are properly rested and preparations can be made, it is desirable that another campaign should be commenced.

We want to keep the enemy continually pressed to the end of the war. If we give him no peace while the war lasts, the end can not be far distant. Now that we have all of Mobile Bay that is valuable, I do not know but it will be the best move for Major-General Canby's troops to act upon Savannah, while you move on Augusta. I should like to hear from you on this matter.

U. S. GRANT,
Lieutenant-General.

HEADQUARTERS DEPARTMENT OF THE CUMBERLAND,
ATLANTA, GA., *September* 14, 1864.

Brigadier-General R. S. Granger, Decatur:

General Sherman informs me that General Smith has been directed to Missouri by orders from Major-General Halleck; also, that he has official information that Forrest and his command reached Mobile on the 8th instant. You must therefore apprehend no trouble from any but Roddy, Wheeler, and the parties which have already been in Tennessee.

GEO. H. THOMAS,
Major-General U. S. V. Commanding.

HEADQUARTERS MILITARY DIVISION OF THE MISSISSIPPI,
IN THE FIELD, ATLANTA, GA., *October* 1, 1864.
Lieutenant-General U. S. Grant, City Point:

Hood is evidently on the west side of Chattahoochee, below Sweetwater. If he tries to get on my road this side of the Etowah, I shall attack him; but if he goes on to the Selma and Talladega road, why would it not do for me to leave Tennessee to the forces which Thomas has and the reserves soon to come to Nashville, and for me to destroy Atlanta, and then march across Georgia to Savannah or Charleston, breaking roads and doing irreparable damage? We can not remain on the defensive.

W. T. SHERMAN,
Major-General.

HEADQUARTERS MILITARY DIVISION OF THE MISSISSIPPI,
IN THE FIELD, ATLANTA, GA., *October* 1, 1864—2 P. M.
General G. H. Thomas, Chattanooga:

I have your dispatch of noon. Use your own discretion as to matters north of the Tennessee river. If I can induce Hood to swing across to Blue Mountain, I shall feel tempted to start for Milledgeville, Millen, and Savannah or Charleston, absolutely destroying all Georgia, and taking either Savannah or Charleston. In that event, I would order back to Chattanooga everything the other side of Kingston, and bring forward all else; destroy Atlanta and the bridge, and absolutely scour the Southern Confederacy. In that event, Hood would be puzzled and would follow me; or if he entered Tennessee he could make no permanent stay. But if he attempts the road this side of Kingston or Rome, I will turn against him. Forrest will not attack our forts—that is manifest; but will try and get possession of Decatur. All the infantry and cavalry not in forts or blockhouses should be directed against him by roads—say the Shelbyville pike and Fayetteville.

W. T. SHERMAN,
Major-General.

[SPECIAL FIELD ORDERS, NO. 68.]

HEADQUARTERS MILITARY DIVISION OF THE MISSISSIPPI,
IN THE FIELD, ATLANTA, GA., *October* 3, 1864.

The following movements are ordered:

I. Major-General Slocum, with Twentieth Corps, will hold Atlanta and the Chattahoochee bridge, and all detachments of other troops or corps will report to him and be assigned by him to posts looking to the security of the depot.

II. All the rest of the army, provided with ten (10) days' rations, will move by the Chattahoochee bridge to Smyrna Camp-ground—the Army of the Cumberland, Major-General Stanley on the center, looking west; the

Army of the Ohio, Brigadier-General Cox, on the right, and the Army of the Tennessee, Major-General Howard, on the left.

III. The commanding general will be near the center.

By order of General W. T. Sherman.

(Signed,) L. M. DAYTON,
Aid-de-Camp.

[SPECIAL FIELD ORDERS, NO. 85.]

HEADQUARTERS MILITARY DIVISION OF THE MISSISSIPPI,
IN THE FIELD, KENESAW MOUNTAIN, *October* 6, 1864.

I. Major-General Stanley, Army of the Cumberland, will occupy a strong defensive position across the Marietta and Burnt Hickory, and Marietta and Dallas roads, his right near Pine Hill and left behind Nose's creek.

II. Major-General Howard, Army of the Tennessee, will join on to the left of Stanley, and make a line covering the Powder Spring road, and the cavalry on the flank; General Kilpatrick will prevent the enemy from reaching the railroad below Marietta.

III. Brigadier-General Cox, Army of the Ohio, will move on the Burnt Hickory road, via Pine Hill and Mount Olivet Church, west, until he strikes the road by which the enemy have moved on Allatoona. He will have his columns ready for a fight, but not deployed. He will park his wagons near Kenesaw.

IV. General Elliott will send cavalry to-day to Big Shanty, Acworth, and Allatoona, and bring official reports.

V. . . .

By order of Major-General W. T. Sherman.

L. M. DAYTON,
Aid-de-Camp.

[SPECIAL FIELD ORDERS, NO. 87.]

HEADQUARTERS MILITARY DIVISION OF THE MISSISSIPPI,
IN THE FIELD, KENESAW, *October* 8, 1864.

I. The armies will march at once toward Allatoona—that of the Ohio by the roads southwest of Acworth; that of the Cumberland by roads south and west of Kenesaw Mountain, leading through Acworth, and that of the Tennessee by roads north and east of Kenesaw, via Big Shanty and Acworth.

II. The Army of the Ohio will halt for orders near good grass and water, two or three miles this side of Allatoona; that of the Cumberland, this side Acworth, and that of the Tennessee this side of Big Shanty, all giving attention to the grazing of their animals when not on the march.

IV. Until further orders, General Elliott will keep his cavalry force watching the enemy, but ready to march rapidly to Stilesboro and the Etowah bridge, if the enemy turns north toward Rome or Kingston; otherwise the cavalry will remain at the front or left flank of the army.

V. Should the enemy attempt our road about Kingston or to invest Rome, the army must be prepared to leave at Allatoona the principal wagon trains, and to march rapidly to the points threatened; but if the enemy simply moves off toward Jacksonville or Blue Mountain, the army will remain, its right at Alatoona and left at Kenesaw, until our roads are repaired.

By order of Major-General W. T. Sherman.

L. M. DAYTON,
Aid-de-Camp.

HEADQUARTERS MILITARY DIVISION OF THE MISSISSIPPI,
IN THE FIELD, ALLATOONA, GA., *October 9, 1864.*

Lieutenant-General Grant, City Point, Va.:

It will be a physical impossibility to protect the roads, now that Hood, Forrest, Wheeler, and the whole batch of devils are turned loose without home or habitation. I think Hood's movements indicate a diversion to the end of the Selma and Talladega railroad at Blue Mountain, about sixty (60) miles southwest of Rome, from which he will threaten Kingston, Bridgeport, and Decatur, Alabama.

I propose that we break up the railroad from Chattanooga, and strike out with wagons for Milledgeville and Savannah. Until we can repopulate Georgia, it is useless to occupy it; but the utter destruction of its roads, houses, and people will cripple their military resources. By attempting to hold the roads, we will lose a thousand men monthly, and will gain no result. I can make the march and make Georgia howl. We have over eight thousand (8,000) cattle and three million rations of bread, but no corn; but we can forage in the interior of the state.

W. T. SHERMAN,
Major-General Commanding.

HEADQUARTERS MILITARY DIVISION OF THE MISSISSIPPI,
IN THE FIELD, CARTERVILLE, *October 10, 1864.*

General Grant, City Point:

Dispatch about Wilson received. Hood is now crossing Coosa, twelve (12) miles below Rome, bound west. If he passes over to the Mobile and Ohio road, had I not better execute the plan of my letter sent by Colonel Porter, and leave General Thomas with the troops now in Tennessee, to defend the state? He will have an ample force when the reinforcements ordered reach Nashville.

W. T. SHERMAN,
Major-General Commanding.

[SPECIAL FIELD ORDERS, NO. 89.]

HEADQUARTERS MILITARY DIVISION OF THE MISSISSIPPI,
IN THE FIELD, KINGSTON, GA., *October 11, 1864.*

The army will move to-morrow morning early on Rome—the Armies of the Ohio and Tennessee by the river roads, and the Army of the Cumberland by a detour via Woodland; all to reach Rome to-morrow night.

Trains will be taken to Rome.

By order of Major-General W. T. Sherman.

L. M. DAYTON,
Aid-de-Camp.

[SPECIAL FIELD ORDERS, NO. 90.]

HEADQUARTERS MILITARY DIVISION OF THE MISSISSIPPI,
IN THE FIELD, ROME, GA., *October* 12, 1864.

Orders for to-morrow, October 13th, will be as follows:

I. General Corse will dispatch his division and the brigade of the Fifteenth Corps attached to his garrison, and the First Alabama Cavalry, down the Coosa river, on its east bank, toward Coosaville, to develop the force guarding the bridge by which the enemy crossed. He will send one (1) battery with the expedition, and equip the whole party light.

II. General Elliott will, at the same time, dispatch down the west bank of the Coosa a division of cavalry for the same purpose—viz., to develop the force guarding the bridge by which the enemy crossed.

III. All the armies will be held ready to move at a moment's warning.

By order of Major-General W. T. Sherman.

L. M. DAYTON,
Aid-de-Camp.

BY TELEGRAPH FROM "WASHINGTON, 12 M., NASHVILLE, OCTOBER 13, 1864."

Major-General Geo. H. Thomas, Nashville:

Two old regiments from General Pope and several new ones from Ohio and Indiana are on their way to Nashville. Schofield and Burbridge are ordered to send to you everything that can be spared from Kentucky. Put yourself in communication with them. General Grant directs that you collect your forces, and be prepared to meet Hood wherever he may present himself on the Tennessee, and that you take the supplies of the country without compunction. By thus supplying your own army, you will leave none for him.

H. W. HALLECK,
Major-General.

CITY POINT, VA., *October* 13, 1864.

Major-General Halleck:

For Major-General Thomas' information:

I think it will be advisable for Major-General Thomas now to abandon all the railroad from Columbia to Decatur, thence to Stevenson. This will give him much additional force.

LIEUTENANT-GENERAL GRANT.

WASHINGTON, *October* 14, 1864.

Major-General Thomas:

Lieutenant-General Grant suggests the abandonment of the railroad from Columbia to Decatur, and thence to Stevenson, in order to give you more force against Hood.

MAJOR-GENERAL HALLECK.

[SPECIAL FIELD ORDERS, NO. 91.]

HEADQUARTERS MILITARY DIVISION OF THE MISSISSIPPI,
IN THE FIELD, RESACA, GA., *October* 14, 1864.

The first movement will be to free the Snake Creek Gap.

I. General Howard will bring up all the men of his command he can get at 7 A. M. to-morrow, and move direct on Snake Creek Gap, approaching carefully, and holding his column ready to pass through when relieved by General Stanley's movement.

II. General Stanley will cross over to the hills about two (2) miles north of the gap, somewhere south of Tilton, and with infantry, reach the summit, and, if possible, find a way across into the valley toward Villanow.

III. General Cox will come up and follow General Howard.

* * * * * * * * *

V. General McCook will send all the cavalry he can raise boldly to Buzzard Roost Pass, to threaten the enemy in that quarter, and to give General Stanley notice of any force in that vicinity. As soon as General Garrard comes up, he will be dispatched in the same direction.

* * * * * * * * *

By order of Major-General Sherman.

L. M. DAYTON,
Aid-de-Camp.

[SPECIAL FIELD ORDERS, NO. 92.]

HEADQUARTERS MILITARY DIVISION OF THE MISSISSIPPI,
IN THE FIELD, *October* 15, 1864.

The movement to-morrow will be on Lafayette, the primary object being to secure possession of Ship's Gap.

I. General Howard will move rapidly on Villanow and Ship's Gap, to secure the summit, and mass to the right.

II. General Stanley will follow and mass to the left of the gap.

III. General Cox will halt for orders at Villanow, guarding roads north and south.

IV. General Garrard's cavalry will come through Snake Creek Gap and guard the trains. General Elliott will dispatch Colonel Watkins' cavalry and scouts to open communication with Chattanoogo, to let them know that this army is in pursuit of Hood, and to inform me of the state of facts along the road and at Chattanooga.

* * * * * * * * *

By order of Major-General W. T. Sherman.

L. M. DAYTON,
Aid-de-Camp.

HEADQUARTERS MILITARY DIVISION OF THE MISSISSIPPI,
IN THE FIELD, SHIP'S GAP, GA., *October* 16, 1864.

General Thomas, Nashville:

Send me Davis' and Newton's old divisions. Re-establish the road, and I will follow Hood wherever he may go. I think he will move to Blue Mountain. We can maintain our men and animals on the country.

W. T. SHERMAN,
Major-General.

ATLANTA, *October* 17, 1864.

Major-General Sherman:

I have a Montgomery paper of the 12th. The dispatches from Hood, as well as the editorials, state that Beauregard is with Hood, and that the army is going to cross the Tennessee river.

H. W. SLOCUM,
Major-General.

HEADQUARTERS MILITARY DIVISION OF THE MISSISSIPPI,
IN THE FIELD, SHIP'S GAP, GA., *October* 17, 1864.

General Thomas, Nashville:

Hood won't dare go into Tennessee. I hope he will. We now occupy Ship's Gap and Lafayette, and Hood is retreating toward Alpine and Gadsden. I am moving General Garrard to-day to Dirttown, and will move General Corse out to Coosaville, and with the main army move on Summerville.

If Hood wants to go into Tennessee, west of Huntsville, let him go, and then we can all turn on him and he can not escape. The gunboats can break any bridge he may attempt above Decatur. If he attempts to cross, let him do so in part, and then let a gunboat break through his bridge. I will follow him to Gadsden, and then want my whole army united for the grand move into Georgia.

W. T. SHERMAN,
Major-General.

NEW ORLEANS, *October* 18, 1864.

Major-General Sherman:

I learn by an intercepted dispatch from Jeff. Davis to Kirby Smith, dated at Montgomery on the 30th, that the orders to cross the Mississippi had been received. I presume that duplicate of this dispatch has reached Kirby Smith, as Magruder's force, about eighteen or twenty thousand (18,000 or 20,000) men, suddenly left General Steele's front and moved in the direction of the Washita river. I have sent a fast boat to communicate this intelligence to the troops and gunboats on the river, and as I have now about eight thousand (8,000) troops afloat, and will at once increase the number, I think the crossing can be prevented. The crossing will probably be attempted in the neighborhood of Gaines' Landing.

ED. R. S. CANBY,
Major-General.

HEADQUARTERS MILITARY DIVISION OF THE MISSISSIPPI,
IN THE FIELD, SUMMERVILLE, GA., *October* 19, 1864—12 M.
Major-General Halleck, Washington, D. C.:

Hood has retreated rapidly by all the roads leading south. Our advance columns are now at Alpine and Melville Post-office. I shall pursue him as far as Gaylesville. The enemy will not venture toward Tennessee, except around by Decatur. I propose to send the Fourth Corps back to General Thomas, and leave him that corps, the garrisons and new troops, to defend the line of the Tennessee, and with the rest to push into the heart of Georgia, and come out at Savannah, destroying all the railroads of the state.

The break at Big Shanty is repaired, and that about Dalton should be in ten (10) days. We find abundance of forage in the country.

W. T. SHERMAN,
Major-General Commanding.

HEADQUARTERS MILITARY DIVISION OF THE MISSISSIPPI,
IN THE FIELD, SUMMERVILLE, GA., *October* 19, 1864.
General G. H. Thomas, Nashville, Tenn.:

Make a report to me as soon as possible of what troops you now have in Tennessee, what are expected, and how disposed. I propose, with the Armies of the Tennessee, the Ohio, and two corps of yours, to sally forth and make a hole in Georgia and Alabama that will be hard to mend. Hood has little or no baggage, and will escape me. He can not invade Tennessee, except to the west of Huntsville. I want the gunboats and what troops are on the Tennessee to be most active up at the head of navigation. I want General Wilson and General Mower with me, and would like General McCook's division made up to twenty-five hundred (2,500) men mounted. I will send back into Tennessee the Fourth Corps, all dismounted cavalry, all sick and wounded, and all incumbrances whatever, except what I can haul in our wagons, and will probably, about November 1st, break up the railroad and bridges, destroy Atlanta, and make a break for Mobile, Savannah, or Charleston. I want you to remain in Tennessee, and take command of all my division not actually present with me. Hood's army may be set down at forty thousand (40,000) of all arms fit for duty; he may follow me or turn against you. If you can defend the line of the Tennessee in my absence of three (3) months, is all I ask.

W. T. SHERMAN,
Major-General.

MARCH TO THE NORTH, ETC. 181

HEADQUARTERS MILITARY DIVISION OF THE MISSISSIPPI,
IN THE FIELD, GAYLESVILLE, ALA., *October* 26, 1864.

Major-General Thomas, Nashville, Tenn.:

A reconnoissance pushed down to Gadsden to-day reveals the fact that the rebel army is not there, and the chances are it has moved west. If it turns up at Guntersville, I will be after it; but if it goes, as I believe, to Decatur and beyond, I must leave it to you at present, and push for the heart of Georgia. All I want is to get my sick and wounded back to a safe place. I start the Fourth Corps back to-morrow, via Muston's and Valley Head, ordering it to Bridgeport or Chattanooga, according to what orders Stanley may have from you. Stanley will have about fifteen thousand (15,000) men. Beaureguard may attempt Tennesse from the direction of Muscle Shoals, but when he finds me pushing for Macon, Milledgeville, etc., he will turn back. I send you a copy of my order giving you supreme command in my absence.

W. T. SHERMAN,
Major-General Commanding.

NASHVILLE, *October* 26, 1864—2 P. M.

Major-General Sherman:

General Granger telegraphs me again, to-day, that Hood's army is threatening to cross the Tennessee river at various places between Guntersville and Decatur. I have sent down to him all the reinforcements I have to spare at this time. Have you any information that Hood has moved with his army in the direction indicated in these reports?

GEO. H. THOMAS,
Major-General.

[SPECIAL FIELD ORDERS, NO. 105.]

HEADQUARTERS MILITARY DIVISION OF THE MISSISSIPPI,
IN THE FIELD, GAYLESVILLE, ALA., *October* 26, 1864.

In the event of military movements or the accidents of war separating the general in command from his military division, Major-General Geo. H. Thomas, commanding the Department of the Cumberland, will exercise command over all troops and garrisons not absolutely in the presence of the general-in-chief. The commanding generals of the departments, Armies of the Ohio and Tennessee, will forthwith send abstracts of their returns to General Thomas, at Nashville, in order that he may understand the position and distribution of troops; and General Thomas may call for such further reports as he may require, disturbing the actual condition of affairs and mixing up the troops of separate departments as little as possible consistent with the interests of the service.

By order of Major-General W. T. Sherman.

L. M. DAYTON,
Aid-de-Camp.

182 MARCH TO THE NORTH, ETC.

HEADQUARTERS DEPARTMENT OF THE CUMBERLAND,
NASHVILLE, *November* 1, 1864—9.30 A. M.

Brigadier-General Jno. F. Croxton, Shoal Creek, via Pulaski:

Your dispatch of yesterday, reporting your position on Shoal creek, received. Hold that position as long as possible, so as to enable General Stanley to get into position at Pulaski. Should you be compelled to fall back, do so with the view of covering Stanley's march from Athens. I have ordered General Hatch to co-operate with you. Acknowledge receipt and report state of affairs.

GEO. H. THOMAS,
Major-General U. S. V. Commanding.

NASHVILLE, *November* 1, 1864—7 P. M.

Major-General Halleck, Washington, D. C.:

Your dispatch of 11.30 A. M. this date, received. General Croxton reports that last night he held the fords of Shoal creek, eight miles east and nine miles north of Florence, and that he will retard the enemy as long as possible. Stanley's troops are now arriving at Pulaski. I hope they will all be there at 12 M. to-morrow.

I have halted General Hatch at Pulaski, and he is co-operating with General Croxton against the enemy. If I had General Schofield, should feel perfectly easy. I have given such instructions as ought to expedite his arrival. It will be necessary to hold the usual guards on the railroad until the troops can pass over. I will give instructions to have them concentrated as soon as the troops have passed. I despair of getting any troops from Missouri in time to be of any service. None of my telegrams have been answered by General Rosecrans. Be assured I will do the best I can.

GEO. H. THOMAS,
Major-General U. S. V. Commanding.

HEADQUARTERS MILITARY DIVISION OF THE MISSISSIPPI,
IN THE FIELD, ROME, GA., *November* 1, 1864.

Lieutenant-General U. S. Grant, City Point, Va.:

As you foresaw, and as Jeff. Davis threatened, the enemy is now in the full tide of execution of his grand plan to destroy my communications and defeat this army. His infantry, about thirty thousand (30,000), with Wheeler's and Roddy's cavalry, from seven to ten thousand (7,000 to 10,000), are now in the neighborhood of Tuscumbia and Florence, and the water being low, are able to cross at will. Forrest seems to be scattered from Eastport to Jackson, Paris, and the lower Tennessee, and General Thomas reports the capture by him of a gunboat and five transports. General Thomas has near Athens and Pulaski, Stanley's corps, about fifteen thousand (15,000) strong, and Schofield's corps, ten thousand (10,000), en route by rail, and has at least twenty to twenty-five thousand (20,000 to 25,000) men, with new regiments and conscripts arriving all the time; also, General Rosecrans promises the two divisions of Smith and Mower, belonging to me, but I doubt if they can reach Tennessee in less than ten (10) days. If I were to let go Atlanta and North Georgia, and make for Hood, he would, as he did here, retreat to the southwest, leaving his militia, now assembling at Macon and Griffin, to occupy our conquests, and the work of last summer would be lost. I have retained about fifty thousand (50,000) good troops, and have sent back full twenty-five thousand (25,000), and have instructed General Thomas to hold defensively Nashville, Chattanooga, and Decatur, all fortified and provisioned for a long siege. I will destroy all the railroads of Georgia, and do as much substantial damage as is possible, reaching the seacoast near one of the points hitherto indicated, trusting that Thomas, with his present troops, and the influx of new regiments promised, will be able in a few days to assume the offensive.

Hood's cavalry may do a good deal of damage, and I have sent Wilson back with all dismounted cavalry, retaining only about four thousand five hundred (4,500). This is the best I can do, and shall, therefore, when I get to Atlanta the necessary stores, move south as soon as possible.

W. T. SHERMAN,
Major-General.

CITY POINT, *November* 1, 1864—6 P. M.

Major-General Sherman:

Do you not think it advisable, now that Hood has gone so far north, to entirely ruin him before starting on your proposed campaign? With Hood's army destroyed, you can go where you please with impunity. I believed, and still believe, if you had started south while Hood was in the neighborhood of you, he would have been forced to go after you. Now that he is so far away, he might look upon the chase as useless, and he will go in one direction while you are pushing the other. If you can see the chance for destroying Hood's army, attend to that first, and make your other move secondary.

U. S. GRANT,
Lieutenant-General.

HEADQUARTERS MILITARY DIVISION OF THE MISSISSIPPI,
IN THE FIELD, KINGSTON, GA., *November* 2, 1864.

Lieutenant-General U. S. Grant, City Point, Va.:

If I turn back, the whole effect of my campaign will be lost. By my movements, I have thrown Beauregard well to the west, and Thomas will have ample time and sufficient troops to hold him until reinforcements meet him from Missouri and recruits. We have now ample supplies at Chattanooga and Atlanta to stand a month's interruption to our communications, and I do n't belive the Confederate army can reach our lines, save by cavalry raids, and Wilson will have cavalry enough to checkmate that. I am clearly of opinion that the best results will follow me in my contemplated movement through Georgia.

W. T. SHERMAN,
Major-General.

CITY POINT, VA., *November* 2, 1864—11.30 A. M.
Major-General Sherman:

Your dispatch of 9 A. M. yesterday is just received. I dispatched you the same date advising that Hood's army, now that it had worked so far north, ought to be looked upon more as the object. With the force, however, you have left with General Thomas, he must be able to take care of Hood, and destroy him. I really do not see that you can withdraw from where you are, to follow Hood, without giving up all we have gained in territory. I say, then, go on as you propose.

U. S. GRANT,
Lieutenant-General.

HEADQUARTERS MILITARY DIVISION OF THE MISSISSIPPI,
IN THE FIELD, KINGSTON, GA., *November* 10, 1864.
General Thomas, Nashville:

Your dispatch of 5 P. M. is received. All will be ready to start from here the day after to-morrow. Keep me well advised. I think you will find Hood marching off, and you should be ready to follow him. Decatur, Tuscaloosa, Columbus, and Selma are all good points to forage and feed an army.

Let me keep Beauregard busy, and the people of the South will realize his inability to protect them.

W. T. SHERMAN,
Major-General.

HEADQUARTERS MILITARY DIVISION OF THE MISSISSIPPI,
IN THE FIELD, KINGSTON, GA., *November* 11, 1864.
Major-General Thomas, Nashville, Tenn.:

Dispatch of to-night received. All right. I can hardly believe Beauregard would attempt to work against Nashville, from Corinth as a base, at this stage of the war, but all information seems to point that way. If he does, you will whip him out of his boots; but I rather think you will find commotion in his camp in a day or two. Last night we burned Rome, and in two more will burn Atlanta, and he must discover that I am not retreating, but, on the contrary, fighting for the very heart of Georgia. About a division of rebel cavalry made its appearance this morning south of the Coosa river, opposite Rome, and fired on the rear-guard, as it withdrew. Also, two days ago, some of Iverson's cavalry—about eight hundred (800)—approached Atlanta from the direction of Decatur, with a section of guns, and swept round toward Whitehall, and disappeared in the direction of Rough and Ready. These also seem to indicate that Beauregard expected us to retreat. I hear of about fifteen hundred (1,500) infantry down at Carrollton, and also some infantry at Jonesboro, but what numbers I can not estimate. These are all the enemy I know to be in this neighborhood, though a rumor is that Breckinridge has arrived with some from West Virginia. To-morrow I begin the movement laid down in my Special Field Order No. 115, and shall keep things moving thereafter. By to-morrow morning all trains will be at or north of Kingston, and you can have the exclusive use of all the rolling stock. By using detachments of recruits and dismounted cavalry in your fortifications, you will have Schofield and Stanley and A. J. Smith, strengthened by eight or ten new regiments and all of Wilson's cavalry. You can safely invite Beauregard across the Tennessee, and prevent his ever returning. I still believe, however, that the public clamor will force him to turn, and follow me; in which event, you should cross at Decatur, and move directly toward Selma, as far as you can transport supplies. The probabilities are the wires will be broken to-morrow, and that all communication will cease between us; but I have directed the main wire to be left, and will use it if possible, and wish you to do the same. You may act, however, on the certainty that I sally from Atlanta on the 16th, with about sixty thousand (60,000) men, well provisioned, but expecting to live liberally on the country.

W. T. SHERMAN,
Major-General.

CHAPTER XXXIV.

THE RESISTANCE TO GENERAL HOOD'S ADVANCE FROM THE TENNESSEE RIVER, CULMINATING IN THE BATTLE OF FRANKLIN.

THE responsibility of repelling General Hood was now thrown upon General Thomas, and the most stupendous interests turned upon his success. Not in figure, but in fact, the territory gained by all the battles in Kentucky, Tennessee, and Georgia was in jeopardy. The peril was not such as is inevitable when two equal armies meet in battle, but such as is intertwined with the contingencies of improvising an army against a bold invasion. It is true that General Thomas expressed himself hopefully in his last dispatch to General Sherman, but his assurance was based upon the fact that General Smith's forces were then due at Nashville, and the expectation that his cavalry would be speedily remounted, and that the coming of the promised reinforcements from the North would not be delayed. In these expectations he was disappointed, and the situation in Tennessee was most unpromising during the month of November. General Hood's army was stronger than when, under General Johnston, in May, it boldly confronted a hundred thousand men. His three corps of infantry, under Generals Lee, Cheatham, and Stewart, comprised from forty to forty-five thousand men, and his cavalry corps from ten to fifteen thousand, under Forrest, one of the boldest generals in the South. Against this compact army, at least fifty thousand strong, General Thomas had a movable army of twenty-two thousand infantry and four thousand three hundred cavalry. He had, in addition, the garrisons at Chattanooga, Bridgeport, Stevenson, Huntsville, Decatur, Murfreesboro, and Nashville, and the detachments in block-houses on the railroads; but it was not considered safe to withdraw the troops from either of the two railroads leading from Nashville to the Tennessee river, until General Hood should indicate his line of advance. General Hood, with the exception of Forrest's raid in West Tennessee, confined himself to operations near Florence, during the first half of the month. His main reason for clinging to the Tennessee river was doubtless the uncertain attitude of General Sherman in Georgia. He may have still hoped that reinforcements from the other side of the Mississippi might join him as previously anticipated. But though refraining from positive offense, he was preparing for it. His forces which crossed the Tennessee river on the 29th of October, drove back General Croxton and covered the laying of a pontoon bridge. Lee's corps soon after crossed and intrenched, having cavalry in front. November 4th, General Croxton was driven across Shoal creek, but the enemy advanced no farther. General Hatch, with his division of cavalry, joined General Croxton on the line of Shoal creek on the 7th, and these officers then watched closely and reported the movements of the enemy. Wishing to ascertain the enemy's strength in his front, General Hatch crossed the creek on the 11th, and drove back the enemy's cavalry upon the infantry, and ascertained that there was a large force on the Waynesboro road. The next day telegraphic communication between General Sherman and General Thomas was severed; and as soon as it was thus known that General Sherman had started on his great expedition, there was the most anxious watching in Hood's front, in the endeavor to ascertain how the "march to the sea" would affect the situation in Tennessee. The alternative to General Thomas and his little army was the defensive in Tennessee, or the offensive in Alabama, accordingly as Hood should advance or retreat, and all were eager for the development of his intentions. Generals Hatch and Croxton watched closely for decisive indications, and although the high stage of water in the Tennessee delayed a general advance, it was soon evident that such a movement was meditated. To delay Hood's advance as much as possible, General Hatch obstructed the roads crossing Shoal creek, and sent rafts down the swollen river to break his bridges. Reports were current, subsequently, that his bridges did part, and from this or other causes, he did not complete the transfer of his army to the north bank until the 19th, when his movement was completely developed. Colonel Coon, commanding General Hatch's right brigade, crossed Shoal creek, which still separated the opposing cavalry, had a severe conflict, and did not return until he had discovered the advancing infantry. The possibility of General Hood following General Sherman was now at an end.

Up to this time General Thomas had hoped that the enemy would be so delayed, that he could concentrate his forces to give battle south of Duck river, but this was now plainly impossible. General Smith had not arrived, new regiments had not come as fast as old ones had been discharged upon expiration of terms of service, and the dismounted cavalry had made but little headway in securing horses, arms, and accouterments. His only resource then was to retire slowly, and delay the enemy's advance, to gain time for reinforcements to arrive and concentrate. It was hoped that the state of the roads would prevent the advance of infantry, but Hood appreciated the effect of delay, and pressed forward. He advanced on the 19th, on the Waynesboro and Butter Creek roads, with his cavalry mainly on his left. The direction of his advance indicated that he would strike Columbia, rather than Pulaski, and General Thomas authorized General Schofield to move to the former place, if Hood's approach to that point should be developed. General Hatch concentrated his division at Lexington, and on the 21st, withdrew to Lawrenceburg, where he was attacked the following morning.

A severe fight continued through the day, but General Hatch held the position against a heavy force of cavalry, with nine pieces of artillery in action. The same day, General Schofield commenced the removal of the public property from Pulaski, preparatory to falling back to Columbia, and moved with the divisions of Generals Cox and Wagner to Lynnville, the latter covering the passage of the trains. The next day General Cox advanced ten miles toward Columbia, and General Stanley, with the divisions of Generals Wood and Kimball, reached Lynnville. Colonel Capron was before the enemy on the Mount Pleasant road, and Generals Hatch and Croxton covered the movement from Pulaski, the latter having a severe fight at the junction of the roads to Pulaski and Campbellsville, maintaining his position and retiring at leisure by night to Campbellsville.

In the meantime, General Thomas made dispositions looking to the defense of the line of Duck river, and the Nashville and Chattanooga railroad. He ordered the two brigades of General Ruger's division of the Twenty-third Corps to move from Johnsonville—one by rail through Nashville to Columbia, and the other by road through Waverly—to occupy the crossings of Duck river at Williamsport, Gordon's ferry, and Centerville. General Granger was instructed to withdraw his command from Decatur, Athens, and Huntsville, and reinforce the garrisons of Stevenson and Murfreesboro, to protect the Nashville and Chattanooga railroad. He sent Colonel Von Schrader, his inspector-general, to Chattanooga to assist in the organization of the detached troops belonging to General Sherman's army, and another officer—Lieutenant M. J. Kelley—to Paducah, to hasten the coming of General Smith. His engineers were busy with the construction of fortifications at various points, especially at Nashville, while effort was made to provide pontoon trains in room of those which had gone to Savannah.

General Hood's rapid advance from Florence had been made with the hope of cutting off General Schofield from Columbia, and barely failed in this object, as the national troops gained the place by a night march. General Stanley, having been informed after midnight that Colonel Capron had been driven from Mount Pleasant by an infantry force, roused his corps and hastened toward Columbia, twenty-one miles distant. General Cox started at the same hour, and reached Columbia in time to save Capron from defeat and the town from capture. When within three miles of Columbia, General Cox crossed to the Mount Pleasant road and intercepted the enemy's forces, which were pressing Capron back upon the town. As the divisions of the Fourth Corps arrived, they formed in line of battle south of Duck river and intrenched. General Hatch was attacked at Campbellsville by cavalry supported by infantry. Colonel Wells, commanding first brigade, at first repulsed the enemy, but subsequently the whole command was compelled to retire to Lynnville; there the fighting was continued until after dark, when General Hatch withdrew to Columbia.

With a view to check the enemy and hold the place, heavy works were thrown up before Columbia, and the cavalry, General Wilson commanding in person, was disposed to watch against turning movements up and down the river. Hatch's division and Croxton's brigade were stationed on the Shelbyville road, six miles east of Columbia, and Capron's brigade at Rally Hill, on the Lewisburg turnpike. Colonel Stewart, with three regiments from Hatch's division, was sent to the right to the fords between Columbia and Williamsport; Capron's brigade, and the Eighth Iowa and Seventh Ohio Cavalry regiments were here formed into a provisional division under command of General R. W. Johnson.

During the 24th and 25th, the enemy skirmished before Columbia, but showed nothing but dismounted cavalry, until the 26th, when his infantry appeared, and during that day and the next he pressed the lines, but made no assault. General Schofield constructed an interior line of works, but these were soon regarded as untenable, as the enemy manifested an intention to pass round the position. An effort was made to cross to the north bank the night of the 26th, but failed on account of a severe storm and entire darkness. The night following, the movement was accomplished, and General Schofield left General Ruger to hold the crossing at the railroad bridge; placed General Cox's division before the town, and directed General Stanley to station his corps on the Franklin turnpike, in readiness to meet the enemy should he attempt to cross near Columbia. These dispositions were made by General Schofield in hope that he could hold the line of Duck river, until reinforcements should arrive; but the promised reinforcements had not reached Nashville. General Thomas had received twelve thousand raw troops, and had sent North, either on final discharge or to vote, fifteen thousand veterans. General Smith had not come, and only one thousand cavalry had found horses and the front. General Thomas had obtained permission to call upon the governors of the Western States for troops, but was cautioned to use such troops sparingly.

The 28th was passed in quietness, at Columbia, though there were palpable indications that quietness there meant activity in another quarter. At noon the enemy's cavalry appeared at various fords, between Columbia and the Lewisburg turnpike, in such force as to indicate plainly the purpose to cross. General Hood's cavalry was especially massed at Huey's Mills, eight miles above Columbia, and having there driven in General Wilson's pickets, began to pass over the river. At 2.10 P. M. General Wilson notified General Schofield of the enemy's movements, and informed him that he would concentrate his cavalry at Hunt's creek, on the Lewisburg turnpike, expressing the belief that the enemy would swing in between them and strike the road to Franklin, at Spring Hill.

General Wilson's cavalry detachments, at the various fords, held their respective positions as long as possible, but all were finally driven back, and it was then evident that three divisions of cavalry—Chalmers', Buford's, and Jackson's—had crossed Duck river. By 7 P. M. General Wilson had concentrated his command, as far as practicable, at Hart's Cross-roads. Major Young, of the Fifth Iowa Cavalry, commanding detachments, was intercepted, but cut his way through the enemy's lines with trifling loss. During the night General Wilson ascertained that General Forrest was moving toward Franklin, and also that General Hood's infantry forces were expected to cross before morning. In view of the palpable peril, he advised General Schofield to withdraw to Franklin, and suggested that his command should be at Spring Hill by 10 A. M. the next day. When General Thomas was informed of the probable state of things at Columbia, he directed General Schofield to withdraw to Franklin, as soon as he should gain certain knowledge of the reported movements of the enemy. And very soon afterward, at 3.30 A. M. on the 29th, he directed him to withdraw from Columbia, as by this time he was convinced that General Hood had turned General Schofield's position.

The situation at Columbia on the morning of the 29th, and during that day, was exceedingly critical. General Hood's infantry forces were crossing the river during all the early hours, at Huey's Mills, on a road leading directly to Spring Hill; his cavalry forces had very early cut off all communication between Generals Schofield and Wilson, and were pressing the latter back upon Franklin, on the Lewisburg turnpike, General Wilson having chosen this line of retreat as the one upon which he could best resist General Forrest, and cover the retirement of the infantry on the direct road from Columbia to Franklin.

To develop the facts fully, before withdrawing altogether from Columbia, General Schofield directed General Wood to send a brigade up the river to watch the enemy; ordered General Stanley to move with two of his divisions to Spring Hill, to hold that point and cover the trains and spare artillery; left General Cox to guard the crossing at Columbia, and ordered Ruger's division to take position on the turnpike, in rear of Rutherford's creek, leaving one regiment to hold the ford at Columbia, near the railroad bridge—this bridge having been partially destroyed and all the others entirely.

General Wood sent Post's brigade early, to reconnoiter up the river; and at 8 A. M. General Stanley moved toward Spring Hill with Wagner's and Kimball's divisions. Before reaching Rutherford's creek, four miles distant, he learned that the enemy was crossing infantry and trains above Columbia, and was moving to the north on a converging road which touched General Schofield's line of retreat at Spring Hill. Apprehending that the forces that Colonel Post reported to be crossing the river might make a flank attack upon the troops between Duck river and Rutherford's creek, he halted Kimball's division and formed it facing east, and then proceeded to Spring Hill with Wagner's division. When within two miles of the place, at 11.30 A. M., he was informed that the enemy's cavalry was approaching from the direction of Rally Hill. The noise of firing east of the village immediately called the division to rapid motion, and the town was gained in time to meet the enemy, who was driving back a small force of national toops, composed of infantry and cavalry. Colonel Opdycke immediately deployed his brigade and drove back the enemy's cavalry, when General Stanley threw forward the division to hold the town and protect the trains. Opdycke's

BATTLE OF FRANKLIN, ETC. 193

and Lane's brigades were deployed to cover such space as served to park the wagons, and Bradley's was advanced to hold a wooded knoll nearly a mile to the east, which commanded the approaches from that direction.

At the time these dispositions were made, it was not known that heavy forces of infantry were near; but this fact was soon after developed by a fierce assault upon General Bradley. The nature of the attack, confirming the first reports of the advance of the Confederate army to the east of Columbia, gave demonstration of the greatest peril, not only to General Stanley, but to the four divisions behind him. General Hood's columns had now passed General Schofield's left flank, and were enveloping a single division, twelve miles in his rear, or twelve miles in advance, when he should face to the north to retreat.

When the enemy's infantry attacked General Bradley from the east, his cavalry on the west of the town threatened the railroad station, and then fell upon a small train, composed of some baggage-wagons, at Thompson's Station, three miles north. About the same time, General Stanley received a dispatch from General Schofield, confirming the reports that had first indicated the strategy of General Hood, and led him to fear that a heavy force was enveloping his position. He could not therefore reinforce General Bradley, lest he should thereby expose his trains to capture or destruction.

General Bradley repulsed two fierce attacks, but in the third his right flank was overlapped by the enemy's line, and he was compelled to fall back to the town, where his shattered brigade was rallied and reformed. The enemy followed, but fell under the fire of eight pieces of artillery, at good range for spherical case shot, and was also taken in flank by a section on the turnpike, south of the town. A portion of the attacking troops then fled to the rear, and other portions sought cover in a ravine between the opposing lines. General Stanley reported Bradley's loss at one hundred and fifty men killed and wounded, and the enemy's at five hundred. General Bradley received a severe wound while encouraging his men to resist the last attack, and the command of the brigade passed to Colonel Conrad.

As darkness fell, the enemy's lines were extended until a corps of infantry was in order of battle facing the Franklin road. Two other corps were near a little later, one deployed also, and Forrest's troopers were on the main road, both north and south of Spring Hill. It seemed hardly possible in this posture of affairs that General Schofield's forces and trains could elude this involution by General Hood's army, and yet this result was achieved without a serious contest.

During the day, the enemy covered his movement past General Schofield's left to his rear by earnest efforts, as General Schofield believed, to force a crossing and lay a pontoon bridge at Columbia, that he might thus secure a passage for his artillery, which was impracticable at Huey's Mills. His repeated attacks were all repulsed by General Cox, and at 3 P. M. General Schofield became satisfied that the enemy would not attack on Duck river, but was moving two corps directly to Spring Hill. He then gave orders for the withdrawal of all the troops when darkness would cover the movement, and with General Ruger's division hastened forward to open communications with General Stanley. At dark, he brushed away the enemy's cavalry from the road, three miles south of Stanley, and joined him at 7 P. M. Whittaker's brigade of Kimball's division followed Ruger's closely from Rutherford's creek, and upon arrival was posted parallel to the turnpike, where the enemy's left rested within eight hundred yards of the road, to cover the passage of the troops still in the rear. General Schofield, leaving the management of the march and the safety of the trains to General Stanley, then moved again with Ruger's division to clear the road to Franklin. As he approached Thompson's Station, the enemy's cavalry disappeared, and then the road was open from Columbia to Franklin, though an army of at least fifty thousand men was in closest proximity to it, and along its front four divisions and an immense train were at rest or in motion, and yet there was only slight skirmishing here and there, and occasional picket-firing. There was momentary expectation that this great army would take a step forward, and press troops, artillery, and trains from the road in confusion and rout; but still the movement went on without interruption by the enemy.

Having cleared the road at Thompson's Station, General Schofield returned to Spring Hill to make arrangements and dispositions to avert his extreme peril. He did not anticipate the possibility of his getting his army out of the reach of the enemy that night, and feared that he would be forced to fight a general battle the next day, or lose his wagon train. In the emergency he had dispatched a staff officer to Franklin to bring forward the command of General A. J. Smith, which he supposed had reached Franklin.

At 11 P. M. General Thomas, believing that General Schofield had, in obedience to his order of 3.30 A. M., withdrawn from Columbia earlier in the day, telegraphed to him at Franklin to withdraw from that place also, should the enemy attempt to get on his flank with infantry. As General Smith's troops had not yet arrived at Nashville, he considered it necessary, should the enemy advance quickly upon General Schofield, to concentrate his forces at Nashville.

General Cox left Columbia at 7 P. M., followed by General Wood, and the latter by General Kimball. There was some delay at Rutherford's creek, as the bridge was inadequate for the emergency, but nevertheless the divisions, one after another, arrived at Spring Hill—the foremost of the three at 11 P. M. The enemy's pickets fired into the column frequently, but when they did not come upon the road, the national troops gave no response. The enemy was so close to the road, that when a column was not moving upon it, it was difficult for a single horseman to pass.

The danger did not end with the arrival of the last division at Spring Hill. It was 1 A. M. before a train of eight hundred wagons, including artillery and ambulances, could move toward Franklin, in rear of Cox's division, as at starting the wagons had to pass singly over a bridge. This caused delay, and consequently peril, as an attack was inevitable, unless the train and troops could be put on the road and in motion before daylight. General Stanley was advised to burn at least a portion of the wagons, to avoid an attack, but he determined to save all, if practicable. At 3 A. M. an attack upon the head of the train, north of Thompson's, was reported, and all wagons on the road were stopped until General Kimball could rush forward to clear the road, and General Wood deploy his division on the east of the road. The attack was repulsed by Major Steele, with stragglers that he had gathered together, and then the train, bereft of ten wagons burned by the enemy, moved on, with Wood's division on the right and Wagner's in the rear. At 5 A. M. the last wagon crossed the bridge, and then all was in motion. The enemy's cavalry was on the hills to the right for awhile, and made one or two dashes, but these were easily repulsed by Wood's skirmishers, with the help, at one time, of a section of Canby's battery. Colonel Opdycke's brigade formed the rear-guard, and though skirmishing with the pursuing forces of the enemy, kept them so well in check as to save the weary and lame from capture. Rarely has an army escaped so easily from a peril so threatening. It has been accepted as true that General Hood ordered one corps general and then another to attack the national troops when passing so near the front of his army, at Spring Hill; but these generals disobeyed the orders, so plainly imperative from the situation itself, as well as from the voice of the commander-in-chief. From whatever cause the failure resulted, the opportunity of the campaign was lost to the Confederate army.

General Schofield, with the head of his column, reached Franklin before daylight, and he immediately made preparation to pass the Harpeth river, as he had been ordered by General Thomas to fall behind this stream. The railroad bridge was fitted as rapidly as possible for the passage of wagons, and a foot-bridge was constructed, which also proved adequate for them. General Schofield's aim was to get his train and artillery over the river before the enemy could attack him, but he nevertheless instructed General Cox to put the troops in line around the town, as the several divisions should arrive. The Twenty-third Corps formed the left and center—Cox's division on the left with its left flank on the river, Ruger's on its right, and Kimball's completing the circuit to the river on the right. Wood's division crossed to the north bank to be directed to the support of either flank in the event of a turning movement, and Wagner's was left in front to check the enemy, should he form his army to attack. Colonel Opdycke reached the heights two miles south of the town at noon, and was ordered to halt to observe the enemy. Croxton's brigade of cavalry was pushed back by infantry on the Lewisburg turnpike, and at 1 P. M. Colonel Opdycke reported heavy columns of infantry advancing on the Columbia and Lewisburg roads, when the division was withdrawn to the more immediate front of the army on the Columbia road. Colonel Opdycke, at his own notion, came inside the main line, and halted his brigade on the Columbia road in rear of the junction of the right and left flanks of Cox's and Ruger's divisions of the Twenty-third Corps.

The line as formed, was about one mile and a half long, inclosing the town, except on the north where the Harpeth river was the boundary, with its flanks touching the river. The line rested on a slight elevation, or series of low hills, which encompassed the town. The troops threw up breastworks, and a slight abatis was also constructed in places. The artillery of the Twenty-third Corps was on the north side of the river, and a portion of it placed in Fort Granger—a fortification previously constructed so as to command the railroad, which leaves the town near the river, and runs in parallelism with it for some distance. The batteries of the Fourth Corps were held on the south side, some of them having been placed on the line and others in reserve. The Sixth Ohio Light Artillery and the First Kentucky battery were in position on the right and left of the Columbia road, before the battle opened. Battery "M," Fourth United States Artillery, and battery "G," First Ohio Light Artillery, were placed with the left brigade of the Twenty-third Corps, and Bridge's battery, Illinois Light Artillery, was posted in the center of Strickland's brigade of Ruger's division. The position was a good one for defense, and the undulations of the ground in front exposed the enemy in approaching. The key-point was Carter's Hill on the Columbia road, and was opposite the center of General Hood's army, which was advancing on the Lewisburg, Columbia, and Carter's Creek turnpikes.

General Croxton resisted the enemy's infantry on the Lewisburg road until 2 P. M., when, having learned that Forrest was moving to his left, as if to cross at Hughes' ferry, he crossed at McGarock's ford. He had hardly gained the north bank before it was reported that the enemy's cavalry were endeavoring to cross at several points above Franklin. General Wilson now threw his whole force before General Forrest, and held him in check during the day and following night, in some cases driving back detachments after they had succeeded in crossing the river. Had General Forrest succeeded in crossing with his whole force, he could have caused a heavy detachment of forces from the little army to protect the trains already in motion toward Nashville, in anticipation of the withdrawal of the army from Franklin at 6 P. M., should General Hood make no attack.

At the time that General Croxton was forced to cross the river, General Hood's infantry began to appear in great force in front of Wagner's two brigades, but it was not believed by the ranking generals of the national army, until 4 P. M., that he would attempt to carry the position by assault. But at this hour his army emerged from the woods, in splendid array, heavily massed on the Columbia road, two corps in front and one in reserve, and soon brushed away the two brigades of Wagner's division, posted in extreme exposure on the plain, opposite the massive center of the Confederate army. General Wagner had been instructed to check the enemy with these brigades, without involving them in an engagement with superior forces, but had, notwithstanding, directed their commanders, Colonels Conrad and Lane, to hold their position as long as possible. Conscious of their extreme peril they threw up barricades, and when General Hood finally advanced against them with his main lines, uncovered by skirmishers, their effort to check him precipitated a conflict so unequal as to have been hopeless from the first. When broken by the attack of an army, they fell back in great haste and disorder, and formed a shield for the enemy following upon their steps. The veteran troops mainly succeeded in reaching the main line of the national army, but a large portion of the raw troops were captured. The pursued and the pursuers broke through the intrenched line in company, carrying away portions of Reilley's brigade, on the right of General Cox's division, and Strickland's, on the left of General Ruger's. And thus, without conflict on the immediate front of the national army or on the parapet, General Hood gained a lodgment at the key-point of the position, and commanded the direct approach to the bridges. He had gained this advantage, almost without firing a shot, after the rout of Conrad and Lane, and without receiving one, except that a portion of the troops of the brigade of the latter, having loaded guns, wheeled and fired as they crossed the intrenchments. Such an advantage, to an army of more than double the strength of the divisions holding the position, according to the precedents of war, was decisive of complete victory. But in this case it was not, though at first it seemed to be entirely so. The enemy's center, made strong to thrust itself through the national line, had gained its immediate objective, and commenced at once to use two captured batteries in enfilading the national line, right and left, to double each fraction upon the flanks, and grasp the bridges between them. Two of the three brigades of Wagner's division, the only troops south of the river not in the main line, were so shattered that they could not be rallied for the emergency, and every moment of delay in attacking the enemy's forces that had gained the center, permitted their reinforcement from his rear lines. The teams from the captured batteries galloped to the rear, and intensified the impression that the disaster was fatal. Conrad's brigade had entered the intrenchments near the Columbia road, and on the right of this road the enemy gained at the first dash three or four hundred yards of the line. Lane's brigade had crossed the parapet several hundred yards to the right, without disturbing the troops at that point, and its volley had a marked effect upon the enemy. Toward the breach, the enemy's heavy central lines began at once to press, and to it his lateral lines were turned, in seemingly overwhelming convergence. To General Hood, the advantage so easily gained, promised the capture or destruction of the national army, and he and his army were inspired to quickest action to maintain and utilize it for this grand achievement. And he certainly could have maintained his hold of the national line, and used it for extreme success, had time been given him to thrust into the breach his rapidly-advancing and massive rear lines; and as it was, he began to gain ground right and left from the Columbia road.

When General Stanley first heard the noise of battle, he was with General Schofield, at his headquarters on the north bank of the river, a fifteen minutes' ride from Carter's Hill, and was entertaining the conviction, from the strength of the position and the former course of the enemy, that an assault was entirely improbable. But as soon as an attack was indicated to him and others, in their distant view, he rode rapidly to his troops, and reached the left of Opdycke's brigade to find that a disaster, seemingly prophetic of the overthrow of the army, had came with the first onset of the enemy. In quick provision for the emergency, he approached this one reserve brigade, to order it to charge the enemy in the breach; but seeing its gallant commander in front of its center leading it forward, he gave no orders, for none were needed, and taking position on the left of the line, the corps and brigade commanders, with common purpose to hurl back the enemy and restore the continuity of the line, cheered as they led this heroic brigade. When Colonel Opdycke had first seen the enemy within the intrenchments, he turned to his men from the front of the center of his brigade, to find they had already fixed bayonets for the encounter, which they plainly foresaw would be desperate and decisive; for they were veterans who had charged the enemy on other fields, and yet they had never been called by orders, soldierly instincts, or patriotism to such a conflict as was now plainly before them. Their commander saw, in this unbidden act of preparation, and in their eyes and attitude, the response to his own purpose, and his ringing order, "First brigade forward to the lines," was in harmony with the stern will of every officer and man of that brigade. And when he dashed on the breach, he gave expression to the courage and purpose of every man in that self-appointed forlorn hope, while those near General Stanley shouted: "We can go where the general can." Opdycke rode forward until he reached the enemy, followed closely by his brigade. He first emptied his revolver, then clubbed it in the hand-to-hand conflict, and as the deadly struggle raged more fiercely, he dismounted and clubbed a musket. His men fought as did their leader, and with bayonets baptized in blood, they hurled the enemy from the intrenchments and saved the army. This was one of the supreme moments of battle which heroes recognize, and by which only the bravest of the brave are inspired to deeds of daring, transcendent from motive and momentous results. Four regimental commanders fell in the charge, but other officers of similar temper maintained the gallant leadership. Colonel Opdycke, foremost in the charge and throughout the ensuing conflict in the intrenchments, escaped injury. General Stanley also escaped for a time, but in leaving this brigade to look after other dispositions, was pierced in the neck by a bullet, and was compelled to leave the field.

Colonel Opdycke's brigade recaptured eight pieces of artillery, and with them four hundred prisoners; wrenched ten battle-flags from the hands of the enemy, and left the ground behind them strewn with a greater number, which dropped under their blows. The number of prisoners and battle-flags, shows most plainly that General Hood was holding the position with an exceedingly strong force.

The recaptured guns again changed the direction of their missiles of death, while the sheet of flame from Opdycke's brigade and others in reach revealed to the enemy the necessity of other charges upon new and less promising conditions, or the abandonment of the conflict. Opdycke's charge regained nearly all the line that had been lost, but the enemy still held a small salient to the right of the Columbia road, and to maintain this point and widen the breach, General Hood and his subordinate commanders exerted themselves to the utmost. In counter effort, small portions of Conrad's and Lane's brigades were directed to Opdycke's support. The enemy's first heavy line in his front was not more than fifty yards distant, and in addition to a direct fire from this line, he was subjected to an enfilading one from the troops still in the intrenchments on his right. It was next to impossible for his brigade to maintain position under this deadly cross-fire, but yet, in twenty minutes, through the vigorous support of troops on right and left, the enemy was entirely expelled, and the continuity of the line re-established. Then, in seeming retribution for General Schofield's escape at Spring Hill, and his own dislodgment from his hope-giving grasp of the key-point of the national line, General Hood repeated his assaults with the expression of frenzied vengeance and valor. His subordinates, with a recklessness of life in keeping with the charge of Opdycke and his heroic brigade, led their columns to the muskets of the national troops, charging repeatedly, mainly at Carter's Hill, and only desisted with the fall of night. In leading a charge, General Cleburne, the most dashing division commander in the Confederate army, fell upon the parapet in front of Opdycke's brigade, and in the whole contest, five other generals were killed, six wounded, and one captured—a fact which reveals how the columns of the enemy were led; while the loss of thirty-three battle-flags manifests the strength of the columns which gained the national lines.

The defensive fire was so rapid from 4 P. M. to nightfall that it was difficult to supply the troops with ammunition. One hundred wagon-loads of artillery and infantry ammunition were used from the Fourth Corps train alone, and this expenditure wrought fearful havoc in the ranks of the enemy, whose boldness placed them much of the time at short range.

Firing, of more or less severity, was maintained until nearly midnight, the enemy continuing his activity to determine the time of the withdrawal of the national army, and to embarras such a movement.

General Hood buried seventeen hundred and fifty men on the field. He had three thousand eight hundred so disabled as to be placed in hospitals, and lost seven hundred and two captured—an aggregate of six thousand two hundred and fifty-two, exclusive of those slightly wounded.

General Schofield lost one hundred and eighty-nine killed, one thousand and thirty-three wounded, and one thousand one hundred and four missing—an aggregate of two thousand three hundred and twenty-six. More than half of this loss was from Wagner's division, from the exposure of Conrad's and Lane's brigades, and from the charge and subsequent fighting of Opdycke's brigade.

The battle of Franklin, for its proportions, was one of the

grandest of the war. The salient features of this battle were the position and action of the two brigades posted in front of the main line, and the gallantry of the third, after the enemy had carried the intrenchments on Carter's Hill.

The reports of Generals Schofield, Stanley, and Cox declare that it was not the expectation that the brigades in front should resist until they should be compromised in an engagement with superior forces, and that General Wagner was so instructed. Nevertheless, the two brigade commanders were instructed by General Wagner to hold their position as long as possible, and having been thus impressed with the necessity of extreme resistance, they did not abandon their position until forced to do so by the bayonets of the enemy, and then their hurried retreat brought disaster to their own army. Their resistance, if not prudent, was exceedingly gallant, and veterans and new troops alike displayed the highest qualities of soldiers in confronting in actual conflict an army of three corps, and deserve mention in history as brave and heroic, under circumstances of extreme trial and peril.

With regard to the second prominent feature of this battle, it may be said that seldom in the history of war has a single brigade* made itself so conspicuous in saving an army, and its transcendent action must be accepted as proof that its previous training and experience, and the manhood of its members had given the morale—the *elan* requisite for such an emergency. It was no new experience for Colonel Opdycke to ride in a charge in advance of his men, for this he did in developing the enemy in front of General Thomas' right, after the great disaster at the battle of Chickamauga. He charged, too, with a demi-brigade on Missionary Ridge, and with his regiment, the One Hundred and Twenty-fifth Ohio, on Rocky Face Ridge, and the officers and men of his brigade were meet for such a leader. And General Stanley, sick as he was, manifested his appreciation of the emergency as well as his personal gallantry, in descending from the command of a corps to take the left

---

* This brigade comprised the One Hundred and Twenty-fifth Ohio; the Twenty-fourth Wisconsin; the Thirty-sixth, Fourty-fourth, Seventy-third, Seventy-fourth, and Eighty-eighth Illinois regiments.

of a brigade, in an action plainly decisive of the battle. For beyond all power of generalship to mold the battle or control its issue, the simple charge of Opdycke's brigade stands in boldest relief.

The enemy having been repulsed and the trains transferred to the north bank of the Harpeth river, the problem to solve. was the safe withdrawal of the army to Nashville. It was still in General Hood's power, having great superiority in both infantry and cavalry, to cross the river above General Schofield's position, and unless prevented by battle or withdrawal, to throw his army between Franklin and Nashville. As to the propriety of withdrawal, there was no question, either with the general officers at Franklin, including General Schofield, or with General Thomas. So that the movement to the rear, meditated before the battle, was commenced as soon as the quietness of the enemy permitted. During the early part of the night the artillery was transferred to the north bank, and at midnight the army crossed the river without loss or special hinderance. General Wood retained his position until 3 A. M., and then moved northward as the rear-guard of the army. General Hood perceived the retirement early, and though following closely, wrought no damage. General Wood had destroyed the bridges before leaving position, and his division in rear of the army, with Wilson's cavalry on its flanks, was able to beat back General Hood's head of column, which he could not under the circumstances make strong in time, even to greatly harass so strong a force. With the exception of a brush between Hammond's brigade of cavalry and some portion of Forrest's command at Brentwood, the enemy provoked no engagement, and the army marched quietly to Nashville. The rear column reached that city at 1 P. M., and the different corps were assigned to positions on the defensive line which General Thomas had selected. The Twenty-third Corps, under General Schofield, was assigned to the left, extending to the Nolensville turnpike; the Fourth Corps, General Wood commanding, in room of General Stanley, disabled by his wound, took position in the center; and the corps from the "Army of the Tennessee," General A. J. Smith commanding, having arrived the day before, held the right, with its flank touching the river below the city.

In view of General Hood's superiority of force, his operations thus far had fallen behind just expectations. He had allowed General Schofield to pass safely before his army, after he had touched his communications, while he was yet at Columbia, and he had met most disastrous defeat at Franklin, in assaults that could not be repeated with greater vigor. The consequent depression in his army was doubtless excessive. Thus far, none of the grand results of his northward march, as announced with prophetic emphasis by Mr. Davis, had been achieved, although General Sherman had swept southward from Northern Georgia and on toward Savannah, with sixty-five thousand men; and the Confederate army, of which so much had been expected, was now far from its base, thus far defeated in the accomplishment of its great aims, with the consciousness that the conditions of ultimate success were passing day by day beyond the range of possibilities. To go back would express total defeat; and before General Hood was a fast-increasing army, posted on a strong defensive line, with a deep river behind, and its key-points fortified early in the war; and as he could not at once go round Nashville, he sat before the city and extended his lines in semblance of a siege, which should last until General Thomas should be fully ready to throw him upon the defensive.

General Thomas had hoped to deliver battle at some point farther to the south; but his reinforcements had come too slowly, and his cavalry horses had come as tardily as his accessions of troops. His forces were not fully in hand, and those that had fought their way from Columbia were physically exhausted beyond the ordinary experience of veterans on long marches and months under fire. During the seven days of Hood's advance from the Tennessee, he had hurried his preparations for the battle now palpably imminent. On the 29th of November, he had ordered General Milroy to abandon Tullahoma and retire to Murfreesboro, leaving a garrison in the block-house at Elk River bridge. The same day, he had ordered General Steedman, with a provisional division of five thousand men, composed of detachments from the corps with

General Sherman and a brigade of colored troops, to move to Nashville. Nashville had been placed in a state of defense; additional fortifications had been constructed under the direcsion of Brigadier-General Tower, and the whole had been manned by the regular garrison, reinforced by a provisional force, under Brevet Brigadier-General Donaldson, chief quartermaster, composed of the employes of the quartermaster and commissary departments. No other forces were now expected, except the brigade of General Cooper, of Ruger's division, which having watched the fords of Duck river, below Columbia, was now marching to Nashville by a detour to evade the enemy. With the cavalry remounted, and this heterogeneous force organized, General Thomas proposed to assume the offensive and dispute with General Hood the possession of Tennessee.

NASHVILLE, *November* 12, 1864—8.30 A. M.
Major-General Sherman:

Your dispatch of 12 o'clock last night received. I have no fears that Beauregard can do us any harm now, and if he attempts to follow you I will follow him as far as possible. If he does not follow you, I will then thoroughly organize, and, I believe, shall have men enough to ruin him, unless he gets out of the way very rapidly. The country of Middle Alabama, I learn, is teeming with supplies this year, which will be greatly to our advantage. I have no additional news to report from the direction of Florence. I am now convinced that the greater part of Beauregard's army is near Florence and Tuscumbia, and that you will at least have a clear road before you for several days, and that your success will fully equal your expectations.

GEORGE H. THOMAS,
Major-General.

VICKSBURG, *November* 8, 1864, VIA CAIRO, *November* 14, 1864.
Major-General Sherman:
Major-General Thomas:

Your dispatch of October 30th was received yesterday. Hatch's division of cavalry was at the Tennessee river at last account. Two infantry divisions under General A. J. Smith, and a brigade of cavalry, are in Missouri in pursuit of Price. They have been ordered to Memphis by nearest route, but this is contingent on where the orders may reach them, and the time uncertain. The effective field force left on the river is very light, and the posts from Cairo to Natchez are held by small garrisons, but I will, to the extent of my force, carry out your instructions. A demonstration of three thousand cavalry from Baton Rouge promised into Lower Mississippi. Magruder is moving in force on Major-General Steele, at Little Rock. The enemy is threatening to (move on) cross to the east side of the Mississippi, at Gaines' Landing, where Major-General Reynolds is ready for them.

N. J. P. DANA,
Major-General.

HEADQUARTERS DEPARTMENT OF THE CUMBERLAND,
NASHVILLE, *November* 10, 1864—9 A. M.

Adjutant-General U. S. A., Washington, D. C.:

Please direct the return to this department immediately of all convalescents belonging to the Fourteenth, Fifteenth, Seventeenth, and Twentieth Army Corps, to report at Chattanooga, and those of the Fourth and Twenty-third Army Corps to report at Decatur, Alabama. These men were furloughed by direction of the War Department to permit them to vote in their several States.

GEORGE H. THOMAS,
Major-General U. S. V. Commanding.

HEADQUARTERS DEPARTMENT OF THE CUMBERLAND,
NASHVILLE, *November* 11, 1864—11 A. M.

Major-General Stanley, Pulaski:

Have Capron make a scout out in the direction of Clifton, and ascertain the truth of rumors which are constantly coming to these headquarters, that a large force of the enemy's cavalry is on the Lawrenceburg road, between Lawrenceburg and Columbia.

GEORGE H. THOMAS,
Major-General U. S. V. Commanding.

NASHVILLE, *November* 14, 1864.

Brigadier-General Hatch, Tyler Springs via Pulaski:

Your telegram of 2 A. M. to-day is received. Keep a good lookout. Report all you observe, to General Schofield, at Pulaski, as well as myself.

GEORGE H. THOMAS,
Major-General U. S. V. Commanding.

NASHVILLE, *November* 14, 1864.

Major-General W. S. Rosecrans, St. Louis:

Your dispatch received. Please send a courier to overtake Colonel Winslow and direct him to this place, via Louisville, as rapidly as he can.

GEORGE H. THOMAS,
Major-General.

CITY POINT, *November* 15, 1864—11 A. M.
Major-General Thomas, Nashville:
If Hood commences falling back, it will not do to wait for the full equipment of your cavalry to follow. He should, in that event, be pressed with such forces as you can bring to bear upon him.
U. S. GRANT,
Lieutenant-General.

HEADQUARTERS DEPARTMENT OF THE CUMBERLAND,
NASHVILLE, *November* 15, 1864—4 P. M.
Lieutenant-General Grant, City Point, Va.:
Your telegram of this morning just received. I am watching Hood closely, and, should he move after General Sherman, will follow him with what force I can raise at hand. The reports this morning are that he is moving in the direction of Waynesboro. A cavalry force has been sent to ascertain the true state of facts.
GEO. H. THOMAS,
Major-General U. S. V. Commanding.

HEADQUARTERS DEPARTMENT OF THE CUMBERLAND,
NASHVILLE, *November* 16, 1864—10 A. M.
Major-General Schofield, Pulaski:
Your dispatch of yesterday just received. Send me the first reliable news you have from Hatch. Smith telegraphed me two days ago, that his troops had been delayed by bad roads and impassable streams, but that he would make all possible speed. I can not say when he will be here.
GEO. H. THOMAS,
Major-General U. S. V. Commanding.

HEADQUARTERS MILITARY DIVISION OF THE WEST,
TUSCUMBIA, *November* 17, 1864.
General J. B. Hood, Commanding, etc., General:
General Beauregard directs me to say that he desires you will take the offensive at the earliest practicable moment, and deal the enemy rapid and vigorous blows, striking him whilst thus dispersed, and by this means distract Sherman's advance into Georgia. . . .
Respectfully, your obedient servant,
GEORGE W. BRENT,
Colonel and Assistant Adjutant-General.

CHEROKEE, ALA., *November* 17, 1864—3.30 P. M.
Major-General Howell Cobb, Macon or Griffin, Ga.:
Have ordered General Taylor to send at once all troops he can possibly spare, and General Hood to send immediately one brigade of Jackson's

cavalry division, or the whole division, if it can possibly be spared at this juncture. A victory in Tennessee will relieve Georgia.

* * * * * * * * *

G. T. BEAUREGARD,
General.

PULASKI, *November* 18, 1864.

Major-General Thomas.

I have received no report from General Hatch this evening. His report yesterday indicated that Hood was about to move, but I think there is no probability of his moving this way while this weather continues.

J. M. SCHOFIELD,
Major-General.

HEADQUARTERS DEPARTMENT OF THE CUMBERLAND,
NASHVILLE, *November* 19, 1864.

Major-General A. J. Smith, or commanding officer of troops en route for Nashville, Paducah, Ky.:

Start for Nashville, via Cumberland river, as soon as possible after receiving this, with what troops you have, and leave orders for the balance to follow the same route.

Acknowledge receipt,

GEO. H. THOMAS,
Major-General U. S. V. Commanding.

HEADQUARTERS DEPARTMENT OF THE CUMBERLAND,
NASHVILLE, *November* 19, 1864—2.30 P. M.

Major-General Schofield, Pulaski:

If the enemy advance in force, as General Hatch believes, have everything in readiness to fight him at Pulaski, if he advances on that place, or cover the railroad and concentrate at Columbia. Should he attempt to turn your right flank, in the latter case—that is, the attempt to turn your right flank—General Hatch should cover the fords and ferries across Duck river, and hold them when you concentrate at Columbia. Report to me at once, should you be compelled to leave Pulaski, that I may give the necessary orders for the concentration of the troops on the Nashville and Chattanooga railroad. I can hardly think, however, that the enemy will attempt to advance in such weather as we now have. I shall send an officer to-morrow morning to hurry General Smith's troops along as fast as possible to this place. Give the necessary orders to Hatch and Croxton, in case of a decided advance of the enemy.

GEO. H. THOMAS,
Major-General U. S. V. Commanding.

VOL. II—14

PULASKI, *November* 19, 1864.
Major-General Thomas:
Your dispatch of 2.30 P. M. is received. I have already given the necessary preliminary instructions to Hatch, and will have everything ready to carry out your orders in the event of Hood's advance. I do not believe he will attempt to move his infantry in this state of roads, but Forrest may make a raid on our railroads.

J. M. SCHOFIELD,
Major-General.

HEADQUARTERS DEPARTMENT OF THE CUMBERLAND,
NASHVILLE, *November* 20, 1864—2.30 P. M.
Major-General Schofield, Pulaski:
If Forrest makes a decided advance, I think it would be best for you to go to Lynnville with two divisions, leaving Stanley two at Pulaski. In order to have everything out of your way, the construction party which went to Pulaski a few days since had better come back to Columbia, and all surplus stores should be prepared to be sent back in case Hood's army advances. Give Hatch instructions according to your movements, and urge upon him the necessity of getting the most reliable information he can. I will order Ruger with one brigade to Columbia.

GEO. H. THOMAS,
Major-General U. S. V. Commanding.

NASHVILLE, *November* 20, 1864—5.30 P. M.
Major-General A. J. Smith, St. Louis, Mo.:
Your dispatch of this date just received. I wish you to make every exertion to reach this place with all possible dispatch. Bring with you all the troops ordered to report to you at Paducah, as well as all others belonging to your command. You will come to Nashville, via the Cumberland river. I have sent an officer with orders to bring Winslow's cavalry to this place without delay.

GEO. H. THOMAS,
Major-General U. S. V. Commanding.

HEADQUARTERS DEPARTMENT OF THE CUMBERLAND,
NASHVILLE, *November* 21, 1864.
Major-General Schofield, Pulaski:
Have you seen General Hatch's dispatch from Lexington at 8 A. M. to-day? It is very detailed, and he thinks it reliable. I have just received your two telegrams of 11 A. M. and 12 M., and approve the move. I have sent General Wilson out to take general charge of the cavalry, and directed him to report to you. He will reach Lynnvillé to-morrow morning.

GEO. H. THOMAS,
Major-General U. S. V. Commanding

NASHVILLE, TENN., *November* 23, 1864—10 P. M.

Major-General H. W. Halleck, Washington, D. C.:

It has occurred to me since my last dispatch was sent to you that it might be advisable to call on the governor of Indiana for some of the militia of that state, and I would like to know whether I am authorized to make the application. There are no available troops in Kentucky.

GEO. H. THOMAS,
Major-General U. S. V. Commanding.

NASHVILLE, TENN., *November* 23, 1864—1 P. M.

Major-General W. S. Rosecrans, St. Louis, Mo.:

Has General Smith and command embarked for this place yet? If so, when? They should hurry forward as rapidly as possible. Please answer on receipt of this.

GEO. H. THOMAS,
Major-General U. S. V. Commanding.

NASHVILLE, *November* 23, 1864.

Colonel Wm. E. Merrill, Chattanooga:

The major-general commanding directs that you organize a pontoonier battalion out of your regiment. Yours about the canvas received; will be attended to.

WM. D. WHIPPLE,
Brigadier-General.

COLUMBIA, *November* 24, 1864.

Major-General Thomas:

I now have your dispatch of 9 A. M. I do not believe Forrest has had time to get across Duck river yet, and hope the troops you have sent will be in time to prevent him. Capron was driven in very rapidly, and by a pretty large force. Cox arrived just in time to beat it back, and punished it very severely. Hood had ten miles the start of Stanley at noon yesterday, but Stanley outmarched him, and reached here at 10 o'clock to-day. His troops are all here and in position. Colonel Moore got here last night. My orders to Hatch are as you suggested. I have not heard from him to-day.

J. M. SCHOFIELD,
Major-General.

COLUMBIA, *November* 24, 1864—1.30 P. M.

Major-General G. H. Thomas:

Do you think it important to hold Columbia? My force is not large enough to cover the town and the railroad bridge. I can hold a shorter line covering the railroad bridge, leaving the town and the railroad depot outside; but in any case the enemy can turn the position by crosssing above or below, and rendering withdrawal to the north bank very difficult. Please give me your views soon.

             J. M. SCHOFIELD,
                Major-General.

       HEADQUARTERS DEPARTMENT OF THE CUMBERLAND,
         NASHVILLE, *November* 24, 1864—3 P. M.

Major-General Schofield, Columbia :

If you can not hold Columbia, you had better withdraw to the north bank of the river. From the description given, I supposed the line was sufficiently short to enable you and Stanley to hold it securely and have a reserve. But it is better, of course, to substantially check the enemy than to run the risk of defeat by resisting too much. Where is Stanley? Is he with you?

             GEO. H. THOMAS,
            Major-General U. S. V. Commanding.

        WASHINGTON, *November* 25, 1864—12 M.

Major-General Thomas :

Secretary war authorizes you, if you deem it necessary, to call upon the governor of Indiana and of any other Western states for troops. As this force is very expensive, if compared with its value against an enemy, it should be used as sparingly as circumstances will admit. Dispatches just received from Hilton Head indicate that General Sherman has captured Milledgeville and Macon, and that Beauregard has been recalled from Tennessee to fall on General Sherman's rear. This is also indicated through Beauregard's proclamation to the people of Mississippi, sent from Corinth through Selma.

             H. W. HALLECK,
           Major-General and Chief of Staff.

       CITY POINT, VA., *November* 24, 1864—4 P. M.

Major-General Geo. H. Thomas, Nashville :

Following proclamation just taken from papers of 21st. Do not let Forrest get off without punishment.

              U. S. GRANT,
               Lieutenant-General.

       HEADQUARTERS DEPARTMENT OF THE CUMBERLAND,
           NASHVILLE, *November* 25, 1864.

Lieutenant-General Grant, City Point, Va. :

Your dispatch of 4 P. M. yesterday just received. Hood's entire army is in front of Columbia, and so greatly outnumbering mine at this time, that I am compelled to act on the defensive. None of General Smith's troops have arrived yet, although they embarked at St. Louis on Tuesday last. The transportation of General Hatch's and Grierson's cavalry was

BATTLE OF FRANKLIN, ETC. 213

ordered by General Washburne, I am told, to be turned in at Memphis, which has crippled the only cavalry I have at this time. All of my cavalry was dismounted to furnish horses to Kilpatrick's division, which went with General Sherman. My dismounted cavalry is now detained at Louisville, awaiting arms and horses. Horses are arriving slowly, and arms have been detained somewhere en route for more than a month. General Grierson has been delayed by conflicting orders in Kansas and from Memphis, and it is impossible to say when he will reach here. Since being in charge of affairs in Tennessee, I have lost nearly fifteen thou sand men, discharged by expiration of service, and permitted to go home to vote. My gain is probably twelve thousand of perfectly raw troops; therefore, as the enemy so greatly outnumbers me, both in infantry and cavalry, I am compelled for the present to act on the defensive. The moment I can get my cavalry, I will march against Hood, and if Forrest can be reached, he will be punished.

GEO. H. THOMAS,
Major-General U. S. V. Commanding.

HEADQUARTERS DEPARTMENT OF THE CUMBERLAND,
NASHVILLE, *November* 25, 1864—11.20 A. M.
Major-General Schofield, Columbia:

In case you have to move to the north bank of Duck river, I wish you to keep some cavalry on the south side of it, to observe and delay Hood's advance on Chattanooga railroad as much as possible. I hope to have five (5) regiments of Granger's troops in Murfreesboro to-day. Have made arrangements for Milroy to fall back to Murfreesboro on this side of Duck river; also, if the enemy advances, the cavalry on the south side of Duck river should cover the approaches to Shelbyville, and cross at that place, and hold the bridge in case of an advance in force. I have asked Steedman how large a force he can raise to threaten the enemy's rear, should he get on the Chattanooga road, and expect an answer soon. About one thousand of Hatch's cavalry have arrived here from Memphis dismounted, and they will be mounted here as soon as possible, and sent to the front. Three regiments should start to-day, making about one thousand men. Have not heard of any of Smith's troops yet. Some of them will surely be here to-day. If Hood moves on the Chattanooga road, I will send Smith to Murfreesboro, as we shall be enabled thereby to concentrate more rapidly. If you can hold Hood on the south side of Duck river, I think we shall be able to drive him back easily after concentrating. Answer, giving your views.

GEO. H. THOMAS,
Major-General U. S. V. Commanding.

HEADQUARTERS DEPARTMENT OF THE CUMBEBLAND
NASHVILLE, *November* 26, 1864.
Rear-Admiral Lee, Mound City :
If you have any iron-clads which can resist heavy shot, I will be obliged if you will order them up the Tennessee river as far as they can go, on a reconnoissance. Hood is threatening Columbia, and I am anxious to know positively whether he has all his force with him or not.

GEO. H. THOMAS,
Major-General U. S. V. Commanding.

WASHINGTON, *November* 26, 1864—12 M.
Major-General Thomas :
All troops ordered from Missouri are under your orders, and will be subject to your disposal. Any others, embracing all officers and troops belonging to Sherman's force in the field, left behind by their commands, will be under your orders till they can again join their proper corps. If you call for any militia, notify adjutant-general's office.

H. W. HALLECK,
Chief of Staff.

HEADQUARTERS DEPARTMENT OF THE CUMBERLAND,
NASHVILLE, *November* 27, 1864.
Major-General Schofield, Columbia, via Franklin :
Your dispatch of 10 A. M. yesterday received. I will send you all the available infantry I can raise. I expect some of Smith's command here to-day, and will send it forward as rapidly as possible. Sent you two regiments of cavalry day before yesterday, two yesterday, and will send another to-day. If you can hold Hood in check until I can get Smith up, we can whip him.

GEO. H. THOMAS,
Major-General U. S. V. Commanding.

PADUCAH, *November* 27, 1864.
Major-General Thomas :
I have just arrived at this point. The brigade, Seventeenth Army Corps, and First division, Sixteenth Army Corps, will proceed immediately to destination, in obedience to your telegram of the 19th inst. The Third division will be up early in the morning. Telegraph me at Smithland.

A. J. SMITH,
Major-General.

DUCKTOWN, *November* 27, 1864—12.30 P. M.
Major-General Thomas :
The enemy has made no real attack, and I am satisfied he does not mean to attack. My information, though not very satisfactory, leads me to believe that Hood intends to cross Duck river above Columbia, and as near it as he can. I shall withdraw to the north bank to-night, and en-

deavor to prevent him from crossing. Wilson is operating mainly on my left, with a portion of his command south of the river. I have no late information from him. I have succeeded in getting your cipher of the 25th translated. I believe your dispositions are wise.

J. M. SCHOFIELD,
Major-General.

NEAR COLUMBIA, *November* 28, 1864—3.30 P. M.

Major-General Thomas:

The enemy has crossed in force a short distance this side of the Lewisburg pike, at noon to-day, and has driven our cavalry back across the river on that pike at the same time. The force is reported to be infantry, but I do not regard it as being probable. Wilson has gone with his main force to learn the facts, and drive the enemy back, if possible.

J. M. SCHOFIELD,
Major-General.

NASHVILLE, *November* 28, 1864.

Major-General Schofield, near Columbia:

Your dispatch of 3.30 is just received. If General Wilson can not succeed in driving back the enemy, should it prove true that he has crossed the river, you will necessarily have to make preparations to take up a new position at Franklin, behind Harpeth, immediately, if it becomes necessary to fall back.

GEO. H. THOMAS,
Major-General U. S. V. Commanding.

NASHVILLE, *November* 28, 1864.

Major-General Schofield:

You can have some of the pontoons you used at Columbia sent to Franklin, to lay a bridge there. I will answer your other telegram in a few moments.

GEO. H. THOMAS,
Major-General U. S. V. Commanding.

NEAR COLUMBIA, *November* 28, 1864—11 A. M.

Major-General Thomas:

I am in doubt whether it is advisable, with reference to future operations, to hold this position or retire to some point from which we can move offensively. Of course, we can not recross the river here. I could have easily held the bridge-head at the railroad, but it would have been useless, as we could not possibly advance from that point. Please give me your views and wishes.

J. M. SCHOFIELD,
Major-General.

NEAR COLUMBIA, *November* 28, 1864—6 P. M.

Major-General Thomas:

The enemy's cavalry in force has crossed the river on the Lewisburg pike, and is now in possession of Rally Hill. Wilson is trying to go on the Franklin road ahead of them. He thinks the enemy may swing in between him and me and strike Spring Hill, and wants Hammond's brigade halted there. Please give orders, if you know where it is.

J. M. SCHOFIELD,
Major-General.

NEAR COLUMBIA, *November* 28, 1864—9 P. M.

Major-General Thomas:

If Hood advances on the Lewisburg and Franklin pike, where do you propose to fight him? I have all the force that is necessary, and Smith's troops should be placed with reference to the proposed point of concentration.

J. M. SCHOFIELD,
Major-General.

NASHVILLE, *November* 29, 1864—3.30 A. M.

Major-General Schofield, near Columbia:

Your dispatches of 6 P. M. and 9 P. M. yesterday are received. I have directed General Hammond to halt his command at Spring Hill, and report to you for orders, if he can not communicate with General Wilson, and also instructing him to keep you well advised of the enemy's movements. I desire you to fall back from Columbia, and take up your position at Franklin, leaving a sufficient force at Spring Hill to contest the enemy's progress until you are securely posted at Franklin. The troops at the fords below Williamsport, etc., will be withdrawn, and take up a position behind Franklin. General A. J. Smith's command has not yet reached Nashville. As soon as he arrives, I will make immediate disposition of his troops, and notify you of the same. Please send me a report as to how matters stand, upon your receipt of this.

GEO. H. THOMAS,
Major-General U. S. V. Commanding.

HEADQUARTERS, HART'S CROSS-ROADS, ON FRANKLIN AND LEWISBURG PIKE,
November 29, 1864—3 A. M.; VIA FRANKLIN, 9.30 A. M.

Major-General Thomas:

Forrest's cavalry, Buford's, Chalmers', and Jackson's brigades, a part of Hanley's and Biffle's regiments, crossed Duck river on this road, and at several fords between it and Huey's Mills, seven miles above Columbia, yesterday. A pontoon train, sufficient for three bridges, had arrived at Huey's just before dark. The bridges were expected to be ready by 11 o'clock last night, and their infantry across by daylight this morning. The cavalry began crossing about noon, at Davis' fords, near Huey's, but could not get across at Hardison's, on the pike. Capron's and Garrard's brigades were struck in flank and rear by rebels, at Rally Hill. I have kept Major-General Schofield fully informed, and, at 1 A. M., sent him the information above, advising him to get back to Franklin at once. I have all of my command, except Hammond's and Hatch's first brigade, here. I do n't know where the former is. The latter has been watching the river at Knobgrass creek, and was ordered, at sunset last night, to join him at Spring Hill. I shall delay the enemy all in my power, if he presses me, and follow him wherever he goes. I have information from Franklin's Hill to-day. The Sixth Illinois is now probably near that place to-night, having gone to Shelbyville on a scout. I am sure, from what prisoners tell me, that the enemy is aiming for Nashville, via Franklin; his present direction, location of his bridge, and other circumstances point clearly to that conclusion. This being so, I shall probably cross the Harpeth midway between Triune and Franklin, and aim for Nolensville. Everything should be got off the railroad to-day. Hurry forward all cavalry, via Nolensville. I think everything should be concentrated at Nashville.

J. H. WILSON,
Major-General.

HEADQUARTERS ARMY OF THE OHIO, *November* 29—8.30 A. M.
Major-General Thomas:

The enemy's cavalry has crossed in force, on the Lewisburg pike, and General Wilson reports the infantry crossing above Huey's Mills, about five miles from this place. I have sent an infantry reconnoissance to learn the facts. If it prove true, I will act according to your instructions received this morning. Please send orders to General Cooper,* via Johnsonville; it may be doubtful whether my messenger from here will reach him.

J. M. SCHOFIELD,
Major-General.

HEADQUARTERS, 4½ MILES SOUTHEAST OF FRANKLIN,
November 29, 1864—2 P. M., VIA FRANKLIN.
Major-General Thomas:

The enemy pressed the rear of my column closely as far as the Ridge Meeting-house, and by marching around my left prevented me from getting upon the Fayetteville road. My impression is that Forrest is aiming for Nashville, via Triune and Nolensville. A part of his force may have cut into Spring Hill. Heavy artillery firing heard in that direction since 11 A. M. I can not hear from Schofield, but fear he may not have reached Franklin. I shall hold Hatch's second brigade and

---

* Commanding a brigade of General Ruger's division.

Hammond's here till I know all is clear. In the meantime, Johnson and Croxton are crossing the Harpeth at Henderson's ford, with orders to push strong parties to Triune Zend Grove, and thereby to push on to Nolensville to-night, if they find the enemy moving in that direction. I shall go in the same direction as soon as I can leave here with safety. You had better look out for Forrest at Nashville to-morrow noon. I'll be there before, or very soon after he makes his appearance.

J. H. WILSON,
Brevet Major-General.

NASHVILLE, *November* 29, 1864—11 P. M.
Major-General Schofield, Franklin:

General Wilson has telegraphed me very fully the movements of the enemy yesterday and this morning. He believes Forrest is aiming to strike this place, while the infantry will move against you, and attempt to get on your flank. If you discover such to be his movement, you had better cross Harpeth at Franklin, and then retire along the Franklin pike to this place, covering your wagon train and the railroad. I directed General Cooper, in accordance with your wishes yesterday, to withdraw from Centreville, by the Nashville road, crossing Harpeth at widow Dean's, and to report to you from that place for further orders. You had better send orders to meet him.

GEO. H. THOMAS,
Major-General U. S. V. Commanding.

FRANKLIN, *November* 29, 1864—10 P. M.
Major-General Thomas:

Major-General Schofield directs me to inform you that the enemy's cavalry crossed Duck river in force at daylight this morning, at Huey's Mills, six miles from Columbia, and pushed at once for Spring Hill. Their cavalry reached that point at 4 P. M., and their infantry came in before dark, and attacked General Stanley, who held the place with one division very heavily (engaged?). General Schofield's troops are pushing for Franklin as rapidly as possible. The general says he will not be able to get farther than Thompson's Station to-night, and possibly not farther than Spring Hill. He regards his situation as extremely perilous, and fears he may be forced into a general battle to-morrow, or lose his wagon train. General Wilson's cavalry have been pushed off toward the east, and do not come with our infantry, nor cover the pike. Thinking that the troops under General A. J. Smith's command had reached Franklin, General Schofield directed me to have them pushed down the Franklin pike to Spring Hill, by daylight to-morrow. I left General Schofield two hours ago, at Thompson's Station.

W. J. TWININGS,
Captain, Aid-de-Camp, and Chief Engineer, Army of Ohio.

BATTLE OF FRANKLIN, ETC.

EXTRACT FROM GENERAL THOMAS' REPORT.

The important result of this signal victory can not be too highly appreciated, for it not only seriously checked the enemy's advance and gave General Schofield time to move his troops and all his property to Nashville, but it also caused deep depression among the men of Hood's army, making them doubly cautious in their subsequent movements. Not willing to risk a renewal of the battle on the morrow, and having accomplished the object of the day's operations—viz., to cover the withdrawal of his trains—General Schofield, by my advice and direction, fell back during the night, to Nashville; in front of which city, line of battle was formed, by noon of the 1st of December, on the heights immediately surrounding Nashville.

EXTRACTS FROM GENERAL SCHOFIELD'S REPORT.

The troops rested in this position on the 28th, and I had strong hopes of being able to hold the line of Duck river until reinforcements should arrive; but I learned from General Wilson, about 2 A. M. on the 29th, that the enemy's cavalry had forced a crossing near the Lewisburg pike, and about daylight in the morning, that his infantry was also crossing at Huey's Mills, five miles above Columbia, from which a road leads into the Franklin pike, at Spring Hill. The enemy might endeavor to reach the latter place in advance of me, and thus cut off my retreat, or strike me in flank near Duck river, or both. He had already forced a column of cavalry between General Wilson and me, and cut off all communication between us. I therefore sent General Stanley with a division of infantry to Spring Hill, to hold that point and cover the trains; General Cox was left in his position, to hold the crossing at Columbia; Generals Wood and Kimball were put in line facing Huey's Mills, with a brigade thrown forward to reconnoiter, and General Ruger was ordered to move on to the pike, in rear of Rutherford's creek, leaving one regiment to hold the ford near the railroad bridge, the bridges having been destroyed.

* * * * * * * *

About 3 P. M. I became satisfied that the enemy would not attack my position on Duck river, but was pushing two corps direct for Spring Hill. I then gave the necessary orders for the withdrawal of the troops after dark, and took General Ruger's troops and pushed for Spring Hill, to reopen communication with General Stanley, and was followed at a short distance by the head of the main column. I struck the enemy's cavalry at dark, about three miles from Spring Hill, but we brushed them away without difficulty, and reached Spring Hill about seven o'clock. . . .

I arrived at Franklin with the head of the column a little before daylight on the 30th, and found no wagon-bridge for crossing the river, and the fords in very bad condition. I caused the railroad bridge to be prepared for crossing wagons, and had a foot-bridge built for infantry, which fortunately proved available for wagons, and used the ford as much as possible. I hoped, in spite of the difficulties, to get all my material, including the public property and a large wagon train, across the river, and move the army over before the enemy could get up force enough to attack me; but I put the troops in position as they arrived on the south side—the Twenty-third Corps on the left and center, covering the Columbia and Lewisburg pikes, and General Kimball's division of the Fourth Corps on the right, both flanks resting on the river. Two brigades of Wagner's division were left in front to retard the enemy's advance, and General Wood's division, with some artillery, was moved to the north bank of the river, to cover the flanks, should the enemy attempt to cross above or below. The enemy followed close after our rear-guard; brought up and deployed two full corps with astonishing celerity, and moved rapidly forward to the attack. Our outposts, imprudently brave, held their ground too long, and hence were compelled to come in at a run. In passing over the parapet, they carried with them the troops of the line for a short space, and permitted a few hundred of the enemy to get in; but the reserves sprang forward, regaining the parapet, and capturing those of the enemy who had passed it. The enemy assaulted persistently and continuously with his whole force, from about 3.30 P. M. until after dark, and made numerous intermittent attacks at a few points until about 10 o'clock P. M. He was splendidly repulsed along the whole line of attack. . . .

It is to be observed that more than half our loss occurred in Wagner's division of the Fourth Corps, which did not form part of the main line of defense. This loss arose in two brigades of that division, from their remaining in front of the line after their proper duty as outposts had been accomplished, and after they should have taken their position in reserve; and in the other brigade (Colonel Opdycke's), in its hand-to-hand encounter with the enemy over the parapet, which had been temporarily lost by the precipitate retreat of the other two brigades.

* * * * * * * * *

My experience on the 29th had shown how entirely inferior a force my cavalry was to that of the enemy, and that even my immediate flank and rear were insecure, while my communication with Nashville was entirely without protection. I could not even rely upon getting up ammunition necessary for another battle. To remain longer at Franklin, was to seriously hazard the loss of my army, by giving the enemy another chance to cut me off from reinforcements, which he had made three desperate futile attempts to accomplish. I had detained the enemy long enough to enable you to concentrate your scattered troops at Nashville, and had succeeded in inflicting upon him very heavy losses, which was the primary object. I had found it impossible to detain him long enough to get reinforcements at Franklin. Only a small portion of the infantry and none of the cavalry could reach me in time to be of any use in battle, which must have been fought on the 1st of December, for these reasons. After consulting with corps and division commanders, and obtaining your approval, I determined to retire the night of the 30th toward Nashville.

EXTRACT FROM GENERAL STANLEY'S REPORT.

From 1 o'clock until 4 P. M. in the evening, the enemy's entire force was in sight, and forming for attack; yet, in view of the strong position we held, and reasoning from the former course of the rebels during the campaign, nothing appeared so improbable as that they would assault. I felt so confident in this belief, that I did not leave General Schofield's headquarters until the firing commenced. About 4 o'clock the enemy advanced with his whole force, at least two corps, making a bold and persistent assault, which, upon part of the line, lasted forty minutes, when Wagner's division fell back from the heights south of Franklin. Opdycke's brigade was placed in reserve, in rear of our main line on the Columbia pike; Lane's and Conrad's brigades were deployed, the former on the right, the other on the left of the pike, and about three hundred yards in advance of the main line. By whose mistake I can not tell, it certainly was never a part of my instructions, but these brigades had orders from General Wagner not to retire to the main line until forced to do so by the fighting of the enemy.

Speaking of the effect of their retreat, General Stanley said: "It was at that moment I arrived at the scene of disorder, coming from the town on the Columbia pike. The moment was critical beyond any I have ever known in battle. Could the enemy hold that part of the line, he was nearer our two bridges than the extremities of our line. Colonel Opdycke's brigade was lying down about one hundred yards in rear of the works. I rode quickly to the left regiment and called to them to charge; at the same time I saw Colonel Opdycke near the center of his line, urging his men forward. I gave the colonel no order, as I saw him engaged in doing the very thing to save us, namely, to get possession of our line again."

EXTRACT FROM GENERAL J. H. WILSON'S REPORT.

At 1 A. M. (November 29), I sent a dispatch to General Schofield, informing him that the force at Huey's Mill was Forrest's cavalry, consisting of Chalmers', Jackson's, and Buford's divisions, and Biffle's regiment; that the rebel infantry were to have began crossing two hours before, by three pontoon bridges under construction at the same place. Believing the information to be perfectly correct, I therefore suggested that our infantry should reach Spring Hill by 10 A. M. of that day.

CHAPTER XXXV.

BATTLE OF NASHVILLE AND PURSUIT OF THE ROUTED ENEMY.

THE arrival of General Steedman with his command from Chattanooga, December 1st, in the evening, completed the concentration of forces, which had been so unexpectedly delayed. Three lines of defence had been abandoned because the promised troops had not appeared in Tennessee. And now that the concentration had been effected, the improvised army contained three corps, each one of which represented a distinct department; a provisional division made up of detachments from almost every organization, large and small, embraced in the sixty-five thousand men, then on "the march to the sea;" an infusion of raw infantry regiments; the greater portion of the cavalry of the Military Division of the Mississippi, but still largely dismounted; and colored soldiers, who were to have their first opportunity in the central theater of war, to fight by brigades.

General Thomas had held General Steedman's command, on the line of the Nashville and Chattanooga railroad for two reasons—one, the complications in East Tennessee, of which a narrative will be given in another chapter; and the other, the probability that General Hood would strike that important railroad south of Nashville. Having arrived, General Steedman took position about a mile in advance of the left center of the main line, and east of the Nolensville turnpike. General Wilson, with his cavalry, had previously taken a strong position at Thomson's Chapel, on the Nolensville turnpike, covering the space between General Schofield's left and the Cumberland river.

General Hood being still greatly superior in cavalry, there

was danger that he would detach a large portion of it to interrupt the vital communications with Louisville. To guard against the passage of his cavalry over the Cumberland, above Nashville, General Hammond's brigade of cavalry was sent to Gallatin on the 2d, to watch the river as far up as Carthage. And the day following General Thomas threw all the remaining cavalry across to Edgefield, and then General Steedman's command covered the space between General Schofield's left and the river.

General Hood's infantry, did not approach Nashville until the 3d, when General Thomas' outposts were driven in, and soon after the enemy began to establish his main line. The next morning his salient was seen on Montgomery Hill, within six hundred yards of the center of the national line. General Hood's investing lines occupied the high ground on the southeast side of Brown's creek, extending from the Nolensville turnpike, across the Granny White and Franklin turnpikes, in a southwesterly direction, to the hills south and southwest of Richland creek, and down that creek to the Hillsboro turnpike. From his right, on the Nolensville road to the river, above the city, and from his left, on the Hillsboro road to the river below, his cavalry were posted. Intent upon completing and strengthening his line, General Hood made no response to the fire of artillery, which opened upon him from several points. It was doubtless necessary, too, that he should be economical in the use of his ammunition, as it was difficult for him to replenish from his base at Corinth.

Although not active at Nashville, General Hood was enterprising in other directions. He sent Bate's division of Cheatham's corps to reduce Murfreesboro and other minor points in the vicinity, and on the 4th the block-house, at Overall's creek, five miles north of Murfreesboro, was attacked by this force. But such was the strength of the block-house constructed for the defense of the railroad bridge, that although seventy-four artillery shots were fired against it, the garrison held out until General Milroy arrived with reinforcements from Murfreesboro, consisting of three regiments of infantry, four companies of cavalry, and a section of artillery. General Bate was then attacked and driven away. During the 5th,

6th, and 7th, having been reinforced by a division from Lee's corps, and twenty-five hundred cavalry, General Bate demonstrated heavily against Fortress Rosecrans, near Murfreesboro, held by eight thousand men, under General Rousseau. The enemy declining to make a direct attack, General Milroy was sent against him on the 8th, with seven regiments of infantry. He was found on the Wilkinson turnpike behind rail barricades, which were carried by assault—General Milroy capturing two hundred and seven prisoners and two guns, and suffering a loss of thirty men killed, and one hundred and seventy-five wounded. The same day Buford's cavalry, after shelling Murfreesboro, entered the town, but were driven out by a regiment of infantry and a section of artillery. The whole force then moved to Lebanon and down the bank of the Cumberland river to Nashville, threatening to cross, to interrupt the Louisville and Nashville railroad.

A portion of the enemy's cavalry, under General Lyon, succeeded in crossing the Cumberland river above Clarksville, on the 9th. The object of the movement was to reach the Louisville and Nashville railroad, at some point in Kentucky, and to prevent its accomplishment General Thomas directed General McCook, who was in Kentucky, to remount Watkins' and La Grange's brigades of cavalry, and to look after Lyon with these brigades.

During the first half of December, General Grant felt great uneasiness with regard to the situation in Tennessee, fearing that General Hood would pass round Nashville and march into Kentucky reproducing the scenes and issues of the summer and autumn of 1862. Believing that General Thomas should have delivered battle immediately after the engagement at Franklin, he urged him thereafter, from day to day, to attack General Hood. General Thomas, on the other hand, thought it advisable to remount his cavalry and make other preparations, that he might be assured of victory, before assuming the offensive, and at the same time gain the full results of victory by a vigorous pursuit of the enemy, when defeated and routed. He was confident of final success, and was vigilant in guarding the river with his cavalry, and secured the services of the gunboats of the Eleventh Division of the Mississippi Squadron, under Lieutenant-Commander Leroy Fitch, to patrol the river above and below the city. During the first eight days of the month, General Wilson had raised his cavalry to good strength, by the influx of new horses and by ransacking the corrals for convalescent animals, and in this time much had been done to supply the army with the transportation essential to successful pursuit, and with pontoons for the full rivers. But delay for any cause was displeasing to General Grant, as besides the supposed danger to Kentucky, the troops under General Canby on the Mississippi river, intended for co-operation with General Sherman, were detained to prevent the trans-Mississippi Confederate forces, from joining General Hood, and on the 9th of December at the suggestion of the lieutenant-general, an order was issued by the President, relieving General Thomas, and placing General Schofield in command. General Thomas himself preferred to be relieved rather than be responsible for a battle fought under unfavorable conditions. The order relieving him, however, was subsequently suspended; but there was no respite to the urgent communications requiring the deliverance of battle without delay.

General Thomas at first hoped to be ready for battle on the 7th, but on account of delay in remounting his cavalry, he was not ready until the 9th. But with the completion of his preparations there came a sleet which rendered the movement of troops for any purpose, especially for battle, an impossibility. Reconnoissances on the 11th and 13th—the first by Colonel J. G. Mitchell, and the second by Colonel A. G. Malloy—developed the fact that infantry could move only with the greatest difficulty upon the surface of the uneven ground. On the 9th, General Thomas ordered General Wilson to move his command to the south side of the river to take position between the Hillsboro and Harding turnpikes, to be in readiness to participate in the attack, projected for the next day; but even this movement could not be executed upon the ice with cavalry, except with horses shod expressly for such a surface. As the refusal of General Thomas to give battle, after a peremptory order on the 6th to attack without waiting longer for a remount for his cavalry, called for the order relieving him from command, with General Schofield as his successor, so his unwillingness to attack upon the ice first elicited an order from General Grant, on the 11th, to delay no longer for weather or reinforcements, and then another on the 13th, directing Major-General John A. Logan to proceed to Nashville, reporting arrival at Louisville and Nashville. And on the 15th, General Grant reached Washington, on his way to Nashville to take command in person.

However, by midday on the 14th, the ice had so far melted that General Thomas resolved upon attacking the enemy the next day, and at 3 P. M. he called together his corps commanders to announce to them his plan of battle, and give them instructions with regard to the specific action of their respective commands in its execution. The following is the text: "Major-General A. J. Smith, commanding detachment of the Army of the Tennessee, after forming his troops on and near the Harding pike in front of his present position, will make a vigorous assault upon the enemy's left. Major-General Wilson, commanding the cavalry corps Military Division of the Mississippi, with three divisions, will move on and support General Smith's right, assisting as far as possible in carrying the left of the enemy's position, and be in readiness to throw his force upon the enemy the moment a favorable opportunity occurs. Major-General Wilson will also send one division on the Charlotte pike, to clear that road of the enemy and observe in the direction of Bell's landing, to protect our right rear until the enemy's position is fairly turned, when it will rejoin the main force. Brigadier-General T. J. Wood, commanding Fourth Corps,*after leaving a strong skirmish line in his works from Lawrens' Hill to his extreme right, will form the remainder of the Fourth Corps on the Hillsboro pike to support General Smith's left, and operate on the left and rear of the enemy's advanced position on Montgomery Hill. Major-General Schofield, commanding Twenty-third Army Corps, will replace Brigadier-General Kimball's division of the Fourth Corps with his troops, and occupy the trenches from Fort Negley to Lawrens' Hill with a strong skirmish line. He will move with the remainder of his force

---

*Gen. D. S Stanley was absent on account of wounds received at Franklin.

in front of the works, and co-operate with General Wood, protecting the latter's left flank against an attack by the enemy. Major-General Steedman, commanding District of Etowah, will occupy the interior line in rear of his present position, stretching from the reservoir on the Cumberland river to Fort Negley, with a strong skirmish line, and mass the remainder of his force in its present position, to act according to the exigencies which may arise during these operations. Brigadier-General Miller, with troops forming the garrison of Nashville, will occupy the interior line from the battery on hill 210, to the extreme right, including the inclosed work on the Hyde's Ferry road. The quartermaster's troops, under the command of Brigadier-General Donaldson, will, if necessary, be posted on the interior line from Fort Morton to the battery on hill 210. The troops occupying the interior line will be under the direction of Major-General Steedman, who is charged with the immediate defense of Nashville during the operations around the city. Should the weather permit, the troops will be formed to commence operations at 6 A. M. on the 15th, or as soon thereafter as practicable."

General Thomas modified this plan, by ordering General Steedman to make a most positive feint against the enemy's right, to divert his attention from the dominant movement against his left, and also by calling General Schofield's corps, first to the reserve, and afterward directing it to move upon General Smith's right, after other movements had been successfully accomplished.

The weather and the ice, which from the 9th had prevented General Thomas from assuming the offensive, had also for six days barred all activity on the part of the enemy, who was meditating a movement* round Nashville from the consciousness that he could not successfully assault the army intrenched before it. The morning of the 15th being favorable for the tactical dispositions required by General Thomas' plan of operations, the two armies were thrown into deadly conflict,

---

*This statement is not supported by official testimony, but upon the declarations of prisoners and citizens within General Hood's lines. He, too, was delayed by the ice-covered ground.

to contest not only the possession of Tennessee, but to decide the supremacy of the national arms in all the West.

At 4 A. M. on the 15th, the provisional division composed of troops from corps and other organizations of General Sherman's army, under command of Brigadier-General Cruft, moved forward and relieved the Fourth and Twenty-third Corps, occupied their exterior line of works, and picketed the front of this line from the Acklin place to Fort Negley, commanding the approaches to the city by the Granny White, Franklin, and Nolensville turnpikes. At the same hour, General J. F. Miller occupied the works with the garrison of the city, from Fort Negley to the Lebanon turnpike, covering the approaches by the Murfreesboro, Chicken, and Lebanon turnpikes. Brigadier-General Donaldson, with his command, occupied the defenses from General Cruft's right to the Cumberland river, commanding the approaches by the Harding, Hillsboro, and Charlotte turnpikes. General Steedman was instructed to support General Wood's left, when his corps should take position, and make a vigorous demonstration in his front to cover the grand effort to turn the enemy's left flank.

About daylight the other commands began to move to their several positions as prescribed in the modified plan of battle. General Smith advanced his second division, Brigadier-General Garrard commanding, on the Harding turnpike, and deployed to the left of that road; he threw forward his first division, Brigadier-General J. McArthur commanding, on the Harding and Charlotte turnpikes, and formed it on the right of Garrard; his third division, Colonel J. B. Moore, Thirty-third Wisconsin commanding, he held in reserve opposite the junction of the right and left flanks of the other two divisions. Owing to the divergence of the roads upon which he moved, and the stubborn resistance of the enemy, McArthur did not get into position until 8 A. M. He silenced a batttery, and skirmished heavily as he advanced.

General Wood formed the Fourth Corps, with the Second division, Brigadier-General Elliott commanding, on the right; the First division, Brigadier-General Kimball commanding, in the center; and the third division, Brigadier-General S.

Beatty commanding, on the left. Elliott's right was refused, in echelon with Smith's left. The other divisions were formed in similar manner—the right of each in echelon—to facilitate the wheel of the whole line to the right, on the left of the Fourth Corps as a pivot. The formation of the Fourth Corps was a double battle-line—the first deployed, and the second in column, by division, opposite the intervals in the first. The front was covered with a line of skirmishers, and a similar force remained in the works in the rear.

The Twenty-third Corps, when relieved from position on the left of the Fourth, moved to the right of Wood. The Third division, Brigadier-General J. D. Cox commanding, excepting one brigade left to support General Steedman, moved by the Hillsboro turnpike, and formed in the rear of Elliott's right; the Second (recently General Ruger's), Major-General D. N. Couch commanding, advanced on the Harding turnpike, and took position in rear of Garrard's left.

When the infantry on the right had given room for the movements of the cavalry, General Wilson at once assumed position. The Fifth division, Brigadier-General E. Hatch commanding, took position on the right of McArthur, of Smith's corps. General Croxton, with his brigade of the First division, formed on the right of Hatch. The Seventh division, one brigade mounted, Brigadier J. F. Knipe commanding, was held in reserve, to render aid wherever emergency might demand. The Sixth division, Brigadier R. W. Johnson commanding, one brigade mounted, was ordered to move by the Charlotte turnpike, to clear that road of the enemy, and keeping connection with Croxton by skirmishers or patrols, to push as far as Davidson's house, eight miles from the city, so as to cover the remainder of the corps from the enemy's cavalry, and look well to the guns of the enemy at Bell's landing, commanding the Cumberland river, and the force supporting them.

A dense fog hung over the two armies during the early morning, which, with the undulations of the ground, concealed the movements of the national army, though from these causes the evolutions were also greatly retarded. When, about noon, the fog lifted, there was doubtless to General

Hood an unexpected revelation. He had thus far in the campaign monopolized the offensive, and during the days of enforced inaction, he had been maturing his plans to turn Nashville and move into Kentucky. This would have been an exceedingly rash adventure, and after his experience at Franklin, where three divisions beat back his army, with the help of extemporized intrenchments, he could not, even in the wildest forecast of the consequences of an attempt to carry Nashville, with its elaborate fortifications, held by an army of equal strength, decide to take such a risk. Neither could he stay long before the city, and supply his army. It was imperative that he should move in some direction, and in his desperate extremity, he no doubt meditated an early advance into Kentucky, hoping, despite all the dangerous contingencies, that he could at least escape destruction. He had not anticipated the necessity of so soon acting on the defensive, and even when he saw an army deployed before him in aggressive attitude, he did not expect an attack upon his left flank. The troops opposite his right, during the twelve days of his nominal investment, alone had made the pretense of aggression, in contesting the defenses which General Steedman had constructed when he was before Wilson, on the left of the national line. And now, while the strength of the Army of the Cumberland was on his left, he was to be still further misled by a feint, which, from its spirit and force, might easily be mistaken for a positive assault.

When, the combination to turn General Hood's left had been fully completed, Brigadier-General Whipple, chief of staff to General Thomas, bore an order to General Steedman to advance against his right, in semblance of actual assault. General Steedman had previously formed a column for this movement, composed of three strong detachments—the first under Colonel T. J. Morgan, embracing his own regiment, the Fourteenth Colored, the Seventeenth, Forty-fourth, and a detachment of the Eighteenth; the second under Colonel Thompson, including his own regiment, the Twelfth Colored, and the Thirteenth and One Hundredth; and the third under Lieutenant-Colonel Grosvenor, of the Eighteenth Ohio, composed of his regiment, the Sixty-eighth Indiana, and the Second battalion of the Fourteenth Army Corps; and in addition, the Eighteenth Ohio and Twentieth Indiana batteries. At 8 A. M. the detachments of Morgan and Grosvenor, the former commanding both, moved forward from the Murfreesboro turnpike to Riddle's hill, drove in the enemy's pickets, and assaulted his works, between the turnpike and the Nashville and Chattanooga railroad. These troops gained a lodgment in the works, but were exposed, while holding them, to a severe fire from General Hood's massed forces on that flank, and General Steedman withdrew them. The charge was so gallantly made, that General Hood was so deceived as to its ultimate aim, that he drew troops from his center and left to give strength to his seemingly endangered flank.

Soon after this action on the extreme left, the forces on the opposite flank moved forward on the Harding and Hillsboro roads with resistless force, in executing the grand initiative of the battle. McArthur's division moved rapidly behind its skirmishers, who were soon sharply engaged, and gradually wheeling to the left, the direction of the line, was parallel to the Harding road. Advancing thence a short distance, the division was before a detached earthwork of the enemy, situated on the top of a hill, and inclosing four brass guns. This fort was covered by a stronger one, some four hundred feet to the right, and containing the same number of guns. In the meantime, Hatch's division of cavalry, with its left connected with McArthur's right, had swept round on a longer curve and was in readiness to co-operate in assaulting the forts. Hatch had previously engaged Ecton's brigade of infantry beyond Richland creek, and had driven it past Harding's house, near which Colonel Spalding, commanding the Twelfth Tennessee Cavalry, charged and captured forty-three prisoners and the headquarter-train of Chalmers' division. Hatch's right brigade, under Colonel Coon, having diverged too far from the direction of the general movement, was now moved by the left flank till it joined his other brigade on the flank of the four-gun redoubt, which covered the extremity of the enemy's line. Here, by direction of General Hatch, Coon's brigade dismounted to charge, planting its battery—"I," First Illinois Artillery—so as to enfilade the enemy's line. Four batteries then opened upon the guns in the redoubt and soon silenced them, and Coon's brigade charged the supporting infantry force, and though under the fire of the second redoubt, captured the four guns. The skirmishers of McMillen's and Hubbard's brigades of McArthur's division were also charging from an opposite direction, and entering the redoubt at the same moment contributed to the successful issue. One hundred and fifty prisoners were taken with the guns.

The two divisions immediately moved to the right, cavalry and infantry vieing with each other in the effort to carry the stronger redoubt on a hill whose acclivity greatly increased the hazard of an assault. This position, however, was carried in the same manner as the other. Coon's brigade, armed with the Spencer rifle, supported by two fresh brigades, charged up the hill and drove the enemy from position; while McArthur's brigades were in such close proximity, in a sweeping charge, as to lay claim to the guns and two hundred and fifty prisoners.

During these successful movements, by the direction of General Thomas, General Schofield moved his corps to the right of General Smith, and formed it for battle. This change became necessary, as the latter had moved farther to the left than had been anticipated, and the enemy's true flank had not been found. General Schofield was directed to attack his flank, which rested upon a group of hills near the Hillsboro turnpike, that the cavalry might operate in his rear. In order to preserve continuity of line, General Smith threw Ward's brigade of his reserve division to the front, to fill a space of a half mile between his right and Schofield's left; and to give full space to General Schofield, General Hatch moved to the right, across the Hillsboro turnpike, and with his other brigade attacked the enemy on another range of hills, drove him from it, and captured a battery in the valley beyond. In the meantime, Generals Schofield and Smith advanced their lines. Colonel Hill's brigade of McArthur's division carried a small earthwork containing two guns, but lost its commander in the assault. Colonel Wolf's brigade of Garrard's division crossed the Hillsboro turnpike and gained the works on the left. General Schofield moved to the right of the two redoubts first captured, crossed the Hillsboro road and a valley beyond, and carried a series of hills overlooking the Granny White turnpike—one of the two remaining lines of retreat available to the enemy. The charge was made by General Cooper's brigade of Couch's division. The enemy here made his first attempt on his left to give a counter-blow. He had previously massed a heavy force on his left to hurl it against General Thomas' right flank. When General Cooper had crossed the valley to carry the hills beyond, this force appeared in his rear in the low ground. General Couch then sent Mehringer's brigade against it, and though the enemy was of superior strength, Colonel Mehringer checked him until Doolittle's and Casement's brigades of Cox's division advanced in his support. The engagement was continued with sharp fighting until dark.

The action of the Fourth Corps was equally successful. As soon as General Smith became engaged on General Wood's right, the latter moved his corps toward Montgomery Hill, the salient of the enemy's defensive line. This position was very strong, being an irregular cone rising about one hundred feet above the general level of the country. The ascent, except on the left and rear, is quite abrupt, and was covered with forest trees. The intrenchments concealed the hill a little below the crest, and the approaches were covered with abatis and sharpened stakes firmly planted in the ground. During the formation of the corps for assault, the guns in position expressed defiance, and in response and menace General Wood's guns opened with vigor. As the corps advanced, it swung to the left, in order that the more easy ascent should be in front of Beatty's division, which had been required to furnish an assaulting column, of which Colonel Post's brigade was designated for the front and Colonel Streight's for immediate support. At 1 P. M. Colonel Post dashed up the hill and over the intrenchments on the summit, and held the enemy's stronghold This action was anterior to the more positive success of Smith and Wilson on the right, and opened the way for General Schofield to move to the right of General Smith. When the Twenty-third Corps was transferred to the right, General Thomas directed General Wood to throw his reserves on his right, to extend his line to as great an extent as was compatible with the security of his front. In obedience, General Wood put the reserve brigade of each division on his right, and then engaged the enemy with his entire corps. He brought three batteries into play and pressed forward a strong skirmish line, but at first made no threat of assaulting. Soon, however, he made preparations to carry the enemy's works in his front; moving his right division, whose right had extended in rear of General Smith's left, farther to his own left, and then advanced it and his central division, so as to bring Kimball's division opposite a fortified hill near the center of General Hood's main line. Placing two batteries so as to throw a converging fire upon the hill, he used them vigorously for an hour, and then ordered General Kimball to charge with his whole division. With loud cheers, the division ascended the hill and leaped over the intrenchments, capturing several pieces of artillery, stands of colors, and a large number of prisoners. At the same time, General Elliott carried the intrenchments in his front, and General Beatty crowned the enemy's works before his division with captures of artillery and prisoners. In this general advance, the right of General Wood's line became involved with the left of General Smith's, and conflicting claims for the fruits of victory were preferred. At 5 P. M. General Wood received an order from General Thomas to move to the Franklin turnpike, two and a half miles distant, and facing southward, to drive the enemy across it. The corps moved as directed, but the night fell too soon for it to reach its destination, but it bivouacked on a line parallel to the Granny White turnpike connecting with General Smith's left.

On the extreme left, other advantages were gained after the feint of the morning. Colonels Morgan and Grosvenor pressed the enemy from Raine's house and held the position, using the buildings for defense. Colonel Thompson, with his detachment, advanced across Brown's creek, between the Murfreesboro and Nolensville turnpikes, and carried the left of the front line of fortifications on the latter road, holding his ground firmly. In this succession of aggressive movements, the colored troops were prominent and successful.

During the day the enemy had been driven from his original

line of works, and forced back to a position on the Harpeth hills, and his left had been completely turned, though he still held two lines of retreat—one on the Granny White road, and the other on the direct road to Franklin. Seventeen pieces of artillery had been taken from him, also twelve hundred prisoners and several hundred small arms. The cavalry had cleared its front, covered the extremity of the infantry line, enveloped the enemy's left flank and taken it in reverse, and had only failed in the extreme possibility of reaching the Franklin turnpike in rear of Hood's army. General Wilson at dark directed General Hatch to bivouac on the Hillsboro road, to cover General Smith's right flank. He placed General Knipe's division on Hatch's right; Hammond's brigade had reached the six-mile post on the Hillsboro road, and turned thence up a branch of Richland creek for three miles, bivouacking on the Granny White turnpike. General Johnson's division had moved far to the right during the day, to co-operate with the gunboats in dislodging the enemy from Bell's landing, and bivouacked in the vicinity, in prospect of co-operating with Lieutenant-Commander Fitch in an attack the next morning. General Croxton had moved on Johnson's left for several miles, and having turned to the left, rested for the night at the six-mile post on the Charlotte turnpike. The brigade of dismounted cavalry took position on the Hillsboro turnpike, to cover Hatch and Hammond against a possible advance of the enemy's cavalry on that road.

The whole army bivouacked with assurance of complete victory on the morrow. The authorities at Washington and the people of the country, after ten days of impatience at General Thomas' delay in preparation for a battle now so gloriously begun, were in full sympathy with the troops lying on their arms before the defeated enemy. General Grant, on his way to Nashville from City Point, Virginia, stopped at Washington, while General Logan, farther advanced toward the same destination, halted at Louisville. Official congratulations from the President, Secretary of War, and Lieutenant-General sped their swift way to General Thomas and his army. The defeat, total and immediate, of one of the two great armies upon which the existence of the rebellion depended was now assured, and the reaction from the historic uneasiness which had obtained throughout the country with regard to the situation at Nashville to the extreme of hopefulness with respect to the immediate issue and the ultimate consequences of the battle, was one of the most marked revulsions of opinion and feeling during the war. The army had felt no uneasiness, and now looked forward with calm assurance to the result which had been anticipated during all the days of peparation for battle.

During the night, General Hood drew back his center and right to a stronger position, his right then resting on Overton hill, and his left remaining on the Harpeth or Brentwood range. His line extended along the base of the hills, his artillery was massed at points most available for its effective use, and his troops spent the night in fortifying the position. The battle-front now presented by the enemy was on its left nearly perpendicular in trend to the right of the national line, the latter having so far wheeled to the left that its direction was nearly at right angles to its original linear course. This relation of the army lines made General Schofield fearful with regard to his right flank, and during the night he requested reinforcements from General Smith, who sent to him Colonel Moore's division. Before daylight, Colonel Moore was in reserve on General Schofield's right.

As General Hood's retreat was now probable, General Thomas gave orders for movements on the 16th having reference to attack should he accept battle, and to pursuit should he retreat. Each corps was ordered to move forward rapidly at 6 A. M. until the enemy should be met. As General Hood's left remained in proximity to General Schofield's line, he did not move early in the morning. The Fourth Corps advanced promptly as ordered toward the Franklin road. The enemy's skirmishers were soon encountered, but were speedily driven back, and the Franklin road was gained. Here the corps was deployed—Elliott's division across the road facing southward, Beatty's on the left, and Kimball's in reserve behind Elliott. It then advanced rapidly three-fourths of a mile, and met a strong skirmish line behind barricades, the main line being plainly in view a half mile beyond. Simultaneously with the movement of the Fourth Corps, General Steedman advanced on the left, and General Smith on the right. The former soon found that the enemy had left his front, and pressing forward, took position between the Nolensville turnpike and General Wood's left, his own right resting on the railroad, and his left on the Nolensville road. To cover his rear against dashes of cavalry, he ordered Mitchell's brigade of Cruft's division from the defenses, to occupy Riddle's hill. General Smith advanced with two divisions, Garrard's and McArthur's, going into position under the fire of the enemy's artillery, about eight hundred yards from his main line. The Twenty-third Corps was still at right angles with this his new offensive line, facing eastward. General Smith's right was opposite very strong intrenchments of the enemy—in fact, was at the base of the hill upon which they rested. He simply held position until 1 P. M., waiting for General Schofield, who was to take the initiative againt General Hood's left. There being an interval between his left and General Wood's right, the latter threw into it Kimball's division, and completed the continuous alignment of the infantry from left to right. In the meantime, the artillery from all parts of the line kept up a measured fire, and even muskets were used freely to induce the enemy to expend his limited ammunition.

Pending the movements of the infantry to perfect their array, General Wilson was active in the formation of the cavalry on the right. Early in the morning, Hammond's pickets on the Granny White turnpike had been attacked and driven back; but in compliance with orders, General Hammond had strengthed his line and regained his position. During this action, Hatch's division had been directed to the enemy's rear, passing to Hammond's left. The country being hilly and covered with a dense forest, was impracticable for the movement of cavalry, mounted, and hence the whole force was dismounted and pushed forward. General Croxton moved to the front to support either Hatch or Hammond, and General Johnson, who had ascertained early in the morning that the enemy had abandoned Bell's landing, had been ordered to move across to the Hillsboro turnpike. By noon, the cavalry formed a continuous line from General Schofield's right to the Granny White turnpike. General Thomas' object now was to turn both flanks of the enemy. His flanks were stronger than his center, but success in turning either or both promised better results than to break through his center, as they covered his lines of retreat. Could one or the other be turned, there was the possibility of reaching his rear and cutting off his retreat, and could both be turned at once, he would be thrown in confusion on his only line of retreat through the Brentwood Pass, and the probability would be doubly strong of cutting him off. Having rode along his line from Wood to Schofield, he ordered the latter and Smith to attack the enemy's left, and the former and Steedman to move against Overton hill.

The Brentwood hills, rising about three hundred and fifty feet above the level of the country, consist of two ranges trending from their northernmost summits, on the one hand to the southeast, and on the other to the southwest, and terminating on opposite sides of the Brentwood Pass, through which the direct road to Franklin courses, and situated about nine miles from Nashville. These hills were the background for General Hood's army; his battle line coursed over the detached hills in front, covered in great part with native forests. Overton hill commanded the Franklin turnpike, running along its base, and was intrenched around its northern slope, half-way from base to summit, with a flank running round its eastern descent, and the approaches were obstructed by abatis and other entanglements. This position was exceedingly strong, and the troops holding it had been heavily reinforced during the forenoon.

General Wood sent Colonel Post to reconnoiter the position, who reported that the northern slope was most favorable for assault. As before, his brigade was chosen to form the head of the assaulting column, with Streight's in support. General Steedman designated Thompson's brigade of colored troops, and Grosvenor's, to co-operate in the assault. As preparatory to the advance of these columns, Major Goodspeed, chief of artillery of the Fourth Corps, was ordered to pour a converging fire upon the enemy's batteries, and continue it as long as it could be done with safety to the advancing troops. At 3

P. M. the assaulting columns moved up the steep ascent, covered with a strong line of skirmishers, to draw the enemy's fire and annoy his gunners. The instructions required that the columns should move steadily until near the intrenchments, and then to dash up the ascent and leap the abatis and parapets. The movement promised success until the moment of final issue. The leading men in each column reached the parapets, and a few had gained the works, when the enemy's reserves opened a fire so destructive as to drive back both lines with heavy loss. The colored soldiers suffered equally with the veteran white troops, and with them shared the glory of a gallant but unsuccessful assault. The survivors were reformed at the base of the hill, in readiness for another attack; but Colonel Post was not for the third time to lead, as had received a severe wound.

The advance on the right soon followed the attack upon Overton hill. It had been anticipated that the Twenty-third Corps, facing east, would first advance; but there was so much delay that General McArthur requested permission to carry the strong position before him and General Schofield equally, and although General Thomas desired him to wait until he could hear from General Schofield, and went himself to the right, McArthur, fearing that an opportunity would be lost, directed Colonel McMillen to charge with his brigade and take by storm, the hill upon which rested the left flank of the main line of the enemy. McMillen was directed to ascend from the west, while the other brigades of the division should attack in front, when he should be half-way up to the summit. Colonel McMillen ordered his men to refrain from firing a shot, and from all cheering, until they had gained the works. The One hundred and Fourteenth Illinois, Ninth Indiana, and Eighth Minnesota formed his first line, and the Seventy-second Indiana and the Ninety-fifth Ohio his second. A heavy line of skirmishers moved rapidly forward, and as it advanced, the artillery, in sympathy, gave roar after roar with·quick repetition, while between these sheets of flame and smoke, in the stern silence of desperate valor, the brigade moved up the hill. Hubbard, "eager in emulation," started directly up, followed by Hill's brigade with another leader, and all by Garrard's division. The enemy opened with musketry, and the death-dealing short-range missiles of his artillery; but on, without halt or waver, moved the columns, and soon the position was carried, with three general officers and a large number of lower grades, and a corresponding number of men as prisoners, and twenty-seven pieces of artillery, and twelve stands of colors. The shout of these divisions in victory called forth responsive cheers from those charging on right and left. Wilson, with his dismounted troopers, swept eastward, and, with Coon's brigade, gained the hill, against which the Twenty-third Corps was advancing. Soon after, Doolittle's brigade of Cox's division crowned a fortified position on the right of the salient of the enemy's left flank, the division capturing eight guns and from two hundred and fifty to three hundred prisoners. The noise of Smith's victory moved Wood and Steedman to renew their assault upon Overton hill—their entire commands rushing forward and sweeping all before them, on the summit and beyond as they moved in rapid pursuit. Beatty's division crowned the hill, and captured four pieces of artillery, a large number of prisoners, and two stands of colors; Kimball's cleared the intrenchments in its front, and captured a large number of prisoners and small arms; and Elliott's carried the line throughout its front, and captured five guns and several hundred prisoners and small arms. This general charge was resistless, and the enemy was hurled from every position in utter rout and demoralization. The success of the first day was the inspiration of the second, and officers and men vied with each other in personal daring and persistent, steady courage. General Hood must have regarded his second position stronger than his first, or he would not have attempted to hold it, for all other conditions of the second battle were much more unfavorable to successful resistance than those of the first. The prestige was with the national army, and, on the second day of his last battle, he ought to have known that a victorious iniatitive by a Northern army had more significance than when attained by a Southern one. The Northern armies seldom lost a battle which had a promising beginning, and they often gained them, after the Southern people had been electrified by the rash assumption of victory by their generals, when afterward, on the same field, their initial success was turned into positive defeat, by the pluck and persistence of Northern soldiers.

When General Wilson's command had gained their saddles, which unfortunately was delayed in consequence of the fact, that they had gone far from their horses, as those leading them made slow progress over the broken ground and dense forests, Hatch and Knipe hurried in pursuit. General Hatch was directed to move on the Granny White road and make effort to reach the Franklin turnpike that night. He had, however, proceeded but a short distance, when he met Chalmers' division, strongly posted across the road behind a barricade of rails. Dismounting a portion of his command, he deployed on both sides of the road. While his skirmishers were advancing, Colonel Spalding charged, broke the line, and scattered the force in all directions, capturing Brigadier-General Rucker, for the time in command of the division. The cavalry then bivouacked for the night—Hatch, Knipe, and Croxton on the Granny White road, and Johnson on the Hillsboro road, near the Harpeth river.

The Fourth Corps followed the enemy on the Franklin turnpike, and the frequent discharges of its artillery increased the confusion of the retreat. At dark the corps bivouacked a mile from the village of Brentwood. The line of retreat revealed the fact that General Hood's army had abandoned itself to a most disorderly withdrawal. Small arms and accouterments were strewn thickly along the road, while no effort was made to carry off the wounded or dispose of the dead. The army was not only defeated, but it was broken and crushed, and had the conditions of pursuit proved favorable, even the fragments would have been gathered in capture.

The action of the 15th removed from all in the North the fear of disaster at Nashville, or the invasion of Kentucky. That of the 16th announced the overthrow of the rebellion in the West, and foretold its speedy utter annihilation. There was now no formidable Confederate army between the Mississippi river and Virginia. One of the two armies, upon whose organic life, strength and activity the rebellion rested, was fleeing southward in disorganization and dismay. On no other field of the war had two armies of equal proportions fought with similar issue. Drawn battle or indecisive victory had usually resulted. But now, the Confederate Army of the Tennessee, which had fought with historic honor at Donelson, Shiloh, Perryville, Murfreesboro, Chickamauga, Lookout Mountain, Missionary Ridge, Resaca, New Hope Church, Kenesaw Mountain, Peachtree Creek, Atlanta, Jonesboro, in all the minor battles of "the hundred days under fire," and at Franklin and Nashville, found its grave on a field in close proximity to its first line of defense. Neither was its demoralization rife before its last conflict. There were too many officers and men captured with swords, guns, and colors, within their intrenchments, to warrant the supposition that this historic army, with its traditions of valor and unity on every previous field, came far north in the mere semblance of the boldest aggression, to throw down its arms in shameless disregard of its glorious antecedents. There was, indeed, less loss of life to the victors than usual, but may not this result find explanation in the nice adjustment of strategic and tactical combinations and the almost unprecedented vigor of assault. Successful assaults are never as costly as those which fail, all other things being equal. Thompson's brigade of colored troops lost twenty-five per cent. of its strength in thirty minutes, on the slope of Overton hill; but had not the gallant leader of the main column fallen at the critical moment when a leader's presence and heroism is the ruling condition of successful assault, the soldiers who fell on the parapets and within the enemy's lines might have lived to plant their banners in room of those of treason and rebellion. The story is half told, and the philosophy of the victory is half revealed, by the declaration of a captured general officer, "that powder and lead were inadequate to resist such a charge." The other half of the history of the battle, and the cause of victory, come to light in the palpable co-operation of the chief subordinates with the commander-in-chief in the execution of a definite plan of battle, and the personal supervision of the vital movements by General Thomas. There were no exposed flanks, and no opportunities for stunning offensive returns.

There was only one unsuccessful assault, and that was upon the strongest position of the enemy, manned by the heaviest concentration on his line. No battle of the war manifests more complete prevision of contingencies, or more full provision for emergencies and possibilities. This battle moved on gloriously from its initial feint to the final charge, in the revelation of the highest type of generalship and the highest martial virtues of an entire army. Its immediate fruits were four thousand four hundred and sixty-two prisoners, including one major-general and three brigadiers, and two hundred and eighty officers of lower grades, all the wounded upon the field, fifty-three pieces of artillery, thousands of small arms, and twenty-five battle-flags.

General Thomas and the officers and men of his army were fully alive to the importance of vigorous pursuit. But it had been impossible to make full preparations before the battle, and the bridges on the line of retreat being at the mercy of the enemy, the difficulties in prospect were by no means slight. It was the season of rain, and there were bad roads, and the rivers and creeks which crossed the line of pursuit were full, as well as bridgeless in prospect. In the conduct of the pursuit, General Thomas was put under orders and exhortations, as he had previously been to fight the battle before he considered himself prepared and the conditions promising. During the evening of the 16th, he gave orders for the movements of the next day, and in one single direction to a staff officer he failed to express what he intended. Being roused from rest in his tent, by an officer who was to receive instructions regarding the movement of the pontoon train, he directed it upon the Murfreesboro road instead of the one to Franklin. He did not discover his mistake until the next morning, when he asked as he was riding on the latter road, if the train had passed to the front. It was immediately recalled from the wrong road, and hurried forward, but nevertheless a serious delay resulted.

Having given orders for the care of the wounded, and the collection of the captured and abandoned property, General Thomas commenced the pursuit early in the morning of the 17th. The Fourth Corps pushed on to Franklin through

Brentwood, and the cavalry followed the Granny White road to the junction of the two roads, and then General Wilson hurried past the infantry. In moving upon Franklin, General Wilson kept General Knipe's command on the direct road, and sent Generals Hatch and Croxton to cross the Harpeth above the town.

General Knipe found the enemy strongly posted at Hollow Tree Gap, four miles north of Franklin, and charging him, front and flank, carried the position, and captured four hundred and thirteen men and three flags. At Franklin, he again made a show of resistance, but upon Johnson's approach on the south bank of the river, he retreated toward Columbia.

Beyond the town, Generals Knipe and Hatch moved in parallel columns on the Columbia and Carter's Creek roads, while Johnson followed Knipe, and Croxton advanced on the Lewisburg road. The extreme flanking columns were instructed to press round the flanks of the enemy's rear-guard, composed almost entirely of infantry, while a strong line of skirmishers should attack in the rear—the object being to break up the last organized force which was covering the fugitive and broken columns in rapid retreat. This rear-guard, however, proved very efficient and subtle, preventing any successful flanking, and skirmishing with spirit in the rear, while moving rapidly. Late in the evening, the enemy took a strong position in the open field, about one mile from the West Harpeth. The rapid movement of the cavalry had thrown them into some confusion and intervolution with the enemy, which, with the fog and falling darkness, caused some doubt as to the fact that the force in front was the rear-guard of the enemy. The consequent hesitation gave the enemy opportunity to form his line and post his batteries. As soon as the true state of affairs was ascertained, General Wilson ordered Hatch and Knipe to charge both flanks. The batteries from both sides opened briskly, when Lieutenant Hedges, commanding the Fourth United States Cavalry, with his regiment in column by fours, dashed forward in a saber charge, and broke through the battery. Hatch's division and Hammond's brigade, dismounted, charged at the same time, and the enemy was completely routed. Lieutenant Hedges was three times captured, but escaped at last. The pursuit was vigorous, notwithstanding the darkness. General Hatch, with the Tenth Indiana Cavalry, forded the West Harpeth, and struck the enemy in flank. Being pressed on all sides, the enemy abandoned his guns, and fled in disorder, under cover of the darkness. This rear-guard was Stevenson's division of Lee's corps, under Forrest.

The Fourth Corps reached Franklin a little after noon, but the river had risen so rapidly after the cavalry had crossed, that the infantry were delayed to extemporize a bridge. General Steedman followed General Wood, and encamped near by on the north bank of the Harpeth; the other two corps were in the rear. Trains followed, with rations for ten days, and a hundred rounds of ammunition to each man.

Early on the 18th, General Wilson pursued and endeavored, with Johnson's and Croxton's commands, to strike the enemy at Spring Hill, but he had passed on over Rutherford's creek, destroying the bridges behind him. The roads, even the turnpikes, had become exceedingly bad from the heavy rains and their use by the enemy, and in consequence the pursuit was greatly retarded. General Wood crossed the Harpeth in the morning, and joined General Wilson at night at Rutherford's creek.

The difficulties of the pursuit were now fully apparent, and anticipating the failure of all efforts to intercept Hood's army with his own in direct advance, General Thomas, on the 18th, ordered General Steedman to march his command to Murfreesboro; that passing through Stevenson by rail, he should take the troops of General R. S. Granger, including the former garrisons of Huntsville, Athens, and Decatur, and proceed to the latter place. His instructions required that he should reoccupy the important posts on that line, abandoned at the time of General Hood's advance, and with the remainder of his forces cross the Tennessee river, and threaten the enemy's communications west of Florence.

On the morning of the 19th, Generals Wilson and Wood advanced to Rutherford's creek, whose deep swift current formed a better rear-guard for the enemy than his dispirited infantry and cavalry. During the day, several efforts were made to cross the stream, but all were fruitless. The rain continued and the pontoon train was still in the rear. While the leading columns were thus detained, General Smith reached Spring Hill, and General Schofield crossed the Harpeth at Franklin.

The next morning, General Hatch formed a floating bridge from the debris of the railroad bridge, and crossing with his division advanced rapidly to Columbia, to find that the enemy had succeeded, the evening previous, in passing Duck river and lifting his pontoon bridge. General Wood also crossed by various expedients and encamped near Columbia.

The pontoon train reached Rutherford's creek at noon on the 21st. A bridge was immediately thrown, and the troops and trains passed over and moved to Columbia. The weather now changed from excessive rain to extreme cold; and this greatly retarded the throwing of the bridge over Duck river. The rapid subsidence of the water caused repeated alterations in the length of the bridge, and protracted the delay. General Wood, however, crossed in the evening of the 23d, and encamped two miles south of Columbia. The cavalry crossed the next day and the pursuit was resumed; but by this time General Hood had reformed his rear-guard, and this accomplishment was one of the conditions of his escape. All his best troops had been thrown to his rear, and the interval between his disorganized forces and their pursuers had been greatly increased. Such, too, was the topography of the country, that a small force could compel the deployment of the leading troops, with loss of time. Another difficulty was the impossibility of moving the cavalry off the turnpike on the flanks of the infantry column, as General Thomas had directed, on account of the softness of the soil. As a consequence, the infantry fell in rear of the cavalry; and in this order Generals Wilson and Wood moved toward Pulaski. The former encountered the enemy in the vicinity of Lynnville, and the country being open he was driven rapidly. At Buford's Station, while Hatch was pressing directly forward, Croxton struck the enemy's flank, when he was thrown into rapid retreat. A number of prisoners were captured, and General Buford was wounded.

The enemy moved hurriedly through Pulaski, closely followed by Colonel Harrison's brigade. Harrison's quick movement compelled the enemy to leave the bridge over Richland creek, and hurrying forward he found him intrenched at the head of a ravine through which the road passed. Here his infantry leaped quickly from the intrenchments, brushed back Harrison's skirmishers, and captured one gun of Smith's battery—"I," Fourth United States Artillery. The enemy retained the gun, but left fifty prisoners when Hatch and Hammond moved upon his flanks. On the 26th, the pursuit was continued to Sugar creek, where the enemy was again found in intrenchments, but which he abandoned upon the development of a line of attack.

Here the pursuit was abandoned, as it had been ascertained that General Hood's infantry forces had effected the passage of the Tennessee river at Bainbridge. The gunboats under Admiral Lee had reached Chickasaw, Mississippi, on the 24th, and soon after captured two guns from a battery at Florence. General Steedman reached Decatur on the 28th, having met resistance in crossing the river at that place.

When the pursuit terminated, General Thomas gave orders for the disposition of his forces in winter cantonments, on the line of the Tennessee river, having ulterior aggressive aims. His orders located the Fourth Corps at Huntsville and Athens, Alabama; the Twenty-third Corps at Dalton, Georgia; General Smith's corps at Eastport, Mississippi, and General Wilson's cavalry at Huntsville and Eastport. On the 30th, he announced in orders the conclusion of the campaign, and congratulated his army upon its eminent success.

This was the last invasion of the State of Tennessee by the Confederate Army of the Tennessee, composed largely of troops from that state, many of whom, in the final rout, scattered in all directions, and never again stood under their banners. Indeed, the banners of this army, as such, were never again borne in battle. Exclusive of the multitudes who wandered from his army, General Hood lost by capture thirteen thousand one hundred and eighty-nine men, including seven general officers, sixteen colonels, and nearly one thousand of lower grades, and two thousand by formal desertion. He lost seventy-two pieces of serviceable artillery, seventy stands of colors, and immense quantities of small arms, wagons, pontoons, and other material. If, to the fifteen thousand men reported as prisoners and deserters, there should be added his losses in battle and the never-reported desertions, it is safe to conclude that scarcely one-half of his army recrossed the Tennessee river. The portion of it which did cross, was too dispirited to give further support to the sinking cause.

In the whole campaign, General Thomas lost, in all the forms of casualty, about ten thousand men, a large portion of this aggregate having been slightly wounded.

This campaign, as also the Atlanta campaign, had intimate relations with the operations of General Canby on the Mississippi river. Twice had the Confederate President ordered the armies under Generals Smith and Magruder, west of the great river, to cross to the east—once to aid General Johnston against General Sherman, and again, to join General Hood in his projected advance through Kentucky. General Canby's success in preventing the transfer of these forces in the two cases, eliminated from each the ruling condition of success. He achieved this result by holding the best crossings with strong detachments, and keeping a floating army, in conjunction with the gunboat fleet, in constant motion up and down the river.

NASHVILLE, *November* 29, 1864.
Major-General Steedman, Stevenson:

Your dispatch of 11,30 A. M. to-day received. Concentrate your troops at Cowan, as previously directed, and if the enemy moves over to the N. & C. railroad, act according to instructions given in my telegram of the 25th. When General Smith arrives, and he begins to push the enemy back, you can then proceed to execute the Tuscumbia expedition.

GEO. H. THOMAS,
Major-General U. S. V. Commanding.

NASHVILLE, *November* 30, 1864—3 P. M.
Admiral S. P. Lee:

As soon as the iron-clads return to Paducah, please order them into the Cumberland river, to patrol that river and convoy transports up and down. Hood at present has a cavalry force so much larger than mine that I have been compelled to fall back and concentrate on Nashville. But as soon as I can get my cavalry back from Louisville, I feel confident I can drive him back.

GEO. H. THOMAS,
Major-General U. S. V. Commanding.

BATTLE OF NASHVILLE, ETC. 249

NASHVILLE, *December* 1, 1864—9.30 P. M.
Admiral S. P. Lee:
Your communication by Commander Fitch and telegram of 1 P. M., this date are received, and I am much indebted to you for having changed the destination of the iron-clads. Commander Fitch thinks if the iron-clads you expect at Smithland were stationed at Clarksville, the river then would be made perfectly safe. Will you please order them to Clarksville?

GEO. H. THOMAS,
Major-General U. S. V. Commanding.

NASHVILLE, *December* 3, 1864.
Admiral S. P. Lee, Mound City:
Your telegram of yesterday received last night. My force of cavalry and infantry at Franklin being so much less than that of the enemy, I determined to fall back to this place to concentrate my infantry and give time to General Wilson to arm and equip sufficient cavalry to meet Forrest. I have here now nearly as much infantry as Hood, and in a few days hope to have cavalry enough to enable me to assume the offensive. In the meantime, Captain Fitch has cheerfully complied with my request to patrol the river above and below the city. I am therefore in hopes we shall, in a few days, be able to take the offensive on pretty even terms with the enemy. I regret much that my telegram of the 30th implied an order to you, which was not intended. With many thanks for your previous prompt co-operations,

I am, yours truly,

GEO. H. THOMAS,
Major-General U. S. V. Commanding.

HEADQUARTERS DEPARTMENT OF THE CUMBERLAND,
December 9, 1864.
Major-General J. M. Schofield, Commanding Twenty-third Army Corps:
Owing to the severity of the storm raging to-day, it is found necessary to postpone the operations designed for to-morrow morning until the breaking up of the storm. I desire, however, that everything be put in condition to carry out the plan contemplated as soon as the weather will permit it to be done, so that we can act instantly when the storm clears away. Acknowledge receipt.

GEO. H. THOMAS,
Major-General U. S. V. Commanding.

Sent to Major-General A. J. Smith, commanding detachment Army of Tennessee; Major-General J. B. Steedman, commanding District of Etowah, and Brigadier-General Thomas J. Wood, commanding Fourth Army Corps.

HEADQUARTERS DEPARTMENT OF THE CUMBERLAND,
December 10, 1864.
Brigadier-General Thomas J. Wood, Commanding Fourth Army Corps:
What is the condition of the ground between the enemy's line and your own? Is it practicable for men to move about on it with facility? I would like your opinion about it.

GEO. H. THOMAS,
Major-General U. S. V. Commanding.

NASHVILLE, *December* 11, 1864.
Major-Generals Schofield, Steedman, Smith, and Brigadier-General Wood:
Have your commands put in readiness to-morrow for operations. I wish to see you at my headquarters at 3 P. M. to-morrow. Acknowledge receipt.

GEO. H. THOMAS,
Major-General U. S. V. Commanding.

NASHVILLE, *December* 1, 1864—9.30 P. M
Major-General Halleck, Washington, D. C.:
After General Schofield's fight of yesterday, feeling convinced that the enemy very far outnumbered him both in infantry and cavalry, I determined to retire to the fortifications around Nashville, until General Wilson can get his cavalry equipped. He has now but about one-fourth the number of the enemy, and consequently is no match for him. I have two iron-clads here with several gunboats, and Commander Fitch assures me that Hood can neither cross the Cumberland nor blockade it. I therefore think it best to wait here until Wilson can equip all his cavalry. If Hood attacks me here, he will be more seriously damaged than he was yesterday. If he remains until Wilson gets equipped, I can whip him, and will move against him at once. I have Murfreesboro strongly held, and therefore feel easy in regard to its safety. Chattanooga, Bridgeport, Stevenson, and Elk river bridges have strong garrisons.

(Signed,) GEO. H. THOMAS,
Major-General U. S. V. Commanding.

WAR DEPARTMENT,
WASHINGTON, *December* 2—10.30 A. M.
Lieutenant-General Grant, City Point:
The President feels solicitous about the disposition of Thomas, to lay in fortifications for an indefinite period "until Wilson gets equipments." This looks like the McClellan and Rosecrans strategy of do nothing, and let the enemy raid the country. The President writes you to consider the matter.

EDWIN M. STANTON,
Secretary of War.

CITY POINT, VA., *December 2, 1864*—11 A. M.

Major-General Geo. H. Thomas, Nashville:

If Hood is permitted to remain quietly about Nashville, we will lose all the roads back to Chattanooga, and possibly have to abandon the line of the Tennessee river. Should he attack you, it is all well, but if he does not, you should attack him before he fortifies. Arm and put in the trenches your quartermaster's employes, citizens, etc.

    (Signed,)   U. S. GRANT,
                  Lieutenant-General.

CITY POINT, VA., *December 2, 1864*—1.30 P. M.

Major-General Geo. H. Thomas, Nashville:

With your citizen employes armed, you can move out of Nashville with all your army, and force the enemy to retire or fight upon ground of your own choosing. After the repulse of Hood at Franklin, it looks to me that instead of falling back to Nashville, we should have taken the offensive against the enemy, but at this distance may err as to the method of dealing with the enemy. You will suffer incalculable injury upon your railroads, if Hood is not speedily disposed of. Put forth, therefore, every possible exertion to attain this end. Should you get him to retreating, give him no peace.

    (Signed,)   U. S. GRANT,
                  Lieutenant-General.

HEADQUARTERS DEPARTMENT OF THE CUMBERLAND,
NASHVILLE, TENN., *December 2, 1864*—10 P. M.

General U. S. Grant, City Point, Va.:

Your two telegrams of 11 A. M. and 1.30 P. M. to-day are received. At the time Hood was whipped at Franklin, I had at this place but about five thousand (5,000) men of General Smith's command, which, added to the force under General Schofield, would not have given me more than twenty-five thousand (25,000) men. Besides, General Schofield felt convinced that he could not hold the enemy at Franklin until the five thousand could reach him. As General Wilson's cavalry force also numbered only about one-fourth that of Forrest, I thought it best to draw the troops back to Nashville, and await the arrival of the remainder of General Smith's force, and also a force of about five thousand (5,000) commanded by General Steedman, which I had ordered up from Chattanooga. The division of General Smith arrived yesterday morning, and General Steedman's troops arrived last night. I now have infantry enough to assume the offensive, if I had more cavalry; and will take the field anyhow as soon as the remainder of General McCook's division of cavalry reaches here, which I hope it will in two or three days.

We can neither get reinforcements nor equipments at this great distance from the North very easily, and it must be remembered that my command was made up of the two weakest corps of General Sherman's

army, and all the dismounted cavalry except one brigade; and the task of reorganizing and equipping has met with many delays, which have enabled Hood to take advantage of my crippled condition. I earnestly hope, however, in a few more days, I shall be able to give him a fight.
    (Signed,)   GEO. H. THOMAS,
        Major-General U. S. V. Commanding.

      CITY POINT, VA., *December 5, 1864—6.30 P. M.*
Major-General Geo. H. Thomas, Nashville, Tenn.:
 Is there not danger of Forrest's moving down the Tennessee river where he can cross it? It seems to me, while you should be getting up your cavalry as rapidly as possible to look after Forrest, Hood should be attacked where he is.
 Time strengthens him, in all probability, as much as it does you.
    (Signed,)   U. S. GRANT,
        Lieutenant-General.

      NASHVILLE, *December 6, 1864.*
Lieutenant-General U. S. Grant, City Point:
 Your telegram of 6.30 P. M., December 5th, is just received. As soon as I get up a respectable force of cavalry I will march against Hood. General Wilson has parties out now pressing horses, and I hope to have some six or eight thousand cavalry mounted in three days from this time. General Wilson has just left me, having received instructions to hurry the cavalry to remount as rapidly as possible. I do not think it prudent to attack Hood with less than six thousand (6,000) cavalry to cover my flanks, because he has under Forrest at least twelve thousand (12,000). I have no doubt Forrest will attempt to cross the river, but I am in hopes the gunboats will be able to prevent him. The enemy has made no new developments to-day. Breckinridge is reported at Lebanon with six thousand (6,000) men, but I can not believe it possible.
    (Signed,)   GEO. H. THOMAS,
        Major-General U. S. V. Commanding.

      CITY POINT, VA., *December 6, 1864—4 P. M.*
Major-General Geo. H. Thomas, Nashville:
 Attack Hood at once, and wait no longer for a remount for your cavalry. There is great danger in delay, resulting in a campaign back to the Ohio.
    (Signed,)   U. S. GRANT,
        Lieutenant-General.

      NASHVILLE, *December 6, 1864—9 P. M.*
Lieutenant-General U. S. Grant, City Point:
 Your dispatch of 4 P. M. this day received. I will make the necessary disposition and attack Hood at once, agreeably to your orders, though I

believe it will be hazardous with the small force of cavalry now at my service.
(Signed,) GEO. H. THOMAS,
Major-General U. S. V. Commanding.

WAR DEPARTMENT,
WASHINGTON, *December* 7, 1864—10.20 A. M.
Lieutenant-General Grant:
You remember that when Steele was relieved by Canby he was ordered to Cairo, to report to this department. What shall be done with him? The order superseding Rosecrans by Dodge has been issued. Thomas seems unwilling to attack because it is hazardous, as if all war was any but hazardous. If he waits for Wilson to get ready, Gabriel will be blowing his last horn.
EDWIN M. STANTON.

CITY POINT, VA., *December* 8, 1864.
Major-General Halleck, Washington:
Please direct General Dodge to send all the troops he can spare to General Thomas. With such an order, he can be relied on to send all that can properly go. They had probably better be sent to Louisville, for I fear either Hood or Breckinridge will go to the Ohio river. I will submit whether it is not advisable to call on Ohio, Indiana, and Illinois, for 60,000 men for thirty days. If Thomas has not struck yet, he ought to be ordered to hand over his command to Schofield. There is no better man to repel an attack than Thomas, but I fear he is too cautious to take the initiative.
U. S. GRANT,
Lieutenant-General.

WAR DEPARTMENT,
WASHINGTON, D. C., *December* 8, 1864.
Lieutenant-General Grant, City Point:
If you wish General Thomas relieved, give the order. No one here will, I think, interfere. The responsibility, however, will be yours, as no one here, so far as I am informed, wishes General Thomas removed.
H. W. HALLECK,
Major-General, Chief of Staff.

NASHVILLE, TENN., *December* 7, 1864—9 P. M.
Major-General H. W. Halleck, Washington, D. C.:
The enemy has not increased his force on our front. Have sent gunboats up the river above Carthage. One returned to-day, and reported no signs of the enemy on the river bank from forty miles above Carthage to this place. Captain Fitch, U. S. navy, started down the river yesterday, with a convoy of transport steamers, but was unable to get them down, the enemy having planted three batteries on a bend of the river, between this and Clarksville. Captain Fitch was unable to silence all

three of the batteries yesterday, and will return again to-morrow morning, and, with the assistance of the Cincinnati, now at Clarksville, I am in hopes will now be able to clear them out. So far the enemy has not materially injured the Nashville and Chattanooga railroad.

     (Signed),   GEO. H. THOMAS,
            Major-General U. S. V. Commanding.

        CITY POINT, VA., *December* 8, 1864—7.30 P. M.
Major-General Geo. H. Thomas, Nashville:

Your dispatch of yesterday received. It looks to me evidently the enemy are trying to cross the Cumberland, and are scattered. Why not attack at once? By all means avoid the contingency of a foot-race to see which, you or Hood, can beat to the Ohio. If you think necessary, call on the governors of states to send a force into Louisville to meet the enemy if he should cross the river. You clearly never should cross, except in rear of the enemy. Now is one of the fairest opportunities ever presented of destroying one of the three armies of the enemy. If destroyed, he can never replace it. Use the means at your command, and you can do this and cause a rejoicing from one end of the land to the other.

     (Signed,)   U. S. GRANT,
              Lieutenant-General.

        CITY POINT, VA., *December* 8, 1864—10 P. M.
Major-General Halleck, Washington:

Your dispatch of 9 P. M. just received. I want General Thomas reminded of the importance of immediate action. I sent him a dispatch this evening, which will probably urge him on. I would not say relieve him until I hear further from him.

               U. S. GRANT,
              Lieutenant-General.

       NASHVILLE, TENN., *December* 8, 1864—11.30 P. M.
Lieutenant-General U. S. Grant, City Point, Va.:

Your dispatch of 7.30 P. M. is just received. I can only say, in further extenuation why I have not attacked Hood, that I could not concentrate my troops, and get their transportation in order, in shorter time than it has been done, and am satisfied I have made every effort that was possible to complete the task.

              GEO. H. THOMAS,
             Major-General Commanding.

        WASHINGTON, *December* 9, 1864—10.30 A. M.
Major-General George H. Thomas, Nashville, Tenn.:

Lieutenant-General Grant expresses much dissatisfaction at your delay in attacking the enemy. If you wait till General Wilson mounts all his cavalry, you will wait till doomsday, for the waste equals the supply. Moreover, you will be in the same condition that Rosecrans was last year, with so many animals that you can not feed them. Reports already come in of a scarcity of forage.

(Signed,)   H. W. HALLECK,
Major-General and Chief of Staff.

CITY POINT, VA., *December* 9, 1864—11 A. M.
Major-General Halleck, Washington, D. C.:

Dispatch of 8 P. M. last evening, from Nashville, shows the enemy scattered for more than seventy miles down the river, and no attack yet made by Thomas. Please telegraph orders relieving him at once, and placing Schofield in command. Thomas should be ordered to turn over all orders and dispatches received since the battle of Franklin, to Schofield.

U. S. GRANT,
Lieutenant-General.

[GENERAL ORDERS NO. —.]

WAR DEPARTMENT, ADJUTANT-GENERAL'S OFFICE,
WASHINGTON, *December* 9, 1864.

The following dispatch having been received from Lieutenant-General Grant, viz, "Please telegraph orders relieving him (General Thomas) at once, and placing (General) Schofield in command," the President orders:

I. That Major-General J. M. Schofield relieve at once Major-General G. H. Thomas in command of the Department and Army of the Cumberland.

II. General Thomas will turn over to General Schofield all orders and instructions received by him since the battle of Franklin.

E. D. TOWNSEND,
Assistant Adjutant-General.

NASHVILLE, *December* 9, 1864—2 P. M.
Major-General H. W. Halleck, Washington, D. C.:

Your dispatch of 10.30 A. M. this date is received. I regret that General Grant should feel dissatisfaction at my delay in attacking the enemy. I feel conscious that I have done everything in my power to prepare, and that the troops could not have been gotten ready before this. And if he should order me to be relieved, I will submit without a murmur.

A terrible storm of freezing rain has come on since daylight, which will render an attack impossible till it breaks.

(Signed,)   GEO. H. THOMAS,
Major-General U. S. V. Commanding.

NASHVILLE, TENN., *December* 9, 1864—1 P. M.
Lieutenant-General U. S. Grant, City Point:
Your dispatch of 8.30 P. M. of the 8th is just received. I have nearly completed my preparations to attack the enemy to-morrow morning, but a terrible storm of freezing rain has come on to-day, which will make it impossible for our men to fight to any advantage. I am therefore compelled to wait for the storm to break, and make the attack immediately after. Admiral Lee is patrolling the river above and below the city, and I believe will be able to prevent the enemy from crossing. There is no doubt but Hood's forces are considerably scattered along the river, with the view of attempting a crossing, but it has been impossible for me to organize and equip the troops for an attack at an earlier time. Major-General Halleck informs me that you are very much dissatisfied with my delay in attacking. I can only say I have done all in my power to prepare, and if you should deem it necessary to relieve me, I shall submit without a murmur.
(Signed,) GEO. H. THOMAS,
Major-General U. S. V. Commanding.

WAR DEPARTMENT, WASHINGTON, *December* 9, 1864—4 P. M.
Lieutenant-General Grant, City Point:
Orders relieving General Thomas had been made out when his telegram of this P. M. was received. If you still wish these orders telegraphed to Nashville, they will be forwarded.
H. W. HALLECK,
Chief of Staff.

CITY POINT, VA., *December* 9, 1864—5.30 P. M.
Major-General Halleck, Washington:
General Thomas has been urged in every possible way to attack the enemy; even to the giving the positive order. He did say he thought he should be able to attack on the 7th, but he did not do so, nor has he given a reason for not doing it. I am very unwilling to do injustice to an officer who has done so much good service as General Thomas has, however, and will therefore suspend the order relieving him until it is seen whether he will do anything.
U. S. GRANT,
Lieutenant-General.

CITY POINT, VA., *December* 9, 1864—7.30 P. M.
Major-General Thomas, Nashville:
Your dispatch of 1 P. M. to-day is received. I have as much confidence in your conducting the battle rightly as I have in any other officer, but it has seemed to me you have been slow, and I have had no explanation of affairs to convince me otherwise. Receiving your dispatch to Major-General Halleck of 2 P. M. before I did the first to me, I telegraphed to

BATTLE OF NASHVILLE, ETC. 257

suspend the order relieving you, until we should hear further. I hope most sincerely that there will be no necessity of repeating the order, and that the facts will show that you have been right all the time.
(Signed,) U. S. GRANT,
Lieutenant-General.

CITY POINT, VA., *December* 11, 1864—4 P. M.
Major-General Geo. H. Thomas, Nashville:
If you delay attacking longer, the mortifying spectacle will be witnessed of a rebel army moving for the Ohio, and you will be forced to act, accepting such weather as you find. Let there be no further delay. Hood can not stand even a drawn battle so far from his supplies of ordnance stores. If he retreats and you follow, he must lose his material and most of his army. I am in hopes of receiving a dispatch from you to-day announcing that you have moved. Delay no longer for weather or reinforcements.
U. S. GRANT,
Lieutenant-General.

NASHVILLE, TENN., *December* 11, 1864—10.30 P. M.
Lieutenant-General U. S. Grant, City Point, Va.:
Your dispatch of 4 P. M. this day is just received. I will obey the order as promptly as possible, however much I may regret it, as the attack will have to be made under every disadvantage. The whole country is covered with a perfect sheet of ice and sleet, and it is with difficulty the troops are able to move about on level ground. It was my intention to attack Hood as soon as the ice melted, and would have done so yesterday had it not been for the storm.
(Signed,) GEO. H. THOMAS,
Major-General U. S. V. Commanding.

NASHVILLE, TENN., *December* 12, 1864—10.30 P. M.
Major-General Halleck, Washington, D. C.:
I have the troops ready to make the attack on the enemy as soon as the sleet which now covers the ground has melted sufficiently to enable the men to march. As the whole country is now covered with a sheet of ice so hard and slippery, it is utterly impossible for troops to ascend the slopes, or even move over level ground in anything like order. It has taken the entire day to place my cavalry in position, and it has only been finally effected with imminent risk, and many serious accidents, resulting from the numbers of horses falling with their riders on the road. Under these circumstances, I believe that an attack at this time would only result in a useless sacrifice of life.
(Signed,) GEO. H. THOMAS,
Major-General U. S. V. Commanding.

[SPECIAL ORDERS, NO. 149.]

HEADQUARTERS OF THE ARMIES OF THE UNITED STATES,
CITY POINT, VA., *December* 13, 1864.

I. Major-General John A. Logan, United States Volunteers, will proceed immediately to Nashville, Tennessee, reporting by telegraph to the lieutenant-general his arrival at Louisville, Kentucky, and also his arrival at Nashville, Tennessee.

* * * * * * * * *

By command of Lieutenant-General Grant.
(Signed,) T. S. BOWERS,
Assistant Adjutant-General.

Major-General Geo. H. Thomas, Nashville:

It has been seriously apprehended that while Hood, with a part of his forces, held you in check near Nashville, he would have time to co-operate against other important points, left only partially protected. Hence, Lieutenant-General Grant was anxious that you should attack the rebel forces in your front, and expresses great dissatisfaction that his order had not been carried out. Moreover, so long as Hood occupies a threatening position in Tennessee, General Canby is obliged to keep large forces on the Mississippi river to protect its navigation, and to hold Memphis, Vicksburg, etc., although General Grant had directed a part of these forces to co-operate with Sherman.

Every day's delay on your part, therefore, seriously interferes with General Grant's plans.

(Signed,) H. W. HALLECK,
Major-General and Chief of Staff.

NASHVILLE, *December* 14, 1864—8 P. M.

Major-General H. W. Halleck, Washington, D. C.:

Your telegram of 12.30 M. to-day is received. The ice having melted away to-day, the enemy will be attacked to-morrow morning. Much as I regret the apparent delay in attacking the enemy, it could not have been done before with any reasonable prospect of success.

(Signed,) GEO. H. THOMAS,
Major-General U. S. V. Commanding.

NASHVILLE, TENN., *December* 15, 1864—9 P. M.

Major-General Halleck, Chief of Staff:

Attacked enemy's left this morning; drove it from the river, below city, very nearly to Franklin pike, distance about eight miles.

(Signed,) GEO. H. THOMAS,
Major-General.

BATTLE OF NASHVILLE, ETC. 259

WASHINGTON, *December* 15, 1864—11.30 P. M.
Major-General Geo. H. Thomas, Nashville:
I was just on my way to Nashville, but receiving a dispatch from Van Duzen, detailing your splendid success of to-day, I shall go no farther. Push the enemy now, and give him no rest until he is entirely destroyed. Your army will cheerfully suffer many privations to break up Hood's army, and make it useless for future operations. Do not stop for trains or supplies, but take them from the country, as the enemy has done. Much is now expected.
    (Signed,)   U. S. GRANT,
                                 Lieutenant-General.

[GENERAL ORDERS, NO. 160.]
        HEADQUARTERS DEPARTMENT OF THE CUMBERLAND,
        NEAR NASHVILLE, TENN., *December* 16, 1864.
The major-general commanding, with pride and pleasure, publishes the following dispatches to the army, and adds thereto his own thanks to the troops for the unsurpassed gallantry and good conduct displayed by them in the battles of yesterday and to-day. A few more examples of devotion and courage like these, and the rebel army of the West, which you have been fighting for three years will be no more, and you may reasonably expect an early and honorable peace:

WASHINGTON, D. C., *December* 16—11.20 A. M.
To Major-General Thomas:
Please accept for yourself, officers, and men the nation's thanks for your work of yesterday. You made a magnificent beginning. A grand consummation is within your easy reach. Do not let it slip.
                                 A. LINCOLN.

WASHINGTON, *December* 15, 1864—12 MIDNIGHT.
Major-General Thomas:
I rejoice in tendering to you, and the gallant officers and soldiers of your command, the thanks of this department for the brilliant achievement of this day, and hope that it is the harbinger of a decisive victory that will crown you and your army with honor, and do much toward closing the war. We shall give you a hundred (100) guns in the morning.
                                 E. M. STANTON,
                                     Secretary of War.

WASHINGTON, *December* 15, 1864—12 MIDNIGHT.
Major-General Geo. H. Thomas, Nashville:
Your dispatch of this evening just received. I congratulate you and the army under your command for to-day's operations, and feel a conviction that to-morrow will add more fruits to your victory.
    (Signed,)   U. S. GRANT,
                                 Lieutenant-General.
By command of Major-General Thomas.
                         WM. D. WHIPPLE,
                             Assistant Adjutant-General.

HEADQUARTERS DEPARTMENT OF THE CUMBERLAND
SIX MILES FROM NASHVILLE, *December* 16, 1864.

The President of the United States, Hon. E. M. Stanton, and General U. S. Grant, Washington, D. C.:

This army thanks you for your approbation of its conduct yesterday, and to assure you that it is not misplaced, I have the honor to report that the enemy has been pressed at all points to-day on his line of retreat through the Brentwood hills, and Brigadier-General Hatch, of Wilson's corps of cavalry, on the right, turned the enemy's left and captured a large number of prisoners; number not yet reported. Major-General Schofield's troops, next on the left of cavalry, carried several heights, captured many prisoners and six pieces of artillery. Brevet Major-General Smith, next on the left Major-General Schofield, carried the salient point of the enemy's line, with McMillen's brigade of McArthur's division, capturing sixteen pieces of artillery, two brigadier-generals, and about two thousand prisoners. Brigadier-General Garrard's division of Smith's command, next on the left of McArthur's division, carried the enemy's intrenchments, capturing all the artillery and troops on the line. Brigadier-General Wood's corps, on the Franklin pike, took up the assault, carried the enemy's intrenchments in his front, captured eight (8) pieces, something over six hundred prisoners, and drove the enemy within one mile of the Brentwood Pass. Major-General Steedman, commanding detachments of the Military Division of the Mississippi, most nobly supported General Wood's left, and bore a most honorable part in the operations of the day. I have ordered the pursuit to be continued in the morning at daylight, although the troops are very much fatigued. The greatest enthusiasm prevails. I must not forget to report the operations of Brigadier-General Johnson, in successfully driving the enemy, with co-operation of the gunboats, under Lieutenant-Commander Fitch, from their established batteries on the Cumberland river below the city of Nashville, and the of services of Brigadier-General Croxton's brigade, in covering and relieving our right and rear in the operations of yesterday and to-day. Although I have no report of the number of prisoners captured by Johnson's and Croxton's commands, I know they have made a large number. I am glad to be able to state that the number of prisoners captured yesterday greatly exceeds the number reported by me last evening. The roads, fields, and intrenchments are strewn with the enemy's abandoned small arms, abandoned in their retreat. In conclusion, I am happy to state that all this has been effected with but a very small loss to us. Our loss does not probably exceed three thousand, very few killed.

GEO. H. THOMAS,
Major-General U. S. V. Commanding.

WASHINGTON, *December* 18, 1864—12 M.
Major-General Thomas:

The armies operating against Richmond have fired two prolonged guns in honor of your great victory. Sherman has fully established his base on Ossabaw Sound, with Savannah fully invested. I hope to be able to fire a salute to-morrow in honor of the fall of Savannah. In all your operations, we hear nothing of Forrest. Great precaution should be taken to prevent him crossing the Cumberland or Tennessee rivers below Eastport. After Hood is driven as far as possible to follow him, you want to re-occupy Decatur and all other abandoned points.

U. S. GRANT,
Lieutenant-General.

WASHINGTON, *December* 21, 1864—12 M.
Major-General Geo. H. Thomas:

Permit me, general, to urge the vast importance of a hot pursuit of Hood's army. Every possible sacrifice should be made, and your men for a few days will submit to any hardships and privations to accomplish the great result. If you can capture or destroy Hood's army, General Sherman can entirely crush out the rebel military force in all the Southern States. He begins a new campaign about the first of January, which will have the most important results if Hood's army can now be used up. A most vigorous pursuit on your part is therefore of vital importance to General Sherman's plans. No sacrifice must be spared to obtain so important a result.

(Signed,) H. W. HALLECK,
Major-General and Chief of Staff.

IN THE FIELD, *December* 21, 1864.
Major-General Halleck, Washington, D. C.:

Your dispatch of 12 M. this day is received. General Hood's army is being pursued as rapidly and as vigorously as it is possible for one army to pursue another. We can not control the elements, and you must remember that, to resist Hood's advance into Tennessee, I had to reorganize and almost thoroughly equip the force now under my command. I fought the battles of the 15th and 16th insts. with the troops but partially equipped, and notwithstanding the inclemency of the weather and the partial equipment, have been enabled to drive the enemy beyond Duck river, crossing two streams with my troops, and driving the enemy from position to position, without the aid of pontoons, and with but little transportation to bring up supplies of provisions and ammunition. I am doing all in my power to crush Hood's army, and, if it be possible, will destroy it. But pursuing an enemy through an exhausted country, over mud roads completely sogged with heavy rains, is no child's play, and can not be accomplished as quickly as thought of. I hope, in urging me to push the enemy, the department remembers that General Sherman took with him the complete organization of the Military Division of the Mississippi, well equipped in every respect, as regards ammunition, supplies, and transportation, leaving me only two corps, partially stripped of their transportation, to accommodate the force taken with him, to oppose the advance into Tennessee of that army which had resisted the advance of the army of the Military Division of the Mississippi on Atlanta, from the commencement of the campaign till its close, and which is now in addition aided by Forrest's cavalry. Although my progress may appear slow, I feel assured that Hood's army can be driven from Tennessee, and eventually driven to the wall by the force under my command. But too much must not be expected of troops which have to be reorganized, especially when they have the task of destroying a force, in a winter's campaign, which was able to make an obstinate resistance to twice its numbers in spring and summer. In conclusion, I can safely state that the army is willing to submit to any sacrifice to oust Hood's army, or to strike any other blow which may contribute to the destruction of the rebellion.

  (Signed,)   GEO. H. THOMAS,
                               Major-General.

                CITY POINT, *December* 22, 1864.
Major-General Geo. H. Thomas:

You have the congratulations of the public for the energy with which you are pushing Hood. I hope you will succeed in reaching his pontoon bridge at Tuscumbia before he gets there. Should you do so, it looks to me that Hood is cut off. If you succeed in destroying Hood's army, there will be but one army left to the so-called Confederacy capable of doing us harm. I will take care of that, and try to draw the sting from it, so that in the spring we shall have easy sailing. You have now a big opportunity, which I know you are availing yourself of. Let us push and do all we can before the enemy can derive benefit either from the raising of negro troops on the plantations, or white troops now in the field.

  (Signed,)   U. S. GRANT,
                              Lieutenant-General.

              WASHINGTON, *December* 22, 1864—9 P. M.
Major-General Geo. H. Thomas:

I have seen to-day General Halleck's dispatch of yesterday, and your reply. It is proper for me to assure you that this department has the most unbounded confidence in your skill, vigor, and determination to employ to the best advantage all the means in your power to pursue and destroy the enemy. No department could be inspired with more profound admiration and thankfulness for the great deed which you have already performed, or more confiding faith that human effort could do no more, and no more than will be done by you and the accomplished gallant officers and soldiers of your command.

  (Signed,)   E. M. STANTON.

WASHINGTON, *December* 22, 1864—9 P. M.
Major-General Thomas:
In order that the department may, as fully as the case will permit, award due promotions to your army, please forward, some time before the 5th of next month, a list of such promotions as you desire to recommend. There is no vacancy in the number of major-generals by law, and only two— but brevets can be granted, and some vacancies may be created by mustering out useless officers.

E. M. STANTON,
Secretary of War.

HEADQUARTERS DEPARTMENT OF THE CUMBERLAND,
COLUMBIA, *December* 23, 1864—8 P. M.
Major-General II. W. Halleck, Washington, D. C.:
The troops are still crossing Duck river, and all close up to the enemy's rear-guard, on the Pulaski road. I hope to get the whole force across to-morrow, and continue the pursuit. The railroad bridges between Spring Hill and this place, five in number, have been destroyed, but the construction corps is hard at work, and I am in hopes will have the road repaired up to Columbia in the course of four or five days. The railroad between Chattanooga and Murfreesboro is in running order, and I am assured that the road between Nashville and Murfreesboro will be repaired in a few days. General McCook has routed and scattered the rebel General Lyon, who succeded in crossing the Cumberland river, and with General Long, will soon join General Wilson, thus increasing my cavalry force sufficiently to enable me to completely destroy Forrest, if I can overtake him, which I shall make every exertion to do.

GEO. H. THOMAS,
Major-General U. S. V. Commanding.

HEADQUARTERS DEPARTMENT OF THE CUMBERLAND,
December 23, 1864—8 P. M.
Hon. E. M. Stanton, Secretary of War, Washington, D. C.:
Your two dispatches of 9 P. M., 22d, are received. I am profoundly thankful for the hearty expression of your confidence in my determination, and desire to do all in my power to destroy the enemy, and put down the rebellion; and in the name of this army, I thank you for the complimentary notice you have taken of all connected with it, for the deeds of valor they have performed. I will forward the list of meritorious officers to-morrow or next day.

GEO. H. THOMAS,
Major-General U. S. V. Commanding.

HEADQUARTERS MILITARY DIVISION OF THE MISSISSIPPI,
IN THE FIELD, SAVANNAH, GA., *December* 23, 1864.

DEAR GENERAL:—Major Dixon arrived last night, bringing your letter of the 10th December, for which I am very much obliged, as it gives me a clear and distinct view of the situation of affairs at Nashville up to that date. I have also from the War Department a copy of General Thomas' dispatch, giving an account of the attack on Hood on the 15th, which was successful, but not complete. I await further accounts with anxiety, as Thomas' complete success is necessary to initiate my plans for this campaign, and I have no doubt that my calculation, that Thomas had in hand (including A. J. Smith's troops) a force large enough to whip Hood in fair fight, was correct. I approved of Thomas' allowing Hood to come north far enough to enable him to concentrate his own men, though I would have preferred that Hood should have been checked about Columbia. Still, if Thomas followed up his success of the 15th, and gave Hood a good whaling, and is at this moment following him closely, the whole campaign in my division will be even more perfect than the Atlanta campaign, for at this end of the line I have realized all I had reason to hope for, except in the release of our prisoners, which was simply an impossibility.

December 24.—I have just received a letter from General Grant, giving a detail of General Thomas' operations up to the 18th, and I am gratified beyond measure at the result.

Show this letter to General Thomas, and tell him to consider it addressed to him, as I have not time to write more now. I want General Thomas to follow Hood to and beyond the Tennessee, and not hesitate to go on as far as Columbus, Mississippi, or Selma, Alabama, as I know that he will have no trouble whatever in subsisting his army anywhere below Sand Mountain, and along the Black Warrior. In the poorest part of Georgia, I found no trouble in subsisting my army and animals, some of my corps not issuing but one (1) day's bread from Atlanta to Savannah.

Keep me fully advised by telegraph, via New York, of the situation of affairs in Tennessee. I will be here probably ten (10) days longer, and in communication for a longer time.

I am, very truly yours,
W. T. SHERMAN,
Major-General.

General J. D. *Webster, Nashville, Tenn.*

HEADQUARTERS DEPARTMENT OF THE CUMBERLAND,
PULASKI, TENN., *December* 28, 1864.

Major-General Steedman, Decatur, Ala.:

Your dispatch of the 27th received. I am very much gratified with your operations against Decatur. The roads from here to Florence are in an almost impassable condition, and the country is so completely devastated that we scarcely get any supplies; but the enemy has been as vigorously pursued as circumstances will admit. It is reported that Hood crossed at Lamb's ferry and Bainbridge, with what force he could get off. He is represented as being in a most deplorable condition. I shall try to intercept him at Iuka, if he retreats that way, and I want you to push a strong reconnoissance toward Lamb's ferry, to see if he has retreated by way of Courtland and Moulton.

GEO. H. THOMAS,
Major-General U. S. V. Commanding.

[GENERAL ORDERS, NO. 169.]

PULASKI, *December* 29, 1864.

SOLDIERS:—The major-general commanding announces to you that the rear-guard of the flying and dispirited enemy was driven across the Tennessee river, on the night of the 27th instant. The impassable state of the roads, and consequent impossibility to supply the army, compels a closing of the campaign for the present.

Although short, it has been brilliant in its achievements, and unsurpassed in its results by any other of this war, and is one of which all who participated therein may be justly proud. That veteran army which, though driven from position to position, opposed a stubborn resistance to much superior numbers during the whole of the Atlanta campaign, taking advantage of the absence of the largest portion of the army which had been opposed to it in Georgia, invaded Tennessee, buoyant with hope, expecting Nashville, Murfreesboro, and the whole of Tennessee and Kentucky to fall into its power, an easy prey, and scarcely fixing a limit to its conquests. After having received, at Franklin, the most terrible check that army has received during this war, and later, at Murfreesboro, in its attempt to capture that place, it was finally attacked at Nashville, and, although your forces were inferior to it in numbers, was hurled back from the coveted prize, on which it had been permitted to look from a distance, and finally sent flying, dismayed and disordered, whence it came, impelled by the instinct of self-preservation, and thinking only of how it could relieve itself for short intervals from your persistent and harassing pursuit, by burning the bridges over the swollen streams, as it passed them, until, finally, it had placed the broad waters of the Tennessee river between you and its shattered, diminished, and discomfited columns, leaving its artillery and battle-flags in your victorious hands—lasting trophies of your noble daring, and lasting monuments of the enemy's disgrace and defeat.

You have diminished the forces of the rebel army since it crossed the Tennessee river to invade the state, at the least estimate, fifteen thousand men, among whom were killed, wounded, and captured eighteen general officers.

Your captures from the enemy, as far as reported, amount to sixty-eight pieces of artillery, ten thousand prisoners, as many stand of small arms—

several thousand of which have been gathered in, and the remainder strew the route of the enemy's retreat—and between thirty and forty flags, besides compelling him to destroy much ammunition and abandon many wagons; and, unless he is mad, he must forever abandon all hope of bringing Tennessee again within the lines of the accursed rebellion.

A short time will now be given you to prepare to continue the work so nobly begun.

By command of Major-General Thomas.

W. D. WHIPPLE,
Assistant Adjutant-General.

EXTRACTS FROM GENERAL GEO. H. THOMAS' REPORT.

On the morning of the 15th of December, the weather being favorable, the army was formed, and ready at an early hour to carry out the plan of battle promulgated in the special field orders of the 14th. The formation of troops was partially concealed from the enemy by the broken nature of the ground, as also by a fog, which lifted toward noon.

* * * * * * * * *

Finding General Smith had not taken as much distance to the right as I expected he would have done, I directed General Schofield to move his command (the Twenty-Third Corps) from position in reserve, to which it had been assigned, over to the right of General Smith, enabling the cavalry thereby to operate more freely to the enemy's rear. This was rapidly accomplished by General Schofield, and his troops participated, in the closing operations of the day.

* * * * * * * * *

Our line at nightfall was readjusted, running parallel to and east of the Hillsboro pike—Schofield's command on the right, Smith's in the center, and Wood's on the left, with cavalry on the right of Schofield, Steedman holding the position he had gained early in the morning. The total result of the day's operations was the capture of sixteen pieces of artillery and twelve hundred prisoners, besides several hundred stands of small arms, and about forty (40) wagons. The enemy had been forced back at all points with heavy loss. Our casualties were unusually light. The behavior of the troops was unsurpassed for steadiness and alacrity in every movement, and the original plan of battle, with but few alterations, strictly adhered to. The whole command bivouacked in line of battle during the night, on the ground occupied at dark, while preparations were made to renew the battle at an early hour on the morrow.

* * * * * * * * *

Immediately following the effort of the Fourth Corps, Generals Smith's and Schofield's commands moved against the enemy's works in their respective fronts, carrying all before them, irreparably breaking his lines in a dozen places, and capturing all his artillery and thousands of prisoners— among the latter, four (4) general officers. Our loss was remarkably small, scarcely mentionable. All of the enemy that did escape were pur sued over the tops of Brentwood and Harpeth hills. General Wilson's cavalry, dismounted, attacked the enemy simultaneously with Schofield and Smith, striking him in reverse, and gaining firm possession of Granny White pike, cut off his retreat by that route. Wood's and Steedman's troops hearing the shouts of victory coming from the right, rushed impetuously forward, renewing the assault on Overton's hill, and although meeting a very heavy fire, the onset was irresistible, artillery and many prisoners falling into our hands. The enemy, hopelessly broken, fled in confusion through Brentwood Pass, the Fourth Corps in close pursuit, which was continued for several miles, when darkness closed the scene, and the troops rested from their labors.

* * * * * * * *

During the two days' operations there were 4,462 prisoners captured, including 287 officers of all grades from that of major-general, fifty-three pieces of artillery, and thousands of small arms. The enemy abandoned on the field all of his dead and wounded.

EXTRACT FROM GENERAL SCHOFIELD'S REPORT.

On the night of the 15th I waited upon the major-general commanding, at his héadquarters, and received his orders for the pursuit of the enemy on the following day. Our operations during the 15th had swung the right and center forward, so that the general direction of the line was nearly perpendicular to that before the attack, only the right was in contact with the enemy, and was therefore much exposed. Apprehensive that the enemy, instead of retreating during the night, would mass and attack our right in the morning, I requested that a division of infantry be sent to reinforce the right, which was ordered accordingly from Major-General Smith's command. In response to this order, General Smith sent five regiments and a battery (about 1,600 men), which were put in reserve near the right. In the morning it was found that the enemy still held his position in our front, of which the hill in front of General Couch was the key, and had thrown up considerable breastworks during the night. He had also increased the force on his left during the night, and continued to mass troops during the early part of the day. During the morning, therefore, our operations were limited to preparations for defense and co-operation with cavalry, which was operating to strike the Granny White pike, in rear of the enemy.

About noon, the troops on my left (Generals Smith and Wood) having advanced and come in contact with the enemy in his new position, the enemy again withdrew from his 'left a considerable force to strengthen his right and center, when I ordered General Cox to advance, in conjunction with cavalry, and endeavor to carry a high wooded hill beyond the flank of the enemy's intrenched line and overlooking the Granny White pike. The hill was occupied by the enemy in considerable force, but was not intrenched. My order was not executed with the promptness or energy which I had expected, yet probably with as much as I had reason to expect, considering the attenuated character of General Cox's line and the great distance and rough ground over which the attacking force had to move. The hill was, however, carried by General Wilson's cavalry (dismounted), whose gallantry and energy on that and other occasions, which came under my observations, can not be too greatly praised. Almost simultaneously with this attack on the extreme right, the salient hill, in front of General Couch, was attacked and carried by General Smith's troops, supported by a brigade of General Couch's division, and the fortified hill in front of General Cox, which constituted the extreme flank of the enemy's intrenched line, was attacked and carried by Colonel Doolittle's brigade of General Cox's division, the latter capturing eight pieces of artillery and two to three hundred prisoners.

EXTRACT FROM GENERAL SMITH'S REPORT.

During the night a request coming from General Schoefield, commanding Twenty-third Corps, for reinforcements, I sent him the Third division, Colonel J. B. Moore commanding, just before daylight. On the morning of the 16th, advancing my line in the same order as on the previous day, the First on the right and the Second divison on the left, it was discovered that the enemy had taken position at the base of a chain of hills, called the Brentwood hills, with a front nearly perpendicular to our lines, and had strongly intrenched themselves by throwing up breastworks and massing artillery in every available position. Changing my front by a half-wheel, by brigades the command moved slowly in echelon from the right, so as not to break connections with the Fourth Corps, and took a position directly in front of the enemy, at a distance of about six hundred yards, my right resting at the base of a hill, on the top of which was the enemy's left, and my line being the whole front of the two divisions, extending about one mile. The enemy opening a heavy artillery fire upon my brigades, as they went into position, all the batteries of the First and Second divisions, six in number, were brought into action at a distance of about eight hundred yards, and after a fierce cannonading of about two hours, succeeded in quieting the enemy's guns in our front. The Twenty-third Corps was on my right in the intrenchments, thrown up by them the night before, and nearly at right angles with my present line. Expecting that corps to take the initiative, as they were on the flank of the enemy, I held the command in its present position, keeping up a slow artillery fire at their line without eliciting any reply. About 1 o'clock I received a request from General Schofield, and a few minutes later an order from you, to send another division to his assistance, he having retained the one sent at daylight that morning, not having any reserve, and my whole line being in front of the enemy, and liable to be attacked and broken at any point wherever a brigade should be withdrawn, I therefore sent a staff officer to him to state the condition of my command, and ascertain if he could not get along without my division. The officer reported to me that General Schofield's line was not engaged, and upon my condition being reported to him, he said he did not need the additional force, consequently it was not sent. About 3 o'clock P. M. General McArthur sent word that he could carry the hill on his left by assault. Major-General Thomas being present, the matter was referred to him, and I was requested to delay the movement until he could hear from General Schofield, to whom he had sent. General McArthur not receiving any reply, and fearing if the attack should be longer delayed the enemy would use the right to strengthen his works, directed the First brigade, Colonel N. L. McMillen, Ninty-fifth Ohio Infantry, to storm the hill on which was the left of the enemy's line, and the Second and Third brigades of the division to attack in front, when the first should be half-way up the hill.

* * * * * * * * *

CHAPTER XXXVI.

MINOR OPERATIONS HAVING RELATIONS MORE OR LESS INTIMATE WITH THOSE OF THE MAIN ARMY DURING NOVEMBER AND DECEMBER.

GENERAL STEEDMAN knew, upon reaching Decatur, that it was too late to embarrass the enemy in crossing the Tennessee river, but he determined to move toward his line of retreat south of the river. He had been joined at Stevenson by Colonel W. J. Palmer, of the Fifteenth Pennsylvania Cavalry, with a force composed of his own regiment and detachments from the Second Tennessee, and the Tenth, Twelfth, and Thirteenth Indiana Cavalry, in all about six hundred and fifty men. At 8 P. M. on the 28th, Colonel Palmer moved from Decatur toward Courtland. He encountered the enemy at a point two miles distant, and attacking with his advance of thirty men pressed him back. The force was Colonel Wines' regiment of Roddy's command, and this commander was resisting to cover his artillery, but against thirty men, yielded his position and two pieces of artillery. Colonel Palmer the next day divided his force, sending Colonel Prosser with the detachments on the main road, and moving with his own regiment on the Brown's Ferry road. Colonel Prosser soon met Roddy's whole force drawn up in two lines, and without hesitation charged, broke his lines, captured forty-five men, and drove the enemy through Courtland.

At Leighton, on the 30th, Colonel Palmer learned that General Hood's pontoon train of two hundred wagons had passed through the day before en route for Columbus, Mississippi. General Roddy was in the rear to protect this train, and although Colonel Palmer felt safe in disregarding him in making an effort to capture it, it was necessary that he should shun another cavalry force under General Armstrong, which was also near. Making the venture, he moved to the rear of a portion of Roddy's command, and captured Colonel Warren and other prisoners. At Russellville, another portion was met and routed, and Palmer then pressed on after the train and soon captured it, consisting of two hundred wagons and seventy-eight boats with appointments complete. Such was the condition of the roads and the teams that it was not considered safe to attempt its removal from the presence of the enemy, and hence it was destroyed. Then having heard that a supply train was moving from Barton Station to Tuscumbia, Colonel Palmer moved to capture it. On the 1st of January, this train, consisting of one hundred and ten wagons and five hundred mules, was also taken in Itawamba county, Mississippi, and mules enough saved to mount one hundred and fifty prisoners. Losing one man killed and two wounded, Colonel Palmer returned to Decatur.

In the meantime, General Steedman had been ordered to Chattanooga. He put his sick men and his artillery on transports, and started his infantry by rail, under General Cruft. When the force reached Huntsville, Colonel Mitchell's brigade was hurried forward to Larkinsville, to intercept, if possible, General Lyon, who, with a portion of his command, was in retreat from Kentucky. His expedition had proved disastrous in the extreme in its general issue. He captured Hopkinsville, but was met near Greenbury by General McCook, who had been detached from the main army to protect the Louisville and Nashville railroad, and to pursue this raiding force. Colonel La Grange first met Lyon with his brigade. Engaging him with spirit, after a short conflict he threw his troops into confusion and rout, capturing one gun and some prisoners. General Lyon then made a detour through Elizabethtown and Glasgow, and crossed the Cumberland river at Burksville, and thence proceeded through McMinnville and Winchester to the Memphis and Charleston railroad. On the 7th of January, General Cruft's command was disposed to capture him or drive him across the Tennessee river at the approaches to Bellefont, Larkinsville, and Scottsboro; but he succeeded in eluding all the detachments on the watch, and crossed the Tennessee river.

He was finally intercepted and captured, with one hundred of his men and his remaining gun, at Red Hill. He, however, escaped, having shot the soldier in charge of him.

As General Thomas was in command of all the troops within the limits of the Military Division of the Mississippi, the operations in East Tennessee were subject to his direction. There had been complications there during the summer and early autumn, and General Schofield had left his corps at Atlanta, to give attention to affairs in that region. General J. H. Morgan had been killed by General Gillem's troops, but infantry had been subsequently sent there, and when General Hood was menacing Tennessee from Florence, General Breckinridge, supported by Duke and Vaughn, appeared before General Gillem at Bull's Gap. At this period, General Gillem, commanding three regiments of Tennessee cavalry and a battery, was acting under the immediate instructions of Governor Johnson, having been detached for this duty. On the 13th of November, General Breckinridge, with a force estimated at three thousand men, attacked and routed the fifteen hundred under General Gillem, capturing about one third, including his battery. General Gillem had repulsed two attacks of the enemy, but reinforcements having come, he concluded to withdraw, and while retreating was attacked in rear. There was a lack of co-operation between General Gillem and General Ammen, which General Thomas considered the cause of the disaster. General Gillem fell back upon Knoxville with the remainder of his force, followed closely by General Breckinridge.

In the emergency, General Thomas directed General Steedman to hold troops in readiness to support General Ammen, at Knoxville; and General Stoneman, in command of the Department of the Ohio, in the absence of General Schofield, ordered a concentration of forces in Kentucky, to advance from Lexington to Cumberland Gap, either to repel the enemy, should he advance into Kentucky, or to advance into East Tennessee, should he continue to operate there.

On the 18th, General Breckinridge withdrew from the vicinity of Knoxville, and General Ammen, reinforced by fifteen hundred men from Chattanooga, reoccupied Strawberry Plains the same day. About the same time, General Stoneman left

Louisville to take the direction of affairs in East Tennessee, and on his way received his instructions from General Thomas, at Nashville. He was directed "to concentrate the largest force possible against Breckinridge, and either destroy his force or drive it into Virginia, and, if possible, destroy the salt-works at Saltville, and the railroad from the Tennessee line as far into Virginia as he could go without endangering his command." On the 6th of December, General Thomas repeated his instructions upon the receipt of information that General Breckinridge was retreating.

General Stoneman had been delayed in consequence of the deficiency of his command in the essential appointments for the service proposed. On the 9th, he was ready for active operations. His command comprised the infantry and dismounted cavalry under General Ammen, General Gillem's force, and the mounted troops under General Burbridge, forty-two hundred men. He first sent the Fourth Tennessee and Third North Carolina regiments to Paint Rock, to hold the pass over the mountains into North Carolina. December 9th, he moved two regiments of Ohio artillery from Strawberry Plains to Blair's Cross-roads, and with General Gillem proceeded to that point the next day. At Bean's Station these forces were joined on the 11th by General Burbridge's command. Hitherto the commander alone knew the service and destination of the troops, but here the men were supplied with all the ammunition and rations that they could carry on themselves and horses. On the 13th, at daylight, General Gillem reached the north fork of the Holston river, opposite Kingston. Here was General John Morgan's command, under his brother, in the temporary absence of General Duke. After a sharp conflict, General Gillem crossed the river and totally defeated the enemy, capturing Morgan and a portion of his command, and killing or dispersing the remainder. During the afternoon, Burbridge was pushed on to Bristol, in the endeavor to intercept Vaughn, who had held Greenville for some time with a force estimated at twelve hundred men. At night, Generals Stoneman and Gillem followed, arriving at Bristol early on the 14th.

Fearing that Vaughn would pass in the night and join

Breckinridge, Burbridge was sent to Abingdon with instructions to send a regiment forward to strike the railroad at some point between Saltville and Wytheville. When General Gillem had completed the destruction of Bristol, which General Burbridge had commenced, he moved to Glade Springs, followed by Burbridge. At 2 A. M. on the 16th, General Stoneman learned that the Twelfth Kentucky Cavalry, sent forward from Abingdon, after threatening the salt-works, had destroyed two trains which had brought Breckinridge from Wytheville with reinforcements, and decided to press on to Wytheville, destroy it and the salt-works on New river, and give attention to the destruction of Saltville on his return. He therefore put his forces in motion eastward, and soon General Gillem overtook Vaughn at Marion, and attacking, routed him, pursuing rapidly to Wytheville, capturing his trains, artillery, and one hundred and ninety-eight men, and destroying the town. General Burbridge reached Mount Airy the next day, where Buckley's brigade was dispatched by order of General Stoneman to destroy the lead mines twenty-five or thirty miles beyond. Nothing now remained but the destruction of Saltville, and General Stoneman, by a quick return, interposed his command so that General Breckinridge was cut off and forced to retreat into North Carolina. The two main columns were then ordered to converge upon Saltville. When they were near, and General Stoneman was waiting for General Burbridge, he sent Colonel Stacy with his regiment, the Thirteenth Tennessee, to dash into the town and commence the work of destruction with all possible noise. The brilliant dash of Stacy put the enemy into retreat, and then the celebrated salt-works with all their machinery and supplies were destroyed.

This expedition brought defeat to the enemy at every step, and destruction to important manufactories of the material of war, to vast quantities of material of every kind, and to railroads and rolling-stock. General Burbridge destroyed five trains filled with supplies, a thousand stand of arms, a vast amount of fixed ammunition, and a large number of wagons and ambulances, and captured seventeen officers and two hundred and sixty privates; Buckley ruined the lead-works in

Wythe county; Major Harrison, of the Twelfth Kentucky Cavalry, captured two railroad trains, destroyed all the railroad bridges from Glade Springs to Marion, and the large iron-works at the latter place, and captured several hundred fine horses; General Gillem's brigade, reinforced by the Eleventh Michigan and the Eleventh Kentucky Cavalry, drove Vaughn beyond Wytheville, destroyed that town, all the railroad bridges from Marion to Reedy creek, vast amounts of stores and supplies of all kinds, several hundred wagons and ambulances, two locomotives and several cars, and captured ten pieces of field artillery, and over two hundred prisoners. This command made an average march of forty-two and a half miles per day, completing its work of destruction on the 22d of December. Then General Burbridge returned to Kentucky by way of the Big Sandy valley, and General Gillem to Knoxville.

WASHINGTON, *November* 5, 1864—2 P. M.

Major-General Thomas:
How much force and artillery had Gillem?

A. LINCOLN,
President United States.

HEADQUARTERS DEPARTMENT OF THE CUMBERLAND,
NASHVILLE, *November* 15, 1864—10 P. M.

President A. Lincoln, Washington:
General Gillem's force consisted of three regiments of Tennessee cavalry, and one battery of six guns, belonging to the Governor's Guards—about fifteen hundred men.

GEO. H. THOMAS,
Major-General U. S. V. Commanding.

NASHVILLE, *November* 17, 1864.

Major-General Stoneman, Louisville, Ky.:
Your dispatch of this date just received. Your intention and order to General Burbridge to concentrate his mounted force is perfectly satisfactory, and I wish you to report to me as soon as he has the concentration of his troops completed.

GEO. H. THOMAS,
Major-General U. S. V. Commanding.

HEADQUARTERS DEPARTMENT OF THE CUMBERLAND,
NASHVILLE, *November* 17, 1864—4.30 P. M.
Major-General Stoneman, Louisville, Ky.:
Your dispatch of yesterday is received. I wish you to send all the mounted force you can raise to East Tennessee. I have directed General Steedman to send all the infantry he can spare from Chattanooga.
GEO. H. THOMAS,
Major-General U. S. V. Commanding.

HEADQUARTERS DEPARTMENT OF THE CUMBERLAND,
NASHVILLE, *November* 19, 1864.
Brigadier-General Ammen, Knoxville:
Do not send the reinforcements from Chattanooga further than Knoxville, unless it is absolutely necessary, as they are not able to march. Return them to Chattanooga as soon as you can dispense with their services.
GEO. H. THOMAS,
Major-General U. S. V. Commanding.

CITY POINT, *November* 27, 1864—9 P. M.
Major-General Thomas:
Savannah papers, just received, state that Forrest is expected in the rear of General Sherman, and that Breckinridge is already on his way to Georgia from East Tennessee. If this proves true, it will give you a chance to take the offensive against Hood, and to cut the railroad up in Virginia with a small cavalry force.
U. S. GRANT,
Lieutenant-General.

NASHVILLE, *November* 28, 1864—10 A. M.
Lieutenant-General Grant, City Point, Va.:
Your dispatch of 9 P. M. yesterday received. We can as yet discover no signs of the withdrawal of Forrest from Tennessee, but he is closely watched, and our movements will commence against Hood as soon as possible, whether Forrest leaves Tennessee or not. My information from East Tennessee leads me to believe that Breckinridge is either falling back to Virginia, or is on his way to Georgia. He now holds Bull's Gap, but Stoneman is moving on that place from Knoxville, and Burbridge from Cumberland Gap. Stoneman already has orders to destroy the railroad into Virginia if he possibly can.
GEO. H. THOMAS,
Major-General U. S. V. Commanding.

KNOXVILLE, *November* 28, 1864.
Major-General G. H. Thomas:
As near as I can learn from scouts and deserters, all the mounted force Breckinridge brought with him is now in the vicinity of Bull's Gap, say 2,500; a portion of his dismounted force, under Palmer, say 700, has gone

back to Asheville, and Breckinridge, with the rest of the force, say 700, with captured wagons and artillery, has gone back to Wytheville. Burbridge's troops will all be through Cumberland Gap to-morrow. They have been detained by high water. I wrote you at length yesterday. Have you received the letter?

            GEO. STONEMAN,
              Major-General.

KNOXVILLE, *November* 28, 1864—10.30 P. M.

Major-General Thomas:

Your telegram of 3 P. M. is received. A scout, a woman, and a negro came in this evening, and report Breckinridge's force at Morristown and in that vicinity. Breckinridge is no doubt with his command. He had not left yesterday in pursuit of General Sherman, nor do I think he intends to. His command is not formidable, and he can not get much the start of us if he leaves this section to cross the mountains. I will keep you informed. Burbridge is ordered forward.

            GEO. STONEMAN,
              Major-General.

CITY POINT, VA., *November* 30, 1864—11.30 A. M.

Major-General Thomas:

The Richmond *Enquirer* of yesterday says that it is no longer contraband to state that Breckinridge's command is now marching on a campaign that will fill Kentucky with dismay, and that probably by this time Burbridge has felt the shock. The Richmond papers of the 28th state that Breckinridge was at Bristol on the 28th.

              U. S. GRANT,
              Lieutenant-General.

NASHVILLE, *December* 6, 1864—8.30 P. M.

Major-General Stoneman, Knoxville:

Your dispatches of 10.30 P. M., 5th inst., and 12.30 P. M. to-day, are just received. If you can effectually destroy the railroad for twenty-five or thirty miles beyond the Virginia line, East Tennessee will, I think, then be perfectly secure from further invasion. After destroying the railroad and the salt-works, if you can, you had better draw your main force back to the vicinity of Knoxville, for the defense of East Tennessee.

              GEO. H. THOMAS,
            Major-General U. S. V. Commanding.

CHAPTER XXXVII.

THE MARCH TO THE SEA, AND THE CAPTURE OF THE CITY OF
SAVANNAH, GEORGIA.

GENERAL SHERMAN'S forces selected for his march to the seacoast comprised sixty thousand infantry and five thousand five hundred cavalry, and one piece of artillery for every thousand men. These troops had been so thoroughly sifted that they really represented a much larger army than this aggregate, with the usual percentage of ineffective men. They were organized into right and left wings; the former embracing the Fifteenth and Seventeenth Corps, under the command of Major-General O. O. Howard, and the latter the Fourteenth and Twentieth Corps, under Major-General H. W. Slocum. The Fifteenth and Seventeenth Corps, from the Army of the Tennessee, were commanded respectively by Major-Generals P. T. Osterhaus and F. P. Blair, and the Fourteenth and Twentieth, from the Army of the Cumberland, were commanded respectively by Brevet Major-General J. C. Davis and Brigadier-General A. S. Williams. The appointments were ample beyond precedent, as selection had been made from the material of the Military Division of the Mississippi; in fact, each corps had complete army appointments, that each might have the independence of a separate army.

The last ten days of October and the first days of November had been devoted to preparation. Supplies had been accumulated at Atlanta in such quantities that there were forty days' rations of beef, sugar, and coffee, twenty days' of bread, and a double allowance of salt for forty days. The amount of ammunition was ample for all possibilities. There was little forage, only for three days in grain; but it was known that the lines of march penetrated regions abounding in corn and fodder, and also in substantial supplies for men, and those delicacies in great abundance which do not often fall to soldiers. All the material at Atlanta not needed for the expedition was sent to the rear, or devoted to destruction with a large portion of the city. The garrisons north of Kingston moved to Chattanooga, and the rails were lifted from the railroad track from Resaca north; but those between Resaca and the Etowah river were left in place in view of the probable occupancy of the country as far forward as the line of that river.

November 11th, General Corse, in obedience to orders, destroyed the bridges, foundries, mills, shops, machines, and all property useful in war, at Rome, Georgia. The next day, the telegraph wires extending northward from Kingston were cut; and the several corps moved rapidly toward Atlanta. On the 14th, the four corps and cavalry were grouped around that city, and on the 15th, the Fifteenth, Seventeenth, and Twentieth Corps moved out upon their respective lines of march, and that night the conflagration of a large portion of Atlanta gave emphatic announcement that the grand movement had begun.

As the great objects of this expedition were an illustration of the weakness of the Confederacy behind its defensive and offensive lines, and the diminution of its remaining resources by the destruction of railroads and all property useful in war, the lines of march diverged widely. Besides, there was another end to be secured by this broad divergent front in moving from Atlanta—the concealment of the ultimate objective, that the enemy might not know where to concentrate his forces. The right wing, with Kilpatrick's division of cavalry on its right flank, marched by Jonesboro and McDonough, under orders to make a strong feint upon Macon, and then turn eastward and rendezvous at Gordon on the 23d. The Twentieth Corps advanced by Decatur, Stone Mountain, Social Circle, and Madison, to turn southward to Milledgeville, under instructions to tear up the railroad from Social Circle to Madison, and burn the railroad bridge over the Oconee in the same period. On the 16th, the Fourteenth Corps advanced upon Milledgeville, through Lithonia, Covington, and Shady Dale.

On the 23d, the right wing and the cavalry reached Gordon and the left wing Milledgeville; and this first stage of the campaign was the realization of all anticipations. General Sherman had interposed his army between Macon and Augusta, and the enemy, in his doubt as to his destination and his utter inability to oppose him wherever he might go, was paralyzed completely. He had not, in the eight days, shown any great strength at any point, and it was evident that no strong force was opposing either of the two main columns. His cavalry, under General Wheeler, which had been dispatched as a corps of observation, had engaged General Kilpatrick several times, and General Cobb's militia and regular troops, from Macon and Savannah, had sallied from the former place to receive severe punishment from Walcutt's brigade; and besides these feeble demonstrations there had been no opposition, and it was manifest that no serious resistance could be organized in Central Georgia. The veteran troops were either with General Hood, in Tennessee, or in the large cities on the seaboard, and General Sherman's plans had been discerned too late for any troops in force to be directed to his front. When General Beauregard, who was at Corinth directing the great concentration of forces which was to march in triumph to the Ohio river, learned that General Sherman with a large army was marching southward from Atlanta, he committed to General Hood the conduct of the Tennessee campaign, and hastened to Georgia to arouse the people, by frantic proclamations, to resist this overwhelming invasion. His own second great plan of aggression from Corinth, Mississippi, was now, as far as he was personally concerned, as palpabale a failure as was his first, when he evacuated Corinth in May, 1862, with an army embracing all the available Confederate troops in the West. Appeals of similar fervor and futility were issued by the Confederate authorities at Richmond, including the President and Congress—at least by the congressional representatives from Georgia—and from the governor of the invaded state. While there was a veteran army between the homes of the people and the invader, there was some basis for appeal; but now the hopelessness of the situation was so apparent that the people were paralyzed with fear and despair, and noisy proclamations were as impotent as the cry of women and children.

The orders for the second stage of the campaign sent the two wings on parallel lines toward Millin, and Kilpatrick to destroy the railroad between Milledgeville and Augusta, and then to hasten to Millin, to rescue the prisoners supposed to be there confined. On the 26th, the heads of columns of the left wing gained Sandersville, and then swept eastward toward the Georgia Central railroad, and the right wing moved from Gordon, on the line of the railroad. December 2d, the central columns of the two corps were at Millin, and the extreme corps were abreast. Immense damage had been done to the railroads, mills, cotton-mills, and gins, and some fighting had occurred on the flanks, especially by the cavalry—Kilpatrick having had several brushes with Wheeler, but had been victorious, whether in offense or defense, The heads of columns had also been slightly annoyed, but not to an extent to greatly embarrass their movements. The greatest obstacles on the way to Millin were the Ogeechee and Oconee rivers, and an army behind these streams might have been successful in resistance, but the enemy's slender forces were easily dislodged, and the army passed over without delay. There had been no rescue of prisoners from the enemy, as all had been removed from Millin too soon.

Instructions for the third and last stage required the convergence of the wings upon Savannah—the left wing and the Seventeenth Corps moving on parallel roads, and the Fifteenth Corps deflecting to the right, on the right bank of the Ogeechee, to cross at Eden Station. General Wheeler followed the columns on the east bank, but their rear was protected by Kilpatrick's cavalry and Baird's division of the Fourteenth Corps. As the army approached Savannah, the country became more marshy, and the roads more obstructed by fallen trees, especially where the roads crossed the swamps on causeways that traverse the lowlands, which are overflowed artificially for the culture of rice. When within fifteen miles of the city, the columns were confronted by earthworks and artillery, in addition to the ordinary obstructions of the roads and causeways. But these defenses were easily turned, and on the 10th of December, the enemy was driven within the fortifications of Savannah, and its investment in great part accomplished. The right and left wings closed in with connected lines near the main defenses of the city. The left of the Twentieth Corps rested on the Savannah river, and the right of the Fourteenth Corps connected with the left of the Seventeenth, beyond the canal, near Lawson's plantation. General Slocum held the bridge of the Charleston railroad and the river itself, and General Howard controlled the Gulf railroad and the Ogeechee down toward Fort McAllister. Thus General Sherman held firmly all the railroads centering in Savannah, and the two rivers forming the main channels of supply, and all the roads leading out from the city, except the Union causeway, over which the road to Hardeeville and Charleston, passes from the shore of the river opposite the town.

General Slocum grasped the Savannah river firmly with his left flank, at a point about five miles from the city, and planted batteries so as to command the channel. He was scarcely in position, when Captain Gildersleeve, of the One Hundred and Fiftieth New York, in command of a foraging party, captured the steamer Ida, having on board Colonel Lynch of General Hardee's staff, bearing dispatches to the gunboats up the river. This boat was burned, to prevent recapture by the gunboats patrolling the river below. Near General Slocum's left flank were two river islands, Hutchinson and Argyle, whose possession was essential to his complete mastery of the river. These he promptly seized. During the evening of the 16th, Colonel Hawley, of the Third Wisconsin, from Carman's brigade, by order of General Williams, sent over two companies of his regiment to Argyle Island, and the next morning six more. While he was crossing with the latter, he discovered three steamers descending the river. He hastened across, while Winegar's battery from the Georgia shore opened upon them. The boats were driven back, and in turning the two gunboats disabled their armed tender, which fell into Hawley's hands, at the head of the island. The next day, General Geary, commanding First division Twentieth Corps, was directed to occupy the upper end of Hutchinson Island with a detachment, to prevent the approach of the enemy's gunboats. A sunken battery was also established on the Georgia shore, whose guns commanded the river above and below the island, and ranged over the island to the Carolina shore.

The defenses of the enemy had by this time been thoroughly developed by reconnoissances along the whole front of the investing lines, and it was apparent that by means of irrigating canals, traversing the rice plantations, the whole region could be so flooded as greatly to embarrass the advance of assaulting columns. It was equally apparent that there were but two ways to take the city, by assault between the rivers, or the completion of the investment by closing the road to Charleston, which was General Hardee's only avenue of escape, and force a capitulation by starvation.

Before, however, attempting either an assault or the completion of the investment, General Sherman made a successful effort to open communications with the fleet known to be in waiting for his coming, to secure supplies by the passage of the boats on the Ogeechee river, to the rear of his encampments. He was not yet in need, as he had large herds of cattle, and his trains were filled with supplies, which had been gathered on the march from Atlanta and with what had been loaded in that city, and there was an open country for foraging in his rear. Still he deemed communication with the fleet to be of paramount importance. The barrier to this was Fort McAllister, a redoubt on the right bank of the Ogeechee, holding heavy guns, and to its reduction he addressed himself, while he intrusted the immediate investment to his subordinate commanders. On the 13th, General Kilpatrick was sent over the Ogeechee on a pontoon bridge, under instructions to reconnoiter Fort McAllister and the inlets in that vicinity, and if practicable to take the fort; subsequently he was directed by General Sherman to examine St. Catherine's Sound and open communication with the fleet. General Kilpatrick having reported that Fort McAllister was manned by two hundred men, and the bridge over the Ogeechee, known as "King's Bridge," having been repaired in an incredibly short time by Colonel Buell and his regiment—the Fifty-eighth Indiana, famous in the Army of the Cumberland for such exploits—General Hazen, commanding the Second division of the Fifteenth Army Corps, was ordered to be in readiness to move against the fort. Early on the 13th, General Hazen crossed King's bridge, and deployed his division before the position, with its flanks resting on the river. Having at 3 P. M. signaled his readiness for assault to General Sherman, who, with General Howard, had taken post at Chase's rice-mill for observation and direction, he received orders to make the attack. In compliance, General Hazen assaulted at 5 P. M.; his troops broke through the abatis and leaped over the parapet, announcing their victory by shouts and the elevation of the national flag. While observing Hazen's operations, General Sherman caught sight of a steamer, which came to herald the proximity of the fleet at the very moment that the Ogeechee was opened for its use. Supplies were now assured, and the reduction of Savannah was the immediate problem for solution.

The day following, Generals Sherman and Foster, the latter commanding the forces in South Carolina, met Admiral Dahlgren in conference, and arranged for co-operative movements against Savannah. Siege-guns were to be brought from Hilton Head; the fleet was to bombard the lower forts, and the investing forces were to carry the landward defenses of the city. At this time General Sherman thought that he could reach the "Union Causeway"—General Hardee's only way of escape from his left flank—by throwing a column across the Savannah river. He therefore returned from the fleet, with announced determination to assault the lines of the enemy as soon as the promised siege-guns should arrive.

On the 17th, General Sherman demanded the surrender of the city; but on the next day received a positive refusal from General Hardee, who reminded him that his investment was not complete, that his guns were four miles from Savannah, and that there would be no justification for capitulation while he had an open road to Charleston. He had probably less than fifteen thousand men, a force that was inadequate for successful defense against the armies and fleet that were converging upon him, but the issue proved that the necessity of surrender did not exist.

The problem of reducing Savannah was not the only one which now engrossed the attention of General Sherman, as a greater one had been devolved upon him by General Grant—one in comparison with which the other was merely incidental. This was the movement of General Sherman's army, to assist in the reduction of Richmond. But as this enterprise was contingent upon the accumulation of vessels sufficient to transport fifty or sixty thousand men, the operations against Savannah were continued as though its capture was paramount, except that the ulterior objective induced General Sherman to refrain from throwing one of General Slocum's corps across to South Carolina.

Pending the opening of the Ogeechee and the coming of the siege-guns, there was some activity on the left flank of the army, and General Slocum was urgent to throw one of his corps into South Carolina, to close General Hardee's only avenue of escape. On the 15th, Colonel Hawley crossed to the Carolina shore from Argyle Island, with five companies, drove the enemy from Izzard's plantation, and made a reconnoissance of the country two miles farther. Being isolated, he thought it prudent to return, and in doing this he was vigorously pressed by the enemy, but recrossed to the island in safety. Upon his return, he was reinforced by the Second Massachusetts regiment, and on the next day the remainder of the brigade, Colonel Carman commanding, and a section of artillery, crossed to the island and took position on the eastern point near the South Carolina shore. During the night, Colonel Carman received orders from General Williams to cross to South Carolina and take position near the river, threatening the Savannah and Charleston road. This was not accomplished immediately for want of small boats, and barges could not be used on account of low tide. In the meantime, General Wheeler appeared on the opposite shore, and opened with his light guns upon Carman's troops, the latter responding during the 17th and 18th, but made no effort to cross.

In view of these revelations, General Sherman abandoned the idea of closing the road to Charleston by operations from his left flank, as the enemy held the river opposite the city with iron-clad gunboats, and could, as was conjectured, destroy pontoons between Hutchinson Island and the Carolina shore, and isolate any force sent from that flank.

Upon the abandonment of this movement, General Slocum was ordered to get the siege-guns into position and make preparations for assault. The approaches to the city were upon the narrow causeways, which were commanded by artillery; but nevertheless the reconnoissance from the left wing had convinced General Slocum and his subordinate commanders that the works in their front could be carried. Two of General Howard's division commanders were confident they could attack successfully, though the conditions of assault on their portion of the line was less favorable than on the left.

In abandoning the purpose to close the Charleston road from his left flank, General Sherman did not forego the attempt to shut it from another direction, as it was then threatened by one of General Foster's divisions from the head of Broad river, and on the 19th he set sail for Port Royal to arrange with General Foster for a movement upon the causeway, so vital to General Hardee. His instructions, at departure, to Generals Howard and Slocum were to get ready, but not to strike until his return.

At daybreak on the morning of the 19th, by order of General Williams, commanding the Twentieth Corps, Colonel Carman threw the Third Wisconsin, the Second Massachusetts, and the Thirteenth New York regiments, under Colonel Hawley, to the South Carolina shore. These troops landed without opposition, and advancing to Izzard's mill, skirmished into a good position. The enemy expressed his appreciation of the position, which he had lost, by charging with his cavalry to regain it, but suffered repulse. During the afternoon and evening, Colonel Carman sent forward the remaining regiments of his brigade, and assumed command at Izzard's mill. His position was a strong one for defense, but the ground before him presented marked obstacles to an advance. His front was a rice plantation, traversed by canals and dikes, the fields being overflowed to the depth of eighteen inches. To move forward under these circumstances, it was necessary to follow the dikes, and these were easily defended. During the night he intrenched his line, which extended from the Savannah river, on his right, two and a quarter miles, to an inlet near Clyesdale creek.

The next morning, in obedience to orders from General Jackson, his division commander, Colonel Carman detailed twelve companies under Colonel Hawley, and directed in person a reconnoissance to determine the relation of his line to Clyesdale creek. This creek was reached, with loss of one man. Works were then constructed for a regiment; two companies were left to hold them, and with the remainder of the force an effort was made to reach the Charleston road. This movement had been anticipated by the enemy, and a strong force had been thrown before Carman. As he could not advance without crossing a canal under fire, he withdrew, but remained sufficiently near the road to observe the passage of vehicles of all descriptions, in motion toward Charleston. During the afternoon he was shelled by a gunboat, and at 4 P. M. he was reinforced by three regiments. He was so near the enemy's pontoon bridge, at Savannah, that from 7 P. M. to 3 A. M. he could distinctly hear the retreating army crossing upon it. This noise was also heard by General Geary from his position below Hutchinson's Island. These facts were duly reported.

Thus, under the mantle of darkness, during a moonless and windy night, General Hardee withdrew his entire force along the front of a brigade of the investing army. The approach of this brigade to his only line of retreat may have hastened his withdrawal; but his final haste, whatever its immediate cause, was his salvation, and his stay at Savannah for ten days with such possibilities in his rear, vindicates him from the charge of abandoning his post before there was absolute need.

General Sherman returned on the 22d, to find the city of Savannah in the quiet possession of his army. General Hardee had destroyed as much of his material as the security of his retreat permitted; but he left his guns unspiked, three steamboats, his railroad rolling-stock, twenty-five thousand bales of cotton belonging to the Confederate government, and vast quantities of other public property of great value, uninjured.

Except the failure to capture General Hardee's army at Savannah and release the prisoners at Millin, the march from Atlanta to that city was a triumphant success—the full realization of all anticipated possibilities. It illustrated with fearful emphasis the weakness of the rebellion, for no force able to resist one of General Sherman's thirteen divisions was met on the way. It left a track of desolation forty miles wide; broke up the railroad system of Georgia and of the South, by the destruction of three hundred miles of track, all workshops, station-houses, tanks, and warehouses; crippled the industries of the empire state of the South, by burning all the mills and factories on the broad belt of ruin, and made otherwise a heavy draft upon the resources of the people, in consuming and transporting supplies in immense quantities, and by the destruction of twenty thousand bales of cotton. The general significance of these results spread gloom and despair over the South. Coupled with the victory at Nashville, "The March to the Sea" brought near the collapse of the rebellion. The death-throes of treason, organized in magnitude most grand, were subsequently in harmony with its proportions and persistence; but all doubt of its quick destruction was now removed. When General Lee should surrender, the end would come; and to hasten this result, the victorious Western armies were under orders to move northward by sea or land, as circumstances should determine.

[SPECIAL FIELD ORDERS, NO. 115.]

HEADQUARTERS MILITARY DIVISION OF THE MISSISSIPPI,
IN THE FIELD, KINGSTON, GA., *November* 4, 1864.

I. In view of the contemplated movement, the commanding generals of the Fourteenth, Fifteenth, Seventeenth, and Twentieth Corps will hold their commands prepared, on short notice, to march, provided with as much bread, salt, sugar, coffee, and ammunition as they can transport with their present means—each corps independent of all others, and in dependent of the general supply train. . . .

II. The general plan of movement will be as follows: As much notice as possible will be given in advance to General Eaton at Atlanta, and

General Steedman at Chattanooga, who are charged with the responsibility of causing all the rolling-stock of the railroad to be removed to and north of Resaca, from which point General Steedman will cover its removal into Chattanooga. The railroad lying between Resaca and the Etowah bridge will be left substantially undisturbed. The bridge at Resaca and the iron north of it will be removed by cars into Chattanooga, and stored for future use. The railroad from the Etowah bridge into Atlanta will be destroyed. The Fourteenth Corps will be charged with the destruction of that road from Etowah to Big Shanty; the Fifteenth and Seventeenth Corps with that from Kenesaw to Chattahoochee bridge; and the Twentieth Corps from the Chattahoochee into and including Atlanta. . . .

III. The army commanders are enjoined to observe as much caution and secrecy as possible, and to act with the utmost energy, as, after our railroad communication is broken, every hour of our time is essential to success.

By order of Major-General W. T. Sherman.

L. M. DAYTON,
Aid-de-Camp.

[SPECIAL FIELD ORDERS, NO. 120.]

HEADQUARTERS MILITARY DIVISION OF THE MISSISSIPPI,
IN THE FIELD, KINGSTON, GA., *November* 9, 1864.

I. For the purpose of military organization, this army is divided into two wings, viz:

The right wing, Major-General O. O. Howard commanding, the Fifteenth and Seventeenth Corps.

The left wing, Major-General H. W. Slocum commanding, the Fourteenth and Twentieth Corps.

II. The habitual order of march will be, wherever practicable, by four roads, as near parallel as possible, and converging at points hereafter indicated in orders. The cavalry, Brigadier-General Kilpatrick commanding, will receive special orders from the commander-in-chief.

* * * * * * * * *

By order of Major-General W. T. Sherman.

L. M. DAYTON,
Aid-de-Camp.

HEADQUARTERS MILITARY DIVISION OF THE MISSISSIPPI,
IN THE FIELD, KINGSTON, GA., *November* 11, 1864.

Major-General Halleck, Headquarters United States Army, Washington, D. C.:

My arrangements are now all complete, and the railroad cars are being sent to the rear. Last night we burned all foundries, mills, and shops of every kind in Rome, and to-morrow I leave Kingston with the rear-guard for Atlanta, which I propose to dispose of in a similar manner, and to start on the 16th on the projected grand raid. All appearances still indicate that Beauregard has got back to his old hole at Corinth, and I hope he will enjoy it. My army prefers to enjoy the fresh sweet-potato fields of the Ocmulgee. I have balanced all the figures well, and am satisfied that General Thomas has in Tennessee a force sufficient for all probabilities; and I have urged him, the moment Beauregard turns south, to cross the Tennessee at Decatur, and push straight for Selma. To-morrow our lines will be broken, and this is probably my last dispatch. I would like to have Foster to break the Savannah and Charleston road about Pocotaligo, about the 1st of December. All other preparations are to my entire satisfaction.

W. T. SHERMAN,
Major-General

[SPECIAL FIELD ORDERS, NO. 124.]

HEADQUARTERS MILITARY DIVISION OF THE MISSISSIPPI,
IN THE FIELD, ATLANTA, GA., *November* 14, 1864.

The armies will begin the movement on Milledgeville and Gordon to-morrow, the 15th November, as follows:

I. The right wing will move via McDonough and Monticello to Gordon.

II. The left wing (General Slocum's) will move via Covington, Social Circle, and Madison to Milledgeville, destroying the railroad in a most thorough manner, from Yellow river to Madison.

III. The cavalry (General Kilpatrick commanding) will move in concert with the right wing, feigning strong in the direction of Forsyth and Macon, but will cross the Ocmulgee on the pontoon bridge of General Howard.

IV. Each column will aim to reach its destination—viz., Gordon and Milledgeville—on the seventh day's march, and each army commander will, on arrival, communicate with the other wing and the commanding general, who will accompany the left wing.

By order of Major-General W. T. Sherman.

L. M. DAYTON,
Aid-de-Camp.

TUSCUMBIA, ALA., *November* 16, 1864.

General S. Cooper, Adjutant and Inspector-General, Richmond, Va.:

Reports of General Wheeler indicate that Sherman is about to move with three corps from Atlanta to Augusta or Macon; thence probably to Charleston or Savannah, where a junction may be formed with the enemy's fleet.

The threatened attack on Wilmington, in that event, must be intended for Charleston. I would advise that all available forces which can be spared from North and South Carolina, be held ready to move to defense of Augusta, or crossing of Savannah river, in conjunction with forces in the State of Georgia.

THE MARCH TO THE SEA.

Should Sherman take Charleston, or reach Atlantic coast, he might then reinforce Grant. General Taylor has been ordered to move with his available forces into Georgia, and assume command of all troops operating against Sherman, should he move as reported.

G. T. BEAUREGARD.

CORINTH, *November* 18, 1864—VIA SELMA.

To the People of Georgia:

Arise for the defense of your native soil! Rally around your patriotic governor and gallant soldiers. Obstruct and destroy all roads in Sherman's front, flank, and rear, and his army will soon starve in your midst. Be confident and resolute. Trust in an overruling Providence, and success will crown your efforts. I hasten to join you in defense of your homes and firesides.

G. T. BEAUREGARD.

HEADQUARTERS MILITARY DIVISION OF THE MISSISSIPPI,
IN THE FIELD, COBB'S PLANTATION, *November* 22, 1864.

GENERAL:—I am directed by the general-in-chief to write you as follows: The march of this wing has been, since leaving Atlanta, in two columns, and very successful up to this time. The Fourteenth Corps is now on the Hillsboro road, ten (10) ten miles west of Milledgeville, and the Twentieth Corps must now be in the capital, having marched by the Eatonton road. The Georgia railroad, from and including the Oconee bridge, west of Lithonia, is well destroyed. Troops in fine condition, having fed high on sweet potatoes and poultry. Stock is also doing well, though the roads have been very heavy. The general desires you will report to him at Milledgeville to-morrow (where he will go early), in detail, your operations since leaving Atlanta, and also the position of your command, in view of his making further orders. In the meantime, you can not do too much permanent damage to that railroad east of Macon and about Gordon. You will also notify General Kilpatrick a similar report is desired of him.

I am, general, respectfully yours, etc.,

L. M. DAYTON,
Aid-de-Camp.

General Howard, Commanding Army of the Tennessee.

[SPECIAL FIELD ORDERS, NO. 127.]

HEADQUARTERS MILITARY DIVISION OF THE MISSISSIPPI,
IN THE FIELD, MILLEDGEVILLE, GA., *November* 23, 1864.

The first movement of this army having proved perfectly successful, and the weather now being fine, the following will constitute the second stage of the campaign, and the movement will commence to-morrow, November 24th:

I. General Kilpatrick, with his cavalry command, unincumbered by wagons, will move, via Milledgeville, by the most practicable route eastward, break the railroad between Millin and Augusta, then turn and strike the railroad below Millin; after which he will use all possible effort to rescue our prisoners of war now confined near Millin. He will communicate back to the wings of the army, as often as it is safe, any information of roads and the enemy that may be of interest to them.

II. The right wing, General Howard, will move substantially along, but south of the railroad, to a point opposite Sandersville, breaking and destroying in the most thorough manner the railroad and telegraph; at which point further orders will be issued.

III. The left wing, General Slocum, will move directly from Milledgeville to the railroad opposite Sandersville, and at once commence destroying the railroad forward to the Ogeechee.

IV. Great attention should be paid to the destruction of this road, as it is of vital importance to our cause. Besides burning bridges and trestles, the iron should be carefully twisted and warped, so that it will be impossible ever to use it again; to this end, the rate of travel will be reduced to ten miles a day.

* * * * * * * * *

VI. The general-in-chief will accompany the left wing until it reaches Sandersville, when he will join the Army of the Tennessee.

By order of Major-General W. T. Sherman.

L. M. DAYTON,
Aid-de-Camp.

HEADQUARTERS MILITARY DIVISION OF THE MISSISSIPPI,
IN THE FIELD, MILLEDGEVILLE, GA., *November* 23, 1864.

Major-General Howard, Commanding Army of the Tennessee:

By instructions of the general-in-chief, I give you the following directions: Continue to destroy the railroad eastward to the Oconee, in the most complete and thorough manner, burning and twisting every rail, and the same for a distance to the west toward Macon; also destroy the Oconee bridge. You may lay your pontoon over the Oconee, but do not cross any of your command until further orders. Hardee has probably swung around, via Albany, for Savannah, which, the general says, is all right, and he do n't care particularly. Kilpatrick will be moved here or in this vicinity for the present. The probability is we will concentrate at or near Sandersville. Prosecute the railroad destruction in the most thorough manner, and communicate with the general-in-chief frequently.

I am, general, respectfully yours, etc.,

L. M. DAYTON,
Aid-de-Camp.

THE MARCH TO THE SEA. 293

HEADQUARTERS MILITARY DIVISION OF THE MISSISSIPPI,
IN THE FIELD, NEAR MILLIN, GA., *December* 2, 1864.

GENERAL:—The army will move on Savannah, delaying only to continue the destruction of the railroad from Millin as far as Ogeechee Church. General Howard will continue to move along the south bank of the Ogeechee, General Blair along the railroad, and General Slocum by the two roads lying north of the railroad, between it and the Savannah river. The general wishes you to confer with General Slocum, to make a strong feint up in the direction of Waynesboro, and then to cover his rear from molestation by dashes of cavalry. I send you copies of two letters from members of Wheeler's staff, which will interest you. After reading, please return them for file in this office.

I am, general, respectfully yours, etc.,
L. M. DAYTON,
Aid-de-Camp.

General Kilpatrick, Commanding Cavalry Division.

HEADQUARTERS ARMIES OF THE UNITED STATES,
CITY POINT, VA., *December* 3, 1864

GENERAL:—The little information gleaned from the Southern press indicating no great obstacle to your progress, I have directed your mails, which previously had been collected in Baltimore, by Colonel Markland, special agent of the post-office department, to be sent as far as the blockading squadron off Savannah, to be forwarded to you as soon as heard from on the coast. Not liking to rejoice before the victory is assured, I abstain from congratulating you and those under your command until bottom has been struck. I have never had a fear, however, for the result.

Since you left Atlanta, no very great progress has been made here. The enemy has been closely watched though, and prevented from detaching against you. I think not one man has gone from here, except some twelve or fifteen hundred dismounted cavalry. Bragg has gone from Wilmington. I am trying to take advantage of his absence to get possession of that place. Owing to some preparations Admiral Porter and General Butler are making to blow up Fort Fisher, and which, while I hope for the best, do not believe a particle in, there is delay in getting this expedition off. I hope they will be ready to start by the 7th, and that Bragg will not have started back by that time.

In this letter I do not intend to give you anything like directions for future action, but will state a general idea I have, and will get your views after you have established yourself on the sea-coast. With your veteran army I hope to get control of the only two through routes from east to west, possessed by the enemy before the fall of Atlanta. This condition will be filled by holding Savannah and Augusta, or by holding any other post to the east of Savannah and Branchville. If Wilmington falls, a force from there can co-operate with you.

Thomas has got back into the defenses of Nashville, with Hood close upon him. Decatur has been abandoned, and so have all the roads, except the main one leading to Chattanooga. . . .

I hope Hood will be badly crippled or destroyed. After all becomes quiet, and the roads up here so bad that there is likely to be a week or two that nothing can be done, I will run down to the coast and see you.

U. S. GRANT,
Lieutenant-General.

Major-General W. T. Sherman, Commanding Armies near Savannah.

HEADQUARTERS ARMIES OF THE UNITED STATES,
CITY POINT, VA., *December* 6, 1864.

GENERAL:—On reflection, since sending my letter by the hands of Lieutenant Dunn, I have concluded that the most important operation toward closing out the great rebellion will be to close out Lee and his army. You have now destroyed the roads of the South, so that it will probably take them months, without interruption, to re-establish a through line from east to west. In that time, I think, the job here will be effectually completed. My idea now is, that you establish a base on the coast, fortify and leave it to your artillery and cavalry, and enough infantry to protect them, and at the same time so threaten the interior that the militia of the South will have to be kept at home. With the balance of your command come here by water, with all dispatch. Select yourself the officer to leave in command, but you I want in person. Unless you see objections to this plan which I can not see, use every vessel going to you for the purpose of transportation.

Very respectfully, your obedient servant,

U. S. GRANT,
Lieutenant-General.

Major-General W. T. Sherman, Commanding Military Division of the Mississippi.

HEADQUARTERS MILITARY DIVISION OF THE MISSISSIPPI,
IN THE FIELD, NEAR SAVANNAH, *December* 11, 1864—2 A. M.

GENERAL:—Your dispatch of December 10th, and also Special Field Order 191, are just received. The general-in-chief wishes you to secure the trains cut off on the Gulf road, and also describe to him what is the position of King's bridge and Dillon's ferry; neither are on the map. I have had couriers looking for you since 5 P. M., with orders, but they are unable to find your headquarters. I send inclosed another copy. The general understands the trains to be between Way's and Fleming's Station.

I am, general, very respectfully, etc.,

L. M. DAYTON,
Aid-de-Camp.

Major-General O. O. Howard, Commanding Army of the Tennessee.

THE MARCH TO THE SEA.

HEADQUARTERS MILITARY DIVISION OF THE MISSISSIPPI,
IN THE FIELD, NEAR SAVANNAH, *December* 16, 1864.

GENERAL:—I received day before yesterday, at the hands of Lieutenant Dunn, your letter of December 3d, and last night, at the hands of Colonel Babcock, that of December 6th. I had previously made you a hasty scrawl from the tugboat Dandelion in Ogeechee river, advising you that the army had reached the sea-coast, destroying all railroads across the State of Georgia, and investing closely the city of Savannah, and had made connection with the fleet.

Since writing that note, I have in person met and conferred with General Foster and Admiral Dahlgren, and made arrangements which I deemed essential to reduce the city of Savannah to our possession; but since the receipt of yours of the 6th, I have initiated measures looking principally to coming to you with fifty or sixty thousand (50,000 or 60,000) infantry, and incidentally to take Savannah, if time will allow. At the time we carried Fort McAllister so handsomely by assault, with twenty-two (22) guns and its entire garrison, I was hardly aware of its importance; but since passing down the river with General Foster, and up with Admiral Dahlgren, I realize how admirably adapted are Ossabaw Sound and Ogeechee river to supply an army operating against Savannah. Sea-going vessels can easily come to King's bridge, a point on the Ogeechee river, fourteen and a half (14½) miles due west from Savannah, from which point we have roads leading to all our camps. The country is low and sandy, and cut up with marshes, which in wet weather will be very bad, but we have been so favored with weather that they are all now comparatively good, and heavy details are constantly employed in double corduroying the marshes, so that I have no fear of a bad spell of weather. Fortunately, also, by liberal and judicious foraging, we reached the sea-coast abundantly supplied with forage and provisions, needing nothing on arrival except bread. Of this we started from Atlanta with from eight to twenty (8 to 20) days' supply for corps, and some of the troops had only one (1) day's issue of bread during the trip of thirty (30) days, and yet they did not want, for sweet-potatoes were very abundant, as well as corn-meal, and our soldiers took to them naturally. We started with about five thousand (5,000) head of cattle, and arrived with over ten thousand (10,000); of course consuming mostly turkeys, chickens, sheep, hogs, and the cattle of the country. As for our mules and horses, we left Atlanta with about two thousand five hundred (2,500) wagons, many of which were drawn by mules which had not recovered from the Chattanooga starvation; all of which were replaced, the poor mules shot, and our transportation is now in superb condition. I have no doubt the State of Georgia has lost by our operations fifteen thousand (15,000) first-rate mules. As to horses, Kilpatrick collected all his remounts, and it looks to me, in riding along our columns, as though every officer has three or four led horses, and each regiment seems to be followed by at least fifty (50) negroes and foot-sore soldiers, riding on horses and mules. The custom was for each brigade to send out daily a foraging party of about fifty (50) men on foot, who invariably returned mounted, with several wagons loaded with poultry, potatoes, etc., and as the army is composed of about forty (40) brigades, you can estimate approximately the quantity of horses collected. Great numbers of these were shot by my orders, because of the disorganizing effect on our infantry of having too many idlers mounted. General Easton is now engaged in collecting statistics on this subject; but I know that the government will never receive full accounts of our captures, although the result aimed at was fully attained, viz., to deprive our enemy of them. All these animals I will have sent to Port Royal, or collected behind Fort McAllister, to be used by General Saxton in his farming operations, or by the quartermaster's department, after they are systematically accounted for.

While General Easton is collecting transportation for my troops to James river, I will throw to Port Royal Island all of our means of transportation I can, and collect the balance near Fort McAllister, covered by the Ogeechee river and intrenchments to be erected, and for which Captain Poe, my chief engineer, is now reconnoitering the grounds; but, in the meantime, I will act as I have begun, as though Savannah city were my only objective—namely, the troops will continue to invest Savannah closely, making attacks and feints wherever we have firm ground to stand upon; and I will place some thirty (30) pounder Parrots, which I have got from General Foster, in position near enough to reach the center of the city, and then will demand its surrender. If General Hardee is alarmed, or fears starvation, he may surrender; otherwise, I will bombard the city, but not risk the lives of my own men by assaults across the narrow causeways, by which alone we can reach it. If I had time, Savannah, with all its dependent fortifications, is already ours, for we hold all its avenues of supply. The enemy has made two desperate efforts to get boats from above to the city, in both of which he has been foiled; General Slocum, whose left flank rests on the river, capturing and burning the first boat, and in the second instance driving back two gunboats and capturing the steamer Resolute, with seven naval officers and a crew of twenty-five seamen. General Slocum occupies Argyle Island and the upper end of Hutchinson Island, and has a brigade on the South Carolina shore opposite, and he is very urgent to pass one of his corps over to that shore. But in view of the change of plan made necessary by your orders of the 6th, I will maintain things *in statu quo* till I have got all my transportation to the rear and out of the way, and until I have sea transportation for the troops you require at James river, which I will accompany and command in person. Of course, I will leave Kilpatrick with his cavalry, say five thousand three hundred (5,300), and, it may be, a division of the Fifteenth Corps; but before determining this, I must see General Foster, and may arrange to shift his force—now over about the Charleston railroad, at the head of Broad river—to the Ogeechee, where, in co-operation with Kilpatrick's cavalry, he can better threaten the State of Georgia than from the direction of Port Royal. Besides, I would much prefer not to detach from my regular corps any of its veteran divisions, and would even prefer that other less valuable troops should be sent to reinforce Foster, from some other quarter. My four (4) corps, full of experience and full of ardor, coming to you *en masse*, equal to sixty thousand (60,000) fighting men, will be a reinforcement that Lee can not disregard. Indeed, with my present command, I had expected, after reducing Savannah, instantly to march to Columbia, South Carolina, thence to Raleigh, and thence to report to you. But this would consume, it may be, six weeks' time, after the fall of Savannah, whereas, by sea, I can probably reach you with my men and arms before the middle of January.

As to matters in the Southeast, I think Hardee in Savannah has good artillerists, some five thousand (5,000) or six thousand (6,000), good infantry, and it may be, a mongrel mass of eight thousand or ten thousand (8,000 or 10,000) militia and fragments. In all our marching through Georgia, he has not forced me to use anything but a skirmish line, though at several points he had erected fortifications and made bombastic threats. In Savannah, he has taken refuge in a line constructed behind swamps and overflowed rice-fields, extending from a point on the Savannah river, about three miles above the city, around to a branch of the Little Ogeechee, which stream is impassable from its salt marshes and boggy swamps, crossed only by narrow causeways or common corduroy roads. There must be twenty-five thousand (25,000) citizens, men, women, and children, in Savannah, that must also be fed, and how he is to feed them beyond a few days, I can not imagine, as I know that his requisitions for corn, on the interior counties of Georgia were not filled, and we are in possession of the rice fields and mills, which alone could be of service to him in this neighborhood. He can draw nothing from South Carolina, save from a small corner down in the southeast, and that by a disused wagon-road. I could easily get posession of this, but hardly deem it worth the risk of making a detachment, which would be in danger by its isolation from the main army.

Our whole army is in fine condition as to health, and the weather is splendid. For that reason alone I feel a personal dislike to turning northward.

I will keep Lieutenant Dunn here until I know the result of my demand for the surrender of Savannah; but, whether successful or not, shall not delay my execution of your orders of the 6th, which will depend alone upon the time it will require to get transportation by sea.

W. T. SHERMAN,
Major-General U. S. A.

Lieutenant-General U. S. Grant, Commander-in-Chief, City Point, Va.

HEADQUARTERS MILITARY DIVISION OF THE MISSISSIPPI,
IN THE FIELD, NEAR SAVANNAH, GA., *December* 17, 1864.

GENERAL:—You have doubtless observed from your station at Rosedew that sea-going vessels now come through Ossabaw Sound and the Ogeechee to the rear of my army, giving me abundant supplies of all kinds, and more especially of heavy ordnance necessary to the reduction of Savannah. I have already received guns that can cast heavy and destructive shot as far as the heart of your city; also, I have for some days held and controlled every avenue by which the people and garrison of Savannah can be supplied, and I am therefore justified in demanding the surrender of the city of Savannah and its dependent forts, and shall await a reasonable time your answer before opening with heavy ordnance. Should you entertain the proposition, I am prepared to grant liberal terms to the inhabitants and garrison; but should I be forced to resort to assault, or the slower and surer process of starvation, I shall then feel justified in resorting to the harshest measures, and shall make little effort to restrain my army burning to avenge the great national wrong they attach to Savannah and other large cities, which have been prominent in dragging our country into civil war.

I inclose you a copy of General Hood's demand for the surrender of the town of Resaca, to be used by you for what it is worth.

I have the honor to be, your obedient servant,

W. T. SHERMAN,

Major-General.

General William J. Hardee, Commanding Confederate Forces in Savannah.

HEADQUARTERS DEPARTMENT SOUTH CAROLINA AND GEORGIA AND FLORIDA,
SAVANNAH, GA., *December* 17, 1864.

Major-General W. T. Sherman, Commanding Federal Forces near Savannah:

GENERAL:—I have to acknowledge receipt of a communication from you of this date, in which you demand "the surrender of Savannah and its dependent forts," on the ground that you "have received guns that can cast heavy and destructive shot into the heart of the city;" and for the further reason that you "have for some days held and controlled every avenue by which the people and garrison can be supplied." You add, that should you "be forced to resort to assault, or to the slower and surer process of starvation, you will then feel justified in resorting to the harshest measures, and will make little effort to restrain your army," etc., etc.

The position of your forces half a mile beyond the outer line for the land defense of Savannah is, at the nearest point, at least four miles from the heart of the city. That and the interior line are intact.

Your statement that you have for some days held and controlled every avenue by which the people and garrison can be supplied is incorrect. I am in free and constant communication with my department.

Your demand for the surrender of Savannah and its dependent forts is refused.

With respect to the threats conveyed in the closing paragraph of your letter, of what may be expected in case your demand is not complied with, I have to say that I have hitherto conducted the military opera-

THE MARCH TO THE SEA. 299

tions intrusted to my direction in strict accordance with the rules of civilized warfare, and I should deeply regret the adoption of any course by you that may force me to deviate from them in future.

I have the honor to be, very respectfully,
Your obedient servant,
W. J. HARDEE,
Lieutenant-General.

HEADQUARTERS DIVISION OF THE MISSISSIPPI,
IN THE FIELD, NEAR SAVANNAH, GA., *December* 18, 1864.

GENERAL:—I wrote you at length by Colonel Babcock on the 16th instant. As I therein explained my purpose, yesterday I made a demand on General Hardee for the surrender of the city of Savannah, and to-day received his answer refusing. Copies of both letters are herewith inclosed. You will notice that I claim that my lines are within easy range of the heart of Savannah, but General Hardee claims we are four and a half miles distant. But I myself have been to the intersection of the Charleston and Georgia railroad and the three (3) mile post is but a few yards beyond, within the line of our picket. The enemy has no pickets outside of his fortified line, which is a full quarter of a mile within the three (3) mile post, and I have the evidence of Mr. R. R. Cuyler, president of the Georgia Central railroad, who was a prisoner in our hands, that the mileposts are measured from the Exchange, which is but two squares from the river. . . . General Slocum feels confident that he can make a successful assault at one or two points in front of the Twentieth Corps and one or two in front of General Davis' (Fourteenth) Corps. But all of General Howard's troops, the right wing lie behind the Little Ogeechee, and I doubt if it can be passed by troops in the face of an enemy. Still we can make strong feints, and if I can get a sufficient number of boats, I shall make a co-operative demonstration up Vernon river or Wassaw Sound. I should like very much to take Savannah before coming to you; but, as I wrote to you before, I will do nothing rash or hasty, and will embark for the James river as soon as General Easton, who is gone to Port Royal for that purpose, reports to me that he has an approximate number of vessels for the transportation of the contemplated force. . . .

In relation to Savannah you will remark that General Hardee refers to his still being in communication with his war department. This language he thought would deceive me, but I am confirmed in the belief that the route to which he refers—namely, the Union plank-road, on the South Carolina shore—is inadequate to feed his army and the people of Savannah, for General Foster assures me that he has his force on that very road near the head of Broad river, and that his guns command the railroad, so that cars no longer run between Charleston and Savannah. We hold this end of the Charleston road, and have destroyed it from the three (3) mile post back to the bridge, about twelve (12) miles above. . . .

I do sincerely believe that the whole United States, North and South, would rejoice to have this army turned loose on South Carolina, to devastate that state in the manner we have done in Georgia, and it would have a direct and immediate bearing on your campaign in Virginia.

I have the honor to be, your obedient servant,

W. T. SHERMAN,
Major-General Commanding.

Lieutenant-General U. S. Grant, City Point, Va.

HEADQUARTERS MILITARY DIVISION OF THE MISSISSIPPI,
IN THE FIELD, NEAR SAVANAH, GA., *December* 19, 1864.

GENERAL:—The general-in-chief has gone to the bay. He wishes you to push the preparations for attacking Savannah with all possible speed, but to await orders for the attack. He will see General Foster and the admiral before returning, and will get co-operation from both, if possible. Should anything occur that you would like to communicate to the general, I will forward for you.

I am, general, with great respect,

L. M. DAYTON,
Aid-de-Camp.

Major-General O. O. Howard, Commanding Army of the Tennessee.

HEADQUARTERS MILITARY DIVISION OF THE MISSISSIPPI,
IN THE FIELD, NEAR SAVANNAH, GA., *December* 19, 1864.

GENERAL:—The general-in-chief has gone to the bay. He directs me to further instruct you to push preparations for the attack on the defenses of Savannah as rapidly as possible, and then await further directions before doing more.

He will endeavor to get co-operation from Admiral Dahlgren and General Foster, with whom he will confer before returning. If, in the meantime, anything should occur you would wish to communicate to him, please to send to me, and I will forward.

I am, general, with respect,

L. M. DAYTON,
Aid-de-Camp.

Major-General Slocum, Commanding Left Wing.

EXTRACT FROM GENERAL SHERMAN'S REPORT.

In the meantime, further reconnoissances from our left flank had demonstrated that it was impracticable or unwise to push any considerable force across the Savannah river, for the enemy held the river opposite the city with iron-clad gunboats, and could destroy any pontoons laid down by us between Hutchinson's Island and the South Carolina shore, which would isolate any force sent over from that flank. I therefore ordered

THE MARCH TO THE SEA.

General Slocum to get into position the siege-guns, and make all the preparations necessary to assault, and to report to me the earliest moment when he could be ready, whilst I should proceed rapidly round by the right, and make arrangements to occupy the Union causeway, from the direction of Port Royal. General Foster had already established a division of troops on the peninsula or neck between the Coosawhatchie and Tullifinney rivers, at the head of Broad river, from which position he could reach the railroad with his artillery.

I went to Port Royal in person, and made arrangements to reinforce that command by one or more divisions, under a proper officer, to assault and carry the railroad, and thence turn toward Savannah, until it occupied the causeway in question.

EXTRACT FROM GENERAL HOWARD'S REPORT.

It having been intimated that our future plans would be modified by specific instructions from the commander-in-chief, General Sherman and his officers became anxious to crown our success by the capture of Savannah. In order to accomplish this, every exertion was made. Heavy guns were brought from Hilton Head and McAllister, and placed in position; the lines were worked up closer to the enemy, along the dikes; good batteries constructed for small guns, and every part of the front of General Osterhaus and General Blair thoroughly reconnoitered; light bridges were constructed, and fascines made, so as to span the streams and fill up the ditches; in brief, every possible preparation was made to assault the enemy's works. The same was the case along General Slocum's front.

While these preparations were going on, the general-in-chief, having demanded the surrender of Savannah on the 18th instant, and having been refused, had gone to the fleet, in order to secure co-operation from the admiral and General Foster, in the contemplated attack. He left directions to get ready, but not to strike till his return.

Two at least of my division commanders felt perfectly confident of success, in case the assault should be made.

EXTRACT FROM GENERAL SLOCUM'S REPORT.

Our line was established as close as possible to that of the enemy, and the time spent in preparations for an assault upon his works. Batteries were established on the river, in such positions as prevented any boats from passing. The steamer Ida, while attempting to pass up from Savannah, on the 10th of December, was captured and burned. On the 12th, two gunboats and the steamer Resolute attempted to pass our batteries from above, but both gunboats were driven back by Winegar's battery, and the steamer was so disabled that she fell into our hands. She was soon repaired, and has since been transferred to the quartermaster's department.

On the 18th, a brigade of the First division, Twentieth Corps, was thrown across the river, and established near Izzard's plantation, on the South Carolina shore, in a position which threatened the only line of communication still held by the enemy. A bridge, in the meantime, had been constructed by the enemy from the city to the South Carolina shore, and on the evening of December 20th he commenced the evacuation of the city.

EXTRACT FROM THE REPORT OF GENERAL WILLIAMS.

During the day of the 20th, the fire from the enemy's works and gunboats was unusually-heavy and continuous. Reports from Carman's brigade, that large columns were crossing to the Carolina shore, either to cover their only line of communication, or preparatory to a final evacuation of the city. In the night, General Geary reported to me that the movements across the river were still apparently going on.

EXTRACT FROM GENERAL GEARY'S REPORT.

I ascertained this morning, the 20th, that the enemy had completed a pontoon bridge across to the South Carolina shore, from Savannah, and notified the general commanding the corps of the discovery. This bridge was about two and a half miles from my left. The usual artillery fire was kept up by the enemy during the day and night. During the night, I heard the movement of troops and wagons across the pontoon bridge before mentioned, and sent a report of the fact to the general commanding the corps.

EXTRACT FROM GENERAL JEFF. C. DAVIS' REPORT.

During the intervening days between the 12th and 21st, at which time the enemy evacuated his position, my troops were assiduously engaged in skirmishing with the enemy, reconnoitering his position, and making general preparations for an attack. Five (5) points in my front had, several days before the evacuation, been reconnoitered, and pronounced accessible to an attacking party. This information was duly forwarded to the commanding general.

EXTRACTS FROM COLONEL CARMAN'S REPORT.

I then moved the remaining regiment of the brigade—One Hundred and Fiftieth New York Volunteers—to the South Carolina shore, and established there my headquarters at Izzard's mill. The position occupied by the brigade was strong for defense, but the nature of the ground was such that an advance was difficult. . . .

During the night, I transported the two pieces of artillery across the river, and put them in position in the center of the line. The line as then formed and held by my brigade was two and a quarter miles long, the left resting on the Savannah river, and the right on an inlet near Clyesdale creek. . . .

December 20. . . . During the day, a great number of vehicles of all descriptions were seen passing our front, moving from Savannah toward Hardeeville, which was reported to the headquarters of the division. In the afternoon, a rebel gunboat came up the river in our rear, and threw about thirty shells into my brigade, killing one man of the One Hundred and Fiftieth New York. I could reach it with my artillery. At 4 P. M. the enemy was reinforced by three regiments of infantry from Savannah.

From 7 P. M. until 3 A. M. the noise of the retreating enemy could plainly be heard as they crossed the bridges from Savannah to the South Carolina shore.

CHARLESTON, S. C., *December* 8, 1864.

Lieutenant-General Hardee, Savannah, Ga.:

Having no army of relief to look to, and your forces being essential to the defense of Georgia and South Carolina, whenever you shall have to select between their safety and that of *Savannah*, sacrifice the latter, and form a junction with General Jones, holding the left bank of the Savannah river and the railroad to this place as long as possible.

G. T. BEAUREGARD.

HEADQUARTERS OF THE ARMY,
WASHINGTON, *December* 16, 1864.

GENERAL:—Lieutenant-General Grant informs me that in his last dispatch sent to you, he suggested the transfer of your infantry to Richmond. He now wishes me to say that you will retain your entire force, at least for the present, and, with such assistance as may be given you by General Foster and Admiral Dahlgren, operate from such base as you may establish on the coast. General Foster will obey such instructions as may be given by you. Should you have captured Savannah, it is thought that by transferring the water-batteries to the land side, that place may be made a good depot and base for operations on Augusta, Branchville, or Charleston. If Savannah should not be captured, or if captured and not deemed suitable for this purpose, perhaps Beaufort would serve as a depot. As the rebels have probably removed their most valuable property from Augusta, perhaps Branchville would be the most important point at which to strike in order to sever all connections between the Virginia and the Northwestern railroads. General Grant's wishes, however, are that this whole matter of your future actions should be left entirely to your discretion.

We can send you from here a number of complete batteries of field artillery, with or without horses, as you may desire. Also, as soon as General Thomas can spare them, all the fragments, convalescents, and furloughed men of your army. It is reported that Thomas defeated Hood yesterday near Nashville, but we have no particulars nor official reports, telegraphic communications being interrupted by a heavy storm. Our last advices from you were in General Howard's note, announcing his approach to Savannah.

Yours truly,
H. W. HALLECK,
Major-General, Chief of Staff.

Major-General Sherman, via Hilton Head.

HEADQUARTERS OF THE ARMY,
WASHINGTON, *December* 18, 1864.

MY DEAR GENERAL:—Yours of the 13th, by Major Anderson, is just received. I congratulate you on your splendid success, and shall very soon expect to hear of the crowning work of your new campaign, in the capture of Savannah. Your march will stand out prominently as the great one of this great war. When Savannah falls, then for another wide swath through the center of the Confederacy. But I will not anticipate. General Grant is expected here this morning, and will probably write you his own views.

* * * * * * * *

Orders have been issued for all officers and detachments, having three months or more to serve, to rejoin your army, via Savannah. Those having less than three months to serve will be retained by General Thomas. Should you capture Charleston, I hope that by *some* accident the place may be destroyed; and if a little salt should be sown upon its site, it may prevent the growth of future crops of nullification and secession.

Yours truly,
H. W. HALLECK,
Major-General, Chief of Staff.

Major-General W. T. Sherman, Savannah.

HEADQUARTERS MILITARY DIVISION OF THE MISSISSIPPI,
IN THE FIELD, SAVANNAH, *December* 24, 1864.

GENERAL:—I had the pleasure of receiving your two letters of the 16th and 18th instant to-day, and I feel more than usually flattered by the high encomiums you have passed on our recent campaign, which is now completed by the occupation of Savannah.

I am very glad that General Grant has changed his mind about embarking my troops for James river, leaving me free to make the broad swath you describe through South and North Carolina, and am still more gratified at the news from Thomas in Tennessee, because it fulfills my plans, which contemplated his being fully able to dispose of Hood in case he ventured north of the Tennessee river. So I think, on the whole, I can chuckle over Jeff. Davis' disappointment in not turning my Atlanta campaign into a Moscow disaster.

* * * * * * * *

THE MARCH TO THE SEA. 305

I will bear in mind your hint as to Charleston, and do n't think "salt" will be necessary. When I move, the Fifteenth Corps will be on the right of the right wing, and their position will naturally bring them into it first; and if you have watched the history of that corps, you will have remarked that they do their work up pretty well. The truth is, the whole army is burning with an insatiable desire to wreak vengeance upon South Carolina. I almost tremble at her fate, but feel that she deserves all that is in store for her. Many and many a person in Georgia asked me why we did not go to South Carolina; and when I answered that I was en route for that state, the invariable reply was, "Well, if you make those people feel the severities of war, we will pardon you for your desolation of Georgia." I look upon Columbia as quite as bad as Charleston, and I doubt if we shall spare the public buildings there as we did at Milledgeville.

* * * * * * * * *

I felt somewhat disappointed at Hardee's escape from me, but really am not to blame. I moved as quick as possible to close up the "Union Causeway," but intervening obstacles were such, that before I could get my troops on the road, Hardee slipped out. Still, I know that the men that were in Savannah will be lost in a·measure to Jeff. Davis; for the Georgia troops under G. W. Smith declared they would not fight in South Carolina, and they have gone north en route for Augusta, and I have reason to believe North Carolina troops have gone to Wilmington—in other words, they are scattered.

* * * * * * * * *

W. T. SHERMAN,
Major-General.

Major-General H. W. Halleck, Chief of Staff, Washington, D. C.

VOL. II—20

CHAPTER XXXVIII.

MARCH THROUGH THE CAROLINAS, FROM SAVANNAH TO GOLDSBORO AND RALEIGH; THE BATTLES OF AVERYSBORO AND BENTONVILLE.

SOON after the occupation of Savannah by General Sherman, the movement of his army by sea was abandoned, and its march through the Carolinas was adopted instead. General Sherman had indicated to General Grant, in his letter of December 16th, his preference for the overland movement, and in subsequent communications emphasized his choice. And in view of the apparent advantages of this approach to Virginia, General Grant authorized General Sherman, December 27th, to move his army northward through the Carolinas as soon as practicable. It was anticipated that this movement would prevent, in great measure, the union of the fragments of the defeated Confederate armies in the West and South, while it would repeat and intensify the effect produced by the march from Atlanta to Savannah. The plan adopted, compassed the permanent occupancy of Savannah by troops from a distance, that General Sherman might keep his army intact to be able to resist General Lee until General Grant could give him help from Virginia, should that general abandon the capital of the Confederacy to oppose him.

The river defenses of Savannah, with slight modifications, were deemed adequate. Forts Pulaski, Thunderbolt, and McAllister were put in complete order. The forts bearing upon the approaches by water were dismantled, and their heavy guns sent to Fort Pulaski and Hilton Head. The obstructions, including torpedoes, were removed from the adjacent waters, and Admiral Dahlgren had the channels staked out and indicated by buoys. Preparations were promptly commenced and energetically prosecuted, that the army might move northward by the 15th of January.

A portion of General Sherman's forces did move before the 15th of January; but rain, swollen rivers, and flooded lowlands so delayed co-operative columns, that they did not cross the Savannah river until the first week of February. On the 14th, General Howard, with General Blair's corps, crossed from Beaufort Island to the main land, flanked the enemy at Gordon's Corner, and followed him to Pocotaligo, and on the following morning took possession of the vacant fort at that place. This movement was a feint upon Charleston, to deceive the enemy as to General Sherman's first and second objectives, which were Columbia, South Carolina, and Goldsboro, North Carolina.

A pontoon bridge had been thrown at Savannah for the passage of the left wing, and the Union causeway had been repaired; but the flood in the river had borne away the bridge and submerged the causeway, and General Slocum was compelled to move up the river to find a crossing. Jackson's and Ward's divisions of the Twentieth Corps crossed at Purysburg, and on the 19th were at Hardeeville, in communication with General Howard at Pocotaligo. The Fourteenth Corps, and Geary's division of the Twentieth Corps, which had been relieved from garrison duty at Savannah, by General Grover's division of the Nineteenth Corps from Virginia, did not leave Savannah until the 26th of January. These troops then moved up to Sister's Ferry, and succeeded in crossing the river during the first week of February. In the meantime, the Fifteenth Corps, General John A. Logan commanding, had crossed the river and lowlands, and joined General Howard at Pocotaligo.

General Sherman's forces were now in readiness to enter upon a campaign which involved strategic combinations of widest range. When the northward march was first indicated, Generals Bragg, Beauregard, and Hardee were intent upon concentrating all fragments of armies far and near to oppose it. Generals Beauregard and Hardee were in Charleston, and General Bragg was in North Carolina.

North Carolina was open to attack from the coast, and

thither General Schofield's corps of twenty-one thousand men from the West and other forces were to move. General Sherman had an offensive army of sixty-five thousand men, and forces in his rear to hold Savannah and garrison such other fortified places as should fall into his hands. Acting aggressively on a broad field, with possible objectives in front, or right or left, their antagonist could conceal his purposes, and strike vital points uncovered by invitation of feints in other directions. The disposition of his forces from Sister's Ferry to Pocotaligo menaced equally Charleston, Columbia, and Augusta, and which was General Sherman's immediate objective, the Confederate generals could not discern with certainty. And if they could have ascertained his aims, he could change them with pleasure with crushing effect. Having passed by Augusta in his march from Atlanta that he might menace that city with his left flank while feigning against Charleston with his right, to concentrate between the divided forces of the enemy upon Columbia as his first objective, he proposed that his two wings should shake hands where secession first found positive expression through the convention of South Carolina, and then stride on to Goldsboro and Richmond.

The inevitable delay at Savannah was favorable to the enemy, as it had given time for a sweeping conscription in the states immediately threatened, for the fragments of Hood's army to move far toward the Carolinas, and for Wheeler to obstruct the roads before General Sherman's columns, and destroy the bridges that could not be utilized for defense. These obstructions, the depth of the rivers, and the breadth of the immediate lowlands on their margins, doubtless gave hope to the enemy that the invasion of the Carolinas would be greatly delayed, if not defeated. But though the obstacles were almost insurmountable, General Sherman's victorious troops did not hesitate to make causeways in the deep cold waters for miles, nor to make roads through the swamps of South Carolina in midwinter, and made a march not inferior to the celebrated passage of the Alps, except in the low lines of advance.

The infantry forces of the enemy occupied the line of the

Salkehatchie river, while Wheeler's cavalry hovered around the heads of column or on the flanks of the two wings. The left wing, with Kilpatrick on its left flank, moved upon Barnwell, threatening Augusta; the right wing, accompanied by General Sherman, moved westward to the Salkehatchie, touching the river at Beaufort and Rivers' bridges, flanking Charleston, and neutralizing the elaborate fortifications of that city, which had so long defied the heavy guns of iron-clads and land-batteries. The bridges of the Salkehatchie were defended with spirit, but in vain; and General Howard soon forced the passages, when the enemy retired to Branchville, burning all bridges behind him. These movements spread alarm everywhere. The Confederate forces were feeble at best, and there were now so many possibilities to General Sherman, all fruitful of ruin, that extreme uncertainty and foreboding of crushing disasters palsied the courage of troops and citizens. They could only guess at General Sherman's objective, and so many were possible' and his strategy so bewildering that no positions were held with adequate strength for temporary resistance, and Columbia was uncovered almost entirely.

General Sherman threw the Fifteenth and Seventeenth Corps on the Orangeburg road—the latter by Binnaker's bridge over the south fork of Edisto, and the former by Holman's. Having reached Orangeburg, the right wing moved on the direct road to Columbia. The enemy was driven from all points where resistance was made, and on the 16th, the head of column approached the capital of South Carolina. The left wing advanced steadily by Barnwell and Lexington as the general direction, and destroyed the Charleston and Augusta railroad for several miles. After a well-sustained menace to Augusta, General Slocum gathered his forces and touched the Saluda river above Columbia simultaneously with the arrival of General Howard on the bank of the river opposite the city.

General Sherman's maneuvers resulted in marked success. Throwing his columns in diverging lines from Savannah, and then converging them upon Columbia, he caused the evacuation of Charleston, and drove General Cheatham, moving eastward with the remnant of Hood's army, to the north of his projected line. It now remained to reach Goldsboro through repetition of the same confusing strategy; but the conditions of its success were now greatly changed, as the garrisons of Charleston, Columbia, and Augusta could be united with the Western troops and other forces on the Atlantic coast, and endanger isolated columns. Besides, a great strategist, General Joseph E. Johnston, had been appointed to the command of all the forces available to resist General Sherman, in tacit recognition of the fact that his management of defensive campaigns promised better results than that of any other general who could be assigned to command in the Carolinas; but General Johnston's conduct of the defensive was now to be subject to conditions radically different from those of the Atlanta campaign. His army, as before, was inferior to that of General Sherman's, and was composed of fragmentary troops, whose morale was in harmony with the condition of the cause which they represented; and, besides, he was to meet his old antagonist, with an army whose spirit had risen, if possible, with its successive triumphs, and not now, as before, restrained in maneuver by connection with a railroad as its only channel of supply. General Johnston could therefore have no hope of success, unless he could strike unsupported columns and defeat General Sherman in detail; and past experience did not give promise of such an opportunity.

In advancing from Columbia, General Sherman, as before, covered his real object by a menace in a different direction. He now directed General Slocum to threaten Charlotte, North Carolina, to create the impression that he would strike that point on his way to Virginia, while in reality directing his army to Goldsboro. Accordingly, General Slocum resumed motion on the 17th, crossed the Saluda at Mount Zion Church on the 19th, and Broad river at Freshley's mills the day following, and arrived at Winnsboro on the 21st. On this march the left wing and cavalry destroyed several miles of railroad north and south of Alston. The right wing, General Sherman accompanying, left Columbia on the 20th, on the direct road to Winnsboro, and destroyed the railroad between the two places. Eighty squares in Columbia were left in ashes from a conflagration whose origin and progress has been a matter of historical controversy.

From Winnsboro the two wings again diverged. General Slocum moved to the north with his troops well spread out and then turned east, crossed the Catawba, and advanced to Sneedsboro. The cavalry on his left demonstrated toward Charlotte, and then followed to Sneedsboro. The right wing, in the meantime, advanced to Cheraw—the Seventeenth Corps entering that place on the 2d of March. The enemy offered some resistance, but did not retard a single column. Wheeler's cavalry and the forces from Charleston appeared at times before the columns. The other forces, including Cheatham's from the West, were directed to Charlotte, under the impression that this was the objective.

From Pedee river the two wings moved toward Fayetteville, crossing near Sneedsboro and at Cheraw—the corps moving on separate roads, and the cavalry maintaining position on the left flank. On the 9th of March, General Hampton surprised one of General Kilpatrick's brigades, and gained a temporary advantage over his whole force. General Kilpatrick barely escaped capture on foot. The enemy, however, stopped to plunder the camps, and this gave time for the national cavalry to rally; and having done this, General Kilpatrick charged and recaptured his camps and repelled all subsequent attacks. General J. G. Mitchell, with his brigade of infantry, reached the scene of conflict just as the enemy abandoned his effort to regain his lost advantage.

On the 11th, the Fourteenth and Seventeenth Corps arrived at Fayetteville and skirmished with Hampton's cavalry, which covered General Hardee as he withdrew from the town on the bridge spanning Cape Fear river, which he succeeded in burning. It was anticipated that General Hardee would contest the possession of this place, but he abandoned it without resisting and with it a vast amount of public property, including an immense arsenal. At Fayetteville, General Sherman was met by the army tug Davidson, Captain Ainsworth commanding, and the gunboat Eolus, Lieutenant-Commander Young, with the first intelligence of the fall of Wilmington, and he then dispatched orders to Generals Schofield and Terry to move upon Goldsboro.

The march through South Carolina had left a track of desolation more than forty miles wide. That state's special guilt in taking the initiative in secession, was assumed by officers and men as the justification of its devastation. As many of the Southern people who were originally opposed to secession, blamed South Carolina for precipitating the movement, and having themselves experienced the terrible retributions of the war which resulted, desired that South Carolina should feel war's heavy hand before peace should come, it was not strange that the national troops in marching through the state which originally suggested secession, and studiously endeavored to induce the Southern States to withdraw from the Union, should leave behind them the fearful evidences of vengeance achieved. But it was easier for the veterans of the war to find justification for sweeping desolation in their own feelings than it is for others to find grounds for its historical vindication.

As General Johnston had now lost a large number of important places without losing their garrisons, and had been joined by several thousand troops from the West, it was now possible for him to unite all to resist General Sherman between Fayetteville and Goldsboro. Altogether they did not constitute an army equal to General Sherman's, yet, when united, were formidable against either wing or a smaller fraction. Referring to these forces, General Sherman thus wrote: "These made up an army superior to me in cavalry, and formidable enough in artillery and infantry to justify me in extreme caution in making the last step necessary to complete the march I have undertaken." In a letter to General Schofield, of March 12th, he said that General Johnston might concentrate at Raleigh from forty to forty-five thousand men, and wrote: "I can whip that number with my present force, and with yours and Terry's added, we can go wherever we can live." To General Grant, the same day, he wrote: "Joe Johnston may try to interpose between me and Schofield about Newbern; but I think he will not try that, but concentrate his scattered armies at Raleigh, and I will go straight at him as soon as I get my men reclothed and our wagons reloaded."

General Sherman's maneuvers, after leaving Fayetteville, were, in type, a repetition of his former strategy. He moved his cavalry toward Raleigh, and followed immediately with four divisions of the left wing, and more remotely with four of the right, throwing all his trains and the four remaining divisions farther to the east. He commenced these movements on the 15th. At 3 A. M. General Kilpatrick advanced on the direct road to Averysboro to make the feint on Raleigh, and then strike the railroad near Smithfield. General Slocum followed with four unincumbered divisions. General Howard held four divisions in trim to march to General Slocum's help should there be need. The trains of the left wing, with two divisions, moved on the direct road to Goldsboro, and the trains and two divisions of the right wing, toward Faison Station on the Wilmington and Goldsboro railroad. General Sherman accompanied the left wing.

The heavy rains made quagmires of the roads, and it became necessary to corduroy them for the artillery. So much of this work had been done in the swamps of South Carolina, that great facility had been attained, and the army moved on without serious delays. During the evening of the 15th, General Kilpatrick met a strong force of infantry near Taylor's Hole creek, under the command of General Hardee. He skirmished with the rear-guard and captured some prisoners, among whom was Colonel Rhett of the heavy artillery. The next morning General Slocum advanced his infantry columns to the vicinity of Averysboro, and found General Hardee intrenched on a narrow neck of swampy land between the Cape Fear and South rivers. General Hardee's position was in front of the point where the Goldsboro road through Bentonville leaves the main road leading in the direction of Raleigh. This was the first positive resistance which had been offered by infantry in strong force north of Savannah, and was doubtless intended to retard General Sherman's advance, until General Johnston could prepare for still stronger opposition at some point farther north or east. At this time the conjecture was that he would concentrate at Raleigh, Smithfield, or Goldsboro; but his point of intended concentration was much nearer than either of these towns. But the execution of General Sherman's plan, wherever General Johnston might offer battle, required that General Hardee should be dislodged. Without this, the feint on Raleigh could not be sustained or even fully initiated, and the ultimate reunion of the columns, as contemplated, could not be effected, as General Hardee barred the diverging road to Goldsboro.

General Slocum was therefore ordered to advance against General Hardee, whose position was not strong, except from intrenchments and the softness of the ground before it, which scarcely admitted the deployment and advance of infantry, and rendered the movement of horses almost impossible. Notwithstanding this obstacle, General Slocum advanced, Williams' corps leading and Ward's division deployed. General Ward's skirmishers soon developed Rhett's brigade of artillery, acting as infantry, behind slight intrenchments, whose trend was at right angles to the road, and was sustained by a battery, which enfiladed the line of direct approach. Direct attack being perilous, General Williams threw a brigade on the left of the enemy's line, when the quondam artillerymen, in complete rout, fell back to a stronger position. This success opened the way for a general attack, to accomplish which Jackson's division formed on the right of Ward and General Davis' two divisions of the Fourteenth Corps on his left. General Kilpatrick was directed to reach out beyond Jackson's right flank and grasp the Bentonville road. One brigade of cavalry gained the road, but was attacked furiously by McLaw's division, and driven back. After this repulse, General Slocum's whole line advanced, pushed General Hardee within his intrenchments, and pressed him there so heavily that during the following dark and stormy night he retreated. The next morning, General Ward followed through Averysboro, but soon rejoined the main force, in motion on the Goldsboro road, which the engagement had opened. General Slocum lost about eighty killed and four hundred and eighty wounded. The enemy left one hundred and seventy-eight dead on the field, and lost one hundred and seventy-five men and three guns by capture. The number of his wounded was not ascertained. General Ward's pursuit developed the fact that General Hardee had retreated toward Smithfield.

The night previous, General Kilpatrick crossed South river, and on the 17th advanced toward Elevation, on the east bank. General Slocum built a bridge over the swollen stream, and then advanced on the Goldsboro road. General Sherman continued with the left wing, and encamped with the head of column, on the night of the 18th, on the Goldsboro road, twenty-five miles from Goldsboro, and five from Bentonville, at a point where the road from Clinton to Smithfield crosses the one to Goldsboro. General Howard reached Lee's store, a few miles distant, the same night, and the two wings were sufficiently near to give support in battle, and were upon roads which united a short distance to the east.

Up to this time, General Sherman had anticipated an attack upon his left flank; but he was now led to believe that General Johnston would not attack, as it was supposed that he had retreated to Smithfield, and he gave orders for the two columns to move upon Goldsboro—General Howard, on the new Goldsboro road, by Falling Creek Church, to give the direct road to General Slocum. His object was to concentrate his forces at Goldsboro as soon as practicable, and he moved to General Howard's head of column, to open communication with Generals Schofield and Terry—the former coming to meet him from Newbern, and the latter from Wilmington, having conjointly from thirty to thirty-five thousand men. It was not known that General Johnston's whole army was in immediate proximity, but it was supposed that only cavalry would be met on the way to Goldsboro.

Scarcely had General Carlin's division of the Fourteenth Corps, in the advance of the left wing, wheeled into the road to push on to Goldsboro, when Dibbrell's division of cavalry was met, whose stubborn resistance indicated that there was support, or that its courage had given a new type to the conflict of cavalry with infantry. Being under orders to press on, and supposing that cavalry alone was in his front, General Carlin engaged the enemy vigorously, and soon the responsive roar of artillery announced the opening of a battle which General Johnston was delivering, in expectation of crushing the Fourteenth Corps at least. But the magnitude of the conflict was not yet apparent. As the resistance of the enemy became more stubborn, Colonels Hobart's and Miles' brigades were deployed, the former on the right, and Colonel Buell was sent, by order of General Slocum, some distance to the left to develop the enemy's line. The resistance offered by the enemy was supposed at first to be done by cavalry, and General Slocum so reported to General Sherman, who had gone to the right to join General Howard, whose columns were moving toward Goldsboro.

As resistance increased, General Morgan was directed to move to the right of Carlin in support. The former threw General Mitchell's brigade to the right of Miles' brigade and the road, and General Fearing's to the right and rear of Mitchell—both in double lines. The Seventy-eighth Illinois of the former was sent forward to skirmish. Under this stronger formation, both division generals were directed to press the enemy closely, and compel him to reveal his position and strength.

General Slocum soon became convinced that he had before him a force more formidable than a division of cavalry. While still in doubt as to the strength of the enemy, a deserter came to him, who had been a national soldier, who gave information that General Johnston had, by forced marches, massed his entire army in his front. This statement being supported by actual developments, induced General Slocum to prepare for defense, and immediately ordered General Williams to throw his train to the right, gather his forces, and hasten to the support of General Davis. He then sent a messenger to General Sherman to announce that there was evidence that an army was before him.

The direction of General Hardee's retreat from Averysboro, had led to the belief that the way to Goldsboro was open. And this was the impression that General Johnston desired to make by all his movements. General Hardee meanwhile had changed direction not far from Averysboro, and by a detour, had united his command with the other forces concentrated and intrenched near Bentonville. Apparently, the coveted conditions of the battle assured the success of General

Johnston's strategy, for two divisions in isolation were within his reach; two more were distant a few miles, and the four divisions of the right wing, intended for the support of the left, in the event of battle, were in rapid motion toward Goldsboro, far to the right. General Williams' defeat, in prospect, was to follow that of General Davis, and the other corps and detached divisions were to be defeated in turn, and the trains destroyed. The plan miscarried, mainly, from two unexpected causes—the resistance of two divisions until the Twentieth Corps could give support, and the lack of complete concert of action in General Johnston's army, composed of the commands of Generals Bragg, Hardee, S. D. Lee, and Cheatham.

When General Slocum first ordered the Twentieth Corps to move quickly to the field, it was his intention to form it on the right of the Fourteenth, but when he became fully convinced that General Johnston's army was in his front, he directed General Williams to form his corps, as the several fractions should reach the field, on the left of General Davis. Robinson's being in the advance, was the first to come up, and was placed in support of Carlin's division.

Anticipating that Colonel Buell would need support in his movement, General Carlin was directed by General Davis to move Hobart's brigade to the left, and place Robinson's brigade in its place in the line, and support a battery, located on the main road, which had been responding to the enemy's artillery.

Colonel Buell, in advancing as directed, soon struck the enemy's intrenchments, which he assaulted furiously. After a somewhat protracted struggle, resulting in heavy loss, Colonel Buell was forced to withdraw his brigade, which had been badly broken, when the enemy sallied from his works in strong force in pursuit, and pressed him back, until checked by Hobart's brigade, which offered most stubborn resistance.

When the action commenced, the small train of the corps, in charge of General Vanderveer's brigade, was moved to the right, until this brigade had reached the right of General Mitchell, where the troops were formed in double lines, with their right resting on a swamp. This was a timely disposition, as the advance of the enemy against Colonel Buell was merely an incident in General Johnston's plan of aggression, which was to wheel his whole line upon its left to envelop and capture General Davis' two divisions. Colonel Hobart, first, after Colonel Buell, felt the force of this general attack, but he was not entirely encompassed, as Buell's attack had broken the continuity of the enemy's movement, and General Johnston's troops on the right of the point assaulted by Buell failed to move forward promptly. This failure gave time for General Davis to make such dispositions as were essential to his safety, and afforded General Slocum opportunity to bring up his reserve artillery and locate it with reference to the arrest of the enemy and the formation of a new line to the left and rear.

The front attack upon Hobart and Robinson on his right, was so vigorous as to involve them speedily in the severest conflict, and soon after in retreat upon the artillery, put in position far to the rear, on the main road. The recession of these brigades exposed the artillery on the right of Robinson, three pieces of which were captured, and also caused the retirement of Miles' brigade between Mitchell's left and the road. There were now only two brigades, Mitchell's and Vanderveer's, on the original line, and the flank of the former was in air.

At this juncture, General Davis rode to his right and ordered General Fearing's brigade to move to the left, forming line of battle as it advanced, and facing the Bentonville road. This brigade moved quickly and was soon lost to view in the thickly wooded swamp. General Morgan now directed General Mitchell to throw his second line on his left, but this movement had been anticipated by the brigade commander in provision for the stability of his left flank. Mitchell's brigade was now in single line, bent at right angles in the center.

The full weight of the enemy's attack was soon after felt by all the troops on the field. The forces that had driven back Carlin's division and Robinson's brigade, pursued toward the batteries in the rear, and heavy columns assaulted Mitchell and Vanderveer with great impetuosity. General Slocum had been active in forming a new line near his artillery, which covered the re-formation of the troops that had been driven back on the left. To this result General Fearing rendered timely co-operation, as he advanced against the flank of the columns in parallelism to the road, and brought upon himself a counter attack by overwhelming numbers. Wounded himself, and his brigade decimated, he persisted in holding his position for a time, but was finally compelled to give ground, to the exposure of Mitchell's flank. In the emergency, General Morgan threw Vanderveer's second line to Mitchell's left; but his line thus extended, was soon overlapped, and the two brigades, in single line, were exposed to attacks in front and rear, as they were cut off from all support and from all communication with the corps commander, and each brigade was separately surrounded. Repulsing the enemy in front repeatedly, they leaped their barricades and reversing the direction of their fire repelled the enemy from their rear. In this state of affairs, General Davis put into the action his escort and a train-guard of four companies under Lieutenant-Colonel Topping. General Hoke and a part of his division were captured in the rear of Mitchell and Vanderveer, but as a guard could not be spared from the engagement, the prisoners passed round Vanderveer's right flank and escaped.

In the meantime, the new line had been formed at right angles to the road, at the batteries, and Fearing's brigade and portions of Carlin's division faced the road, but not in connection with Mitchell's left. The general line was now bent twice at right angles—an improvised formation, but the most effective possible for defense; for the enemy's columns of attack to the left of Mitchell's salient angle were taken in flank in assaulting either the line parallel to the road or the one at right angles to it, while batteries enfiladed the road between the two angles of the line, and to some extent covered the opening between Mitchell and the troops on his left, and also swept a wide open space to the left of the road. The firmness of Mitchell and Vanderveer contributed largely to break the offensive force of General Johnston's army.

Late in the evening, Cogswell's brigade of the First division, Twentieth Corps, moved into the space between Fearing and

Mitchell, and drove the enemy back until nearly all the lost ground was recovered.

Viewed in relation to the magnitude of the army, successfully resisted by eight brigades of infantry, and Kilpatrick's division of cavalry, which held position on the left and rear, the objects and hopes of the enemy and the character of the fighting by Morgan's division, this engagement takes rank amongst the great decisive battles of the war. The defense, under such unequal conditions, was triumphantly successful, and General Johnston here failed in the only special aggressive effort against General Sherman in his march from Atlanta to Raleigh. That the issue turned upon the action of the brigades of Mitchell, Vanderveer, and Fearing, can not be doubted. The two former did not give an inch of ground to the enemy, though thrown into single lines, cut off from support, surrounded, and compelled to fight in front and rear. The action of Fearing's brigade was not less important, as it disturbed and defeated General Johnston's combination to utilize for complete success his first advantage. General Fearing fought in complete isolation for some time, without defenses, and when his right flank was struck by the enemy with such force as to shatter it, he changed front upon his left, rallied his shattered troops, and held the ground essential to the stability of the new line. The later dispositions and resistance by the whole command gave a symmetry and brilliancy to the conflict which have seldom found expression in such urgent improvision.

To the enemy the issue must have been dispiriting in the extreme. Sadly and hopelessly must the Confederate chieftain have witnessed the failure of his initiative, in destroying General Sherman's corps consecutively, in their isolation. He had constructed his fortifications, which were strong and elaborate, to accomplish this object. His intrenchments crossed the main Goldsboro' road at right angles, then extended to the west one mile, and then curved more than two miles to the west-northwest, nearly parallel to the road, but concealed by distance and forests. He then resisted strongly on the Bentonville road to conceal his fortifications at that point, that he might throw his whole army around the Fourteenth Corps and interpose between it and the Twentieth, which, at the first, was nearly ten miles in the rear, and restrained from swift motion by exceedingly boggy roads, made almost impassable by the wagons and artillery of the Fourteenth Corps. The failure of the initiative of this elaborate plan, was therefore entirely unexpected to General Johnston, and was doubtless as much a surprise to himself as was the presence of his army at Bentonville to General Sherman, who scattered his columns the morning before the battle, believing that the Confederate army was far to the north, having abandoned the purpose of offering further resistance to his advance to Goldsboro.

In the evening the remainder of the Twentieth Corps reached the field, and was placed on the left of the line of battle, with Kilpatrick's troopers covering that flank.

When General Sherman was informed by General Slocum, through a messenger late in the day, that General Johnston's army had been developed, he directed him to call up his two divisions guarding the wagon trains, and also General Hazen's division of the Fifteenth Corps, then in the rear of the right wing, but several miles distant, and to act defensively until he could direct the remaining divisions of the right wing to the enemy's left and rear, from the direction of Cox's bridge over the Neuse river. At the time, General Howard's advance was near this bridge, about ten miles from Goldsboro. General Sherman did not give full credit to General Slocum's reports of General Johnston's concentration at Bentonville, as he did not believe that he would accept or invite battle with the Neuse river in his rear.

On the morning of the 20th, Generals Baird and Geary, each with two brigades, and General Hazen, with his entire division, arrived on the field. General Hazen, by direction of General Slocum, formed his command on the right of General Morgan, and General Baird moved out in front of the line of battle of the preceding day. These three generals received orders to press the enemy, and General Morgan gained a portion of his line on the right.

At 2 A. M., on the 20th, General Sherman informed General

Slocum that he would go to his support with his whole army. He turned back the right wing from the Neuse river, ordered General Schofield to push for Goldsboro and then move toward Smithfield, and instructed General Terry to move on Cox's bridge and establish a crossing. By daylight, General Howard's columns were in motion toward Bentonville. Cavalry was encountered earlier, but the first infantry was found behind barricades near Bentonville, three miles east of the battle-field. General Logan, in moving forward, ascertained that General Johnston's left was refused behind a parapet, connecting with the intrenchments before General Slocum, with a salient on the main Goldsboro road between the two wings. His flanks rested on Mill creek, covering the road to Smithfield, which crosses the stream on a bridge. General Sherman directed General Howard to approach cautiously, who connected his left flank with General Slocum's right at 4 P. M., and then a strong line was presented to the enemy.

On the 21st, General Sherman gave orders to press the enemy with skirmishers, use artillery freely, but not give battle unless at an advantage. The same day, General Schofield reached Goldsboro, and General Terry laid a pontoon bridge at Cox's bridge, and then the three armies, in the aggregate nearly one hundred thousand men, were virtually united.

During the day, General Mower's division of the Seventeenth Corps worked round the enemy's left flank, and nearly reached the bridge so essential to General Johnston. This movement and the approach of Generals Schofield and Terry induced General Johnston to abandon his position the following night. General Johnston, in this case as in all others during the war, made a safe retreat. He sacrificed his pickets and left his wounded in hospitals, but lost nothing of value besides.

General Slocum lost nine officers and one hundred and forty-five men killed, fifty-one officers and eight hundred and sixteen men wounded, and two hundred and twenty-three captured. The aggregate loss was twelve hundred and forty-seven. He buried on the field one hundred and sixty-seven of the enemy, and captured three hundred and thirty prisoners.

General Howard's total loss was three hundred and ninety-nine, and he captured twelve hundred and eighty-seven.*

General Johnston was pursued at dawn the next morning, but the troops were soon recalled, when General Sherman renewed his orders for the concentration at Goldsboro.

After the armies had been placed in encampments, General Sherman visited General Grant to confer with regard to the final operations of the war on the Atlantic coast. He returned with the impression that General Lee would unite with General Johnston after abandoning Richmond. But whatever the specific action of the two Confederate generals might be, he was to co-operate with General Grant by advancing against General Johnston and then moving north.

At Goldsboro, General Sherman proposed a new organization for his combined armies, giving General Schofield the command of the "center," and thus designating his forces, retaining for the right wing its old designation, Army of the Tennessee, and styling the two corps of the Army of the Cumberland, the Fourteenth and Twentieth, the "Army of Georgia." The left wing had informally borne this name during the march through Georgia and the Carolinas, but these corps were only really detached from the Army of the Cumberland after they had fought their last battle.

This fact gives the Fourth, Fourteenth, and Twentieth Corps a community of fame and glory achieved at Nashville and Bentonville. General Sherman had assigned them separate fields of operation, but had not formally separated them until it was too late to give them new historic relations. The fame of "Bentonville," quite as much as that of "Franklin" and "Nashville," belongs to the Army of the Cumberland. At Bentonville, the Fourteenth Corps, long under the personal command of General Thomas, and the Twentieth, of more recent connection with the Army of the Cumberland, but of friendly alliance, achieved a great victory. Indeed, all the achievements of these three corps, in union or separation, are portions of the history of the same army, as by hearty consent each has an interest in the aggregate glory. They have an

---

* General Sherman's statement in official report.

undivided tenure in the fame of the army, achieved in all the battles from Lookout Mountain to Jonesboro; not less do they hold in common the glory of the fields so widely separated. The shouts of the Fourteenth and Twentieth Corps at Savannah for victory at Nashville, in which the Fourth and their own representatives had a share, and their beloved commander the chief glory, was answered in glad response from every camp in Tennessee and Alabama for the repulse of General Johnston in his attempt to bring defeat and disgrace to the oldest corps of the unequaled Army of the Cumberland.

On the 9th of April, General Lee surrendered himself and his army to General Grant, and on the following morning, General Sherman's armies moved from the vicinity of Goldsboro toward Smithfield and Raleigh, against the only remaining Confederate army east of the Mississippi river. General Johnston knew well that he could not resist the hundred thousand men moving against him, but to make the most of his slender possibilities, he retreated through Raleigh as General Sherman advanced, and fell back to Greensboro. His objects were to avoid the crime of waging a hopeless warfare, to get the best possible terms in a surrender which would terminate it, and disband his troops on such conditions as would prevent their plundering their friends as they sought their homes. The last campaigns had inflicted upon the South losses of a magnitude transcending approximate estimation and a desolated country, wasted resources and the traditions of a lost cause (but a cause which, during the bloody trial of its existence and supremacy, had commanded the persistent efforts and strongest aspirations of millions) were now the sad inheritance of a proud people. And General Johnston sought to save what material resources remained, and to return his soldiers to their homes with as little demoralization as possible.

At Smithfield, General Sherman heard of the surrender of General Lee, and pressed forward with the conviction that he would soon give the final blow. At Raleigh, he dropped his trains, and directed General Howard to follow the line of retreat, and General Slocum to take a route to the south through Pittsville and Ashboro, in expectation that General Johnston would follow the railroad to Salisbury. On the 14th, he received a note which opened negotiations and resulted in a convention embracing conditions of peace as well as the surrender of the remaining Confederate forces and armies, and declaring a truce until after notice should be given of its discontinuance, on account of the disapproval of the government of the terms agreed upon. The government did disapprove, and the stipulated notice of forty-eight hours, as the limit of the truce, was given on the 24th. Two days later, there was a second conference at General Johnston's request, which resulted in the surrender of all the forces of the Confederacy east of the Chattahoochee river. The next day General Sherman announced in orders the cessation of hostilities, and made provision for the relief of the people. He then directed Generals Howard and Slocum to move their armies through Richmond to Washington.

HEADQUARTERS MILITARY DIVISION OF THE MISSISSIPPI,
IN THE FIELD, FAYETTEVILLE, N. C., *March* 12, 1865.

GENERAL:—

* * * * * * * * *

We must not lose time for Joe Johnston to concentrate at Goldsboro. We can not prevent his concentrating at Raleigh, but he shall have no rest. I want General Schofield to go on with his railroad from Newbern as fast as he can, and you do the same from Wilmington. If we can get the roads to, and secure Goldsboro by April 10th, it will be soon enough, but every day is worth a million of dollars. I can whip Joe Johnston, provided he don't catch one of my corps in flank; and I will see that my army marches hence to Goldsboro in compact form.

* * * * * * * * *

W. T. SHERMAN,
Major-General.

Major-General Terry, Commanding United States Forces, Wilmington, N. C.

HEADQUARTERS MILITARY DIVISION OF THE MISSISSIPPI,
IN THE FIELD, FAYETTEVILLE, N. C., *March* 12, 1865.

DEAR GENERAL:—

* * * * * * * * *

I hope you have not been uneasy about us and that the fruits of this march will be appreciated. It had to be made not only to secure the valuable depots by the way, but its incidents, in the necessary fall of Charleston, Georgetown, and Wilmington. If I can add Goldsboro to the list without too much cost, I will be in position to aid you materially in the spring campaign.

Joe Johnston may try to interpose between me here and Schofield about Newbern; but I think he will not try that, but concentrate his scattered armies at Raleigh, and I will go straight at him as soon as I get my men reclothed and our wagons reloaded.

Keep everybody busy and let Stoneman push toward Greensboro or Charlotte from Knoxville; even a feint in that quarter will be most important. . . .

I expect to make a junction with General Schofield in ten days.

Yours truly,
W. T. SHERMAN,
Major-General.

Lieutenant-General U. S. Grant, Commanding United States Army, City Point.

HEADQUARTERS MILITARY DIVISION OF THE MISSISSIPPI,
IN THE FIELD, OPPOSITE FAYETTEVILLE, N. C., TUESDAY, *March* 14, 1865.

GENERAL:—I am now across Cape Fear river, and to-morrow will draw out ten miles, and next day, if weather is favorable, will begin to maneuver on Goldsboro. I shall feign on Raleigh, by approaching, and it may be striking the railroad half-way between Goldsboro and Raleigh; then, as soon as the wagons are well toward Faison's, will swing rapidly in front of Goldsboro, but will not cross the Neuse till I hear from you. You must push vigorously toward Kingston and Goldsboro, with the absolute certainty that I will engage the attention of Joe Johnston's army to the west and southwest of Goldsboro. . . .

I take it for granted Joe Johnston now has S. D. Lee's corps, four thousand (4,000); Cheatham's, five thousand (5,000); Hoke's, eight thousand (8,000); Hardee's, ten thousand (10,000); and detachments, about ten thousand (10,000); making thirty-seven thousand (37,000), with near eight thousand (8,000) cavalry. Our duty is to effect a junction south of the Neuse; but if you can get Kingston whilst Joe Johnston is engaged with me, do so, and push on toward Goldsboro. I will attack the Raleigh road. . . .

I am, yours truly,
W. T. SHERMAN,
Major-General Commanding.

Major-General Schofield, Commanding at Newbern.

HEADQUARTERS MILITARY DIVISION OF THE MISSISSIPPI,
IN THE FIELD, OPPOSITE FAYETTEVILLE, TUESDAY, *March* 14, 1865.

DEAR GENERAL:—I am now across Cape Fear river with nearly all my army, save one division, with orders to cross at daylight to-morrow. I shall then draw out ten miles, and begin my maneuvers for the possession of Goldsboro, which is all important for our future purposes.

I was in hopes that I could get some shoes and stockings at Wilmington, but the tug Davidson has returned with Brigadier-General Dodge, chief quartermaster, with word that there is no clothing there; but he brings us some forage, sugar, and coffee. I can get along for ten days, having forced the army to collect plenty of beef and a good deal of cornmeal.

I shall to-night move my cavalry (5,000) straight toward Raleigh, and follow it with four divisions infantry, without trains, and keep the trains off toward the right rear. I will hold another four divisions in close support, and move toward Smithfield, or to strike the railroad half way between Goldsboro and Raleigh; then, when my trains are well across toward the Neuse, will move rapidly to Bentonville, and afterward, at leisure, move opposite Goldsboro, and open direct communication with General Schofield, who is ordered to push against Kingston and Goldsboro. I may cross the Neuse about Cox's bridge, and move into Goldsboro; but will not attempt it till within close communication with General Schofield. I have sent full orders to Schofield. It will not do to build any determinate plan until I am in full possession of Goldsboro. I have ordered Generals Schofield and Terry to push toward Goldsboro as hard as possible from the east, as I advance from the southwest. The enemy is superior to me in cavalry, but I can beat his infantry man for man; and I do n't think that he can bring forty thousand (40,000) men for battle. I will force him to guard Raleigh until I have interposed between it and Goldsboro.

Weather is good now, but threatens rain. We are all well. Keep all parts busy, and I will give the enemy no rest.

Yours truly,
W. T. SHERMAN,
Major-General.

Lieutenant-General U. S. Grant, City Point.

HEADQUARTERS MILITARY DIVISION OF THE MISSISSIPPI,
IN THE FIELD, OPPOSITE FAYETTEVILLE, N. C., *March* 14, 1865.

GENERAL:—I have notified General Howard that to-morrow night your head of column will be near the cross-roads above Kyle's landing; the next day across Black river, near Mingo, and third day near Bentonville; and have instructed him to have four (4) divisions in easy support, and a little in advance of you—say, five or six miles—so that, on receiving orders or hearing battle, he may come promptly up on your right.

I think Colonel Garber can promise you another boat, in which case it would be well to send to Wilmington your prisoners of war You might leave them to-morrow where the gunboat lies, two (2) miles below General Howard's bridge, and the guard, if unable to overtake you the day after to-morrow, could follow direct to Bentonville. I want the first marches to be made with prudence and deliberation. I am willing to accept battle with Johnston's concentrated force, but would not attack him in position until I make a junction with General Schofield.

I am, truly yours,
W. T. SHERMAN,
Major-General Commanding.

Major-General Slocum, Commanding Left Wing.

HEADQUARTERS MILITARY DIVISION OF THE MISSISSIPPI,
IN THE FIELD, OPPOSITE FAYETTEVILLE, *March* 14, 1865—7 P. M.

GENERAL:—I think I have studied the problem of the next move, and will give you in confidence its analysis.

We must make a strong feint on Raleigh, and strike with cavalry, if possible, the railroad near Smithfield. I take it for granted that the bridge will be too strongly guarded for General Kilpatrick to surprise, and therefore I will leave him to disable that road, of course only partially, between the Neuse and Eureka. To this end the cavalry will move to-night across the bridge, beginning at 3 A. M., and will push up the plank-road to about Averysboro, General Slocum following up with four disincumbered divisions to near the forks of the road, moving his trains by a cross-road toward Bentonville. The next move will be the cavalry to Elevation, and General Slocum will cross Black river. The next move will bring General Slocum to Bentonville, and Kilpatrick, supported by a division of infantry, will make a dash for the railroad. This is as far as I will now determine.

I want you to be as near in support as possible. I do think it is Johnston's only chance to meet this army before an easy junction can be effected with General Schofield.

I would like you to have four (4) divisions free to move rapidly to the sound of battle in the direction of Mingo creek and Elevation, and, at any event, to make a junction by head of column with General Slocum at Bentonville. The weather looks bad, and I fear we may have swamps about South river. I think it would be well for you to have four divisions to get ahead of General Slocum's trains on the direct road from Fayetteville to Bentonville, and keeping ahead of him about five or six miles, so as, in case of action, to come up on his right.

* * * * * * * *

Yours truly,
W. T. SHERMAN,
Major-General Commanding.

Major-General O. O. Howard, Commanding Right Wing.

HEADQUARTERS MILITARY DIVISION OF THE MISSISSIPPI,
IN THE FIELD, 18 MILES NORTHEAST FAYETTEVILLE, *March* 17, 1865—7 A. M.

GENERAL:—General Slocum found the enemy covering the narrow neck from Taylor's creek to Goldsboro road. He drove them from two successive positions, taking three guns, some prisoners, wounded, but losing himself pretty severely—I think as many as three hundred in all; but the enemy lost heavily also, from appearances. . . .

General Slocum will feel out toward Averysboro, but move his column on the Goldsboro road, which is that which crosses Black and Mingo creeks, just ahead of where we are. Our true tactics would be to push all our columns to Smithfield, but I will only follow Hardee far enough to give him impulse, when we must resume our course.

I want you to-day to get to where the Goldsboro road crosses Mingo, and have that bridge well repaired. You need not come on to General Slocum unless you hear him engaged. We might cut his column at Elevation, but it will be enough to think of that to-night.

General Blair is getting too far off; better draw him and all your trains toward Troublefield's Store.

* * * * * * * * *

Yours, etc.,

W. T. SHERMAN,
Major-General Commanding.

Major-General O. O. Howard, *Commanding Right Wing.*

HEADQUARTERS MILITARY DIVISION OF THE MISSISSIPPI,
IN THE FIELD, CAMP BETWEEN NORTH RIVER AND MINGO CREEK,
March 17, 1865.

GENERAL:—

* * * * * * * * *

I have examined your order, and it will do, only get on a right-hand road as soon as possible, that you may not delay General Slocum's troops, who will all be forced on the one road. Try and keep around the head of Falling Water creek, viz., to the south. I will push General Slocum to-morrow and next day, and think by day after to-morrow we will be in position—viz., you directly in front of Goldsboro, and General Slocum at Cox's bridge.

At the time I sent Colonel Ewing to you yesterday, the enemy had brought General Slocum up all standing, and it was on the theory that he would hold General Slocum there, that I wanted you at Mingo bridge. But the enemy retreated in the night on Smithfield, and we are again on the march, feigning to the left, but moving trains and troops as rapidly as the roads admit on Goldsboro. You may do the same.

* * * * * * * * *

Yours truly,

W. T. SHERMAN,
Major-General

Major-General Howard, *Commanding Right Wing.*

HEADQUARTERS MILITARY DIVISION OF THE MISSISSIPPI,
IN THE FIELD, TWENTY-SEVEN MILES FROM GOLDSBORO, N. C.,
March 18, 1865.

GENERAL:—The Fourteenth Corps is here, but the Twentieth is well back. It started from Averysboro and North river, with General Kilpatrick to the north of the road. We heard some musketry and artillery in that direction, but Colonel Poe left Mingo creek, which he bridged, at 11 A. M., at which time the Twentieth Corps was a half mile behind.

We can not get any farther to-day. General Davis may go a couple of miles farther to the forks of the road. I think this road, the Averysboro and Goldsboro road, will lead to Cox's bridge, though it is represented as passing three (3) miles south of Bentonville.

Get on the right-hand road, so that General Geary and his trains may take that to Goldsboro, via Cox's bridge.

I think the enemy is concentrated about Smithfield, and I can not make out whether Goldsboro is held in force or not. I think it probable that Joe Johnston will try to prevent our getting to Goldsboro.

* * * * * * * * *

I fear General Slocum will be jammed with all his trains in a narrow space; but, at the same time, I do n't want to push you too far till his flank is better covered by the Neuse. General Slocum is back with the Twentieth Corps, and as soon as I hear from him I will send over to you.

General Morgan's division found a couple of Hampton's regiments here, but they cleared out to the north as soon as he deployed skirmishers.

I am, general, very respectfully, etc.,
W. T. SHERMAN,
Major-General Commanding.

Major-General O. O. Howard, Commanding Right Wing.

HEADQUARTERS MILITARY DIVISION OF THE MISSISSIPPI,
IN THE FIELD, *March* 18, 1865.

GENERAL:—General Slocum is up. The firing you heard was General Kilpatrick, who found parties picketing the roads to the north. He reports Hardee retreating on Smithfield, and Joe Johnston collecting his old Georgia army this side of Raleigh. I know he will call in all minor posts, which embraces Goldsboro. You may therefore move straight for Goldsboro, leaving General Slocum the river road, and, if possible, the one from Lee's Store toward Falling Waters. Make a break into Goldsboro, from the south, and let your scouts strike out for General Schofield, at Kingston, though I hope to meet him at Goldsboro.

Our roads are very bad, but I think the Fourteenth Corps will be at Cox's bridge to-morrow night, and will aim to strike the railroad to the northwest of Goldsboro. If any change occurs, I will notify you to-night.

Yours,
W. T. SHERMAN,
Major-General Howard, present.   *Major-General.*

HEADQUARTERS MILITARY DIVISION OF THE MISSISSIPPI,
IN THE FIELD, TEN MILES SOUTHWEST OF GOLDSBORO,
SUNDAY, March 19, 1865—2 P. M.

Major-General Schofield, Kingston:

To-night my left wing will be at Cox's bridge, and my right within ten miles of Goldsboro. To-morrow we will cross the Neuse river at Cox's bridge, and be near Goldsboro, to prevent the enemy from occupying Goldsboro in force.

The scout Pike has arrived with dispatch of 17th. Continue to extend to the right as fast as possible, and I expect you to move toward Goldsboro, even if it be unnecessary, as I do n't want to lose men in direct attack, when it can be avoided. . . .

We whipped Hardee easily about Averysboro. All retreated on Smithfield and Raleigh.

W. T. SHERMAN,
Major-General.

HEADQUARTERS MILITARY DIVISION OF THE MISSISSIPPI,
IN THE FIELD, FALLING CREEK CHURCH, March 19, 1865—2 P. M.*

GENERAL:—General Howard, with one division, is now at this point, which is just three miles south from Cox's bridge and ten from Goldsboro. A scout is just in from General Schofield, who writes that he will leave Kingston for Goldsboro to-day or to-morrow. I have sent him a courier with orders to march straight for Goldsboro. General Howard's four (4) divisions are strung out, but he will push them through to-night. We occupy a position dangerous to the enemy, if he thinks he is in front of the whole army. You may strengthen your position, but feel the enemy all night. If he is there at daylight we will move to Cox's bridge, and then turn toward you. I think you will find him gone in the morning. General Howard has sent a regiment to Cox's bridge. It has not reported yet. He has the bridge across Falling Creek, two miles east of this, toward Goldsboro, and has some mounted men opposite Goldsboro, where they find a *tete-de-pont* occupied by the enemy. General Blair is about five miles south of this with his trains.

I will order General Kilpatrick to remain with you. Get up your trains between Lee's Store and your camp, and keep the enemy busy until we can get up the Fourth division of the Fifteenth Corps.

If you hear firing to your front, not explained by your own acts, you must assault or turn the enemy, for it will not do to let him fight us separately.

Yours,
W. T. SHERMAN,
Major-General.

Major-General Slocum, Commanding Left Wing.

---

*The date of this dispatch is thus given in the "Report of the Committee on the Conduct of the War," Supplement, Part I., Second Session, Thirty-eighth Congress, page 358. But this must be an error, for the P. S. mentions the reception of a dispatch of 2 P. M. from General Slocum, from the battle-field of Bentonville.

P. S.—Your note of 2 P. M. is just received. General Howard's regiments drove the pickets from the cross-roads, one mile this side of Cox's bridge. That will disturb the force to your front. General Howard can better help you from this quarter than by returning by Lee's Store.

SHERMAN.

HEADQUARTERS MILITARY DIVISION OF THE MISSISSIPPI,
IN THE FIELD, FALLING CREEK CHURCH, *March* 19, 1865—5 P. M.

GENERAL:—Your report of to-day is received. General Slocum thinks the whole rebel army is in his front. I can not think Johnston would fight us with the Neuse to his rear. You may remain with General Slocum until further orders, or until the two wings come together.

If that force remain in General Slocum's front to morrow, I will move straight on its rear.

Yours truly,
W. T. SHERMAN,
Major-General.

General Kilpatrick, Commanding Cavalry.

HEADQUARTERS MILITARY DIVISION OF THE MISSISSIPPI,
IN THE FIELD, FALLING CREEK CHURCH, *March* 20, 1865—2 A. M.

GENERAL:—Yours of 8 P. M., 19th, is just received, and I acknowledge receipt by the direction of the general-in chief, who instructed me to say that the whole army is moving to your assistance as rapidly as possible. Upon its approach he wishes you to be prepared to assume the offensive against the enemy.

* * * * * * * * *

L. M. DAYTON,
Assistant Adjutant-General.

Major-General Slocum, Commanding Left Wing.

HEADQUARTERS MILITARY DIVISION OF THE MISSISSIPPI,
IN THE FIELD, NEAR BENTONVILLE, *March* 20, 1865—2 P. M.

GENERAL SCHOFIELD:—Your dispatch of yesterday is received. You can march into Goldsboro without opposition. General Terry is at Faison's, and I have ordered him to Cox's bridge until the present action is over. I am now within two miles of Slocum, but Johnston is between us. We are now skirmishing.

After occupying Goldsboro, if you hear nothing to the contrary, join a part of your force with General Terry's, and come to me wherever I may be.

W. T. SHERMAN,
Major-General.

HEADQUARTERS MILITARY DIVISION OF THE MISSISSIPPI,
IN THE FIELD, NEAR BENTONVILLE, N. C., *March* 22, 1865—10 A. M.
GENERAL:—Your dispatch of yesterday is just received. We whipped all of Joe Johnston's army yesterday, and he retreated in disorder in the night. We are in possession of the field, and our skirmishers are after his rear-guard, two miles north of Mill creek. We are not in condition as to supplies, to follow up, but will gradually draw back to Goldsboro, and refit. . . .

W. T. SHERMAN,
Major-General Commanding.
General Schofield, Goldsboro.

HEADQUARTERS MILITARY DIVISION OF THE MISSISSIPPI,
IN THE FIELD, COX'S BRIDGE, NEUSE RIVER, N. C., *March* 22, 1865.
GENERAL:—
* * * * * * * *
We resumed the march toward Goldsboro. I was with the left wing until I supposed all danger passed; but when General Slocum's head of column was within four miles of Bentonville, after skirmishing as usual with cavalry, he became aware that there was infantry at his front. He deployed a couple of brigades, which, on advancing, sustained a partial repulse, but soon rallied, and he formed a line of the two leading divisions, Morgan's and Carlin's, of Jeff. C. Davis' corps. The enemy attacked these divisions with violence, but was repulsed. This was in the forenoon of Sunday, the 19th. General Slocum brought forward the two divisions of the Twentieth Corps, and hastily disposed them for defense and General Kilpatrick moved his cavalry on the left.

General Joe Johnston had, the night before, marched his whole army—Bragg, Cheatham, S. D. Lee, Hardee, and all the troops he had from every quarter—determined, as he told his men, to crush one of our corps, and then defeat us in detail. He attacked General Slocum in position from 3 P. M. on the 19th till dark, but was everywhere repulsed, and lost fearfully. At the time, I was with the Fifteenth Corps, marching on a road more to the right; but on hearing of General Slocum's danger, directed that corps toward Cox's bridge, and that night brought Blair's corps over, and on the 20th marched rapidly on Johnston's flank and rear. We struck him about noon, and forced him to assume the defensive, and fortify. Yesterday we pushed him hard, and came very near crushing him.
* * * * * * * *

W. T. SHERMAN,
Major-General.
Lieutenant-General U. S. Grant, Commander-in-Chief, City Point, Va.

HEADQUARTERS MILITARY DIVISION OF THE MISSISSIPPI,
IN THE FIELD, GOLDSBORO, N. C., *March* 31, 1865.

DEAR SIR:—I had the honor and satisfaction to receive your letter and telegram of welcome when at City Point and Old Point Comfort.

I am back again at my post, possessed of the wishes and plans of the general-in-chief, and think, in due time, I can play my part in the coming campaign. All things are working well, and I have troops enough to accomplish the part assigned me, and only wait the loading our wagons, patching up and mending made necessary by the wear and tear of the past winter. . . .

W. T. SHERMAN,
Major-General.

Hon. E. M. Stanton, Secretary of War.

HEADQUARTERS MILITARY DIVISION OF THE MISSISSIPPI,
IN THE FIELD, GOLDSBORO, N. C., *April* 5, 1865.

DEAR GENERAL:—I can hardly help smiling when I contemplate my command. It is decidedly mixed. I believe, but am not certain, that you are in my jurisdiction, but I certainly can not help you in the way of orders or men, nor do I think you need either. General Cruft has just arrived with his provisional division, which will at once be broken up, and the men sent to their proper regiments, as that of Meagher was on my arrival. You may have some feeling about my asking that General Slocum should have command of the two corps that properly belonged to you—viz., Fourteenth and Twentieth; but you can recall that he was but a corps commander, and could not legally make orders of discharge, transfer, etc., which was imperatively necessary. I therefore asked that General Slocum be assigned to command " an army in the field," called the "Army of Georgia," composed of the Fourteenth and Twentieth Corps. The order is not yet made by the President, though I have recognized it, because both General Grant and the President sanctioned it, and promised to have the order made. . . .

W. T. SHERMAN,
Major-General.

Major-General Geo. H. Thomas, Commanding Department of the Cumberland.

HEADQUARTERS MILITARY DIVISION OF THE MISSISSIPPI,
IN THE FIELD, GOLDSBORO, N. C., *April* 7, 1865.

GENERAL:—The capture of Richmond, and the retreat of Lee's army to the west (Danville and Lynchburg), necessitates a change in our plans. We will hold fast to Goldsboro and its lines, and move rapidly on Raleigh. I want you to be all ready to move early on Monday, straight on Smithfield and Raleigh, by the most direct road. General Schofield will support you, with the Twenty-third Corps following you, and on the 10th the cavalry will move from Mount Olive and Faison's, by Bentonville and Turner's bridge, the right wing by Pikesville and Whitely's mill, with a division around by Nahunta and Folk's bridge. If the enemy declines to fight this side of the Neuse, I will of course throw the right wing up to Hinton's bridge.

Yours,
W. T. SHERMAN,
Major-General Commanding.

Major-General Slocum, Commanding Army of Georgia.

[SPECIAL FIELD ORDERS, NO. 44.]

HEADQUARTERS MILITARY DIVISION OF THE MISSISSIPPI,
IN THE FIELD, GOLDSBORO, N. C., *April* 1, 1865.

* * * * * * * * *

VI. The following is announced as the organization of this army:

Right wing—Army of the Tennessee, Fifteenth and Seventeenth Corps, Major-General O. O. Howard commanding.

Left Wing—Army of Georgia, Fourteenth and Twentieth Corps, Major-General H. W. Slocum commanding.

Center—Army of Ohio, Tenth and Twenty-third Corps, Major-General J. M. Schofield commanding.

Cavalry—Brevet Major-General J. Kilpatrick commanding.

VII. Each of these commanders will exercise the powers prescribed by law for a general commanding a separate department or army in the field.

* * * * * * * * *

By order of Major-General W. T. Sherman.

L. M. DAYTON,
Aid-de-Camp.

HEADQUARTERS MILITARY DIVISION OF THE MISSISSIPPI,
IN THE FIELD, RALEIGH, *April* 14, 1865.

GENERAL:—The general-in-chief has arranged for a meeting with General J. E. Johnston, near Durham's Station, North Carolina railroad, at 12 M., April 27th, and to accomplish it will leave here at 8 A. M. to-morrow, by railroad. Until further orders he directs that all troops will remain as they are at this time, the movements as directed in Special Field Orders No. 55, being for the time suspended.

I am, general, with great respect,
L. M. DAYTON,
Assistant Adjutant-General.

General H. W. Slocum, Commanding Army of Georgia.

HEADQUARTERS MILITARY DIVISION OF THE MISSISSIPPI,
IN THE FIELD, RALEIGH, N. C., *April* 24, 1865—6 A. M.

General Johnston, Commanding Confederate Army, Greensboro:

You will take notice that the truce or suspension of hostilities agreed upon between us, will cease in forty-eight hours after this is received at your lines, under first article of our agreement.

W. T. SHERMAN,
Major-General.

HEADQUARTERS MILITARY DIVISION OF THE MISSISSIPPI,
IN THE FIELD, RALEIGH, *April* 24, 1865.

General Johnston, Commanding Confederate Armies:

I have replies from Washington to my communication of April 18th. I am instructed to limit my operations to your immediate command, and not to attempt civil negotiations. I therefore demand the surrender of your army on the same terms as were given General Lee at Appomattox, of April 9th instant, purely and simply.

W. T. SHERMAN,
Major-General Commanding.

CHAPTER XXXIX.

GENERAL GEORGE STONEMAN'S CAVALRY OPERATIONS IN TENNESSEE AND NORTH CAROLINA.

IN terminating the pursuit of General Hood's army, General Thomas' first thought was to put his forces in winter cantonments to rest after their severe service since early spring, and to prepare for such operations as the future movements of the enemy might render necessary, or such as might promise the entire supremacy of the national government within the limits of the Military Division of the Mississippi or throughout the Southern States; but General Grant ordered otherwise, and on the 31st of December the troops of the military division were disposed with a view to immediate active operations. General A. J. Smith's corps, and four divisions of cavalry under General Wilson, were ordered to Eastport, Mississippi, and the Fourth Corps to take post at Huntsville, Alabama, according to previous arrangement, for a different purpose, and the Twenty-third Corps was left at Columbia, instead of taking position at Dalton, Georgia.

General Sherman was desirous that General Thomas should conduct a campaign in Northern Alabama and Georgia, and expressed this wish to General Grant; but the latter had formed other plans before this wish had been expressed, and had ordered General Schofield's corps, and the detachments from the corps with General Sherman, to North Carolina, to co-operate with him. Subsequently, he directed General Thomas to send General A. J. Smith's forces and five thousand cavalry, by river, to report to Major-General Canby, at New Orleans, to take part in the operations against Mobile. Accordingly, General Smith's troops started from Eastport on the

6th of February, and General Knipe's division of cavalry from Eastport and Nashville on the 12th. These transfers of forces reduced the troops under General Thomas to the Fourth Corps, the infantry and artillery garrisons of the military division, the cavalry divisions under General Wilson, and the one under General Stoneman in East Tennessee.

Early in February, General Thomas ascertained from various sources that a remnant of General Hood's army, under Generals Cheatham and S. D. Lee, were on their way from Mississippi to South Carolina, moving through Selma and Montgomery, Alabama, to reinforce the army opposing General Sherman, and that other fragments of the Confederate Army of the Tennessee—a skeleton corps—under General Richard Taylor, and seven thousand cavalry, under General Forrest, remained in Mississippi, with headquarters at Meridian.

February 6th, General Grant directed that General Stoneman should be sent on an expedition to penetrate North Carolina and well down toward Columbia, South Carolina, to destroy the enemy's railroads and military resources which were out of the reach of General Sherman; and on the 13th, General Grant directed General Thomas to prepare a cavalry expedition to penetrate Northern Alabama and co-operate with General Canby in his movement against Mobile. Preparations for both expeditions were completed about the same time, and on the 22d of March Generals Stoneman and Wilson moved as respectively directed.

The cavalry division in East Tennessee, commanded by Brigadier-General A. C. Gillem, comprised three brigades, under the respective command of Colonel Palmer, Brigadier-General Brown, and Colonel Miller. It was concentrated at Mossy creek on the 22d of March, in readiness for movement into North Carolina under the personal direction of General Stoneman. It was known at this time that General Sherman had captured Columbia, South Carolina, and was moving into North Carolina. Rumors were current that General Lee's army would evacuate Richmond and Petersburg, and might force a passage through Lynchburg to Knoxville. To guard against such a contingency, General Stoneman was directed to move toward Lynchburg, to destroy the railroad and resources of that region, and then sweep through Western North Carolina with the same destructive intent; and the Fourth Corps was ordered by General Thomas to advance from Huntsville as far into East Tennessee as it could supply itself, to repair the railroad as it advanced, and form at last with General Tillson's division of infantry, a strong support to General Stoneman, should he meet the enemy in such force as to drive him back.

On the 24th, General Stoneman moved to Morristown, and there detached the Third brigade, Colonel Miller commanding, to make a detour from Bull's Gap, to reach the railroad between Jonesboro and Carter's Station, in the rear of a force reported to be in the vicinity of the former place. The other two brigades advanced directly forward, and encamped on the night of the 25th ten miles west of Jonesboro. Here all incumbrances were left, save one ambulance, one wagon, and four guns with their caissons.

At noon on the 26th, the division was reunited at Jonesboro. Colonel Miller had complied with his instructions, but the Confederate general, Jackson, had fled in haste the night previous. General Stoneman then moved forward, and reached the Watauga river on the 27th, and the town of Boone, North Carolina, on the 28th. At the latter place, Major Keogh, of General Stoneman's staff, with a detachment of the Twelfth Kentucky, routed a company of home guards, capturing sixty. Here the brigades again separated—General Stoneman, with Palmer's brigade, moving on Wilkesboro, by Deep Gap, and General Gillem, with the other two brigades and the artillery, to the same point, by the Flat Gap road. From Wilkesboro, the whole command moved through Mount Airy, and over the Blue Ridge, to Hillsville, Virginia, with no incidents, save the capture of a small forage train. At Hillsville, Colonel Miller, with five hundred picked men, moved on Wytheville, destroyed a depot of supplies there, and a bridge over Reedy creek, and another at Max Meadows. The command then advanced to Jacksonville, where Major Wagner, of the Fifteenth Tennessee, with two hundred and fifty select men, dashed on to Salem, Virginia, and destroyed bridges and the railroad track extensively. On the 6th of April, two brigades were at Christianburg, and had possession of ninety miles of the Virginia and Tennessee railroad, from Wytheville to Salem. From Christianburg, after destroying twenty miles of railroad, and several bridges over Roanoke river, and disabling the bridge over New river, Colonel Palmer moved to Martinsville, and General Brown to Taylorsville, and at 10 A. M. on the 8th, Palmer and Brown united at that place, and then the whole command converged upon Danbury, North Carolina, arriving there on the 9th. At Germantown, beyond, Colonel Palmer was detached, and ordered to Salem, North Carolina, to destroy the large factories, which were supplying the Confederate armies with clothing, and then to send parties to destroy the railroad south of Greensboro, and between that place and Danville, the main column turned south from Germantown toward Salisbury, bivouacking at night on the 11th, twelve miles north of Salisbury. A little after midnight, the South Yadkin river was crossed, without opposition, as had not been expected. From the river, the main force advanced on a new road on the left, while a battalion of the Twelfth Kentucky was sent on the road to the right, to demonstrate strongly at the crossing of Grant creek, and, if successful in passing that stream, to attack in rear the forces defending the upper bridge. At daylight, the head of the main column met the enemy's pickets, who were driven back to the bridge over Grant creek, and his artillery and musketry opened from the other side. A reconnoissance developed the fact that a portion of the floor of the bridge had been taken up from two spans of the bridge, and trains could be heard leaving the town on the South Carolina and Morgantown railroads. General Gillem now ordered Colonel Miller and General Brown to close up their brigades, and a section of Reagan's battery to move forward. At this juncture, General Stoneman directed that a detachment should cross the creek two and a half miles above, cut the railroad, and, if practicable, capture the train, and then get in the rear of the town, and annoy the enemy as much as possible. Lieutenant-Colonel Slater, of the Eleventh Kentucky, was designated with his regiment for this service, and Captain Morrow, of General Stoneman's staff, joined the detachment. At the same time, Major Donnelly, of the Thirteenth Tennessee, with one hundred men, and Lieutenant-Colonel Smith, with a party of dismounted men, were ordered to cross at lower points. As soon as these parties engaged the enemy across the stream, and the rattling fire of the Spencer rifles of the Eleventh Kentucky announced that the enemy's left had been turned, Colonel Miller's brigade was ordered to advance on the main road. A detachment of the Eighth and Thirteenth Tennessee regiments restored the floor of the bridge, and Miller charged across. By this time the enemy was falling back along his entire line. Brown was thrown forward to support Miller, who continued to press the enemy back. The retreat soon terminated in rout. Major Keogh, who had led the charge of the Eleventh Kentucky on the right, having been joined by Major Sawyer's battalion of the Eighth Tennessee, charged the enemy again at the intersection of the Statesville road with the one upon which Colonel Miller was advancing, and captured all the artillery which had been used on the enemy's left flank. The pursuit was continued until the enemy's troops lost even the semblance of organization, and all who escaped capture, hid themselves in the woods. Three thousand men, under command of Major-General W. M. Gardener, with eighteen pieces of artillery, in charge of Colonel J. C. Pemberton, recently a lieutenant-general, were thus routed. Nearly thirteen hundred prisoners were captured, eighteen pieces of artillery, and public property of immense value, most of which was destroyed. At 2 P. M. Major Barnes, to whom the destruction of public property had been committed, reported having destroyed ten thousand stand of small arms, one million pounds of (small) ammunition, ten thousand pounds of artillery ammunition, six thousand pounds of powder, three magazines, six depots, ten thousand bushels of corn, seventy-five thousand suits of uniform clothing, two hundred and fifty thousand blankets (English manufacture), twenty thousand pounds of leather, six thousand pounds of bacon, one hundred thousand pounds of salt, twenty-seven thousand pounds of rice, ten thousand pounds of saltpetre, fifty thousand bushels of wheat, eighty barrels of turpentine, fifteen million of Confederate money, and medical stores worth over one hundred thousand dollars in gold. Besides the detachments which had been sent to Virginia, destroyed the railroad nearly to Lynchburg, seven thousand bales of cotton and two large factories, and captured four hundred prisoners. The railroad south of Salisbury having been destroyed for some distance, and it having been determined to send the prisoners, and captured artillery, not destroyed, to East Tennessee, the forces withdrew on the 13th, and reached Lenoir on the 15th.

Here General Stoneman turned over the command to General Gillem, with instructions as to the disposition and service of the troops. Colonel Palmer was to take post at Lincolnton, and scout down the Catawba; General Brown, at Morgantown, to connect with Colonel Palmer on the Catawba, and Colonel Miller, at Asheville, to open communications through to Greenville, Tennessee. The objects in leaving the cavalry on this side of the mountains, were to obstruct, intercept, or disperse any troops moving south, and to capture trains.

When General Gillem, with Brown's and Miller's brigades, reached the Catawba, two and a half miles from Morgantown, he found the bridge torn up, the ford blockaded, and his passage of the stream disputed by Major-General McCown, with about three hundred men and one piece of artillery. He then sent Major Kenner, of the Eighth Tennessee, to cross up the river and reach the enemy's rear, and threw forward another battalion of the same regiment as directly toward the bridge as shelter could be found. Opening with his artillery, he disabled the enemy's gun and drove him from his defenses, and the dismounted men charging over the sleepers of the bridge, drove him from the ford, and captured his gun and fifty men.

On the 19th, General Gillem moved toward Asheville, by way of Swananoa Gap. He found the gap the nex day, to be held by about five hundred men, with four pieces of artillery. Leaving Colonel Miller to make feints, he moved rapidly to Rutherford, forty miles distant, and at sundown on the 22d, he passed the Blue Ridge, at Hammond's Gap, and was in the rear of the enemy, who retreated through Andersonville, pursued by Slater, who, in a charge, captured the four guns and seventy men At this time he learned that Colonel Palmer had not moved as he had been ordered, in consequence of information through

General Echols, that a truce had been proclaimed. Deeming it essential to the safety of his command that he should hold one of the gaps of the Blue Ridge, General Gillem ordered Palmer to move as previously directed, and advanced with his own column to attack Asheville. At 3 P. M. on the 23d, he received a flag of truce from Asheville, covering a communication from General Martin, which stated that he had received official notification of a truce. Later, General Martin proposed a meeting for the next day. That night at 11 o'clock, the fact of the existence of a truce was established by an official announcement, coming from General Sherman, and at 11 P. M. he received an order from him, directed to General Stoneman, requiring the command to move to Durham Station or Hillsboro. Being convinced that this order had been issued by General Sherman, under the conviction that this cavalry division was at or near Salisbury, he decided to draw back to his base at Greenville, Tennessee, rather than advance two hundred miles to Durham's Station. At the meeting with General Martin, he announced this decision, and requested three days' rations for his men, to save the people on his route from supplying his wants by constraint. General Martin furnished supplies, but demanded the rendition of the artillery which had been captured the day before; but General Gillem positively refused to do this, as the capture had been made prior to his reception of any authentic announcement of a truce.

This expedition was ably conducted and eminently successful. General Stoneman's strategy put the enemy under positive disadvantage, at each objective, in receiving the intended blow. When the Blue Ridge was first passed, the enemy supposed that Salisbury was menaced. This supposition placed the Tennessee and Virginia railroad at General Stoneman's mercy, and the advance for its destruction was a surprise, and cost the enemy three trains, and the loss of more than two hundred wagons, and twenty-one pieces of artillery, spiked and abandoned, while the troops that were separated from the main body by this movement, returned to Kentucky. Again, when the column turned south, Colonel Palmer's divergence toward Danville and Greensboro, by Martinsville, caused the enemy to withdraw troops from Salisbury, which fell more easily in consequence when it was attacked, as the paramount object of the advance southward. The enemy discovered his mistake, and made effort to reinforce Salisbury when the danger was apparent, but the railroad being cut in five places south of Danville, the effort miscarried, as the reinforcing division of infantry and brigade of cavalry did not reach the vicinity of the town until after the destruction of the depots, magazines, and stores. And at last a brigade held the enemy at Swananoa Gap, until another passed to the rear and surprised and captured a large portion of his force. The captures were twenty-five guns taken in action, twenty-one abandoned in Southwest Virginia, and over six thousand prisoners and seventeen battle-flags.

WASHINGTON, *December* 31, 1864—11.30 A. M.
Major-General Thomas:

Lieutenant-General U. S. Grant directs all of your available force not essential to hold your communications, be collected on the Tennessee river—say, at Eastport and Tuscumbia—and be made ready for such movements as may be ordered. It is supposed that a portion of the troops in Louisville, and other parts of Kentucky and Tennessee, can now be available for active operations elsewhere. They should be made ready for that purpose. General Dodge wishes you to return to St. Louis the Thirty-ninth Missouri Infantry, now at Louisville, so that he may complete its organization. Please give us the earliest possible notice of Hood's line of retreat, so that orders may be given for the continuance of the campaign. Lieutenant-General Grant does not intend that your army should go into winter-quarters. It must be ready for active operations in the field.

H. W. HALLECK,
Major-General.

EXTRACT FROM GENERAL THOMAS' REPORT.

On the 6th of February, a communication was received from Lieutenant-General Grant, directing an expedition, commanded by General Stoneman, to be sent from East Tennessee to penetrate North Carolina and well down toward Columbia, South Carolina, to destroy the enemy's railroads and military resources in that section, and visit a portion of the state beyond the control or reach of General Sherman's column. As the movement was to be merely for the purpose of destruction, directions were given General Stoneman to evade any heavy engagements with the enemy's forces.

Again, on the 13th of February, General Grant telegraphed me to prepare a cavalry expedition of about ten thousand strong, to penetrate Northern Alabama, acting as a co-operative force to the movement on Mobile by General Canby. Before leaving Eastport, Mississippi, I had directed General Wilson to get his command in readiness for just such a campaign, of which the above was simply an outline—my instructions being for him to move on Selma, Montgomery, and Tuscaloosa, Alabama, and to capture those places if possible, after accomplishing which he was to operate against any of the enemy's forces in the direction of Mississippi, Mobile, or Macon, as circumstances might demand.

CLIFTON, TENN., *January* 14, 1865.
H. W. Halleck, Major-General, Washington, D. C.:
I arrived here this morning, and from all I can learn, Hood has gone south of Corinth. Accordingly, Schofield's corps, in obedience to your orders, has been ordered to Annapolis, and will commence embarking tomorrow.

GEO. H. THOMAS,
Major-General Commanding.

EASTPORT, MISS., *February* 2, 1865.
H. W. Halleck, Major-General, Washington, D. C.:
A telegram just received from Louisville, from General Allen, states that your order to me of the 26th January, means five thousand cavalry instead of five divisions, as I have informed him. Which is correct—five thousand or five divisions? Are they and General Smith to take their wagon transportation with them?

GEO. H. THOMAS,
Major-General U. S. A.

NASHVILLE, TENN., *February* 16, 1865.
U. S. Grant, Lieutenant-General, City Point, Va.:
It seems to be now pretty certain that Cheatham's and Lee's corps of Hood's army have left Mississippi, and gone eastward. They left Columbus and Tupelo about the 17th of January last, and I have traced them through different persons so regularly, that I can no longer doubt their having gone. The last person reported their having passed Opelika on the 27th of January, and all agree in reporting that they were going to South Carolina. I have also received two or three reports during the past week, that Forrest is about to remove his troops to Georgia, if he has not already started. I think my cavalry expedition from Eastport will overtake him. It will be ready about the 20th inst. I have taken measures to equip General Stoneman as rapidly as possible, and have substituted another regiment for the Fourth Missouri Cavalry, but would like to get that regiment as soon as possible, as I could make it very useful south of Chattanooga, as there are a number of scouting parties of

the enemy about Rome, Resaca, Lafayette, and other towns in that region.

GEO. H. THOMAS,
Major-General U. S. A. Commanding.

NASHVILLE, TENN., *February* 27, 1865.
U. S. Grant, Lieutenant-General, City Point, Va. :
Your telegram of the 26th inst. is just received. General Stoneman has not yet started, but informed my chief of staff a few days since at Louisville, that he would be ready to start about the 1st of March. I will notify you as soon as he gets off. He has been delayed for want of horses. I have just returned from Eastport, having completed the arrangements for the cavalry expedition from that point. Owing to the recent stormy and rainy weather, General Wilson will be delayed a few days for the roads to dry up. He will be able to start in a few days with at least ten thousand men.

GEO. H. THOMAS,
Major-General U. S. A. Commanding.

CHAPTER XL.

GENERAL J. H. WILSON'S CAVALRY OPERATIONS IN ALABAMA AND GEORGIA.

GENERAL WILSON'S column of cavalry, comprising Generals McCook's, Long's, and Upton's divisions, having crossed the Tennessee river on the 18th of March, was put in motion southward on the 23d. General Hatch's division not having a full remount, was deprived of all horses for the other divisions, and left at Eastport, to join the column subsequently, should horses be obtained in time. General Wilson's wagon and pontoon trains, including about two hundred and fifty teams, were put under the direction of Captain Brown, protected by fifteen hundred dismounted men, under Major Archer. The destitution of forage, in the region immediately south of the Tennessee river, imposed the necessity of starting the troops in detachments to glean over a broad belt of country, what little produce might be left, where war had so long and so heavily laid its hand. This diffusion, however, involved no hazard, as General Forrest's command was at West Point, Mississippi, one hundred and fifty miles south of Eastport, and General Roddy's forces were holding Montevallo, on the Alabama and Tennessee railroad, as remote, to the southeast. There was, besides, an important advantage in this divergence in the beginning of the enterprise, as thereby the enemy was put in doubt as to the first objectives, and was compelled to watch equally the roads to Selma, Tuscaloosa, and Columbus.

General Grant's orders required the movement of a force of five or six thousand men, to demonstrate against Tuscaloosa and Selma, to co-operate with General Canby. General

Wilson expressed the conviction that he could capture these places and conduct other decisive operations, and General Thomas gave him permission to take with him all his available force, giving him such freedom of action as the nature and proposed objects of the expedition, positive and contingent, demanded. Thus, by General Grant's instructions, the license given by General Thomas, and the conditions of his enterprise, General Wilson became an independent commander, at least as far as all special combinations and minor objectives were concerned. He was subject still to General Thomas, as actual commander of all the forces within the geographical limits of the military division; but he had discretion within exceedingly extended limits.

General Upton's division, followed by his train, moved rapidly on the most easterly route, passing Barton's Station, Throgmorton's Mills, Russellville, Mount Hope, and Jasper, to Sanders' Ferry, on the west fork of the Black Warrior river. General Long's division marched through Cherokee Station, Frankfort, and Russellville, and then followed the Tuscaloosa road to the Black Water creek, twenty-five miles from Jasper. General McCook's division followed Long's to the Upper Bear creek, then moved on the Tuscaloosa road to Eldridge, afterward turning east to Jasper. The crossing of the Black Warrior river was beset with difficulties, but the knowledge that General Chalmers was moving to Tuscaloosa, and the danger of a full river, permitted no delay, and the corps was hurried across, with the loss of a few horses, and then, with pack-mules bearing supplies, wagons and artillery being far in the rear, the command moved rapidly through Elyton to Montevallo. At Elyton, General Croxton was detached with his brigade to advance to Tuscaloosa, to burn the public stores, military school, bridges, foundries, and factories at that place, and then join the main column at Selma, if practicable. The direction of Croxton's movement somewhat covered the trains and artillery in the rear, and was intended to develop any movement of the enemy in that quarter. On the march, General Upton destroyed the Red Mountain, Central, Bibb, and Columbiana iron-works, Cahawba rolling-mills, and much valuable property. The other divisions followed, and when General Wilson reached Montevallo, on the 31st of March, General Upton was ready to move forward. And for this there was need, as the enemy had appeared on the Selma road, and General Upton, with General Alexander's brigade leading, was sent against him. Alexander soon provoked a sharp conflict, which he terminated by a charge, driving the enemy, a portion of Roddy's division and Crossland's Kentucky brigade, in confusion toward Randolph. General Roddy attempted to make a stand five miles south of Montevallo, when General Upton threw Winslow's brigade to the front, and opened Rodney's battery, Fourth United States Artillery, causing the retreat of the enemy and loss of fifty prisoners in the pursuit by Winslow. This action gave the type of the campaign.

At night, General Upton bivouacked fourteen miles from Montevallo, and the next day advanced to Randolph. Here he turned to the east by Maplesville to the old Selma road, while General Long pushed forward on the new road. A message from General Croxton to the effect that he was in the rear of General Jackson's division, near Trion, and dispatches captured from the enemy revealing his plans and the dispositions of his forces, called for new combinations and their prompt execution. General Forrest, with a portion of his command, was in the front of the main column; Jackson's division was involved with Croxton.

General Chalmers was under orders to cross from Union, to join Forrest, either in Wilson's front or in the works at Selma, and the enemy's dismounted men were holding an important bridge over the Cahawba, at Centreville. To secure this bridge and prevent the junction of Jackson's division with Forrest, General Wilson directed General McCook to strengthen the battalion en route to Centreville, by a regiment, and to follow with La Grange's brigade with all speed, leaving even his pack trains, to seize the bridge, and then hasten to support Croxton against Jackson. Having provided for his right flank, he next looked to the protection of his rear, against the traditional strategy of Forrest, by ordering Upton and Long to push him without rest toward Selma. These officers moved forward rapidly, without changing roads, and brushing back small parties, developed Forrest in position for battle, on the north bank of Bigler's creek, his right resting on Mulberry creek, and left on a high wooded ridge, covered by a battery of artillery. A portion of his front was covered by slashed timber and rail barricades. His force comprised Crossland's brigade, Armstrong's brigade of Chalmers' division, Roddy's division, and a battalion just arrived from Selma, in all about five thousand men. Perceiving the enemy in strength in his immediate front, General Long reinforced his vanguard by a battalion of the Seventy-second Indiana Mounted Infantry, with the remainder of the regiment dismounted, and formed on the left of the road. This regiment drove back the enemy in broken ranks. At this juncture General Long ordered forward four companies of the Seventeenth Indiana, Lieutenant-Colonel Frank White commanding, with drawn sabers. These companies drove the enemy to his works, dashed against his main line, broke through it, rode over his guns, and finally turning to the left cut their way out, but leaving one officer and sixteen men with the enemy. In this charge Captain Taylor lost his life, having led his men into the midst of the enemy, and engaged in a running fight for two hundred yards with General Forrest himself.

Hearing the noise of this preliminary fighting, Alexander's brigade of Upton's division hurried up on the trot, and formed on the left of General Long, and as soon as everything was in readiness, the brigade advanced, dismounted. In less than an hour, although Forrest resisted stubbornly, his forces were completely routed. Alexander captured two guns and about two hundred prisoners. Long's division took one gun. Winslow's brigade pressed forward in pursuit, but could not bring the enemy to a stand. At sundown the corps bivouacked near Plantersville, in sharp conflict with the enemy, who had been driven twenty-four miles during the day.

At daylight the next day, the columns were in motion toward Selma. General Long advanced to the town and crossed to the Summerville road. General Upton moved on the Range Line road, sending a squadron on the Burnsville road. Lieutenant Rundlebrook, with a battalion of the Fourth United States Cavalry, followed the railroad, burning stations and bridges to Burnsville. By 4 P. M. the troops were in position and ready to assault. General Wilson had previously obtained a complete description of the defenses, and having corroborated its correctness by observation and formal reconnoissance, he gave orders for the assault. General Long was instructed to move across the road, upon which his troops were posted, and General Upton was permitted, as he had requested, with three hundred picked men, to penetrate a swamp on his left, and break the line covering it, thus to turn Forrest's right, while the remainder of his division should conform to his movements.

A single gun from Rodney's battery was to be the signal for a general advance, and this was to be given as soon as Upton's success was revealed. Before this signal gun could be fired, General Long was informed that a heavy force of cavalry was skirmishing with his rear-guard, and threatening an attack from that quarter. He left six companies well posted at the creek, in anticipation of the movement which General Chalmers was now making in obedience to orders from General Forrest. This force was known to have been the day before at Marion, and fearing that its appearance on the road, as had been expected, might compromise the assault upon the town, General Long determined not to wait for the development of General Upton's turning movement. He simply strengthened his rear with a regiment, and then dismounting four regiments from the brigades of Miller and Minty, he, with these officers, led them in charging over an open space for six hundred yards, over a stockade, a deep ditch, and the parapet, and drove the enemy in confusion to the city. At the moment of victory, General Wilson reached that part of the field, and directed Colonel Minty, who had assumed command of the division in consequence of a severe wound to General Long, to advance toward the town. He ordered Colonel Vail to place his own regiment, the Seventeenth Indiana, and the Fourth Ohio, in line inside the works, and the Fourth United States Cavalry and the Board of Trade battery to participate in the attack. When the division again advanced, the enemy was occupying unfinished defenses near the town. The Fourth Cavalry, Lieutenant O'Connell commanding, was repulsed, but formed again on the left. In the meantime, General Upton had succeeded in his movement, and was now advancing on the left of Minty. A charge was again made by the Fourth Ohio, Seventeenth Indiana, and Fourth Cavalry dismounted, and the whole line participating with wildest enthusiasm, the enemy was hurled from position, and the city was penetrated in all directions.

The charge of General Long, his brigade commanders leading with him, and fifteen hundred and fifty men following, was brilliant in the extreme. A single line without support advanced in utmost exposure for five or six hundred yards, leaped a stockade five feet high, a ditch five feet deep and fifteen wide, and a parapet six to eight feet high, and drove Armstrong's brigade, the best of Forrest's command, over fifteen hundred strong, in rout from works of great strength and advantages of wonderful superiority, and this was done while sixteen field-guns were playing upon them. In the charge, Colonel Dobbs, of the Fourth Ohio, was killed. General Long, and Colonels Miller, McCormick, and Biggs were wounded. The general loss of the division was forty killed, two hundred and sixty wounded, and seven missing.

The fruits of the victory were in correspondence with the gallantry of the troops that won it. Thirty-one field-guns and one thirty-pounder Parrott, two thousand seven hundred prisoners, including one hundred and fifty officers, and public property of great value. Lieutenant-General Taylor sought safety in flight early in the afternoon, and under cover of the darkness, Generals Forrest, Roddy, Armstrong, and Adams escaped with a number of men. A portion of Upton's division pursued on the Burnsville road till late in the night, capturing four guns and many prisoners. The enemy destroyed twenty-five thousand bales of cotton, but left the foundries, machine-shops, arsenals, and warehouses of this immense depot of war material, for the torch.

General Wilson placed Brevet Brigadier-General Winslow in command of the city, and instructed Lieutenant Haywood, engineer officer, to press the construction of pontoons for a bridge over the Alabama river. The next day at daylight, General Upton marched to draw General Chalmers to the west side of the Cahawba river and open communications with General McCook, who was expected with the train from Centerville. This movement looked to an advance of the whole command toward Montgomery as soon as it could be gathered together and other conditions were favorable. The capture of Selma and so large a portion of Forrest's force gave General Wilson the assurance of successful movements whatever objectives he might choose.

Generals McCook and Upton arrived at Selma, April 5th, with the train. The former had been successful against Centreville, but on reaching Scottsboro had found General Jackson so strongly posted that he did not attack him, but burning the cotton factories and the bridge, turned toward Selma. General Croxton had not been found nor even heard from; but his protracted separation from the corps did not cause uneasiness, as it was confidently believed that he had taken care of himself and gone in a new direction.

On the 6th, General Forrest requested a conference with General Wilson, with reference to an exchange of prisoners. His arrogance and manifest hope that he could recapture his men made the interview brief, but through it, General Wilson learned that General Croxton had had an engagement two days before with General Adams at Bridgeville, forty miles southwest of Tuscaloosa. His safety being assured, as also General Canby's ability to take Mobile without support, there was no barrier to the movement to Montgomery but the Alabama river, whose deep, swift current gave an unsteady resting to a pontoon bridge eight hundred and seventy feet long. Three times the bridge was broken, but Major Hubbard, aided by Generals Upton and Alexander and the staff of General Wilson, succeeded in connecting the banks by the floating bridge, and the command passed safely over by daylight on the 10th of April Selma had been so far destroyed as to be of no use to the enemy for military purposes; and Forrest's force had been so greatly diminished and so thoroughly demoralized that General Wilson moved fearlessly forward toward Montgomery, intending to destroy railroads and army supplies and material, and then sweep on to the theater of operations in North Carolina. His mounted force was now stronger than at starting, as he had captured horses for all his dismounted men, and he now disincumbered himself of all wagons and pontoons which could be spared, to give him facility for quick movement. The able-bodied negroes who had joined his column were organized into regiments under efficient officers. These men, in the first flush of freedom, became soldiers, keeping pace with the troopers, gathering supplies from the country, and marching thirty-five miles per day.

The march from Selma to Montgomery was retarded by bad roads and bridgeless streams; but at 7 A. M. on the 12th, Colonel La Grange, whose brigade was in advance, received the surrender of the capital of the State of Alabama, and the first capital of the Southern Confederacy. But how great had been the changes of four years of civil war! On the 4th of March, 1861, the insurgent Congress had asserted, with the pomp and circumstance befitting a nation's birth, the independence of seven slaveholding states. The national government was boldly defied, and blindly ignoring the contingencies of their venture, the members of this Congress boldly assumed the independence of the South as an actuality, and talked of war as if its invocation involved no guilt, and its progress compassed naught but victories and speedy triumph. The outlying crowds of men drawn to Montgomery by the culmination of Southern frenzy in the assumption of a new nationality, echoed the bold utterances of the provisional President and Congress in jubilant ecstasy through the streets. The illuminated city was a blazing type of the fire that was burning in the Southern heart, and all the assumptions of prospective empire, in the frenzy of the moment, were removed beyond the sphere of doubt. Now, the mayor of the city—the dispirited representative of a conquered people—comes meekly forth from the provisional capital of the war-broken Confederacy and tenders its surrender to a commander of brigade. How different the beginning and end of Montgomery in the "great conflict!" The burning of ninety thousand bales of cotton, the ideal king of commerce, is now the illumination which betokens the loss of his crown and the loyalty of his subjects, for it is they who, in their desperation, set fire to this immense mass of royalty. The quiet streets and silent halls, the fleeing troopers and hiding citizens, are in striking antithesis to the pomp, the boast, and the maddened multitude of a former day.

Having destroyed five steamboats, several locomotives, one armory, and several foundries, General Wilson resumed motion on the 14th. General Upton moved through Mount Meigs and Tuskegee, toward Columbus, Georgia, and Colonel La Grange followed the railroad through Opelika, to West Point. Two days later, General Upton, with three hundred dismounted men, assaulted and carried the breastworks at Columbus, saving by the impetuosity of his attack the bridges over the Chattahoochee, and capturing fifty-two guns in position, and twelve hundred prisoners. The ram Jackson, nearly ready for the sea, and carrying six seven-inch guns, was destroyed; also the navy-yard, foundries, arsenal, armory, sword and pistol factory, accouterment-shops, paper-mills, four cotton factories, fifteen locomotives, two hundred cars, and one hundred and fifteen thousand bales of cotton. The assault was made at night, by men from the Third Iowa, Colonel Noble commanding, the Fourth Iowa and Tenth Missouri being held in support. Generals Upton and Winslow directed the movement in person. The enemy opened a heavy artillery and musketry fire as the troops advanced, but their Spencer rifles gave response as they rushed through the abatis and over the parapet. When this had been accomplished, General Upton sent Captain Glassen, with two companies of the Tenth Missouri, to get possession of the bridge over the Chattahoochee. The captain passed through the inner line of defenses, under cover of the darkness, and seized the bridge before the enemy was aware of his movement. Then General Upton made a general charge, swept away all opposition, seized the bridges, and stationed his troops thoughout the city. The fortifications were held by three thousand men, and yet three hundred penetrated the main line, and this primal success was followed by overwhelming victory, with a loss in all of twenty men killed and wounded.

Colonel La Grange had spirited skirmishing on the way to

West Point, but reached the vicinity with his advance at 10 A. M., April 16th. Beck's Indiana battery and the Second and Fourth Indiana held the attention of the enemy until the arrival of the remainder of the brigade. Then after a reconnoissance, preparations were made for an assault. Detachments from the First Wisconsin, Second Indiana, and Seventh Kentucky regiments were dismounted to make the charge. At 1 P. M. the signal was given, and these troops moved forward, drove into the fort the skirmishers, and reached the ditch, which was too wide to leap and too deep to pass. Sharpshooters kept the enemy down until materials for bridges were gathered, when the charge was sounded again, and the detachments rushed over the parapets, on three sides of the square fort and captured the entire garrison of two hundred and sixty-five men, General Tyler commanding, and eighteen officers and men were killed and twenty-eight wounded. Colonel La Grange lost seven killed and twenty-nine wounded. He captured three guns and five hundred stand of small arms. Simultaneously with the storming of the fort, the Fourth Indiana dashed through the town, scattered a superior cavalry force which had just arrived, and burned five locomotives and trains; also securing the bridges over the Chattahoochee. Colonel La Grange here destroyed two bridges, nineteen locomotives, and two hundred and forty-five cars loaded with quartermaster, commissary, and ordnance stores. Before departure, he established a hospital for the wounded of both sides, and left for them ample supplies with the mayor. He then moved toward Macon, through La Grange, Griffin, and Forsyth, breaking the railroad at these points.

April 17th, General Wilson commenced his movement on Macon, giving Minty's division the advance, and instructing that commander to send forward a detachment to seize the double bridges over Flint river. Captain Hudson, of the Fourth Michigan, was put upon this service, and, at 7 A. M. the next day, gained the bridges, scattering the guards, and capturing forty prisoners. The whole command followed the detachment on the 18th. Two days later, Colonel White, of the Seventeenth Indiana in the advance, encountered two hundred cavalrymen, and driving them rapidly toward Macon, saved the Echconnee and Tobesofke bridges. When within thirteen miles of Macon, he met a flag of truce in charge of General Robinson, bearing a written communication addressed to the commanding officer United States forces. Colonel White halted and sent the communication to Colonel Minty, his division commander, who, having read it, sent it to General Wilson, but instructed Colonel White to resume his advance, and so informed General Robinson. The communication was from General Cobb, inclosing a dispatch from General Beauregard, advising that a truce was existing, which was applicable to all the forces under Generals Sherman and Joseph E. Johnston, and declaring that he was ready to comply with the terms of the armistice, and proposing a meeting with the commander of the United States forces, to make arrangements for a more perfect enforcement of the armistice.

Without giving entire credence to the communication, General Wilson rode rapidly forward to halt his troops at the defenses of Macon, and by seeing General Cobb to convince himself with regard to the questions at issue, before acknowledging the armistice. But Colonel White had been too quick, and had dashed into the city and received its surrender before General Wilson overtook him. The garrison made a show of resistance, but promptly laid down their arms at the demand of Colonel White. When, however, General Wilson arrived, General Cobb protested against what he termed a violation of the armistice, overlooking the fact that he could not claim to be an authoritative channel of communication for a message of such importance, and demanded that he should withdraw his forces to the point where General Robinson had met his advance. General Wilson had no reason to doubt the existence of the truce, but he was unwilling to give it recognition, until he had received notice and instructions from proper authority authentically transmitted, especially as his subordinate officers had captured the city before he could respond to the message which had been sent under the flag of truce. His force, though known as the cavalry corps of the Military Division of the Mississippi, and organized under General Sherman's order, had not yet served under his personal command, but had, by his direction, reported to General Thomas, as commander of all the forces of the military division not present with the commanding general, and all his orders subsequently had either originated with General Thomas or had been transmitted by him from General Grant. Without authentic instructions from either General Grant, General Sherman, or General Thomas, he hesitated to recognize the application of the armistice to his command. He therefore determined to hold Generals Cobb, Smith, Mackall, Robinson, and Mercer, and the garrison of Macon, as prisoners of war, until his conduct was disapproved by competent authority, after full investigation. However, to relieve himself from suspense, at the earliest possible moment, he sent a dispatch in cipher to General Sherman, the evening of the 20th of April, and the next day received an official notification from him of the existence of the armistice. Upon receiving it, he suspended all operations until he should receive orders to renew them, or until circumstances should justify independent action.

On the 1st of May, General Croxton, who during his separation from the main column, had made a tortuous ride of six hundred and fifty miles, arrived at Macon. He skirmished with General Jackson near Trion, on the 2d of April, and finding that his force was double his own, he declined battle and moved rapidly in simulated flight to the Black Warrior river, crossed to the west side, and reached Northport, April 4th. Fearing that his presence might be known, he moved at midnight, surprised the force at the bridge, crossed into Tuscaloosa, captured three guns and one hundred and fifty prisoners, scattered the state militia and cadets, and destroyed the military school edifice, and the public works and stores. Here he tried to communicate with General McCook, but failed. He then abandoned Tuscaloosa, and moved to the southeast to avoid Jackson and Chalmers. When near Eutaw, he heard of the arrival of Adams' division, and fearing to risk an engagement with a force of cavalry more than double his own strength, supported by militia, he countermarched toward Tuscaloosa; then diverging to the left, moved through Jasper, crossed the Coosa, and marched to Talladega. Near this place he defeated General Hill, capturing one gun and one hundred and fifty prisoners, and then marched through Carrollton, Newnan, and Forsyth, to Macon. During the period of his isolation, he had no knowledge of the movements of the main column, but having faith in the success of the general plan, he sought General Wilson at Macon.

NASHVILLE, TENN., *March 6, 1865.*
J. H. Wilson, Major-General, Eastport, Miss.:

Your note of the 26th February received. You remember the plan of operations you propose in your note is essentially what I mentioned to you last winter I should adopt if permitted. But General Grant wants all my infantry held in readiness for operations in East Tennessee, and has given directions accordingly.

He expects Canby to take Montgomery and Selma, and hold them afterward, and has directed your expedition as a co-operative one, which is also expected to seize either Montgomery or Selma, or both, if you find it can be done when the enemy is opposing the progress of Canby. After Canby gets to Montgomery, your command will then be relieved from further operations in that quarter.

GEO. H. THOMAS,
Major-General U. S. A. Commanding.

NASHVILLE, TENN., *March 9, 1865.*
U. S. Grant, Lieutenant-General, City Point:

General Canby telegraphs me, March 1st, from New Orleans, that, in consequence of the continued rains during the month of February, that he can not start the cavalry expedition from Vicksburg, as he intended, and has ordered Knipe to New Orleans. These heavy rains having extended as far north as this state, have also swollen the streams to an impassable condition, and General Wilson will be somewhat delayed thereby, but will be able to move in time to co-operate with General Canby against Mobile, Selma, and Montgomery. . . .

GEO. H. THOMAS,
Major-General U. S. A. Commanding.

CHATTANOOGA, TENN., *March 14, 1865.*
J. H. Wilson, Major-General, Eastport, Miss.:

Your telegram of 9 A. M. 12th inst. received. If the report made to you by the railroad man be true, then your expedition should be successful. Canby will march against Selma the moment he gets to Mobile. He will have over forty thousand infantry. General Hatch will get his horses in time to have enough to do this summer. I am now on my way to Knoxville to get Stoneman off, and concentrate all my available infantry at Bull's Gap, after which I may move on Lynchburg.

GEO. H. THOMAS,
Major-General U. S. A. Commanding.

CHATTANOOGA, TENN., *March* 19, 1865.
Geo. Stoneman, Major-General, Knoxville, Tenn. :
Your telegram of 8.10 P. M. yesterday received. From our present knowledge of the situation of affairs in Southwestern Virginia, I believe the route agreed upon by us for your forces to take will be the most effective that can be adopted—viz., to go down the New River valley, strike the railroad beyond Christiansburg, unless you learn that Sheridan has possession of Lynchburg; then, should you learn the force at Danville is weak, attack that place, and destroy the railroad as far as you can with safety toward Richmond, and then withdraw toward Tennessee, and observe and report all movements of the enemy to me promptly.

GEO. H. THOMAS,
Major-General U. S. A.

HEADQUARTERS DEPARTMENT TENNESSEE AND GEORGIA,
MACON, *April* 20, 1865.
GENERAL:—I have just received from General G. T. Beauregard, my immediate commander, a telegraphic dispatch, of which the following is a copy:
" GREENSBORO, *April* 19, 1865, VIA COLUMBIA, 19; VIA AUGUSTA, 20.
"*Major-General H. Cobb:*
" Inform general commanding enemy's forces in your front that a truce for the purpose of a final settlement was agreed upon yesterday between Generals Johnston and Sherman, applicable to all forces under their command. A message to that effect from General Sherman will be sent to him as soon as practicable. The contending forces are to occupy their present position, forty-eight hours' notice being given in the event of the resumption of hostilities.
" G. T. BEAUREGARD,
"*General, Second in Command.*

My force being a portion of General Johnston's command, I proceed at once to execute the terms of the armistice, and have accordingly issued orders for the carrying out of the same. I will meet you at any intermediate point between our respective lines for the purpose of making the necessary arrangements for a more perfect enforcement of the armistice. This communication will be handed to you by Brigadier F. H. Robinson.
I am, general, very respectfully yours,

HOWELL COBB,
Major-General Commanding, etc.
The Commanding General of the United States Forces.

HEADQUARTERS CAVALRY CORPS MILITARY DIVISION MISSISSIPPI,
MACON, GA., *April* 20, 1865—9. P. M.

Major-General W. T. Sherman, through headquarters General Beauregard, Greensboro, N. C.:

My advance received the surrender of this city this evening. General Cobb had previously sent me, under flag of truce, a copy of a telegram from General Beauregard, declaring the existence of an armistice between all troops under your command and those under Johnston. Without questioning the authenticity of this dispatch, or its application to my command, I could not communicate orders to my advance in time to prevent the capture of the place. I shall therefore hold its garrison, including Major-Generals G. W. Smith and Cobb, and Brigadier-General Mackall, prisoners of war. Please send me orders. I shall remain here a reasonable length of time to hear from you.

J. H. WILSON,
Major-General Commanding Cavalry Corps.

HEADQUARTERS, GREENSBORO, N. C., *April* 21, 1865—2 P. M.

Major-General Wilson, Commanding Cavalry Army United States, through Major-General H. Cobb:

The following is a copy of a communication just received, which will be sent to you to-day by an officer:

"HEADQUARTERS MILITARY DIVISION OF THE MISSISSIPPI,
"RALEIGH, *April* 20, 1865.

"*Major-General Wilson, Commanding Cavalry United States Army in Georgia:*

"General Joseph E. Johnston has agreed with me for a universal suspension of hostilities, looking to a peace over the whole surface of our country. I feel assured that it will be made perfect in a few days. You will therefore desist from acts of war and devastation until you hear that hostilities are resumed. For the convenience of supplying your command, you may either contract for supplies down about Fort Valley or the old Chattahoochee arsenal; or, if you are south of West Point, Georgia, in the neighborhood of Rome or Kingston, opening up communication and a route of supplies into Chattanooga and Cleveland. Report to me your position through General Johnston, as also round by sea. You may also advise General Canby of your position, and the substance of this, which I have sent round by sea.

" W. T. SHERMAN,
"*Major-General Commanding.*"

Please communicate above to the Federal commander.

J. E. JOHNSTON.

CHAPTER XLI.

CAPTURE OF THE CONFEDERATE PRESIDENT.

THE two cavalry columns were arrested about the same time, by the armistice established by Generals Sherman and Johnston, under circumstances of embarrassment to the generals commanding them, though fortunately there were no conditions of great hazard, in suspending their operations, as each had swept through the enemy's country in ceaseless success and triumph. Their orders were so positive as to allow no discretion, even had the suspension of their operations given advantage to the enemy, through whom the knowledge of the truce was communicated. Neither did the embarrassments produced by the truce stop with the commanders in the field, but reached General Thomas, who was charged with the management of the affairs of the Military Division of the Mississippi, and who had organized these expeditions under orders from Lieutenant-General Grant. For, although telegraphic communications did not reach either General Wilson or General Stoneman, General Thomas heard of the armistice through each of these generals before he received official information of its existence from the lieutenant-general. Referring to the time of receiving information from his subordinates, he thus, in his official report, mentioned his own embarrassments in relation to the armistice and the manner of its announcement: " Up to that period I had not been officially notified of the existence of any armistice between the forces of Generals Sherman and Johnston, and the information only reached me through my sub-commanders, Generals Wilson and Stoneman, from Macon, Georgia, and Greenville, East Tennessee, almost simultaneously. The question naturally arose in my mind, whether the troops acting under my direction, by virtue of General Sherman's Special Field Order No. 105, series of 1864, directing me to assume control of all the forces of the Military Division of the Mississippi, 'not absolutely in the presence of the general-in-chief,' were to be bound by an armistice or agreement made at a distance of several hundred miles from where those troops were operating and of which they were advised through an enemy, then in such straitened circumstances that any ruse, honorable at least in war, was likely to be practiced by him to relieve himself from his difficult position. Then, again, General Sherman was operating with a movable column, beyond the limits of his territorial command, viz., the Military Division of the Mississippi, and far away from all direct communication with it; whereas 'the troops not absolutely in the presence of the general-in-chief,' were operating under special instructions and not even in co-operation with General Sherman against Johnston, but, on the contrary, General Stoneman was dismantling the country to obstruct Lee's retreat and General Wilson was moving independently in Georgia or co-operating with General Canby. Before I could come to any conclusion how I should act under the circumstances, and without disrespect to my superior officer, General Sherman, Secretary Stanton telegraphed to me from Washington, on the 27th of April, and through me to my sub-commanders, to disregard all orders except those coming from General Grant or myself, and to resume hostilities at once, sparing no pains to press the enemy firmly, at the same time notifying me that General Sherman's negotiations with Johnston had been disapproved."

Having now full authority for independent action, and having learned that President Davis with a party had started south from Charlotte, North Carolina, on the cessation of the armistice, General Thomas at once made dispositions to capture the fugitive President, and those who still clung to him and his fortunes. He directed General Stoneman to send the brigades of Miller, Brown, and Palmer, to concentrate at Anderson, South Carolina, and scout down the Savannah river to Augusta, Georgia, in search of the fugitives. General Gillem was absent from the command at the time, and Colonel

W. F. Palmer, of the Fifteenth Pennsylvania Cavalry, assumed direction of the expedition. By rapid marching, he reached and crossed the Savannah river in advance of Mr. Davis, and so disposed his troops as to change the direction of the flight, from the west toward the Mississippi river, to the Atlantic coast. General Thomas also notified General Wilson, at Macon, Georgia, of the issue of the negotiations in North Carolina, and ordered him to resume hostilities at once, with special reference to the capture of Mr. Davis.

These orders had scarcely been issued before the surrender of the Confederate forces east of the Chattahoochee river, to General Sherman, by General Johnston, was officially announced to both General Thomas and General Wilson, and the latter at once adopted measures looking to the surrender of the enemy's military establishments at Atlanta, Georgia, and Tallahassee, Florida, and to throw a cordon of cavalry across the State of Georgia to intercept and capture Mr. Davis and his party. He sent General Upton to Augusta; General Winslow, with the Fourth division, to march to Atlanta " for the purpose of carrying into effect the terms of the convention, as well as to make such a disposition of his forces, covering the country northward, from Forsyth to Marietta, so as to secure the arrest of Jefferson Davis and party;" General McCook, with five hundred men of his division, to move to Tallahassee, Florida, " to receive the surrender of the enemy in that state;" Colonel Minty, " to extend his troops along the line of the Ocmulgee and Altamaha rivers, as far as Jacksonville; and General Croxton, commanding a division (the First), " to distribute it along the line of the Ocmulgee," connecting with Winslow, and reaching to Macon. Besides, General Wilson directed that detachments should watch the crossings of Flint river, and the stations on the railroad from Atlanta to Eufala, as well as Columbus, West Point, and Talladega. These general and special dispositions, with thorough scouting, promised the interception of all large parties and the arrest of prominent persons.

Evading the terms of General Johnston's surrender, Mr. Davis moved south from Charlotte, North Carolina, through Yorkville, toward Unionville and Abbeville, South Carolina, with evident purpose of passing through to the trans-Mississippi Department, with a vague hope that he could there continue the war. He was, at first, accompanied by his staff and cabinet, under escort of cavalry, from the commands of Ferguson, Duke, Harris, and Butler. Finding, upon reaching the Savannah river from Abbeville, where his last council of war was held, which expressed the utter despair of all but himself, that he was enveloped by the national cavalry, Mr. Davis dismissed his retinue, and with a few friends pushed on to Washington, reaching that place on the morning of the 3d of May. In dismissing his escort, he abandoned the idea of fighting his way to the west, and attempted to accomplish the passage by the most secret means. During the day, he left Washington, by rail, for Atlanta, but abandoned his car at Union Point, and started southwest on horseback. Colonel Palmer having ascertained this fact, scattered his forces to intercept him, and at the same time gather up the fragments of the Confederate forces roaming over the country. But, notwithstanding great vigilance and activity, Mr. Davis slipped through Palmer's detachments, to be caught by Wilson's troopers, farther west and south. On the 7th of May, Colonel Harnden, of the First Wisconsin, with one hundred and fifty men, having advanced from Macon, ascertained that Mr. Davis had crossed the Oconee at Dublin, fifty-five miles southeast of Macon, and had fled on the Jacksonville road. He pursued rapidly, marching forty miles on the 8th on the footsteps of the fugitive. On the 9th he crossed the Ocmulgee, at Brown's ferry, and at Abbeville learned that Mr. Davis had left that point at 1 A. M. on the road to Irwinsville. Hastening forward, he reached the vicinity of Irwinsville at nightfall, and awaited daylight to make the capture.

Having learned at Abbeville of the approach of Colonel Pritchard of the Fourth Michigan, Colonel Harnden went, after halting, to meet him and inform him of his success in tracing the steps of Mr. Davis. The former stated that he had been sent to Abbeville to watch for Mr. Davis, but that he would go no farther that night. However, after making this stipulation, he moved into Irwinsville during the night, and at dawn captured Mr. Davis in disguise, and the small party with him.

Soon after this accomplishment, Colonel Harnden approached, and having been hailed by Colonel Pritchard's detachment, answered "friends," and fell back. In the mutual uncertainty as to the identity of the two commands, several shots were fired, killing several men—a sad issue of a misunderstanding that should not have existed. The pursuit had been conducted with great vigor by all the parties from the two general commands. A reward had been offered of which they were ignorant, from a conjecture that Mr. Davis was remotely connected with the assassination of Mr. Lincoln, President of the United States.

Mr. Davis would have made a better appearance in history, had he met the final issue with General Johnston in preference to seeking, by stealthy flight, the preservation of the life which he had often declared should not survive the fall of his country. This termination of his vaunted presidency, and the disgrace of his flight, were foreign to his grand promises and lofty aspirations. His humiliation and helplessness were, however, the fitting symbols of the cause and the government, of which in the days of his glory and power he was the most prominent representative. His descent from power was as sudden and as marked as the oft-repeated transfer of kings and emperors from thrones to dungeons, but history furnishes no parallel to such emphatic loss of a cause which commanded the real and nominal allegiance of so many millions of men. And the philosophical historian must ask the question, could it have collapsed so suddenly, had its foundation been laid at the beginning in the hearts of the Southern people?

The overthrow of the rebellion was doubtless due to a variety of causes, which were strictly subjective. The maladministration of the Confederate government was a prominent cause, but could not have been the most potential one. It has been claimed, however, by Southern historians, that it had this rank, as it demoralized the people and divorced them from the cause which they at first so earnestly espoused.

The palpable immediate cause of the collapse of the rebellion was the lack of soldiers to fight for it, not of supplies or strict war material. And this need of soldiers did not result from the failure of the conscription more than from the desertion of both volunteers and conscripts; for, at the last, nearly a moiety of those who had borne arms were deserters. The first armies had been formed from volunteers, but soon mere enlistment was abandoned, and then soldiers and supplies could only be secured by despotic constraint. And it has been assumed that the final despotic measures of the government produced a fatal disaffection, which did not originally exist. But it should be considered, in estimating the force and exact influence of the severe measures of the government—the conscription which enrolled for military service all able-bodied male persons between the ages of eighteen and fifty-five years, and the sweeping impressment of supplies—that there was need of these expedients, or the government would never have adopted them, and that consequently the potential cause of failure produced the state of things from which originated the objectionable demands of the government. Mr. Davis and the Confederate Congress would never have ignored the rights of the states, for the maintenance of which they invoked the war, had it been possible to maintain the conflict without trenching upon the sovereignty of the individual states composing the Confederacy. It was a pleasant doctrine for days of harmony and peace, but unsuited to those of war. The despotism of the government, then, was only a secondary cause of the failure of the rebellion.

The ruling cause was that the war on the part of the South was the expression of an insurrection and not a true revolution; and the inherent vices of a false revolution may be traced from the very beginning of the despotic measures of the government. All true revolutions of popular expression have their foundation and force in the sentiments of the masses engaged in them, and will be maintained to the direst extremity. No insurrection that is impressed upon a people by a few leaders or by an influential or powerful minority, can command the perpetual support of the masses. The people may be deceived for a time by false issues and delusive hopes, and the enthusiasm which may thus be called forth may take on the appearance of genuine revolutionary sentiment, but it will not survive the revelation of the real issues or the disappointments that follow groundless hopes. To say that the Southern people were deprived of their moral force and patriotism by their government, through mere errors in the conduct of the war or absolute despotism, is to attribute to them character too weak to warrant any movement which would involve a protracted war of immense proportions; and the only supposition that gives room for the existence of manhood and strong character in the Southern people is, that the masses were beguiled into insurrection against a good government by a few men of great influence, and that they abandoned it when they discovered the deception.

The original opposition to secession by a party of great numerical strength, but of feeble and incomplete organization, may be cited as evidence that the movement toward disunion was not supported by the people generally with such heartiness and spontaneous purpose as indicated a true revolution. A fallacy, glaring in absurdity when strictly analyzed, yet subtle, imposing, and of momentous force, when accepted, swept a multitude of originally sincere Union men into the rebellion, inducing their allegiance to the several seceding states and to the Confederate government formed by them. The fallacy was that a formal act of secession, though unconstitutionally enacted and pronounced, bound all citizens of a state to serve the state in the extreme consequences of the act. Its force prevented all organization in opposition to the resulting war in any stage of its progress, and long enforced its support; but it did not and could not create the foundations of a true revolution, and when the awakening to the grand mistake did occur, the seeming revolution failed in default of the general support of the Southern people.

The want of sympathy between the leaders and the masses was never so apparent as during the later campaigns of the war, especially during the last operations of the national cavalry, when perhaps hundreds of millions of property might have been saved from destruction if the leaders of the rebellion had recognized the fact that the majority of the Southern people had abandoned it.

CHAPTER XLII.

THE DISSOLUTION OF THE ARMY—SUMMARY OF ITS ACHIEVEMENTS.

THE surrender of the remaining Confederate armies and forces east and west of the Mississippi river soon followed the capitulation of General Johnston and the capture of Mr. Davis. Preparations were then promptly made to disband the national armies, with the retention of such forces only as were necessary to prevent political and social chaos in the Southern States.

The formal unity of the Army of the Cumberland was restored before its dissolution by the return of the Fourteenth and Twentieth Corps within the territorial limits of the Department of the Cumberland. This reunion of the grand units under their revered commander was eminently appropriate as well as historically imperative. Their dismemberment at Goldsboro, North Carolina, occurring after their last battle had been fought, did not really impair the historical unity of this great army. Still, there would have been a painful lack of complete roundness in its mere organic unity, had two corps been disbanded outside the territorial limits of the department.

During the summer of 1865, the Fourth Corps was also temporarily detached, and sent upon a mission to Texas under General Sheridan. But it, too, was soon remanded to the Department of the Cumberland, to be disbanded, as were the Fourteenth and Twentieth, by General Thomas.

From the 1st of June, 1865, to February 1, 1866, there were mustered out of the service of the United States, from the Army of the Cumberland, five thousand and eighty-three commissioned officers and one hundred and thirty-seven thousand five hundred and thirty-three enlisted men, exclusive of sixteen regiments of cavalry, whose strength was not definitely reported. About twenty thousand volunteer troops were retained within the Military Division of the Tennessee, under the command of Major-General George H. Thomas, until a later period. From the data given, the strength of the Army of the Cumberland, at the close of the war, may be placed, with approximate correctness, at one hundred and seventy-five thousand men. And when these heroic citizen soldiers were remanded to the duties of civil life, the Army of the Cumberland passed from organic existence to live in history as an army unsurpassed, if equaled, by any of the great armies which participated in our gigantic civil war—as one of the grandest that ever battled for country or freedom.

This army fought, unaided, the battles of "Mill Springs," "Perryville," "Stone River," "Chickamauga," "Wauhatchee," and "Bentonville;" gave essential aid to the Army of the Tennessee, at "Fort Donelson" and "Pittsburg Landing;" in combination with that army, but in twofold strength, gained the decisive victories on Lookout Mountain and Missionary Ridge; furnished more than half the forces for the Atlanta campaign, placing upon its banners the historic fields of "Buzzard's Roost," "Resaca," "Rome," "New Hope Church," "Kenesaw Mountain," "Peachtree Creek," "Atlanta," and "Jonesboro;" at Jonesboro, represented by the Fourteenth Corps, made the only successful assault, in force, during the Atlanta campaign, carrying intrenchments held by Hardee's corps; formed the left wing of the army which marched from Atlanta to Savannah, and then swept through the Carolinas to Richmond and Washington; divided the glory of "Franklin" with the Army of the Ohio, and that of "Nashville" with the Armies of the Tennessee and Ohio; and, represented by the troopers of Generals Wilson and Stoneman, rushed through Alabama, Georgia, Tennessee, and North Carolina, in swift and brilliant sequence to the great central battles of the war. This army, in its unity, never gave but one field to the enemy. But when it yielded the bloody ground of Chickamauga, it had revealed, under conditions of battle greatly unequal, its invincibility within fair terms of conflict. But even here it gained the fruits of victory, under the semblance of defeat, as it held Chattanooga, the objective of the campaign.

[GENERAL ORDERS, NO. 108.]
WAR DEPARTMENT, ADJUTANT-GENERAL'S OFFICE,
WASHINGTON, D. C., June 2, 1865.

Soldiers of the Armies of the United States:

By your patriotic devotion to your country in the hour of danger and alarm, your magnificent fighting, bravery, and endurance, you have maintained the supremacy of the Union and the constitution, overthrown all armed opposition to the enforcement of the laws, and of the proclamation forever abolishing slavery—the cause and pretext of the rebellion—and opened the way to the rightful authorities to restore order and inaugurate peace on a permanent and enduring basis, on every foot of American soil.

Your marches, sieges, and battles, in distance, duration, resolution, and brilliancy of result, dim the luster of the world's past military achievements, and will be the patriot's precedent in defense of liberty and right in all time to come.

In obedience to your country's call, you left your homes and families, and volunteered in its defense. Victory has crowned your valor, and secured the purpose of your patriot hearts; and with the gratitude of your countrymen, and the highest honors a great and free nation can accord, you will soon be permitted to return to your homes and families, conscious of having discharged the highest duty of American citizens. To achieve these glorious triumphs, and secure to yourselves, your fellow-countrymen, and posterity, the blessings of free institutions, tens of thousands of your gallant comrades have fallen, and sealed the priceless legacy with their lives. The graves of these a grateful nation bedews with tears, honors their memories, and will ever cherish and support their stricken families.

U. S. GRANT,
Lieutenant-General.

[SPECIAL FIELD ORDERS, NO. 76.]
HEADQUARTERS MILITARY DIVISION OF THE MISSISSIPPI,
IN THE FIELD, WASHINGTON, D. C., May 30, 1865.

The general commanding announces to the Armies of the Tennessee and Georgia that the time has come for us to part. Our work is done, and armed enemies no longer defy us. Some of you will go to your homes, and others will be retained in military service until further orders.

And now that we are all about to separate, to mingle with the civil world, it becomes a pleasing duty to call to mind the situation of national affairs when, but little more than a year ago, we were gathered about the cliffs of Lookout Mountain, and all the future was wrapped in doubt and uncertainty.

Three armies had come together from distant fields, with separate histories, yet bound by one common cause—the union of our country and the perpetuation of the government of our inheritance. There is no need to recall to your memories Tunnel Hill, with Rocky Face Mountain and Buzzard Roost Gap, and the ugly forts of Dalton behind.

We were in earnest, and paused not for danger and difficulty, but dashed through Snake-Creek Gap and fell on Resaca; then on to the Etowah, to Dallas, Kenesaw, and the heats of summer found us on the banks of the Chattahoochee, far from home, and dependent on a single road for supplies.

Again we were not to be held back by any obstacle, and crossed and fought four hard battles for the possession of the citadel of Atlanta. That was the crisis of our history. A doubt still clouded our future, but we solved the problem, destroyed Atlanta, struck boldly across the State of Georgia, severed all the main arteries of life to our enemy, and Christmas found us at Savannah.

Waiting there only long enough to fill our wagons, we again began a march, which, for peril, labor, and result, will compare with any ever made by an organized army. The floods of the Savannah, the swamps of the Combahee and Edisto, the high hills and rocks of the Santee, the flat quagmires of the Pedee and Cape Fear rivers, were all passed in mid-winter, with its floods and rains, in the face of an accumulating enemy; and after the battles of Averysboro and Bentonville, we once more came out of the wilderness to meet our friends at Goldsboro. Even then we paused only long enough to get new clothing, to reload our wagons, again pushed on to Raleigh and beyond, until we met our enemy, suing for peace instead of war, and offering to submit to the injured laws of his and our country. As long as that enemy was defiant, nor mountains, nor rivers, nor swamps, nor hunger, nor cold had checked us; but when he who had fought us hard and persistently offered submission, your general thought it wrong to pursue him farther, and negotiations followed, which resulted, as you all know, in his surrender.

How far the operations of this army contributed to the final overthrow of the Confederacy, and the peace which now dawns upon us, must be judged by others, not by us; but that you have done all that men could do, has been admitted by those in authority, and we have a right to join in the universal joy that fills our land because the war is over, and our government stands vindicated before the world, by the joint action of the volunteer armies and navy of the United States.

To such as remain in the service, your general need only remind you that success in the past was due to hard work and discipline, and that the same work and discipline are equally important in the future. To such as go home, he will only say that our favored country is so grand, so extensive, so diversified in climate, soil, and productions, that every man may find a home and occupation suited to his tastes; none should yield to the natural impatience sure to result from our past life of excitement and adventure. You will be invited to seek new adventures abroad; do not yield to the temptation, for it will lead only to death and disappointment.

Your general now bids you farewell, with the full belief that, as in war you have been good soldiers, so in peace you will make good citizens; and if, unfortunately, new war should arise in our country, "Sherman's army" will be the first to buckle on its old armor, and come forth to defend and maintain the government of our inheritance.

BY ORDER OF MAJOR-GENERAL W. T. SHERMAN.

L. M. DAYTON,
Assistant Adjutant-General.

[GENERAL ORDERS, NO. 30.]

HEADQUARTERS DEPARTMENT OF THE CUMBERLAND,
NASHVILLE, TENN., *May* 10, 1865.

The general commanding the department takes pride in conveying to the Fourth Army Corps the expression of his admiration, excited by their brilliant and martial display at the review of yesterday.

As the battalions of your magnificent corps swept successively before the eye, the coldest heart must have warmed with interest in contemplation of those men who had passed through the varied and shifting scenes of this great modern tragedy, who had stemmed with unyielding breasts the rebel tide threatening to engulf the landmarks of freedom, and who, bearing on their bronzed and furrowed brows the ennobling marks of the years of hardship, suffering, and privation, undergone in defense of freedom and the integrity of the Union, could still preserve the light step and wear the cheerful expression of youth.

Though your gay and broidered banners, wrought by dear hands far away, were all shred and war-worn, were they not blazoned on every stripe with words of glory—Shiloh, Spring Hill, Stone River, Chickamauga, Atlanta, Franklin, Nashville, and many other glorious names, too numerous to mention in an order like this? By your prowess and fortitude you have ably done your part in restoring the golden boon of peace and order to your once distracted but now grateful country, and your commander is at length enabled to give you a season of well-earned rest.

But, soldiers, while we exult at our victories, let us not be forgetful of those brave, devoted hearts, which, pressing in advance, throbbed their last amid the smoke and din of battle, nor withhold our sympathy for the afflicted wife, child, and mother, consigned, far off at home, to lasting, cruel grief.

BY COMMAND OF MAJOR-GENERAL THOMAS.

WM. D. WHIPPLE,
Assistant Adjutant-General.

[GENERAL ORDERS, NO. 15.]

HEADQUARTERS ARMY OF GEORGIA,
WASHINGTON, D. C., *June* 6, 1865.

With the separation of the troops composing this army, in compliance with recent orders, the organization known as "the Army of Georgia" will virtually cease to exist. Many of you will at once return to your homes. No one now serving as a volunteer will probably be retained in service against his will but a short time longer. All will soon be permitted to return and receive the rewards due them as the gallant defenders of their country.

While I can not repress a feeling of sadness at parting with you, I congratulate you upon the grand results achieved by your valor, fidelity, and patriotism.

No generation has ever done more for the permanent establishment of a just and liberal form of gevernment—more for the honor of their nation—than has been done during the past four years by the armies of the United States, and the patriotic people at home, who have poured out their wealth in support of these armies with a liberality never before witnessed in any country.

Do not forget the parting advice of that great chieftain who led you through your recent brilliant campaigns. "As in war you have been good soldiers, so in peace be good citizens."

Should you ever desire to resume the honorable profession you are now about to leave, do not forget that this profession is honorable only when followed in obedience to the orders of the constituted authority of your government.

With feelings of deep gratitude to each and all of you for your uniform soldierly conduct, for the patience and fortitude with which you have borne all the hardships it has been necessary to impose upon you, and for the unflinching resolution with which you have sustained the holy cause in which we have been engaged, I bid you farewell.

H. W. SLOCUM, *Major-General Commanding.*

[GENERAL ORDERS, NO. 17.]

HEADQUARTERS FOURTEENTH ARMY CORPS,
WASHINGTON, D. C., *June* 15, 1865.

Soldiers of the Fourteenth Army Corps:

Since he assumed command of the corps, your general has seen many occasions when he was proud of your endurance, your courage, and your achievements. If he did not praise you then, it was because your labors and triumphs were incomplete. Whilst the enemies of your country still defied you, whilst hardships and dangers were yet to be encountered and overcome, it seemed to him premature to indulge in unnecessary praise of deeds being enacted, or to rest upon laurels already won. But now, when the battle and the march are ended and the victory yours; when many of you are about to return to your homes, where the sound of the hostile cannon—now silenced, let us trust, forever in our land—will soon be forgotten amidst the welcoming plaudits of friends; when the heavy armor of the soldier is being exchanged for the civic wreaths of peace, he deems it a happy occasion to congratulate you upon the part which you have borne, in common with your comrades of the armies of the Union, in the mighty struggle for the maintenance of the unity and integrity of your country. You will join heartily in the generel rejoicing over the grand result and the termination of the nation's peril. While the country is welcoming her defenders home, and their noble deeds are being commemorated, you will ever remember with proud satisfaction that at Chickamauga yours were the invincible battalions with which the unyielding Thomas hurled back the overwhelming foe and saved the day; that at Mission Ridge you helped, with your brothers of the Armies of the Cumberland and of the Tennessee, to plant the banners of your country once more on the cloud-clad heights of Chattanooga; that at Jonesboro your resistless charge decreed the final fate of proud Atlanta; that at Bentonville you for hours defied the frenzied and determined efforts of the rebel hosts to crush *seriatim* the columns of the victorious Sherman. Years hence, in the happy enjoyment of the peace and prosperity of your country, whose preservation your valor on many hard-fought fields secured, it will be among your proudest boasts that you fought with Thomas and marched with Sherman from the mountains to the sea; that you toiled and skirmished in midwinter through the swamps of Georgia and the Carolinas; that after years of bloody contest you witnessed the surrender of one of the enemy's proudest armies, no longer able to withstand your irresistible pursuit. Now the danger past, and the victory won, many of you turn homeward. Let the same generous spirit, the same pure patriotism that prompted your entry into your country's service, be cherished by you, never forgetting that the true soldier is always a good citizen and Christian.

Some remain yet for a time as soldiers. The same country that first called you needs your further services and retains you. Let your future record be a continuation of the glorious past, and such that as long as a soldier remains of the Fourteenth Corps it shall continue bright and untarnished.

Many of the noblest, bravest, and best who came out with us will not return. We left them on the hills and by the streams of the South, where no voice of mother, sister, or wife will ever wake them—where no kind hand will strew flowers upon their graves. But, soldiers, by us they will never be forgotten. Their heroic deeds and last resting-places will often be brought to mind in fond remembrance. Though dead, they will live in the affections of their countrymen and their country's history. Whilst passing events are fast changing our past associations and requiring us to form new ones, let us seek to extend a warm greeting and the hearty hand of congratulation to all who rejoice in our country's preservation and return to peace.

By command of Brevet Major-General Jeff. C. Davis.

A. C. McCLURG,
Brevet Colonel A. A. G. and Chief of Staff.

[GENERAL ORDERS, NO. 39.]
HEADQUARTERS CAVALRY CORPS, M. D. M.,
MACON, GA., *July* 2, 1865.

To the Officers and Men of the Cavalry Corps, Military Division of the Mississippi:

Your corps has ceased to exist! The rebellion has terminated in the re-establishment of your country upon the basis of nationality and perpetual unity. Your deeds have contributed a noble part to the glorious result; they have passed into history and need no recital from me. In the nine months during which I have commanded you, I have heard no reproach upon your conduct—have had no disaster to chronicle!

The glowing memories of Franklin, Nashville, West Harpeth, Ebenezer Church, Selma, Montgomery, Columbus, West Point, and Macon may well fill your hearts and mine with pride.

You have learned to believe yourselves invincible, and, contemplating your honorable deeds, may justly cherish that belief. You may be proud of your splendid discipline no less than your courage, zeal, and endurance. The noble impulses which have inspired you in the past, will be a source of enduring honor in the future. "Peace has her victories no less renowned than war." Do not forget that clear heads, honest hearts, and stout arms, guided by pure patriotism, are the surest defense of your country in every peril. Upon them depend the substantial progress of your race and order of civilization, as well as the liberty of all mankind.

Let your example in civil life be an incitement to industry, good order, and enlightenment, while your deeds in war shall live in the grateful remembrance of your countrymen.

Having discharged every military duty honestly and faithfully, return to your homes with the noble sentiment of your martyr President deeply impressed upon every heart: "With malice against none and charity for all, strive to do the right as God gives you to see the right."

J^S. H. WILSON,
Brevet Major-General.

CHAPTER XLIII.

THE DEAD AND THEIR DISPOSITION.

THE history of the Army of the Cumberland would not be complete was the disposition of its heroic dead omitted; for never, in the history of war, have the slain of any other army been so honored in burial.

The first permanent National Cemetery for soldiers established by military order, was the one founded by General George H. Thomas, near Chattanooga, Tennessee. The circumstances under which this site was selected, have historic interest far transcending the mere fact of priority of establishment.

During the battle, which resulted in the dislodgment of General Bragg's army from Missionary Ridge, a reserve force, in line over a hill near the field position of General Thomas, revealed its beautiful contour and suggested its use as a National Cemetery. This hill, conical in general outline, but fruitful in lateral hillocks and varied in expression from every point of view, is located equidistant from Cameron hill, which rises abruptly from the Tennessee river, where it turns toward Lookout Mountain and Missionary Ridge on the east, and is central between General Hooker's point of attack on Lookout Mountain, and General Sherman's, on the northern summit of Missionary Ridge. Thus it is the center of this complex battle-field.

Soon after the battle, General Thomas issued the following order:

[GENERAL ORDERS, NO. 296.]

CHATTANOOGA, TENN., *December* 25, 1863.

It is ordered that a National Cemetery be founded at this place, in commemoration of the battles at Chattanooga, fought November 23d, 24th,

25th, 26th, and 27th, and to provide a proper resting-place for the remains of the brave men who fell upon the fields fought over upon those days, and for the remains of such as may hereafter give up their lives in this region in defending their country against treason and rebellion.

The ground selected for the cemetery is the hill lying beyond the Western and Atlantic railroad, in a southeasterly direction from the town.

It is proposed to erect a monument upon the summit of the hill, of such materials as are to be obtained in this vicinity, which, like all the work upon the cemetery, shall be exclusively done by the troops of the Army of the Cumberland.

Plans for the monument are invited to be sent in to these headquarters. When the ground is prepared, notice will be given, and all interments of soldiers will thereafter be made in the cemetery, and all now buried in and around the town removed to that place.

By command of Major-General George H. Thomas.
(Signed,)   WM. D. WHIPPLE,
                             Assistant Adjutant-General.

The exigencies of war prevented the execution of all the work upon this cemetery by the troops of the Army of the Cumberland, and the monument contemplated has never been erected. Neither was it subsequently practicable to obtain a brief history of the many thousands interred in this classic ground, as at first contemplated. However, while the war lasted, troops from the Army of the Cumberland continued the work of burial and embellishment. When the volunteers were mustered out of the service, employes of the quartermaster's department completed the enterprise as far as practicable.

The establishment of the Chattanooga National Cemetery was followed, first, by one upon the battle-field of Stone River, and later, by one at Nashville, Tennessee, and another at Marietta, Georgia. Chaplain William Earnshaw was charged with the burial of the dead and the ornamentation of the grounds at Stone River and Nashville, and another chaplain sustained a similar relation to the cemeteries at Chattanooga and Marietta. In these four cemeteries were finally interred the remains of more than forty thousand soldiers. Many smaller cemeteries were established within the limits of the Department of the Cumberland, within the States of Kentucky, Tennessee, Mississippi, Alabama, and Georgia, and more than one hundred thousand soldiers were interred in cemeteries commemorative, often, of great battles, and always of the nation's gratitude to those who gave their lives to maintain the nation's life.

In expression of the value of each citizen who fell in the war, the body of each was placed in a separate grave. And so thorough was the search for the dead upon every battle-field and over the whole country, that their friends may be assured that, whether identified or not, all rest in grounds consecrated for their abode forever.

[EXTRACT FROM GENERAL ORDERS, NO. 8.]

HEAD-QUARTERS ARMY OF THE CUMBERLAND,
CHATTANOOGA, TENN., *January* 8, 1864.

Commanding officers of regiments in this department will furnish, on the application of Chaplain Thomas B. Van Horne, 13th O. V. I., in charge of the Mortuary Record of the National Cemetery at this place, full information in regard to the full name, rank, company, native state, date, age, marital state, date of enlistment, address of nearest friends, number of engagements participated in, soldierly character, special circumstances of death, if killed in action, and whatever else is worthy of their history of record, of all soldiers who may be interred in the National Cemetery at Chattanooga.

BY COMMAND OF MAJOR-GENERAL THOMAS:

WM. D. WHIPPLE, *Assistant Adjutant-General.*
Official: WM. MCMICHAEL, *Assistant Adjutant-General.*

APPENDIX.

ORGANIZATION DEPARTMENT OF THE CUMBERLAND.

[OFFICIAL.]

Organized August 15, 1861 (G. O. No. 57, W. D.), embracing states of Kentucky and Tennessee. Brigadier-General ROBERT ANDERSON, U. S. A., to command. Discontinued November 9, 1861 (G. O. No. 97, W. D.), and the states embraced therein assigned as follows: Kentucky, west of Cumberland river, to DEPARTMENT OF THE MISSOURI; Kentucky, east of Cumberland river, to DEPARTMENT OF THE OHIO; Tennessee, to the DEPARTMENT OF THE OHIO.

Reorganized October 24, 1862 (G. O. No. 168, W. D.), embracing State of Tennessee, east of the Tennessee river, and such parts of Northern Georgia and Alabama as are taken possession of by United States forces.

ORGANIZATION DEPARTMENT OF THE CUMBERLAND, MILITARY DIVISION, AND DEPARTMENT OF THE TENNESSEE, ETC.

DEPARTMENT OF THE CUMBERLAND.

Organized, and Major-General W. S. ROSECRANS assigned to the command, October 30, 1862 (G. O. No. 168, W. D., October 24, 1862), consisted of the Fourteenth Army Corps, the troops of which were subsequently divided into three (3) army corps—the Fourteenth, Twentieth, and Twenty-first—as follows: The "Center," under command of Major-General G. H. THOMAS, to constitute the Fourteenth Army Corps; "Right Wing," under Major-General A. McD. McCOOK, the Twentieth; and the "Left Wing,"

382   APPENDIX.

under Major-General T. L. CRITTENDEN, the Twenty-first Army Corps. (See G. O. No. 9, W. D., February 2, 1863.)

The Twentieth and Twenty-first Army Corps were consolidated October 9, 1863, to constitute one corps, to be known as the Fourth Army Corps. Major-General GORDON GRANGER to command (G. O. No. 228, D. C., 1863).

Major-General ROSECRANS relieved from command of the Department, October 19, 1863; General G. H. THOMAS assumed command October 20, 1863. General J. M. PALMER to command Fourteenth Army Corps, vice THOMAS, assigned to command DEPARTMENT OF THE CUMBERLAND, October 28, 1863 (G. O. No. 350, W. D., 1863).

The Eleventh and Twelfth Corps, consolidated, to constitute the Twentieth Corps, April 4, 1864. Major-General JOSEPH HOOKER assigned to the command (G. O. No. 144, W. D., Series of 1864).

By same order, General GORDON GRANGER relieved from command of the Fourth Army Corps, and General O. O. HOWARD assigned in his stead.

Major-General J. HOOKER relieved from, and Major-General SLOCUM assigned to, command Twentieth Army Corps; and General HOWARD transferred from, and General STANLEY assigned to, command Fourth Army Corps (G. O. No. 238, W. D., July 30, 1864).

Brevet Major-General JEFF. C. DAVIS assigned to command the Fourteenth Army Corps (G. O. No. 241, W. D., August, 1864).

The Twentieth and Fourteenth Army Corps accompanied General SHERMAN on his march to the sea.

By direction of the President (contained in telegram from W. A. NICHOLS, Assistant Adjutant-General, January 17, 1865), the DEPARTMENT OF THE OHIO was united to the DEPARTMENT OF THE CUMBERLAND, to embrace such parts of Mississippi, Georgia, and Alabama as were occupied by troops of General THOMAS' command. On the 12th of February, the Department was divided into the following Districts and Subdistricts, viz :

DISTRICT OF WEST TENNESSEE, headquarters at Memphis, Tennessee, Major-General C. C. WASHBURNE to command.

DISTRICT OF MIDDLE TENNESSEE, headquarters at Nashville, Major-General L. H. ROUSSEAU.

DISTRICT OF NORTHERN ALABAMA, headquarters at Decatur, Brigadier-General R. S. GRANGER.

FIRST SUBDISTRICT OF MIDDLE TENNESSEE, headquarters at Tullahoma, Major-General R. H. MILROY.

SECOND SUBDISTRICT OF MIDDLE TENNESSEE, headquarters at Pulaski, Brigadier-General R. W. JOHNSON.

THIRD SUBDISTRICT OF MIDDLE TENNESSEE, headquarters at Kingston Springs, Colonel C. R. THOMPSON.

FOURTH SUBDISTRICT OF MIDDLE TENNESSEE, Colonel JAMES GILFELLAN, Eleventh Minnesota Volunteers.

FIFTH SUBDISTRICT OF MIDDLE TENNESSEE, headquarters at Clarksville, Colonel A. A. SMITH, Eighty-third Illinois Volunteers.

DISTRICT OF ETOWAH, Major-General J. B. STEEDMAN; and DISTRICT OF EAST TENNESSEE, Major-General GEORGE STONEMAN.

By order of the Lieutenant-General commanding Armies of the United States, dated May 27, 1865, Northern Mississippi was embodied in DISTRICT OF WEST TENNESSEE, DEPARTMENT OF THE CUMBERLAND discontinued, and MILITARY DIVISION OF THE TENNESSEE organized, June 20, 1865.

THE MILITARY DIVISION OF THE TENNESSEE

Consisted at its organization of five (5) Departments, viz:

DEPARTMENT OF KENTUCKY, Major-General J. M. PALMER to command, headquarters at Louisville, Kentucky.

DEPARTMENT OF TENNESSEE, Major-General GEORGE STONEMAN to command, headquarters at Knoxville, Tennessee.

DEPARTMENT OF GEORGIA, Major-General J. B. STEEDMAN to command, headquarters at Augusta, Georgia.

DEPARTMENT OF ALABAMA, Major-General C. R. WOODS to command, headquarters at Mobile, Alabama.

DEPARTMENT OF FLORIDA and DISTRICT OF KEY WEST, Major-General A. A. HUMPHREYS to command, Tallahasse, Florida.

The DEPARTMENT OF MISSISSIPPI, Major-General H. W. SLOCUM commanding, added to the MILITARY DIVISION OF THE TENNESSEE, by direction of the President (G. O. No. 2, M. D. T., 1865).

By direction of the President, the orders annexing the Departments of Florida and Mississippi were revoked, in General Orders No. 4, M. D. T., 1865.

APPENDIX.

DEPARTMENT OF THE TENNESSEE.

Organized August 13, 1866, consisting of the following Districts and Subdistricts, viz:

DISTRICT OF THE CUMBERLAND, Major-General STONEMAN, headquarters at Memphis, to embrace Kentucky and Tennessee.

SUBDISTRICT OF KENTUCKY, Brevet Major-General J. C. DAVIS.

SUBDISTRICT of TENNESSEE, Brevet Major-General C. B. FISK.

DISTRICT OF MISSISSIPPI, Major-General THOMAS J. WOOD.

DISTRICT OF THE CHATTAHOOCHEE, Brevet Major-General C. R. WOODS, to embrace Subdistricts of Georgia and Alabama.

SUBDISTRICT OF ALABAMA, Major-General W. SWAYNE.

SUBDISTRICT OF GEORGIA, Brevet Major-General DAVIS TILLSON.

MILITARY DIVISION OF TENNESSEE was divided into DEPARTMENT OF THE CUMBERLAND, consisting of the Districts (late Departments) of Tennessee and Kentucky, Major-General GEORGE STONEMAN to command, Memphis (organized by G. O. No. 36, W. D., June 5, 1866); DEPARTMENT OF THE SOUTH, consisting of the Districts (late Departments) of Georgia and Alabama, Major-General C. R. WOODS to command, Macon, Georgia (organized by G. O. No. 32, W. D., May 19, 1866); DEPARTMENT OF MISSISSIPPI annexed to Department by G. O. No. 142, W. D., October 7, 1865, Major-General H. W. SLOCUM to command.

General T. J. WOOD assigned to command of the Department November 3, 1865 (G. O. No. 159, W. D.)

APPENDIX. 385

ORGANIZATION OF THE DEPARTMENT OF THE OHIO.

[OFFICIAL.]

Organized May 3, 1861 (G. O. No. 14, W. D.), embracing States of Ohio, Indiana, and Illinois. Major-General GEO. B. MCCLELLAN to command. Headquarters, Cincinnati, Ohio.

Extended May 9, 1861 (G. O. No. 19, W. D.), to embrace portions of West Virginia and Pennsylvania.

Extended June 6, 1861 (G. O. No. 30, W. D.), to embrace State of Missouri.

Reorganized September 9, 1861 (G. O. No. 80, W. D.), embracing States of Ohio, Indiana, and so much of Kentucky as lies within fifteen miles of Cincinnati, Ohio. Brigadier-General MITCHELL to command.

Reorganized November 9, 1861 (G. O. No. 97, W. D.), embracing States of Ohio, Michigan, Indiana, Kentucky, east of the Cumberland river, and Tennessee. Brigadier-General D. C. BUELL to command. Headquarters, Louisville.

Extended August 19, 1862 (G. O. No. 112, W. D.), to embrace Ohio, Michigan, Indiana, Illinois, Wisconsin, and Kentucky, east of the Tennessee river. Major-General H. G. WRIGHT to command.

Extended September 19, 1862 (G. O. No. 135, W. D.), to embrace West Virginia.

Major-General BURNSIDE assumed command of the Department March 25, 1863.

Major-General J. G. FOSTER relieved General BURNSIDE from command December —, 1863.

Department to embrace Kentucky, north of the Tennessee river, and such portions of Tennessee as may be occupied by troops of the Department.

Major-General J. M. SCHOFIELD assumed command February 9, 1864.

Department annexed to the Department of the Cumberland by direction of the President, contained in telegram from W. A. NICHOLS, dated January 17, 1865.

LIST OF OFFICERS OF ARMY OF THE CUMBERLAND WHO WERE KILLED IN ACTION OR DIED OF WOUNDS OR DISEASE DURING THE WAR, MAINLY COMPILED FROM THE "ARMY REGISTER."

CONNECTICUT.

Fifth Connecticut Infantry.

First Lieut. James P. Henderson. Killed March 16, 1865.

Twentieth Connecticut Infantry.

Captain Oliver R. Post. Died, July 21, 1864, of wounds in action before Atlanta, Ga.
First Lieut. Edward A. Doolittle. Died of disease, December 20, 1863.
First Lieut. Henry Lewis. Died December 26, 1864.
First Lieut. Wellington Barry. Died March 17, 1865.

ILLINOIS.

Brigadier-General E. N. Kirk. Died ——, 1863, of wounds received at Stone River, December 31, 1862.

Battery B, Second Illinois Light Infantry.

First Lieut. William Bishop. Killed at Chickamauga, September 20, 1863.
Second Lieut. Franklin Seeborn. Died, November 11, 1864, of wounds received in action.

Battery C, Second Illinois Artillery.

First Lieut. Elijah V. Moore. Died, February 5, 1863, of wounds received at Fort Donelson.

Battery I.

First Lieut. Alonzo W. Coe. Killed near Savannah, Ga., December 9, 1864.

Tenth Illinois Infantry.

First Lieut. William W. Rice, Adjutant. Died at Chattanooga, Tenn., June 16, 1864, of wounds.

Sixteenth Illinois Infantry.

Major Samuel M. Hayes. Died, August 6, 1862, at Monticello, Ill.
Captain David Wells. Died of disease, at Macomb, Ill., April 7, 1862.
Captain Calvin H. Wilson. Died at Quincy, Ill., June 16, 1864.
Captain Eben White. Died, May 18, 1865, of wounds received at Averysboro, N. C.
First Lieut. James Donaldson. Died, July 17, 1864, of wounds received at Vining's Station, Ga.

Nineteenth Illinois Infantry.

Colonel Joseph Scott. Died, July 8, 1863, of wounds received at Stone River.
Captain Bushrod B. Howard. Killed by railroad accident, September 17, 1871.
Captain Charles H. Shepley. Died, March 23, 1862, from accident with his revolver.
Captain Knowlton H. Chandler. Killed at Stone River, January 2, 1863.
First Lieut. Willington Wood. Died, January 5, 1863, of wounds received at Stone River.
Second Lieut. Thomas L. Job. Killed accidentally July 18, 1861.
Second Lieut. John H. Hunter. Died, January 9, 1863, of wounds received at Stone River.
Chaplain Augustus H. Conant. Died February 8, 1863.

Twenty-first Illinois Infantry.

Colonel John W. S. Alexander. Killed at Chickamauga, September 20, 1863.
Captain Benjamin F. Reed. Died, September 23, 1863, of wounds received at Chickamauga.
Captain Andrew George. Died, January 15, 1864, of wounds received at Chickamauga.
First Lieut. Charles L. Smedel. Died at Nashville, Tenn., April 27, 1863, of disease.
Second Lieut. Emanuel M. Weigle. Killed at Stone River, December 31, 1862.
Second Lieut. John F. Weitzel. Killed at Chickamauga, September 19, 1863.
Assistant Surgeon Carl Muntz. Died, January 31, 1862, at Ironton, Mo.

Twenty-second Illinois Infantry.

Lieut. Colonel Harrison E. Hart. Died of disease at Alton, Ill., July 25, 1862.
Captain Milton French. Died, September 27, 1863, of wounds received at Chickamauga.
Second Lieut. Cyrus M. Galloway. Died, January 24, 1863, of wounds received at Stone River.

Twenty-fourth Illinois Infantry.

Colonel Geza Mihalotzy. Died, March 11, 1864, of wounds received at Buzzard's Roost, Ga.
Captain Ernst F. Pletschke. Died, October 9, 1861, at Louisville, Ky.
Captain Fred. Hartman. Died, November 9, 1862, of wounds received in action.
Captain George Heinricks. Killed at Chickamauga, September 20, 1863.
Second Lieut. Ami Smith. Died, October 15, 1862, at Bowling Green, Ky.

Twenty-fifth Illinois Infantry.

Colonel Thomas D. Williams. Killed at Stone River, December 31, 1862.
Captain Charles A. Clark. Killed in quelling mutiny, November 25, 1863.
Second Lieut. David M. Richards. Died, December 10, 1863, of wounds received in action.
Second Lieut. James K. Weir. Died, June 21, 1864, of wounds received in action.

APPENDIX.

Twenty-seventh Illinois Infantry.

Colonel Fazelo A. Harrington. Died, January 1, 1863, of wounds received at Stone River.
Captain William S. Bryan. Killed at Chickamauga, September 19, 1863.
First Lieut. William Shipley. Killed at Belmont, Mo., November 7, 1861.
First Lieut. Joseph Voellinger. Died, October 18, 1863, of wounds received in action.
First Lieut. Hugh M. Love. Killed at Missionary Ridge, November 25, 1863.
First Lieut. Andrew J. Slides. Killed at Kenesaw Mountain, June 27, 1864.
First Lieut. Alexander M. Boggs. Killed accidentally, near Atlanta, Ga., July 23, 1864.
Second Lieut. Herbert Weyman. Killed at Missionary Ridge, November 25, 1863.

Thirty-fourth Illinois Infantry.

Lieut. Colonel Amos Bosworth. Died, April 23, 1862, of disease.
Major Charles H. Levanway. Killed at Shiloh, April 7, 1862.
Captain Mabry G. Greenwood. Died of wounds received December 31, 1862, at Stone River.
Captain John A. Parrott. Killed at Resaca, May 14, 1864.
Captain Amos W. Hostetter. Died, July 26, 1864, of wounds received at Atlanta.
First Lieut. Daniel Riley. Died at Nashville, January 20, 1863, of wounds.
First Lieut. Henry D. Wood, Adjutant. Died, October 12, 1864, at Atlanta, of disease.
First Lieut. Edward B. Hamer. Killed near Haywood, N. C., April 15, 1865.
Second Lieut. Henry Miller. Died of wounds, May 1, 1862.
Second Lieut. John M. Smith. Killed at Stone River, December 31, 1862.

Thirty-fifth Illinois Infantry.

Major John McIlvain. Killed near Kenesaw Mountain, June 22, 1864.
Captain Collins P. Jones. Killed at Chickamauga, September 20, 1863.
First Lieut. Joseph Moore. Died, April 7, 1862, of wounds received at Pea Ridge.
First Lieut. Humphrey M. McConnell. Died, January 3, 1863, of wounds received in action.
First Lieut. Moses C. Snook. Died, March 9, 1863, of disease.
First Lieut. George F. Dietz. Died, July 8, 1863, of disease.
First Lieut. John W. Snyder. Killed at Chickamauga, September 19, 1863.
First Lieut. Daniel H. Kagay. Died, February 10, 1864, of disease.
Second Lieut. Joseph F. Clise. Died, October 7, 1861, of disease.
Second Lieut. James P. Butler. Killed at Chickamauga, September 19, 1863.
Second Lieut. Benjamin F. Smith. Died, November 9, 1864, of disease.

Thirty-sixth Illinois Infantry.

Colonel Silas Miller. Died, July 27, 1864, of wounds received at Kenesaw Mountain.
Lieut. Colonel Porter C. Olson. Died, November 30, 1864, of wounds received at Franklin.

Captain Theodore G. Griffin. Died, November 24, 1862, of wounds received at Perryville.
Captain Aaron C. Holden. Died, December 1, 1862, of wounds received in action.
Captain Sanford H. Wakeman. Died, September 20, 1863, of wounds received at Chickamauga.
Captain James B. McNeal. Died, September 4, 1864, of wounds received in action.
First Lieut. Edward S. Chappell. Died, October 16, 1861, at Rolla, Mo.
First Lieut. Orison Smith. Killed at Chickamauga, September 20, 1863.
First Lieut. Charles F. Chase. Died, December 18, 1864, of wounds received at Franklin.
Second Lieut. Soren L. Olson. Killed at Stone River, December 31, 1862.
Second Lieut. Myron A. Smith. Killed at Chickamauga, September 20, 1863.
Second Lieut. Sidney M. Abbott. Killed at Missionary Ridge, November 25, 1863.

Thirty-eighth Illinois Infantry.

Lieut. Colonel Daniel H. Gilmer. Killed at Chickamauga, September 20, 1863.
Lieut. Colonel William T. Chapman. Died, November 23, 1864, at Pulaski, Tenn., of disease.
Captain James P. Mead. Killed at Stone River, December 31, 1862.
Captain Thomas Cole. Killed at Chickamauga, September 19, 1863.
Captain William C. Harris. Died, July 13, 1864, of wounds received at Kenesaw Mountain.
First Lieut. Arthur Lee Bailhache, Adjutant. Died of disease, January 2, 1862.
First Lieut. John L. Dillon. Killed at Stone River, December 31, 1862.
First Lieut. Benjamin G. Humes. Died, January 6, 1865, of wounds received in action.
Second Lieut. Peter N. Scott. Died, January 8, 1863, of wounds received at Stone River.
Chaplain William M. Brown. Died at Springfield, Ill., November 23, 1863, of disease.

Forty-second Illinios Infantry.

Colonel William A. Webb. Died, December 24, 1861, at Smithton, Mo.
Colonel G. W. Roberts. Killed at Stone River, December 31, 1862.
Major James Leighton. Killed at Chickamauga, September 20, 1863.
Major D. Woodman Norton. Killed at New Hope Church, June 3, 1864.
Captain George Varden. Died, September 19, 1862, at Nashville, Tenn., of disease.
Captain Levi Preston. Died, at Chattanooga, Tenn., December 31, 1863, of disease.
Captain Charles A. Seaver, Killed before Atlanta, Ga., August 3, 1864.
Captain Gilbert A. Parshall. Died, December 3, 1864, of wounds received at Spring Hill, Tenn.
First Lieut. Ezra A. Montgomery. Killed at Chickamauga, September 20, 1863.
First Lieut. Edward H. Brown, Adjutant. Killed at Chickamauga, September 20, 1863.
First Lieut. George C. Smith. Died, December 7, 1863, of wounds received at Missionary Ridge.

First Lieut. Alfred O. Johnson. Died, December 8, 1863, of wounds received at Missionary Ridge.
First Lieut. Edward Hurson. Died, May 18, 1864, of wounds received at Resaca.
Second Lieut. Gilbert L. Barnes. Died, October 24, 1861, of disease.
Second Lieut. Julius Lettman. Killed at Stone River, December 31, 1862.
Second Lieut. Jacob Y. Elliott. Died, December 7, 1863, of wounds received at Missionary Ridge.

Forty-fourth Illinois Infantry.

Captain Andrew I. Hosmer. Killed at Stone River, December 31, 1862.
Captain Ernst Moldenhauser. Died, February 27, 1863, of wounds received in action.
Captain Carl R. Harnisch. Killed, at Chattanooga, in action, November 25, 1863.
Captain Benjamin F. Knappen. Died, July 4, 1864, of wounds received in action.
First Lieut. Martin Reminger. Died, August 20, 1862, of disease.
First Lieut. Peter Weyhrich. Died, July 6, 1864, of wounds.
Second Lieut. Silas L. Parker. Died, January 19, 1863, of wounds received in action.

Fifty-first Illinois Infantry.

Captain John T. Whitson. Died, July 15, 1862, at Chicago, Ill.
Captain George L. Bellows. Killed at Missionary Ridge, November 25, 1863.
First Lieut. Otis Moody. Killed at Chickamauga, September 19, 1863.
First Lieut. Thomas T. Lester. Killed at Resaca, May 14, 1864.
First Lieut. Henry W. Hall, Adjutant. Killed at Kenesaw Mountain, June 27, 1864.
First Lieut. Archibald L. McCormick. Killed at Kenesaw Mountain, June 27, 1864.
First Lieut. Calvin H. Thomas. Killed at Franklin, November 30, 1864.
Second Lieut. Albert G. Simmons. Killed at Chickamauga, September 19, 1863.

Fifty-ninth Illinois Infantry.

Captain David M. Bailey. Died, October 10, 1864, of disease.
First Lieut. Albert H. Stookey. Died, March 14, 1862, of disease.
First Lieut. John Kelley. Died, September ——, 1862, at Iuka, Miss., of disease.
First Lieut. Charles F. Adams. Died, October 16, 1862, of wounds received at Perryville.
First Lieut. Robert Gooding. Killed at Nashville, December 16, 1864.
Second Lieut. Andrew R. Johnson. Killed at Perryville, October 8, 1862.
Surgeon J. D. S. Haslett. Killed at Perryville, October 8, 1862.
Assistant Surgeon, James W. Gaston. Died, September 13, 1864, of disease.

Sixtieth Illinois Infantry.

Captain John Coleman. Killed at Peach Tree Creek, July 20, 1864.
First Lieut. Amzi Kniffen. Died, May 17, 1864, of wounds received before Dalton, Ga.

APPENDIX. 391

Seventy-third Illinois Infantry.

Major William E. Smith. Killed at Chickamauga, September 20, 1863.
Major Thomas W. Motherspaw. Died, December 18, 1864, of wounds received in action.
Captain Edwin Alsop. Killed at Stone River, December 31, 1862.
First Lieut. Julian R. Winget, Adjutant. Killed at Chickamauga, September 20, 1863.
First Lieut. William R. Wilmer, Adjutant. Killed at Franklin, November 30 1864.

Seventy-fourth Illinois Infantry.

Lieut. Colonel James B. Kerr. Died, July 3, 1864, of wounds, when prisoner.
Captain Henry C. Barker. Killed at Kenesaw Mountain, June 27, 1864.
Captain Frederick W. Stegner. Killed at Kenesaw Mountain, June 27, 1864
Captain David O. Buttolp. Died, June 29, 1864, of wounds received at Kenesaw Mountain.
Captain Bowman W. Bacon. Died, July 21, 1864, of wounds received at Kenesaw Mountain.
First Lieut. Lewis Williams, R. Q. M. Died November 25, 1862.
First Lieut. Cyrenius N. Woods. Died, August 12, 1863, at Winchester, Tenn.
Assistant Surgeon Sherman C. Ferson. Killed, October 7, 1864, by railroad accident.

Seventy-fifth Illinios Infantry.

Captain Robert Hale. Killed in action, July 4, 1864.
Captain Addison S. Vorrey. Died, August 13, 1864, of disease.
First Lieut. Franklin H. Eels. Killed at Perryville, October 8, 1862.
First Lieut. William H. Thompson. Died, February 25, 1864, of disease.
Second Lieut. James Blean. Killed at Perryville, October 8, 1862.
Second Lieut. Ezekiel J. Killgour. Died, December 26, 1862, of disease.
Second Lieut. Thomas G. Bryant. Died, April 12, 1863, of disease.
Second Lieut. Alfred K. Buckaloo. Died, March 14, 1864, of disease.

Seventy-eighth Illinois Infantry.

Colonel Carter Van Vleck. Died of wounds, August 23, 1864.
Major William L. Broaddus. Killed at Chickamauga, September 20, 1864.
Captain Robert M. Black. Killed at Jonesboro, September 1, 1864.
First Lieut. Tobias E. Butler. Died, May 29, 1864, of wounds.
First Lieut. George A. Brown. Died, June 30, 1864, of wounds received in action.
First Lieut. Daniel W. Long. Killed at Jonesboro, September 1, 1864.
First Lieut. George T. Beers. Killed at Bentonville, March 19, 1865.
First Lieut. William E. Summers. Killed at Bentonville, March 21, 1865.

Seventy-ninth Illinois Infantry.

Lieut. Colonel Sheridan P. Read. Killed at Stone River, December 31, 1862.
Captain John H. Patton. Killed at Liberty Gap, June 25, 1863.
Captain Hezekiah D. Martin. Died, July 3, 1863, of wounds received at Liberty Gap.
First Lieut. Martin L. Linninger. Killed by fall of tree, November 19, 1862.

Eightieth Illinois Infantry.

Captain Edmund R. Jones. Killed at Sand Mountain, Ala., April 30, 1863.
First Lieut. James C. Jones. Killed at Sand Mountain, Ala., April 30, 1863.
Second Lieut. Alex. Van Kendle. Killed in action, October 8, 1862.
Second Lieut. Samuel G. Andrews. Died, November 22, 1862, of wounds received in action.
Second Lieut. John A. Armour. Died, June 11, 1864, of wounds received in action.
Second Lieut. Harvey Clendenin. Died, July 17, 1864, of wounds received in action.

Eighty-second Illinois Infantry.

First Lieut. Frederick Bechstein. Killed at Peach Tree Creek, July 20, 1864.

Eighty-third Illinois Infantry.

Captain Philo. E. Reed. Killed in action at Fort Donelson, February 3, 1863.
Captain John McClanahan. Died, February 23, 1863, of wounds received at Fort Donelson.
Captain William W. Turnbull. Killed at Pine, Bluff, Ark., in action, August 20, 1864.
First Lieut. H. D. Bissell, R. Q. M. Killed in action, Fort Donelson, February 3, 1862.
Second Lieut. John Morton. Died, June 19,1864, at Fort Donelson.

Eighty-fourth Illinois Infantry.

Captain Moses W. Davis. Died, January 20, 1863, of wounds received at Stone River.
Captain Thomas D. Adams. Died, September 21, 1863, of wounds received at Chickamauga.
First Lieut. Luther T. Ball. Killed at Stone River, December 31, 1862.
Second Lieut. Thomas F. Kendrick. Died, November 17, 1862, at Bowling Green, Ky., of disease.
Second Lieut. Henry E. Abrocombie. Killed at Stone River, December 31, 1862.

Eighty-fifth Illinois Infantry.

Captain Charles H. Chatfield. Killed at Kenesaw Mountain, June 27, 1864.
Captain John Kennedy. Killed at Peach Tree Creek, July 19, 1864.
Captain Samuel Young. Died, November 22, 1864, of disease.
First Lieut. Clark N. Andrews, Adjutant. Died, July 23, 1864, of wounds received in action.

Eighty-six Illinois Infantry.

Colonel David D. Irons. Died, August 11, 1863, of disease, at Nashville, Tenn.
Captain Edward Vanantwerp. Died, July 15, 1864, of wounds received in action.
Captain John F. French. Killed at Averysboro, N. C., March 16, 1865.
Captain William B. Bogardus. Died, April 13, 1865, of wounds received at Bentonville.

APPENDIX. 393

Eighty-eighth Illinois Infantry.

Lieut. Colonel George W. Chandler. Killed at Kenesaw Mountain, June 27, 1864.
First Lieut. Thomas F. W. Gullich. Killed at Stone River, December 31, 1862.
First Lieut. Joshua S. Ballard, Adjutant. Died, April 9, 1863, of disease, at Murfreesboro, Tenn.
First Lieut. Charles H. Lane. Killed at Missionary Ridge, November 25, 1863.
First Lieut. John P. D. Gibson. Killed accidentally at Loudon, Tenn., April 17, 1862.
First Lieut. Noah W. Rae. Died, June 2, 1864, of wounds received at Adairsville, Ga.
Second Lieut. Henry W. Meacham. Died, April 1, 1863, of disease, at Murfreesboro, Tenn.
Second Lieut. Henry L. Bingham. Killed at Missionary Ridge, November 25, 1863.
Surgeon George Coatsworth. Died, June 9, 1863, of disease, at Murfreesboro, Tenn.

Eighty-ninth Illinois Infantry.

Lieut. Colonel Duncan J. Hall. Killed at Chickamauga, September 20, 1863.
Captain Henry S. Willett. Killed at Stone River, December 31, 1862.
Captain Herbert M. Blake. Killed at Liberty Gap, June 25, 1863.
Captain William H. Rice. Killed at Chickamauga, September 19, 1863.
Captain Thomas Whiting. Killed at Chickamauga, September 19, 1863.
Captain John W. Spink. Killed at Chickamauga, September 19, 1863.
Captain Henry L. Rowell. Died, December 3, 1863, of wounds received at Missionary Ridge.
First Lieut. Nathan Street. Died, August 6, 1964 (?), of wounds received in action at Nashville, Tenn.
First Lieut. Peter G. Tait. Killed at Nashville, December 16, 1864.
Second Lieut. Amory P. Ellis. Died, October 4, 1863, of wounds received at Chickamauga.
Second Lieut. Erastus O. Young. Killed at Missionary Ridge, November 25, 1863.
Second Lieut. William Harkness. Killed in action at Kenesaw Mountain, Ga., June 21, 1864.
Captain James D. Hill. Died, January 14, 1863, of disease.

Ninety-second Illinois Infantry.

Captain William Stauffer. Died of disease, January 21, 1863, at Danville, Ky.
First Lieut. David B. Colehour. Died, March 17, 1863, of disease, at Nashville, Tenn.
First Lieut. James Daubon. Died, September 21, 1864, of wounds received at Jonesboro.

Ninety-sixth Illinois Infantry.

Lieut. Colonel Isaac L. Clack. Died, September 22, 1863, of wounds received at Chickmauga.
Captain Evangelist J. Gillmore. Killed at Kenesaw Mountain, June 23, 1864.
Captain David James. Died, July 20, 1864, of wounds received at Kenesaw Mountain.

First Lieut. Caleb A. Montgomery. Died, January 28, 1863, of disease, at Danville, y.

First Lieut. Nelson R. Sims. Died, September 29, 1863, of wounds received at Chickamauga.

Captain George F. Barnes. Died, October 3, 1863, of wounds received at Chickamauga.

Ninety-eighth Illinois Infantry.

Captain Orville L. Kelley. Killed September 8, 1862, by railroad accident, at Bridgeport, Ill.

First Lieut. Lindsay D. Law. Died, January 26, 1863, of disease.

First Lieut. William Tarrant. Died, April 19, 1863, of disease, at Murfreesboro, Tenn.

First Lieut. Silas Jones. Died, April 19, 1863, of disease, at Murfreesboro, Tenn.

Second Lieut. George W. Boggess. Died, March 3, 1864, at Charleston, Tenn.

One Hundreth Illinois Infantry.

Colonel Frederick A. Bartleson. Killed at Kenesaw Mountain, June 23, 1864.

Major Rodney S. Bowen. Died, December 3, 1864, of wounds received at Franklin.

Captain John A. Bunell. Killed near Dallas, Ga., in action, May 30, 1864.

First Lieut. George W. Rouse, Adjutant. Died, August 3, 1864, of wounds received before Aslanta, Ga.

First Lieut. George C. Shoonmaker. Killed before Atlanta, in action, August 5, 1864.

Second Lieut. Morris Worthington. Killed at Stone River, December 31, 1862.

Second Lieut. Charles F. Mitchell. Died, January 4, 1863, of wounds received at Stone River.

One Hundred and First Illinois Infantry.

Captain Thomas B. Woof. Killed before Atlanta, July 20, 1864.

First Lieut. William S. Wright. Died, October 6, 1862, at Franklin, Ill.

First Lieut. Ferdinand A. Dimm. Killed skirmishing near Kenesaw, June 27, 1864.

First Lieut. Josiah H. Belt. Died, June 29, 1864, of wounds received near Dallas, Ga.

One Hundred and Fourth Illinois Infantry.

Captain John S. H. Doty. Killed at Peach Tree Creek, July 20, 1864.

Captain David C. Rynearson. Killed at Peach Tree Creek, July 20, 1864.

Captain Joseph P. Fitzsimmons. Killed in action before Atlanta, August 7, 1864.

First Lieut. Moses M. Randolp. Died, December 9, 1862, of wounds received at Heartsville, Tenn.

First Lieut. William E. Brush. Died, April 13, 1863, at Chicago, Ill.

First Lieut. Orrin S. Davidson. Died, December 5, 1863, of wounds received at Missionary Ridge.

Assistant Surgeon Thomas B. Hamilton. Died, March 17, 1865, at Nashville, Tenn.

APPENDIX. 395

One Hundred and Fifth Illinois Infantry.

Second Lieut. August H. Fischer. Killed on picket line, before Atlanta, August 13, 1864.
Surgeon Horace S. Potter. Killed near Acworth, Ga., June 2, 1864.

One Hundred and Tenth Illinois Infantry.

Captain John F. Day. Died, January 27, 1863, of disease, at Nashville, Tenn.
Captain James L. Parks. Died, March 8, 1863, of disease, Readyville, Tenn.
Second Lieut. Jesse G. Payne. Killed at Stone River, December 31, 1862.

One Hundred and Fifteenth Illinois Infantry.

Lieut. Colonel William Kinman. Killed at Chickamauga, September 20, 1863.
Captain S. Barlow Espy. Killed at Chickamauga, September 20, 1863.
Captain Stephen M. Huckstep. Died, December 9, 1863, of wounds received in action.
First Lieut. John Beauchamp. Died, March 26, 1863, of disease.
First Lieut. Jacob Porter. Died, May 14, 1864, of wounds received in action.
Second Lieut. Mathew Freeman. Died, March 30, 1863, of disease.
Second Lieut. David Reed. Died, September 27, 1863, of wounds received in action.
Assistant Surgeon James A. Jones. Killed by Guerrillas, July 9, 1864.

One Hundred and Twenty-third Illinois Infantry.

Colonel James Monroe. Killed at Farmington, October 7, 1863.
Captain Samuel Coblentz. Died November 30, 1862.
Captain Abram C. Van Buskirk. Killed in action, March 20, 1863.
First Lieut. Otho J. McManus. Killed at Selma, April 9, 1865.

One Hundred and Twenty-fifth Illinois Infantry.

Colonel Oscar F. Harmon. Killed at Kenesaw Mountain, June 27, 1864.
Captain William W. Fellows. Killed at Kenesaw Mountain, June 27, 1864.
Captain Marion Lee. Killed at Kenesaw Mountain, June 27, 1864.
Captain Edward B. Kingsbury. Died, August 19, 1864, of wounds received before Atlanta, Ga.
Captain Jackson Charles. Killed at Jonesboro, September 2, 1864.
Captain Andrew W. Ingraham. Died, February 15, 1865, of disease, at Savannah, Ga.
Second Lieut. William Hart. Died, April 2, 1863, at Nashville, Tenn.
Second Lieut. James A. McLean. Killed at Kenesaw Mountain, June 27, 1864.
Second Lieut. John L. Jones. Killed in action before Atlanta, July 19, 1864.
Second Lieut. John J. White. Killed in action before Atlanta, August 7, 1864.
Chaplain Levi W. Sanders. Killed in action at Caldwell's Ford, Tenn., November 17, 1863.
Chaplain George K. Buesing. Died, October 13, 1864, at Atlanta, Ga.

One Hundred and Twenty-ninth Illinois Infantry.

First Lieut. John Haldeman. Died, November 15, 1864, prisoner, at Columbia, S. C.
Second Lieut. Stephen K. Kyle. Died, December 1, 1862, at Bowling Green, Ky.

APPENDIX.

INDIANA.
Second Indiana Cavalry.

Major Samuel Hill. Died, April 6, 1863, of disease.
Captain Levi Ross. Died, March 8, 1863, at Louisville, Ky.
First Lieut. Henry H. Dunlap. Died, May 25, 1863, of disease.
First Lieut. William D. Stover. Killed in action at Indian Creek, Tenn., July 28, 1864.
First Lieut. Asa S. Smith. Killed near Scottville, Ala., April 2, 1865.
Second Lieut. John G. Myers. Killed in action at Vinegar Hill, Ky., September 22, 1862.
Second Lieut. William C. Blaine. Killed in action, June 11, 1863.

Third Indiana Calvary.

Second Lieut. Thomas G. Sheaffer. Killed at Resaca, Ga., August 25, 1864.

Fourth Indiana Cavalry.

Major Joseph P. Leslie. Killed in action, at Fair Garden, Tenn., January 27, 1864.
Captain Jesse Keethley. Died at Madisonville, Ky., March 3, 1863.
Captain Christopher C. Mason. Killed in action at Fayetteville, Tenn., November 1, 1863.
First Lieut. George Lydick. Died, February 3, 1863, of disease, at Munfordsville, Ky.
First Lieut. John Jackson. Died, in prison, at Columbia, S. C., November 20, 1864.
Second Lieut. Edmund J. Davis. Died, September 24, 1862, of disease, at Louisville, Ky.
Second Lieut. Johnson M. Webb. Killed in action at Madisonville, Ky., October 5, 1862.
Second Lieut. Enoch S. Boston. Died, November 7, 1862, of disease, at Bowling Green, Ky.

Eighth Indiana Cavalry.

Captain Joseph C. Potts. Died, October 5, 1863, of wounds received in action.
First Lieut. John A. Stockdell. Died, April 1, 1862, of disease, at Columbia, Tenn.
First Lieut. William R. Phillips, Killed at Shiloh, April 7, 1862.
First Lieut. William H. Garboden. Died, October 28, 1863, of wounds received in action.
First Lieut. Wiley Baker. Killed in action at Puluski, Tenn., September 27, 1864.
First Lieut. James A. Gray. Died of wounds, October 2, 1864, at Nashville, Tenn.
First Lieut. Clinton Lennen. Killed in action at Black River, N. C., March 16, 1865.
Second Lieut. Gabriel Woodmansee. Died, January 9, 1863, of wounds received in action.
Second Lieut. Moses M. Neal. Died, January 8 1863, of wounds received in action.

APPENDIX. 397

Fifth Indiana Battery.
Captain Peter Simonson. Killed at Kenesaw Mountain, June 16, 1864.

Seventh Indiana Battery.
Second Lieut. Frank W. Backmar. Died, January 16, 1863, of wounds received at Stone River.

Eleventh Indiana Battery.
Second Lieut. Charles R. Scott. Died January 5, 1864.

Twelfth Indiana Battery.
First Lieut. Moody C. Dustin. Died March 16, 1863.
Second Lieut. Benjamin F. Lutz. Died April 18, 1862.

Eighteenth Indiana Battery.
First Lieut. Martin J. Miller. Killed in action, near Selma, Ala., April 2, 1865,

Nineteenth Indiana Battery.
First Lieut. Samuel W. Webb. Died, May 20, 1865, of wounds received in action.

Sixth Indiana Infantry.
Colonel Philomen G. Baldwin. Killed at Chickamauga, September 19, 1863.
Captain Samuel Russell. Killed at Chickamauga, September 19, 1863.
Captain Frank P. Strader. Died, December 15, 1863, of wounds received in action.
Captain Andrew F. Connor. Killed in action near Dallas, Ga., May 27, 1864.
Captain Andrew J. Newland. Killed in action near Dallas, Ga., May 27, 1864.
Captain Samuel F. McKeehan. Died of wounds, July 15, 1864.
First Lieut. Alanson Solomon. Died, May 11, 1862, of disease, at Washington, Ind.
First Lieut. George B. Green. Died, October 28, 1863, of wounds.
First Lieut. William A. Cummings. Killed at Allatoona Ridge, Ga., May 27, 1864.
Second Lieut. Jerome P. Holcomb. Died, June 12, 1863, of accidental wounds.
Second Lieut. Charles Neal. Died June 22, 1864.

Ninth Indiana Infantry.
Captain James Houghton. Died, April 8, 1862, of wounds received at Shiloh.
Captain Isaac M. Pettit. Died, March 19, 1863, of wounds received at Stone River.
Captain De Witt C. Hodsden. Died, July 27, 1864, of wounds received in action.
First Lieut. Thomas J. Patton, Adjutant. Killed at Shiloh, April 7, 1862.
First Lieut. Joseph S. Turner. Died, April 16, 1862, of wounds received at Shiloh.
First Lieut. James J. Drum, R. Q. M. Died May 31, 1863.
First Lieut. Lewis S. Nickerson. Killed at Chickamauga, September 19, 1863.
First Lieut. William H. Criswell. Died, September 23, 1863, of wounds received in action.
Second Lieut. Henry Kessler. Killed at Stone River, December 31, 1862.
Second Lieut. Seth B. Parks. Killed at Chickamauga, September 19, 1863.

Second Lieut. Benjamin Franklin. Died, October 17, 1863, of wounds received in action.
Second Lieut. Leander C. Shipherd. Died, October 20, 1863, of wounds received in action.
Assistant Surgeon Alexander W. Gilmore. Died, May 13, 1863, of disease, at Nashville, Tenn.

Tenth Indiana Infantry.

Colonel William B. Carroll. Died, September 20, 1863, of wounds received at Chickamauga.
Captain Samuel H. Shortle. Died, October 13, 1863, of disease, at Frankfort, Ind.
Captain John W. Perkins. Died, November 16, 1863, of accidental wounds at Chickamauga.
First Lieut. James H. McAdams. Killed at Mill Springs, January 19, 1862.
First Lieut. Martin T. Jones. Killed at Chickamauga, September 19, 1863.
Second Lieut. Israel H. Miller. Died, March 7, 1862, of disease, at Nashville, Tenn.
Second Lieut. Jeremiah Batterton. Died, September 27, 1862, of disease, at Bowling Green, Ky.

Fifteenth Indiana Infantry.

Captain Robert J. Templeton. Killed at Stone River, December 31, 1862
Captain Joel W. Foster. Killed at Stone River, December 31, 1862.
Captain John F. Monroe. Died, November 26, 1863, of wounds received at Missionary Ridge.
Second Lieut. William D. Sering. Killed at Missionary Ridge, November 25, 1863.

Seventeenth Indiana Infantry. (Mounted.)

Captain James D. Taylor. Killed near Plantersville, Ala., April 1, 1865.
First Lieut. James T. Mooreland. Died, July 12, 1863, of wounds received at Stone River.
First Lieut. George B. Covington, Adjutant. Died, June 1, 1864, of wounds.
Chaplain John L. Craig. Died, July 11, 1865, of disease.

Twenty-second Indiana Infantry.

Lieut. Colonel Squire Isham Keeth. Killed at Perryville, October 8, 1862.
Captain Robert K. Smith. Killed at Perryville, October, 8, 1862.
Captain Alonzo J. Moss. Died, June 29, 1864, of wounds received in action.
First Lieut. Lewis W. Daily. Died, March 2, 1862, of wounds.
First Lieut. Samuel H. McBride. Died, December 9, 1862, of wounds received at Perryville.
Second Lieut. Tyrus Tolbert. Killed at Perryville, October 8, 1862.
Second Lieut. Francis L. M. Sibbitt. Killed at Perryville, October 8, 1862.
Second Lieut. George R. Ridlen. Killed at Perryville, October 8, 1862.
Second Lieut. David G. Linson. Killed at Jonesboro, September 1, 1864.
Second Lieut. David R. Runzan. Killed at Jonesboro, September 1, 1864.
Second Lieut. Nicholas Moser. Killed at Bentonville, March 19, 1865.

APPENDIX.   399

Twenty-seventh Indiana Infantry.
First Lieut. George T. Chapin. Killed at Resaca, May 15, 1864.

Twenty-ninth Indiana Infantry.
Major Joseph P. Collins. Died, October 5, 1864, of disease, at Chattanooga, Tenn.
Captain Frank A. Hardman. Died March 5, 1862.
Captain Frank Stebbins. Killed at Stone River, December 31, 1862.
Captain Thomas J. Henderson. Died, July 6, 1863, at Murfreesboro, Tenn.
Captain N. Palmer Dunn. Killed at Chickamauga, September 19, 1863.
First Lieut. Asa H. Mathews, R. Q. M. Died April 21, 1862.
First Lieut. John Cutler. Killed at Chickamauga, September 19, 1863.
Second Lieut. Elijah A. Macomber. Died, September 19, 1864, of wounds received in action.

Thirtieth Indiana Infantry.
Colonel Sion S. Bass. Died, April 7, 1862, of wounds received at Shiloh.
First Lieut. Edwin B. Scribley. Killed at Stone River, December 31, 1862.
First Lieut. Douglas L. Phelps. Died, September 19, 1863, of wounds received in action.
First Lieut. Joshua Eberly. Died, September 20, 1863, of wounds received in action.
Assistant Surgeon Delos W. Rupert. Died, October 2, 1862, of disease.

Thirty-first Indiana Infantry.
Lieut. Colonel Francis L. Neff. Killed at Kenesaw Mountain, June 25, 1864.
Major Frederick Arn. Killed at Shiloh, April 6, 1862.
Captain John S. Welch. Died December 26, 1861.
Captain George Harvey. Killed at Shiloh, April 6, 1862.
Captain William I. Leas. Killed at Chickamauga, September 19, 1863.
Captain Jeremiah Mewhinney. Died, June 24, 1864, of disease, at Chicago, Ill.
Captain Richard M. Waterman. Died, August 23, 1864, of disease.
Second Lieut. James W. Peckins. Died, January 7, 1863, of wounds received at Stone River.
Second Lieut. John N. Pike. Died, April 16, 1863, of disease.
Second Lieut. Lucien Ray. Died, April 11, 1864, of disease.

Thirty-second Indiana Infantry.
Colonel Henry Von Trebra. Died, August 6, 1863, of disease, at Arcola, Ill.
Major Jacob Glass. Killed at Missionary Ridge, November 25, 1863.
Captain Fred. A. Mueller. Killed at Shiloh, April 7, 1862.
Captain Frank Kodalle. Killed at Shiloh, April 7, 1862.
Captain John D. Ritter. Killed at Chickamauga, September 20, 1863.
Captain Henry Seyffert. Killed at Allatoona, Ga., May 27, 1864.
First Lieut. Max Sachs. Killed in action, at Rowlett's Bridge, Ky., December 17, 1861.
First Lieut. Max Hupfauf. Killed at Allatoona Ga., May 27, 1864.

APPENDIX.

Thirty-third Indiana Infantry.

Captain Israel C. Dille. Killed by Guerrillas, at Fosterville, Tenn., July 17, 1863.
Captain James L. Banks. Died, June 22, 1864, of wounds received at Dallas, Ga.
Captain George L. Scott. Killed on picket, before Atlanta, July 23, 1864.
First Lieut. Estees Wallingford, Adjutant. Died, April 21, 1864, of disease.
First Lieut. Charles H. Porter, Adjutant. Killed near Kenesaw Mountain, June 22, 1864.
Second Lieut. Eli M. Adams. Died, December 8, 1861, of disease.

Thirty-fifth Indiana Infantry.

Major John P. Dufficy. Killed at Kenesaw Mountain, June 20, 1864.
Captain Frank Baggot. Died, January 5, 1863, of wounds received at Stone River.
Captain Henry Prosser. Died, January 9, 1863, of wounds received at Stone River.
First Lieut. Bemald R. Mullin, Adjutant. Killed near Nashville, in action, December 9, 1862.
First Lieut. William Kilroy. Died, January 10, 1863, of wounds received at Stone River.

Thirty-sixth Indiana Infantry.

Captain Abram D. Shultz. Killed at Stone River, December 31, 1862.
Captain James H. King. Killed at Stone River, December 31, 1862.
Captain George M. Graves. Died, September 28, 1863, of wounds.
First Lieut. Addison M. Davis. Killed at Shiloh, April 7, 1862.
First Lieut. Joseph W. Connell, R. Q. M. Died, May 26, 1862, of disease, near Corinth, Miss.
First Lieut. William H. Fentress. Killed at Dallas, Ga., May 31, 1864.
First Lieut. George W. Bowman. Killed before Atlanta, Ga., July 19, 1864.
First Lieut. Mahlon Hendricks. Killed at Kenesaw Mountain, June 23, 1864.
First Lieut. George O. Williard. Killed before Atlanta, Ga., August 5, 1864.
Second Lieut. William Butler. Died, September 24, 1863, of wounds received at Chickamauga.
Second Lieut. James Patterson. Died, September 24, 1863, of wounds received at Chickamauga.
Second Lieut. Salathiel D. Colvin. Died, October 9, of wounds.

Thirty-seventh Indiana Infantry.

Captain James H. Burk. Died, July 9, 1864, of wounds, at Nashville, Tenn.
Captain Frank Hughes. Died, July 28, 1864, at Nashville, Tenn.
First Lieut. Isaac N. Abernethy. Killed at Stone River, December 31, 1862.
First Lieut. Jesse B. Holman. Killed at Stone River, December 31, 1862.
Second Lieut. James M. Hartley. Died, April 26, 1862, of disease.
Second Lieut. William Speer. Killed in action, at Dallas, Ga., May 27, 1864.

APPENDIX. 401

Thirty-eighth Indiana Infantry.

Captain John Sexton. Died, November 10, 1862, of wounds received at Perryville.
Captain James E. Fouts. Killed at Stone River, December 31, 1862.
Captain Joshua B. Jenkins. Died, November 13, 1864, of wounds received at Jonesboro.
Captain James H. Low. Died, March 20, 1865, of wounds received at Bentonville.
First Lieut. Rufus H. Peck. Killed at Chickamauga, September 20, 1863.
First Lieut. John B. Southern. Died, October 13, 1863, of wounds received at Chickamauga.
First Lieut. Joseph H. Reeves. Died, March 15, 1864, of disease.
First Lieut. Adam Osborn. Killed at Jonesboro, September 1, 1864.
First Lieut. Charles S. Deweese. Killed at Bentonville, March 19, 1865.
Second Lieut. Thomas S. W. Hawkins. Died, January 23, 1863, of wounds received at Stone River.

Fortieth Indiana Infantry.

Lieut. Colonel James N. Kirkpatrick. Drowned near Iuka, Miss., June 8, 1862.
Captain James K. Kiser. Died, May 17, 1862, of disease, near Corinth, Miss.
Captain Charles T. Elliott. Killed at Kenesaw Mountain, June 27, 1864.
Captain Absalom Kirkpatrick. Killed at Kenesaw Mountain, June 27, 1864.
Captain William L. Coleman. Killed April 27, 1865, by explosion of steamer "Sultana."
Captain Henry L. Hazelrigg. Killed April 27, 1865, by explosion of Steamer "Sultana."
First Lieut. Jeremiah C. Brower. Killed at Franklin, November 30, 1864.
Second Lieut. John H. Holmes. Died, June 24, 1864, of wounds, at Chattanooga, Tenn.
Chaplain Allen D. Beaseley. Died, June 30, 1864, of disease, at Murfreesboro, Tenn.

Forty-second Indiana Infantry.

Lieut. Colonel James M. Shanklin. Died, May 23, 1863, at Evansville, Ind.
Captain Charles G. Olmsted. Killed at Perryville, October 8, 1862.
First Lieut. Edmund M. Knowles. Killed, January ——, 1864, when prisoner of war, at Augusta, Ga.
First Lieut. John D. A. Steel. Killed at Bentonville, March 19, 1865.
First Lieut. Ephraim Rutledge. Died, March 22, 1865, of wounds.
Second Lieut. Emory Johnson. Killed, before Atlanta, July 22, 1864.

Forty-fourth Indiana Infantry.

Lieut. Colonel Baldwin J. Crosswait. Died, February 18, 1862, at Angola, Ind.
Lieut. Colonel Simeon C. Aldrich. Died, August 15, 1864, of disease.
Lieut. Colonel Joseph C. Hodges. Died, September 28, 1864, of injury by railroad.
Captain John Murray. Died, April 9, 1862, of wounds received at Shiloh.
Captain William H. Cuppy. Died July 15, 1862.
Captain John Gunsenhouser. Killed at Chickamauga, September 20, 1863.
First Lieut. Marcus W. Bayless, R. Q. M. Died June 9, 1862.

First Lieut. Sedgwick Livingston. Died, January 25, 1864, at Nashville, Tenn.
Second Lieut. J. Delta Kerr. Died, March 25, 1862, at Evansville, Ind.
Second Lieut. Charles M. Hinman. Died April 27, 1863.
Second Lieut. David K. Stopher. Died, January 18, 1864, of disease, Knoxville, Tenn.
Assistant Surgeon Edward B. Speed. Died, September 14, 1864, of disease.

Fifty-first Indiana Infantry.

Lieut. Colonel James W. Sheets. Died, June 30, 1863, of wounds.
Captain Samuel Lingeman. Died, March 18, 1864, at Danville, Ind.
Captain Adolphus H. Wonder. Died, September 24, 1862, at Charleston, S. C.
First Lieut. Albert Light. Died, February 24, 1862, at Lebanon, Ky.
Second Lieut. Harvey Slavens. Died, March 21, 1862, at Nashville, Tenn.
Second Lieut. Samuel C. Owen. Died, February 26, 1863, at Murfreesboro Tenn.
Second Lieut. Jeremiah Sailor. Died, March 19, 1863, near Murfreesboro, Tenn,

Fifty-seventh Indiana Infantry.

Lieut. Colonel George W. Lennard. Killed at Resaca, May 14, 1864.
Captain William S. Bradford. Died May 16, 1862,
Captain Joseph S. Stidham. Killed in action, June 28, 1864.
Captain Addison M. Dunn. Killed at Franklin, November 30, 1864.
First Lieut. Benjamin F. Beitzell. Killed in action, June 18, 1864.
First Lieut. Robert F. Callaway. Died, July 4, 1864, of wounds received in in action.
First Lieut. Charles W. T. Minesinger. Died, September 13, 1864, of wounds received in action.
Surgeon Issac S. Collings. Died, September 10, 1865, of disease.

Fifty-eighth Indiana Infantry.

Captain Charles H. Bruce. Killed at Chickamauga, September 19, 1863.
First Lieut. William Overlin. Died, March 19, 1862, of disease, at Nashville, Tenn.
First Lieut. James D. Foster. Killed at'Chickamauga, September 19, 1863.
First Lieut.. George Raffan, R. Q. M. Died, May 13, 1864, at Nashville, Tenn.
Second Lieut. Francis B. Blackford. Killed at Stone River, December 31, 1862,
Second Lieut. Hugh J. Barnett. Died, September 24, 1863, of wounds received at Chickamauga.

Sixty-eighth Indiana Infantry.

Colonel Edward A. King. Killed at Chickamauga, September 20, 1863.
Captain Charles C. Wheeler. Died, August 22, 1864, of wounds, at Dalton, Ga.
First Lieut. Robert J. Price. Killed at Chickamauga, September 19, 1863.
First Lieut. John Reese. Killed at Missionary Ridge, November 25, 1863.

Seventieth Indiana Infantry.

First Lieut. Edward B. Colestock. Died, May 30, 1864, of wounds, at Resaca, Ga.
Second Lieut. Jeptha F. Bunta. Died, May 14, 1863, at Gallatin, Tenn.

Second Lieut. Josiah E. Lewes. Killed before Atlanta, July 20, 1864.
Assistant Surgeon John M. White. Died, August 31, 1863, of disease.

Seventy-second Indiana Infantry.

Captain William H. McMurtry. Killed at Rock Spring, September 12, 1863.
First Lieut. Liews C. Priest. Died June 24, 1864.
Second Lieut. John W. Gaskill. Killed at Hoover's Gap, in action, June 24, 1863.
Chaplain John R. Eddy. Killed in action, at Hoover's Gap, June 24, 1863.

Seventy-third Indiana Infantry.

Colonel Gilbert Hathaway. Killed at Blount's farm, Ala., May 2, 1863.
Captain Miles H. Tibbitts. Killed at Stone River, December 31, 1862.
Captain Peter Doyle. Killed at Stone River, December 31, 1862.

Seventy-fourth Indiana Infantry.

Lieut. Colonel Myron Baker. Killed before Atlanta, August 5, 1864.
Captain Philip F. Davis. Died, February 6, 1863, of disease.
Captain Everett F. Abbott. Killed at Jonesboro, September 1, 1864.
First Lieut. Stephen Hamlin. Died, December 27, 1862, of disease, at Gallatin, Tenn.
First Lieut. Thomas Bodley. Killed at Chickamauga, September 19, 1863.
First Lieut. Ananias Davis. Died, October 11, 1863, at Chattanooga, Tenn.
Second Lieut. Richard H. Hall. Killed at Chickamauga, September 19, 1863.

Seventy-fifth Indiana Infantry.

Captain Francis M. Bryant. Died, December 2, 1863, of wounds received at Missionary Ridge.
Captain William McGinness. Died, August 31, 1864, at Savaunah, Ga.
First Lieut. John B. Frazer. Died, July 4, 1863, near Tullahoma, Tenn.

Seventy-ninth Indiana Infantry.

First Lieut. Thompson Dunn, Adjutant. Killed at Lovejoy's Station, September 2, 1864.
Second Lieut. John S. McDaniels. Died, December 2, 1862, of disease, at Nashville, Tenn.
Second Lieut. Benjamin T. Poynter. Killed at Stone River, January 2, 1863.
Second Lieut. George W. Clark. Died, September 28, 1863, of wounds received at Chattanooga, Tenn.
Chaplain Perry T. Hall. Died, October 26, 1862, of disease, at Indianapolis, Ind.

Eightieth Indiana Infantry.

Captain Thomas J. Brooks, Jun. Died, February 26, 1863, of wounds received at Perryville.
Captain Russell J. Showers. Killed at Resaca, May 14, 1864.
Captain William S. Emery. Died, May 28, 1864, of wounds received at Resaca.
First Lieut. William Archer. Killed at Resaca, May 14, 1864.
Second Lieut. Alexander Anderson. Died, October 13, 1862, of wounds received at Perryville.

Second Lieut. James F. Ruark. Died, October 24, 1862, of wounds received at Perryville.
Second Lieut. Lewis C. Turbett. Died, December 31, 1862, of accidental wounds.

Eighty-first Indiana Infantry.

Captain Elijah R. Mitchell. Died, September 20, 1863, of wounds received at Chickamauga.
Captain Eugene M. Schell. Killed at Nashville, December 15, 1864.
First Lieut. William M. Morgan. Killed at Stone River, December 31, 1862.
Second Lieut. Samuel Wilde. Died, January 1, 1863, of wounds received at Stone River.
Second Lieut. John Felkner. Died March 13, 1863.

Eighty-second Indiana Infantry.

Lieut. Colonel Paul P. Slocum. Died, May 3, 1864, of wounds received in action.
Captain George W. Kendrick. Died, January 23, 1863, at Murfreesboro, Tenn.
Captain Harrison McCallister. Killed at Chickamauga, September 20, 1863.
First Lieut. John W. Walker. Killed at Rasaca, May 14, 1864.
First Lieut. Jackson Woods. Died, May 27, 1864, of disease, at Macon, Ga.
First Lieut. Joseph Fraker. Died, September 30, 1864, of disease.
Second Lieut. Samuel Guy. Died, May 22, 1863, of disease, at Triune, Tenn.
Second Lieut. Thomas V. Webb. Died, March 3, 1864, at Madison, Ind.
Assistant Surgeon Mathew Kelley. Died, August 23, 1864, of disease.

Eighty-fourth Indiana Infantry.

Major William A. Boyd. Died, July 11, 1864, of wounds received at Rocky Face Ridge.
Captain John H. Ellis. Killed at Chickamauga, September 20, 1863.
First Lieut. George C. Hatfield. Killed at Chickamauga, September 20, 1863.
First Lieut. Noble B. Gregory. Killed at Nashville, December 16, 1864.
First Lieut. Frank M. Flickenger. Killed accidentally, March 13, 1865.
Second Lieut. William L. Steele. Died at Franklin, Tenn., May 16, 1863.
Second Lieut. Jerome B. Mason. Killed at Chickamauga, September 20, 1864.

Eighty-fifth Indiana Infantry.

Major Robert E. Craig. Died, April 2, 1862, at Murfreesboro, Tenn.
Captain Abner Floyd. Killed at Thompson's Station, Tenn., March 5, 1865.
Captain Wilson T. Stark. Died, March 28, 1863, at Franklin, Tenn.
Captain Caleb Nash. Died, May 20, 1863, at Annapolis, Md.
First Lieut. Mortimer Denny. Died, August 19, 1864, of wounds.

Eighty-sixth Indiana Infantry.

Captain William M. Southard. Killed at Missionary Ridge, November 25, 1864.
First Lieut. George W. Smith. Killed at Stone River, December 31, 1862.
Second Lieut. James T. Doster. Died, December 10, 1863, of disease.

APPENDIX. 405

Eighty-seventh Indiana Infantry.

Captain James M. Holliday. Killed at Chickamauga, September 19, 1863.
Captain George W. Baker. Killed at Chickamauga, September 20, 1863.
Captain Lewis Hughs. Killed at Chickamauga, September 20, 1863.
First Lieut. Sloan D. Martin. Killed at Chickamauga, September 19, 1863.
First Lieut. Fredus Ryland, Adjutant. Killed at Chickamauga, September 20, 1863.
First Lieut. Burr Russell. Died, November 29, 1863, of wounds received at Missionary Ridge.
First Lieut. John Demuth. Killed at Atlanta, August 22, 1864.
Second Lieut. Franklin H. Bennett. Killed at Chickamauga, September 19, 1863.
Second Lieut. Abram C. Andrew. Killed at Chickamauga, September 20, 1863.
Second Lieut. Elisha Brown. Died, September 24, 1863, of wounds received at Chickamauga.
Surgeon Samuel Higinbotham. Died, —— 29, 1863, at Triune, Tenn.
Chaplain Joseph K. Albright. Died, December 5, 1862, at Gallatin, Tenn., of disease.

Eighty-eighth Indiana Infantry.

Major George W. Stough. Died, October 28, 1863, of wounds at Richmond, Va.
Captain Isaac H. Le Fevre. Died, September 21, 1863, of wounds received at Chickamauga.
Captain James H. Steele. Killed at Missionary Ridge, November 25, 1863.
First Lieut. Samuel L. Stough. Died, April 20, 1863, at Waterloo, Ind.
First Lieut. William Forrest. Died, September 20, 1863, of disease, at Nashville, Tenn.
First Lieut. David Caston. Killed in action at Resaca, May 15, 1864.
First Lieut. Walter E. Boley. Killed in action at Resaca, May 15, 1864.
First Lieut. Thomas E. Kimball. Died, October 1, 1864, in Libby Prison, Richmond, Va.
First Lieut. George W. Seelye. Died, March 23, 1865, of wounds received at Bentonville.
First Lieut. Isaac A. Slater. Died, April 26, 1865, of wounds received at Bentonville.
Second Lieut. John G. Goheen. Died, January 24, 1863, of wounds received at Stone River.
Second Lieut. Daniel Little. Died, December 15, 1863, of wounds received at Chickamauga.

One Hundred and First Indiana Infantry.

First Lieut. John H. Ellis. Died, October 20, 1863, of disease, at Chattanooga, Tenn.
First Lieut. Andrew J. Barlow. Died, September 16, 1864, of wounds received in action, at Chattanooga, Tenn.
Second Lieut. Richard H. Busick. Died, October 16, 1863, of wounds received at Chickamauga.
Second Lieut. Henry W. Waterman. Killed at Missionary Ridge, November 25, 1863.

APPENDIX.

IOWA.

Fifth Iowa Cavalry.

Major William Kelsay. Died, February 28, 1862, of disease, at Ft. Heiman, Ky.
Major Shaeffer DeBoernstein.' Died, May 7, 1862, of wounds.
Captain William Curl. Killed in skirmish at Coosa River, July 13, 1864.
First Lieut. Milton S. Summers. Died, August 28, 1862, of wounds received in action.
First Lieut. Michael Gallagher. Killed in action at Garrettsburg, Ky., November 6, 1862.
First Lieut. Andrew Guler. Killed in action near Chattahoochee River, August 3, 1864.
Second Lieut. John W. Watson. Killed at Nashville, December 15, 1864.

Eighth Iowa Cavalry.

Colonel Joseph B. Dorr. Died, May 28, 1865, of disease, at Macon, Ga.
Major H. Isett. Died, April 6, 1865, of disease, at South Bend, Ind.
First Lieut. James Horton. Killed at Lovejoy's Station, Ga., July 29, 1864.
Second Lieut. John B. Loomis. Killed at Newnan, Ga., July 30, 1864.

KANSAS.

Eighth Kansas Infantry.

Captain Edgar P. Trego. Killed at Chickamauga, September 19, 1863.
First Lieut. John L. Graham. Killed at Chickamauga, September 19, 1863.
First Lieut. Zacharias Burckhardt. Died, October 28, 1863, of wounds received in action.
Second Lieut. William Becker. Died of disease, November 21, 1863.
Second Lieut. Seth Foot. Died of disease, at Famesburg, Iowa, May 14, 1864.
Assistant Surgeon Samuel E. Beach. Died of disease, at Nashville, Tenn., November 4, 1863.

KENTUCKY.

First Kentucky Cavalry.

Brigadier-General James S. Jackson. Killed at Perryville, October 8, 1862, commanding division.
Captain Jarrett W. Jenkins. Killed in action, at Perryville, Ky., October 8, 1862.
Captain Jesse M. Carter. Killed at Columbus, Ky., July 3, 1863.
Captain Francis M. Wolford. Killed in action near Hillsboro, Ga., July 31, 1864.
First Lieut. Jonathan P. Miller. Killed in action at Mill Springs, Ky., January 19, 1862.
First Lieut. James Humphrey. Died, September ——, of wounds.
Second Lieut. Alexander Thompson. Died, October 30, 1861, of disease.

Second Kentucky Cavalry.

Major William H. Eifert. Killed in action, September 3, 1864.
Captain Miller R. McCullock. Killed in action at Stone River, Tenn., December 30, 1862.
First Lieut. William G. Jenkins. Killed in action, June 29, 1863.

First Lieut. George A. Hosmer. Died October 6, 1863.
First Lieut. G. W. L. Batman. Died of disease, April 23, 1864.
First. Lieut. William Bradney. Killed in action, July 30, 1864.

Fourth Kentucky Cavalry.

Captain Basil N. Hobbs. Died April 30, 1864.
First Lieut. Frank N. Sheets. Killed in action at Chickamauga, September 20, 1863.

Fifth Kentucky Cavalry.

Colonel William P. Sanders. Died of wounds received in action, November 20, 1863.
Captain John W. Forrester. Died of wounds, November 29, 1864.
First Lieut. W. D. Mitchell, Adjutant. Killed in action, March 10, 1865.
First Lieut. Amos M. Griffin. Killed in action, March ——, 1865.
Second Lieut. Edward Hughes. Died July 17, 1862.
Second Lieut. James Funk. Died, December 4, 1862, of disease.
Second Lieut. Francis B. McAllister. Died of disease, at Huntsville, Ala., July 28, 1863.
Second Lieut. Joseph G. Hardin. Died of disease, at Nashville, Tenn., September 29, 1863.
Second Lieut. George M. Vandover. Died July 9, 1864.

Sixth Kentucky Cavalry.

Colonel D. I. Halisey. Killed in action near New Market, Ky., December 31, 1862.
Major William H. Fidler. Died, April 28, 1865, from injuries by explosion of steamer "Sultana."
Captain Edmund H. Parish. Died, April 28, 1865, from injuries by explosion of steamer "Sultana."
First Lieut. James I. Surber. Died, April 28, 1865, from injuries by explosion of steamer "Sultana."
First Lieut. William Murphy. Killed in action, July 4, 1863.
Second Lieut. William C. Hunter. Died at Louisville, Ky., December 7, 1864.

Seventh Kentucky Cavalry.

Lieut. Colonel Thomas T. Vincent. Died at Dandridge, Tenn., June 16, 1864.
Captain Jesse H. Berry. Died of disease, at Carlisle, Ky., September 18, 1863.
Captain Seneca P. Goulding. Drowned at Benton, Ala., April 10, 1865.
First Lieut. John S. Stodgill. Died of disease, at Nashville, Tenn., March 2, 1864.
Second Lieut. Samuel H. Royce. Killed in action, at Big Hill, Ky., August 23, 1862.
Second Lieut. Alfred Mitchell. Died at Maysville, Ky., September 29, 1862.
Second Lieut. Lewis B. Vimont. Died of disease, at Chattanooga, Tenn., October 28, 1864.

Twelfth Kentucky Cavalry.

First Lieut. Elza C. Smith. Killed by guerrillas while sick at Saltville, Va., October 7, 1864.
Second Lieut. Joseph W. Cartwright. Drowned at Burksville, June 22, 1864.

Battery A.

Second Lieut. William K. Irwin. Died at Nashville, Tenn., August 15, 1864.

First Kentucky Infantry.

First Lieut. Courtland W. King. Drowned in Bear Creek, Ala., June 15, 1562.

Second Kentucky Infantry.

Captain John H. Spellmeyer. Killed at Shiloh, Tenn., April 7, 1862.
Captain James M. Bodine. Killed in action at Chickamauga, Tenn., September 21, 1863.
Second Lieut. Daniel W. Finch. Died of disease, at Camp Lookout, Va., September 26, 1861.
Second Lieut. James A. Miller. Killed in action, at Shiloh, April 7, 1862.

Third Kentucky Infantry.

Colonel Samuel McKee. Killed in action, at Stone River, December 31, 1862.
Captain Henry S. Taylor. Killed in action, at Chickamauga, Ga., September 20, 1863.
First Lieut. Daniel Severance. Died of wounds received at Stone River, January 10, 1863.
First Lieut. Alban D. Bradshaw. Died of wounds received at Chickamauga, Ga., October 8, 1863.
First Lieut. G. D. Hunt, Adjutant. Died of wounds received at Missionary Ridge, November 30, 1863.
Second Lieut. Matthew Cullen. Killed at Stone River, December 31, 1862.

Fourth Kentucky Infantry. (Mounted.)

Captain John L. Williams. Died of disease, at Paris, Ky., April 28, 1864.
Captain E. R. Harrington. Died of disease, at Atlanta, Ga., October 3, 1864.
First Lieut. N. M. Kelley. Died of disease, at Lebanon, Ky., January 12, 1862.
Second Lieut. James M. Kelley. Killed in action near Logan's Cross Roads, January 19, 1862.
Chaplain John W. Jacobs. Died at Lebanon, Ky., January 20, 1862.

Fifth Kentucky Infantry.

Major Charles L. Thomasson. Killed at Chickamauga, September 19, 1863.
Captain Alexander B. Ferguson. Killed at Stone River, December 31, 1862.
Captain Upton Wilson. Killed at Missionary Ridge, November 25, 1863.
Captain John P. Hurley. Killed at Missionary Ridge, November 25, 1863.
Captain Joseph E. Miller. Killed at Resaca, Ga., May 15, 1864.
First Lieut. Richard Jones. Died of disease, near Corinth, Miss., June 9, 1862.
First Lieut. John W. Huston. Killed at Chickamauga, September 20, 1863.
First Lieut. Frank Dissell. Died of wounds received at Stone River, May 12, 1863,
Second Lieut. Milton W. Curray. Died November 20, 1861.
Second Lieut. John Ryan. Died of wounds received at Chickamauga, September 25, 1863.

APPENDIX. 409

Sixth Kentucky Infantry.

Lieut. Colonel George T. Cotton. Killed at Stone River, December 31, 1862.
Captain Peter Enge. Died of disease, at Louisville, Ky., May 17, 1862.
Captain Charles S. Todd. Killed at Stone River, December 31, 1862.
Captain Peter Marker. Killed at Chickamauga, September 19, 1863.
Captain John McGraw. Killed at Chickamauga, September 20, 1863.
Captain Frederick Nierdoff. Killed at Kenesaw Mountain, Ga., June 23, 1864.
First Lieut. Sundsford D. Carrington. Died of disease, January 4, 1862.
First Lieut. William H. Middletown. Died of disease, March 1, 1863.
First Lieut. Richard Rockingham. Killed at Chickamauga, September 20 1863.
Second Lieut. William B. Dunlap. Died of disease, March 10, 1862.
Second Lieut. Anton Hund. Died of wounds received at Shiloh, May 23, 1862.
Second Lieut. Thomas Eubanks. Killed at Chickamauga, September 19, 1863.
Second Lieut. Frederick V. Lochman. Killed at Chickamauga, September 19, 1863.
Second Lieut. William W. Furr. Killed near Dallas, May 27, 1864.
Assistant Surgeon Abner B. Coone. Died of disease, March 4, 1862.

Eighth Kentucky Infantry.

Captain Robert B. Hickman. Killed at Stone River, January 2, 1863.
Captain John H. Benton. Killed at Stone River, January 2, 1863.
Captain Landon C. Minton. Died of wounds received at Stone River, February 15, 1863.
First Lieut. Wade B. Cox. Died of wounds received at Stone River, January 12, 1863.
First Lieut. Newton J. Hughes. Died of disease, Murfreesboro, Tenn., February 9, 1863.

Ninth Kentucky Infantry.

Lieut. Colonel Allen J. Roark. Died of disease, April 10, 1862.
Captain William T. Bryan. Killed at Stone River, January 2, 1863.
Captain Demetrius B. Coyle. Killed at Stone River, January 2, 1863.
First Lieut. Moses L. Norvell. Died March 31, 1862.
First Lieut. Charles R. Tate. Killed at Shiloh, April 7, 1862.
First Lieut. Henry W. Jenkins. Died of disease, July 9, 1862.
First Lieut. Algernon S. Leggett. Killed at Stone River, January 2, 1863.
First Lieut. Turner Hestand. Killed at Lovejoy's Station, Ga., September 2, 1864.
First Lieut. Fred. F. Carpenter. Killed at Stone River, January 2, 1863.
Second Lieut. William S. Barton. Killed at Missionary Ridge, November 25, 1863.

Tenth Kentucky Infantry.

Major Henry G. Davidson. Died of disease, at Louisville, Ky., November 21, 1864.
Captain Seth P. Bevill. Died of wounds received at Chickamauga, September 21, 1863.
Captain Henry Waller. Died March 13, 1864.

Second Lieut. John H. Myers. Killed at Chickamauga, September 20, 1863.
Surgeon Will. Atkinson. Died April 9, 1862.
Assistant Surgeon Thomas M. Knott. Died April 5, 1862.
Assistant Surgeon Charles Hardesty. Died July 7, 1863.

Eleventh Kentucky Infantry.

Captain Elijah C. Phelps. Died at Columbus, Tenn., March 29, 1862.
Captain Isaac W. Sketoe. Killed at Shiloh, April 7, 1862.
Captain Joseph S. Willis. Died February 10, 1863.
Captain Columbus H. Martin. Died of wounds received at Philadelphia, Tenn., December 18, 1863.
First Lieut. Vincent S. Hay, R. Q. M. Died in prison at Atlanta, Ga., March ——, 1863.

Thirteenth Kentucky Infantry.

Captain Wallace Victor. Died, July 13, 1864, of wounds received at Chickamauga.

Fifteenth Kentucky Infantry.

Colonel Curran Pope. Died, November 5, 1862, of wounds received at Perryville.
Colonel James B. Foreman. Killed at Stone River, December 31, 1862.
Lieut. Colonel George P. Jouett. Killed at Perryville, October 8, 1862.
Major William P. Campbell. Killed at Perryville, October 8, 1862.
Captain William T. McCure. Died of disease, July 12, 1862.
Captain Aaron S. Bayne. Killed at Stone River, December 31, 1862.
Captain E. Irvine McDowell. Killed at Resaca, Ga., May 14, 1864.
First Lieut. James A. T. McGrath. Killed at Perryville, October 8, 1862.
First Lieut. L. Frank Todd. Died, of wounds received in action, January 20, 1863.
Second Lieut. Joseph L. McClure. Died, of wounds received in action, October 18, 1862.

Seventeenth Kentucky Infantry.

Captain Henry S. Barnett. Died March 22, 1862.
Captain Preston Morton. Killed at Shiloh, April 6, 1862.
Captain John V. Boyd. Died at Murfreesboro, Tenn., March 22, 1863.
Captain James W. Anthony. Died, October 10, 1863, of wounds received at Chickamauga.
Captain Robert L. Beckham. Died April 13, 1864.
Captain William J. Landrum. Killed at Cassville, Ga., in action, May 19, 1864.
Captain Robert C. Sturgis. Died, August 9, 1864, of wounds received in action.
First Lieut. John M. Williams. Killed at Chickamauga, September 19, 1863.
Second Lieut. Isaac S. Condit. Died December 18, 1861.
Second Lieut. Albert E. Brown. Died, May 18, 1862, of wounds received at Shiloh.

APPENDIX.

Eighteenth Kentucky Infantry.

Major Abram G. Wileman. Killed at Pendleton, Ky., by guerrillas, October 5, 1865.
Captain Orin M. Lewis. Killed in action at Richmond, Ky., August 30, 1862.
Captain W. W. Culbertson. Died, September 22, 1862, of wounds received in action.
Captain Charles S. Williams. Died of disease, January 14, 1865.
First Lieut. James Dunlap. Killed in action at Richmond, Ky., August 30, 1862.
Second Lieut. John W. Washburn. Killed in action at Richmond, Ky., August 30, 1862.

Nineteenth Kentucky Infantry.

Captain Aaron Blakeman. Died, July 11, 1861, at Cumberland Gap, Tenn.

Twenty-first Kentucky Infantry.

Colonel Ethelbert Dudley. Died of disease, February 20, 1862, at Columbus, Ky.
Captain Williamson Irvin. Died of disease, January 21, 1862.
Captain William C. Edwards. Died of disease, January 27, 1862, at Campbellville, Ky.
Captain Zachariah Taylor. Died of disease, February 7, 1862.
Captain G. W. Twyman. Died at Lexington, Ky., February 16, 1865.
First Lieut. Sebastian Stone. Killed at Stone River, January 2, 1863.
First Lieut. Hugh A. Hedger. Killed at Nashville, December 15, 1864.
First Lieut. James I. Dolton. Died at Indianola, Texas, July 17, 1865.
Second Lieut. John H. Bevill. Killed at Stone River, January 2, 1863.

Twenty-third Kentucky Infantry.

Lieut. Colonel James C. Foy. Died of wounds received at Vining's Station, July 24, 1864.
Captain Ephraim P. Mavity. Died at Chattanooga, Tenn., September 17, 1864, of wounds received in action.
First Lieut. John B. Konnan. Died, July 26, 1864, of wounds received in action, at Chattanooga, Tenn.
First Lieut. Joseph C. Hoffman. Killed at Chickamauga, September 19, 1863.

Twenty-eighth Kentucky Infantry.

First Lieut. Granville J. Sinkham. Killed at Franklin, Tenn., in action, November 30, 1864.
Second Lieut. Isaac Everet. Died, January 8, 1863, at Louisville, Ky.

MARYLAND.

Third Maryland Infantry.

First Lieut. Frederick Pringey. Died January 3, 1863.

MASSACHUSETTS.

Thirty-third Massachusetts Infantry.

First Lieut. William P. Mudge, Adjutant. Killed in action, Lookout Valley, October 29, 1863.

First Lieut. Edgar L. Bumpers. Killed in action at Resaca, May 15, 1864.
First Lieut. Henry J. Parker. Killed in action at Resaca, May 15, 1864.
Second Lieut. Joseph P. Burrage. Killed in action, Lookout Valley, October 29, 1863.
Second Lieut. James Hill. Killed in action, Lookout Valley, October 29, 1863.
Second Lieut. Oswego Jones. Died, November 12, 1863, of wounds received in action.

MICHIGAN.

First Michigan Mechanics and Engineers.

Captain James W. Sligh. Died by railroad accident, November 15, 1863.

Second Michigan Cavalry.

Captain Philo. W. Rodgers. Died, May 17, 1862, at Evansville, Ind.
Captain James Hawley. Killed at Chickamauga, September 20, 1863.
First Lieut. Russel T. Dawon. Killed in action, at Florence, Ala., October 7, 1864.
First Lieut. James. P. Scott, R. Q. M. Shot himself accidentally, at Cleveland, Tenn., May 15, 1865.

Fourth Michigan Cavalry.

First Lieut. Edward L. Tucker. Died, October 7, 1863, of wounds received in action.
First Lieut. Theodore W. Sutton. Killed in action, at Noonday Church, June 20, 1864.
Second Lieut. Charles F. McKenzie. Died November 18, 1863.
Second Lieut. Aaron F. Ismon. Died, December 21, 1863, of disease.
Second Lieut. Smith Randolp. Died, May 30, 1864, of wounds received at Kingston, Ga.

Battery "A," Michigan Light Artillery.

First Lieut. George W. Van Pelt. Killed at Chickamauga, September 19, 1863.

Ninth Michigan Infantry.

Captain Albert Nye. Died, June 23, 1862, at Murfreesboro, Tenn.
First Lieut. Joseph H. Jott. Died, March 16, 1862, at Elizabethtown, Ky., of disease.
First Lieut. Charles T. Fox. Died, September 22, 1862, of wounds received in action.
Second Lieut. Lambert Barshite. Died, February 19, 1862, of disease, at Elizabethtown, Ky.
Second Lieut. Alpheus Chase. Killed at Murfreesboro, Tenn., in action, July 13, 1862.

Tenth Michigan Infantry.

Major James J. Scarritt. Died, November 16, 1863, of disease, at Nashville, Tenn.
Major Henry S. Burnett. Killed at Jonesboro, September 1, 1864.
Captain Bradford Cook. Died, June 29, 1864, of wounds received in action.
Captain Hannibal H. Ninus. Died, September 3, 1864, of wounds received at Jonesboro.
First Lieut. Sylvester D. Cowles, Adjutant. Died May 26, 1862.

First Lieut. Daniel Leach. Died, July 7, 1862, of disease.
First Lieut. Frank M. Vanderburgh. Died, April 18, 1863, of wounds received in action.
Second Lieut. Richard Teal. Killed at Peach Tree Creek, July 20, 1864.
Second Lieut. John Knox. Killed at Jonesboro, September 1, 1864.

Eleventh Michigan Infantry.

Major Benjamin G. Bennet. Killed at Missionary Ridge, November 25, 1863.
Captain David Oakes, Jun. Died, January 30, 1863, of disease, at Murfreesboro, Tenn.
Captain Charles W. Newbury. Killed at Chickamauga, September 20, 1863.
First Lieut. Christopher C. Haight. Died, February 5, 1862, of disease, at Bardstown, Ky.
First Lieut. Joseph Wilson. Killed at Stone River, December 30, 1862.
First Lieut. Thomas Flynn. Killed at Stone River, December 31, 1862.
First Lieut. Edward U. Catlin. Died, August 7, 1864, of wounds received before Atlanta, Ga.

Thirteenth Michigan Infantry.

Major Williard G. Eaton. Killed at Bentonville, March 19, 1865.
Captain Clement C. Webb. Died, February 4, 1863, of wounds received in action.
Captain Clark D. Fox. Killed at Chickamauga, September 19, 1863.
Captain Daniel B. Hosmer. Killed at Chickamauga, September 19, 1863.
Second Lieut. Jerome S. Bigelow. Died, May 28, 1862, of disease.

Fourteenth Michigan Infantry.

Captain John C. Lind. Died, August 8, 1863, of disease, at Saginaw, Mich.
Captain James J. Jeffres. Died, July 10, 1864, at Chattanooga, Tenn.
First Lieut. Joseph Kirk. Killed before Atlanta, Ga., August 8, 1864.

Nineteenth Michigan Infantry.

Colonel Henry C. Gilbert. Died, May 24, 1864, of wounds received at Resaca
Major Eli A. Griffin. Died, June 16, 1864, of wounds received at Golgotha Church, Ga.
Captain Charles H. Calmer. Killed at Resaca, May 15, 1864.
Captain Charles W. Bigelow. Died, May 29, 1864, of wounds received at New Hope Church.
Captain Leonard Gibbon. Killed at Averysboro, March 16, 1865.
First Lieut. Charles G. Parsel. Killed at Averysboro, March 16, 1865.
Second Lieut. Charles Mandeville. Killed at New Hope Church, May 25, 1864.

Twenty-first Michigan Infantry.

Lieut. Colonel William L. Whipple. Died November 16, 1862.
Lieut. Colonel Morris B. Wells. Killed at Chickamauga, September 20, 1863.
Captain Leonard O. Fitzgerald. Died, January 8, 1863, of wounds.
Captain Edgar W. Smith. Died, October 16, 1863, of wounds received at Chickamauga.
First Lieut. Herman Hunt. Died, December 16, 1862, of disease.

Twenty-second Michigan Infantry.

Colonel Moses Wisner. Died, January 5, 1863, at Lexington, Ky.
Captain Henry Carlton. Killed on railroad, June 6, 1863.
Captain Elijah Snell. Died, September 25, 1863, of wounds received at Chickamauga.
Captain William Augustus Smith. Died, October 11, 1863, of wounds received in action.
Captain Alexander G. Golbraith. Died, April 1, 1865, of disease.
Second Lieut. John Sackett. Died, January 1, 1863, at Cincinnati, Ohio.
Second Lieut. Joseph R. Nute. Died, October 8, 1864, in prison, at Millen, Ga.

MINNESOTA.
Second Minnesota Battery.

First Lieut. Albert Woodbury. Died, October 29, 1863, of wounds received at Chickamauga.

Second Minnesota Infantry.

First Lieut. Henry C. Simpson. Died December 1, 1861.
First Lieut. Charles Haven. Died, March 4, 1862, at Nashville, Tenn.
First Lieut. Samuel G. Trimble. Killed at Missionary Ridge, November 25, 1863.
Second Lieut. John C. Jones. Killed at Kenesaw Mountain, June 18, 1864.

MISSOURI.
Battery "G," Missouri Light Artillery

First Lieut. R. C. M. Taliaferro. Killed at Stone River, December 31, 1865.

Second Missouri Infantry.

Colonel Frederick Schaefer. Killed at Stone River, December 31, 1862.
Captain Walter Hoppe. Killed at Perryville, October 8, 1862.
Captain Charles Deyhle. Killed at Chickamauga, September 20, 1863.
Captain Herman Hartmann. Died, December 7, 1863, of wounds.
First Lieut. William Aulbach. Killed accidentally, at St. Louis, Mo., December 31, 1863.

Fifteenth Missouri Infantry.

Captain M. Zimmermann. Killed at Stone River, December 31, 1862.
Captain John V. Krebs. Killed at Chickamauga, September 20, 1863.
Captain John G. Rees. Died, December 19, 1863, of wounds received at Missionary Ridge.
Captain William Hark. Killed at Franklin, November 30, 1864.
Captain Joseph B. Vourdon. Killed accidentally, June 12, 1865.
First Lieut. Martin Schroeder, Adjutant. Died, January 19, 1863, of wounds received at Stone River.
First Lieut. Hermann C. Koerner. Killed at Chickamauga, September 20, 1863.
Second Lieut. Christian Guinzius. Killed at Stone River, December 31, 1862.
Second Lieut. Charles Kellner. Killed at Stone River, December 31, 1862.

APPENDIX.   415

Twenty-third Missouri Infantry.
Major John McCullough. Died, October 7, 1863, of disease.
First Lieut. William P. Harlbut. Died, November 24, 1862, of disease.
First Lieut. William O. Seaman. Died, July 31, 1864, of wounds.
First Lieut. N. Judson Camp. Killed accidentally, August 4, 1864.
Chaplain James M. Oyler. Died, December 30, 1862, of disease.

NEW JERSEY.
Thirteenth New Jersey Infantry.
First Lieut. Peter M. Ryerson. Died, July 1, 1864, of wounds received in action.

Thirty-third New Jersey Infantry.
Captain Samuel F. Waldron. Killed in action, November 23, 1863.
Captain William G. Boggs. Died, December 19, 1863, of wounds received in action.
Captain Henry C. Bartlett. Killed, May 8, 1864, at Rocky Face Ridge, Ga.
Captain Charles J. Field. Died, June 5, 1864, of wounds received in action.
First Lieut. Joseph L. Miller. Killed May 8, 1864, at Rocky Face Ridge, Ga.
First Lieut. William H. Cochrane. Killed, June 25, 1864, before Kenesaw Mountain.

Battery "I," New Jersey Light Artillery.
Captain Nicholas Sohm. Died, May 1, 1864, of disease.
Second Lieut. Francis Henchew. Killed before Atlanta, July 27, 1864.

Thirteenth New Jersey Battery.
Captain William Wheeler. Killed at Culp's Farm, June 22, 1864.

NEW YORK.
Fifty-eighth New York Infantry.
Captain Albert Von Rosenburg. Died May 3, 1864.
Chaplain Anthony Zyla. Died, April 5, 1865, of disease, at Nashville, Tenn.

Sixtieth New York Infantry.
First Lieut. John E. Wilson. Killed near Golgotha, Ga., June 18, 1864.

One Hundred and Second New York Infantry.
Major Gilbert M. Elliott. Killed in action at Lookout Mountain, November 24, 1863.

One Hundred and Seventh New York Infantry.
Major Lathrop Baldwin. Died July 30, 1864.
Captain John F. Knox. Died, May 29, 1864, of wounds received near Dallas, Ga.
Second Lieut. John D. Hill. Killed, near Dallas, Ga. (New Hope Church) May 25, 1864.

One Hundred and Nineteenth New York Infantry.
Lieut. Colonel Edward F. Lloyd. Killed at Resaca, May 15, 1864.

One Hundred and Twenty-third New York Infantry.

Colonel Archibald L. McDougall. Died, June 23, 1864, of wounds received at New Hope Church.
Captain Henry O'Wily. Killed at Peach Tree Creek, July 20, 1864.
First Lieut. John H. Daicy. Killed at Peach Tree Creek, July 20, 1864.

One Hundred and Thirty-fourth New York Infantry.

Captain Edwin Forrest. Died, May 20, 1864, of wounds received at Rocky Face Ridge.
First Lieut. C. P. Hunter. Accidentally drowned in North River, March 11, 1864.
First Lieut. Charles A. Ahreetz. Killed at Savannah, Ga., December 13, 1864.

One Hundred and Thirty-sixth New York Infantry.

First Lieut. Charles F. Tresser. Died, December 16, 1863, of wounds received in action at Chattanooga.
First Lieut. William C. Hall. Died, May 27, 1864, at Nashville, Tenn.

One Hundred and Thirty-seventh New York Infantry.

Colonel David Ireland. Died, September 10, 1864, of disease, at Atlanta, Ga.
First Lieut. George C. Owen. Killed at Lookout Mountain, November 24, 1864.
Assistant Surgeon Taylor Elmore. Died, May 25, 1864, at Chattanooga, Tenn.

One Hundred and Forty-first New York Infantry.

Colonel William K. Logie. Killed at Peach Tree Creek, July 20, 1864.
First Lieut. Alfred E. Barber. Killed at Resaca, May 15, 1864.
First Lieut. Theodore M. Warren. Killed at Peach Tree Creek, July 20, 1864.
First Lieut. Eugene Egbert. Died, December 18, 1864, of disease.

One Hundred and Forty-third New York Infantry.

Lieut. Colonel Joseph B. Taft, Killed at Missionary Ridge, November 25, 1863.
First Lieut. William M. Ratcliff, Adjutant. Killed at Peach Tree Creek, July 20, 1864.
First Lieut. Peter L. Waterbury. Died, July 24, 1864, of wounds received at Peach Tree Creek.
First Lieut. R. M. J. Hordenbough. Died, March 15, 1865, of wounds received in action.
Second Lieut. Edward Carrington. Killed in action at Natural Bridge, Fla., March 6, 1865.

One Hundred and Forty-ninth New York Infantry.

Lieut. Colonel Charles B. Randall. Killed at Peach Tree Creek, July 20, 1864.
Captain David J. Lindsay. Killed at Peach Tree Creek, July 20, 1864.

One Hundred and Fiftieth New York Infantry.

First Lieut. Edgar P. Welling. Died, October 21, 1863, at Tallahoma, Tenn.
First Lieut. Henry Gridley. Killed in action at Culp's Farm, June 22, 1864.
First Lieut. David B. Sleight. Killed at Averysboro, March 16, 1865.
Second Lieut. John Sweet. Died August 13, 1864.

APPENDIX. 417

One Hundred and Fifty-fourth New York Infantry.
Captain Alanson Crosby. Died, July 9, 1864, of wounds received in action.

OHIO.

Brigadier General Robert L. McCook. Killed in ambulance, April 1, 1862, near New Market, Tenn.
Brigadier General J. W. Sill. Killed at Stone River, December 31, 1862.
Brigadier General W. H. Lytle. Killed at Chickamauga, September 20, 1863.
Brigadier General C. G. Harker. Killed at Kenesaw, June 27, 1864.

First Ohio Cavalry.
Colonel Minor Millikin. Killed in action at Stone River, December 31, 1862.
Lieut. Colonel Valentine Cupp. Died, September 20, 1863, of wounds received at Chickamauga.
Major David A. B. Moore. Killed in action, December 31, 1862, at Stone River.
Captain Andrew B. Emery. Died, July 15, 1862, of wounds received in action.
Captain John H. Robinson. Died October 31, 1862.
Captain William H. Scott. Died, September 22, 1864, of wounds received in action.
Second Lieut. John M. Renick. Died, May 28, 1862, at Corinth, Miss.
Second Lieut. Ira Stevens. Died, October 31, 1862, at Danville, Ky.
Second Lieut. Timothy L. Condit. Killed at Stone River, December 31, 1862.

Third Ohio Cavalry.
Captain Daniel Gotshall. Died, June 17, 1862, of disease.
Captain William B. Amsden. Died, June 19, 1862, at Fremont, Ohio.
Captain Richard B. Wood. Killed, February 23, 1864, in action, at Dalton, Ga.
Captain J. Samuel Clock. Died, July 2, 1865, of wounds received at Macon, Ga.
Second Lieut. William G. Goodnow. Died, May 27, 1862, of disease.
Second Lieut. Ralf Devereaux. Died, June 21, 1862, of disease.

Fourth Ohio Cavalry.
Lieut. Colonel George W. Dobb. Killed, April 2, 1865, at Selma, Ala.
Captain Jesse P. Wilson. Killed, February 20, 1862, on picket, near Nashville, Tenn.
Captain John C. Stewart. Died, November 18, 1864, at Cincinnati, Ohio.
Captain Frank Robie. Killed, April 2, 1865, in action, at Selma.
First Lieut. Richard W. Neff. Killed, September 20, 1863, at Chickamauga.

Tenth Ohio Cavalry.
Captain Samuel E. Norton. Died, December 5, 1864, at Waynesboro, Ga.
First Lieut. Henry H. Crooks. Killed in action, August 30, 1864.
First Lieut. James S. Morgan. Killed in action, at Bear Creek, Ga., November 16, 1864.
Surgeon James W. Thompson. Died, November 25, 1864, at Wrightsville, Pa.

First Ohio Light Artillery.

Lieut. Colonel W. E. Lawrence. Died, November 26, 1864, of disease, at Murfreesboro, Tenn.

Battery "B."

Second Lieut. George D. Eldridge. Died, March 24, 1863, at Nashville, Tenn.

Battery "F."

Second Lieut. John Lynch. Killed at Chickamauga, September 19, 1863.

Battery "I."

Second Lieut. Charles Kotzebue. Died, July 16, 1864, of wounds received at Kenesaw Mountain.

Sixth Ohio Battery.

First Lieut. Oliver H. P. Ayres. Died, July 8, 1864, of wounds.

Twentieth Ohio Battery.

First Lieut. Charles F. Nitschelm. Died, August 15, 1864, at Chattanooga, Tenn.
First Lieut. John S. Burdick. Killed in action, at Franklin, Tenn., November 30, 1864.

First Ohio Infantry.

First Lieut. John W. Jackson. Killed at Chickamauga, September 19, 1863.
First Lieut. Sylvanus S. Dixon. Killed in action, near Dallas, Ga., May 27, 1864.
First Lieut. George J. Grove. Killed in action, near Dallas, Ga., May 27, 1864.
First Lieut. Alexander Varian. Died, June 2, 1864, of wounds received at Resaca.
Second Lieut. Christopher Wollenhaupt. Killed at Missionary Ridge, November 25, 1863.

Second Ohio Infantry.

Colonel John Kell. Killed at Stone River, December 31, 1862.
Captain Alexander S. Berryhill. Killed at Perryville, October 8, 1862.
Captain John Herrel. Killed at Perryville, October 8, 1862.
Captain John C. Hazlett. Died, June 7, 1863, at Murfreesboro, Tenn.
Captain Jacob Fotrel. Killed in action, at Resaca, May 14, 1864.
First Lieut. Richard S. Chambers. Killed at Stone River, December 31, 1862.
First Lieut. Lafayette Van Horn. Died, January 14, 1863, of wounds received at Stone River.
First Lieut. George W. Landrum. Killed at Chickamauga, September 20, 1863.
First Lieut. John W. Thomas, Adjutant. Killed in action before Atlanta, Ga., July 20, 1864.

Third Ohio Infantry.

Captain Leonidas McDougal. Killed at Perryville, October 8, 1862.
Captain Henry E. Cunard. Killed at Perryville, October 8, 1862.
First Lieut. C. L. Starr. Killed at Perryville, October 8, 1862.
First Lieut. James St. John. Killed at Perryville, October 8, 1862.
Surgeon R. R. McMeens. ——, 1862.

APPENDIX.

Fifth Ohio Infantry

Colonel John H. Patrick. Killed at New Hope Church, Ga., May 25, 1864.
Major Henry E. Symmes. Died July 9, 1864.
First Lieut. Henry A. Fortman, Adjutant. Died, September 28, 1864, of disease.

Sixth Ohio Infantry.

Major Samuel C. Erwin. Killed at Missionary Ridge, November 25, 1863.
Captain Ezekiel H. Tatem. Killed by railroad accident, July 19, 1862.
Captain Henry McAlpin. Died, December 31, 1862, of wounds received at Stone River.
First Lieut. Albert G. Williams, Adjutant. Killed at Stone River, December 31, 1862.
Second Lieut. Charles H. Foster. Killed at Stone River, December 31, 1862.

Seventh Ohio Infantry.

Colonel William R. Creighton. Killed at Ringgold, Ga., November 27, 1863.
Lieut. Colonel Orrin J. Crane. Killed at Ringgold, Ga., November 27, 1863.

Ninth Ohio Infantry.

Captain Gustav Richter. Killed at Chickamauga, September 20, 1863.
Captain Ferdinand Mueller. Died, September 25, 1863, of wounds received at Chickamauga.
Captain John Gansen. Died, October 28, 1863, of disease.
First Lieut. Henry Liedke. Died, September 22, 1863, of wounds received in action at Chickamauga.
First Lieut. Theodore Lammers. Died, October 7, 1863, of wounds received in action at Chickamauga.
Second Lieut. Raymond Hermann. Killed at Chickamauga, September 19, 1863.
Assistant Surgeon James Davenport. Died March 29, 1863.

Tenth Ohio Infantry.

Captain Charles F. Nickel. Died, November 3, 1862, of wounds.
Captain James M. Fitzgerald. Died, November 17, 1863, of disease.
First Lieut. John S. Mulroy. Killed at Perryville, October 8, 1862.
Second Lieut. Sebastian Eustachio. Died, August 1, 1861, of disease.
Second Lieut. William Porter. Killed at Perryville, October 8, 1862.

Eleventh Ohio Infantry.

Captain David K. Curtis. Killed at Missionary Ridge, November 25, 1863.
First Lieut. George E. Peck. Died, November 26, 1863, of wounds received at Missionary Ridge.

Thirteenth Ohio Infantry.

Colonel Joseph G. Hawkins. Killed at Stone River, December 31, 1862.
Lieut. Colonel Elhanon M. Mart. Killed at Chickamauga, September 19, 1863.
Captain Isaac R. Gardner. Died, May 31, 1862, of wounds received at Shiloh.
Captain Thomas F. Murdock. Killed, September 20, 1863, at Chickamauga.
Captain Thomas J. Loudon. Drowned, September 29, 1863, in Mississippi River.

Captain Samuel McCulloch. Died, May 28, 1864, of wounds received in action.
First Lieut. James A. Leisure, R. Q. M. Died, October 17, 1861, at Gallipolis, Ohio.
First Lieut. John Murphy. Died, January 10, 1863, of wounds received at Stone River.
Second Lieut. James C. Whittaker. Killed at Stone River, December 31, 1862.
Second Lieut. John Fox. Died, January 1, 1863, of wounds received at Stone River.

Fourteenth Ohio Infantry.

Major John W. Wilson. Died October 3, 1864.
Captain Wilbur F. Spofford. Killed at Jonesboro, September 1, 1864.
Second Lieut. Walter B. Kirk. Killed at Jonesboro, September 1, 1864.
Second Lieut. Ebenezer C. Tillotson. Died, September 24, 1864, on Lookout Mountain, Tenn.
Second Lieut. Charles B. Mitchell. Died September 28, 1864.
Second Lieut. Nathaniel O. Cobb. Died, October 3, 1864, of wounds received at Jonesboro.

Fifteenth Ohio Infantry.

Captain James C. Cummins. Died, February 19, 1864, of wounds received in action.
First Lieut. Thomas N. Hanson. Killed at Nashville, Tenn., December 16, 1864.
Fist Lieut. Charles J. Rodig. Killed at Nashville, Tenn., December 16, 1864.
Second Lieut. Andrew E. Smiley. Killed in action, June 24, 1863.
Second Lieut. Nicholas M. Fowler. Killed at Chickamauga, September 20, 1863.
Second Lieut. Frank W. Sanders. Died November 26, 1863.
Second Lieut. Andrew L. Hadden. Killed in action, June 14, 1864.
Surgeon Henry Spellman. Died, June 9, 1862, of disease.

Sixteenth Ohio Infantry.

Captain William Spangler. Died, January 19, 1862, of disease.
Captain Joseph Edgar. Killed near Tazewell, Tenn., August 6, 1862.

Seventeenth Ohio Infantry.

Major Benjamin F. Butterfield. Died, December 16, 1863, of wounds received at Missionary Ridge.
Captain Ezra Ricketts. Killed at Chickamauga, September 20, 1863.
First Lieut. Jacob Humphreys. Died, December 21, 1861, of disease.
First Lieut. Theodore C. Stewart. Killed at Resaca, May 14, 1864.
First Lieut. Lyman W. Barnes. Killed in action, August 5, 1864.
First Lieut. Jacob M. Ruffner, Adjutant. Killed before Atlanta, August 9, 1864.
Second Lieut. Richard T. Foster. Died June 15, 1864.

Eighteenth Ohio Infantry.

Captain George Stivers. Died, January 4, 1863, of wounds received at Stone River.
Captain Philip E. Taylor. Died, January 5, 1863, of wounds received at Stone River.

APPENDIX. 421

Captain Ashbel Fenton. Died, April 14, 1863, of wounds received at Stone River.
Captain George W. Dunkle. Died, June 9, 1863, of disease.
Captain Ebenezer Grosvenor. Killed at Nashville, Tenn., December 15, 1864.
Second Lieut. William W. Blacker. Killed at Stone River, December 31, 1862.
Second Lieut. Samuel W. Thomas. Killed at Nashville, Tenn., December 15, 1864.

Nineteenth Ohio Infantry.

Major Timothy D. Edwards. Killed at Shiloh, April 7, 1862.
Captain W. Rakestraw. Died, December 17, 1861, at Columbus, Ky.
Captain Franklin E. Stowe. Died, April 30, 1862, at Pittsburgh Landing, Tenn.
Captain Urwin Bean. Killed at Stone River, January 2, 1863.
Captain Uriah W. Irwin. Died, December 6, 1863, of wounds received at Chickamauga.
Captain Charles Brewer. Killed in action at Picket Mills, May 27, 1864.
First Lieut. Samuel F. Lentz. Died, February 16, 1862, of disease.
First Lieut. Daniel Donovan. Killed at Stone River, December 31, 1862.
First Lieut. Job D. Bell. Killed at Stone River, December 31, 1862.
First Lieut. William F. McHenry. Killed before Atlanta, August 24, 1864.
Second Lieut. D. W. Heldenbrand. Died, July 21, 1862, at Nashville, Tenn.
Second Lieut. J. Stanley Cochran. Died, May 6, 1865, at Nashville, Tenn.
Assistant Surgeon James H. Biteman. Died, September 25, 1865, near San Antonia, Texas.

Twenty-first Ohio Infantry.

Lieut. Colonel Dwella M. Stoughton. Died, November 19, 1863, of wounds received at Chickamauga.
Captain Daniel Lewis. Killed before Atlanta, July 21, 1864.
First Lieut. Amos E. Wood. Died, June 14, 1863, at Murfreesboro, Tenn.
First Lieut. Robert S. Dilworth. Killed June 27, 1864.
Second Lieut. Enoch B. Wiley. Died, June 5, 1863, of wounds received at Stone River.
Second Lieut. Asa C. Spafford. Died, October 14, 1864, at Columbia, S. C.

Twenty-fourth Ohio Infantry.

Colonel Frederick C. Jones. Killed at Stone River, December 31, 1862.
Major Henry Terry. Killed at Stone River, December 31, 1862.
Captain Enoch Weller. Killed at Stone River, January 2, 1863.
Captain Dewitt C. Wadsworth. Died, September 21, 1863, of wounds received at Chickamauga.
Captain Isaac N. Dryden. Died, October 1, 1863, of wounds received at Chickamauga.
First Lieut. Charles R. Harman. Killed at Stone River, December 31, 1862.

Twenty-sixth Ohio Infantry.

Captain William H. Ross. Died, September 20, of wounds received at Chickamauga.
First Lieut. David McClelland. Killed at Stone River, December 31, 1862.
First Lieut. Francis M. Williams. Killed at Chickamauga, September 19, 1863.
First Lieut. James W. Burbridge. Killed at Chickamauga, September 19, 1863.

Second Lieut. John W. Ruley. Killed at Chickamauga, September 19, 1863.
Second Lieut. Samuel G. Platt. Killed near Dallas, Ga., June 4, 1864.

Twenty-ninth Ohio Infantry.

Major Myron T. Wright. Died, January 7, 1865, of wounds received before Savannah, Ga.
First Lieut. Winthrop H. Grant. Killed at Rocky Face Ridge, May 8, 1864.
First Lieut. John W. Dice. Died, June 17, 1864, of wounds received at Kenesaw Mountain.

Thirty-first Ohio Infantry.

Captain David C. Rose. Died, December 26, 1861, of disease.
Captain James A. Cahill. Killed at Kenesaw Mountain, June 23, 1864.
First Lieut. James K. Rochester. Killed at Missionary Ridge, November 25, 1863.

Thirty-third Ohio Infantry.

Major Joshua V. Robinson. Died, March 23, 1862, at Portsmouth, Ohio.
Major Ephraim J. Ellis. Killed at Chickamauga, September 20, 1863.
Captain Samuel A. Currie. Died, April 16, 1862, at Shelbyville, Tenn.
Captain William McKain. Killed at Resaca, May 14, 1864.
First Lieut. Charles R. Pomeroy, Jun. Killed, before Atlanta, August 13, 1864.
Second Lieut. Enos A. Holmes. Died, December 24, 1861, at Elizabethtown, Ky.
Second Lieut. Joseph H. Cole. Killed at Chickamauga, September 19, 1863.
Second Lieut. Edgar J. Higby. Killed at Resaca, May 14, 1864.
Second Lieut. Francis M. Campbell. Died, July 22, 1864, of wounds.
Second Lieut. John E. Sykes. Killed in action, September 6, 1864.

Thirty-fifth Ohio Infantry.

Captain John S. Earhart. Died, August 10, 1863, at Winchester, Tenn.
Captain Oliver H. Parshall. Killed at Chickamauga, September 19, 1863.
Captain Joel K. Deardorf. Died, October 8, 1863, of wounds received at Chickamauga.
Captain David M. Gans. Died, November 25, 1863, of disease.
First Lieut. Thomas M. Harlan. Killed at Chickamauga, September 20, 1863.
First Lieut. James Sabin. Died, June 16, 1864, of wounds received in action.

Thirty-sixth Ohio Infantry.

Colonel William G. Jones. Killed at Chickamauga, September 19, 1863.
Captain James C. Selby. Died, September 14, 1864, of wounds.
Second Lieut. William A. Rhodes. Died, October 11, 1863, of wounds received in action.

Thirty-eighth Ohio Infantry.

Colonel Edward H. Phelps. Killed at Missionary Ridge, November 25, 1863.
Colonel William A. Choate. Died, September 12, 1864, of wounds.
Captain John H. Adams. Died, December 10, 1862, of disease.
Captain Edgar M. Denchar. Died, September 4, 1864, of wounds.
Captain John Crosson. Died, September 10, 1864, of wounds.
First Lieut. James C. Betts. Killed at Jonesboro, September 1, 1864.
Second Lieut. Alphonso L. Braucher. Died, January 29, 1862, of disease.

APPENDIX. 423

Second Lieut. John Lewis. Killed at Missionary Ridge, November 25, 1863.
Second Lieut. Joseph Newman. Died, December 12, 1863, of wounds.
Second Lieut. James McQuillen. Died, October 2, 1864, of wounds.

Fortieth Ohio Infantry.

Major Thomas Acton. Killed at Lookout Mountain, November 24, 1864.
Captain Clements F. Snodgrass. Killed before Atlanta, July 1, 1864.
Captain John C. Meagher. Died, August 15, 1864, at Liberty, Ohio.
First Lieut. Cyrenius Van Mater. Killed at Chickamauga, September 20, 1863.
First Lieut. Daniel Collett. Died, May 30, 1864, of wounds received at Lookout Mountain.
First Lieut. Charles Converse. Killed at Kenesaw Mountain, June 30, 1864.

Forty-first Ohio Infantry.

Captain William W. Munn. Died, December 2, 1863, of wounds received at Missionary Ridge.
Captain William Hansard. Died, January 9, 1865, of wounds.
First Lieut. Franklin E. Pancoast. Died, May 16, 1862, of wounds received at Shiloh.
First Lieut. Calvin C. Hart. Killed at Stone River, December 31, 1862.
First Lieut. Lester T. Patchin. Died, January 18, 1863, of wounds received at Stone River.
First Lieut. Samuel B. Asdel, Adjutant. Died, November 17, 1863, of disease.
First Lieut Henry S. Dirlam. Died, December 18, 1863, of wounds received at Missionary Ridge.
Second Lieut. Chauncey H. Talcott. Killed at Shiloh, April 7, 1862.
Second Lieut. William W. Watson. Killed at Missionary Ridge, November 25, 1863.

Forty-ninth Ohio Infantry.

Lieut. Colonel Levi Drake. Killed at Stone River, December 31, 1862.
Captain Amos Keller. Died, January 1, 1863, of wounds received at Stone River.
Captain Hiram Chance. Killed at Liberty Gap, June 24, 1863.
Captain Shepherd Green. Died, November 27, 1864, of wounds received in action.
First Lieut. Aaron H. Keller. Died, January 27, 1863, of wounds received in action.
First Lieut. Jacob C. Miller. Killed at Missionary Ridge, November 25, 1863.
First Lieut. Silas W. Simons. Killed in action, at Pickett's Mills, May 27, 1864.
First Lieut. John C. Ramsey. Killed in action, at Pickett's Mills, May 27, 1864.
First Lieut. Theodore A. Pesso. Killed, August 25, 1864, at Vining's Station.
First Lieut. John K. Gibson. Died, January 25, 1865, of wounds received in action.
Second Lieut. Henry F. Arndt. Killed at Missionary Ridge, November 25, 1864.
Second Lieut. Issac H. White. Killed at Missionary Ridge, November 25, 1863.

Second Lieut. Jacob Wolf. Died, December 16, 1863, of wounds received in action.
Second Lieut. William F. Gibbs. Killed at Pickett's Mills, May 27, 1864.
Second Lieut. Charles Wallace. Died, June 23, 1864, of wounds received in action.

Fifty-first Ohio Infantry.

Captain William Patton. Died, April 14, 1862, at Nashville, Tenn.
Captain Benjamin F. Heskett. Died, January 4, 1863, of wounds received at Stone River.
Captain Samuel Stephens. Killed at Kenesaw Mountain, June 20, 1864.
First Lieut. Frank Shriver. Died, July 9, 1864, of wounds received in action.
Second Lieut. Willis C. Workman. Killed at Kenesaw Mountain, June 22, 1864.

Fifty-second Ohio Infantry.

Colonel Daniel McCook. Died, July 17, 1864, of wounds received at Kenesaw Mountain.
Captain Salathiel M. Neighbor. Died, July 7, 1864, of wounds.
Captain Peter C. Schneider. Killed at Peach Tree Creek, July 19, 1864.
Captain James M. Summers. Died, April 16, 1865, of wounds.
First Lieut. Ira H. Pool. Died, July 30, 1864, of wounds received at Kenesaw Mountain.
Second Lieut. James H. Donaldson. Killed at Peach Tree Creek, July 19, 1864.
Second Lieut. David F. Miser. Died, August 2, 1864, of wounds received at Kenesaw Mountain.
Assistant Surgeon Arthur J. Rosa. Died February 20, 1864.

Fifty-fifth Ohio Infantry.

Colonel Charles B. Gambee. Killed at Resaca, May 15, 1864.
Major Rodolphus Robbins. Killed at Resaca, May 15, 1864.
Captain Albert E. Peck. Killed at Averysboro, March 16, 1865.
Second Lieut. Edward Bromley. Killed in action, at Missionary Ridge, November 24, 1863.

Fifty-ninth Ohio Infantry.

First Lieut. Frank H. Woods. Killed at Chickamauga, September 19, 1863.
Second Lieut. John W. Shinn. Died, June 17, 1863, at Stone River Ford, Tenn.
Second Lieut. Jesse Ellis. Killed at Chickamauga, September 19, 1863.

Sixty-first Ohio Infantry.

Lieut. Colonel William H. H. Brown. Died, September 5, 1864, of wounds, at Chattanooga, Tenn.
Major David C. Beckett. Killed in action, June 22, 1864.
Captain William H. McGroarty. Killed in Lookout Valley, October 28, 1863.
Captain Edward H. Newcomb. Killed July 21, 1864.

APPENDIX.

Sixty-fourth Ohio Infantry.

Colonel Alexander McIlvaine. Killed at Rocky Face Ridge, May 9, 1864
Captain Joseph B. Sweet. Killed at Stone River, December 31, 1862.
Captain John K. Ziegler. Died, September 20, 1863, of wounds received at Chickamauga.
Captain Henry H. Kling. Killed at Missionary Ridge, November 25, 1863.
First Lieut. Thomas H. Ehlers. Killed at Rocky Face Ridge, May 9, 1864.
First Lieut. George C. Marshall. Killed near Dallas, Ga., May 27, 1864.
Second Lieut. Thomas McGill. Died, March 30, 1862, at Nashville, Tenn.

Sixty-fifth Ohio Infantry.

Major Samuel C. Brown. Died, September 22, 1863, of wounds received at Chickamauga.
Captain Jacob Christophel. Killed at Stone River, December 31, 1862.
Captain Nahan L. Williams. Killed at Kenesaw Mountain, July 27, 1864.
First Lieut. Horace H. Justice, Adjutant. Died, February 14, 1862, of disease.
First Lieut. Clark S. Gregg. Died, May 11, 1862, of disease, at St. Louis, Mo.
First Lieut. William H. Massey, Adjutant. Died, April 7, 1863, of wounds received at Stone River.
First Lieut. Nelson Smith. Killed at Chickamauga, September 19, 1863.
First Lieut. Jonas Smith. Died, June 10, 1865, from accidental injury.
First Lieut. John T. Hyatt. Died, December 16, 1861, of disease.
Second Lieut. George N. Huckins. Died, April 2, 1862, of disease.
Second Lieut. John R. Parish. Died July 31, 1862.
Second Lieut. Dolsen Van Kirk. Killed at Stone River, December 31, 1862.
Second Lieut. Samuel C. Henwood. Killed at Chickamauga, September 19, 1863.
Second Lieut. Eben Bingham. Killed at Big Shanty, Ga., in action, June 18, 1864.

Sixty-sixth Ohio Infantry.

First Lieut. Harrison Davis. Killed at Ringgold, Ga., November 27, 1863.
First Lieut. Joseph W. Hitt. Killed at Dallas, Ga., May 25, 1864.
First Lieut. John R. Organ. Killed before Atlanta, July 20, 1864.

Sixty-ninth Ohio Infantry.

Captain Leonard Counseller. Killed at Stone River, January 2, 1863.
First Lieut. Joseph W. Boynton. Died, June 5, 1863, of wounds received in action.
First Lieut. Jacob S. Pierson. Killed at Jonesboro, September 1, 1864.
First Lieut. Martin V. Bailey. Killed at Jonesboro, September 1, 1864.
Second Lieut. John S. Scott. Killed at Missionary Ridge, November 25, 1863.

Seventy-first Ohio Infantry.

Major James W. Carlin. Perished on Steamer Sultana, April 24, 1865.
First Lieut. Nicholas Eidemiller. Died, May 16, 1862, at Cincinnati, Ohio.
First Lieut. Eliah A. Widener. Killed at Nashville, Tenn., December 16, 1864.
Second Lieut. William S. Hamilton. Drowned August 19, 1862.
Second Lieut. John M. Simmons. Died, August 24, 1863, of disease.
Second Lieut. Everah C. Le Blond. Killed at Nashville, December 16, 1864.

Seventy-third Ohio Infantry.
Captain Luther M. Buchwalter. Killed in Lookout Valley, October 29, 1863.

Seventy-fourth Ohio Infantry.
First Lieut. W. H. H. Moody. Died, September 28, 1864, of disease.
First Lieut. Geosge W. Bricker. Died, September 15, 1864, of wounds received in action.
Second Lieut. John A. McKee. Drowned, February 1, 1864, at Cincinnati, O.
Second Lieut. John Scott. Killed at Jonesboro, September 1, 1864.

Seventy-ninth Ohio Infantry.
First Lieut. Isreal D. Compton. Died, December 31, 1862, of disease.

Eighty-second Ohio Infantry.
Captain William J. Dickson. Killed at Resaca, May 15, 1864.
Captain William Ballentine. Died, March 19, 1865, of wounds received in action.
Second Lieut. Asa H. Gary. Killed at Peach Tree Creek, July 20, 1864.

Eighty-ninth Ohio Infantry.
Captain George H. DeBolt. Died, February 3, 1865, at Savannah, Ga.
First Lieut. J. Riley Dixon. Died, December 18, 1862, of disease.
First Lieut. George W. Penn. Died, January 21, 1863, at Moscow, O.
First Lieut. Granville Jackson. Killed at Chickamauga, September 20, 1863.
First Lieut. Stephen V. Walker. Killed at Chickamauga, September 20, 1863.
First Lieut. Dudly King. Died, August 13, 1864, of wounds received in action.
First Lieut. Otho P. Fairfield. Died, October 8, 1864, at Columbia, S. C., a prisoner of war.
Second Lieut. Clement Thomas. Died, February 20, 1863, of disease.

Ninetieth Ohio Infantry.
Major George Angle. Killed near Marietta, Ga., July 2, 1864.
Captain Robert D. Caddy. Killed at Chickamauga, September 20, 1863.
Captain Thomas Rains. Killed before Atlanta, August 19, 1864.
First Lieut. Daniel N. Kingery, Adjutant. Killed at Chickamauga, September 20, 1863.
Second Lieut. Nelson A. Patterson. Died, October 10, 1863, of wounds received at Chickamauga.

Ninety-second Ohio Infantry.
Captain John Brown. Died, October 7, 1863, of wounds received at Chickamauga,
Captain William B. Whittlesey. Killed at Missionary Ridge, November 25, 1863.
Captain Edward Grosvenor. Died, November 27, 1864, of disease.
First Lieut. George B. Turner, Adjutant. Died, December 1, 1863, of wounds received at Missionary Ridge.
Second Lieut. Hugh Townsend. Killed at Missionary Ridge, November 25, 1863.

APPENDIX. 427

Ninety-third Ohio Infantry.

Colonel Hiram. Strong. Died, October 7, 1863, of wounds received at Chickamauga.
Major William Birch. Died, November 25, 1863, of wounds received at Missionary Ridge.
Captain John Eastman. Killed at Kenesaw Mountain, June 23, 1864.
First Lieut. John M. Patterson. Killed at Nashville, December 16, 1864.

Ninety-fourth Ohio Infantry.

Captain John C. Drury. Killed at Perryville, October 8, 1862.
Captain David Steel. Died, January 5, 1863, of wounds received in action.
First Lieut. John A. Beall. Died, January 2, 1863, of disease.

Ninety-seventh Ohio Infantry.

Captain William Berkshire. Killed at Kenesaw Mountain, June 27, 1864.
Second Lieut. William P. Gardner. Died, November 30, 1862, at Scottsville, Ky.

Ninety-eighth Ohio Infantry.

Colonel George Webster. Killed at Perryville, October 8, 1862.
Lieut. Colonel James M. Shane. Killed at Kenesaw Mountain, June 27, 1864.
Captain William C. Lochary. Killed at Chickamauga, September 20, 1863.
Captain Armstrong J. Thomas. Killed at Chickamauga, September 20, 1863.
Captaid Robert F. Williams. Died, August 10, 1864, of wounds received at Vining's Station, Ga.
First Lieut. Samuel A. Rank. Killed at Perryville, October 8, 1862.
First Lieut. William McMillen. Died, October 27, 1862, of wounds received at Perryville.
First Lieut. John H. Reeves, Adjutant. Killed at Jonesboro, September 1, 1864.
First Lieut. John M. Banum. Killed at Bentonville, March 19, 1865.
Second Lieut. Richard B. McGuire. Died, October 15, 1863, of wounds received at Chickamauga.
Surgeon F. W. Marseilles. Died April 23, 1864.

PENNSYLVANIA.

Seventh Pennsylvania Cavalry.

Captain James Bryson. Died April 1, 1862.
Captain David G. May. Killed at Missionary Ridge, Tenn., September 21, 1863.
Captain James G. Taylor. Killed in action at Lovejoy's Station, August 20, 1864.
Captain Robert McCormick. Died, December 29, 1864, at Bardstown, Ky.
First Lieut. Joseph Castles. Died, March 13, 1862, at Munfordsville, Ky.
First Lieut. Amos B. Rhoads. Killed at Shelbyville, Tenn., June 27, 1863.
First Lieut. Chauncy C. Hermans. Killed in action at Lovejoy's Station, August 21, 1864.
First Lieut. Jacob Sigman. Killed in action at Selma, April 2, 1865.
Second Lieut. Harvey H. Best. Died, March 5, 1862, of disease, at Bardstown, Ky.

Second Lieut. Nicholas Wynkoop. Killed in action at Gallatin, Tenn., August 21, 1862.
Second Lieut. Henry W. Lutz. Died, November 29, 1862, at Nashville, Tenn.
Second Lieut. James Henderson. Died, April 17, 1863, at Murfreesboro, Tenn.
Second Lieut. Henry D. Calkins. Died October 7, 1864.
Surgeon John L. Sherk. Killed by guerrillas at Bardstown, Ky., December 29, 1864.

Ninth Pennsylvania Cavalry.

Lieut. Colonel Thomas C. James. Died, January 13, 1863, at Philadelphia, Pa.
Captain Hugh W. McCullough. Killed in action near Tompkinsville, Ky., June 6, 1862.
Captain Gilbert Waters. Killed in action at Shelbyville, Tenn., June 28, 1863.
Captain John Boal. Killed in action, March 16, 1865.
First Lieut. Theophilus J. Mountz. Killed at Dandridge, Tenn., December 24, 1863.
Second Lieut. Isaac B. Kauffman. Died June 7, 1862.
Second Lieut. David Nissley. Died, July 5, 1862, at Bowling Green, Ky.
Second Lieut. Aaron Sullivan. Killed in action at Tompkinsville, Ky., July 9, 1862.

Fifteenth Pennsylvania Cavalry.

Major Adolph B. Rosengarten. Killed at Stone River, December 29, 1862.
Major Frank B. Ward. Died, January 11, 1863, of wounds received at Stone River.
First Lieut. Harvey S. Lingle. Killed in action at Mossy Creek, December 29, 1863.

Battery "B," Independent Pennsylvania Artillery.

Captain Alanson J. Stevens. Killed at Chickamauga, September 20, 1863.
Captain Samuel M. McDowell. Killed in action, May 27, 1864.

Battery "E," Independent Pennsylvania Artillery.

Captain Charles A. Atwell. Died, November 2, 1863, of wounds received at Wauhatchie.
First Lieut. Edward R. Geary, Killed at Wauhatchie, October 29, 1863.

Twenty-seventh Pennsylvania Infantry.

Major Peter A. McAloon. Died, December 7, 1863, of wounds received at Missionary Ridge.

Twenty-eighth Pennsylvania Infantry.

First Lieut. Peter Kaylor. Died, December 5, 1863, of wounds received at Ringgold, Ga.
Second Lieut. Isaiah B. Robison. Killed at Peach Tree Creek, July 20, 1864.

Twenty-ninth Pennsylvania Infantry.

Second Lieut. William Harrington. Killed by railroad accident, March 4, 1864.
Second Lieut. Ethan O. Fulce. Killed in action, near Fayetteville, N. C., March 14, 1865.

APPENDIX. 429

Forty-sixth Pennsylvania Infantry.

Captain Dennis H. Cheesbro. Killed at New Hope Church, May 25, 1864.
Captain Sefrer T. Kettrer. Died, July 21, 1864, of wounds received at Peach Tree Creek.
First Lieut. John H. Knipe. Died, May 15, 1864, of wounds received at Resaca.
First Lieut. Luther R. Witman, Adjutant. Died, July 20, 1864, of wounds received at Peach Tree Creek.
First Lieut. David C. Selheimer. Died, September 21, 1864, of wounds received at Peach Tree Creek.
Second Lieut. John W. Phillips. Killed at New Hope Church, May 25, 1864.
Second Lieut. Samuel Wolf. Killed at Peach Tree Creek, July 20, 1864.
Second Lieut. Howell J. Davis. Killed at Peach Tree Creek, July 20, 1864.

Seventy-third Pennsylvania Infantry.

Captain Henry Hess. Died, June 19, 1864, of wounds received at Pine Knob, Ga.

Seventy-seventh Pennsylvania Infantry.

Lieut. Colonel Peter B. Housum. Died, December 31, 1862, of wounds received at Stone River,
Captain John E. Walker. Killed before Atlanta, Ga., August 5, 1864.
First Lieut. William H. Thomas. Killed in action at Liberty Gap, June 25, 1863.
First Lieut. Henry B. Thompson. Killed at Lovejoy's Station, September 3, 1864.
First Lieut. Alexander T. Baldwin. Killed at Nashville, December 16, 1864.

Seventy-eight Pennsylvania Infantry.

Captain William S. Jack. Died, February 5, 1863, of wounds received at Stone River.
First Lieut. Adam Lowry, R. Q. M. Died, September 28, 1863, of disease.
Second Lieut. Matthew J. Halstead. Killed at Stone River, January 2, 1863.
Assistant Surgeon William Morrow Knox. Killed accidentally, at Louisville, Ky., April 27, 1862.
Assistant Surgeon T. P. Tomlinson. Died September 7, 1865.

Seventy-ninth Pennsylvania Infantry.

Captain John H. Dysart. Died, February 8, 1862, of disease, at Louisville, Ky.
Captain Samuel J. Boone. Killed at Perryville, October 8, 1862.
Captain Lewis Heidegger. Killed at Chickamauga, September 19, 1863.
Second Lieut. Henry J. Test. Killed at Perryville, October 8, 1862.
Second Lieut. Frederick Strasbaugh. Died, September 20, 1863, of wounds received at Chickamauga.

One Hundred and Ninth Pennsylvania Infantry.

First Lieut. James Glendening. Killed at Wauhatchie, October 29, 1863.

APPENDIX.

One Hundred and Eleventh Pennsylvania Infantry.

Colonel George A. Cobham, Jun. Killed at Peach Tree Creek, July 20, 1864.
Major John A. Boyle. Killed at Wauhatchie, October 29, 1863.
Captain Charles Woeltge. Killed at Resaca, May 15, 1864.
Captain Martellus H. Todd. Killed at New Hope Church, May 25, 1864.
Captain Hiram L. Blodget. Died, August 5, 1864, of disease.
Second Lieut. Marvin D. Pettit. Killed at Wauhatchie, October 29, 1863.

One Hundred and Forty-seventh Pennsylvania Infantry.

Captain Charles S. Davis. Died, November 28, 1863, of wounds received at Taylor's Ridge.
Captain Samuel F. McKee. Died, June 25, 1864, of wounds received in action.

TENNESSEE.

First Tennessee Cavalry.

Captain Alfred J. Lane. Killed in action, July 1, 1863.
Captain Elbert J. Canon. Died, January 3, 1864, of wounds received at Mossy Creek.
Captain Nelson Bowman. Died, October 22, 1864, of wounds, at Bull's Gap, Tenn.
First Lieut. Adam L. Whitehead. Died, ——, 1862.
First Lieut. George W. Cox. Died, December 30, 1863, of wounds received at Mossy Creek.
Second Lieut. John Roberts. Died, July 29, 1864, of wounds received in action.
Second Lieut. Thomas T. Hull. Died, February 9, 1865, at Memphis, Tenn.

Second Tennessee Cavalry.

Captain James H. Morris. Killed at Stone River, January 1, 1863.
Captain Aaron G. McReynolds. Died, October 27, 1864, of wounds received in action.

Third Tennessee Cavalry.

Major Albert C. Catlett. Died, March 24, 1864, of disease, at Nashville, Tenn.
Captain Gid. R. Griffith. Died, July 11, 1863, at Nashville, Tenn.
First Lieut. John W. White. Died, March 16, 1863, at Murfreesboro, Tenn.
First Lieut. George E. Curton. Killed in action, September 25, 1864.
First Lieut. Robert B. Hunter. Died, December 22, 1864, at Nashville, Tenn.
Assistant Surgeon Frederick Wagner. Killed in action, September 25, 1864.

Fourth Tennessee Cavalry.

Captain Daniel Meader. Drowned bathing, August 8, 1863.
Captain Henry C. Kerner. Died, October ——, 1864, of wounds received in action.
Captain Robert W. Ragon. Died, June 4, 1865, of disease.
Second Lieut. John P. Harper. Died April 14, 1865.

Fifth Tennessee Cavalry.

Captain A. T. Julian. Killed in action, March 18, 1863.
Surgeon Joseph B. Moore. Killed by guerrillas, September 5, 1864.

APPENDIX.

Eighth Tennessee Cavalry.
Captain Willey Galyou. Died, at Nashville, Tenn., March 25, 1864.
First Lieut. Pryor L. Mason. Killed in action, July 29, 1863.

Ninth Tennessee Cavalry.
Captain William J. Trotter. Died June 28, 1854.

Tenth Tennessee Cavalry.
Major William P. Story. Died, December 27, 1864, of wounds received in action.
First Lieut. Judson Wise. Died, June 3, 1864, of disease.

Twelfth Tennessee Cavalry.
Major Sater Boland. Died, December 31, 1864, of wounds received in action at Franklin.
Captain Andrew J. Sullivan. Killed by guerrillas, April 20, 1864.
Captain John C. Rodgers. Killed in action, June 14, 1864.
Captain John C. Penoyer. Died, July 14, 1864, at Pulaski, Tenn.
First Lieut. Chauncey Cunningham. Killed in action, at Florence, Ala., August 10, 1864.
First Lieut. William T. Ford. Killed near Shoal Creek, Ala., November 8, 1864.
Second Lieut. William J. Rankin. Died, December 18, 1864, of wounds received in action.

Thirteenth Tennessee Cavalry.
Lieut. Colonel William H. Ingerton. Died, December 8, 1864, of wounds.
Captain Richard H. Luttrell. Died, January 20, 1864, at Camp Nelson, Ky.
Captain James B. Wyatt. Killed in action, December 12, 1864.
Captain William M. Gourley. Killed in action, in Marion, Va., December 13, 1864.

First Tennessee Infantry.
Lieut. Colonel Milton L. Phillips. Died December 25, 1863.
Second Lieut. Thomas Pierce. Died, January 17, 1863, at Murfreesboro, Tenn.

Second Tennessee Infantry
Captain William H. Cowan. Died April 12, 1862.
Captain Elihu E. Jones. Died, May 21, 1862, of disease.
Captain John L. Sneed. Died, February 14, 1863, of wounds received at Stone River.
Captain Francis M. Skaggs. Died, May 19, 1863, of disease.
First Lieut Abraham Meyrs. Died, March 25, 1862, of wounds received in action.
Second Lieut. John Brown. Died February 13, 1863.
Second Lieut. Charles O. McBee. Killed in action, October 14, 1863.

Tenth Tennessee Infantry.
First Lieut. William C. Shelbey. Killed accidentally, August 26, 1863.
Second Lieut. Patrick Sullivan. Died, September 16, 1862, of wounds.
Assistant Surgeon Charles Johnson. Killed by a fall from his horse, April 5, 1863.

WISCONSIN.

First Wisconsin Cavalry.

Second Lieut. Charles Clinton. Died, March 29, 1864, at Murfreesboro, Tenn.
Second Lieut. Sheldon E. Vosburg. Died, April 16, 1865, of wounds received in action.

Fifth Wisconsin Battery.

Captain Oscar F. Pinney. Died, February 17, 1863, of wounds received at Stone River.
Second Lieut. Almon Smith. Died, August 23, 1862, of disease.

Eighth Wisconsin Battery.

Captain Stephen J. Carpenter. Killed at Stone River, December 31, 1862.

First Wisconsin Infantry.

Captain William S. Mitchell. Killed at Chickamauga, September 19, 1863.
Captain Abner O. Heald. Killed at Chickamauga, September 19, 1863.
First Lieut. Robert J. Nickles. Killed at Chickamauga, September 19, 1863.
First Lieut. Charles A. Searles. Killed at Chickamauga, September 19, 1863.
Second Lieut. Jarius S. Richardson. Died, October 5, 1863, of wounds received at Chickamauga.
Second Lieut. Collins C. McVean. Died, June 22, 1864, of wounds received in action.
Assistant Surgeon Egbert Jamieson. Died, June 17, 1863, of disease.

Third Wisconsin Infantry.

Captain James W. Hunter. Died, June 8, 1864, of wounds received in action.
Captain Thomas E. Orton. Died, July 25, 1864, of wounds received before Atlanta, Ga.
First Lieut. John H. Meigs. Died May 7, 1865.
Chaplain John M. Springer. Died, May 29, 1864, of wounds received at Resaca.

Tenth Wisconsin Infantry.

Lieut. Colonel John H. Ely. Died, October 4, 1863, of wounds received in action.
Major Henry O. Johnson. Killed at Perryville, October 8, 1862.
Captain William Moore. Killed by guerrillas, July 4, 1862.
Captain George M. West. Killed at Chickamauga, September 19, 1863.
First Lieut. Robert Rennie. Killed at Chickamauga, September 19, 1863.
First Lieut. Chester A. Burdick. Died, September 17, 1864, of disease, at Charleston, S. C.

Thirteenth Wisconsin Infantry.

Colonel David E. Wood. Died, June 17, 1862, of disease.
Captain George E. Waldo. Killed at Shiloh, April 7, 1862.
Captain Levi W. Vaughn. Killed at Corinth, Miss., October 3, 1862.
Captain Samuel Harrison. Died of wounds received at Corinth, Miss.

APPENDIX.

Fifteenth Wisconsin Infantry.

Colonel Hans C. Heg. Died of wounds received at Chickamauga, September 20, 1863.
Lieut. Colonel David McKee. Killed at Stone River, December 31, 1862.
Captain John Ingmandson. Killed at Stone River, December 30, 1862.
Captain John M. Johnson. Killed at Chickamauga, September 19, 1863.
Captain Haus Hansen. Died, October 13, 1863, of wounds received at Chickamauga.
Captain Henry Hauff. Killed at Chickamauga, September 19, 1863.
First Lieut. Andrew Clement. Died, September 23, 1864, of disease, at Briggsville, Wis.
Second Lieut. Oliver Thompson. Killed at Chickamauga, September 20, 1863.

Twenty-first Wisconsin Infantry.

Major Frederick Schumacher. Killed at Perryville, October 8, 1862.
Captain George Bently. Killed at Perryville, October 8, 1862.
Captain Hiram M. Gibbs. Died, October 15, 1862, of wounds received at Perryville.
Captain John Jewett, Jun. Died, November 21, 1862, of disease, at Mitchellsville, Tenn.
First Lieut. Edward T. Midgley. Killed at Bentonville, March 19, 1865.
Second Lieut. David Mitchell. Killed at Perryville, October 8, 1862.
Second Lieut. Henry C. Taylor. Died, December 12, 1864, at Charleston, S. C., a prisoner.
Surgeon Samuel J. Carolin. Died, November 4, 1862, at Bowling Green, Ky.

Twenty-second Wisconsin Infantry.

Captain Gustavus Goodrich. Died, March 17, 1863, at Racine, Wis.
Captain Marshall W. Patton. Died, May 19, 1864, of wounds received at Resaca.
First Lieut. John E. Holmes, R. Q. M. Died, May 8, 1863, at Annapolis, Md.
Second Lieut. Ephraim K. Newman. Died, December 25, 1862, as Nicholasville, Ky.
Second Lieut. David Flint. Died, May 27, 1864, at Chattanooga, Tenn., of wounds.

Twenty-fourth Wisconsin Infantry.

Captain Gustavus Goldsmith. Died, October 3, 1863, of wounds received at Chickamauga.
Captain Howard Greene. Killed at Missionary Ridge, November 25, 1863.
Captain Frederick A. Root. Died, December 2, 1863, at Chattanooga, Tenn.
Captain Alvah Philbrook. Killed at Franklin, November 30, 1864.
First Lieut. Robert J. Chivas. Killed at Missionary Ridge, November 25, 1863.
First Lieut. Thomas T. Keith. Killed in action at Adairsville, Ga., May 17, 1864.
First Lieut. Frederick Schlenstedt. Killed at Jonesboro, September 1, 1864.
Second Lieut. Christian Nix. Died, January 1, 1863, of wounds received at Stone River.
Second Lieut. George Bleyer. Died, January 25, 1863, of wounds received at Stone River.

APPENDIX.

Twenty-sixth Wisconsin Infantry.

Captain John P. Seeman. Killed at Peach Tree Creek, July 20, 1864.
Captain Robert Mueller. Killed at Peach Tree Creek, July 20, 1864.
Captain Carl Schmidt. Killed at Averysboro, March 16, 1865.
First Lieut. Christian Phillip. Killed at Resaca, May 15, 1864.
First Lieut. Nicholas Wolmer. Died, August 21, 1864, of wounds received at Peach Tree Creek.
First Lieut. Francis Rudolph Klein. Killed at Averysboro, March 16, 1865.

Thirty-first Wisconsin Infantry.

Major William J. Gibson. Died, September 9, 1863, of disease, at Columbus, Ky.
Captain James B. Mason. Died, October 17, 1863, of disease, at Nashville, Tenn.
Second Lieut. Gilbert N. Rodgers. Died, August 12, 1864, of disease.

Twelfth Colored Infantry.

Captain Robert Headin. Died, January 1, 1865, of wounds received at Nashville, Tenn.
First Lieut. William L. Clark. Killed, November 21, 1864.
Second Lieut. David G. Cook. Killed near Murfreesboro, Tenn., December 24, 1864.
Second Lieut. Dennis Dease. Died, December 25, 1864, of wounds received at Nashville.

Thirteenth Colored Infantry.

First Lieut. George Taylor. Killed at Nashville, December 16, 1864.
First Lieut. J. W. Woodruff. Killed at Nashville, December 16, 1864.
Second Lieut. James A. Trom. Killed at Nashville, December 16, 1864.
Second Lieut. Luther L. Parks. Killed at Nashville, December 16, 1864

Fourteenth Colored Infantry.

First Lieut. George W. Apthorp. Died, October 28, 1864, of wounds received at Decatur.
Second Lieut. Frank Gillett. Died, October 28, 1864, of wounds received at Decatur.
Second Lieut. Charles Woodworth. Killed in action at Decatur.

Fifteenth Colored Infantry.

Assistant Surgeon Eli M. Hewitt. Killed by guerrillas, near Springfield, Tenn., July 24, 1864.
Second Lieut. Edward Long. Died, March 15, 1866, of disease, at Nashville, Tenn.

Seventeenth Colored Infantry.

Captain Gideon V. Ayres. Killed in action at Nashville, December 15, 1864.
Captain Job H. Aldrich. Killed in action at Nashville, December 15, 1864.
First Lieut. George L. Clark. Died of wounds received at Nashville, January 7, 1865.

APPENDIX. 435

Eighteenth Colored Infantry.
First Lieut. Leander Martin. Killed in action at Sand Mountain, Ala., January 27, 1865.
Forty-fourth Colored Infantry.
Captain Charles G. Penfield. Murdered, after capture, by Forrest's Command, December 22, 1864.

One Hundredth Colored Infantry.
Assistant Surgeon Edward M. Wash. Died, September 20, 1865, of disease, at Columbus, Tenn.

One Hundred and First Colored Infantry.
Captain Stephen H. Eno. Died, December 16, 1865, of disease, at Nashville, Tenn.

One Hundred and Eleventh Colored Infantry.
Colonel Wm. H. Lathrop. Killed in action at Sulphur Branch Trestle, Ala., September 25, 1864.

NAMES OF OFFICERS APPOINTED BY THE PRESIDENT, IN THE VOLUNTEER SERVICE, WHO FELL IN THE WAR, OR DIED FROM WOUNDS OR SICKNESS.

Major-General William Nelson, U. S. N. Died at Louisville, Ky., September 29, 1862.
Brigadier-General Wm. R. Terrill, Captain U. S. A. Killed at Perryville, October 8, 1862.
Lieutenant-Colonel George E. Flint, A. A. G., Chief of Staff, Fourteenth Corps. Died, 1864.
Surgeon Abraham L. Cox. Died on Lookout Mountain, Tenn., July 28, 1864.
Surgeon R. W. S. Jackson. Died on Lookout Mountain, Tenn., January 18, 1865.
Captain Henry Clay, A. A. G. Died, June 5, 1862, at Louisville, Ky.
Captain Richard Stevenson, A. Q. M. Died, October 5, 1862, at Louisville, Ky.
Captain William C. Russell, A. A. G. Killed at Chickamaugua, September 20, 1863.
Captain Edward D. Saunders, A. A. G. Killed in action at Allatoona Creek, June 2, 1864.
Captain R. J. Waggener, A. A. G. Killed at Dallas, Ga., May 28, 1864.
Captain Oscar O. Muller, A. A. G. Killed at Jonesboro, Ga., September 2, 1864.
Captain John A. Irvine, C. S. Died, March 1, 1865, at Nashville, Tenn.
Captain Samuel A. Bonsall, A. Q. M. Died at Gallatin Tenn., July 19, 1865.
Captain S. H. Sunt, A. Q. M. Died, July 28, 1865, at Mobile, Ala.

NAMES OF OFFICERS OF THE REGULAR ARMY, SERVING ACCORDING TO ARMY RANK, WHO FELL IN BATTLE OR DIED FROM WOUNDS OR DISEASE DURING THE WAR.

Colonel Edward A. King, 6th U. S. Infanty. Killed at Chickamauga, September 20, 1863.

Colonel Julius P. Gareschè, Chief-of-Staff to General Rosecrans. Killed at Stone River, December 31, 1862.

Major S. D. Carpenter, 19th U. S. Infantry. Killed at Stone River, December 31, 1862.

Major Sidney Coolidge, 16th U. S. Infantry. Killed at Stone River, December 31, 1862.

Captain Wm. H. Acker. Killed at Shiloh, April 7, 1862.

Captain Patrick T. Kayes, 16th U. S. Infantry. Died, May 3, 1862, of wounds received at Shiloh.

Captain J. B. Bell, 15th U. S. Infantry. Killed at Stone River, December 31, 1862.

Captain Charles L. Kneass, 18th Infantry. Killed at Stone River, December 31, 1862.

Captain Wm. W. Wise, 15th U. S. Infantry. Died, January 3, 1863, of wounds received at Stone River.

Captain Charles E. Dennison, 18th U. S. Infantry. Died, June 15, 1863, of wounds received at Stone River.

Captain John A. Thompson, 18th U. S. Infantry. Killed at Hoover's Gap, June, 1863.

Captain David Ireland, 15th U. S. Infantry. Died at Atlanta, Ga., September 10, 1864.

Captain Wm. H. Ingerton, 16th U. S. Infantry. Died at Knoxville, Tenn., December 8, 1864.

First Lieut. Irwin W. Wallace, 18th U. S. Infantry. Died at Pittsburgh, Pa., February 19, 1862.

First Lieut. William W. Stevenson, 16th U. S. Infantry. Died, February 27, 1862, at Louisville, Ky.

First Lieut. Edward L. Mitchell, 16th U. S. Infantry. Killed at Shiloh, April 7, 1862.

First Lieut. James W. Bingham, 16th U. S. Infantry. Died at Bardstown Ky., November 9, 1862.

First Lieut. Herman G. Radcliffe, 18th U. S. Infantry. Killed at Stone River, December 18, 1862.

First Lieut. James L. Simonds, 18th U. S. Infantry. Died, June 14, 1863, of wounds received at Stone River.

First Lieut. Joseph McConnell, 18th U. S. Infantry. Died, January 14, 1863, of wounds received at Stone River.

First Lieut. Howard M. Burnham, Battery H, 5th U. S. Artillery. Killed at Chickamauga, September 19, 1863.

First Lieut. Charles L. Truman, 18th U. S. Infantry. Killed at Chickamauga, September 20, 1863.

APPENDIX. 437

First Lieut. Michael B. Fogarty, 19th U. S. Infantry. Killed at Chickamauga, September 20, 1863.
First Lieut. Lucius F. Brown, 18th U. S. Infantry. Died at Chattanooga, October 10, 1863, of wounds received at Chickamauga.
First Lieut. Homer H. Clarke, 16th U. S. Infantry. Died at Nashville, October 21, 1863, of wounds received at Chickamauga.
First Lieut. Tillinghast L'Hommedieu, 4th U. S. Cavalry. Died at Pulaski, Tenn., December 31, 1863, of disease.
First Lieut. William H. Leamy, 19th U. S. Infantry. Died, July 11, 1864, of disease, at Chattanooga, Tenn.
First Lieut. Samuel J. Dick, 18th U. S. Infantry. Died, December 28, 1864, of disease, at Nashville, Tenn.
First Lieut. Edward Fitzgerald, 4th U. S. Cavalry. Died, February 16, 1865, of disease, at Nashville, Tenn.
First Lieut. Elbridge G. Roys, 4th U. S. Cavalry, Killed at Selma, Ala., April 2, 1865.
First Lieut. Arthur N. Thompson, 16th U. S. Infantry. Died July 13, 1865, at New Orleans, La.
First Lieut. George H. Burns, 15th U. S. Infantry. Died, October 15, 1865, of disease, at Mobile, Ala.
First Lieut. William A. Garland, 19th U. S. Infantry. Died, December 1, 1865, of disease, at Augusta, Ga.
First Lieut. Charles M. Reed, 19th U. S. Infantry. Died, December 8, 1865, of disease, at Augusta, Ga.
First Lieut. Douglas Edwards, 19th U. S. Infantry. Died, December 24, 1865, of disease, at Augusta, Ga.
Second Lieut. John F. Hitchcock, 18th U. S. Infantry. Killed at Stone River, December 31, 1862.
Second Lieut. Thomas Healey, 4th U. S. Cavalry. Died of wounds, at Franklin, Tenn., April 23, 1863.
Second Lieut. Francis C. Wood, 4th U. S. Cavalry. Died, May 23, 1863, of wounds received at Middleton, Tenn.
Second Lieut. Charles F. Miller, 19th U. S. Infantry. Died of wounds received at Chickamauga, September 22, 1863.
Second Lieut. John Lane, 18th U. S. Infantry. Died, October 15, 1863, of wounds received at Chickamauga.
Second Lieut. Robert Floyd, 3d U. S. Artillery. Died, September 23, 1863, of wounds received at Chickamauga.
Second Lieut. Henry C. Pohlman, 18th U. S. Infantry. Died, October 15, 1863, at Richmond, Va.
Second Lieut. Peter J. Covenzler, 16th U. S. Infantry. Killed at Missionary Ridge, November 25, 1863.
Second Lieut. Joseph C. Forbes, 15th U. S. Infantry. Killed at New Hope Church, Ga., May 31, 1864.

BLOCK-HOUSES, ETC.

THE ENGINEER SERVICE IN THE ARMY OF THE CUMBERLAND.

(By Brevet-Colonel W. E. Merrill, Major Engineers, late Chief Engineer Army Cumberland.)

The peculiarities of the country in which the Army of the Cumberland campaigned, developed novel modifications of many of the engineering appliances in general use by all fully equipped armies, and some of these are deserving of record, especially in a work that aims to be a complete history of the gallant army by whom they were used and for whom they were devised. In the present article, I will briefly call attention to three points of military engineering in which the experience of this army may be valuable to others that in the future may have to tread in similar paths of difficulty and danger. The three subjects to which I would invite attention are block-houses for railroad defense, canvas pontons, and military maps.

BLOCK-HOUSES FOR RAILROAD DEFENSE.

Among all the American armies that fought in the long civil war, the Army of the Cumberland was exceptional in being the only one that from the beginning to the end of its career fought exclusively along lines of railroad, was supplied wholly by railroad, had its depots at prominent railroad centers, fought for the possession of the railroad centers of the enemy, and in general was compelled to adapt its strategy and its tactics to the novel conditions imposed by the invention of railroads, and the total change in methods of transportation that had occurred since the great Napoleonic wars, from whose records students of the military art had hitherto derived their knowledge. No other American army acquired so great an experience in the art of defending railroads through hostile territory, and therefore it is believed that a brief statement should be made of the means by which these results were attained.

Supplies for the depot at Nashville were mainly received by rail from Louisville (one hundred and eighty-five miles), but whenever the stage of water permitted, the Cumberland and Tennessee rivers (the latter with the aid of the railroad from Johnsonville to Nashville—seventy-eight miles) were used as auxiliaries. South of Nashville, the only communication was by railroad. When the army was at Chattanooga, its only line of supply was the single-track railroad to Nashville (one hundred and fifty-one miles), and when, with the sister armies of the Tennessee and the Ohio, it pressed southward to Atlanta, the narrow iron band that connected them with their main depot at Louisville was lengthened out to four hundred and seventy-three miles, the whole distance being in territory either wholly or partly hostile. The success of the Southern campaigns depended entirely on holding this line with such tenacity that no serious break in it could be made by cavalry raids, or by the disaffected population of the district through which it passed. The destruction of a single important bridge would have made matters in front look very serious. The destruction of a number would have compelled the army to retrace its steps. It was therefore a vital matter to hold the railroads at all hazards, and it was almost equally important to arrange a system of railroad defenses that would require but few men at any one place, otherwise the invading army would soon become too much reduced to continue the offensive.

When, in January, 1864, I was appointed chief engineer of the Army of the Cumberland, which position I held from that time until the close of the war, the headquarters of the Army of the Cumberland was in Chattanooga, that of the Army of the Ohio in Knoxville, and that of the Army of the Tennessee in Huntsville—General Sherman being in chief command at Nashville. As Middle Tennessee, Northern Alabama, and Georgia, and the southern part of East Tennessee composed the Department of the Cumberland, the defenses of the railroads and fortified towns in this territory properly fell to my charge. A very interesting report could be made on the defenses of the three chief towns of Nashville, Murfreesboro, and Chattanooga; but though the works at the first two were very elaborate and highly creditable to the professional skill of General St. Clair Morton, Captain of Engineers, who designed them, there were no marked novelties in construction, and the influence of the works themselves on the campaigns was only indirect. Lack of space unfortunately prevents more than this passing mention. During the long halt of the Army of the Cumberland at Murfreesboro, the seven bridges on the thirty miles of railroad between it and Nashville were defended by heavy stockades built in the form of a Greek cross. These stockades were block-houses in all respects, except the possession of a roof. During the campaigns that culminated in the capture of Tullahoma and Chattanooga, detachments were left at various points on the railroad, but no systematic effort was made to erect engineering structures for railroad defense. The army was so busily occupied in endeavoring to maintain itself east of the Cumberland mountains, that it had no time to pay much attention to perfecting its conquests by permanently holding the country gained. Besides the main line of the Nashville and Chattanooga railroad, the course of events had given us possession of the line from Nashville to Decatur (along which the Army of the Tennessee was supplied), the portion of the Memphis and Charleston railroad between Decatur and Stevenson, the Northwestern railroad to Johnsonville, the railroad to Clarksville, and portions of the railroads extending northeast to Knoxville and southeast toward Atlanta. There was thus suddenly thrown on my hands for defense about six hundred miles of railroad, every foot of which lay in hostile territory, and was exposed to injury, not only from raids of regularly organized commands, but was also in danger from guerilla bands and from nominally peaceful citizens.

A similar problem had fallen to my lot, when, in the fall of 1862, the Army of Kentucky, commanded by General Gordon Granger, advanced from Cincinnati to Lexington, and had to rebuild all the bridges on the Kentucky Central railroad, except the trestle-work at Paris. General Granger ordered me to plan such fortifications as would prevent a recurrence of such a disaster. A brief examination showed me that the bridges as a rule were located at points where the land rose gradually on both sides for long distances, thus making it very difficult to place a fort near enough to protect the bridge, and at the same time to secure its occupants from plunging or reverse fires. Safety from this kind of attack necessitated cover over head, and as the requirements of the service called for the minimum garrisons at bridges which would be consistent with their adequate protection, I was naturally led to select the block-house as the only available means of defense.

It did not seem at all probable that any cavalry command that would be likely to get over the mountains into Central Kentucky would be accompanied by artillery, and therefore the block-houses were only planned to resist attack by musketry. I believe that some of them were captured in 1864 by a cavalry command, but I have the impression that the garrisons either evacuated the block-houses, or else surrendered them without a fight. I was with the army in Georgia at the time, and news from Central Kentucky was very meager. The plans of these Kentucky block-houses are shown in figures 1, 2, and 3, with the exception that the walls were of one thickness of timber, and there were no towers.

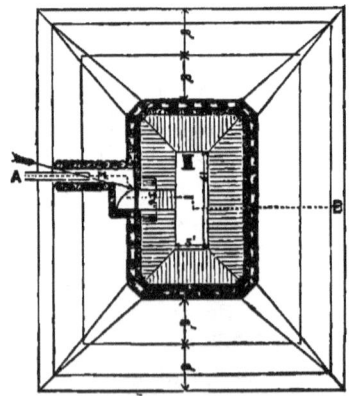

Fig. 1. Plan of Rectangular Block-house.

APPENDIX. 443

Fig. 2. Elevation of Rectangular Block-house.

Fig. 3. Section on A. B. (Fig. 1.)

When General Buell was campaigning in Kentucky and Tennessee his engineers constructed stockades for defending railroad bridges—a favorite form being that of a square redoubt with four circular bastions, the diameter of the latter being made the same as that of a Sibley tent, so that the bastions could be covered by these tents and used as men's quarters. These stockades answered a good purpose against infantry, but were worse than nothing against artillery, becoming at such times mere slaughter-pens. With this experience before me, I determined to endeavor to make my block-houses proof against such light artillery as cavalry might be expected to take with them. The Michigan Engineers (Colonel Innes) were assigned by General Thomas to the work of building the necessary block-houses, and accordingly I started out with Lieutenant-Colonel Huntoon (then commanding the regiment) on a tour of location, stopping at every bridge and selecting the most favorable sites for block-houses. While at Lavergne, I decided to change the location of the heavy stockade which had been built there while the army was at Murfreesboro, and therefore took advantage of the opportunity to try some experiments on its power to resist artillery. After hitting it a number of times with solid shot from a six-pounder, it became apparent that even the heavy timbers (from twenty to twenty-four inches in diameter) of which it was built, would not answer the purpose. I then decided to double the walls, so as to secure at least forty inches of timber.

The tower, or second story of the block-house, was valuable as giving a more elevated point from which to see the enemy, and, if necessary, to look over the railroad bank. It was set diagonally to the lower story so as to cover more thoroughly all the country around. To avoid excessive weight it was made log-house fashion of one thickness of logs, the expectation being that it would be vacated in case of artillery attack. Owing to the amount of work to be done, the construction of towers was left to the garrisons after the engineer troops had finished. As a matter of fact but few were built. The usual course was to employ engineer troops to build the block-houses of a single thickness of timber, without cellar or tower, and to employ the garrisons to finish the work under the direction of the inspectors of railroad defenses.

To resist plunging fire, the roof of the block-house was made of a layer of logs laid side by side and covered with earth. On top of all was a roof of shingles (when they could be procured), or of boards and battens—it being very important to keep the block-house dry, so that the garrison might always live in it. With the same view the block-houses were supplied with ventilators, cellars, water-tanks, and bunks.

It was foreseen from the first that a rectangular plan was not the best for a block-house, but the extra cost and difficulty of making the best form, the octagonal, and the great number that had to be built immediately, made it necessary to use the simplest plan that could be made to answer. Late in the war the octagonal plan, shown in Figs. 4 and 5, was adopted, and the result of my experience is, that this form is the best for an independent block-house. In the rectangular block-house each corner has but one loop-hole, and therefore the block-houses are of little offensive power along the diagonals through the corners. In the octagonal these corners are cut off, and the angles of the loop-holes are such that the fire of two faces

APPENDIX. 445

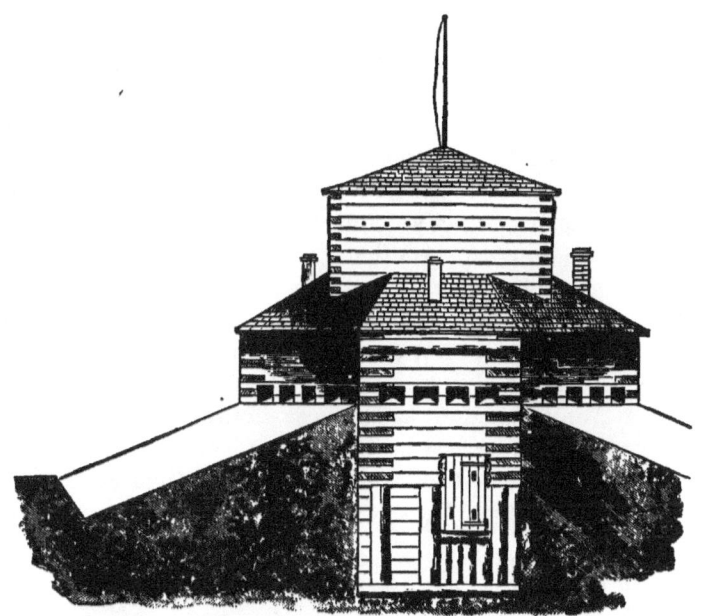

Fig. 4. Elevation of Octagonal Block-house. Bank removed from in front of Entrance.

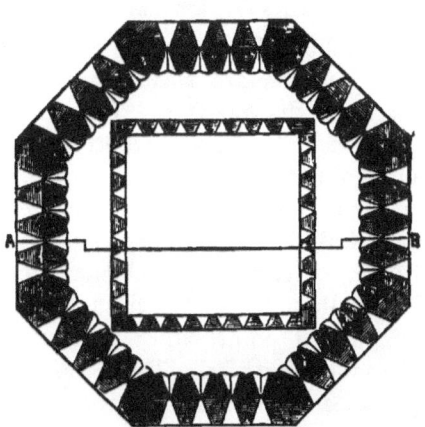

Fig. 5. Plan of Octagonal Block-house with Tower.

can always be concentrated on the diagonal through their intersection; the former weak points are thus made the strongest. I would therefore earnestly advise the use of octagonal

446 APPENDIX.

block-houses for railroad defense. So much time was consumed in making mortises and tenons, that I would advise for future block-houses a greater simplicity of joints and the liberal use of spikes, abolishing, as far as possible, all work requiring skilled labor. Spikes answered admirably on the Kentucky Central block-houses, but I was induced to try tenons in Tennessee, on account of having skilled labor available. I am now satisfied that the first method of construction was greatly preferable.

As a rule, the small railroad bridges had one block-house, and the larger ones two, on opposite sides of the track. At the very high and long trestle-work across the Running Water gorge at Whiteside, four small block-houses were built. For the protection of the east bridge over the Tennessee, at Bridgeport, I thought it best to establish two block-houses for artillery. The design of these works are given in Figs. 6 and 7.

FIG. 6.   ELEVATION OF ARTILLERY BLOCK-HOUSE.

An upper story (not shown in the figure), resting diagonally on the corners of the inner square, was added to the west block-house as quarters for the garrison. To avoid an excess of weight, this story was only made musketry-proof. On top of all was a small lookout. The construction of these block-houses reflected great credit upon the Michigan Engineers by whom they were built. An artillery block-house was also commenced in 1865, at Larkinsville, Alabama, but it was never completed. It was intended to answer as a fort for the garrison at this important point, which was much exposed to attack from the south side of the Tennessee. It is proper to add that my first idea of building a block-house for artillery came from seeing a rude, half-finished work of this kind, which was begun by the Confederates in 1863, at Strawberry Plains, above Knoxville.

An artillery block-house is difficult and costly to build, and is only justifiable in very exceptional localities. I think

APPENDIX. 447

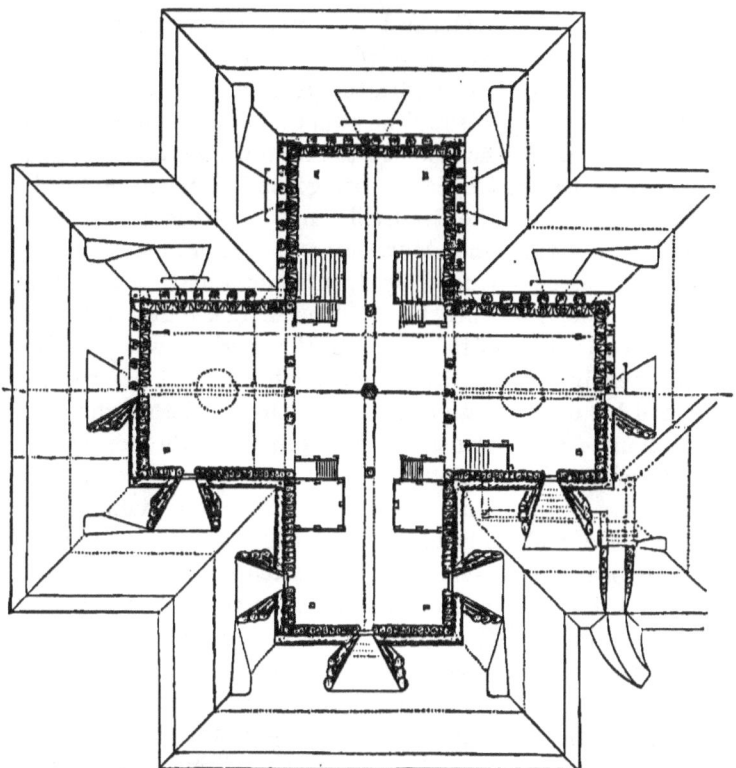

Fig. 7. Plan of Artillery Block-house.

that Bridgeport was such a locality, as the vital importance to the army of the two long bridges over the Tennessee called for defense by artillery, as well on the island as on the main land, and the latter so thoroughly commanded the island that artillery could only remain on it while thoroughly under cover. It may be well to mention that an artillery block-house after my designs was built in 1864, near Alexandria, Virginia, to protect from cavalry raids down the valley of Hunting creek.

The enemy soon found that our block-houses were proof against any ordinary attack, and small bodies never molested them. Injury to the track of the railroad was repaired almost as soon as made, and after a while such annoyances ceased. The only serious assaults received by our block-houses were as follows:

APPENDIX.

In August, 1864, General Wheeler, with a division of cavalry, left Atlanta, traveled north to near Knoxville, thence west to near Nashville, thence southwest to Northern Alabama. During this raid he swept along a large portion of the railroad from Chattanooga to Atlanta, and tore it up in some places, but destroyed no bridge and attacked no blockhouse. He struck the Nashville and Chattanooga railroad between Nashville and Murfreesboro, and attacked blockhouse No. 5, commanded by Lieutenant John S. Orr, One Hundred and Fifteenth Ohio. The artillery fire killed or wounded one-third of the garrison (the garrison was probably thirty men in all), but the gallant lieutenant did not surrender, and his bridge was not injured. One of the neighboring block-houses was commanded by a sergeant, who got demoralized and surrendered after a slight show of resistance. His bridge was burned, but I believe no other was damaged on this railroad, and no bridge at all on the railroad to Decatur.

In October, 1864, General Hood started north from Atlanta with his army, and General Sherman after him. All the blockhouses south of Dalton (except the one at Allatoona creek, which was captured) were evacuated by order and burned by his forces. After the capture of Dalton he wished to go west through Buzzard Roost Gap. In this gap, and at the bridge over Mill creek, was a block-house containing about thirty men. This block-house commanded the wagon-road through the gap, and no wagons or artillery could get through until it was captured. Bate's division of infantry, with three batteries of artillery, were detailed to capture the block-house. The infantry kept up an ineffectual musketry fire, and the artillery, after being driven from many positions, finally got on the diagonal through one corner and concentrated their shot on this corner. The weight of metal thrown soon made a breach in the block-house, but the garrison did not surrender, and at the close of the day they still held their position. During the night it was decided to organize a storming party, part of whom should stop the loop-holes with fence rails, while the other portion were to leap on the roof of the block-house and dig down to the garrison below. At daylight the storming party crept as near the block-house as possible; but before giving the command to charge, the colonel, desirous to save further bloodshed, in a loud voice summoned the garrison to surrender. A white handkerchief was waved in reply, and the block-house surrendered. Fully one-half of the small garrison were killed or wounded, and it seems that during the latter part of the preceding day, after many lives had been lost and the block-house had become entirely untenable, they had tried to surrender, but their signals were not seen and they had concluded that the Confederates were enraged at their obstinacy and were determined to kill them all. I regret that I can not give the names of this heroic garrison, as they were of course sent south with other prisoners, and I never had the fortune to meet any of them afterward. The details given above were obtained long after the war, from Confederate sources.

In a series of articles published in the New Orleans *Times* in the spring of 1874, General Hood reviews "Johnson's Narrative," and speaks as follows of the block-house in Buzzard Roost Gap:

"When *en route* to Tennessee, during the campaign in the fall of 1864, our army, having captured the troops stationed in Dalton, attempted to march through Mill-creek Gap, but was prevented from so doing by a squad of men posted within a little fort, covered with railroad iron and constructed of logs of large size, around which was thrown up an embankment of earth to protect the troops against field artillery; port-holes were cut so as to allow the men to fire in all directions, and especially upon the line of railroad.

"It was reported to me that field artillery had little or no effect upon this impromptu fortification, and that when the men charged up to it, they could not find an entrance; therefore it could not be taken without much loss of time and considerable cost.

"Major Kinlocke Falconer was, I think, severely wounded while experimenting with this little fortress, which obliged me to march some twenty miles around it."

This account differs somewhat from the one which I have given, but I think that General Hood is slightly in error in some of the details. He leaves the impression that the block-house was not captured, while I know that it was. He also speaks of it as an "impromptu" fortification, which it was not, having been carefully built by the Michigan Engineers, and finished before the capture of Atlanta.

It may be proper to add in explanation that the block-houses were not designed to defend bridges against a fully equipped army, but only against cavalry raids, and that a raiding band of cavalry is always too scantily supplied with artillery ammunition to indulge in the luxury of battering down a block-house.

The most serious destruction of block-houses occurred in September, 1864, during a raid made by General Forrest on the road leading south from Nashville to Decatur. The following account of this raid I afterward obtained from General Forrest himself. He first attacked an unfinished block-house near the southern end of the road, and the first shell fired from his battery entered the block-house and injured some of its occupants. They at once surrendered, and the block-house was burned. At the next block-house he ostentatiously paraded the captured commander of the first one; and on this convincing proof that block-houses could be taken, quite a number of them surrendered without a fight, and their bridges were burned. One German captain refused to surrender, but General Forrest had with him several bottles of a kind of Greek fire, and some of his men crept up behind the railroad embankment, and suddenly breaking the bottles on the ends of the bridge, set it on fire, and it was destroyed. The gallant captain and his command held their block-house, but unfortunately lost the bridge which it was to defend.

In all, General Forrest captured and destroyed eleven block-houses.

When General Hood, with his army, advanced to Nashville, the block-houses on the Nashville and Decatur railroad were very sensibly abandoned. Fortunately for us, the Nashville and Decatur railroad was not our main line, and the destruction of its bridges caused no serious loss.

From the time that the block-houses were built until the close of the war, but six bridges (all small) were burned on the Nashville and Chattanooga railroad, our main line of supply. These were the six nearest Nashville, one of them, as recorded above, having been previously burned by General Wheeler, and rebuilt. They were abandoned by order; but the seventh, at Overall's creek, five miles north of Murfreesboro, was ordered to be held. Its garrison consisted of about thirty men of the 115th O. V. I., commanded by Lieutenant H. H. Glosser. Bate's division of infantry (the same that fought the Buzzard Roost block-house), with a large force of cavalry and three twelve-pound guns, operated in its vicinity for two weeks, and fired seventy-two cannon-shot against it. Once during this time, a sortie was made from Murfreesboro, and the garrison's supplies of ammunition and provisions were replenished. The block-house was not captured nor the bridge burned.

To keep the block-houses and their garrisons thoroughly efficient, I organized a special corps of block-house inspectors, and placed at their head Major J. R. Willett, of my own regiment, the First U. S. Vet. Vol. Engineers. To his professional skill, zeal, and efficiency, the excellent results attained were mainly due.

In his Memoirs (vol. 2, pp. 146 and 398), General Sherman thus alludes to this system of railroad defense:

"All the important bridges were likewise protected by good block-houses, admirably constructed, and capable of a strong defense against cavalry or infantry."

"The Atlanta campaign would simply have been impossible without the use of the railroads from Louisville to Nashville, one hundred and eighty-five miles; from Nashville to Chattanooga, one hundred and fifty-one miles; and from Chattanooga to Atlanta, one hundred and thirty-seven miles. Every mile of this 'single track' was so delicate that one man could in a minute have broken or moved a rail, but our trains usually carried along the tools and means to repair such a break. We had, however, to maintain strong guards and garrisons at each important bridge or trestle, the destruction of which would have necessitated time for rebuilding. For the protection of a bridge, one or two log block-houses, two stories high, with a piece of ordnance and a small infantry guard, usually sufficed. The block-house had a small parapet and ditch about it, and the roof was made shot-proof, by earth piled on. These points could usually be reached only by a dash of the enemy's cavalry, and many of these block-houses successfully resisted serious attacks by both cavalry and artillery. The only block-house that was actually captured on the main [line] was the one described, near Allatoona."

General Sherman is mistaken about the piece of ordnance in each block-house. He was too far in front to be familiar with all these details.

He describes the capture of the block-house near Allatoona as follows (Memoirs, vol. 2, p. 149):

" Before finally withrawing [from the attack on Allatoona], General French converged a heavy fire of his cannon on the block-house at Allatoona creek, about two miles from the depot, set it on fire, and captured its garrison, consisting of four officers and eighty-five men."

The usual garrison of a block-house was from twenty to thirty men.

Besides their use in railroad defense, block-houses were freely employed in the defenses of Nashville, Murfreesboro, Stevenson, McMinnville, Chattanooga, and other fortified positions, occasionally as independent works, but usually as citadels or keeps for earthern forts, so that the garrison might have a secure place of retreat should the main work be carried by assault.

Nashville and Chattanooga Railroad, 151 miles. Fifty block-houses were built on this road, two being large block-houses for artillery. The majority of the block-houses had double walls, the chief exceptions being along Crow creek, where the probability of attack by artillery was very slight. One block-house near Nashville was captured by General Wheeler, three by General Hood (one being the first mentioned that had been rebuilt), and three were evacuated. These six had been partly rebuilt at the close of the war.

Nashville, Decatur and Stevenson Railroad, 200 miles. Fifty-four block-houses were built on this road, almost all of which had double walls. Eleven were surrendered to General Forrest, in October, 1864, and burned, the greater number having made no attempt at defense. When General Hood marched north to Nashville, the remaining block-houses, except three near Stevenson and four built in 1865, were abandoned, and the majority were burned by the enemy. Three, near Decatur, were not burned, but they were probably overlooked. When the war closed, a large number of the burned block-houses had been rebuilt on the octagonal plan, and work was under way on the others.

Chattanooga and Atlanta Railroad, 137 *miles*. Twenty-two block-houses were built on this road, all of which had double walls. Three of these were captured by General Hood's army, in October, 1864, and burned. Six others, south of Dalton, were abandoned, by order, when General Sherman tore up the railroad below Dalton, and left Atlanta for the sea. The others were held until the close of the war.

Chattanooga and Knoxville Railroad to Charleston, 42 *miles*. The only bridge on this road (within the limits of the Department of the Cumberland) that required defense was at the crossing of the Hiawassee river. Two block-houses were built here, which were held until the close of the war.

Nashville and Johnsonville Railroad, 78 *miles*. Twenty-three block-houses were commenced on this road, but only a few of them were finished. When Hood's army appeared before Nashville, the road was abandoned and the block-houses were burned, except the one nearest Johnsonville. At the close of the war twenty-five block-houses were under construction.

Louisville and Nashville Railroad to Kentucky line, 44 *miles*. One single-wall block-house was built at Edgefield Junction. The remainder of the road was protected by redoubts and stockades, built in 1862 and 1863. No serious damage was done on this line after Bragg's Kentucky campaign.

Nashville and Clarksville Railroad, 52 *miles*. This line began at Edgefield Junction, went to the Kentucky State line, by the Edgefield and Kentucky Railroad, and thence to Clarksville, by the Memphis Branch of the Louisville and Nashville Railroad. It was opened, as a supply route, in 1864, but was but little used. It was designed to connect at Clarksville with steamboats on the Cumberland River, that were unable to get over Harpath shoals. Eight single-wall block-houses were built on this line, but three of them were never fully completed. No damage was done to this road by the enemy.

CANVAS PONTON-TRAINS.

The canvas ponton-train used by the Army of the Cumberland was somewhat peculiar. The ordinary canvas ponton has long been in use in European armies, especially in Russia, and is made by putting together a skeleton-boat and drawing canvas over it. The usual length of such a boat is twenty-one feet, and this is the length of the two side-frames. These frames are usually carried on very long wagons, specially devised for the purpose; but as the Army of the Cumberland had to campaign in a country where the only dependence was upon a single-track railroad, it was of the utmost importance to devise some way of carrying their pontons in the ordinary army-wagon so as to avoid the cost of keeping up an independent ponton-train, whose services would only occasionally be required.

I believe that General Rosecrans first suggested cutting the frames in two for transportation, and uniting them when needed for use. At all events, when I became chief engineer I found that one such boat had been prepared, and seemed to do well. The two parts were connected by keys. After a careful examination, I decided to adopt such a boat for our army, but to replace the keys by permanent strap-hinges on the outside of the frames. I sent Captain O'Connell, of the Pioneer Brigade, to Nashville, with a detachment of pontoniers, to build a train of such boats, giving him authority to make any additional improvements that he or any one else could suggest. The result was the boat shown in the drawings (Fig. 8), excepting that the framing of the sides has been changed so as to conform more to the usual model. Some minor changes have also been made, but the boat is in essentials the same that was so successfully used to cross General Sherman's army

APPENDIX. 455

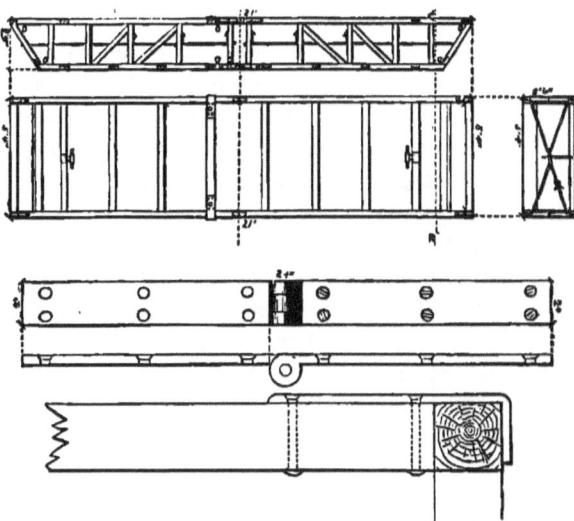

FIG. 8. FRAME OF HINGED CANVAS PONTON, WITH ENLARGED VIEW OF HINGE, AND OF MIDDLE BRACE.

over all the rivers between Chattanooga and Atlanta, and which afterward accompanied the army in its march to the sea and through the Carolinas. It answered its purpose admirably. So many persons contributed their mite toward the development of this boat that it is impossible to apportion the credit properly; but I think that Captain (afterward Major) O'Connell and Lieutenant (afterward Major) Willett deserve special mention.

General Sherman (Memoirs, vol. 2, p. 401) thus speaks of canvas pontons, his reference to the hinge showing that he had specially in mind the pontons of the Army of the Cumberland, as the frames of the other canvas ponton-train had no hinges:

"For the passage of rivers each army corps had a ponton-train with a detachment of engineers, and on reaching a river, the leading infantry division was charged with the labor of putting it down. Generally, the single ponton-train could provide for nine hundred feet of bridge, which sufficed; but when the rivers were very wide, two such trains would be brought together, or the single train was supplemented by a trestle-bridge, or bridges made on crib-work, out of the timber found near the place. The pontons in general use were skeleton frames, made with a hinge, so as to fold back and constitute a wagon-body. In this same wagon were carried the cotton canvas cover, the anchor and chains, and a due proportion of the balks, chesses, and lashings. All the troops became very familiar with their mechanism and use, and we were rarely delayed by reason of a river, however broad. I. saw recently, in Aldershot, England, a very complete ponton-train; the boats were sheathed with wood and felt, made very light; but I think they were more liable to chafing and damage in rough handling than were our less expensive and rougher boats. On the whole, I would prefer the skeleton frame and canvas cover to any style of ponton that I have ever seen."

MAPS.

The topographical department of the Army of the Cumberland consisted of the acting topographical engineers on each brigade, division, and corps staff, and the topographical engineers at department headquarters. The army was so far from Washington that it had to have a complete map establishment of its own. Accordingly, the office of the chief topographical engineer contained a printing press, two lithographic presses, one photographic establishment, arrangements for map-mounting, and a full corps of draughtsmen and assistants.

During the first year of the war, maps for field use were reproduced by photography; but these maps were objectionable on many accounts. Unless a very fine and expensive lens was used they were inaccurate at the borders, and sections of a large map would not join properly; they faded when exposed to sunlight; copies could not be made at night nor on rainy days; nor could a sufficient number be made even on the best days. For these reasons photography was gradually set aside for lithography; but as lithographic stones and presses were too heavy for an active campaign, they were left at the depot nearest to the front, and replaced by a fac-simile photo-printing device invented by Captain Margedant, chief assistant. This consisted of a light box containing several india-rubber baths, fitting into one another, and the proper supply of chemicals. Printing was done by tracing the required map on thin paper and laying it over a sheet coated with nitrate of silver. The sun's rays passing through the tissue paper blackened the prepared paper except under the ink lines, thus making a white map on black ground. By this means copies from the drawing-paper map could be made as often as new information came in, and occasionally there would be several editions of a map during the same day. The process, however, was expensive, and did not permit the printing of a large number of copies; therefore these maps were only issued to the chief commanders.

The map of Northern Georgia, on which the Atlanta campaign was based, was made by first enlarging the best printed map attainable, to the scale of one inch to the mile. This being used as a basis, the details were elaborated by cross-questioning refugees, spies, prisoners, peddlers, and any and all persons familiar with the country in front of us. It was remarkable how vastly our maps were improved by this process. The best illustration of the value of this method is the fact that Snake Creek Gap, through which our whole army turned the strong positions at Dalton and Buzzard Roost Gap, was not to be found on any printed map that we could get, and the knowledge of the existence of this gap was of immense importance to us. Sergeant Finnegan, of the Fourth Ohio Cavalry, had charge of this branch of the office, and became exceedingly expert in extracting information in this manner.

Two days before the army started from Chattanooga on the Atlanta campaign I received notice of the intended march. Up to this moment there was but one copy of the large map of Northern Georgia, and this was in the hands of the draughtsmen. I kept it back until the last moment so as to get on it the latest information that Sergeant Finnegan might be able to extract from the motley crew turned over by the Provost-Marshal General for examination.

The map was immediately cut up into sixteen sections and divided among the draughtsmen, who were ordered to work night and day until all the sections had been traced on thin paper in autographic ink. As soon as four adjacent sections were finished they were transferred to one large stone, and two hundred copies were printed. When all the map had thus been lithographed the map-mounters commenced their work. Being independent of sunlight the work was soon done—the map-mounting requiring the greatest time; but before the commanding generals left Chattanooga, each had received a bound copy of the map, and before we struck the enemy, every brigade, division, and corps commander in the three armies had a copy.

The copies for the cavalry were printed directly on muslin, as such maps could be washed clean whenever soiled and could not be injured by hard service. Many officers sent handkerchiefs to the office and had maps printed on them.

Although our map became less and less accurate as we advanced south from Chattanooga, it was still valuable even where its information was defective, because every subordinate commander had the same map as the commanding general, and therefore knew at once from the nature of his orders what he was expected to do. If a road could not be found, still the general direction and the general object of his march could be divined, and the spirit of the general's orders could be faithfully carried out.

I think that I am warranted in saying that the army that General Sherman led to Atlanta was the best supplied with maps of any that fought in the civil war.

INDEX.

ACKWORTH, GA., U. S. forces at, ii, 82.
ADAMS, GEN., driven from Rodgersville by U. S. forces, i, 131. Defeated by Col. Hambright, i, 132. Repulsed at Stone River, i, 242.
ALABAMA, expedition of Gen. O. M. Mitchell into, i, 130. Gen. J. H. Wilson's campaign in, ii, 347.
ALEXANDER, GEN. J. W. S., charges upon a battery at Stone River, i, 224. Operations of, in Alabama and Georgia, ii, 349.
ALESHIRE'S BATTERY, i, 291.
ALLATOONA PASS, the turning of, ii, 75.
ALTAMONT, concentration of Buell's forces at, i, 156.
AMMON, GEN. J., commands Tenth Brigade, Army of the Ohio, i, 69. In action at Shiloh, i, 107. Operations of, in East Tennessee, ii, 273.
ANDERSON CAVALRY, charge of, upon the enemy, i, 222.
ANDERSON, GEN. P., at battle of Missionary Ridge, i, 425.
ANDERSON, GEN. ROBERT, assigned to command Department of Kentucky, i, 20. Invokes Kentuckians to arm for expulsion of rebel invaders, i, 31. Proclamation of, i, 134. Relieved at his own request, i, 31. General orders of, i, 35.
ANDREWS, J. J., secret expedition of, to destroy railroad bridges in Georgia, i, 136.
ARMY OF THE CUMBERLAND, under Anderson, i, 22. Under Sherman, i, 35. Designation of, changed to "Army of the Ohio," under Buell, i, 46. Assumed its original name under Rosecrans, i, 207. Concentration of, at Nashville, i, 207. Roster of organization of, at battle of Stone River, i, 281. Re-equipment of, at Murfreesboro, i, 288. Roster of organization of, at the battle of Chickamauga, i, 378.

Thomas assigned to command of, i, 394. Attitude and condition of, early in 1864, ii, 13. Important changes made in, at Chattanooga, ii, 28. Strength of, at Chattanooga, ii, 30. Organization of, April, 1864, ii, 31. Loss of, during June, 1864, ii, 95. Casualties of, during the Atlanta campaign, ii, 149. During the campaign against Hood in Tennessee, ii, 248. Dissolution of, and summary of its achievements, ii, 369. Disposition of its heroic dead, ii, 377. See also Appendix as to organization of, ii, 381. List of its officers killed in battle, or who died in the service, ii, 386. Engineer service in, ii, 439.
ARMY OF KENTUCKY, under Gen. G. Granger, i, 290.
ARMY OF THE OHIO, constituted under Buell, i, 46. Strength of, i, 98. Discipline and valor of, at the battle of Shiloh, i, 116. Designation of, changed back to "Army of the Cumberland," i, 207.
ARMY OF THE TENNESSEE, arrives at Chattanooga, i, 410. McPherson assigned to command of, ii, 24. Howard succeeds McPherson in command of, ii, 124.
ASHBOTH, GEN. A., at siege of Corinth, i, 126.
ATHENS, ALA., occupied by Mitchell, i, 132.
ATLANTA, GA., campaign to, commenced, ii, 44. Advance upon, ii, 109. Siege of, ii, 123. Shelling of, ii, 140. Siege of, raised, ii, 140. Abandoned by Hood, ii, 147. Effects of the fall of, ii, 148. A large portion of, destroyed by Sherman, ii, 279.
AVERYSBORO, battle of, ii, 314.
BAIRD, GEN. A., at Stevens' Gap, i, 320. Joins Negley, i, 322. At Chickamauga, i, 334. At Missionary

(459)

Ridge, i, 428. In movement toward Dalton, ii, 20. Advance toward Tunnel Hill, ii, 26. At Ringgold, ii, 45. At New Hope Church, ii, 82. Before Kenesaw Mountain, ii, 88. Before Atlanta, ii, 127. At battle of Jonesboro, ii, 144. At battle of Bentonville, ii, 321.

BAKER, LIEUT. COL. M., killed before Atlanta, ii, 128.

BALDWIN, MAJ. L., mortally wounded at Peachtree Creek, ii, 116.

BALDWIN, COL. P. P., at battle of Stone River, i, 231. Report of the battle, i, 264. At Chickamauga, i, 335.

BATE, GEN. W. B., at battle of Chickamauga, i, 362. On Missionary Ridge, i, 430. At Buzzard Roost, ii, 49. Driven from Overall's Creek, ii, 223.

BARNES, COL. S. M., at battle of Chickamauga, i, 337.

BARNET, CAPT., at battle of Perryville, i, 187.

BARTON, GEN., commands rebel forces at Cumberland Gap, i, 133.

BARDSTOWN, KY., camp of instruction at, i, 72.

BATTLE CREEK, Gen. Mitchell at, i, 144.

BAUM, GEN., refuses to surrender Resaca, ii, 162.

BEATTY, GEN. J., drives the enemy at battle of Stone River, i, 261. At battle of Chickamauga, i, 345. At Missionary Ridge, i, 429.

BEATTY, GEN. S., commands Eleventh Brigade in Kentucky, i, 71. At battle of Stone River, i, 236. At battle of Chickamauga, i, 336. At battle of Nashville, ii, 229.

BEAUREGARD, GEN. G. T., succeeded A. S. Johnston in command at Shiloh, i, 108. Sends jubilant dispatch to Richmond, i, 108. Defeated, i, 114. Extract from report of battle of Shiloh, i, 125. At Corinth, i, 126. Withdraws his army, i, 129. Dispatches of to Hood and Cobb, ii, 208. To the people of Georgia, ii, 291. To Hardee at Savannah, ii, 303. Movements of at Charleston, ii, 307.

BECKET, MAJ. D. C., killed near Kenesaw Mountain, ii, 92.

BENTONVILLE, N. C., battle of, ii, 316.

BIG HILL, engagement at, i, 179.

BIG SHANTY, a depot of supplies for Sherman's army, ii, 88.

BLACKBURN, DR., pledges Kentucky to the rebels, i, 10.

BLAIR, GEN. F. P., at Missionary Ridge, i, 426. On the Knoxville campaign, ii, 1. Ordered to Kingston, ii, 74. Reaches Ackworth, ii, 83. On the march to the sea, ii, 278.

BLOCK-HOUSES, illustrations of, rectangular, ii, 442; octagonal, ii, 445; designs for artillery block-houses, ii, 446, 447; effectiveness of against Hood's forces, ii, 449. For railroad defense, ii, 452–454.

BLOODGOOD, LIEUT. COL., at Peachtree Creek, ii, 113.

BOARD OF TRADE BATTERY, at the battle of Selma, ii, 351.

BOONE, COL., raid into Georgia, ii, 17,

BOWLING GREEN, KY., capture of by Gen. O. M. Mitchell, i, 68.

BOYLE, GEN. J. T., opposed neutrality in Kentucky, i, 15. Placed in command at Columbia, i, 52. Resists Morgan in Kentucky, i, 146.

BRADLEY, GEN. L. P., report of battle of Stone River, i, 270. At battle of Chickamauga, i, 337. Engagement near Spring Hill, ii, 193.

BRAGG, GEN. B., repulsed at Shiloh, i, 107. Succeeds Beauregard, i, 139. Puts his army in motion for Tennessee, i, 140. Invades Kentucky, i, 158. Strength of, i, 158. Moves toward Nashville, i, 158. Gives battle at Perryville, i, 186. Failure of his campaign in Kentucky, i, 198. Extract from report of, i, 204. Line of battle and attack at Stone River, i, 228. Checked at all points, i, 245. Retreat of, i, 251. Strength and losses of at battle of Stone River, i, 252. Report of the battle, i, 255. Evacuates Tullahoma, i, 307. Retreats to Chattanooga, 1, 308. Evacuates Chattanooga, i, 316. Combination of against Negley, i, 320. Position of and plan of attack at Chickamauga, i, 327. Strength of at Chickamauga, i, 360. Losses of, i, 362. Before Chattanooga, i, 386. Part of army driven from Look-

out Mountain by Hooker, i, 399. Detaches Longstreet's corps, i, 403. Entire army on Missionary Ridge, i, 425. Defeat of, i, 433. Strength and loss at Chattanooga, i, 437. Removed from command in Georgia, ii, 14. Operations of in North Carolina, ii, 307. At battle of Bentonville, ii, 317.
BRAMLETTE, COL. T. E., takes arms to Camp Dick Robinson, i, 22. Moves to Lexington, i, 31.
BRANNAN, GEN. J. M., at Chickamauga, i, 333. Chief of artillery, i, 406. At Missionary Ridge, i, 430. Report of guns captured on Atlanta campaign, ii, 150.
BRECKINRIDGE, GEN. J. C., disloyalty of, in Kentucky, i, 6. Entered Rochester and Bowling Green, i, 71. Demands surrender of Nashville, i, 207. At the battle of Stone River, i, 227. At Chickamauga, i, 340. On Missionary Ridge, i, 425. Drives Gillem from Bull's Gap, ii, 272.
BRIDGE'S BATTERY, on Orchard Knob, i, 416.
BRIDGEPORT, ALA., capture of, i, 131.
BROWN, GEN., cavalry operations of, in North Carolina, ii, 342.
BROWN, LIEUT. COL. W. H. H., mortally wounded at Peachtree Creek, ii, 116.
BROWN'S FERRY, operations at, by Gen. W. F. Smith, i, 396.
BROWNLOW, COL., engagement of, at Sparta, ii, 6.
BRUCE, COL. S. D., commands Twenty-second Brigade, Army of the Ohio, i, 70. Routs a rebel force, i, 212.
BUCKNER, GEN. S. B., disloyalty of, i, 3. Inspector-General of militia in Kentucky, i, 9. At Camp Boone, Ky., i, 23. Attempt of to capture Louisville, i, 28. Withdrawal to Bowling Green, i, 29. Surrenders Fort Donelson to Grant, i, 86. At Perryville, i, 192. Moves against Negley in McLemore's Cove, i, 320. At battle of Chickamauga, i, 364. At Missionary Ridge, i, 425.
BUELL, GEN. D. C., assigned to command Department of the Ohio, i, 46. Early operations of, in Kentucky, i, 47. Advance of, to Nashville, i, 69. Sent troops to Grant 'without solicitation, i, 85. Movement of toward Shiloh, i, 100. Reaches Savannah, i, 103. At the battle of Shiloh, i, 109. Loss of, at Shiloh, i, 114. Letters to Halleck, i, 120, 121. Extract from report of battle of Shiloh, i, 124. At siege of Corinth, i, 126. Moving to support Pope, i, 140. Begins transfers of command to East Tennessee, i, 142. Orders his army to Murfreesboro, i, 158. Prepares to offer battle at Altamont, i, 156. Moves toward Louisville, i, 159. Letters to Halleck, i, 162. Letters to Thomas, i, 164-173. Campaign of Perryville, i, 184. Loss at battle of Perryville, i, 192. Dispatches relative to his removal, i, 200. Short report of, i, 201. Extract of letters to Halleck, i, 205. Superseded by Rosecrans, i, 206.
BUELL, COL. G. P., at Chickamauga, i, 337. Operations on Lookout Mountain, ii, 5. At Savannah, ii, 283. At battle of Bentonville, ii, 316.
BUFORD, GEN. A., at Duck River, ii, 191.
BULL's GAP, Gillem defeated at, by Breckinridge, ii, 272.
BURBRIDGE, GEN., operations of, in East Tennessee, ii, 273.
BURKE, LIEUT. COL., at Stewart's Creek, i, 247.
BURNSIDE, GEN. A. E., urged to cooperate with Rosecrans against Bragg, i, 365-367. In critical position at Knoxville, i, 436.
BURNT HICKORY, ii, 74.
BUSH's BATTERY, at Perryville, i, 188. Two guns of captured, i, 237.
BUSCHBECK, COL. A., at Missionary Ridge, i, 427. Near Dallas, ii, 76.
BUTTERFIELD, GEN. D., examination of railroads by, ii, 22. At battle of Resaca, ii, 65. At New Hope Church, ii, 76. Before Kenesaw Mountain, ii, 91.
BUZZARD's ROOST, operations at, ii, 47. Hood's attack of blockhouse at, ii, 452.
CAMP CLAY, established near Cincinnati, i, 14.
CAIRO, strategic importance of, i, 80.

462 INDEX.

CAMP DICK ROBINSON, KY., established i, 16. Efforts to prevent transmission of arms to, i, 21.
CAMP JOE HOLT, established by Rousseau, i, 16.
CAMPBELL, COL. A. P., expedition against Wheeler, i, 388. Action of at Mossy Creek, ii, 16.
CANBY, GEN. E. R. S., intercepts President Davis' order to Smith and Magruder, ii, 157. Dispatch of, to Sherman, ii, 179.
CANDY, COL. C., near Dallas, ii, 76.
CARLIN, GEN. W. P., at Perryville, i, 191. At Nolensville, i, 220. Report of battle of Stone River, i, 267. At Chickamauga, i, 336. At Lookout Mountain, i, 421. At Missionary Ridge, i, 429. Expedition toward Dalton, ii, 19. At Buzzard Roost, ii, 49. At battle of Resaca, ii, 66. At battle of Jonesboro, ii, 144. At battle of Bentonville, ii, 315.
CARMAN, COL., at Savannah, ii, 287. Extract from report of the capture of Savannah, ii, 302.
CARTER, GEN. S. P., ordered to join Thomas in Kentucky, i, 46. At battle of Mill Springs, i, 56. At Cumberland Gap, i, 78. Raid into East Tennessee, i, 216.
CHALMERS, GEN. J. R., demands the surrender of Munfordsville, i, 160. At Duck River, ii, 191.
CHARLESTON, S. C., evacuated, ii, 309.
CHARLOTTE, N. C., threatened by Slocum, ii, 301.
CHATTAHOOCHEE RIVER, Johnston retreats across, ii, 111.
CHATTANOOGA, TENN., Negley's demonstration against, i, 132. Buell's advance toward, i, 139. Importance of, i, 140. Occupied by Bragg, i, 310. Evacuated by Bragg, i, 316. Occupied by Crittenden, i, 318. Battles of, i, 386. Fortifications and topography of, 406. National Cemetery established at, by Thomas, ii, 377.
CHATTANOOGA AND ATLANTA RAILROAD, defenses of, ii, 453.
CHATTANOOGA AND KNOXVILLE RAILROAD, defenses of, ii, 453.
CHATTOOGA MOUNTAIN, ii, 48.
CHEATHAM, GEN. B. F., at Perryville, i, 193. At battle of Stone River, i,
227. At Chickamauga, i, 336. At Missionary Ridge, i, 427. In South Carolina, ii, 309. At battle of Bentonville, ii, 317.
CHERAW, S. C., entered by the Seventeenth Corps, ii, 311.
CHICKAMAUGA CAMPAIGN, and battle of, i, 310–385.
CHILDS, LIEUT. J. W., captures rebel general J. P. M. Maury, i, 136.
CHILDS, COL., i, 177.
CHURCH'S BATTERY, i, 245.
CINCINNATI, O., Anderson's headquarters at, i, 120. Threatened by Gen. E. K. Smith, i, 183.
CLEBURN, GEN. P. R., at Stone River, i, 227. At Chickamauga, i, 337. On Missionary Ridge, i, 423. At Dalton, ii, 21. At New Hope Church, ii, 79. Killed at Franklin, ii, 201.
COBB, GEN. H., routed near Macon by Walcutt, ii, 280. Communication of, to Wilson, ii, 360.
COBHAM, COL., at Lookout Mountain, i, 420. Killed at Peachtree Creek, ii, 116.
COBURN, COL. J., attacks Van Dorn, i, 201. Surrenders, i, 292. Expeditions against guerrilla bands, ii, 6. At battle of Resaca, ii, 68. Enters Atlanta, ii, 147.
COCKERILL'S BATTERY, at Chickamauga, i, 339.
COGSWELL, GEN., at battle of Bentonville, ii, 319.
COLUMBIA, S. C., capture and burning of, ii, 309.
COLUMBIA, TENN., occupied by U. S. troops, i, 131.
COLUMBUS, GA., captured by Wilson's forces, ii, 355.
COLUMBUS, KY., occupation of, by Gen. Polk, i, 33.
CONKLING, MAJ., killed, i, 181.
CONNELL, COL. J. M., at London and Rock Castle Hills, i, 381. At Chickamauga, i, 334.
CONRAD, COL., at battle of Franklin, ii, 198.
COON, COL., engages the enemy at Shoal's Creek, ii, 188. Charge of at battle of Nashville, ii, 232.
COOPER, SURGEON G. E., report of on Atlanta campaign, ii, 150.
COOPER, GEN., at battle of Nashville, ii, 332.

INDEX. 463

CORINTH, importance of position of, i, 97. Siege and fall of, i, 126.
CORSE, GEN. J. M., at Missionary Ridge, i, 427. Ordered to Rome, ii, 158. Attacked at Allatoona, ii, 161. Destroys foundries, mills, etc., at Rome, ii, 278.
COUCH, GEN. D. N., at battle of Nashville, ii, 229.
Cox's BATTERY, i, 243.
Cox, GEN. J. D., takes Kentucky regiments to West Virginia, i, 15. At Lynnville, ii, 188. Intercepts Hood near Columbia, ii, 189. Repulsed enemy's attacks, ii, 194. At battle of Franklin, ii, 196. At battle of Nashville, ii, 229.
CRAIGHILL, LIEUT. W. P., constructs fortifications, i, 176.
CRAWFISH SPRINGS, i, 340.
CREIGHTON, COL., at Lookout Mountain, i, 420. Killed near Ringgold, i, 436.
CRITTENDEN, GEN. GEORGE, in command of Confederates at battle of Mill Springs, i, 55.
CRITTENDEN, GEN. T. L., brigadier-general of Kentucky militia, i, 9. Urges members of the State Guard to enter the U. S. service, i, 31. Proclamation of, i, 34. Assigned to command of Fifth Division, i, 71. Moves to Nashville, i, 72. At battle of Shiloh, i, 109. At Corinth, i, 126. Assigned to command of a corps, i, 184. At Perryville, i, 186. Hotly engaged at Stone River, i, 242. Report of the battle, i, 275. Occupies Chattanooga and Rossville, i, 318. At the battle of Chickamauga, i, 348.
CROOK. GEN. G., at Carthage, Tenn., i, 290. At Dougherty Gap, i, 327. Expedition against Wheeler, i, 387. Saves Murfreesboro, i, 389.
CROXTON, GEN. J. T., at the battle of Chickamauga, i, 334. Attacks Pillow at Lafayette, ii, 95. Near Florence, Ala., ii, 170. Covers movement from Pulaski, ii, 189. At Rally Hill, ii, 190. At battle of Nashville, ii, 229. Operations of in Alabama and Georgia, ii, 348.
CRUFT, GEN. C., commands Thirteenth Brigade, Army of the Ohio, i, 71. Reinforces General Grant at Fort Donelson, i, 72. At battle of Richmond, Ky., i, 180. At battle of Stone River, i, 225. Report of the battle, i, 277. At Chickamauga, i, 336. At Lookout Mountain, i, 417. At Missionary Ridge, i, 428. Expedition toward Dalton, ii, 19. At battle of Nashville, ii, 228.
CUMBERLAND GAP, occupied by rebel forces, i, 133. Evacuated by General Morgan, i, 178.
CUSHING'S BATTERY, at battle of Chickamauga, i, 339.
CUTTER, CAPT., contest of with guerrilla band, ii, 6.
DAHLGREEN, ADMIRAL JOHN A., co-operates with Sherman, ii, 284.
DALLAS, GA., engagements at, ii, 76.
DALTON, GA., movement against, ii, 18. Turning of, ii, 44. Captured by Hood, ii, 162.
DANA, GEN. N. J. T., dispatch to Sherman, ii, 206.
DAVIS, PRESIDENT JEFF., extract from message on battle of Shiloh, i, 125. Announces "grave reverses," ii, 10. Disregarded Johnston's suggestions, ii, 26. Incapacity of, ii, 27. Relieves Johnston, ii, 113. Confers with Western generals, ii, 156. Orders Smith and Magruder to co-operate with Hood, ii, 157. Capture of by Wilson's forces, ii, 362.
DAVIES, GEN. J. A., at siege of Corinth, i, 126.
DAVIS, GEN. JEFF. C., joins Buell at Murfreesboro, i, 158. At Nolensville, i, 220. At battle of Stone River, i, 224. Report of the battle, i, 266. At battle of Chickamauga, i, 336. Sent to Hooker at Lookout Mountain, i, 401. On the Knoxville campaign, ii, 1. At Buzzard Roost, ii, 49. At battle of Resaca, ii, 66. Captures Rome, Ga., ii, 73. Assault of, near Kenesaw, ii, 93. At Peachtree Creek, ii, 112. Before Atlanta, ii, 128. Assigned to command of the Fourteenth Corps, ii, 140. At battle of Jonesboro, ii, 143. On the march to the sea, ii, 278. At Averysboro, ii, 314. At battle of Bentonville, ii, 318. Congratulatory order of. ii, 374.

DECATUR, ALA., capture of, by Turchin, i, 130. Hood's demonstration against, ii, 169.
DE COURCY, COL. J. S., at Cumberland Ford, i. 133. Defeats Stevenson, i, 177.
DELPH, J. M., mayor of Louisville, commander of "Home Guard," i, 11. Demands the keys of state magazine, i, 13.
DICK, COL. G. F., at Chickamauga, i, 336.
DEPARTMENT OF THE CUMBERLAND, constituted, i, 22. Designation of, changed, i, 46. Its original name assumed, i, 207.
DEPARTMENT OF KENTUCKY, constituted, i, 20.
DEPARTMENT OF THE OHIO, constituted, i, 46. Discontinued, i, 207.
DOBBS, COL., killed at the battle of Salem, ii, 351.
DODGE, COL. J. B., at Chickamauga, i, 335.
DONALDSON, GEN., garrisons Nashville, ii, 206. At battle of Nashville, ii, 227.
DOOLITTLE, COL., at battle of Nashville, ii, 240.
DILWORTH, COL., near Kenesaw Mountain, ii, 94. At Peachtree Creek, ii, 111. At Jonesboro, ii, 144.
DUFFIELD, COL., in command at Murfreesboro, i, 99. Pursues Morgan, i, 136. Captures rebel detachments, i, 136. Captured at Murfreesboro, i, 147.
DUNHAM, COL., surrenders Munfordsville, i, 160.
DUNLAP, LIEUT., hung as a rebel spy at Murfreesboro, i, 298.
DUMONT, GEN. E., commands Seventeenth Brigade, Army of the Ohio, i, 67. In command at Nashville, i, 99. Routs Morgan, i, 136. Moves against E. K. Smith, i, 184.
EDGARTON'S BATTERY, captured, i, 230.
EDGEFIELD, TENN., occupied by Buell, i, 69.
EDIE, COL., at Jonesboro, ii, 144.
ELIZABETHTOWN, KY., captured by J. H. Morgan, i, 216.
ELLIOTT, GEN. W. L., on the Knoxville campaign, ii, 1. At Athens, ii, 5. Engagement at Mossy Creek, ii, 16. At battle of Nashville, ii, 228.

ELLIOTT, LIEUT. COL., finds rebel cavalry near Florence, ii, 158.
ELLSWORTH'S BATTERY, i, 237.
ESTE, COL. G. P., at Jonesboro, ii, 144.
ESTEP'S BATTERY, i, 243.
ETOWAH RIVER, advance to, ii, 71.
ETOWAH, DISTRICT OF, created, ii, 95.
FAYETTEVILLE, N. C., entered by the U. S. forces, ii, 311.
FEARING, GEN. B. D., at battle of Bentonville, ii, 316.
FISHER, CAPT., at Perryville, i, 189.
FITZGIBBON, MAJ., defeats guerrilla bands, ii, 6.
FLAT ROCK, GA., engagement at, ii, 124.
FOOTE, COM. A. H., at Fort Henry, i, 85.
FORT DONELSON, surrender of, i, 86. Transferred to Rosecrans' command, i, 288. Attacked by Wheeler, i, 289.
FORT HENRY, surrender of, i, 85. Transferred to Rosecrans' command, i, 288. Abandoned, i, 294.
FORT HEIMAN, transferred to Rosecrans, i, 288. Gunboat No. 55 captured at by Forrest, ii, 171.
FORT MCALLISTER, captured by Hazen's division, ii, 284.
FORT TYLER, captured by La Grange, ii, —.
FOURTH ARMY CORPS, formed by consolidation of the Twentieth and Twenty-first Corps, assigned to Howard, ii, 30. Assigned to Gen. D. S. Stanley, ii, 129. Fame and glory of, ii, 323. See also Appendix, ii, 382.
FOURTEENTH ARMY CORPS, first designation given to troops in the Department of the Cumberland under Rosecrans, i, 207. Designated as the "Center," and Thomas assigned to command of, i, 210. Palmer succeeds Thomas in command of, i, 411. Davis assigned to command of, ii, 140. Fame and glory of, ii, 323. See also Appendix, ii, 382.
FORMAN, COL. J., killed, i, 252.
FORREST, GEN. N. B., cavalry dash to Murfreesboro, i, 145. Captures Murfreesboro, i, 147. Captures Athens, Ala., ii, 163. At Johnsonville, Tenn., ii, 171. Moving

toward Franklin, ii, 191. Held by Wilson at battle of Franklin, ii, 198. Defeated by Wilson at Selma, ii, 352.
FOSTER, GEN. J. G., at Savannah, ii, 284.
FOX, CAPT. P. V., at Brown's Ferry, i, 398.
FRANKFORT, KY., secret meeting of Union men at, i, 12.
FRANKLIN, TENN., battle of, ii, 198.
FRENCH, GEN., S. G., attacks Allatoona, ii, 161.
FRY, COL. J. B., at battle of Perryville, i, 201.
FRY, GEN. S. S., at Camp Dick Robinson, i, 17. Kills Zollicoffer at battle of Mill Springs, i, 57. Crosses river at Decatur, i, 148. At Overall's Creek, i, 245.
FYFFE, COL. J. P., at the battle of Stone River, i, 236.
GALBRAITH, COL., at Fayetteville, i, 309.
GARFIELD, GEN. J. A., Eighteenth Brigade organized for, i, 76. Movements in Eastern Kentucky, i, 76. Defeats Marshall, i, 77. Drives enemy from Eastern Kentucky, i, 78. At battle of Chickamauga, i, 355.
GARRARD, COL. T. T., at Camp Dick Robinson, i, 17. Sent to oppose Zollicoffer's advance, i, 30.
GARRARD, GEN. K., on right of Sherman's army, ii, 71. Engagement of at Flat Rock, ii, 124. At Chattooga Valley, ii, 162. At battle of Nashville, ii, 228.
GARESCHE, LIEUT. COL., killed, i, 251.
GARDENER, GEN. W. M., routed by Stoneman, ii, 341.
GARDNER'S BATTERY AT JONESBORO, ii, 144.
GAY, CAPT. E., commanding cavalry brigade at Perryville, i, 185.
GEARY, GEN. J. W., at Wauhatchie, i, 400. At Lookout Mountain, i, 419. At Missionary Ridge, i, 428. Attempt to scale Chattooga Mountain, ii, 48. Near Kenesaw Mountain, ii, 87. At battle of Resaca, ii, 68. Engagements near Dallas, ii, 76. At Peachtree Creek, ii, 114. At Savannah, ii, 287. Extract from report of the capture of Sa-

vannah, ii, 302. Moves northward from Savannah, ii, 307.
GENERAL VIEW AT CLOSE OF 1863, ii, 8.
GEORGIA, expedition to destroy railroad in, i, 136.
GIBSON, COL. W. H., report of battle of Stone River, i, 264.
GILBERT, GEN. C. C., assigned to command of a corps, i, 184. At Perryville, i, 186. Extract from report of, i, 203. Moves to Franklin, Tenn., i, 290.
GILDERSLEEVE, CAPT., captures a steamer on Savannah River, ii, 282.
GILLEM, GEN. A. C., repulsed at Bull's Gap, ii, 272. Operations of in East Tennessee, ii, 273. In Tennessee and North Carolina, ii,* 338. Defeats McCown, ii, 342.
GIST, GEN. S. R., at Missionary Ridge, i, 425.
GLEASON, COL., before Atlanta, ii, 127.
GOLDSBORO, N. C., occupied by U. S. forces, ii, 322.
GOODING, COL, at Perryville, i, 190.
GOODSPEED, MAJ., at battle of Nashville, ii, 238.
GORDON, GA., entered by Howard, ii, 280.
GRACIE, GEN., at Chickamauga, i, 353.
GRANGER, GEN. G., at Corinth, i, 127. Defending Cincinnati, i, 183. At battle of Chickamauga, i, 253. Commands Army of Kentucky, i, 290. Drives Van Dorn, i, 293. At Missionary Ridge, i, 432. Report of the battle, i, 453. On the Knoxville campaign, ii, 1.
GRANGER, GEN. R. S., at Decatur, ii, 132. Makes a sortie on Hood, ii, 169,
GRANT, GEN. U. S., captures Fort Donelson, i, 85. At battle of Shiloh, i, 103. Order to Nelson, i, 123. Letters to Buell, i, 124. Extract from official report of battle of Shiloh, i, 125. Second in command at Corinth, i, 127. Assigned to command Military Division of Mississippi, i, 394. First order to Thomas, i, 395. Reaches Chattanooga, 395. Letters and orders to Thomas at Chattanooga, i, 440. Report of battle near Chattanooga, i, 448. Projected campaign of. ii, 14. Directs an advance toward

Dalton, ii, 18. Dispatches and orders to Thomas, ii, 39. Appointed lieutenant-general, ii, 40. Orders to advance on Georgia campaign, ii, 45. Extract from official report of, etc., ii, 54. Dispatch to Sherman, ii, 120. Dispatch on fall of Atlanta, ii, 153. Advises against a backward movement, ii, 155. Discussion of Sherman's projected march, ii, 172. Dispatches to Sherman, ii, 173, 183, 184. To Halleck, ii, 177. Urges Thomas to attack Hood, ii, 224. On his way to Nashville to relieve Thomas, ii, 235. Dispatches to Thomas during December, 1864, ii, 251, 252, 254, 257, 259, 261, 262. To Halleck, relative to relieving Thomas, ii, 253–255. To Thomas, relating to Breckinridge's movements, ii, 276, 277. Letters of to Sherman, relating to the march to the sea, ii, 293, 294. Congratulatory order of, ii, 371.

GREEN, GEN., wounded at Wauhatchie, i, 401.

GREEN, MAJ., captured by Col. McCook, i, 388.

GREENVILLE, TENN., occupied by rebels, i, 71.

GRENSEL, COL. N., succeeds Sill at battle of Stone River, i, 232. Report of the battle, i, 269.

GROSE, GEN. W., at Chickamauga, i, 336. At Lookout Mountain, i, 419. At Buzzard Roost, ii, 49.

GROSVENOR, COL. C. H., at battle of Nashville, ii, 230.

GROTER, COL. W. W., fell at Jonesboro, ii, 145.

GUNBOATS TYLER AND LEXINGTON at Shiloh, i, 107.

GUNTHER'S BATTERY, i, 238.

GUTHRIE, COL. JAMES V., authorized to raise a regiment, i, 14. Takes his regiment to West Virginia, i, 15.

HALL, COL. A. S., defeats J. H. Morgan, i, 294.

HALLECK, GEN. H. W., assigned to command of the Western armies, i, 98. Letters to Buell, i, 120, 121. At Pittsburg Landing, i, 126. Organization of army at Corinth, i, 126. Commander-in-chief at Washington, i, 160. Dispatch to Buell, i, 161. Assigns Thomas to command of Army of the Ohio, i, 184. Letter to Buell, i, 205. Relieves Buell of command, i, 206. Orders an advance against Chattanooga, i, 310. Ordered Burnside to support Rosecrans, i, 387. Authorizes Thomas to call on Western States for troops, ii, 212. Places officers and troops at Thomas' disposal, ii, 214. Dispatches to Thomas, ii, 177, 178. Dispatch to Sherman, ii, 120. Dispatch of December 31, 1864, to Thomas, ii, 344. Dispatches to Grant relating to relieving Thomas at Nashville, ii, 253, 256. Dispatches to Thomas, ii, 254, 258, 261. Letter to Sherman at Savannah, ii, 304.

HAMBRIGHT, COL. A., defeats Adams at Jasper, i, 132. In movement toward Dalton, ii, 20.

HAMILTON, GEN. S., at Corinth, i, 127.

HAMMOND, GEN. J. H., fight at Brentwood, ii, 204. At battle of Nashville, ii, 237.

HAMPTON, GEN. W., surprises Kilpatrick, ii, 311.

HATCH, GEN., drives enemy at Shoal Creek, ii, 187. Attacked by Hood at Lawrenceburg, ii, 188. Covers movement from Pulaski, ii, 189. Withdraws to Columbia, ii, 190. At battle of Nashville, ii, 231.

HARDEE, GEN. W. J., at Bowling Green, Ky., i, 41. At Chattanooga, i, 152. At battle of Perryville, i, 193. At Stone River, i, 227. On Missionary Ridge, i, 427. At Dalton, ii, 47. Defeated at Jonesboro, ii, 142. Retreats to Lovejoy Station, ii, 146. At Savannah, ii, 283. Letter to Sherman, refusing to surrender Savannah, ii, 298. Withdraws his forces from Savannah, ii, 287. Movements of at Charleston, ii, 307. Defeated at Averysboro, ii, 314. At battle of Bentonville, ii, 317.

HARDING, COL. A. C., repulses Wheeler, i, 289.

HARKER, GEN. C. G., assigned to command Twentieth Brigade, in Kentucky, i, 73. At battle of Stone River, i, 225. At Chickamauga, i,

348. Before Rocky Face Ridge, ii, 47. Assault at Kenesaw, and mortally wounded, ii, 94.
HARLAN, JAMES, i, 12.
HARMAN, COL., killed, near Kenesaw Mountain, ii, 94.
HARNDEN, COL., in pursuit of Davis, ii, 365.
HARRIS, COL., at Perryville, i, 90.
HARRIS' BATTERY, at Chickamauga, i, 336.
HARBISON, COL. T. J., expeditions against guerrillas, ii, 17. In movement toward Dalton, ii, 20.
HASCALL, GEN. M. S., assigned to command Fifteenth Brigade, in Kentucky, i, 72. Position at Stone River, i, 225. Report of battle of Stone River, i, 278. Before Atlanta, ii, 127.
HART, MAJ. J. H., repulsed enemy at Fort Donelson, i, 151.
HARTSVILLE, KY., captured by J. H. Morgan, i, 214.
HAUGHTALING'S BATTERY, captured, i, 237.
HAWKINS, COL. J. G., killed, i, 252.
HAWLEY, COL., at Savannah, ii, 282.
HAZEN, GEN. W. B., commands Nineteenth Brigade, in Kentucky, i, 69. Captures rebel battery, i, 112. At Stone River, i, 224. Report of battle of Stone River, i, 277. At Chickamauga, i, 336. At Missionary Ridge, i, 415. At New Hope Church, ii, 79. Captures Fort McAllister, ii, 284. At battle of Bentonville, ii, 321.
HAZEL GREEN, KY., occupied by U. S. troops, i, 74.
HECKER, COL., on the Knoxville campaign, ii, 2.
HEG, COL. H. C., at Chickamauga, i, 336. Killed, i, 363.
HELM, GEN., killed, i, 346.
HESCOCK'S BATTERY at Perryville, i, 187.
HESCOCK, CAPT., report of battle of Stone River, i, 271.
HILL, COL., at battle of Nashville, ii, 232.
HINDMAN, GEN. T. C., defeated at Rowlett's Station, i, 66. Threatens Columbia, i, 52. Moves against Negley, i, 320. At Chickamauga, i, 340.

HOBART, GEN. H. C., at battle of Bentonville, ii, 316.
HOBLITZELL, CAPT., at Perryville, i, 189.
HOOD, GEN. J. B., at Dalton, ii, 47. At battle of Resaca, ii, 68. Covering Marietta, ii, 88. Attack of, at Kulp's house, ii, 92. Succeeds General Johnston, ii, 113. Defeated at Peachtree Creek, ii, 115. Abandons Atlanta, ii, 147. Crossing the Chattahoochee, in movement north, ii, 159. Advancing upon Allatoona, ii, 161. Demands the surrender of Resaca, ii, 162. Effect and object of movement north, ii, 167. Makes an attack on Decatur, ii, 168. Withdraws from Decatur, ii, 169. Crossing the Tennessee River, ii, 170. Strength of before Thomas, ii, 186. Checked at Franklin, ii, 198. Broken and routed at Nashville, ii, 227-240. Fragments of his army move toward the Carolinas, ii, 308.
HOOKER, GEN. Jos., joins army of the Cumberland, at Bridgeport, i, 393. Defeats Longstreet at Wauhatchie, i, 398. At battle of Lookout Mountain, i, 417. At Missionary Ridge, i, 429. Assigned to command of Twentieth Corps, ii, 28. At Snake Creek Gap, ii, 50. Advances toward Buzzard's Roost, ii, 47. At battle of Resaca, ii, 64. At New Hope Church, ii, 76. At battle of Peachtree Creek, ii, 112.
HOOVER'S GAP, captured by Wilder, i, 304.
HOTCHKISS' BATTERY, at Knob's Gap, i, 220. At battle of Stone River, i, 234.
HOSKINS, COL., skirmish of his pickets at Mill Springs, i, 48.
HOWARD, GEN. O. O., at Lookout Creek, i, 399. At Missionary Ridge, i, 426. On the Knoxville campaign, ii, 1. Assigned to command of Fourth Corps, ii, 28. Extract from report of, ii, 62. At battle of Resaca, ii, 64. At New Hope Church, ii, 78. Before Kenesaw Mountain, ii, 87. Engagement near Jonesboro, ii, 142. Assigned to command of Army of the Tennessee, ii, 124. Repulses Hood's at-

tack before Atlanta, ii, 125. On the march to the sea, ii, 278. At Savannah, ii, 284. Extract from report of the capture of Savannah, ii, 301. Movement north through the Carolinas, ii, 309.
HUBBARD, COL., at battle of Nashville, ii, 232.
HURLBUT, GEN. S. H., at battle of Shiloh, i, 104. At Corinth, i, 126.
HUNTSVILLE, ALA., capture of, i, 130.
INNIS, COL. W. P., defends La Vergne, Tenn., i, 247.
IRELAND, COL. D., at Lookout Mountain, i, 420. At battle of Resaca, ii, 68. Near Dallas, ii, 76.
JACKSON, GEN. J. S., at Perryville, i, 186. Killed, i, 189.
JACKSON, GEN. N. J., at Savannah, ii, 287. At Averysboro, ii, 314.
JACKSON, GEN. W., at Duck River, ii, 191.
JOHNSONVILLE, TENN., engagement at, ii, 171.
JOHNSTON, GEN. A. S., in command of rebel forces at Bowling Green, i, 41. Retreat from Bowling Green, i, 68. Killed at Shiloh, i, 115.
JOHNSTON, GEN. J. E., relieves Bragg, ii, 14. Position and forces of at Dalton, ii, 21. Extracts from reports of, ii, 42, 62. At battle of Resaca, ii, 64. Moves to Allatoona Pass, ii, 73. At New Hope Church, ii, 78. At Kenesaw and Lost Mountain, ii, 86. Withdraws across the Chattahoochee, ii, 96. Relieved by Hood, ii, 113. Extract from official report of, ii, 118. Operations of against Sherman in the Carolinas, ii, 309, 312. Defeated at battle of Bentonville, ii, 315. Retreats through Raleigh, ii, 324. Surrenders to Sherman, ii, 325.
JOHNSON, GEN. R. W., commands Sixth Brigade, Army of the Ohio, i, 63. Defeated by Morgan, i, 151. At battle of Stone River, i, 224. Report of the battle, i, 263. Engagement at Liberty Gap, i, 304. At Chickamauga, i, 335. At Missionary Ridge, i, 429. In movement toward Dalton, ii, 20. At Ringgold, ii, 45. At battle of Resaca, ii, 66. At New Hope Church, ii, 79. Before Atlanta, ii, 127. Near Columbia, ii, 190. At battle of Nashville, ii, 229.
JONES, COL. F. C., killed at Stone River, i, 252.
JONES, COL. J. G., commands Fourteenth Brigade in Kentucky, i, 72.
JONESBORO, GA., battle of, ii, 144.
JORDAN, COL. T. J., charges the rebels at Thompson Station, i, 291.
JUDAH, GEN. H. M., at Corinth, i, 127.
KENESAW MOUNTAIN, operations near, ii, 86.
KENNETT, COL., enters Huntsville, i, 130. Routs rebel force, i, 213. At Gallatin, i, 207. Recaptures a train, i, 245.
KENTUCKY, legislature affirms armed neutrality, i, 4. Timidity of loyal citizens, i, 4. Opposition to secession, i, 6. Militia organized in, i, 8. Recruiting in for Union and rebel armies, i, 15. Rebel citizens plan the removal of loyal troops from the State, i, 21. Efforts to prevent arms reaching Camp Dick Robinson, i, 21. Abandons neutrality, i, 23. Legislature directs the Governor to order Confederate troops out of the State, i, 24. Committed to support of the National Government, i, 24. Operations in Eastern Kentucky, i, 74. Operations of armies in, i, 159, 218.
KENTUCKY LEGION, recruit of, i, 16.
KNIGHTS OF GOLDEN CIRCLE, propose to control Louisville, i, 21.
KILPATRICK, GEN. J., advance toward Tunnel Hill, ii, 26. Wounded near Resaca, ii, 64. Engagements at Fairburn and Lovejoy, ii, 133. On march to the sea, ii, 279. At Savannah, ii, 283. Movements of in the Carolinas, ii, 309. Surprised by Hampton, ii, 311. At Averysboro, ii, 314. At battle of Bentonville, ii, 320.
KILPATRICK, COL. R. L., at battle of Resaca, ii, 68. Fifth Ohio near Dallas, ii, 76.
KIMBALL, GEN. N., at New Hope Church, ii, 80. Assault of, at Kenesaw, ii, 94. At Lovejoy Station, ii, 146. At Lynnville, ii, 188. At battle of Franklin, ii, 199. At battle of Nashville, ii, 226.

KING, COL. E. A., killed, i, 363.
KING, GEN. J. H., at Chickamauga, i, 334. At battle of Resaca, ii, 66.
KIRBY, COL., near Kenesaw Mountain, ii, 39.
KIRK, GEN. E. N., defeats Wheeler, i, 213. Position at Stone River, i, 220. Mortally wounded, brigade dislodged, i, 230. Report of the battle, i, 265.
KNIPE, GEN. J., at battle of Resaca, ii, 68. At Kulp's house, ii, 91. At Peachtree Creek, ii, 114. At battle of Nashville, ii, 229.
KNOB'S GAP, engagement at, i, 220.
KNOXVILLE CAMPAIGN, ii, 1.
KULP'S HOUSE, engagement at, ii, 91.
LA GRANGE, COL. O. H., action of, at Mossy Creek, ii, 16. Repulsed at Poplar Place, ii, 50. Routs Gen. Lyon in Kentucky, ii, 271. Operations of, in Alabama and Georgia, ii, 349. Receives the surrender of Montgomery, ii, 354. Captures West Point, Ga., ii, 356.
LAIBOLDT, COL. B., at battle of Perryville, i, 187. Report of battle of Stone River, i, 270. At Chickamauga, i, 337. Routs Wheeler, ii, 7. Holds Dalton against Wheeler, ii, 131.
LANDRUM, LIEUT. COL., defends Cynthiana, Ky., i, 140.
LANE, COL., routed at Franklin, ii, 198.
LA VERGNE, cavalry engagement at, i, 247.
LEBANON, KY., captured by Morgan, i, 146.
LEBANON, TENN., Dumont defeats Morgan at, i, 136.
LEE, GEN. R. E., surrender of, ii, 324.
LEE, GEN. S. D., at Jonesboro, ii, 142. At battle of Bentonville, ii, 317.
LESTER, COL., captured at Murfreesboro, i, 147.
LEXINGTON, KY., i, 22.
"LEXINGTON," gunboat, at battle of Shiloh, i, 107.
LIBERTY GAP, engagement at, i, 304.
LIDDELL, GEN., at Chickamauga, i, 334.
LINCOLN, PRESIDENT, first call for troops, i, 3. Reply to Magoffin's letter, i, 18. Issued congratulatory order to Thomas for victory at Mill Springs, i, 57. War order No. 3, i, 122. Dispatch of, on fall of Atlanta, ii, 153. At the suggestion of Grant issues an order relieving Thomas, ii, 225. Congratulatory dispatch to Thomas for the victory at Nashville, ii, 259.
LISTER, COL. F. W., repulses J. H. Morgan, i, 212.
LOGAN, GEN. JOHN A., at Pocotaligo, ii, 307. At Bentonville, ii, 322. On his way to relieve Thomas, stops at Louisville, ii, 235.
LOGIE, COL., killed at Peachtree Creek, ii, 116.
LONG, GEN. E., charges of, on Wheeler, i, 389. Raid in East Tennessee, i, 437. On the Knoxville campaign, ii, 2. In movement toward Dalton, ii, 20. Operations of, in Alabama and Georgia, ii, 347. Charge of, at the battle of Selma, ii, 351.
LONGSTREET, GEN. J., at Chickamauga, i, 343. Defeated at Wauhatchie, i, 400. Sent against Burnside, i, 408. Retreats from Knoxville, ii, 3. Sent to Lee, ii, 26.
LOOKOUT MOUNTAIN, held by Bragg, i, 386. Battle of, i, 418.
LOOMIS, COL. C. O., commands artillery in Kentucky, i, 68. At Perryville, i, 187. At Missionary Ridge, 1, 427.
LORING, GEN. W. W., at Rocky Face Ridge, ii, 52. At battle of Resaca, ii, 64. Holding Kenesaw Mountain, ii, 88.
LOST MOUNTAIN, operations near, ii, 86.
LOUISVILLE, KY., citizens raise national flag, i, 2. Loyal citizens elect mayor of, i, 5. Union club, i, 5. Home guard, i, 11. Primal base of supplies, i, 140. Organization of troops at, i, 184.
LOUISVILLE AND NASHVILLE RAILROAD, defenses of, ii, 453.
LOVEJOY'S STATION, engagement at, ii, 146.
LOWE, COL. W. W., at the Etowah, ii, 74.
LUM, COL., at Jonesboro, ii, 144.
LYON, GEN., expedition of into Kentucky, ii, 271. Captured at Red Hill, ii, 272.
LYTLE, GEN. W. H., at Athens, Ala., i, 132. At Perryville, i, 190. At battle of Chickamauga, i, 340.

470   INDEX.

McARTHUR, GEN. J., at battle of Nashville, ii. 228.
McCLERNAND, GEN. J. A., at battle of Shiloh, i, 104. At Corinth, i, 126.
McCOOK, GEN. A. McD., assigned to command of Second Division, Army of the Ohio, i, 63. At battle of Shiloh, i, 111. At Corinth, i, 126. Assigned to command of a corps, i, 184. At battle of Perryville, i, 189. Extract from report of the battle, i, 203. At battle of Stone River, i, 224. Report of battle, i, 262. At battle of Chickamauga, i, 348.
McCOOK, COL. A. G., at Peachtree Creek, ii, 115.
McCOOK, COL. D., at Perryville, i, 186. At the battle of Chickamauga, i, 361. At New Hope Church, ii, 80. Assault at Kenesaw Mountain, ii, 93. Mortally wounded, ii, 94.
McCOOK, GEN. E. M., expedition against Wheeler, i, 389. Destroys cotton at Rodgersville, i, 390. Engagement with Longstreet, ii, 15. At battle of Resaca, ii, 67. Engagement with Stevenson, ii, 73. Cavalry movements in Georgia, ii, 124. At McLemore's Cove, i, 327. Burns Reed's bridge, i, 331. Operations of in Alabama and Georgia, ii, 347. Moves to Tallahassee, Fla., ii, 364.
McCOOK, GEN. R. L., assigned to command Twelfth Brigade, Army of the Ohio, i, 51. Wounded at Mill Springs, i, 57. Advances to Athens, i, 149. Killed by guerrillas, i, 149.
McCOWN, GEN., at Stone River, i, 227.
McGOWAN, MAJ., routed enemy at Duck River, i, 151.
McKEAN, GEN. J. J., at Corinth, i, 126.
McKEE, COL. S., captures rebel force, i, 212. Killed at Stone River, i, 242.
McLEMORE'S COVE, engagement in, i, 324.
McMILLAN, COL., at battle of Nashville, ii, 232.
McMINNVILLE, Reynolds' expedition to, i, 297. Captured by Wheeler, i, 389.

McPHERSON, GEN. J. B., in command of Army of the Tennessee, ii, 24. At New Hope Church, ii, 81. Near Kenesaw Mountain, ii, 87. Passes through Snake Creek Gap, ii, 50. At battle of Resaca, ii, 65. Killed near Atlanta, ii, 117.
MACK, CAPT. O. A., at Perryville, i, 186.
MACON, GA., surrendered to Wilson's forces, ii, 357.
MAGOFFIN, GOV. B., recommends arming militia of Kentucky, i, 2. Reply to President's proclamation, i, 3. Proclamation of, i, 7. Demanded removal of Camp Dick Robinson, i, 17. Letter to the President, i, 17. Proclamation of to rebel authorities, i, 33.
MANDERSON, COL., at Orchard Knob, i, 416.
MANSON, GEN. M. D., assigned to command Second Brigade, Army of the Ohio, i, 51. At battle of Richmond, Ky., i. 180.
MARSHALL'S BATTERY, at battle of Stone River, i, 237.
MASON, COL. R., surrendered at Clarksville, i, 151.
MARSHALL, GEN. H., invaded Kentucky, i, 74. Defeated by Garfield, i, 77.
MARTIN, GEN. W., defeated at Mossy Creek, ii, 16.
MATTHEWS, COL. STANLEY, defeats Gen. Wheeler near La Vergne, i, 215.
MAURY, M. T., London Times article of, ii, 10.
MAURY, GEN. J. P. M., capture of, i, 136.
MENDENHALL, CAPT. J., battery of supports Nelson, i, 110. At battle of Stone River, i, 249. Report of the battle, i, 280. At Brown's Ferry, i, 397.
MERRILL, COL. W. E., examination of railroads by, ii, 22. Fortifies Chattanooga, ii, 166.
METCALFE, COL., engagement of at Big Hill, i, 179.
MIHALOTZY, COL. G., mortally wounded, ii, 21.
MILES, COL., at battle of Bentonville, ii, 316.
MILITARY DIVISION OF MISSISSIPPI, constituted, i, 394.

INDEX.

MILL SPRINGS, battle of, i, 56.
MILLEDGEVILLE, GA., entered by Fourteenth and Twentieth Corps, ii, 280.
MILLER, COL. A. O., charges through Wheeler's line, i, 390. Defeats rebel brigade, ii, 16. Operations of in Tennessee and North Carolina, ii, 341. At the battle of Selma, ii, 351.
MILLER, GEN. J. F., at La Vergne, i, 210. Position at Stone River, i, 225. Charges across Stone River, i, 250. Report of the battle, i, 273. At battle of Nashville, ii, 227.
MILLIKEN, COL. M., killed at battle of Stone River, i, 244.
MILROY, GEN., drives Bate from Overall's Creek, ii, 223.
MINTY, COL. R. H. G., captures rebel regiment, i, 289. Routs rebels at Unionville, i, 290. Charges into Shelbyville, i, 306. Delays Bragg at Reed's bridge, i, 331. At the battle of Selma, ii, 351. Advances toward Macon, Ga., ii, 356.
MITCHELL, GEN. J. G., at Chickamauga, i, 353. At the battle of Resaca, ii, 66. At Jonesboro, ii, 144. At Kenesaw, ii, 93. At battle of Nashville, ii, 237. At battle of Bentonville, ii, 216.
MITCHELL, GEN. O. M., assigned to command of Third Division, Army of the Ohio, i, 67. Operations of in Tennessee and Alabama, i, 130. Moves against Chattanooga, i, 132. Organized expedition to destroy bridges in Georgia, i, 136. At Athens, i, 142.
MITCHELL, GEN. R. B., joins Buell, i, 158. At Perryville, i, 185. In command of Nashville, i, 217. Expedition of against Wheeler, i, 389.
MITCHELLSVILLE, a depot of supplies, i, 211.
MISSIONARY RIDGE, held by Bragg, i, 386. Battle of, i, 433.
MOCCASIN POINT, i, 397.
MONROE, COL., killed at Fannington, i, 392.
MONTGOMERY, ALA., surrendered to Wilson's forces, ii, 354.
MOORE, COL. A. B., surrenders to J. H. Morgan, i, 214.
MOORE, COL. J. B., at battle of Nashville, ii, 228.

MOORE, COL. L. P., at Catlettsburg, i, 74.
MORGAN, GEN. G. W., at Cumberland Ford, i, 133. Demonstrations against Cumberland Gap, i, 133. Evacuates Cumberland Gap, i, 178. Operations of in Kentucky, i, 176–183.
MORGAN, GEN. J. D., in movement toward Dalton, ii, 20. At Buzzard Roost, ii, 49. Before Kenesaw Mountain, ii, 93. Before Atlanta, ii, 128. At battle of Jonesboro, ii, 144. At battle of Bentonville, ii, 316.
MORGAN, GEN. JOHN H., assembles "State Guards" at armory, i, 22. Joins Buckner, i, 31. Moving toward Lebanon, Tenn., i, 136. Cavalry in Kentucky, i, 145. Defeats Jordan at Tompkinsville— captures Lebanon, i, 145. Repulsed by Col. Lister, i, 212. Defeated by Reynolds, i, 216. Defeated by Stanley and Hall, i, 294. Killed by Gillem's troops, ii, 272.
MORGAN, COL. T. J., captures rebel battery, ii, 169. At battle of Nashville, ii, 230.
MORTON, CAPT. ST. C., at Florence and Decatur, i, 142. Posted on Stone River, i, 225.
MOWER, GEN. J. A., at Bentonville, ii, 322.
MULDRAUGH'S HILL, captured by J. H. Morgan, i, 216.
MUNDY, COL., at Cumberland Gap, i, 177.
MUNFORDSVILLE, capture of by Bragg, i, 160.
MURFREESBORO, TENN., occupied by Gen. A. S. Johnston, i, 88. Under Col. Duffield, i, 99. Captured by Forrest, i, 147. Fortified by Nelson, i, 149. Occupied by Rosecrans, i, 251. Fortification of, i, 288.
NASHVILLE, a base of Confederate supplies, i, 37. Occupied by Army of the Ohio, i, 97. Under command of Dumont, i, 99. Held against Breckinridge by Negley, i, 207. Fortified by Tower, ii, 206. Battle of, ii, 222.
NASHVILLE AND CHATTANOOGA RAILROAD, defenses of, ii, 452.
NASHVILLE, DECATUR AND STEVENSON RAILROAD, defenses of, ii, 452.

472 INDEX.

NASHVILLE AND JOHNSONVILLE RAILROAD, defenses of, ii, 453.
NASHVILLE AND CLARKSVILLE RAILROAD, defenses of, ii, 453.
NAYLOR, CAPT., on Moccasin Point, i, 421.
NEGLEY, GEN. J. S., commands Seventh Brigade, Army of the Ohio, i, 63. Captures Rodgersville, Ala., i, 131. Bombards Chattanooga, i, 132. In command of Nashville, i, 207. Victory of, at La Vergne, i, 210. At battle of Stone River, i, 224. Report of the battle, i, 273. On the Tullahoma campaign, i, 306. Seizes Cooper's and Stevens' Gaps, i, 316. Moves into McLemore's Cove, i, 318. Skillful movements of against overwhelming forces, i, 322. At battle of Chickamauga, i, 331. Letter of to Baird, i, 368.
NELSON, GEN. W., obtains arms for the Home Guards of Kentucky, i, 11. Advice to President Lincoln, i, 12. Made agent for transmission of arms to Kentucky, i, 12. Assigned to command of Fourth Division, Army of the Ohio, i, 69. Movements in Eastern Kentucky, i, 74. At battle of Shiloh, i, 113. Circular of, i, 123. At Corinth, i, 126. Fortifies Murfreesboro, i, 149. At battle of Richmond, Ky., i, 182. Operations of in Kentucky, i, 176–183.
NEW HOPE CHURCH, engagements at, ii, 76.
NEWTON, GEN. J., at Rocky Face Ridge, ii, 52. At battle of Resaca, ii, 66. At New Hope Church, ii, 80. Before Kenesaw Mountain, ii, 88. At battle of Peachtree Creek, ii, 113. At Lovejoy's Station, ii, 146.
NOLENSVILLE, TENN., i, 220.
OPDYCKE, COL. E., drives back enemy's cavalry at Spring Hill, ii, 192. Heroic charge at the battle of Franklin, ii, 200. Brave actions of, ii, 203.
ORCHARD KNOB, captured, i, 416. Grant's position on, i, 426.
ORR, LIEUT. J. S., defends bridge on N. & C. R. R., ii, 448.
OSTERHAUS, GEN. P. J., at Lookout Mountain, i, 417. At Missionary Ridge, i, 428. On the march to the sea, ii, 278.
OVERALL'S CREEK, effectiveness of block-house at, ii, 223.
OWEN, COL., at Munfordsville, Ky., i, 160.
PAINE, GEN. E. A., at Corinth, i, 127.
PALMER, GEN. J. M., at La Vergne, i, 210. At battle of Stone River, i, 235. Report of the battle, i, 276. At Chickamauga, i, 335. At Missionary Ridge, i, 434. Reconnoissance toward Dalton, ii, 19. Drives enemy from Tunnel Hill, ii, 47. At battle of Resaca, ii, 64. Before Kenesaw Mountain, ii, 89. At Peachtree Creek, ii, 111. Before Atlanta, ii, 127. Relieved of command at his own request, ii, 128.
PALMER, COL. W. J., captures two of Hood's trains, ii, 271. Operations in Tennessee and North Carolina, ii, 342. Attempts to intercept Davis, ii, 365.
PARKHURST, GEN. J. G., reports men captured on Atlanta campaign, ii, 150.
PARROTT, JOHN, captured and flogged by rebels, i, 137.
PARSONS' BATTERY, captured at Perryville, i, 191.
PATRICK, LIEUT. COL., engagement of at Sugar Creek, i, 390.
PAYNE, GEN., expeditions against guerrilla bands, ii, 6.
PEACHTREE CREEK, battle of, ii, 113.
PEMBERTON, COL. J. C., routed by Stoneman, ii, 341.
PERRYVILLE, KY., campaign of, i, 184–206.
PILLOW, GEN. G., attacks Lafayette, ii, 95.
PINE MOUNTAIN, operations near, ii, 86.
PINNEY'S BATTERY, at Perryville, i, 190. At Nolensville, i, 220.
PITTSBURG LANDING, U. S. forces at, i, 101.
POCOTALIGO, occupied by Howard, ii, 307.
POLK, GEN. L., in Tennessee and Kentucky, i, 23. At Perryville, i, 193. At battle of Stone River, i, 227. Report of the battle, i, 258. At Chickamauga, i, 324. Defends Rocky Face Ridge, ii, 52. At bat-

tle of Resaca, ii, 65. Position at New Hope Church, ii, 78. Killed on Pine Mountain, ii, 76.
PONTON-TRAINS, description of, ii, 454. Designs of boat of, ii, 455.
POPE, GEN. J., at siege of Corinth, i, 126.
POST, COL. S., at Nolensville, i, 220. At battle of Stone River, i, 233. Report of the battle, i, 266. Near Columbia, ii, 192. At battle of Nashville, ii, 232.
PRENTISS, GEN. B. M., breaks up Confederate camp in Kentucky, i, 20. At battle of Shiloh, i, 104.
PRESCOTT'S BATTERY, at Jonesboro, ii, 144.
PRESTON, GEN., at battle of Stone River, i, 242. At Chickamauga, i, 340.
PRESTONVILLE, occupied by rebel forces, i, 74.
PRESCOTT'S KNOB, Bragg confronting Buell at, i, 161.
PRICE, COL. S. W., at battle of Stone River, i, 236.
PRIME, CAPT., sent to superintend fortifications, i. 48. Captured, i, 52.
PRITCHARD, COL., captures Jefferson Davis, ii, 365.
PULASKI, TENN., repulse of Forrest at by Rousseau, ii, 164.
RALEIGH, N. C., occupied by U. S. forces, ii, 322.
RANDALL, LIEUT. COL., killed at Peachtree Creek, ii, 116.
RAINS, GEN., at Baptist Gap, i, 135.
REED, COL. S. P., killed, i, 252.
REILLY, COL., at Franklin, ii, 199.
RESACA, battle of, ii, 64. Surrender of demanded by Hood, ii, 162.
REYNOLDS, GEN. J. J., defeats J. H. Morgan, i, 216. Expedition of to McMinnville, i, 297. At Chickamauga, i, 335.
RICHMOND, KY., battle of, i, 181.
RINGGOLD, GA., engagement at, i, 436.
ROBERTS, COL. G. W., killed at battle of Stone River, i, 237.
ROBINSON, COL. J. S., at Kulp's house, ii, 91. At Peachtree Creek, ii, 114. At battle of Bentonville, ii, 318.
ROCK CASTLE HILLS, battle of, i, 39.
ROCKY FACE RIDGE, ii, 47.
RODGERSVILLE, ALA., capture of, i,

132. Rebel cotton destroyed at, i, 390.
RODDY, GEN., crosses Tennessee River, ii, 15. Defeated by Upton, ii, 349.
RODNEY'S BATTERY, at the battle of Selma, ii, 351.
ROME, GA., foundries, mills, etc., at, destroyed, ii, 378.
ROSECRANS, GEN. W. S., in command of Department of the Cumberland, i, 207. Reorganizes his army, i, 210. Restricts non-military enemies, i, 217. Orders a move against Bragg, i, 218. Defeats Bragg at Stone River, i, 290. Strength and loss of, i, 251. Enters Murfreesboro, i, 251. Orders at and report of battle of Stone River, i, 253-255. Reasons for not advancing against Bragg, i, 298. Orders a forward movement, i, 300. Tullahoma campaign of, i, 302. Strategy of successful, i, 306. Barriers to the advance of, i, 310. Maneuvers to dislodge Bragg, i, 213. Crosses Tennessee River, i, 314. At battle of Chickamauga, i, 328. Aggregate loss of, at Chickamauga, i, 362. Report of the battle, i, 377. Aim of at Chattanooga, i, 386. Relieved by order of the President, i, 394. Farewell order of, i, 403.
ROSENGARTEN, MAJ., killed, i, 223.
ROSSVILLE, occupied by Crittenden, i, 318.
ROUSSEAU, GEN. L. H., appointed brigadier-general of militia, i, 11. Requests authority to raise U. S. troops in Kentucky, i, 15. In command of Fourth Brigade under Gen. McCook, i, 63. Repulses a charge at Shiloh, i, 113. At Perryville, i, 186. At battle of Stone River, i, 225. Report of the battle, i, 272. Operations of in Alabama, ii, 110. Arrives at Marietta, ii, 117. Drives Buford from Murfreesboro, ii, 224. Drives Forrest from Pulaski, ii, 164.
RUGER, GEN. T. H., at battle of Resaca, ii, 68. Before Kenesaw Mountain, ii, 91. At battle of Peachtree Creek, ii, 114. At Columbia, ii, 190. At battle of Franklin, ii, 199.
RUSSELL'S BATTERY, at Chickamauga, i, 339.

SALEM, N. C., public property at, destroyed, ii, 341.
SALTVILLE, VA., captured and destroyed by Stoneman, ii, 374.
SALT RIVER, bridge of burned, i, 159.
SAVANNAH, GA., capture of, by the U. S. forces, ii, 287.
SELMA, ALA., battle and capture of, by Wilson, ii, 352.
SCHAEFER, COL. F. C., at battle of Stone River, i, 232. Killed, i, 243.
SCHOEPF, GEN. A., camp of bombarded, i, 49. Assigned to command of First Brigade, Army of the Ohio, i, 51. Moves toward Zollicoffer's position, i, 53. Crosses river at Florence, i, 148. At battle of Perryville, i, 189.
SCHULTZ'S BATTERY, at Stone River, i, 237.
SCHURZ, GEN. C., at battle of Wauhatchie, i, 400. At Missionary Ridge, i, 426.
SCHOFIELD, GEN. J. M., relieves Foster at Knoxville, ii, 18. At turning of Dalton, ii, 50. At battle of Resaca, ii, 64. Near Kenesaw Mountain, ii, 88. Before Atlanta, ii, 127. Assumes command at Pulaski, ii, 172. Operations of, at Columbia, ii, 192. At battle of Franklin, ii, 196. Dispatches to Thomas during retreat before Hood, ii, 210-218. Extract from report of battle of Franklin, ii, 219. At battle of Nashville, ii, 226. Extract from report of battle of Nashville, ii, 267. At Goldsboro, ii, 322.
SCOTT, COL., rebel cavalry of, at Munfordsville, i, 159.
SCRIBNER, COL. B. F., at battle of Chickamauga, i, 334. At New Hope Church, ii, 79.
SCULLEY, LIEUT. COL., defeats Hawkins, ii, 6.
SHANE, LIEUT. COL., wounded near Kenesaw, ii, 94.
SHEERER, CAPT., at Nolensville, i, 220.
SHELBYVILLE, TENN., a depot of supplies, i, 130. Sacked by Wheeler, i, 390.
SHEPHERD, COL. O. L., at battle of Stone River, i, 238.
SHERIDAN, GEN. P. H., at Perryville, i, 185. At battle of Stone River,

i, 224. Report of the battle, i, 268. At Chickamauga, i, 337. At Missionary Ridge, i, 415.
SHERMAN, GEN. T. W., at Corinth, i, 126.
SHERMAN, GEN. W. T., assumes command of Department of the Cumberland, i, 31. Relieved by Buell, i, 46. At battle of Shiloh, i, 104. Arrives at Chattanooga, i, 410. At the battle of Missionary Ridge, i, 423. Report of battle of Missionary Ridge, i, 448. On the Knoxville campaign, ii, 1. Assigned to command of Military Division of the Mississippi, ii, 24. Campaign of from Chattanooga to Atlanta, ii, 25-155. Operations of from Atlanta to Gaylesville, ii, 160-166. March from Atlanta to the coast, ii, 168-305. Letter to Gen. Webster at Nashville, ii, 264. Operations of in the Carolinas, ii, 309-325. Dispatch of to Wilson at Macon, ii, 361. Congratulatory order of, ii, 371.
SHILOH, battle of, i, 106. Rebel loss at, i, 114. National loss at, i, 114.
SLOCUM, GEN. H. W., assigned to command of Twentieth Crops, ii, 141. On the march to the sea, ii, 278. Dispatch to Sherman, ii, 179. At Savannah, ii, 282. Extract from report of the capture of Savannah, ii, 301. At Averysboro, ii, 314. At battle of Bentonville, ii, 316. Moves through Richmond to Washington, ii, 325. Congratulatory order of, iii, 374.
SILL, COL. J. W., commands Ninth Brigade, Army of the Ohio, i, 67. Captures Stevenson, i, 130. Moves against Kirby Smith, i, 184. At battle of Stone River, i, 226. Killed, i, 232.
SIMONSON'S BATTERY, enters Huntsville, i, 130. At Perryville, i, 186. At battle of Resaca, ii, 67. A shot from kills Lieut. Gen. Polk, ii, 86.
SIRWELL, COL. W., at Chickamauga, i, 348.
SISTER'S FERRY, on Savannah river, ii, 307.
SLADE, LIEUT. COL., repulses Buford at Huntsville, ii, 164.
SMITH, GEN. A. J., at Corinth, i, 126.

Defending Cincinnati, i, 183. At battle of Nashville, ii, 226.
SMITH, GEN. C. F., enterprise of a failure, i, 101. Debarks at Pittsburg Landing, i, 101. At battle of Shiloh, i, 104
SMITH, GEN. E. K., at Bridgeport, i, 131. Moves to relieve Chattanooga, i, 132. At Knoxville, i, 152. Moving to Central Kentucky, i, 153. Defeats Nelson, i, 182. Advances toward Cincinnati, i, 183.
SMITH, GEN. G. C., in pursuit of J. H. Morgan, i, 136. Opposes Morgan in Kentucky, i, 146. At Brentwood, Tenn., i, 290.
SMITH, GEN. M. L., assault of at Fort Donelson, i, 86. At Missionary Ridge, i, 426.
SMITH, GEN. J. E., at Missionary Ridge, i, 426. At Chattanooga, ii, 95.
SMITH, GEN. W. F., operations of at Chattanooga, i, 396. Success of at Brown's Ferry, i, 398. Activity of at Chattanooga, i, 421.
SMITH, GEN. W. S., at Perryville, i, 196.
SMITHFIELD, N. C., occupied by U. S. forces, ii, 322.
SOUTH CAROLINA, desolate track through, ii, 312.
SOUTHERN STATES, character of legislatures of, i, 2.
SPALDING, COL., successful charge of at Nashville, ii, 241.
SPEED, GEN. JAS., patriotic address of, i, 2. Appointed brigadier-general of militia in Kentucky, i, 11.
SPEED, JOSHUA F., i, 12.
SPEERS, GEN. J. G., at Cumberland Ford, i, 133. At Stone River, i, 251. On the Knoxville campaign, ii, 2. Engagement with Wheeler, ii, 7.
STANDART'S BATTERY, at Stone River, i, 240. At Chickamauga, i, 339.
STANLEY, GEN. D. S., at Corinth, i, 127. At battle of Stone River, i, 224. Engagement of at Overall's Creek, i, 245. Attacks Van Dorn at Harpeth River, i, 296. Defeats forces at Middleton, i, 297. Captures Wheeler's artillery, i, 306. Movements in Alabama, i, 309. At Buzzard Roost, ii, 49. At battle of Résaca, ii, 66. Engagement near Cassville, ii, 72. Before Kenesaw Mountain, ii, 88. At Peachtree Creek, ii, 112. Assigned to command of the Fourth Corps, ii, 124. Before Atlanta, ii, 129. Engagement at Lovejoy's Station, ii, 146. At Pulaski, ii, 170. At Columbia, ii, 190. Goes with a brigade into a charge at Franklin, ii, 200. Wounded at battle of Franklin, ii, 201. Extract from report of battle of Franklin, ii, 221. Takes Fourth Corps into East Tennessee, ii, 339.
STANLEY, COL. T. R., at battle of Stone River, i, 250. Report of the battle, i, 273. At Chickamauga, i, 348. At Brown's Ferry, i, 397.
STARKWEATHER, COL. J. C., at Perryville, i, 188. At battle of Stone River, i, 224. At Chickamauga, i, 334.
STANTON, E. M., dispatches to Grant, relating to Thomas at Nashville, ii, 250, 253. Dispatches to Thomas, ii, 259, 262. Directs Thomas to disregard all orders except those coming from Grant and himself, ii, 363.
STEEDMAN, GEN. J. B., at Perryville, i, 190. Defeats Roddy, i, 293. At Chickamauga, i, 353. In command of District of Etowah, ii, 95. Drives Wheeler from Dalton, ii, 131. At battle of Nashville, ii, 227.
STEINWEHR, GEN. A. V., at Wauhatchie, i, 400. At Missionary Ridge, i, 426.
STERN, COL. L., killed, i, 252.
STEVENSON, GEN. C. L., near Baptist Gap, i, 135. Near Cumberland Gap, i, 176. Defeated by De Courcy, i, 177. At Missionary Ridge, i, 427. At Buzzard Roost, ii, 49. At battle of Resaca, ii, 67.
STEVENSON, ALA., capture of, i, 130. Works of defense constructed at, i, 148.
STEWART, GEN. A. P., at Chickamauga, i, 346. At Missionary Ridge, i, 434. At Buzzard's Roost, ii, 49. At Resaca, ii, 67. Retreats from Atlanta, ii, 147. On railroad near Marietta, ii, 160.
STONE'S BATTERY, at Perryville, i, 188.

STONE RIVER, campaign of, i, 219–286.
STONEMAN, GEN. G. D., at Rocky Face Ridge, ii, 52. Movement toward Macon, and capture, ii, 124. Operations in East Tennessee, ii, 273. Cavalry operations in Tennessee and North Carolina, ii, 337.
STOUGHTON, COL., at Missionary Ridge, i, 434.
STRAIGHT, COL. A. D., expedition from Decatur, i, 148. Expedition into Alabama, i, 295. Surrendered to Forrest, i, 296. At battle of Nashville, ii, 232.
STRICKLAND, COL., at Franklin, ii, 199.
SWALLOW'S BATTERY, at Chickamauga, i, 336.
TAFEL, COL., surrenders to J. H. Morgan, i, 214.
TENNESSEE, importance of holding, i, 139.
TERRELL, GEN., at Perryville, i, 188.
TERRELL'S BATTERY, at Shiloh, i, 112.
THOMAS, GEN. GEO. H., in command of Camp Dick Robinson, i, 26. Organized First Brigade, Army of the Cumberland, i, 27. Operations of, in Kentucky, i, 30–54. Victory of, at battle of Mill Springs, i, 56. Moves his command to Nashville, i, 58. Commands the center at Corinth, i, 126. In the movement from Corinth toward Kentucky, i, 139. Letters of, to Buell, i, 164–173. Assigned to command of the Army of the Ohio, i, 184. At the battle of Perryville, i, 186. Report of the battle, i, 202. Commands the center at battle of Stone River, i, 224. Report of the battle, i, 272. On the Tullahoma campaign, i, 302. Operations of, in moving army over the mountains, i, 310. Position of, at battle of Chickamauga, i, 328. Left chief in command, i, 348. Saved the army, i, 358. Assigned to command of the Army of the Cumberland, i, 394. Operations of, at Chattanooga, i, 395, ii, 13. Assaults Bragg's center on Missionary Ridge, i, 429. Orders and reports of, at Chattanooga, i, 445, 451. Suggests movement of his army through Snake Creek Gap, ii, 24.
Dispatches of to Grant, ii, 40. Extract of report of, ii, 43. Operation of in the turning of Dalton, ii, 44. Begins movements of Atlanta campaign, ii, 45. Operations of on the Atlanta campaign, ii, 45–152. Congratulatory order of, at Atlanta, ii, 153. Ordered north to secure communications, ii, 159. Placed in command of all troops not in Sherman's presence, ii, 165. Strength of army left with him to defeat Hood, ii, 186. Dispositions of to repel Hood, ii, 186. Withdraws army from Franklin, ii, 191. Dispatch to Sherman, ii, 181. To Halleck, ii, 182. Dispatches from Nashville in November, 1864, ii, 206–218. Extract from report of battle of Franklin, ii, 219. Preparations of for battle of Nashville, ii, 222. Attacks Hood before Nashville, ii, 227. Routs Hood and drives him from Tennessee, ii, 228–247. Extract from report of battle of Nashville, ii, 266. Dispatches from Nashville to Grant, ii, 251, 252, 254, 256, 257, 261. To Halleck, ii, 253, 255, 257, 258, 261. To President Lincoln, ii, 260. General order of at Pulaski, ii, 265. Dispatches to Grant in relation to East Tennessee movements, ii, 276. Extract from report of, ii, 344. Dispatches from Clifton and Eastport to Halleck, ii, 345. Dispatches to Grant in relation to Hood's movements, ii, 345. Communications of to Wilson, ii, 359. Dispatch to Grant, ii, 359. Dispatch to Stoneman, ii, 360. Directed to disregard all orders except those of Grant and Secretary Stanton, ii, 363. Congratulatory order of, ii, 373. Order of, establishing a national cemetery at Chattanooga, ii, 377.
THOMPSON, COL. C. R., engages Forrest at Johnsonville, ii, 171. At battle of Nashville, ii, 242.
TOPPING, LIEUT. COL., mortally wounded, i, 181.
TOWER, GEN., fortifies Nashville, ii, 206.
TRIUNE, TENN., i, 221.
TULLAHOMA CAMPAIGN, i, 302.
TURCHIN, GEN. J. B., commands

Eighth Brigade, Army of the Ohio, i, 67. Occupies Bowling Green, i, 68. Brigade enters Huntsville, i, 130. Captures Decatur and Tuscumbia, i, 130. At Brown's Ferry, i, 397. At Chickamauga, i, 336. Charges and routs the enemy, i, 355. At Missionary Ridge, i, 429. In movement toward Dalton, ii, 20. At battle of Resaca, ii, 66.

TUSCUMBIA, ALA., capture of, i, 130.

TWELFTH ARMY CORPS, joins Army of the Cumberland at Bridgeport, i, 392. See also Appendix, ii, 382.

TWENTIETH ARMY CORPS, organization of, see Appendix, ii, 381.

TWENTY-FIRST ARMY CORPS, organization of, see Appendix, ii, 381.

"TYLER," gunboat, at battle of Shiloh, i, 107.

TYLER, GEN., killed at West Point, Ga., ii, 356.

TYNDALE, GEN. H., at Wauhatchie, i, 400.

UNDERWOOD, COL. A. B., at battle of Wauhatchie, i, 401.

UPTON, GEN. E., operations of in Alabama and Georgia, ii, 347. At the battle of Selma, ii, 351. Captures Columbus, Ga., ii, 355. At Augusta, ii, 364.

VAN CLEVE, GEN. H. P., at battle of Stone River, i, 224. Engaged at Lee & Gordon's Mills, i, 325. At Crawfish Springs, i, 327. At Chickamauga, i, 336.

VANDERVEER, COL. F., at Chickamauga, i, 334. At Missionary Ridge, i, 429. Advance toward Tunnel Hill, ii, 26. At battle of Bentonville, ii, 317.

VAN DORN, GEN., engagement of, near Spring Hill, i, 292.

VAUGHAN, GEN., evacuates London, ii, 2.

"VETERAN VOLUNTEERS," grand name of, ii, 29.

VON SCHRADER, LIEUT. COL. A., system of pickets, i, 210. Sent to Nashville to organize detached troops, ii, 189.

WAGNER, GEN. G. D., assigned to command of Twenty-first Brigade, i, 73. At Perryville, i, 192. At battle of Stone River, i, 243. Report of the battle, i, 279. At Missionary Ridge, i, 432. Assault at

Kenesaw, ii, 94. At New Hope Church, ii, 80. At Lynnville, ii, 188. At battle of Franklin, ii, 198.

WALCUTT, GEN. C. C., engagement of, near Macon, ii, 278.

WALKER, COL. M. B., at Stewartsboro, i, 224.

WALLACE, GEN. L., at Fort Donelson, i, 86. At battle of Shiloh, i, 109. At Corinth, i, 127. Defending Cincinnati, i, 183.

WALLACE, GEN. W. H. L., at battle of Shiloh, i, 104. Mortally wounded, i, 108.

WARD, GEN. W. T., at battle of Resaca, ii, 68. At Peachtree Creek, ii, 113. Moves northward from Savannah, ii, 307. At Averysboro, ii, 314.

WATKINS, COL. L. D., captures part of Texas Legion, i, 297. Posted at Rossville, ii, 5. Dash of upon Lafayette, ii, 7. Holds Lafayette, ii, 95.

WAUHATCHIE, battle of, i, 400.

WEBSTER, COL., at Perryville, i, 188.

WELLS, COL., attacked at Campbellsville, ii, 189.

WEST LIBERTY, KY., occupied by U. S. troops, i, 74.

WEST POINT, GA., captured by Col. La Grange, ii, 356.

WHARTON, GEN. J. A., raid of in Tennessee, i, 388.

WHEELER, GEN. J., defeated by Kirk, i, 213. Defeated by Col. S. Matthews, i, 215. Captures Coburn, i, 292. Artillery of captured, i, 306. Expedition of in Tennessee, i, 387. Defeats of, 1, 391. Defeated at Calhoun, ii, 7. Driven by Palmer, ii, 19. Attack of on Dalton repulsed, ii, 131. At Savannah, ii, 285. Operations of in the Carolinas, ii, 308.

WICKLIFFE, C. A., i, 12.

WICKLIFFE, CAPT., at Perryville, i, 187.

WHIPPLE, GEN. W. D., at battle of Nashville, ii, 230.

WHITE, COL., receives the surrender of Macon, ii, 357.

WHITAKER, GEN. W. C., at Chickamauga, i, 353. At Lookout Mountain, i, 419. Near Kenesaw Mountain, ii, 89.

WILDER, COL. J. T., declines to sur-

render Munfordsville, i, 160. Drives enemy from Hoover's Gap, i, 304. Captures Manchester, i, 306. Delays Bragg at Alexander's bridge, i, 331. Engagement at Leet's tanyard, i, 325. At Chickamauga, i, 337.
WILLIAMS, GEN. A. S., at battle of Resaca, ii, 68. At New Hope Church, ii, 76. Before Kenesaw Mountain, ii, 89. At Peachtree Creek, ii, 114. On the march to the sea, ii, 278. At Savannah, ii, 285. Report of on the capture of Savannah, ii, 302. At Averysboro, ii, 314.
WILLIAMS, COL. L. A., hung as a rebel spy, i, 298.
WILLIAMS, COL. T. D., killed, i, 252.
WILLICH, GEN. A., defeats enemy at Rowlett's Station, i, 65. At battle of Shiloh, i, 113. At Stone River, i, 226. At Chickamauga, i, 335. At Missionary Ridge, i, 415.
WILSON, GEN. J. H., at Chattanooga, i, 422. Chief of cavalry, Military Division of the Mississippi, ii, 192. At Hart's Cross-roads, ii, 191. Covers retirement of the infantry, ii, 192. At the battle of Franklin, ii, 198. Dispatches of from Hart's Cross-roads and Franklin, ii, 216. Extract of report of November 29, 1864, ii, 221. At battle of Nashville, ii, 222, 226. Pursues retreating enemy, ii, 241. Cavalry campaign of in Alabama and Georgia, ii, 347. Captures Selma, Ala., ii, 353. Moves toward Montgomery, ii, 353. Advance of upon Macon, Ga., ii, 356. Dispatch of, from Macon, to Sherman, ii, 361. Suspends operations in compliance with the Sherman-Johnston armistice, ii. 357. Adopts measures to capture Davis, etc., ii, 364. Congratulatory order of, ii, 376.
WINEGAR'S BATTERY, at Kulp's house, ii, 91.
WINSLOW, GEN. E. F., at the battle of Selma, ii, 352. At Columbus, Ga., ii, 355. Operations of, in Alabama and Georgia, ii, 349.

WITHERS, GEN., at Stone River, i, 227.
WOLF, COL., at battle of Nashville, ii, 232.
WOLFORD, COL. FRANK, organizes First Kentucky Cavalry, i, 17. Wounded at Lebanon, Ky., i, 136.
WOOD, COL. J., at battle of Resaca, ii, 68.
WOOD, GEN. T. J., assigned to command Sixth Division, i, 72. At battle of Shiloh, i, 114. At Corinth, i, 126. At Perryville, i, 192. At Stone River, i, 241. At Chickamauga, i, 347. Drives enemy from Orchard Knob, i, 415. At Rocky Face Ridge, ii, 52. At battle of Resaca, ii, 66. At New Hope Church, ii, 73. Before Kenesaw Mountain, ii, 88. At Peachtree Creek, ii, 112. Wounded at Lovejoy's Station, ii, 146. At battle of Franklin, ii, 199. At battle of Nashville, ii, 226.
WOOD, LIEUT. COL., of Morgan's rebel command, captured, i, 136.
WOODBURY'S BATTERY, at Kulp's house, ii, 91.
WOODRUFF, COL. W. E., loyalty of, i, 3. Authorized to raise a regiment, i, 14. Takes regiment to West Virginia, i, 15. At Nolensville, i, 220. At battle of Stone River, i, 231. Report of the battle, i, 267.
WRIGHT, GEN. H. G., relieves Nelson, i, 153.
WYNCOOP, COL., Seventh Pennsylvania Cavalry, i, 136.
WYTHEVILLE, VA., captured and destroyed by Gillem, ii, 274.
YARGER, MAJ. J., wounded near Kenesaw, ii, 94.
YOUNG, LIEUT. COM., at Fayetteville with gunboat Eolus, ii, 311.
ZAHM, COL. L., at battle of Stone River, i, 244.
ZOLLICOFFER, GEN. F. R., occupies Cumberland Gap, i, 23. Advanced to Cumberland Ford, i, 30. Repulsed by Gen. Schoepf's command, i, 39. Retreated to London, i, 39. Issues proclamation to Kentuckians, i, 53. Killed at battle of Mill Springs, i, 57.

www.ingramcontent.com/pod-product-compliance
Lightning Source LLC
Chambersburg PA
CBHW051843300426
44117CB00006B/253